RESEARCH HANDBOOK ON THE THEORY AND HISTORY OF INTERNATIONAL LAW

RESEARCH HANDBOOKS IN INTERNATIONAL LAW

This highly original series offers a unique appraisal of the state-of-the-art of research and thin[king] in international law. Taking a thematic approach, each volume, edited by a prominent expert, cov[ers] a specific aspect of international law or examines the international legal dimension of a particul[ar] strand of the law. A wide range of sub-disciplines in the spheres of both public and private law ar[e] considered; from international environmental law to international criminal law, from international economic law to the law of international organisations, and from international commercial law to international human rights law. The *Research Handbooks* comprise carefully commissioned chapters from leading academics as well as those with an emerging reputation. Taking a genuinely international approach to the law, and addressing current and sometimes controversial legal issues, as well as affording a clear substantive analysis of the law, these *Handbooks* are designed to inform as well as to contribute to current debates.

Equally useful as reference tools or introductions to specific topics, issues and debates, the *Handbooks* will be used by academic researchers, post-graduate students, practicing lawyers and lawyers in policy circles.

Titles in this series include:

Handbook of Research on International Consumer Law
Edited by Geraint Howells, Iain Ramsay and Thomas Wilhelmsson with David Kraft

Research Handbook on International Environmental Law
Edited by Malgosia Fitzmaurice, David M. Ong and Panos Merkouris

Research Handbook on International Criminal Law
Edited by Bartram S. Brown

Research Handbook on the Law of International Organizations
Edited by Jan Klabbers and Åsa Wallendahl

Research Handbook on the Theory and History of International Law
Edited by Alexander Orakhelashvili

Research Handbook on the Theory and History of International Law

Edited by

Alexander Orakhelashvili

University of Birmingham, UK

RESEARCH HANDBOOKS IN INTERNATIONAL LAW

Edward Elgar
Cheltenham, UK • Northampton, MA, USA

Published by
Edward Elgar Publishing Limited
The Lypiatts
15 Lansdown Road
Cheltenham
Glos GL50 2JA
UK

Edward Elgar Publishing, Inc.
William Pratt House
9 Dewey Court
Northampton
Massachusetts 01060
USA

A catalogue record for this book
is available from the British Library

Library of Congress Control Number: 2011924163

MIX
Paper from
responsible sources
FSC® C018575

ISBN 978 1 84844 354 9 (cased)

Typeset by Servis Filmsetting Ltd, Stockport, Cheshire
Printed and bound by MPG Books Group, UK

Contents

Contributors

Jean Allain, Reader in Law, Queen's University of Belfast, Northern Ireland; Extraordinary Lecturer, Centre for Human Rights, Faculty of Law, University of Pretoria, South Africa

William E. Butler, John Edward Fowler Distinguished Professor of Law, the Dickinson School of Law, State University of Pennsylvania, USA; Academician, National Academy of Sciences, Ukraine; Emeritus Professor of Comparative Law, University of London

Patrick Capps, Reader in Law, University of Bristol, England

Robert Cryer, Professor of International and Criminal Law, University of Birmingham, England

Carlo Focarelli, Professor of International Law, University of Perugia and at the Luis University of Rome, Italy

Jörg Kammerhofer, Research Fellow, Hans Kelsen Research Group, University of Erlangen, Germany

Randall Lesaffer, Dean and Full Professor of Legal History, Tilburg University, the Netherlands; part-time Professor of Cultural and Legal History, Faculty of Law, Catholic University of Leuven, Belgium

Amnon Lev, Assistant Professor in Law, University of Copenhagen, Denmark

Lauri Mälksoo, Professor of Law, University of Tartu, Estonia

Frédéric Mégret, Assistant Professor, McGill University, Canada

Alexander Orakhelashvili, Lecturer in Law, University of Birmingham, England

Iain Scobbie, Sir Joseph Hotung Research Professor of Law, SOAS, England

Alain Wijffels, Professor of Law, University of Louvain, Belgium, and University of Leiden, the Netherlands

Katja S. Ziegler, Reader in European and Comparative Law, Faculty of Law, and Tutorial Fellow, St Hilda's College, Oxford, England

Foreword

It was unexpected, but inevitable. It was not easy to suppose that the intellectual discipline of International Law would, at last and so readily, recognise the shameful poverty of its theoretical superstructure. When it happened, it was not surprising, given the spectacular increase in the volume and density and complexity and diversity of substantive International Law since 1945. Large-scale social phenomena – religions, political systems, economic systems – generate the ideas necessary to explain and justify them. And the ideas become part of the life of the phenomena, each energising the other in their further development.

Law, as a large-scale social phenomenon, has been in such a mutually creative relationship with transcendental ideas throughout the whole of recorded human history. Law, evidently a natural and necessary social phenomenon, has needed an exceptional volume of socially effective ideas to explain and justify its highly coercive actual power in given societies. A law governing governments was obviously something less than a natural or necessary social phenomenon. But, intermittently, the prestige of the word *law* was borrowed tentatively, defensively, paradoxically, metaphorically – natural law, the law of nations, international law. But it was out of the question that a law governing governments might be able simply to appropriate, for its own purposes of explanation and justification, the vast age-old accumulation of transcendental thinking about the universal phenomenon of law.

International Law was obviously an anomaly in relation to that perennial and universal tradition. For some observers, it was too anomalous to be treated seriously as law. For others, the wish had to father the thought that International Law might, at least, be useful, if its vestigial law-like characteristics were emphasised, and if the behaviour of governments were, occasionally and generously, interpreted as manifesting some sort of law-consciousness.

Since 1945 there has been what can only be described as a revolution in the social organisation of the human world. The international dimension of human existence has overwhelmed the national dimension of human existence. Bland, easily-spoken words – interdependence, international community, globalisation – do not do justice to the social reality of a world in which there is now a seamless web of causes and effects stretching from the remotest village to the totality of human social phenomena. Social organisation is now stratified, vertically and horizontally, in social and political and legal forms which are often old in their systematic forms (states, governments, law-making and law-applying institutions, public administrations) but which are new in their fields of action and interaction. There is a new global distribution of social power, a new global constitutional reality.

International Law does not merely reflect these new social phenomena. It embodies and enacts and enforces them. No one can now deny that this new kind of human world demands a new effort to generate the ideas necessary to explain and justify it – not least, to explain and justify the new social role of International Law.

Responding to that urgent and intimidating and exciting summons, this *Handbook* reflects three kinds of intellectual strategy. One may look again at the inheritance of transcendental thinking about a law governing governments, and treat it now with the intellectual seriousness that it deserves, given that it was the work of thinkers who were deeply immersed in the perennial and universal tradition of transcendental social and legal philosophy. One might even seek to extrapolate a particular tradition within that philosophy to inspire and direct the new revolutionary social challenge.

One might also engage in the kind of intellectual endeavour which has been at the heart of higher-level thinking about social phenomena at the national level – seeking to unravel the conceptual implications of particular aspects of the new international legal reality, with a view to understanding them and evaluating them and influencing the development of public policy.

Finally, one might try to establish a better understanding of how we have come to be where we are. The past is present in the present, and so is the future. We must bring the sophistication of national historiography at its best to our understanding of the strange story of the troubled co-existence of intensely diverse and competitive societies and cultures, of which we are the more or less grateful heirs.

It is a good time in which to be a thinker about the remarkable present and the daunting future of the human world. This *Handbook* will encourage more thinkers and more thought. It could not be more timely or more necessary.

Philip Allott
Cambridge
December 2010

Preface

In 1992, Professors Philip Allott and James Crawford introduced 'The History and Theory of International Law' as an LLM course at Cambridge University, taking up the challenge of exploring the widest possible intellectual and historical background of international law. I was in a privileged position to be part of that course over the 2000/2001 academic year; its high-level and inspiring discussions highlighting the complexity of theoretical argument, coupled with voluminous sets of photocopied materials, covering thinkers and works ranging from Plato to Morgenthau, and including the actual texts of history-changing documents, provided me with the enthusiasm to engage with theoretical questions of timeless value, ultimately culminating in the preparation of this *Handbook*.

This *Handbook* brings together the scholarly input of a group of academics with an acknowledged expertise in the relevant areas of the theory and history of international law. It is also an effort conducted against the background that, despite the multiplication and diversification of theoretical scholarship of international law, there is still no such work that would locate this subject in a relatively comprehensive perspective, whether in purely legal or inter-disciplinary terms, and thus enable scholars and students to refer to it as a useful starting point for identifying and examining the relevant issues of theory and history.

This *Handbook* has also been prepared against the background that the past two or three decades have witnessed the emergence of many different theories, combining jurisprudential, socio-political and ethical approaches. One single volume obviously cannot accommodate all of them. Given that every publication format is limited, the aim is to focus on the most durable elements of international legal theory and ensure the proper representation of those theories and issues whose timeless relevance has been demonstrated through long experience.

The first part of the *Handbook* is dedicated to the essence and development of international legal theory and focuses on major theoretical developments since the era of classical scholarship of international law. The second part focuses on theorising particular branches, or areas, of international law. The third part focuses on the history of international law from the medieval age to the present day.

Given such a wide profile, this *Handbook* is intended to fill a wide doctrinal gap resulting from the lack of an equivalent contribution so far; and to provide a framework for doctrinal discourse that will enable focusing on the theory and history of international law in its complexity, as opposed to isolated treatment of individual theories or historical periods. Individual chapters provide a thoughtful and focused analysis of pertinent issues and demonstrate how international legal discourse can benefit from historical and interdisciplinary perspectives to enable us to comprehend the multiple aspects of the complex system of international law. They also provide perspectives as to the limits of such analysis and the need to focus on the legal dimension in the first place so that the legal nature of international law is not obscured. While individual chapters serve a common purpose as part of the single comprehensive scholarly effort, they are still individually pursued scholarly efforts; no homogenisation or unification of methods and approaches has been attempted. This is all the more important as the first comprehensive effort in theory and history of international law also has to benefit from its representation of the richness of multiple methods and approaches and thereby gain an enhanced importance to provide a platform for further enhancing the discourse on theory and history of international law.

A Orakhelashvili
Birmingham
August 2010

PART I

THE ESSENCE AND DEVELOPMENT OF INTERNATIONAL LEGAL THEORY

1 The relevance of theory and history – the essence and origins of international law

Alexander Orakhelashvili

1.1 LAW AND SCHOLARSHIP

The international legal argument focuses on the analysis of legal rules and instruments, and their application to facts. The ultimate aim of studying international legal theory is to understand the principal systemic and structural categories of the international legal system. Theory enables us to transcend the context of individual situations in which the international legal argument develops and to indentify general patterns that characterise this legal system in its entirety. Theory also provides a starting-point for studying international law in an interdisciplinary perspective, analysing its interaction with ethics, morality, politics, culture and economy, which include factors that influence the choice of States to accept or reject a particular rule, or decisions whether or not to comply with rules that they have accepted. These considerations cannot, however, replace those that underlie the validity of the rules in question and consequently the lawfulness of the relevant decisions. Therefore, to remain a valid exercise in international legal argument, theory has to tangibly relate to principal categories through which the international legal system operates in terms of creation, implementation and modification of international legal rules. Consequently, one of the principal tasks of theoretical analysis is to separate that part of theory which accurately reflects the nature and content of international law from that which merely constitutes a product of theoretical conjecture and of over-theorising.

Over-theorising has a significant history. As Onuf explained, in the nineteenth century 'the legal order was all the scholar saw around him, for it was an order of his own making, an artifactual order'.[1] As WE Hall observed at the end of the nineteenth century, given the 'standards so different in origin' worked out by writers 'without reference to that body of international usage which always insensibly exerts its wholesome influence whenever particular rules are under consideration, there would be almost as many distinct codes as there are writers of authority'.[2] Scholarship operated through doctrinal paradigms. Writers would 'seise on oracular pronouncements and reiterate them for generations'. Impressions would then emerge

> in the minds of those same writers that the rule exists simply because they are writing about it as if it exists. The relevant practice is largely the opinions of earlier writers, salted with the occasional instances of supportive State behaviour that have come along. Instances of contrary behaviour are dismissed in footnotes as irrelevant to the consensual view of scholars, if they are acknowledged at all.

[1] N Onuf, 'Global Law-Making and Legal Thought' in N Onuf (ed.), *Law-Making in the Global Community* (1982) 1 at 44.

[2] WE Hall, *A Treatise on International Law* (1895) 2–3.

An example is provided by what Onuf calls a putative rule on the three-mile limit of the territorial sea, adding that 'Scholars were shocked when a substantial number of States resisted codification of the three-mile limit at the Hague Codification Conference in 1930.' Then, with the bureaucratisation of foreign policy in the nineteenth century, diplomat-bureaucrats replaced writers as an integrative feature of the system, jurists began to replace writers as law-making catalysts, and codification which initially was a private affair gradually became an inter-State exercise. Thus,

> As the 1930 Hague Conference eloquently testified, scholars found not only that they could no longer make oracular law but that the oracular pronouncements of earlier centuries were not nearly so much cherished by States as they were by successive generations of scholars.[3]

Therefore, 'The chronic upheaval of the twentieth century has all but destroyed the credibility of the legal order invented by scholars. . . . Gone is the scholar's preeminent role in the articulation of a renewed legal order.'[4]

Such privileged role of scholars was due to their privileged position in addressing the audience of those who taught, researched and practised international law, or were interested in it. This enabled scholars to present, or even re-invent, international law as they deemed fit, as their philosophical, ethical, social or political convictions required. A scholar motivated by extra-legal considerations ran a greater risk of losing scholarly independence. Each generation of theorists was guided by principal theoretical categories adopted as the dominant trends of legal theory of their and preceding academic generations. Thus theory could both advance beyond the actual state of development of international law, and stay behind it. On the other hand, legal advisers whose role by definition is to advance the viewpoint of a particular government cannot always give an impartial view either. A practising lawyer can similarly be influenced by political, strategic, economic and ideological considerations, ending up with asserting legal positions or attacking established legal positions to reinforce those considerations.

The relative demise of the role of scholars has been reflected in Oscar Schachter's articulation of the theme of an 'invisible college' of international lawyers. This 'invisible college' was not meant to justify subjectivism in legal reasoning and substitution of agreement of States by a doctrinal judgment. The scholars' role was instead to ensure a representative expression of legal views that would be independent of views of particular governments, and would bring such independent legal expertise to the process of law-making, especially treaty-making. Lawyers not bound by views of a particular govern-

---

[3] Onuf in Onuf, 21–22; Gidel goes as far as to suggest that 'l'absence de possibilité d'accord sur la fixation à trois milles de la largeur de la mer territoriale démontre que la prétendue "règle des trois milles", si fréquemment mise en avant comme un axiome, ne saurait être considérée comme une règle de droit international maritime positif actuel', '*La mer territoriale et la zone contigue*', 48 *RdC* (1934) 133 at 138.

[4] Onuf in Onuf, 44–45; the ILC then superseded the scholar, Onuf, 43. Obviously, Onuf's suggestion should be qualified to the extent that in many instances the ILC codification projects ended up as multilateral treaties widely adhered to by States. To the extent these treaties apply, the need to examine State practice in detail does not arise. But this need persists where the relevant State has refused to accept a particular treaty.

ment could, even if having diverse views, form an objective legal judgment regarding international legal questions.[5]

The problem has thus invariably consisted in projecting, imagining or imitating the agency that can tell us what international law is and how it is supposed to work. The solution to this problem lies solely with understanding that there is not anyone specifically and distinctly suited to this task to the exclusion of anyone else. The real question is not 'who' but 'what', 'how' and 'why'. These real questions relate to methods and evidence as opposed to the agency – methods that require considering international law as a body of rules consensually agreed by States, placing an emphasis on evidence as opposed to perception. The over-theorising of international law is due to projecting particular legal positions as desirable or necessary whenever they suit the particular agency's interests, goals, values and ideology. The only proper remedy against over-theorising is the focus on proper ways of identifying international law – the evidence that States have indeed agreed on a particular rule or principle as binding.

The proper study and analysis of international law should therefore aim at separating legal issues from those of morality, politics, ideology and social interest. Confusing socio-political factors – based on subjective appreciation – with the analysis of legal rules inevitably leads to ignoring the basic nature of international law as the body of rules agreed upon by States. It cannot be over-emphasised that, when agreeing on rules of international law through a treaty or custom, by that very agreement States manifest their judgment as to political, ideological and social considerations attendant on the operation of the agreed rule. Doctrinal attempts to assess or re-appraise agreed rules against the background of political, social and ideological factors essentially amount to attempts to replace the judgment of States embodied in agreed rules by the writers' own judgment. The actual value of theories thus depends on the degree of their reflection of the agreed content of international law. Critical and analytical theories can usefully explain various aspects of operation of the international legal system and point to its social implications, drawbacks and options for improvement. Such theories are not, however, supposed to re-appraise, depending on the writers' political and ideological preferences, what the actual content of international law is; if they attempt to do so, they risk becoming theories for the sake of it, with little or no relevance to how the international legal system actually works.

States need certainty as to whether or not they are bound by a particular rule of international law. The line separating non-law and law is thus crucially significant. Identifying this line was not on the doctrinal agenda prior to the eighteenth century when international law was mainly explained by immemorial custom, natural law and natural reason: these can acquire or consolidate their validity by virtue of States having either observed or not contradicted their existence and relevance, notably by falling short of adopting a contrary rule or practice.[6]

The problem of non-law arises once international law is identified with consensually agreed positive law.[7] In terms of the difference between established rules of law and

---

[5] O Schachter, 'The Invisible College of International Lawyers', 72 *Northwestern University Law Review* (1977–1978), 217.

[6] A D'Amato, 'What "Counts" as Law?' in Onuf (ed.), 83 at 98.

[7] See, on multiple aspects of the relationship between law and non-law, A Orakhelashvili, *Interpretation of Acts and Rules in Public International Law* (2008), chapters 5 to 8.

aims of the legal system, Fitzmaurice has observed that law aims at ultimate justice, but achieves it indirectly, by methods the immediate object of which is 'not so much justice as such, but order, stability, certainty, and the elimination of that subjective element that cannot fail to enter into any attempt to apply justice directly, and which often vitiates it'. Law is obeyed not because it is just but because it is unjust not to obey law.[8] As Kelsen observes in a way similar to Fitzmaurice, goodness or badness of a particular behaviour depends on its compliance with the presupposed legal norm; the relevant value-judgment can only relate to the conformity with that norm. For,

> Without presupposing a general norm prescribing (or forbidding) something, we cannot make a value judgment in the objective sense of this term. The value attributed to an object is not given with the properties of this object without reference to a presupposed norm. The value is not inherent in the object judged as valuable, it is the relation of this object to a presupposed norm. . . . the question as to the highest value in the subjective sense of the term can be decided only emotionally, by the feelings or the wishes of the deciding subject. One subject may be led by his emotions to prefer personal freedom; another, social security; one, the welfare of the single individual; the other, the welfare of the whole nation. By no rational consideration can it be proved that the one is right or the other wrong.[9]

1.2 THEORETICAL OPTIONS FOR DEMONSTRATING THE LEGAL CHARACTER OF INTERNATIONAL LAW

Historically, two options have been deemed conceptually acceptable to explain international law in the society where, unlike national law, there is no government: to link international law to natural law or to deny its existence by reference to the nature of statehood and sovereignty. This dilemma had caught scholars and significantly impacted the range of intellectual choices they could adopt. John Austin denied that international law is law; some nineteenth-century scholars have insisted that international law is external public law of States (*äusseres Staatsrecht*). G-F von Martens adopted the view that this external public law was based on a pre-positive natural law which applies to State conduct before, as it were, the State enacts its positive laws. In relation to external relations with foreigners, a State as a legal person conserves its natural relations ('conserve son rapport naturel') to those who are not its members, whether other States, peoples or individuals. Therefore, natural law applies to the State's external relations (*droit public exterieur*). Such external public law is a branch of the law of nations.[10] An 'external public law' also constitutes a doctrinal construct enabling the State to unilaterally project its political, strategic, economic or ideological visions as binding international law, or its replacement.

In the alternative, Georg Jellinek has suggested the theory of self-obligation (*Selbstverpflichtung*) to explain the binding force of international law. The process of 'self-obliging' could not, however, create sustained legal rights and obligations unless

---

8 G Fitzmaurice, 'The Foundations of the Authority of International Law and the Problem of Enforcement', 19 *Modern Law Review* (1956) 1 at 12–13.

9 H Kelsen, 'The Natural-Law Doctrine before the Tribunal of Science', 2 *Western Political Quarterly* (1949) 481 at 483–485.

10 G-F Martens, *Précis du droit des gens moderne de l'Europe* (1831) 40.

something external to and independent of that 'self-obliging' would determine that it was meant to have that effect. If self-obliging were the ultimate source of international obligations, it would not be possible to objectively ascertain in relation to what that self-obligation is made; every State could then auto-interpret its 'self-obliged' commitments.

Jellinek's two initial options of analysis are either to logically deduce the existence of international law above and over States, or to establish its existence by referring to those legal concepts that are necessary for the existence of all law whether national or international. Jellinek specified the aim of his analysis as locating the existence of rules that inherently follow from the nature of international transactions. Jellinek further observes that the very nature and permissibility of treaties in international relations militated against viewing international law as external public law of States (*äusseres Staatsrecht*).[11] Jellinek's principal thesis, however, is that there can be not merely State will but such State will that can bind the State; States can arguably bind themselves in the sense that the one who obliges is identical with the one who is obliged. In order to establish this, Jellinek considers it necessary first to prove that the State can bind itself in its own legal system towards private legal entities. If the State can subject itself to itself, then it can also set the law internationally ('wenn er sich selbst unterordnen kann, ist er im Stande, sich ein Recht nach Aussen zu setzen').[12]

But Jellinek still accepted that the ultimate basis of international law, even if 'self-obliged' by States, stems from the necessities of inter-State relations, and recognised that treaties cannot have legal effect in the absence of legal rules that stand above treaties and from which treaties obtain their legal validity.[13] This anticipated the argument of Brierly and Anzilotti regarding the fundamental and non-consensual rule from which treaties derive their legal force, thereby underlining the importance of this factor for scholarly legal thought across different theoretical quarters.

Jellinek alluded to Kant that being bound by a treaty is based on the categorical imperative which is seen as an indication that States see themselves as bound.[14] Still, Jellinek's further effort to prove that States can bind themselves internationally is not that straightforward. One option is to suggest that the domestic law of obligations can be applied by analogy to the process of international treaty-making and constitute part of *jus gentium* the way it was understood in Roman law, among others as part of *naturalis ratio*. But this option stumbles at the difficulty of making analogies with principles that do not form part of the same legal system.[15] Then Jellinek demonstrates the existence of international law by reference to obvious facts that States keep agreeing internationally with each other and regard these agreements as binding, as has been manifested in the 1871 London Protocol.[16] This emphasises the relevance of agreement as the basis of international law in line with the classical consensual positivist tradition.

Jellinek's analysis illustrates how the intellectual tradition of international law of his day was caught between the pressures of visions of power politics as ultimately

---

11 G Jellinek, *Die Rechtliche Natur der Staatenverträge* (1880), iii–iv, 1.
12 Ibid., 5–7.
13 Ibid., 4.
14 Ibid., 17.
15 Ibid., 47–51.
16 Ibid., 58–59.

determinative of the outcome of legal claims, and the extreme theories of denial of international law. Jellinek's identification of his principal tasks seems to be to justify the binding force of international law through the use of intellectual categories that would be acceptable to the audience whose thinking was shaped by the nineteenth-century German scholarship of international law, as opposed to demonstrating the essence of international law in a way that would have a durable scientific value.

In England the above dilemma produced the theory of the denial of international law advocated by John Austin. This intellectual platform is to some extent curious because it relies only on part of the intellectual heritage that was available at that time: it is compatible with the vision of Hobbes who, in the absence of an international government, denies that international law is law, and with that of Pufendorf who admits the existence of international law but only as natural law because positive international law allegedly cannot exist for the very same reasons as are emphasised by Hobbes. This platform does not consider the tradition of Grotius, Wolff and Vattel, which applies the idea of law to inter-State relations, later to be voiced in the writings of JL Brierly and Hersch Lauterpacht. Thus the perspective of the particular scholarly tradition and the audience it dominates is not always necessarily the same as the actual state of the international legal system. The task of studying theory and history of international law is meant to focus more on the latter than on the former.

The principal discrepancy in Austin's reasoning relates to his identification of the nature of positive law with the need of a structural subordination through commands between the law-maker and entities to which that law applies.[17] It is however difficult to see how the positiveness of law – that is its postulation in an externally intelligible manner to repeatedly apply to facts covered by its content – inherently includes the element of subordination through command. It is right to say that such subordination is one way of creating positive law but portraying such subordination as the necessary condition for that would entail a logical and conceptual overstretch. If the point of departure is formal legitimacy, then the question of what ultimately entitles national governments to legislate for individuals over generations is not less acute than that of the ultimate basis of international law. Much as national legal systems operate through elected legislatures that often derive their authority from written or unwritten constitutions, the ultimate basis for the authority to make and enact those constitutions can also involve fictions. According to Fitzmaurice, the problem of the ultimate foundation of the binding character of law is in no way peculiar to international law. It is a general legal problem, and arises just as much with regard to national law as it does for international law. Fitzmaurice's reasoning on that point is worth pursuing at some length:

> A man is told he cannot ride a bicycle along a certain footpath. He asks why, and is told because it is forbidden by a certain by-law. He asks what is the authority for the by-law, and is told that it is made under an Act of Parliament. But if he asks what is the authority for the Act of Parliament, and what is the source of the rule that Acts of Parliament have the force of law, there is, and can be, no final answer. As Salmond says, no Statute can confer this authority on Parliament, for that would be to assume the power that has to be accounted for. Whence would that Statute itself derive its validity? No doubt the legal force of Acts of Parliament derives

---

[17] J Austin, *The Province of Jurisprudence Determined* (1954) 141–142, 201–202.

> from the Constitution, written or unwritten. But then it must be asked what is it that gives the Constitution legal force? In some countries the Constitution has itself been enacted: but what gave that enactment validity? If those who enacted it had the legal as distinct merely from the physical, power to do so, whence did they derive it, what is the rule of law that conferred the power on them, and whence did it derive its validity? And so on. Ultimately there can be no answer, or there can only be a series of answers, no one of which can be absolutely final. The reason why the difficulty is less obtrusive in the national than in the international field, is that in the national field the interim terms in the series afford a sufficiently satisfying practical basis for the obligatory force of the law to make the average person feel it unnecessary to go further – for instance, it is usually enough that the law has been enacted by the proper method, without inquiring what it is that confers legal force on enactment by that particular method. In the international field, however, there are no interim terms of quite the same kind. The absence of any patent and obvious source of obligation, such as might exist if there were an international legislature, deprives the international jurist of any manifest point at which he can rest, and which he can regard as a satisfactory terminal point beyond which there is no practical necessity to go.[18]

The difference between national and international legal reasoning is thus merely a difference in (the lack of) established clichés. The difference between legal orders is then no more than, as Brierly called it, that of social organisation.

JB Scott engaged with Austin's argument by pointing out that 'a violation of rights under the treaty would lead to a "command" from the injured State to the State guilty of the infraction'.[19] This command would be enforced not by a public authority but by public opinion. By analogy to English criminal law, Scott argued that the evil threatened is not necessarily imprisonment but social ostracism, which is in the end responsible for many individuals refraining from committing a crime.[20] The feasibility of this approach within the international legal system would stumble at major hurdles. The international legal system operates on the basis of the consensual imperative and is thus inherently pluralistic. It is difficult to find any indication of an overwhelming social opinion that would be accepted in the same way by States adhering to diverse political and economic systems. Moreover, social opinion is at times played against the law with a view to imitating an alternative to the existing legal position. One example of this relates to claims of 'humanitarian intervention'. The NATO attack on the Federal Republic of Yugoslavia in 1999 commanded a substantial socio-political support, but its legality has been rejected by the world at large, as demonstrated by the position expressed by the overwhelming majority of States.[21] An emphasis on social opinion and social ostracism actually imitates alternatives to consensual explanation of international law. The explanation of the basis of international law has instead to fit with the decentralised inter-State nature of the international legal system allowing of no possibility of States being bound without their consent.

---

18 G Fitzmaurice, 'The Foundations of the Authority of International Law and the Problem of Enforcement', 19 *Modern Law Review* (1956) 1 at 9–10.

19 JB Scott, 'The Legal Nature of International Law', 1 *AJIL* (1907) 831 at 837.

20 Ibid. at 844.

21 *Cf* Statement by the Non-Aligned States (132 States), 24 September 1999, in I Brownlie, *Principles of Public International Law* (2008) 744; Statement by the Rio Group, Letter dated 26 March 1999 from the Permanent Representative of Mexico to the United Nations addressed to the Secretary-General, A/53/884, S/1999/347, 2; see also S/PV.3988, 23 March 1999 for the positions of India and China.

If, on the other hand, Austin's reference to subordination relates to national governments having power to coerce individuals, that would place Austin's argument on the same footing with those of Hobbes. It does not seem, however, that Austin's intention was to identify the legitimacy of national legal systems with the physical power of governments to coerce individuals. The same applies essentially to HLA Hart's emphasis on 'secondary' rules[22] – Hart made no genuine effort to identify whether international law included those 'secondary' rules. As it happens, it does include them in abundance. The rules on law-making, law of treaties and law of State responsibility constitute a firm and predictable background against which substantive international legal rules can be created, interpreted, implemented and modified.

All this demonstrates that 'structural' objections to the legal character of international law, although routinely given attention in textbooks, are essentially irrelevant. The principal – and more acute – theoretical question relates to the substantive aspect of the legal character of international law, that is to its ability to consistently, predictably and indiscriminately apply to facts that its rules cover by their content. The substantive difference between international and national law has partly been projected by reliance on the structural difference between national and international law. The perception that the validity of international law differs from that of national law was articulated as early as by Bentham, claiming that 'a treaty between two nations is an obligation which cannot possess the same force as a contract between two individuals'. Custom and treaty in inter-State relations could thus be denoted as law only 'by extending the meaning of the term, and by metaphor', for the organisation on which they were premised was defective and incomplete.[23] Therefore, unless the legal nature of international law is located in its substantive as opposed to structural aspect, its binding force cannot be explained at all and Austin's objections to the legal character of international law become insurmountable.

The legal character of international law cannot thus be explained by factors external to the overall nature of law. International law being grounded in the agreement between States must be good enough to explain the validity and legal character of this legal system, for this approach essentially focuses on the inherent value that the expression of will and agreement of States has. This approach is premised on the inherency of international law in inter-State relations to enable States to properly conduct their business, but it also stresses that being inherent that way, international law is also consensual. Its consensual nature is, in the end, the rationale for its inherency. As Fitzmaurice observed, 'If law is *necessary*, that necessity must lie precisely in the need for *obligatory* rules as between members of a society, and it would involve an inherent contradiction to propound law as necessary, if it was not also necessarily binding.'[24]

The above Benthamite perception of international law being less law due to its structural background has been widely held by international law scholars over a long period of time, until the fallacy of this myth was exposed by JL Brierly and Hersch Lauterpacht.[25] Lauterpacht warned against identifying the conception of law exclusively with more

---

22 HLA Hart, *The Concept of Law* (1961) 209.

23 Quoted in JB Scott, 'The Legal Nature of International Law', 1 *AJIL* (1907) 831 at 834.

24 Fitzmaurice, *MLR*, 11 (emphasis original).

25 On which see, in general, A Orakhelashvili, *The Interpretation of Acts and Rules in Public International Law* (2008) chapter 1.

'developed' legal systems, and provided for a consistent doctrinal approach demonstrating the full-fledged legal character of international law through the thesis of completeness and effectiveness of international legal regulation.[26] Lauterpacht's core argument is that international law may be structurally different but it is not less law than is national law. Lauterpacht never tried to re-appraise or re-invent the fundamentals of international law; he took international law as he found it. The distinctive impact of his scholarship is that he discerned and identified the pertinent elements of this legal system in a more complex way and thus better than many other preceding or contemporary scholars.

Brierly's remedy against the absence of centralised law-making and law-enforcement machinery is to appeal to extra-consensual factors, to some extent natural law, for addressing the issue of imperfection and incompleteness of international law. It was true that a new rule of international law could not be imposed on a dissentient State by any process compatible with the legislative act which imposes a rule of law on a dissentient individual within the State. But this was a difference, however, merely of social organisation.[27] Brierly's analysis also emphasises the extra-consensual principle of *pacta sunt servanda* as the basis on which international law binds States along with the consensual pattern. There is thus an inherent extra-consensual rule that validates the essence and binding force of international law as consensually agreed rules. If such extra-consensual rule was lacking, the consensually agreed international law would also lack binding force.

The question then arises as to the basis of validity of this extra-consensual rule – what makes it so inherent in the nature of the society of States: is this the nature of this society, nature of States, or simply the fact that States accept it? This question obviously has implications for the discourse as to the relationship between naturalism and positivism. But the question is how to justify the inherency of international law in the society of States which is pluralistic and hence divided along with the political and ideological differences between States, there being no ideology common to the entire world, no generally accepted socio-ideological basis on which the goodness or badness of States and their conduct could as such be determined. For the consensual foundation of international law is necessarily premised on the sameness of the legal capacity of States.

Kelsen draws on Pufendorf's thesis that the law of nature can be identified by reference to the nature, condition and desires of human beings, but that men are often malicious, petulant and perverse and think that they can secure greater good from the violation than from the observance of law.[28] Kelsen asks how the law of nature could then be deduced from the nature of man, and clarifies that

> It is not from the nature of man as it actually is that Pufendorf – and all other writers – deduce what they consider to be the natural law; it is from the nature of man as it should be, and as it would be if it would correspond to the natural law. It is not the law of nature which is deduced from the nature, the real nature, of man, it is the nature of man, an ideal nature of man, which is deduced from a natural law presupposed in some way or another.[29]

---

26 H Lauterpacht, *The Function of Law in the International Community* (1933) 433; for analysis see Orakhelashvili (2008), chapter 1.

27 JL Brierly, *The Basis of Obligation in International Law* (1958) 10–14, 16–17.

28 Pufendorf, Book VII, quoted in Kelsen, 487.

29 Kelsen, 487–488.

This produces a conceptual dilemma, requiring identifying the ways that would explain the inherency of international law. One way is Kant's categorical imperative, requiring men to act the way that one would like to see becoming universal law, and reinforces the principle of the legal equality of States based on the reciprocity of rights and obligations. This has further been expressed in Vattel's Golden Rule of Sovereigns, which requires that States treat other States the way they wish to be treated themselves. In other words, the key is not whether one wants to behave in a particular way but whether one wants to see the same conduct performed in relation to oneself. On the basis of reciprocity inherent to the categorical imperative, it is States who decide what they want to see done to them and therefore give or withhold consent in relation to creating international legal rules. This refers not to reciprocity in terms of what States actually do to each other, but reciprocity as a normative principle requiring that States do to others what they desire to be done to them. If this is taken as a premise, then Pufendorf's emphasis on desires and interests of States as the basis for natural law can be understood the way that could reinforce the inherency of international law grounded on legal equality of States. International law can thus be seen as a legal system based on reciprocity and consent.

It is, however, not impossible to interpret Pufendorf's thesis as ultimately pointing to the propensity of States to enforce their political and ideological agenda just because this is required by their interest and nature. Ideological inputs into the international legal reasoning would thus be premised on some being better than others and thus being entitled to enforce their interest, ideology and political agenda even by using means that they would never wish to be applied to themselves. This then points to theories of exclusivity and domination from 'European international law' to modern liberalism, premised on the postulate that some States are better than others;[30] they can therefore be excused with violating international law if their superior cause so requires. If international law is a body of rules agreed upon as between States, such theories can have no validity.

1.3 NATURAL LAW AND POSITIVE LAW

If, as demonstrated, international law is a body of consensually agreed rules, the relevance of natural law can be examined only against that background. Natural law may be unpopular in some quarters, which may also serve as a deterrent for its doctrinal use. But, as Kelsen observed,

> The reason why the natural-law doctrine, in spite of its obvious fallacies, has had, and probably always will have, great influence on social thinking is that it satisfies a deeply rooted need of the human mind, the need for justification.[31]

The need for the ultimate – and extra-consensual – justification of international law has also been reflected in Brierly's fundamental norm and to some extent in Kelsen's own *Grundnorm*.

The doctrinal understanding of positivism varies according to a theoretical framework:

---

[30] See on this Chapter 11 below.

[31] H Kelsen, 'The Natural-Law Doctrine before the Tribunal of Science', 2 *Western Political Quarterly* (1949) 481 at 501.

it can refer to the importance of sanctions, or to the Austinian 'command' theory. D'Amato describes the essence of positivism in existential, and prejudicial, terms, claiming that 'a legal positivist believes that a rule is or is not a rule of law, and if it is a rule of law, then what it commands, however absurdly, gives rise to a legal obligation'. In this context, D'Amato links the positivist–naturalist dichotomy to the problem of interpretation. A court believing in naturalism would correct a meaningless provision in a statute, while a 'positivist' court would enforce the statute as it stands, as only the legislature can 'remedy the mischief'. Such 'pragmatic' approach specifies that a naturalist is a human interpreter of law; law is not as much an aim for itself but a means towards the attainment of human ends. Natural law, according to D'Amato, combines two great substantive principles: survival of the human race and justice to individuals. Any artificial entity, such as a State, standing in the way of the attainment of these goals is contrary to natural law.[32] But this approach does not clarify who determines what the 'human ends' in question are; these 'human ends' can be seen as a policy-oriented '*Grundnorm*' to deny the consensual foundations of international law.

This approach construes naturalism as referring to anything that is not positive law, including political, social and ideological considerations. Natural law has been used, expressly or impliedly, to describe anything that opposes consensual positivism – from George Scelle's social interest theory to the New Haven policy-oriented school. But this is a perverted meaning of naturalism. Its genuine meaning focuses not on interests, policies or ideologies, but on elements that are inherent to the legal system in question; it is not about using extra-legal, above all political, argument to adversely affect the legal reasoning and justify deviation from positive law, but instead aims to clarify the basis of that very legal argument by focusing on fundamentals of the relevant legal system.[33]

Confusion could also ensue to identify 'standards of review' of positive laws on the basis of natural law. What is the threshold warranting the intervention of natural law? Should the 'reviewable' positive law be meaningless, unworkable, immoral, unethical, self-contradictory, undesirable, unsound, or merely something that could be improved? Writers adhering to such 'remedial' and interventionist doctrine of natural law have not provided a clear answer to this question.

1.4 DEVELOPMENT OF THE NATURAL LAW THEORY

Ius gentium derives from natural law as established by the natural reason among all nations. To illustrate this natural reason, Vitoria actually referred to whatever is widely practised by all nations, such as treating strangers humanely. In the beginning of the world, when all things were held in common, everyone was allowed to visit and travel through any land, which intercourse was not intended to be suppressed through the establishment of national boundaries.[34] As explained, Vitoria took the conception of

---

[32] D'Amato, 'What "Counts" As Law?' 88–91.

[33] See for detail of such aspects of natural law, Orakhelashvili (2008), chapter 3.

[34] F de Vitoria, '*De Indis*' in A Pagden and J Lawrence, *Francisco de Vitoria – Political Writings* (1991) 278.

ius gentium from the Roman jurisprudence and applied it to the relations of peoples. International law was the body of rules which natural reason had established between all nations. However, natural law is now associated not with the human nature but with the rules allegedly established by nature to deal with relations between nations (*inter omnes gentes*). This constituted a fundamental departure from older versions of natural law. *Ius gentium* means the law of nations; *ius inter gentes* means the law between nations; international society is then a *societas naturalis gentium*. This implies a recognition, at one time, of the independence and of the interdependence of States, and of their reciprocal rights and obligations. It points to the existence of a juridical tie between nations, which constitute an international society, to the inherency of international law to international society along the lines of the maxim *ubi societas ibi ius*. This interdependence then entails the limits on sovereign powers of States. The underlying philosophy is the same as that of the transition from the 'state of nature' to 'social contract'. The formation of national groups on more clearly defined territories does not imply the intention of these nations to suppress all intercourse natural to men; the 'rights' incidental to the state of nature are thus preserved and perpetuated.[35]

Vitoria reasons from the viewpoint of universality in explaining why Spaniards can travel to the countries of native Indians. As 'it would not be lawful for the French to prohibit Spaniards from travelling or even living in France, so long as it caused no sort of harm themselves; therefore it is not lawful for barbarians either'. Similarly, 'barbarians themselves admit all sorts of other barbarians from elsewhere, and would therefore do wrong if they did not admit Spaniards'. Barbarians cannot prohibit Christians to trade with them any more than Christians can do that to other Christians. All that would be against natural and divine law. A human enactment (*lex*) to that effect would also contradict natural law, and on that account be inhumane, unreasonable and without force of law.[36] This illustrates an early statement of natural law as the body of principles that controls, *in toto*, the substance that positive law can permissibly and validly have. Such substantive view of natural law sees it as shadowing the process of positive law-making. At the same time, Vitoria opposes any cultural or religious exclusivity to impact any legal position, and subscribes to the universality of international law, by way of articulating an early version of natural law as the basis of international law, if the latter is to apply to inter-State relations.

Suarez drew a clear distinction between natural law and *ius gentium*. Natural law is based on the necessity following solely from the nature of the case, while *ius gentium* derives from some other source. *Ius gentium* does not prohibit things because they are evil, but renders them evil by prohibiting them. *Ius gentium* is therefore positive and human.[37] This mirrors the modern distinction between natural law and positive law.

However, Suarez then distinguishes between natural law and *ius gentium* the way that the latter 'came into existence not through [natural] evidence but through probable

---

[35] C Phillipson, 'Franciscus a Victoria (1480–1546). International Law and War', 15 *Journal of the Society of Comparative Legislation* (1917) 175 at 180–181.

[36] Vitoria, 278–280.

[37] F Suarez, '*De legibus, ac deo legislatore* (1612)' in G Williams *et al.*, *Selections from Three Works of F Suarez* (Volume ii, 1944) 342, 344.

inferences and the common judgment of mankind'.[38] It is not immediately clear whether this is the same common judgment of mankind that has to acknowledge the content of natural law.

In 1753 the British Government in its communication to the Prussian Government specified that 'The Law of Nations [is] founded upon justice, equity, convenience, and the reason of the thing, and confirmed by long usage.'[39] This is similar to the approach of Pufendorf in that the natural reason is the basis of international law, further reflected in the long usage.[40] There is no obvious emphasis on State consent. It is noteworthy that this position is expressed in the historical period dominated by nationalism, sovereignty and tradition of the *raison d'Etat*.

The premise inevitably underlying the British statement is that there is such 'justice, equity, convenience, and the reason of the thing' that Britain is relying on and at the same time it will be intelligible and acceptable for Prussia. Much as natural law is conceptually derived from a transcendent reason and justice, in the context of the international system it necessarily requires the reliance on such principles of reason and justice as will be both objectively intelligible to States that have different national interest and political tradition, and also be such as to be subjectively understood by those States as constituting the basis of reason and justice that underlies natural law. As is clear from Vitoria's reasoning, the natural law of nations is the one that suits the nature of the inter-State society; if so, then it must be the natural law that States understand and acknowledge in their mutual intercourse, in relation to which they have a shared understanding.

One way of comprehending natural law from this perspective is to focus on principles underlying multiple national legal systems, as partly reinforce the concept of 'general principles of law' under Article 38(1)(c) of the International Court's Statute. If States accept and apply the principles in question in their own legal systems, they thus recognise that these are just and reasonable. This in fact sounds similar to Jellinek's 'self-obligation' argument, which referred to States binding themselves, towards private entities, in their own national legal systems. As FA Mann has pointed out, a principle is a general one if it is being applied by most representative systems of municipal law; the general principles are determined and defined by comparative law.[41] FA Mann further develops the notion of a commercial law of nations that can arguably be explained partly by transnational natural law as articulated by Lord Asquith, and partly as a modern version of *jus gentium* as was known in ancient Rome.[42]

But this approach leaves two questions unresolved. In the material sense, principles accepted in domestic legal systems may not always be indicative of what the international legal position is. In the formal sense, 'general principles of law' include not only principles accepted *in foro domestico* but also those that relate to the international system and inter-State relations. This, then, transfers the whole reasoning from the area of justice and reasonableness into that of evidence and requires referring to and understanding the attitudes of States in their mutual relations. The principal tools international law is

---

38 Suarez, 344.
39 R Phillimore, *Commentaries upon International Law* (I 1879) 15.
40 See below Chapter 4.
41 FA Mann, 'Reflections on a Commercial Law of Nations', 33 *BYIL* (1957) 20 at 36–38.
42 Mann (1957), 40.

familiar with in this sense are State practice, whereby States act and react, and *opinio juris*, whereby States manifest their positions as to the legality or illegality of particular acts or practices. Once, then, the natural law reasoning would be moved into the area of evidence, it would stumble at the fact that there is no other tool to infer the judgment of States as to the propriety, justice and legitimacy of particular rules, acts and practices other than State practice and *opinio juris*, which constitute the basis of customary international law. Imagining tools alternative to these is simply not feasible.

From here, the reasoning can be conducted by asking two questions. In the first place, is natural law simply another version of customary law? In the second place, how necessary is the requirement of *opinio juris* for the formation of customary law and if it is, to what does it give an expression – to agreement of States, or merely manifests the acknowledgment by States of some inherent natural justice and reason? To answer these questions, the precise essence of *opinio juris* as part of custom-generation must be identified.[43]

This conceptual problem can also be resolved by identifying the proper scope of relevance of natural law in the international legal system, that is in a way consistent with the consensual foundations of this legal system. As Kelsen specifies, if 'natural law is considered to be a system of substantive rules, not a formalistic authorization of any positive law, then the contradiction between a human nature from which this natural law is deduced and a human nature which makes positive law necessary is inevitable'.[44]

The relationship between natural law and positive law has been handled by the international law doctrine for a very long time. Inter-State relations are, according to Phillimore, governed 'partly by Divine, and partly by positive law. Divine Law is either (1) that which is written by the finger of God on the heart of man, when it is called Natural Law; or (2) that which has been miraculously made known to him, when it is called revealed, or Christian law.' Furthermore, 'it is of great practical importance to mark the subordination of the law derived from the consent of States to the law derived from God'.[45] Phillimore used his natural law approach to justify the universality of international law and to demonstrate that international law applied both to the European and non-European world:

> whenever communities come into contact with each other, before usage or custom has ripened into a quasi contract, and before positive compacts have sprung up between them, their intercourse is subject to a Law. . . . if the precepts of Natural Law are obligatory upon Heathen States in their intercourse with each other, much more are they binding upon Christian Governments in their intercourse with Heathen States.[46]

Even more pertinently, it was 'clear that the occasional vicious practice cannot affect the reality of the permanent duty'.[47] Furthermore, natural law sets limits to positive law-making:

---

[43] This cannot feasibly be done here; see instead A Orakhelashvili, 'Natural Law and Customary Law', 69 *ZaöRV* (2008) 61–100.

[44] Kelsen, 486.

[45] Phillimore, *Commentaries upon International Law* I (1879) 15.

[46] Ibid., 20–22.

[47] Ibid., 23.

> the Law derived from the consent of Christian States is restricted in its operation by the Divine Law; and just as it is not morally competent to any individual State to make laws which are at variance with the law of God, whether natural or revealed, so neither is it morally competent to any assemblage of States to make treaties or adopt customs which contravene that Law. Positive Law, whether National or International, being only declaratory, may add to, but cannot take from the prohibitions of Divinc Law.[48]

WE Hall posed the question as to whether there is 'an absolute right, applicable to human relations', whether deriving from the law of God or 'law of nature inductively reached', or 'erected metaphysically'.[49] States, however, are independent beings, subject to no superior. No 'person or body of persons exists to whom authority has been delegated to declare law for the common good; a state is only bound by rules to which it feels itself obliged in conscience after reasonable examination to submit'. A transcendent absolute right 'can only be a source of confusion and mischief when it is regarded as a test of the legal value of existing practices'.[50]

Having ascertained that much, Hall then proceeds to examine the nature of 'usages' which constitute international law, and observes that

> A large part of international usage gives effect to principles which represent facts of state existence, essential under the conditions of modern civilised state life. . . . Another portion of international usage gives effect to certain moral obligations, which are recognised as being the source of legal rules with the same unanimity as marks opinion with respect to the facts of state existence. No third basis of legislation can be found of such solid value as are the essential facts of existence of a society and the moral principles to which that society feels itself obliged to give legal effect. Of both the foregoing kinds of usage, therefore, it can be affirmed unhesitatingly that they possess a much higher authority than any other part of international law.[51]

This sounds like a postulation of the 'absolute right' which Hall has just rejected, and moreover the attribution to that 'absolute right' of a greater normative force than positive law can possess. Hall therefore rejects natural law in a principled sense, but essentially offers a covert natural law reasoning ridden by socio-ideological underpinnings that the author in question professes and upholds. Hall is not a positivist, as his reasoning consistently avoids an emphasis on consent, agreement of States; instead of custom he speaks of 'usage' expressing the pre-existing superior principles.

While both Hall and Phillimore profess that natural law reasoning can influence the state of positive law, none of them go as far, expressly at least, as Lorimer in advocating the role of doctrine in shaping the content and legal force of international law. Lorimer refers to 'the branch of positive law which we call the law of nations', but then asserts that 'the law of nations is the law of nature, realised in the relations of separate political communities'.[52] Given that enforcing international law in the absence of a central government and judiciary involves difficulties,

---

48 Ibid., 26.
49 WE Hall, *A Treatise on International Law* (1895) 2–3.
50 Hall, 4–5.
51 Hall, 6.
52 J Lorimer, *The Institutes of the Law of Nations* (1883) volume I, 19.

> Natural law, in this, as in the other departments of positive law, would then retreat into the arsenal or the armoury of jurisprudence, and the jurist would not be called upon to wield it in his daily work, but only when, in the higher capacity of a scientific discoverer, he sought to indicate what was amiss, or as a legislator to supply what was defective in the positive system which it was his business to expound, to administer, or to reform.
>
> But the case is very different where the object of the law is itself indefinite or disputed, where its general doctrines have as yet no fixed and recognised meaning, and where the questions which arise are not questions of means but questions of ends. Here, unless practice be contented to wait indefinitely on the terrible and often unintelligible teaching of experience, it must still invoke the aid of theory: the positive international jurist has no firm standing-ground of his own: there is no progressive or consistent history to record, and the day for dogmatism has not yet arrived.
>
> These considerations explain to us the exceptional dependence of the law of nations on the law of nature. In dealing with the law of nations, the jurist has always a preliminary function to perform, and as it is natural law that determines the objects of positive law in all its departments, the function is one which he can perform only by keeping it steadily in view.[53]

International law is thus presented as an underdeveloped legal system where the proper use of the evidentiary legal method has to be deemed unhelpful. The doctrinally projected indeterminacy of the actual legal position has then, according to Lorimer, to be remedied through ideological inputs. Consequently, according to Lorimer, there can 'be little question of the justice of the opinion which regards the law of nations rather as a branch of scientific inquiry than as a discovered system, or of the prudence of the academical arrangement which maintains its connection with natural law'.[54] Lorimer's 'natural law' has no revealed or demonstrated systemic dimension – it is instead a product of the writer's subjective appreciation. This essentially amounts to a denial of international law as a system of positive rules and insistence of the relevance of ideology coated as 'natural law' to explain the rights and obligations of States.

This approach is further reflected in Lorimer's treatment of sources of international law. Customary law would matter only if consistent with the doctrinally projected natural law.[55] Therefore, Lorimer asserts that:

> There is no direction in which it is more necessary that we should keep the subjective channel to natural law distinctly before us than when we are called upon to distinguish between good and bad customs, because customs themselves claim to be objective witnesses to the very law by which their qualities must be tested.[56]

Permanent laws of human nature have predominant importance, and 'a custom, or a treaty, which is at variance with these laws, offers no contribution to the positive law of nations in the absolute or scientific sense'.[57] Ideological, social and political views ultimately constitute criteria against which the relevance and propriety of international law should be judged, and those rules of international law which are at variance with those theory-imposed criteria – albeit being based on proper sources of international law – have to be treated as irrelevant. The outcome is thus that the sources of positive law do not

---

53 Ibid., 21–22.
54 Ibid., 26.
55 Ibid., 32–34.
56 Ibid., 34–35.
57 Ibid., 54–55.

contribute to positive law, and consistently a theorist could arrogate to himself a power to declare the relevant positive law as irrelevant, or redefine it in terms of social, political or ideological premises which he represents.

The idea of positive law reflecting natural or generally binding law was also put forward by JC Bluntschli. When civilised States assemble at international congresses, they intend not to enact treaty law that binds its signatories, but general legal norms, above all for the European world to be respected by all European States. They do not wish to create voluntary law (*Willkürrecht*) but to acknowledge the necessary law (*notwendiges Recht*) that is grounded in the nature of legal relations and in duties of civilised nations towards humanity as a whole ('. . . ein notwendiges Recht anerkennen, welches in der Natur der Verhältnisse und in den Pflichten der civilisirten Völker gegen die Menschheit seine eigene Begründung hat').[58]

The perusal of doctrinal views thus expresses the insoluble contradiction between the consensual positivist background of international law and such version of natural law as imagines substantive legal regulation shadowing, replacing or prevailing upon the rules and principles of consensually agreed positive law. Kelsen has therefore got it absolutely right 'That the natural-law doctrine, as it pretends, is able to determine in an objective way what is just, is a lie.'[59]

1.5 THE ORIGINS OF INTERNATIONAL LAW AND THE HISTORICAL SCOPE OF THE INTERNATIONAL LEGAL SYSTEM

For a long time, international legal scholarship has been dominated by the perception that international law has been developed in the Western World and then exported to other places, above all Asia. The analysis of doctrine from Vitoria onwards above has demonstrated that the classical tradition of international law has never contemplated that international law was essentially European, still less that States should have different rights and obligations depending on the region they belong to. The ideology of 'European international law' emerged and became dominant in the nineteenth century to provide the ideological legitimacy to the agenda of colonisation. This ideology chose not to focus on international legal relations that have over the centuries been conducted between European and non-European States on the basis of the international legal system that all of them shared, and instead propagated the cultural and racial superiority of Europeans over non-Europeans that ideologically justified the colonisation and annexation of the latter by the former.[60]

International relations theory has also been influenced by the idea that international society has initially been Western, and then expanded to the East, bringing to the East the frameworks of international relations including international law. International law

---

58 J-C Bluntschli, *Das moderne Völkerrecht der civilisirten Staaten* (1868) 4–5.

59 Kelsen, 513.

60 For detail see A Orakhelashvili, 'The Idea of "European International Law"', 17 *EJIL* (2006) 315.

thus exported, so Adam Watson claimed, has ensured that the relations between States would be predictable.[61] Much as doctrinally influential, such views have constituted a fallacy, always asserted without confronting the evidence accumulated in the centuries-long experience. As Brownlie has aptly observed, 'It is the current cliché to say that the law of nations has been "europocentric" in nature. In a long retrospect this is true but only in the sense that *it happened* that a certain group of States were to become politically dominant in the world as a whole. This is a fact and not a qualitative assertion.'[62] The actual history of international law demonstrates that there has been nothing inherently European in its development. First instruments and institutions of international law identified so far originate from outside Europe. Sumer cities in the third and second millennia BC had a system of treaty law and recognised the immunities of diplomatic representatives.[63] The Treaty between the Kingdoms of Lagash and Umma, concluded near 2500 BC, established boundaries between Lagash and Umma, as well as providing for arbitration on possible differences, and designated the ruler of a third country as an arbitrator. The Treaty of friendship between Lagash and Uruk was concluded in the same period.[64]

The wars in the ancient Middle East brought about a treaty system among the regional powers whereby they terminated wars, concluded peace and apportioned spheres of influence among themselves. Such a treaty was concluded between the Hittite Kingdom and the Rulers of Amuru and provided for the mutual trade embargo against Assyrians.[65] Middle Eastern powers also had reciprocal treaty obligations regarding extradition of political prisoners such as, for example, the treaty concluded in the fourteenth century BC between the Hittites and the Happala Kingdom.[66] Treaties between Egypt and the Hittite Kingdom in 1354 and 1312 BC dealt with the division and allocation of the spheres of influence.[67]

The wars between the Hittite Kingdom and Egypt at the end of the fourteenth century BC ended with the 1280 Peace Treaty which was a quite complex arrangement covering the several fields of international legal cooperation as well as reciprocal respect for the interests of the two States. The Treaty divided the spheres of influence, established a military alliance between the two States, and provided for the reciprocal obligation to provide military assistance against the external enemy or rebels. Refugees and border trespassers were to be extradited but not punished after extradition. These treaty obligations were laid down as reciprocal obligations.[68] No doubt, such treaties embodied full-fledged legal

---

[61] A Watson, 'European International Society and Its Expansion' in H Bull and A Watson (eds), *The Expansion of International Society* (1985) 13 at 24.

[62] I Brownlie, 'The Expansion of International Society: The Consequences for the Law of Nations' in Bull and Watson (eds), 357 at 358 (emphasis original), further illustrating by examples that the range of States engaged in the international legal system in the seventeenth to eighteenth centuries proves the illusory nature of 'European international law'.

[63] D Bederman, *International Law in Antiquity* (2001) 23.

[64] Wegner, *Geschichte des Völkerrechts* (1936) 2; Ziegler, *Völkerrechtsgeschichte* (1994) 15; Bederman, 139–140.

[65] Wegner, 2; Bederman, 145.

[66] Wegner, 3.

[67] Bederman, 27.

[68] Wegner, 4–5; Verdross, 35; for a detailed analysis see Bederman, 28, 146–150.

obligations providing for legal certainty in inter-State relations, in which the States concerned could place confidence.

Ancient China, from the eighth century BC onwards, was familiar with international law and extensively conducted treaty relations; hundreds of treaties were concluded in that period. The legal system then and there was familiar with nearly the whole field of the modern law of treaties, and placed predominant emphasis on the principle of good faith. Wang Tieya poses the question whether this system can be properly called international law, given that in that period the whole of China was united under the rule of the Qin Emperor.[69] Those structural factors notwithstanding, however, the evidence adduced by Wang Tieya himself clearly demonstrates that the Chinese political world was familiar with international law as a system, much as it had to apply to such inter-State relations that cannot straightforwardly be seen as based on sovereign equality and independence of States. The idea of law was still there and operated through specific rules applicable to the making, operation, termination and violation of treaties. These rules operated in the Chinese political world without having been imported into it from elsewhere.

A similar legal environment persisted in the Middle Ages, as evidenced by Chinese treaty practice. The 783 Treaty of Peace, Friendship and Border between China and Tibet provided for Chinese territorial cessions to Tibet. This was reaffirmed in the 822 Treaty between China and Tibet which recognised the equality of both parties as international legal persons. The common legal conviction of both parties as to the binding force of such treaties is recorded. They pledged to observe the agreement and transfer it to future generations. Most impressively, the 783 Treaty provided that if any party, Tibet or China, acts in breach of the Treaty, then nothing that the other party undertakes for retaliation shall be viewed as a breach of the Treaty.[70] This is an amazing anticipation of the modern law regarding the reciprocal non-compliance with treaty obligations, either as a matter of the law of treaties as embodied in Article 60 of the 1969 Vienna Convention on the Law of Treaties regarding the reciprocal termination of a treaty in case of material breach, or as a matter of counter-measures in the law of State responsibility.

Chinese treaty practice in the eleventh to thirteenth centuries included treaties dealing with a variety of international legal issues from extradition to territorial arrangements, such as the 1005 Peace Treaty between Sung and Kitan or the 1142 Peace Treaty between Chin and Sung.[71]

Wang Tieya has raised the question regarding the introduction of international law into China from the seventeenth century onwards, focusing on translation into Chinese of international law works written by Suarez, Vattel, Wheaton and others.[72] But this was merely a process of introducing to the Chinese the Western writings of international law, which is not the same as introducing to them international law as a body of rules applicable to inter-State relations the Chinese had not hitherto been familiar with.

In terms of treaty-making, China had intensive treaty relations outside the context of 'European international law'. As illustrated,

---

69 Wang Tieya, 'International Law in China: Historical and Contemporary Perspectives', 221 *RdC* (1990) 195 at 212–213.

70 Preisner, *Frühe Völkerrechtliche Ordnungen der Aussereuropäischen Welt* (1976) 175–178.

71 Ibid., 178–182.

72 Wang Tieya, 226–231.

> More than 150 years before the Treaty of Nanjing was signed, China had concluded the first modern treaty with Imperial Russia, the Treaty of Nerchinsk, in 1689, delimiting certain portions of the boundary between the two countries. After that treaty, several others had followed, among which were the Kiahta Boundary Treaty of 1727, the Supplementary Treaty of Kiahta of 1768 and the Protocol relating to trade at Kiahta of 1792. These treaties of the pre-Nanjing Treaty period, from the end of the seventeeth century to the end of the eighteenth century, were concerned mainly with border problems: the demarcation of boundaries, the border system, etc. They were principally equal in nature.[73]

The implication is that the treaties concluded in the Opium War period in the nineteenth century did not manifest any distinctly new era of bringing China into the international legal system.[74]

Examples both from the ancient period and the Middle Ages could be further multiplied. But the above is sufficient to demonstrate that the international legal system has always been premised on universality, whether in terms of natural or positive law.

[73] Ibid., 238.
[74] See on this Chapter 4 below, and see further Orakhelashvili, 17 *EJIL* (2006) 315.

2 Early-modern scholarship on international law

Alain Wijffels

The development of international law scholarship from the 16th until the 18th century can be attributed to different changes in a wider context[1]. One major factor was the continuing development of legal scholarship in general, which, on the European continent, maintained its roots in the civil law tradition[2]. Another was the establishment of the territorial sovereign state as the new paradigm of political power. In both cases, the influence was incremental: early-modern legal scholarship evolved from late-medieval legal methods, and, similarly, the early-modern state retained until the end of the *Ancien Régime* many

[1] Most general surveys on the history of international law include sections on international law scholarship, sometimes in greater detail than in the present chapter. Among the older works which are still quoted: A. Nussbaum, *A Concise History of the Law of Nations*, New York, The Macmillan Company, 1954 (revised edn.); *History of International Law* in *Encyclopedia of Public International Law*, Amsterdam, New York, Oxford, North Holland, 1984, vol. 7, esp. the entries on 'History of the Law of Nations: Ancient Times to 1648', and 'History of the Law of Nations: 1648 to 1815', pp. 132–179; A.C.G.M. Eyffinger (ed.), *Compendium rechtsgeschiedenis*, Deventer, Kluwer, 1991 (2nd edn.); W.G. Grewe, *The Epochs of International Law. Translated and revised by Michael Byers*, Berlin, New York, Walter de Gruyter, 2000 (based on the older, original version in German). More recent surveys include: C. Focarelli, *Lezioni di Storia del Diritto internazionale*, Perugia, Morlacchi Editore, 2002; S. Laghmani, *Histoire du droit des gens du jus gentium impérial au jus publicum europaeum*, Paris, Éditions A. Pedone, 2003; D. Gaurier, *Histoire du droit international. Auteurs, doctrines et développement de l'Antiquité à l'aube de la période contemporaine*, Rennes, Presses Universitaires de l'Université de Rennes, 2005; and perhaps the most useful, a brief but comprehensive textbook including a wealth of bibliographical references both to primary and secondary sources: K.-H. Ziegler, *Völkerrechtsgeschichte. Ein Studienbuch*, Munich, Verlag C.G. Beck, 2007 (2nd edn.); see also several articles by the same author, collected in one volume: *Fata iuris gentium*, Baden-Baden, Nomos Verlag, 2008. (The multi-volume *opus magnum* by J.H.W. Verzijl, *International Law in Historical Perspective*, considers international law by subject-matter and is less useful for a specific discussion of scholarship and its development.) See also the useful bibliography offered by P. Macalister-Smith and J. Schwietzke, 'Literature and Documentary Sources Relating to the History of Public International Law: A Bibliographical Survey', JHIL 1999, 136–212. Throughout this chapter, the abbreviation JHIL stands for *Journal of the History of International Law*.

[2] In the present contribution, only Western international law scholarship, mainly anchored in civil law scholarship, will be considered, and specifically from the internal vantage-point of the early-modern developments of that scholarship. This entails, for example, that it will not be envisaged as a specific Western, or 'Christian' scholarship, in contrast to other traditions. For a different perspective, see (e.g.) C.A. Stumpf, 'Christian and Islamic Traditions of Public International Law', JHIL 2005, 69–80. To readers who prefer a thematic approach to international law, where scholarship is only one of the (often, minor) sources, two recent monographs by S.C. Neff should be recommended: *War and the Law of Nations. A General History*, Cambridge, Cambridge University Press, 2005; *The Rights and Duties of Neutrals. A General History*, Manchester, Manchester University Press, Juris Publishing, 2000. For an analysis from the vantage-point of the theory of international relations: R. Tuck, *The Rights of War and Peace, Political Thought and the International Order From Grotius to Kant*, Oxford, Oxford University Press, 1999.

features and institutions inherited from the medieval political order. Around 1500, legal scholarship throughout Western Europe[3] – including in the English universities – was still governed by the 'Italian method' (*mos italicus*) and produced, in Italy and beyond, a mass of legal literature based on a methodology which was followed in the teaching in the law faculties and in legal practice, wherever graduates of law faculties were admitted as counsel or were appointed as judges. The Italian method maintained its hold on university-educated lawyers until the late 16th and early 17th centuries as the mainstream approach to legal reasoning and arguments in most universities and in civil law courts. Until the first years of the 17th century, it also continued to be, if not an innovative, at least a living tradition. Many of the great works of reference, such as the Accursian Gloss, some of the authoritative commentaries, collections of consultations and other legal literature produced between the mid 13th and the late 15th century, remained in print until 1600 and beyond. Throughout the 16th century, new, often less authoritative, epigones were writing and publishing works following closely the Italian method's standards. The 16th century also saw the rise of legal humanism, which produced its own new genres in legal literature, often highly critical of the Italian method and its canons. Legal humanism succeeded in eroding the authority of the Italian method by restoring an historically more authentic reading of the main collections of Roman law and by establishing that many of the doctrines of the late-medieval authors were founded on an erroneous reading or interpretation of the Roman law texts. However, it does not appear that legal humanism managed to replace the Italian method as the mainstream approach among lawyers: it gained some strongholds in a few universities and inspired some highly productive and influential authors; it changed the outlook of the editions of the *Corpus iuris civilis* (and to a lesser degree of the *Corpus iuris canonici*); and it diversified the genres of legal literature, but its direct impact on legal practice seems to have been limited. During the second half of the 16th century, a new development in legal literature had become perceptible, which borrowed some of its materials from both the Italian method and legal humanism, but which also had its own distinctive features. By the mid 17th century, it had superseded the Italian method as the standard (or 'mainstream') approach among teaching and practising lawyers and it was well on its way towards marginalizing legal humanism as a discipline belonging to antiquarian studies. This new approach, which may be referred to as the early-modern method or *usus modernus*, more or less prevailed in legal literature until the end of the 18th century, when it was itself supplanted by new paradigms in legal scholarship at a time when national legislation and codification were giving a new orientation to legal studies. However, *usus modernus* remained mostly a 'practical' form of jurisprudence. By the second half of the 17th century, a more theoretical jurisprudence had appeared as a meta-juristic foundation for legal thinking, a legal theory reflecting the rationalist and natural law theories of that age, and which can be referred to as the Law of Reason (*Vernunftrecht*) or (at least, in its distinctively 18th-century sense) School

---

3 The standard analysis of the history of (early-modern) Western legal science, which should serve as a reference to legal scholarship in any field, is J. Schröder, *Recht als Wissenschaft: Geschichte der juristischen Methode vom Humanismus bis zur historischen Schule (1500–1800)*, Munich, C.H. Beck Verlag, 2001. A more general and conventional overview is that by J.M. Kelly, *A Short History of Western Legal Theory*, Oxford, Clarendon Press, 1992, which includes for each period a brief section on international law.

of Natural Law. Each of these four approaches substantially influenced not only early-modern civil law scholarship in general, but also early-modern international law scholarship in particular.

Before turning to international law scholarship as it evolved through those four models of legal thinking, the contemporaneous influence of new political paradigms on international relations and international law should briefly be mentioned. What is commonly identified, albeit in general terms, as the emergence of the concept of early-modern sovereignty and of the early-modern state refers primarily to a model of political power which has been contrasted to the model of political power in the late Middle Ages – even if some of its features may already be recognized in late-medieval political thinking and practice. That contrast sees late-medieval sovereignty primarily as a multi-layered concurrence of legitimate political actors within a wider territory or polity, each of which had to some extent a capacity to manage independently its own affairs, including the capacity to interact with other actors within or without that territory or polity. Thus, within the notional unity of Latin Christianity (sometimes referred to as *Res publica Christiana*), the emperor and the pope may have had a universal jurisdiction, but such universal authority was rejected or qualified by some actors within Western Christianity. Within several realms (such as the Kingdom of France until the end of the Middle Ages, or, more permanently, the Holy Roman Empire), the king or emperor was not able to impose his authority in those territories which were not directly under his control. The diversity of autonomous political actors was also reflected in the structure of the Western European international community, where war and peace, and international relations in general, were a matter of interest pursued by the emperor and the pope, various territorial rulers, cities, religious and secular orders, groups of merchants, commanders of mercenary troops and other actors. By the 16th century, the diversity of political actors, or at least the legitimate capacity of those actors to act independently, was being challenged and curtailed. A concept of exclusive sovereignty attributed to one ruler or a particular body within a particular territory replaced the former acceptance of concurrent legitimate authorities. This was true within specific territories, but it also inspired political theories which focused on the question of supreme authority in a new perspective, reflecting the idea that the holder of that supreme authority within a territory also held both exclusive internal and external sovereignty. Whereas political theories in the Middle Ages had been mostly elaborated within the conventions and the curriculum of the university faculties (mainly theology, but also in the Arts and in Roman and canon law), it became apparent during the 16th century that political theory was progressively becoming a field of study which could be pursued outside those established academic disciplines[4]. Thus, although

---

4 During early-modern times, canon law and canonistic scholarship became progressively far less relevant for international law scholarship than they had been in late-medieval centuries, while Roman law influence remained important: canon law studies were still being prominently referred to in the early *usus modernus*, but had become marginal by the mid 17th century. See (a.o.) A.Z. Hertz, 'Medieval Treaty Obligation', *Connecticut Journal of International Law* 1991, 425–443; J. Muldoon, 'Medieval Canon Law and the Formation of International Law', ZSSKan. LXXXI (1995), 64–82; R. Lesaffer, 'The Medieval Canon Law of Contract and Early Modern Treaty Law', JHIL 2000, 178–198, with references to all the main earlier literature on canon law influence on international law. For an influential 16th-century canonist's contribution to *ius gentium* doctrines

although it encompasses a much wider European range of publications on international law; as regards its historical perspective, it highlights Antiquity (characteristically represented by ancient Israel, Greece and Rome) and various stages of development since the early 17th century[9]. In the first part of the bibliography, which discusses the 'history of the law of nations', Ompteda mentions works deemed to be representative of the successive stages of the development of international law (specific historiography on the subject was still, in his day, a rare occurrence[10]). That first part is subdivided into three sections: ancient times (ending with Justinian's compilations in 529–534); intermediate times; and modern times, starting with Grotius's *De iure belli ac pacis* (1625). The latter section is further subdivided into three periods: from Grotius to Pufendorf (1625–1673); from Pufendorf to Wolff and Moser (1673–1740); and from these authors to 1785. The 'intermediate times', in this general survey, receive short shrift: barely one page out of the 125 pages which make up the first, historical, part of Ompteda's outline are needed to make the transition between the early 6th century and a handful of 16th-century authors. The author does not hide his lack of interest for the intervening millennium, which he dismisses briefly by stating: 'This period, which stretches from the early 6th century to the beginning of the 17th century, is extremely poor as regards the science of international law. Those were utterly unfavourable times for scholarship in general; and in respect of learning regarding the law of nations there is scarcely anything worth mentioning.' Ompteda's remark is characteristic of the cultural prejudices of his time; it is also revealing, for it completely bypasses the common system of extensive references which was in use by most early-modern authors on international law until about the second quarter of the 17th century, and which still included many references to late-medieval works. Thus, at least half of the legal-doctrinal references in Grotius's major work, which Ompteda highlights as the beginning of his modern era, are not just 'scarcely . . . worth mentioning', but are not mentioned at all.[11]

2.1 THE ENDURING INFLUENCE OF THE ITALIAN METHOD DURING THE 16TH CENTURY

At least two reasons may help to explain why the late-medieval and early-16th century legal literature was lost sight of from the mid 17th century onwards. The first is linked to the prevailing genres of legal literature before the *usus modernus*, the second to the

---

[9] In addition, Ompteda critically assesses late-17th and 18th-century works by analysing to what extent their authors have considered both the natural and positive *ius gentium*.

[10] See (e.g.) A.F. Glafey, *Vollständige Geschichte des Rechts der Vernunft, worin die in dieser Wissenschaft erschienenen Schriften nach ihrem Inhalt und wahren Wert beurteilt werden: Nebst e. Bibliotheca juris naturae et gentium* (reprint of the Leipzig 1739 edn.: Aalen, Scientia Verlag, 1965); a few years after Ompteda's bibliography: R. Ward, *An Enquiry into the Foundation and History of the Law of Nations in Europe, from the Time of the Greeks and Romans, to the Age of Grotius* (reprint of the Dublin 1795 edn.: N.J. Clark, Lawbook Exchange, 2005); on the latter, see D. Panizza, *Genesi di una ideologia, il conservatorismo moderno di Robert Ward*, Padua, Cedam, 1997.

[11] A. Wijffels, 'Ompteda Revisited: The Metamorphoses of Scholarship on International Law', *The Irish Jurist* 38 (2003) 312–330.

shifting political context which had formed the ideological and theoretical backdrop of late-medieval doctrines on issues of international law.

The abundant literature of the Italian method included comparatively few monographic studies by subject-matter.[12] Its main genre was the commentary, which closely followed, in the same way as the curriculum of the teaching in the law faculties, the sequence of sections of the fundamental legal collections of the *corpora iuris*.[13] Civil law commentaries thus proceeded along the *ordo legalis*, i.e. the sequence of books, titles and sections (*leges*) of the collections of Roman law which made up the medieval *Corpus iuris civilis*. The order of the two main Roman law collections, the Digest and Justinian's Code, was not based on a general systematization of the law; the Institutes, which had a more systematic outline, were a relatively minor collection in medieval civil law scholarship. The later canon law collections (from the *Liber Extra* onwards) adopted a general division of subjects in five parts, but there was no overall systematization upon which the *Corpus iuris canonici* or its individual collections were based. All collections, by the last centuries of the Middle Ages, appeared in general as a combination of the text itself and a running commentary displayed (in manuscript form, later copied in incunabula and 16th-century imprints) around the text as a (standard) set of glosses. Commentaries, in civil law and canon law literature, were copied (and later, printed) in separate volumes. Their presentation assumed that the reader was fully familiar with the sequence and the contents of the glossed collection which was the object of the commentary. Within those collections,

---

[12] For the late-medieval and the beginning of the early-modern periods, the first two volumes of the standard textbook on civil law literature published under the general editorship of H. Coing, although specifically focused on private law, are still relevant for any scholar in the history of international law: it does not include works specifically dealing with *ius gentium* or topics on international law, but because, especially in the legal literature of the Italian method and legal humanism, most works did not address a specific branch of the law, and because many issues of international law were dealt with by transposing private law principles and doctrines, much of the literature and its typology should be included in any bibliography of the history of international law, at least for works predating the *usus modernus* in private law. Cf. H. Coing (ed.), *Handbuch der Quellen und Literatur der neueren europäischen Rechtsgeschichte*, vol. 1 *Mittelalter (1100–1500), Die gelehrten Rechte und die Gesetzgebung*, Munich, C.H. Beck'sche Verlagsbuchhandlung, 1973; vol. 2, *Neuere Zeit (1500–1800), Das Zeitalter des gemeinen Rechts*, vol. 2/1, *Wissenschaft*, Munich, C.H. Beck'sche Verlagsbuchhandlung, 1977. For the same reason, H. Coing's presentation of early-modern private law methodology in the civil law tradition (until the beginning of the 17th century) is also relevant for understanding some contemporary developments in international law scholarship: *Europäisches Privatrecht*, vol. 1, *Älteres Gemeines Recht (1500 bis 1800)*, Munich, C.H. Beck'sche Verlagsbuchhandlung, 1985, esp. pp. 15–25. Early *usus modernus* authors such as Gentili and Grotius were steeped in the civil law tradition and also wrote on private law topics.

[13] The course of civil or Roman law (*corpus iuris civilis*) included, in the late-medieval and 16th-century tradition: the Digest (abbr. D., often sub-divided in three parts), Justinian's Code (abbr. C., books 1–9), and the so-called 'small volume' which contained miscellaneous texts, *viz.* Justinian's Institutes (I.), the books 10–12 of the Code, a selection of Novels in a Latin translation (Auth.), a collection on feudal law (*Libri Feudorum*, L.F.), and various smaller texts, among which *De Pace Constantiae* (a version of the Peace of Constance, 1183, commented by medieval civil lawyers) is the most important for later international law scholarship. The course of canon law (*corpus iuris canonici*) included Gratian's *Concordia discordantium canonum* (*ca.*1145), the *Liber extra* of Pope Gregory IX (1234, abbr. X.), the *Liber Sextus* of Pope Bonifatius VIII (1298), the *Clementinae* (1317), and various smaller collections of *extravagantes*, esp. by Pope John XXII (1325), and miscellaneous *extravagantes communes*.

there was not a particular part or subdivision dealing specifically with international law. Notable exceptions were a few titles such as those on *postliminium* and prisoners of war,[14] and on military issues[15] in the Digest and the Code, on truces and peaces in the *Liber Extra*,[16] a few titles on peaces in the *Libri Feudorum* (a medieval feudal law accretion to the Roman law collections, often to be found in the last volume of the *Corpus iuris civilis*),[17] and the text of the 'Peace of Constance' of 1183, together with a gloss by Odofredus and a running commentary by Baldus de Ubaldis, also regularly included in the last volume of the civil law course.[18] In addition, some genres of the late-medieval legal literature, mostly also related to teaching methods in the law faculty, took a particular section (a *lex* in the Roman law collections, a *canon* or *capitulum* in the canon law collections) as their starting point for a more extensive discussion of a particular topic. A 'repetition', for example, might deal at greater length with a specific issue related to the law of war. The repetition was in some ways the elaborate form of a more simple and common device of the commentaries, which sometimes linked a particular section, or short passage of a section, to an issue which, at that point of the commentary became the specific *locus* for discussing a topic in greater detail. Such texts which served as a conventional *locus* for a particular topic became known as *sedes materiae*.[19] A second important genre of the Italian method literature was the collections of *consilia* or consultations. Most of these collections were a compilation of legal opinions given in real-life cases by an individual – usually, academic – lawyer (sometimes by a college of lawyers or a law faculty). As for commentaries, there was obviously a continuing demand for such collections, for many of the late-medieval handwritten collections were printed and reprinted during the 16th century (and later), and new collections by more recent authors continued to appear long after 1500. In some collections, individual opinions were ordered by titles which more or less recalled the rubrics of the *corpora iuris*, but usually, the sequence of the opinions was haphazard. As for the commentaries, 16th-century printers began to edit the texts by adding brief tags (*summaria*) at the beginning of each consultation (or section in the case of a commentary), providing the reader with some of the main principles or issues discussed in the text, usually in the form of a one-liner for each issue; and those were also used for a more or less reliable alphabetical index at the end of the volume. Depending on the case and on the strategy of the consultant, some consultations dealt specifically and entirely with issues

---

14 *De postliminio et de redemptis ab hostibus* (*De postliminio reversis, et redemptis ab hostibus*), C. 8.50; *De captivis, et de postliminio, et de redemptis ab hostibus*, D. 49.15.

15 See (e.g.) *De re militari*, C. 12.35, D. 49.16.

16 *De treuga et pace* (X. 1.34).

17 See (e.g.) *De pace tenenda, et eius violatoribus* (L.F. 2.27).

18 G. Dolezalek, 'I commentari di Odofredo e Baldo alla Pace di Costanza (1183)', *Atti del convegno internazionale tenuto a Milano e Piacenza, 27–30 aprile 1983*, Bologna, 1985, 59–75; M. Ascheri, 'La pace di Costanza: da Odofredo a Baldo e oltre', in: M. Ascheri, M. Heckel and A. Padoa-Schioppa, W. Pöggeler, F. Ranieri and W. Rütten (eds), *'Ins Wasser geworfen und Ozeane durchquert'. Festschrift für Knut Wolfgang Nörr*, Köln-Weimar-Wien, Böhlau, 2003, 1–9; the same, 'La "pace" di Costanza, fondamento delle autonomie municipali, e il suo uso nelle opere dei giuristi', in: G. Andenna (ed.), *I giorni che hanno fatto la Lombardia* (Legnano, Banca di Legnano, 2007), 347–366.

19 A typical example may be gathered from the commentaries and some repetitions on the passage 'item bello capta' at D. 41.2.1.1 and I. 2.1.17.

of international law relevant for deciding the case at hand; in many other consultations, a variety of issues were discussed. Although the argumentative registers of commentaries and consultations differed, they both shared the same conventions with regard to legal methods and the use of authorities. Commentaries (more or less closely reflecting the *lecturae* or reported teaching) and consultations formed the bulk of the Italian method literature. Legal monographs on a particular subject, for example treatises (*tractatus*), were mostly a minor genre, and medieval works labelled as *tractatus* covered essays of varying length and coherence. A handful dealt with international law issues: among the most famous of these were Joannes de Legnano's series of treatises collected as a single work on the law of war;[20] Bartolus de Saxoferrato's treatise on reprisals;[21] and a few smaller treatises (in the form of collected questions) by Martinus Garratus, in particular on ambassadors and on treaties.[22] During the 16th century, many of the medieval treatises we know were printed in multi-volume collections of such works on all legal topics, and through those printed collections, those treaties became widely known throughout Europe.[23] Other genres of legal literature played a lesser role, though some of them were indirectly relevant to international law. For example, one of the subjects which did inspire its own tradition of monographic legal literature during the Middle Ages was procedural

---

[20] T.E. Holland (ed.), *Tractatus De Bello, De Represaliis et De Duello by Giovanni da Legnano*, Printed for the Carnegie Institution of Washington at the Oxford University Press, 1917 [reprint of the edn. Bononie ad instantiam Sigismundi de libris per me magistrum Henricum de Colonia xvi kal. Jan. (1477), edition of the *Tractatus de bello* based on Ms. Bologna Ms. Miscell. B.1393, and translated by J.L. Brierly]. This was vol. 8 of the series Classics of International Law published during the first half of the 20th century under the general editorship of J.B. Scott, and perhaps the most important series of reprints of pre-1800 works on international law. For most works, both a reprint of a pre-1800 edition, an introduction and an English translation were published. Some of these reprints, which are to be found in most academic libraries, were later printed again by other publishers, recently (*ca.*1995) by William S. Hein & Co.: for a convenient overview, see www.lawbookexchange.com/carnegie.htm and the website of W.S. Hein & Co. It should be stressed, however, that, in spite of the enormous merits of that series, it is highly selective and that the selection was inevitably determined by early-20th century concepts of legal scholarship. Thus, only monographs dealing specifically with international law topics were included, ruling out most of the relevant medieval and 16th-century legal literature. For the later early-modern literature, works on 'natural law' and the 'natural law of nations' tend to overshadow the works on positive international law. As a result, the series, however useful, gives a distorted view of late-medieval and early-modern international law scholarship as a whole. Nevertheless, since the publications of the Carnegie Institution are the most widely available, I shall refer here to their reprints (the reader should bear in mind, that in each case, a corresponding English translation is available in the same series, which I shall not mention explicitly).

[21] For a recent reprint: Bartolus de Saxoferrato, *Consilia, questiones, et tractatus* [. . .], Venetiis, per Baptistam de Tortis, 1529, *Tractatus represaliarum*, fol. 115vb–120va (repr. Rome, Il Cigno Galileo Galilei, 1996).

[22] V. Hrabar, *De legatis et de legationibus tractatus varii*, Dorpat, 1905; A. Wijffels, 'Martinus Garatus Laudensis on Treaties', in: R. Lesaffer (ed.), *Peace Treaties and International Law in European History. From the Late Middle Ages to World War One*, Cambridge, Cambridge University Press, 2004, 184–197 (with further references to literature on Garratus) and, in the same volume, a provisional edition of Garratus's *Tractatus de confederatione, pace et conventionibus principum*, pp.412–447.

[23] The most important are the collections printed at Lyons in 1535, 1544, 1549 and the (most extensive, but somewhat more conservative) Venice 1584 collection.

law. The *Speculum iudiciale* by Guilelmus Durand, one of the most important procedural treatises, was the object of commentaries by Baldus de Ubaldis and Joannes Andreae; in at least one case, an addition by Joannes Andreae discussing the capture and recapture of goods in the course of warfare between rival cities became a common authority on the subject.[24] During the 16th century, legal authors steeped in the Italian method remained attached to those genres and further developed some others. The collections of reported cases (*Decisiones*), for example, although initiated during the last centuries of the Middle Ages, became much more popular during the 16th century and survived the passing of the Italian method in legal literature.[25] These collections, not unlike the collections of consultations, reflected a wide variety of cases and legal issues, as they were usually based on the practice of a superior court which had a general, non-specialized jurisdiction. Similarly to what has been observed about consultations, sometimes a particular reported case became a standard reference on a particular issue, and occasionally, on an issue of international law.

From this general survey of the typology of legal literature produced by authors of the Italian method, it may be evident that very few of those works are immediately identifiable as works relevant to international law. Most of the doctrines on international law are scattered throughout the commentaries, in the collections of consultations and in a few other types of works, where they can only be traced if the *loci* are known, which, in 16th-century printed editions, may to some extent be identified through the *summaria* and the corresponding indexes. These difficulties, together with the prejudice against the tradition of the Italian method intensified by the rise of legal humanism, only explain to some degree why, during the 17th century, scholars started to neglect and dismiss the Italian tradition and its works. One of the most striking features of the Italian method, at least from the vantage-point of modern legal science, was that it largely ignored any general systematization of the law. The order of the law, in late-medieval scholarship, was (as already noted) the order offered by the *corpora iuris*. Within the collections of the *corpora iuris*, however, the titles did not fit in an overall systematic plan by subject or otherwise. One of the results of the absence of a general systematization was the strong reliance on general principles and the extensive use of analogical reasoning.[26] Provided conventional principles of logics were followed, a principle or rule borrowed from one particular area could be easily transposed and applied in a legal reasoning pertaining to an entirely different area. Since the *corpora iuris* contained comparatively very few rules with regard to international law, the need to deal with such issues by appropriating principles and concepts from other areas was more urgently felt. And since the general pattern of legal methods facilitated such appropriations, a substantial part of the doctrines developed on

---

24 G. Durand, *Speculum iuris, Ioan. Andreae, Baldi, reliquorumque praestantiss. I. V. Doctorum Theorematib. Illustratum, & ab innumeris erroribus repurgatum*, Pars Prima & Secunda [Pars III. et IIIII.], Basileae, Apud Ambrosium et Aurelium Frobenios fraters, 1574 (reprint Aalen, Scientia Verlag, 1975, 2 vols.): Johannes Andreae ad Lib. IV, Partic. IV, Tit. *De raptoribus, & incendiariis, & violatoribus ecclesiarum*, Addition 'a' ('Primam partem rubricae . . .'), p. 493.

25 For a general survey by country, cf. H. Coing, *Handbuch der Quellen . . ., o.c.*, vol. 2/1.

26 A. Wijffels, 'European Private Law: A New Software-Package for an Outdated Operating System?', in: M. Van Hoecke and F. Ost (eds), *The Harmonization of European Private Law* (Oxford, Hart Publishing, 2000) 101–116.

international issues was based on private law authorities and doctrines. The technique was still widely applied in the early works of the *usus modernus,* which may help to account for the persistence, until the present day, of several international law principles and concepts reminiscent of Roman private law or medieval canonistic doctrines on private law (*occupatio*, *uti possidetis, pacta sunt servanda* etc.).

The Italian method lost much of its direct relevance once a systematized approach to legal reasoning prevailed. Other factors, however, also played a role in undermining its appeal to legal scholarship in the course of the 16th century. In Protestant countries, canonistic learning lost some of its authority because of its association with the papacy and traditional Catholic theology. In general, the decline of canonistic authorities could also be observed in Catholic countries, because of the growing secularization of state power. Directly or indirectly, some of its underlying aims to foster common moral standards between Christian peoples would survive the Reformation and inspire doctrines of restraint in warfare (the *ius in bello*), all the more important since the early-modern state-system made it more difficult to maintain the concept and use of the old just war doctrine in an international order where the individual sovereign was regarded as a supreme judge. Civil law learning had much earlier on shed the constraints of supreme imperial authority. The most important works of the Italian method originated in Northern Italy, which remained notionally part of the Holy Roman Empire (*Reichsitalien*) and therefore in theory under the supreme authority of the emperor. Moreover, in the late-medieval political system of the Italian peninsula, the papacy represented one of the main temporal political actors. The Italian legal scholars had accordingly mastered the reasoning techniques allowing them to preserve the theory of the Empire's supreme legal authority, while acknowledging simultaneously the quasi-sovereignty and law-making power of the autonomous Italian cities and states.[27] In other countries, such as France, late-medieval jurists had at an early stage begun to cast off any remaining imperial authority superior to that of their territorial ruler.[28] By the 16th century, however, the traditional and common approach in Italian works accommodating the independence of territorial jurisdictions with their mainly theoretical subordination to a universal imperial or pontifical authority was too much at odds with both political reality and the new political theories.

Specimen: the Italian method

The *Decisio* 178 by N. Bohier[29] is a typical example of a (French) law report from the first half of the 16th century. It adduces a vast array of legal authorities, mostly from the doctrinal tradition of the Italian method. The central issue of the *decisio* related to a case brought before the *Parlement* (sovereign court) of Bordeaux, which held that a ship from Nantes and

---

[27] M. Bellomo, *Società e istituzioni dal Medioevo agli inizi dell'età moderna*, Roma, Il Cigno Galileo Galilei, 1999, pp. 338–339 and *passim*; E. Cortese, *Le grandi line della storia giuridica medievale*, Roma, Il Cigno Galileo Galilei, 2001, ch. 9.

[28] J. Krynen, *L'empire du roi. Idées et croyances politiques en France, XIIIe–XVe siècle*, Paris, Gallimard, 1993.

[29] I have used the edition: N. Boerius, *Decisiones burdegalenses* [. . .], Lugduni, Sumptibus Pauli Frelon, 1603, pp. 322–325. On Bohier's life and work, see s.v. 'Bohier', in: P. Arabeyre, J.-L. Halpérin, J. Krynen (eds), *Dictionnaire historique des juristes français (XIIe–XXe siècle*), Paris, Quadrige/PUF, 2007.

the whole cargo seized at sea while heading for Spain, at a time when France and Spain were at war, were to be confiscated. The *decisio* became in its own right a frequently quoted reference in *ius commune* literature and arguments, particularly on issues of maritime warfare.

The report considers a variety of issues, mostly relating to licit and illicit trade with countries at war. However, it also addresses several more general questions of international law which were apparently raised by lawyers in the context of this particular case: the recognition of the French king as a sovereign, his capacity to declare war, the legitimacy of defensive acts of warfare, the occurrence of a state of war without any formal declaration, the law and practice with regard to bounty, hostages, ransoms, *postliminium* (the latter only applied to goods), wars between Christian rulers and nations, or against Muslim rulers and polities. Some of these general issues are further developed as a collateral argument, such as the pope's capacity to declare and wage war. The bulk of the report's arguments, however, discuss international trade, operating various distinctions, e.g. whether trade is being pursued with Christian nations or with non-Christians, in peace-time or during war, with declared enemies or other countries, whether the trade involves approved or prohibited goods etc. The opinion to which Bohier appears to subscribe, and which may have been the decision of the Bordeaux court, holds that merchants who trade knowingly with the enemy during wartime are liable to forfeit the whole cargo on board, irrespective of whether the goods are licit or not, or to whom they belong, if the owners were aware of the destination.[30]

Throughout the report, Bohier adduces scores of authorities, mostly civil law and canon law commentaries drawn from a large (yet, conventional) selection of (mostly Italian) late-medieval legists and canonists. Some of these authorities are cited to testify to differences between the practice of warfare (on *postliminium* and captives) in Roman times and '*hodie*' (which stretches from the 14th century to Bohier's day). A few references are made to glosses, repetitions, a famous *quaestio disputata* by Angelus de Ubaldis on the law of war, some treatises, *consilia* and *decisions*.[31] Characteristically, the latter references mention a consultation by Alexander Tartagnus (VI.130) and a report by Guy Pape (Q. 572) which deal specifically with cases on the issue of prohibited exports, and another report by Pape (Q. 191) on the law of war (the requirement of a just war and the capacity to declare war). Each of these consultations and reported cases refer in turn to further references from the *ius commune* literature. Nor does Bohier's format of law reports preclude doctrinal controversies: on the legal issue of which categories of goods may be transported to an enemy country, Bohier takes a more restrictive view than Tartagnus in his *consilium*. Finally, Bohier also includes a few arguments and references which refer specifically to the French context of the case. The sovereign status of the French king had been a recurrent topic, sometimes as an obiter, in many works of the Italian method, and Bohier buttresses his point with a selection of some of the most prominent authorities. On the French king's supreme authority and exclusive capacity, among the political actors in his realm, to declare and wage war, and on the argument in favour of a general confiscation of all goods shipped to the enemy, Bohier also refers to French royal ordinances (purported to confirm the civil law authorities and the learned *communis opinio*).

While Bohier's reported case may in itself not have been an example of original scholarship – which was not the author's aim – one understands why it became a common reference in later years. Bohier's collection was well known throughout Western Europe and frequently quoted by new authorities. The *Decisio* 178 was a clear argument in favour of general forfeiture of mixed cargoes including licit and prohibited goods being exported to enemy countries – applying, as it were, what would later be known as the *infection hostile* doctrine

---

30 N. Boerius, *Decisiones burdegalenses* [see previous note], p. 324, Nos. 20 ss., and p. 325, No. 34 *in fine*.

31 Bohier's argument on the differences between warfare between Christians and wars with the Turks (regarding the enslaving of prisoners) bears a similarity to A. Alciato's commentary on D. 50.16.117, but such early legal-humanistic learning is not conspicuously mentioned in his *decisio*.

in the case of a transport involving a neutral ship or neutral goods. As the text of the *decision* makes clear, Bohier considered that his argument was not only applicable to transport by sea, but also by land. The report was also a trove for many further authorities; combined with the other authorities mentioned in the latter, the single, comparatively brief, reported case was a *locus* which informed the reader about many relevant authorities and doctrinal opinions from the 'legal ocean' of literature produced by thc tradition of the Italian method. Because most of Bohier's references and arguments were specifically related to the issues of international trade and war, it could also more easily remain useful during the 17th century, when the *usus modernus* prevailed.

2.2 THE CHALLENGE OF LEGAL HUMANISM

Historians' opinions differ on which authors should qualify as (legal) humanists. Rather than defining a particular class of authors or works as humanistic, it is more useful to identify the essential features associated with legal humanism, as these features appear more or less prominently in the work of certain authors. The boundaries with the Italian method and with the *usus modernus* are often blurred. Admittedly, some of the authors who championed legal humanism made it a point to emphasize the contrast between their approach and the traditional methods; to some extent, legal humanism should even be understood as a reaction against the institutions and ways of thinking the Italian method stood for, and legal historiography has usually taken its cue from the humanistic criticisms of 'Bartolism' to highlight the dichotomy between *mos italicus* and *mos gallicus*. The reality was less contrasted, as many legal teachers and authors tried to uphold the doctrines of the traditional learning while at the same time adjusting to the wide-scale amendments introduced by legal-humanist scholarship.[32] Revisionism should nevertheless not go so far as to play down excessively the difference between traditional scholarship and legal humanism as an attempt to break the mould of the former and to promote a new paradigm of legal learning. More difficult is the case-by-case distinction between humanistic features and early *usus modernus*. By the second half of the 16th century, many legal authors who had integrated humanistic learning were already developing in their work some of the features which would become the defining characteristics of *usus modernus*; and conversely, many of the authors of works which show primarily the features of *usus modernus* were borrowing many characteristics – both in style and substance – of the humanists. Indeed, the same author could, in the same work or in different works, sometimes emulate the humanistic register, sometimes apply his writing with greater determination along the lines of the *usus modernus*. Finally, it should be remembered that although legal humanism may primarily be associated, in the general development of legal scholarship, with the achievements of 16th-century authors, it had a lasting effect on civil law scholarship throughout the early-modern period: well beyond the comparatively small niche of legal-antiquarian studies, few legal scholars of the 17th

---

[32] See for example recent assessments of the work of F. Vázquez (1512–1569), e.g. G.P. van Nifterik, *Vorst tussen volk en wet. Over volkssoevereiniteit en rechtsstatelijkheid in het werk van Fernando Vázquez de Menchaca (1512–1569)* [diss. Rotterdam, Sanders Instituut, Gouda Quint, 1999], pp. 24–28.

and 18th centuries would not retain at least some of the features and achievements of humanistic scholarship.

'Humanism', in this context, is to be understood as a reformist current which expected an improvement of society and its institutions, of the polity and mankind, from the rehabilitation of the culture and values of 'classical' (Greek-Roman) Antiquity. The movement implied a critical, sometimes distinctly negative, assessment of the 'medieval' or 'gothic' heritage. A preliminary step towards revitalizing Western society through ancient models was a proper reconstruction of the Greek and Roman world through their texts – archeological studies being still in their infancy. The first major achievement of humanism consisted therefore in restoring or rediscovering ancient texts in their original, authentic form through philological and historical criticism. The search for ancient textual sources led rapidly to a critical reassessment of the *corpus iuris civilis*, which had to be culled of its medieval accretions and textual misrepresentations, while cuts had to be restored. The results led to the rejection of the prevailing legal doctrinal tradition, which was a typical product of the medieval standards of scholarship and culture. Legal humanism therefore not only contributed to new editions of the Roman law collections, but also to the swift development of a new doctrinal corpus aiming at reinterpreting the texts and the system of Roman law along historical standards. One difficulty and source of controversy was that the bulk of the available texts of the *corpus iuris* had been transmitted in its 6th-century Byzantine version, not, in the eyes of many humanists, the model society of classical Antiquity. To those scholars who wished to reach for the classical model of Roman law, only few texts were available, as the vast majority of fragments from what was deemed to have been the classical age of Roman law were only known through their recycled form in the collections of the *corpus iuris*, in particular the Digest. The reconstruction of classical law primarily consisted, therefore, in a conceptual, rather than a textual, reconstruction, which was bound to be more speculative and controversial.

Humanistic studies in general profoundly influenced the emancipation of political theories from established disciplines. Humanistic historical studies emphasized that classical Antiquity represented several models of political systems. Political theories developed by humanist authors could therefore diverge as they took their inspiration from different regimes or different writers. Regardless of their political views and interpretations, humanist authors shared a method which relied on a wider corpus of ancient sources, to which they applied a more rigorous method of historical criticism than their late-medieval predecessors. Until the end of the 16th century, comparatively few humanist works, in the various new genres of legal literature developed by legal humanists, dealt specifically with international law, but the historical method they promoted pervaded nonetheless the writings of many authors who still held to a more conventional legal format, and of those who sought the more systematic synthesis which eventually matured into the *usus modernus*. Thus, from the second half of the 16th century onwards, legal works discussing topics of international law often included a substantial body of references to ancient history gained from primary ancient sources or from the new historical scholarship. Moreover, some legal authors wrote monographs on particular areas of international law based almost exclusively on ancient historical materials. The distinction of methods between legal humanism and *usus modernus* is therefore a relative one. In the field of international law scholarship particularly, it should not be applied as an absolute divide in order to classify a work or an author into one or the other 'school', but rather so as to recognize the input of both. Similarly, for the same reasons it is not always evident whether a work ought to be categorized as a legal study or as an historical investigation – or as a political-theoretical essay. The sources and authorities may offer an indication, but primarily the concept of the work and the issues it discusses systematically are the most appropriate criteria for its categorization, when a categorization is necessary.

The use of ancient historical sources – from classical Greek-Roman Antiquity, but also from Biblical antiquity, which was a subject with its own antiquarian specialism – may be representative of an author's particular humanist (and therefore, political) agenda, but at a more technical level, it could also operate as evidence of a legal authority in its own right. Antiquity – especially when related to those ancient civilizations which early-modern Western European culture acknowledged as its historical references – was a means to include a degree of universal validity in one's arguments, a need particularly felt in international law scholarship, which had to bridge the political and religious divides, at least within Latin Christianity. In legal terms, one can recognize, in establishing to what extent a particular practice or norm had been observed or not by ancient nations, either a reference to a universal custom or a principle of natural law. In both cases, the historical discourse could serve to argue – or on the contrary, to deny – the validity of the particular practice or norm. This is precisely why the boundaries between humanism and *usus modernus*, or between political and legal discourse, are sometimes blurred. Historical criticism, although a scholarly discipline with its original humanist aim, was bound to be adapted to the purpose of the author's argument. Humanist historical studies nevertheless ensured that the corpus of accepted historical references and their authenticity were mostly conventional and accepted by the wider community of scholars in Western Europe.

Specimen: legal humanism

A comparatively early example of humanist learning applied to international law is K. Braun's work on embassies, published in 1548.[33] Braun (1491–1563) studied civil and canon law at Tübingen, became a judge at the Imperial Chamber of Justice, a counsellor to the bishop of Augsburg and acted as an official at several Diets of the Holy Empire. In the political controversies of his time, he was a strong supporter of the Catholic religion. His book on embassies was part of a publication including two other treatises on 'ceremonies' and 'images', which may both be regarded as an apology of Catholic doctrines against Lutheranism. The treatise on embassies does not embrace humanism radically, but it belongs to the moderate German humanist movement through its extensive use of ancient sources. Legal authorities play a secondary role in comparison to ancient historical, political, philosophical and literary sources, except in a small number of chapters where Braun develops a legal argument. On those occasions, he refers to both Roman and canon law texts, but also to

[33] I have used the edition: C. Brunus, *De legationibus libri quinque: cunctis in repub. versantibus, aut quolibet magistratu fungentibus perutiles, et lectu iucundi. De caeremoniis libri sex: ad veram pietatem Deique cultum, contra errores et abusus, viam ostendentes. De imaginibus liber unus: ex omni disciplinarum genere copiose disserens* [. . .]. Ex officina Francisci Behem, Typographi Moguntiae apud S. Victorem, 1548 (CD Rom including the part on embassies in: *Conrad Braun, Les cinq livres sur les ambassades à destination de ceux qui sont totalement appliqués à la Chose publique, ou très utiles à ceux qui remplissent une quelconque magistrature, et agréables à la lecture* [Traduction, introduction et notes de D. Gaurier], Limoges, Pulim, 2008).

authors of the Italian method, but he also occasionally takes into account G. Budé's corrections and discusses Greek phrases. Law, however, is not the main theme in Braun's treatise. Much more prominent is his approach to international relations with its considerations of both morality and expediency. The perspective is that of an ambassador, who is expected to reconcile in his actions the ethical demands of his office and the constraints of *Realpolitik*. Two passages may illustrate Braun's approach. In chapter II.9 of the treatise, he discusses the sense of justice supposed to guide the ambassador as the first quality of the virtue (understood here with conventional references to Cicero and Aristotle) which the exercise of his office requires. The definition of justice brings Braun to analyse the laws that will apply. He thereby follows the distinction between positive laws, i.e. customs and written statutes, and natural law. The latter is prescribed by an innate interior force, not as the result of an intellectual process. Natural law's prescriptions are articulated around six motifs: *religio*, *pietas* (towards one's country and family), *gratia* (the reward of those from whom we benefit), *vindicatio* (self-defence against violence and revenge), *observantia* (the respect and honour due to those who deserve it), and *veritas* (the acknowledgement and acceptance of what has been, what is and what will be). *Ius gentium*, Braun adds, stems from that natural law: a process which he describes as a strengthening, through the practice and the common approval of the nations, of what has effortlessly been drawn from nature. It follows that positive law cannot be valid if it is contrary to the universal precepts of natural law. The passage shows how a conventional notion of natural law and *ius gentium* could sustain a largely secularized discourse – such as Braun's, and by many later authors on embassies and other international law topics – based on ancient, and possibly also recent, historical evidence. The second passage may be seen – among many others – as a specific application of that method: in chapter IV.2, Braun discusses the penalties incurred by those who ill-treat or kill ambassadors in violation of the law of nations. It is one of the chapters in which Braun adduces several legal texts from the *corpora iuris*, but a closer examination shows that most of these texts neither bear directly on ambassadors nor consider more generally the status of public messengers. Braun's argument, however, is mostly drawn from ancient (and a few medieval) examples of envoys being slaughtered or made prisoner by the ruler to whom they had been sent. Clearly, such violations had been committed by all nations, including the Romans. The ancient and later statutes Braun records express the condemnation of such violations; and in some cases, the practice of handing over the individual perpetrators of the violation to the foreign nation confirms the censure of such acts in the customary law of nations. Moreover, the – mostly pagan – histories quoted in this chapter also tend to establish that the nations or rulers who had allowed or encouraged such violations suffered severe setbacks. Perhaps one can recognize a degree of scepticism in Braun's conclusion when, after recalling those various historical examples, he states: 'And with respect to all those cases, Antiquity believed that those who had violated the status of ambassadors had suffered the rightful wrath and punishment from God. And many other similar stories are recounted by the authors, which we leave to the learning of those who study history.' Whether or not Braun was subscribing to the opinions of the ancient writers who presented the downfall of violators as divine punishment, he takes up the argument in order to show, in a somewhat traditional scholastic register, that Christ himself had expressed the principle of retribution against those who had injured God's agents.

Braun's work was one of the first early-modern treatises on the subject. A handful of medieval legal treatises on the same subject already existed (in addition to the legal literature relating to the titles *De legationibus* in the Digest and the Code), and some of these were given a new lease of life through their incorporation in the larger collections of treatises printed during the 16th century, but it was under the joint influence of humanist studies and the early *usus modernus* that from around the mid 16th century onwards, a new literature on the status of ambassadors appeared,[34] including (in addition to K. Braun) treatises by

[34] A. Wijffels, 'Le statut juridique des ambassadeurs d'après la doctrine du XVIe siècle', *Publication du Centre européen d'Études bourguignonnes (XIVe - XVIe s.)* 32 (1992), 127–142 (with

the Italians T. Tasso[35] and O. Maggi (Magius),[36] the French F. de La Mothe Le Vayer,[37] C. Paschal,[38] J. Hotman,[39] the German H. Kirchner,[40] the Pole K. Warszewicki,[41] the Fleming F. de Marselaer[42] and a few others, among whom, most prominently, the Italian Alberico Gentili, exiled in England.[43] Other new systematic treatments of the subject had appeared in larger works, such as P. Ayrault's law reports. As may be observed from a note by the German jurist C. Besoldus, who also wrote on embassies at the beginning of the 17th century and presented a brief overview of the existing literature,[44] those late-16th century treatises substantially relied on late-medieval scholarship, but at the same time strongly contributed to rendering it obsolete as current authorities.

In Gentili's work on embassies, which he first published at the beginning of his English academic career[45] (apparently following a consultation he and F. Hotman had been asked

further references, also with regard to the successive editions of the works mentioned in the following footnotes). See also the selection of treatises in V.E. Hrabar, *De legatis et legationibus tractatus varii. Bernardi de Rosergio Ambaxiatorum brevilogus, Hermolai Barbari De officio legati, Martini Garrati Laudensis De legatis maxime principum. Ex aliis excerpta qui eadem de re usque ad annum MDCXXV scripserunt*, Dorpati Livonorum, 1905.

35 T. Tasso, *Il Messagiero, dialogo*, Venetia, B. Giunti e fratelli, 1582.

36 O. Magius, *De legato libri duo*, Venetiis, 1566 (I used the edition Hanoviae, Apud Guilielmum Antonium, 1596).

37 F. de La Mothe Le Vayer, *Legatus, seu de legatione legatorumque privilegiis, officio ac munere libellus ad titulos de legatione et legatis in P etc.*, Paris, apud M. de Roigny, 1579.

38 C. Paschalius, *Legatus. Opus* [. . .] *distinctum in capita septem et septuaginta,* Rothomagi, Apud Raphaelem Parvivallium Typographum Regium, 1598; *Altera editio non paucis locupletata*, Parisiis, Ex Officina Plantiniana, Apud Hadrianum Perier, 1612.

39 [J. Hotman] sieur de Vill. H., *L'ambassadeur*, 1603; Sieur de Villiers Hotman, *De la charge et dignité de l'ambassadeur. Seconde édition augmentée*, Paris, Chez Ieremie Perier, 1604; Ian Hotman, sieur de Villiers, *De la charge et dignité de l'Ambassadeur, Troisième édition augmentée, et meilleure. Avec une liste des Auteurs qui ont escrit en ce mesme sujet et un extrait de l'Anti-Colazon*, Dusseldorp, Bernard Bussius, 1613.

40 H. Kirchner, *Legatus*, Lichae, Excudebat Guolphgangus Kezelius, 1604; *Editione altera* [. . .] *emendatus et plurimum auctus*, Marpurgi, Excudebat Guolphgangus Kezelius, 1610; *Legatus, ejusque jura, dignitas et officium, duobus libris explicata* [with a new preface by the author, dated 1613], Marpurgi, Typis Pauli Egenolphi, Typogr. Acad., 1614.

41 I have seen the editions C. Warsevicius, *De legationibus adeundis luculentissima oratio*, Lichae, Typis Guolphgangi Kezelii, 1604; see also under the title *De legato et legatione. Item ejusdem de concilio et consiliariis principis liber, ex F. Frurii Ceriole in Lat. versus. Cui accessit H. a Collibus Consiliarius*, Dantisci, 1646. On the author and work: A. Tamborra, 'Krzysztof Warszewicki e la diplomazia del Rinascimento in Polonia', *Europa orientalis*, I, Rome, 1965, 88; the *editio princeps* was printed at Krakow in 1595, the second edition at Rostock in 1597.

42 F. de Marselaer, Κηευκλου, *sive legationum insignae, in duos libros distributum*, Antverpiae, Apud Guil. a Tongris sub signo Gryphi, 1618; *Legatus libri duo*, Antverpiae, Ex Officina Plantiniana (Balthasaris Moreti), 1626.

43 A. Gentili, *De legationibus, libri tres*, Hanoviae, Apud Guiliелmum Antonium, 1594 (reprint with an Introduction by E. Nys, New York, Oxford University Press, 1924).

44 C. Besoldus, *Spicilegia politico-juridica, De legatis, (2) De sessionis praecedentia, ac item (3) De pacis jure*; *(4) Deque arcanis rerumpublicarum*, Argentorati, Impensis Heredum Lazari Zetzneri, 1624, including the treatise *De legatis, eorumque jure,* pp. 3–98, followed, pp. 98–119, by P. Ayrault [P. Aerodius], *Rerum judicatarum, Lib. X, Tit. XV: De legationibus* (previously published in *Decretorum liv. VI. Itemque liber singularis de origine et auctoritate rerum iudicatarum*, Parisiis, Apud Martinum Iuvenem, 1573, Book VI, pp. 701–709: *De legationibus, tit. XVI*).

45 A. Gentili, *De legationibus libri tres*, Londini, Excudebat Thomas Vautrollerius, 1585; *De legationibus libri tres.* [. . .] *Editio secunda*, Hanoviae, Apud Gulielmum Antonium, 1607. The

to write after a conspiracy by the Spanish ambassador in London against the Queen), the author relies almost exclusively on ancient sources, and comparatively little on legal authorities. Gentili provides a more elaborate justification than Braun for explaining his reliance on (ancient) history in order to deal with a *ius gentium* topic such as the status of embassies. According to this justification, not only does the historical study reveal that the institution of embassies existed among all (ancient) nations, the ancient usages and experiences may also be proof of the universal validity of the law of nations, irrespective of the era in the history of mankind. However, Gentili admits that the facts adduced by history are insufficient by themselves to establish the normative principles of the law of nations, and hence the need to complement the historical approach with moral and political philosophy.[46]

Some of the authors who have been mentioned – such as Braun himself – had had experience in diplomatic practice, and many were also referring to recent or contemporary history. Remarkably, the reliance on ancient (and late-medieval) sources and models appears to have prevailed over their perception of new tendencies in diplomatic practice: for instance, until the 17th century, very few authors ever discussed the system of permanently resident ambassadors.

2.3 FROM THE EARLY *USUS MODERNUS* TO PROTO-POSITIVISTIC INTERNATIONAL LAW DOCTRINES

The general categorization 'early-modern method' or *usus modernus* refers here to the civil law literature which, in various forms, replaced the Italian method as the mainstream method in legal doctrine and which lasted until the late 18th century, when it began to be supplanted by different legal methods which were primarily understood in a national context, such as the commentaries and manuals based on national codes, or the German Science of Pandects inspired by the Historical School. In at least two respects, the new method differed from its Italian predecessor: in the first place, it was governed by a systematization of the law *ratione materiae*, i.e. by subject-matters, which entailed a new discipline in legal reasoning, imposing a much stricter use of legal rules within their own area; in the second place, the new method sought to merge Roman law doctrines with the substantive particular law of a given (usually, territorial) jurisdiction.[47] As a consequence, European *ius commune* doctrines became less homogenous, because they began to differ according to the importance and the nature of the input from the *iura propria* in each jurisdiction. International law scholarship from the late 16th century onwards strongly displayed the features of systematization: indeed, it was partly because it began, as in other branches of the law, to deal extensively, systematically and specifically with topics of international law that later generations would attribute to the first representatives of that literature the beginnings of international law scholarship. The second feature of *usus modernus*, on the other hand, would not seem to make sense in the field of international law. However, the public law scholarship which flourished during the same period in

---

edition reprinted in the series Classics of International Law: *De legationibus, libri tres*, Hanoviae, Apud Guilielmum Antonium, 1594 (reprint New York, Oxford University Press, 1924).

46 A. Gentili, *De legationibus, libri tres* (1594 edn., 1924 reprint), Book III, chapters 8 and 9, esp. at p. 171.

47 Alain Wijffels, 'Early-Modern Literature on International Law and the Usus Modernus', *Grotiana* NS 16/17 (1995–6), 35–54.

the Holy Roman Empire, and which cannot exclusively be classified as the domestic law of the Empire, was arguably also to some extent a regional system of international law, especially when the capacity of the Empire's States to act autonomously in international relations was increasingly recognized.[48] Moreover, if one considers the European state system as a whole, early-modern international law scholarship effectively came close to achieving a synthesis not dissimilar to that of the *usus modernus* in the individual territories and domestic jurisdictions, although that synthesis of the *Droit public de l'Europe* also owed much to the Law of Reason.

Systematization was a main concern in 16th-century legal studies, but it affected all scientific disciplines in search of reasserting their own boundaries and their internal structure. It did not prevent, certainly as long as various keys of systematization were being experimented with, mutual borrowings between different disciplines. Thus, the first developments of the *usus modernus* during the latter part of the 16th century can be regarded in the same – wider – context as the developments of the 'second scholastics' in theology, and, particularly in international law studies, it has become a set piece in every outline of early-modern scholarship to highlight the influence of theologians, in particular moral theologians associated with the 'Spanish scholastics'.[49] The officially advertised Catholic ideology of the Spanish monarchy, the rise of Spain as a major international power in the Mediterranean region opposing the Ottoman empire, and as a colonial power in the New World, were part of the context which induced Spanish theologians to examine the orthodoxy of Spain's foreign and colonial policy. The interest of several theologians in current international issues was partly in keeping with the theological tradition which saw political affairs, including the political affairs of the Western Christian international community, as its legitimate object, but partly also a result of the new impetus of the Catholic Counter-Reformation faced with the political consequences of the Protestant Reformation and the growing secularization of the political regimes in Catholic countries. Their work was also relevant to Protestant legal authors who sought a foundation of international law which could bridge the divide between Catholic and Protestant Europe. Largely in the Thomistic tradition, two Spanish Dominicans were particularly influential: Francisco de Vitoria (c.1483–1546)[50] and Juan de la Peña

[48] M. Stolleis, *Geschichte des öffentlichen Rechts in Deutschland*, vol. 1, *Reichspublizistik und Policeywissenschaft 1600–1800*, Munich, Verlag C.H. Beck, 1988, pp. 186–197; see also Chapter 6 on *ius publicum universale*, including sections on a.o. Grotius, Pufendorf, Thomasius and Wolff, and, in chapter 5, on J.J. Moser's work on international law (p. 264).

[49] H.G. Justenhoven and J. Stüben (eds), *Kann Krieg erlaubt sein? Eine Quellensammlung zur politischen Ethik der Spanischen Spätscholastik*, Stuttgart, Kohlhammer, 2006. J. Thomas, 'The Intertwining of Law and Theology in the Writings of Grotius', JHIL 1999, 61–100. M. Scattola, '*"Wie der König im Krieg nach der wahrscheinlichen Meinung handeln soll"*. Die Kriegslehre des Gabriel Vázquez im Horizont des Probabilismus', in: N. Brieskorn and M. Riedenauer (eds), *Suche nach Frieden: Politische Ethik in der frühen Neuzeit*, vol. 3, Stuttgart, Kohlhammer, 2003, 119–153.

[50] F. de Vitoria, *De Indis et de jure belli relectiones*, cf. J.B. Scott, *The Spanish Origins of International Law. Francisco de Vitoria and his Law of Nations,* Oxford: At the Clarendon Press, London: Humphrey Milford, 1934 [The Classics of International Law]; for an Italian translation of excerpts, with an introduction: C. Galli (ed.), *Francisco de Vitoria, De iure belli*, Rome, Bari, Edizione Laterza, 2005; another important theologian from Salamanca who wrote on war was D. de Soto, see (a.o.) M. Scattola, '*Bellum, dominium ordo*: Das Thema des gerechten Krieges in der

(1513–1565).[51] Vitoria's writings on the war of conquest and colonization in America[52] and on the war against the Turks emphasized the legitimacy, in the law of nations, of non-Western polities, hence the restrictions on the right to wage war against them or to conquer their territories and enslave their population.[53] Peña developed the ideas of Thomas of Aquinas on just war, applied to the Spanish colonial wars of his days. The Jesuit Francisco Suarez (1548–1617)[54] was the author of an extensive philosophical and theological *opus* which both updated and systematized the medieval scholastic tradition. In political theory, Suarez is mainly remembered for his criticism of the doctrine of divine right as foundation of the monarchs' powers and the ensuing protestations by James I.[55] The Spanish scholastic authors not only brought to the forefront of academic discussions on international law the doctrines on political sovereignty and on war inherited from medieval theology, their own controversies focused the attention of legal scholars on issues which, in the context of late-16th and early-17th century international relations, required a minimum degree of consensus if international law was to progress.[56] Thus, Suarez did not agree with Vitoria's doctrine on the possibility of a just war on the part of both belligerents, which, during the 17th and 18th centuries, became at least a theoretical prerequisite for working out systematically the *ius in bello*. Suarez, on the other hand, is credited with fostering the notion of *ius gentium* understood as the law governing the relations between nations, rather than in its traditional sense, which had included both issues of public international law and issues of domestic law which were deemed to be generally applicable in particular legal systems.

As in other branches of the law, one may recognize during the second half of the 16th century the onset of the *usus modernus* literature in international law. In contrast to most other legal subjects, however, the works by Gentili and, above all, Grotius, brought the new genre to maturity already before the mid 17th century: Gentili's final version of *De*

Theologie des Domingo de Soto' in N. Brieskorn and M. Riedenauer (eds), *Suche nach Frieden: Politische Ethik in der frühen Neuzeit*, vol. 1, Stuttgart, Kohlhammer, 2000, 119–137; H.-G. Justenhoven, *Francisco de Vitoria zu Krieg und Frieden*, Stuttgart, Kohlhammer, 1994; for a Latin edition with a German translation: *Vorlesungen I-II (Relectiones), Völkerrecht, Politik, Kirche,* Stuttgart, Kohlhammer, 1995–1997.

51 I have used the modern edition: J. de la Peña, *De bello contra insulanos,* 2 vols. Madrid, CSIC, 1982.

52 See also J. Bordat, *Gerechtigkeit und Wohlwollen. Das Völkerrechtskonzept des Bartholomé de Las Casas*, Aachen, Shaker Verlag, 2006.

53 See also A. Anghie, *Imperialism, Sovereignty and the Making of International Law*, Cambridge, Cambridge University Press, 2005; D. Schwartz, 'The Principle of the Defence of the Innocent and the Conquest of America: "Save Those Dragged Towards Death"', JHIL 2007, 263–291.

54 J. Soder, *Francisco Suárez und das Völkerrecht: Grundgedanken zu Staat, Recht und internationalen Beziehungen*, Frankfurt a.M., Metzner Verlag, 1973; M. Kremer, *Den Frieden verantworten. Politische Ethik bei Francisco Suárez (1548–1617)*, Stuttgart, Kohlhammer, 2008.

55 On his doctrine regarding the *ius belli*: R. Specht, 'Francisco Suárez über den Krieg', in: N. Brieskorn and M. Riedenauer (eds), *Suche nach Frieden: Politische Ethik in der frühen Neuzeit*, vol. 1, *o.c.*, 191–222.

56 For reprints of a selection from his work in the series Classics of International Law: *Selection from three works of Franscisco Suárez, S.J., De legibus, ac Deo legislatore 1612, Defensio fidei catholicae, et apostolicae adversus anglicanae sectae errores, 1613, De triplici virtute theologica, fide, spe, et charitate, 1621*, Oxford: At the Clarendon Press, London: Humphrey Milford, 1944.

iure belli (1598)[57] and Grotius's *De iure belli ac pacis* (1625) could be regarded as general handbooks of the law of nations in the modern sense. As a result, international law, as a general legal subject or as the distinct frame of reference for specific topics, became, earlier than most other legal subjects, a specialized branch of the law in its own right.

The early *usus modernus* – on topics of international law or other areas – was still a transitory genre. Its most distinctive feature was the monographic treatment of a sub-theme of the law of nations, or at least a distinct treatment of such a sub-theme in a larger legal work. The most advanced authors among the early generations of the new genre also contrived to work out a systematic arrangement of their subject, ideally by also subdividing their subject-matter according to separate issues of substantive law. Until the early 17th century, many of them were nonetheless still relying on authorities of the Italian method and handling specific questions by the standards of that method, in particular referring to principles borrowed from different areas of the law.[58] That period of transition was crucial in ensuring the transfer of many late-medieval doctrines, to which, after they had been systematized in the *usus modernus* literature, later authors would habitually no longer refer directly. The same authors also often borrowed from humanist learning, either in order to widen the scope of their (legal) authorities, or to incorporate historical learning based on classical and Biblical ancient sources. Some topics may at first not have been discussed primarily along legal principles and authorities, but once these earlier works became standard references in later legal literature, their arguments were incorporated into the *usus modernus* scholarship. By the beginning of the 18th century, most topics of the law of nations had been covered by a specifically legal literature, both general works and special studies or monographs. During the early stages of the *usus modernus*, some (broad) topics received more sustained attention: as already mentioned, this was the case during the second half of the 16th century for the status of ambassadors (largely, at first, as part of the more general interest for the model courtier and holder of high offices), but also for the law of war (partly linked to the combined interest of rulers and humanists for ancient warfare, *De re militari*). Milestones in the development of monographs on the law of war during that period were the works by Pietrino Belli (1502–1575) and Balthasar de Ayala (1548–1584). In spite of its title, Belli's *De re militari et bello tractatus* (1563),[59] was an uncompromisingly legal work. The scholarship it relied upon belonged

---

57 For a reprint of a later (posthumous) edition: *De iure belli, libri III*, Hanoviae, Apud Haeredes Guilielmi Antonii, 1612, Oxford: At the Clarendon Press, London: Humphrey Milford, 1933. For a critical *apparatus*, together with a modern Italian translation: *Alberico Gentili, Il diritto di Guerra (De iure belli libri, 1598)*, Introduzione di D. Quaglioni, Traduzione di P. Nencini, Apparato critico a cura di G. Marchetto e Christian Zendri, Milan, Dott. A Giuffrè Editore, 2008.

58 An example of the transition is P. Gudelinus, *De iure pacis commentarius. In quo praecipuae de hoc iure quaestiones distinctis capitibus eleganter pertractantur*, Lovanii, Typis Philippi Dormalii, 1620, which formally refers to the text of *De Pace Constantiae* in the last volume of the *Corpus iuris civilis*, but follows a structure governed by the subject-matter (R. Lesaffer, 'An Early Treatise on Peace Treaties: Petrus Gudelinus between Roman Law and Modern Practice', *The Journal of Legal History* 23 (2002), 223–252).

59 For a recent reprint with a modern French introduction and translation by D. Gaurier: P. Belli, *De re militari et bello tractatus, divisus in partes XI* [. . .], Venetiis, excudebat Franciscus de Portonariis, 1563, reprint Alba, Fondazione Ferrero, 2007, 2 vols.; R. Comba and G.S. Pene Vidari (eds), *Un giurista tra principi a sovrani, Pietrino Belli a 500 anni dalla nascita, Atti del convegno di*

still almost entirely to the Italian method, but the book broke new ground by presenting a wide range of topics on the law of war and warfare in one extensive monograph which showed at least an attempt to classify those topics in a general outline. Ayala's *De iure et officiis bellicis et disciplina militari* (1582)[60] is a less homogenous work. The first part deals with classic issues of war, including the authority to wage war, which allows the author to deny at length the legitimacy of rebels – as a martial judge in the Spanish armies in the Low Countries and a counsellor of the Spanish king, a position clearly marked by his experience in the Netherlands during the first years of the Dutch struggle for independence. That first part of the book is subdivided in conventional and recognizable issues of the law of war, and is strongly buttressed with legal authorities, including many late-medieval doctrines. In the second part, Ayala presents various elements of a theory of war, almost exclusively through extensive references to ancient history; to the extent that these historical references may amount to a normative approach, they are not worked out as a legal doctrine. The third part discusses mainly the status and discipline of soldiers. The argument here reverts to a more legal register, but mainly through its references to Roman law texts, without regard to later doctrinal commentaries. Throughout the three parts, ancient history is the author's main source, which gives the book a more humanistic outlook than Belli's, even though Ayala's style remains fairly traditional. Fault-lines, however, are not absolute in this area, and in Ayala's writings, his political background and agenda are always present. For example, in chapter I.5, Ayala strongly rejects an argument attributed to Alciato which denied the *ius belli* (and its effects) between Christians. Ayala, who in a previous chapter (I.2) had given the traditional arguments in favour of the just war doctrine, and highlighted that such a war could only be waged by a *supremus princeps*, recoiled at the idea that Christians sovereigns might not wage a just war against other Christians.[61]

Gentili and Grotius were the first authors to deal comprehensively with the law of nations, at least from the perspective of the law of war and peace. It should be remembered that although the title of Grotius's book was *De iure belli ac pacis*,[62] and the title

---

studi, Alba, 30 novembre 2002, Alba, Fondazione Ferrero, 2004. The same 1563 edition was also reprinted in the series Classics of International Law, with an introduction by A. Cavaglieri, Oxford: At the Clarendon Press, London: Humphrey Milford, 1936.

60 B. Ayala, *De iure et officiis bellicis et disciplina militari, libri III*, Duaci, Ex officina Ioannis Bogardi Typogr. iurati, 1582 (reprint Washington D.C., 1912).

61 R. Schnepf, 'Balthasar de Ayalas Beitrag zum Kriegsrecht und dessen Kritik bei Francisco Suárez und Hugo Grotius', in: N. Brieskorn and M. Riedenauer (eds), *Suche nach Frieden: Politische Ethik in der frühen Neuzeit*, vol. 3, *o.c.*, 319–345.

62 The standard edition of reference with a modern critical apparatus is now the reprint: Hugo Grotius, *De iure belli ac pacis libri tres in quibus ius naturae et gentium item iuris publici praecipua explicantur* [curavit B.J.A. de Kanter – van Hettinga Tromp, Editionis anni 1939 quae Lugduni Batavorum in aedibus E.J. Brill emissa est exemplar photomechanice iteratum, annotationes novas addiderunt R. Feenstra et C.E. Persenaire, adiuvante E. Arps-de Wilde], Aalen, Scientia Verlag, 1993. See also the English translation: *The Rights of War and Peace, Edited and with an Introduction by R. Tuck*, 3 vols., Indianapolis, Liberty Fund, 2005. For an analysis of Grotius's views on *ius belli* which shows how he recycled various sources, including many late-medieval legal authorities: P. Haggenmacher, *Grotius et la doctrine de la guerre juste*, Paris, Presses Universitaires de France, 1983; see also O. Yasuaki, *A Normative Approach to War. Peace, War, and Justice in Hugo Grotius,* Oxford, Clarendon Press, 1993; D. Little, 'Hugo Grotius and the Doctrine of Just

of Gentili's book *De iure belli*, the third and last part of the latter consists in an extensive discussion of peace, whereas such an extensive and distinctive subdivision on the law of peace and peace treaties does not occur in Grotius's work.

Gentili's book on the law of war had been preceded by an earlier draft on the same topic, his commentaries on the law of war;[63] his other monographs on international law issues included the book, already mentioned, on embassies, and another, posthumously published book which partly deals with issues of maritime warfare. He also wrote a dialectical study on the legitimacy of Rome's conquests through wars, in which the author argues in one part why Rome's policy was illegitimate, and in the other part why it was justified.[64] The three main works on international law can each be associated with historical events in Gentili's lifetime: the book on embassies as an offshoot of his consultation on the Spanish ambassador's involvement in a plot against the monarch; the commentaries on the law of war, later developed into the *De iure belli*, were written when England and Spain were effectively in a state of war after the mid 1580s; and the *Hispanica Advocatio*[65] was again based on Gentili's own consultations, mainly in cases of maritime warfare, after the Anglo-Spanish Peace of 1604. As for Grotius's *magnum opus* of 1625, it partly drew on the author's much earlier research around 1604, when he had been commissioned by the Dutch East Indian Company to write a consultation defending the use of violence against the Portuguese in the East Indies. The young Grotius worked out his consultation in a wholesale dissertation on prize-law (*De iure praedae*),[66] which remained unpublished until modern times (except, famously, for a short extract which appeared first anonymously in 1609 under the title *Mare liberum*). Although the general concept and style of Grotius's *De iure praedae* remained argumentative (*viz.* as a work entirely focused on challenging specifically the Portuguese monopoly of trade in the East Indies[67]), the argumentation took a broad view of the issues involved, incorporated an

---

War' in N. Brieskorn and M. Riedenauer (eds), *Suche nach Frieden: Politische Ethik in der frühen Neuzeit*, vol. 1, *o.c.*, 259–273.

63 A. Gentili, *De iure belli commentatio prima* [*-secunda*], London, Johannes Wolfius, 1588; *De iure belli commentationes duae*, [Leiden, Apud Iohannem de la Croy = London, J. Wolfe] 1589; *De iure belli commentatio tertia*, London, Johannes Wolfius, 1589; *De iure belli commentationes tres*, London, Apud Iohannem Wolfium expensis I.C.M., 1589. I have been relying on a draft version of a paper by Prof. I. MacLean, to be published in the proceedings of the 2008 conference on Gentili at San Ginesio, and which offers the best bibliographical survey of Gentili's works. Also, by the same author, chapter II ('Alberico Gentili, his Publishers and the Vagaries of the Book Trade between England and Germany, 1580–1614' in I. MacLean, *Learning and the Market Place*, Leiden, Brill, 2009, 291–338.

64 A. Gentili, *De armis romanis libri duo*, Hanau, Apud Guilielmum Antonium, 1599 (preceded by *De iniustitia bellica actio*, Oxford, Excudebat Isoephus Barnesius, 1590). An English translation of this work is forthcoming.

65 The *editio princeps* is 1613. For a reprint of a later edition: A. Gentili, *Hispanicae advocationis (In quo tractatu diversae illustres quaestiones maritimae secundum jus gentium et hodiernam praxin quam nitide perlustrantur et deciduntur) libri duo*, Amstelredami, Apud Joannem Ravesteinium, 1661 (reprint New York, Oxford University Press, 1921).

66 H.G. Hamaker (ed.), *Hugonis Grotii De jure praedae commentarius.* The Hague, Martinus Nijhoff, 1868.

67 M.J. van Ittersum, *Profit and Principle: Hugo Grotius, natural rights theories and the rise of Dutch power in the East Indies, 1595–1615*, Leiden, Brill, 2006; see also the Introduction by A.

unprecedented host of issues and authorities, and followed a highly systematic plan. In contrast, Gentili's *Hispanica Advocatio*, written around the same time, and also dealing with maritime warfare, remained an unfinished work. Gentili's original consultations have partly survived, as well as some of his handwritten notes in which he started to edit those consultations in order to write a monographic work, presumably on the same lines as his earlier monographs on international law. The notes are an exceptional testimony of the early *usus modernus* while it was still at a developing stage: in the first drafts, Gentili had obviously in mind a conventional collection of *consilia*, from which he then began to separate the sections of his consultations which dealt specifically with issues of international law; the end result of this unfinished work (published posthumously by his brother Scipio, who was a law professor at Altdorf) was a hybrid book, containing in its first part mostly chapters related to maritime warfare, and in its second part chapters on other issues, such as procedure and evidence. In each part, it is still possible to recognize the cases which inspired the consultations, but Gentili was not able – as Grotius had managed in his scholarly and systematic work on prize-law – to work out a subdivision according to a logical plan. Gentili's *Advocatio* therefore expresses the typical concerns of his time for dealing with international law *ratione materiae*, but it also shows that even the most prominent authors were still struggling to work out a satisfactory outline specific to their subject. Similarly, Grotius's systematization in *De iure praedae* is primarily determined by the purpose of his argument, rather than by the nature of the subject-matter.

In their more accomplished and famous books (*De iure belli* for Gentili; *De iure belli ac pacis* for Grotius), both authors were far more successful in presenting a systematic doctrinal overview of the area of international law they were dealing with. In those books, Gentili and Grotius not only wrote works which gave the most comprehensive and systematic general outlines of the subject available at the time, achievements which greatly boosted the later systematic developments of the *usus modernus* in international law, but they also displayed in their work a firm command of the traditional scholastic learning and of humanist studies. Yet, the two books were also markedly different: Gentili's remained within the essential register of a legal work, whereas in Grotius's work, the assimilation of other critical disciplines for the emerging science of international politics and international relations ensured that it reached a much wider audience beyond that of professional jurists, and that it exercised a much deeper and longer influence on the educated political elites.

A conventional distinction in post-Grotian literature on international law is based on the author's doctrines on the foundations of *ius gentium*. The broad division, according to that distinction, is between doctrines which see *ius gentium* primarily based on natural law, and those which see it primarily based on acts expressing the human will (i.e. customs and conventions). Such a distinction between a 'natural law' school and a 'positivist' school is, admittedly, only relative. Natural law, whether as a backdrop for theories on the foundation of the civil society of individuals or the international community of polities, could be understood in various ways, partly depending on an author's optimistic or pessimistic social anthropology. Most authors, in any case, acknowledged both some

---

Eyffinger, *Hugo de Groot, De vrije zee, een uiteenzetting over het recht van de Nederlanders om handel te drijven in Oost-Indië*, The Hague, Jongbloed, 2009.

concept of natural law and positive law as sources of the law of nations. The later (i.e., late-17th century and 18th century) natural law approach (discussed in the following section) reinforced the first feature of the *usus modernus*, *viz.* its detailed systematization of the subject matter; the positivistic approach was in some ways similar to the second feature of the *usus modernus*, *viz.* its blending of *ius commune* principles and *ius proprium*, in so far as it incorporated and generalized within its general systematic scheme the 'particular' rules borrowed from (European) international customs and treaties.

Treaty practice gave rise, during the early-modern period, to comparatively new genres of works. Diplomats wrote extensive literary reports, or published original sources (such as correspondence) with regard to negotiations which they had attended. Collections of treaties, at first mostly with respect to a particular nation, but later including most European nations, grew within a few generations to multi-volume scholarly editions of such primary sources of diplomatic practice and international law. By the 18th century, when the first modern codifications appeared in the domestic legal systems of some Western European countries, these series of collected treaties were sometimes likened to the 'code' or 'statute-book' of the European law of nations. Reports by diplomats on negotiations and collections of treaties were important primary sources for the 'positivist' side of the *usus modernus* and of the *Droit public de l'Europe.*

Two authors usually classified among the 'positivist' writers on *ius gentium* illustrate the different orientations of *usus modernus* writers even during the second half of the 17th century. S. Rachel's (1628–1691) *De jure naturae et gentium dissertationes* (1676)[68] discusses natural law mainly from a philosophical and historical perspective, while his analysis of the law of nations draws from (ancient) history and early-modern legal authorities. The work displays a relatively rare familiarity with English theologians, political philosophers and civil lawyers. Among the latter, Rachel, who emphasized the importance of covenants as the foundation of society by individuals and of the international community by sovereign polities, quotes R. Zouch for his arguments tending to establish that the *ius inter gentes* was founded on covenants and treaties. That view also led him to adopt the distinction between a universal law of nations and a European or Christian law of nations, and, following a fundamental division in civil law scholarship, between a common and a particular law of nations (*ius gentium commune et proprium*). Thus, Rachel, whose 'dissertation' on the *ius gentium* is not aimed at examining systematically its various issues, does nevertheless represent an approach highlighting the 'particular' sources of the law of nations. J.W. Textor (1638–1701), in contrast, wrote a general survey of the law of nations (*Synopsis iuris gentium*, 1680)[69] in a more distinctly legal register. The classification of his work among early-modern positivists is mainly due to his insistence on custom and practice as a source of the law of nations: here, history is adduced as evidence of those international customs, but rather in order to bring to the fore the gradual changes in international law than any atemporal universal principle. *Ius gentium*, in Textor's manual, is still understood in its broader sense, with the effect

68 S. Rachel, *De jure naturae et gentium dissertationes*, Kiloni, Literis Joachimi Reumanni, 1676 (reprint Washington D.C., The Carnegie Institution, 1916).

69 J.W. Textor, *Synopsis juris gentium*, Basileae, Impensis Joh. Michaelis Rüdingeri, Typis Jacobi Bertschii, 1680 (reprint Washington D.C., Carnegie Institution, 1916).

that it includes various issues of private and public domestic law, as well as issues related to conflicts of laws; from his viewpoint, within the Holy Roman Empire, he still refers to the *Christiana respublica* to reprove treaties made with the Turks with the intention of causing harm to other Christian nations. These are not the only indications that Textor was apparently reluctant to cast away all older views and learning, for although most parts of his outline refer to both *usus modernus* authors and to the developing *Vernunftrecht*, and, in the conventional post-humanist fashion, to extensive historical material, these authorities are joined in several sections by much older legal authors, both from the late-medieval Italian school and early humanists. Yet, the *Synopsis* also includes chapters on areas of the law of nations which legal doctrines had been at times slower to develop systematically, such as the law of neutrals or the law of international trade.

The *usus modernus*'s early systematization proved on the whole more successful in the monographic literature dealing with a specific legal topic or area. R. Zouche's work highlights both the progress made and the deficiencies of any attempts at global systematization outside the tracks laid down by Gentili and Grotius. In his *Elementa jurisprudentiae* (*ed.pr.* 1629),[70] Zouche had suggested a general principle of systematization – also applicable to international law – based on the Institutional system.[71] However, in his major work on the law of nations,[72] Zouche applied a highly consistent subdivision between what he considered settled law and legal controversies. Each of these two parts he further subdivided according to the same plan: first by discussing topics relating to peace, then topics relating to war; again, each subdivision, on peace and on war, was further subdivided by addressing the same issues for nations at peace and for belligerents: their status, their property, the modalities of their legal relationship, and infringements of their status, property or the modalities of their relationship. Within that comparatively rigid structure, Zouche's approach to specific issues and questions is characterized by his constant case-method, adducing both in the first and in the second part historical precedents taken from classical and later sources.[73]

---

[70] I have used the edition: R. Zouch, *Elementa jurisprudentiae, definitionibus, regulis et sententiis selectioribus juris civilis, illustrata; accesserunt, descriptiones juris et judicii, sacri, militaris, et maritimi*, Lugd. Batavorum, Apud Johannem et Danielem Elsevirios, 1652.

[71] Ibid., p. 9: '. . . Et denique in Communione generali, quae inter diversos Principes et Respublicas per Legationes, Foedera, et Bella exercetur. In qualibet vero Communione concurrunt, personae, res, et actus humani: unde, omne jus vel ad personas, vel ad res, vel ad actiones pertinet.'

[72] R. Zouch, *Iuris et iudicii fecialis, sive iuris inter gentes, et quaestionum de eodem explicatio. Qua Quae ad Pacem et Bellum inter diversos Principes, aut Populos spectant, ex praecipuis Historico-jure-peritis, exhibentur*, Oxoniae, Excudebat H. Hall, Impensis Tho. Robinson, 1650 (reprint Washington D.C., 1911). For a modern French translation with an introduction by D. Gaurier: *Explication du droit et du droit fécial, ou Explication du droit entre les nations et des questions à son sujet, par laquelle on montre ce qui regarde la paix et la guerre entre les différents princes et peuples à partir des savants en histoire et en droit, par Richard Zouche, auteur des Éléments de jurisprudence.* [Traduction, introduction et notes de D. Gaurier], Limoges, Pulim, 2009 (with a CD-Rom including a reproduction of the Oxford 1650 edition). For a list of the editions, see P. Stein's bio-bibliographical entry s.v. 'Zouche, Richard' in the *Oxford Dictionary of National Biography*.

[73] Among the many monographs on various topics of international law which were written under the later *usus modernus*, and which can partly be traced through Glafey, Ompteda and other

Specimen I: early usus modernus

Grotius's *Mare liberum* is one of the most famous pamphlets of early-modern international law.[74] Its publication inspired at the time several other authors to write on the law of the sea, sparking a 'book-war' which, in turn, proved a catalyst for international law scholarship in general. *Mare liberum*, first published (anonymously) in 1609, was a section of Grotius's unpublished extensive consultation to the Dutch East India Company on the law of prize, an elaborate argumentation intended to establish that the Company's military engagements with the Portuguese in the East Indies qualified as a just war. The *Mare liberum* section was drawn from that part of the argument in which Grotius had challenged the Portuguese claims of a monopoly or exclusive dominion over the maritime routes to the Indies and its trade. Grotius's arguments in favour of the Dutch Company could also be applied by the English, whose East Indian Company was equally bent on breaking the Portuguese monopoly.[75] The first publication of the *Mare liberum* in 1609, however, should be seen as an attempt to assert the same arguments, which were agreeable to the English in their fight against the Portuguese, in the context of the Dutch–British controversy regarding British claims to refuse access to Dutch fishing ships in their coastal waters. Only the context of the first publication of that part of *De iure praedae* may explain how the same arguments used against Portuguese trade and colonial claims in the Indies could now potentially be turned against British claims to protect fishery near their coast in the North Sea: the text of *Mare liberum* remained, as in the original, larger work, a Dutch argument against the Portuguese claims. Hence *Mare liberum* has more the appearance of a polemical pamphlet than that of an objective or impartial treatise on the law of international trade or the law of the seas. Yet, it retains some of the features of a systematic treatise because it addresses and refutes the various substantial legal grounds of the Portuguese claims (discovery, papal concessions, law of war, possession, positive prescription . . .) in separate chapters, some of which are duplicated for discussing severally, in the first place, the claims pertaining to the sea and the navigation routes, and, subsequently, those pertaining to trade with the Indians. The register of Grotius's argument allies a neo-Latin humanistic style based on classical literary and historical sources[76] with medieval theological and legal authorities, together with a few 16th-century legal authorities which may alternatively be categorized as traditional, humanistic or already expressing the early *usus modernus*. These characteristics, and the influence of the pamphlet in generating a specific strand of legal literature on the law of the sea, make of the *Mare liberum* a typical example of the transition achieved by the early *usus modernus* from the converging currents of 16th-century humanism and traditional methods to the later, more accomplished systematization of the *usus modernus*, which could then rely more directly on the body of literature produced by the earlier authors of the *usus modernus*.

---

older bibliographical works of reference (including the *Bibliotheca iuridica* by M. Lipenius), the dissertations (especially in the Germanic countries, and the countries where the academic system was influenced by the German curriculum) take an important place: cf. F. Ranieri (ed.), *Juristische Dissertationen deutscher Universitäten 17–18. Jahrhundert*, Frankfurt a.M., Vittorio Klostermann, 2 vols., 1986, references in the index, vol. 2, p. 1038 (esp. Völkerrecht; Völkerrechtsverträge, Gesandschaftsrecht, Rang, Kriegsrecht, Seerecht, Völkerrechtsstreitfälle).

74 A quasi-critical edition is now available: R. Feenstra (ed.), *Hugo Grotius Mare Liberum 1609–2009*, Leiden, Boston, Brill, 2009, offering a facsimile reprint of the original imprint of 1609, a critical *apparatus* (with a general introduction) of the sources quoted by Grotius, and an introduction to the successive imprints of the book.

75 K. Zemanek, 'Was Hugo Grotius Really in Favour of the Freedom of the Seas?', JHIL 1999, 48–60.

76 B. Straumann, *Hugo Grotius und die Antike. Römisches Recht und römische Ethik im frühneuzeitlichen Naturrecht*, Baden-Baden, Nomos Verlag, 2007.

political, diplomatic and historical approaches contributed to the shaping of a theory of international law that strove to reduce the tension between a normative approach to international relations and *Realpolitik*. The heritage of that theory would, however, soon be eroded and largely lost by 19th-century legal positivism and 20th-century idealism in international law scholarship.

Specimen I: Law of Reason

J.A. Ickstatt (1702–1776)[93] was educated at Marburg, where he first studied mathematics and philosophy under C. Wolff, then law, a subject he pursued at Mainz. From 1731 until 1741, he held the newly created chair in natural law and the law of nations in Würzburg. He published mainly in the area of public law, but also, in 1740, *Elementa juris gentium*.[94] After 1741, he taught at Ingolstadt, where he was also entrusted with the administration of the university. From the 1760s onwards, he was a political counsellor to the Wittelsbach in Bavaria.

His *Elementa* were written for a public academic discussion held in the course of the curriculum of the young count Charles of Colloredo[95] and reflect Wolff's influence on Ickstatt's methods. The bulk of the book (pp. 1–522) deals with the 'natural' law of nations; only the last 20 pages (pp. 523–542) with the 'positive' law of nations. However, the natural law of nations, in Ickstatt's approach, is practically exclusively concerned with questions of international public law (though some sections deal with conflicts of law): the concept of the law of nations and its subdivisions, the international community, its actors and the law of international relations in general, international law in peace-time (including territorial law and treaties), the law of war (both *ius belli* and *ius in bello*), the law of peace treaties (including truces) and the law of embassies. The style is characteristic of the legal-theoretical approach of the

---

de l'abbé de Mably, London, 1789, vols. 5–6 (the oldest edition I have used: *Le droit public de l'Europe fondé sur les traitez conclus jusqu'en l'année 1740*, The Hague, J. Van Duren, 1746, 2 vols.). See also G. de Réal de Curban, *La Science du Gouvernement, ouvrage de morale, de droit et de politique, qui contient les principes du commandement et de l'obéissance, où l'on réduit toutes les matières de gouvernement en un corps unique,* [. . .] *dans chacune de ses parties; et où l'on explique les droits et les devoirs des Souverains, ceux du sujets, ceux de tous les hommes, en quelque situation qu'ils se trouvent*, Paris, Amsterdam, Aix-la-Chapelle, 1762–1764 (German translation: *Die Staatskunst* [. . .], Frankfurt, Leipzig, Göbhardtische Buchhandlung, 1762–1767; Ch.-F. Lefèvre de La Maillardière, *Précis du droit des gens, de la guerre, de la paix et des ambassades, première partie de la Bibliothèque politique à l'usage des sujets destinés aux négociations,* Paris, Quillau, 1775; P.-J. Neyron, *Principes du droit des gens européen conventionnel et coutumier, ou bien Précis historique, politique et juridiques des droits* [. . .] *que les États de l'Europe se sont acquis et imposés*, Bronswic, Librairie des orphelins, 1783. Also, by G.F von Martens (1756–1821), the compiler of one of the major collections of treaties, which was continued during the 19th and 20th centuries, *Primae lineae juris gentium europaearum practice* [. . .], Gottingae, Typis Jo. Christ. Dieterich, 1785, better known in its French version: *Précis du droit des gens moderne de l'Europe, fondé sur les traités et l'usage*, Göttingue, J.C. Dieterich, 1789.

93 For a general outline of his life and work: s.v. 'Ickstatt' in *Neue Deutsche Biographie*, vol. 10, pp. 113–115.

94 J.A. Ickstatt, *Elementa juris gentium*, Wirceburgi, Typis Joannis Jacobi Christophori Kleyer, 1740. Outside Germany, the book is not widely available, but I have selected it as a *specimen* because it is a characteristic work of the Law of Reason covering international law in general, and also because it is freely available on the Internet.

95 See on the title-page: '. . . in Alma ducali Julio-Fridericiana universitate Wirceburgensi publicae disquisitioni submittit illustrissimus atque generosissimus dominus S.R.I. Carolus de Colloredo' (under whose name the book is entered in some library catalogues).

Law of Reason: it remains abstract and conceptual, with only very exceptionally a reference to a specific historical example or case,[96] following a presentation based on general definitions and principles, subdivisions, and supplemented by 'corollaries' and '*scholia*'. It also attempts to be comprehensive, covering the whole subject of international law. References to authorities are sparse: in spite of the obvious background of Roman law science, the author mentions only a handful of Roman law texts; the few footnotes to doctrinal authorities are mainly to Wolff and Grotius, and occasionally to other authors of the Law of Reason or the *usus modernus* (but specifically on international law issues). Repeatedly throughout the work, Ickstatt relies on allegedly self-evident propositions or conclusions ('it is clear that', 'it cannot be denied', 'there is no doubt' etc.).

Ickstatt's approach to the international community is based on a political theory, also applicable to domestic polities, emphasising the *socialitas*, the natural inclination of men, whether in their own political order or on the international scene, to live as an orderly society, as a fundamental principle of the law of nations.[97] The strength of the principle is especially obvious when Ickstatt discusses the *ius in bello*, which, he argues, only allows necessary violence, excluding any unnecessary cruelty, particularly against civilians and vulnerable categories of people. Even as a form of retaliation for cruelty suffered, the harm inflicted on the enemy ought to remain proportional.[98] Moreover, a just war should only be waged as a matter of necessity, when all other means to obtain a remedy or security fail: and even then, a belligerent still owes a duty of charity towards his enemy.[99] The *socialitas* also justifies treaties and alliances, including military alliances, with non-Christians – though such alliances should not bring Christian faith in jeopardy.[100]

Noteworthy is also that Ickstatt incorporates several pages on the system of the balance of power (*aequilibrium inter gentes*).[101] He considers the balance not only between individual states, but also through the system of alliances, for example in order to neutralize the increased power of a particular state or coalition; he also recognises that the balance of power may be envisaged at a wider regional level, such as the *aequilibrium Europae* or the *aequilibrium Asiae*.[102] All nations are bound to secure and maintain the balance of power

---

[96] In spite of the fact that, at the beginning, Ickstatt mentions as authorities (or 'principles') of the law of nations: '1) Jus naturale, potissimum sociale hominum in statu naturali viventium; 2) Jus Publicum universale; 3) Historia populorum ac gentium; 4) Notitiae rerumpublicarum, potissimum formarum regiminis, queis quaelibet regitur; 5) pactionum, foederum, sanctionum pacis, ceremoniorum atque observantiarum inter gentes receptarum haud proletaria cognitio [. . .]' (*o.c.*, p. 11; see also p. 26). For a very rare example of (brief) references to ancient and early-modern historical cases (based on statements by Coccejus and Gentili), p. 122 (on the unjustified use of excessive violence and cruelty in warfare).

[97] See first *o.c.* pp. 18–20 (§ 14 ' [. . .] ex socialitate itaque intelligimus, cur populi officiis erga gentes alias prompte satisfaciant; Proin socialitatem pro Juris Gentium principio fundamentali habendam esse constat', and *passim*, throughout the work.

[98] *O.c.*, p. 323.

[99] *O.c.*, p. 321: '. . . arma igitur licet quis in hostem moveat, eundem tamen amat, aut amare saltem obstringitur', and, *ibidem*, in the *scholion* (with reference to Wolff) '*de amore inimicorum*': 'Falluntur, qui omnem in bello amorem erga hostes cessare autumant. Non etenim mala iisdem inferuntur, quod odio a belligerantibus habeantur, sed quoniam obstacula seu impedimenta Juris consequendi existent, quae removere via quacunque necessum sit'.

[100] *O.c.*, pp. 381–383 ('Adversus infideles, atque sacrorum cultu dissentientes populos officia amoris, socialitatis, atque humanitatis haud cessant, nec pactis eadem ipsis promittere, firmareque juri Gentium repugnat; cum infidelibus itaque foedera pangere, mutuamque armorum societatem inire aequitati, aut Juri Gentium per se nullatenus refragari constat', p. 381).

[101] *O.c.*, pp. 359–367.

[102] *O.c.*, p. 359.

(*custodia aequilibrii*) against hegemony (*praepotentia*).[103] Hegemony, or its menace, should be counterbalanced by diplomacy, alliances, but is also, if need be, a just cause of war:[104] the argument based on the balance of power seems to legitimize both a preventive war and, exceptionally, interference in the political affairs of another country.[105]

The natural law of nations is generally applicable: throughout his work, Ickstatt nevertheless distinguishes between those nations who abide by its standards (*morati*, *moratiores*, a notion which prefigures that of civilized nations) and the 'barbarians', whose defining feature appears to be, precisely, their systematic disregard for such standards.[106]

The detailed outline of natural law does not leave much latitude for a general survey of the positive law of nations, based on treaties and customs. Ickstatt merely gives a brief overview of the types of treaties (without, once again, providing systematically any specific or historical examples): on religious matters (such as concordats, or treaties allowing some degree of religious tolerance), treaties on trade and navigation, alliances and peace treaties, political unions and confederations, border treaties, *Barrière* treaties, treaties of friendship, and treaties with regard to the dynastic succession and possibly the division of various dominions, treaties on the use of arms and on neutrality – all these types of treaties, however, are simply mentioned, without going into any detail or mentioning specific cases.[107] The brief section on customary positive law remains even more general, recalling the standards to be met by customs as legal authorities, and briefly mentioning the variety of objects of customary law in the law of nations. The last section, on 'ceremonial' positive law, again simply outlines in general terms the types of issues dealt with: precedence, the formalities of negotiations, of sending and receiving ambassadors, of war declarations, of treaty-making, etc.

Specimen II: Droit public de l'Europe

The 'Kettle War' of 1785 between Austria and the United-Provinces and the expectation that it might lead to a much wider conflict in Europe triggered the publication of several pamphlets in different countries.[108] Among these, the booklet published by Mirabeau on the Scheldt issue expresses some characteristic features of the *Droit public de l'Europe*, all the more so because its main purpose is arguably neither to discuss the navigation on the

---

[103] 'Gentes atque populos ad introducendum, custodiendumque aequilibrium, nec non ad impediendum potentiae praepondium omni modo obstrictos esse liquescit' (*o.c.*, p. 361).

[104] *O.c.*, p. 364 (and the *scholion*: '[. . .] Securitatis atque tranquillitatis conservatio prima Gentium lex est').

[105] *O.c.*, pp. 364–366.

[106] The distinction is formally introduced at pp. 22 and 40–41, but it occurs *passim* in various other passages, in particular in the chapters on the law of war.

[107] In the context of commercial treaties, Ickstatt mentions exceptionally (e.g.) the *assiento* treaties between Spain, France and England.

[108] F. Magnette, *Joseph II et la liberté de l'Escaut. La France et l'Europe* [Mémoires couronnés et autres mémoires publiés par l'Académie Royale des Sciences, des Lettres et des Beaux-Arts de Belgique, in-8°, T. LV], Brussels, 1896–1898, and some additional source material mentioned in A. Cauchie, 'Le comte L.C.M. de Barbiano de Belgiojoso et ses papiers d'État conservés à Milan', *Bulletin de la Commission Royale d'Histoire*, vol. 81, Brussels, 1912, 147–332. For a useful list of pamphlets published around the 'Kettle-war', see Ch. Terlinden, 'The History of the Scheldt', *History, The Quarterly Journal of The Historical Association*, New Series, vol. IV (1919–1920), 185–197, and vol. V (1920–1921), 1–10; and F. Magnette, 'Un mémoire inédit sur la liberté de l'Escaut', *Compte rendu des séances de la Commission Royale d'Histoire, ou Recueil de ses Bulletins*, Cinquième série, vol. V, Brussels, 1895, 405–417. Mirabeau's pamphlet was partly a reaction against a publication on the issue by Linguet, see A. Wijffels, 'Flanders and the Scheldt Question. A Mirror of the Law of International Relations and its Actors', *Sartoniana* 15 (2002), 213–280, at p. 244.

Scheldt nor the war itself, but to promote Mirabeau's agenda in favour of political reforms and republican regimes inspired by the Enlightenment, and perhaps also a move to enhance French influence.[109] Mirabeau briefly develops a general legal argument at the beginning of his pamphlet, first considering the Emperor's claim to free navigation on the Scheldt Estuary (under control of the United-Provinces) according to natural law, then under the rules of positive international law. He concedes the validity of the claim by the standards of natural law – mainly on the grounds of the natural freedom of navigation and trade – but the natural law he refers to is not the Law of Reason. His concept of natural law is that of the principles which prevail in a natural state between polities, i.e. before they have begun to form an international society. At that stage, anarchy and the right of the mightiest hold sway over international relations. The law of nations based on customs and treaties is the continuous attempt to work out an international order governed by law rather than by unregulated force. The cumulative effect of treaties, to which Mirabeau refers as 'the political code of Europe',[110] is the expression in positive law, often in very specific terms (such as, in this case, the virtual closing of the Scheldt estuary by the Dutch, enshrined in the Peace of Westphalia and later treaties) of the Law of Reason (which Mirabeau does not mention as such) and should therefore prevail over the principles which hold sway as long as an (international) society is not being formed. The argument relies strongly (but mainly implicitly) on the principle of balance of power as a means to regulate otherwise unrestrained force.

CONCLUSION

International law scholarship during the early-modern centuries reflects the various stages of development of civil law scholarship in general, affecting all areas of the law, whether private or public law, or even public international law. The four main approaches which have been discussed in this chapter are not to be seen as distinct 'schools', which would serve the purpose of pigeonholing particular works in each category. They should be understood as successive stages of developments of legal science, mirroring in many ways broader intellectual and scientific developments in early-modern Western Europe. They also superseded each other gradually and partially. At the beginning of the 16th century, the Italian method still prevailed and an alternative approach had not yet become a major issue. Legal humanism, although fundamentally opposed to the Italian method on account of its core principles, was often subject to a compromise by lawyers seeking to steer a middle course between tradition and modernization. It failed to become the mainstream canon of legal science as the Italian method had been during the later Middle Ages, but even beyond the somewhat marginal position of antiquarian studies during the 17th and 18th centuries, its style and many of its essential contributions to the renewal of legal studies – including references to ancient history based on sound historical studies and criticism – were retained by later generations of lawyers until the end of the early-modern era, even if their methods and aims were not those of the 16th-century legal humanists. The *usus modernus* built on the literature of both the Italian method and legal

[109] Mirabeau [H.-G. Riquetti de], *Doutes sur la liberté de l'Escaut Réclamée par l'Empereur; Sur les Causes et sur les Conséquences probables de cette Réclamation*, À Londres, Chez G. Faden [. . .], chez J. Robson [. . .] P. Elmsley [. . .], s.d. [1785].

[110] Mirabeau, *Doutes*. . . [see previous note], p. 12 ('. . . le traité de Munster me paroît justifié; et loin qu'il soit un monument de déraison, je le regarde comme une des loix les plus importantes du code politique de l'Europe').

humanism and superseded both when it became gradually, from the second half of the 16th century until the mid 17th century, the new mainstream legal method among both academic jurists and legal practitioners. When under the influence of rationalist philosophy and sciences, the Law of Reason developed, their authors incorporated features of both legal humanism and *usus modernus* in their distinctive methods. By then, however, both the authorities and the style of reasoning of the Italian method had become obsolete and would no longer appear as visible layers of legal thinking.

By replacing international law scholarship in the context of these successive approaches of legal scholarship in general, the continuity of legal literature, in spite of the emergence of a new typology of works, of the changes in style and in the use of authorities, and, foremost, of a substantial corpus of legal studies dealing specifically with international law as a whole or with some of its specific topics, becomes more intelligible rather than focusing on these monographic works without reference – as in Ompteda's bibliography – to the ongoing *ius commune* tradition since the late Middle Ages. Yet, as it has already been pointed out in the opening paragraph of this chapter, one cannot reduce early-modern scholarship to intellectual history either: beyond legal methods, the changes which at the time marked the political actors, the international community and its actors, and the involvement of European powers overseas, all contributed to influencing the development of the substantive doctrines of the law of nations from the demise of the *Res publica Christiana* to the era of self-professed civilized nations in the early 19th century.

3 Natural law and the law of nations

Patrick Capps

3.1 INTRODUCTION

Modern natural lawyers hold that all legal norms must be practically reasonable if they are to be valid or binding. An act or a norm can be said to be practically reasonable if it is consistent with a set of other-regarding, or moral, constraints. So, natural lawyers make the claim that there is some intimate connection between law and morality. The moral content of law is usually to be found in concepts like the common good or human dignity. Natural law comes in strong and weak varieties. The stronger version has morality performing an analytical or classificatory function: *lex injusta non est lex*. The weaker version has morality performing a normative function: law is defective if it does not correspond to morality.[1] The opposing position, legal positivism, denies a necessary connection between law and morality and holds that law is to be identified with reference to a social source.[2]

All of these positions have found adherents in modern international legal theory. Historically, however, we see positivism emerging in international law as a dominant position in the later part of the nineteenth century, even though its central claims have a longer history. Prior to this, natural law theory can be said to be the dominant theory by which the authority and content of the law of nations was justified. The application of natural law theory to the law of nations became popular in the late sixteenth century.

For Lesaffer, there is an obvious cause of the turn to natural law at the start of this period. The emergence of a set of claims that natural law governed nations coincided with the demise of the authority of the Holy Roman Empire and the subsequent rise of the modern state system around the mid sixteenth century.[3] The empty box left by the Empire's demise was readily filled by natural law theory, which demanded (and structured the content of) self-restraint from states. Natural law, rather than the Pope or the Emperor, was now understood to govern international relations. Treaties and customs between states were binding not because they were legitimated somehow by a temporal authority. Rather, they were binding as a matter of moral necessity and insofar as they were consistent with natural law. The origins of this position are found in the works of Spanish neo-scholastic philosophers such as Suarez, de Soto and Vitoria who were influenced, in turn, by Aquinas. In the early seventeenth century, we see similar sorts of arguments being advanced by Gentili and Grotius relying on humanist (i.e. Roman)

---

[1] See M Murphy, *Natural Law in Jurisprudence and Politics* (Cambridge University Press, Cambridge, 2006), chapter 1.

[2] Of course, legal positivism is not obviously incompatible with weak natural law theory.

[3] See R Lesaffer, 'The Grotian Tradition Revisited: Change and Continuity in the History of International Law' (2002) 73 *BYIL* 103, 105. See also TE Holland, 'Alberico Gentili' (inaugral lecture delivered at All Souls College, Oxford in 1874) 20.

sources.[4] This intellectual tradition instigated by all of these philosophers carries on through Hobbes and Rousseau to Kant and Bentham.[5] The familiar story would have it that the first serious attempts to use positivism to ground the law of nations emerges around the time Kant and Bentham were writing on this subject, and gains popularity thereafter.[6]

In this chapter, the focus is on the early humanist philosophers, Alberico Gentili and Hugo Grotius, and Immanuel Kant. Each wrote extensively on the law of nations, and all are normally understood to have defended natural law. Although it is correct to exercise a degree of caution concerning the credentials of all of these philosophers as natural lawyers, it is true that each recognised that there were universal moral obligations which were binding on all human agents as well as states. Thus each focused intensely on the question of how natural law could be applied to the study of the law of nations. My aim in this chapter is to show how each attempted to ground a conception of natural law and the law of nations in some essential aspect of human nature or human agency by way of a response to the rise of scepticism about the possibility of such a project.

3.2 SCEPTICISM

After the First World War, the major works of Gentili and Grotius, as well as those of many other old thinkers on international law, were translated into English through the Carnegie Endowment for International Peace, under the editorship of James Brown Scott. According to Richard Tuck, the influence of Scott on these translations leaves us with a 'very misleading picture' about the nature of the intellectual endeavour which these early writers on war and peace were undertaking. Scott and his co-editors assumed that the '. . . subject of "international law" was gradually uncovered and understood in increasingly less primitive terms by writers from the Middle Ages onwards in a manner

---

4 There is considerable disagreement between modern scholars as to the relationship between the scholastic philosophers and the early humanists such as Gentili and Grotius. For example, Lesaffer (ibid) finds that the substance of the claims made by Gentili and Grotius is not fundamentally different to the Spanish neo-scholastics. This influence is also acknowledged by P Haggenmacher (see 'Grotius and Gentili: A Reassessment of Thomas E. Holland's Inaugural Lecture' in H Bull, B Kingsbury and A Roberts (eds), *Hugo Grotius and International Relations* (Clarendon Press, Oxford, 1992)). Panizza as well as Tierney argue that Grotius was more influenced by the neo-scholastics than was Gentili (D Panizza, 'Political Theory and Jurisprudence in Gentili's De Iure Belli: The Great Debate between "Theological" and "Humanist" Perspectives from Vitoria to Grotius' (2005) International Law and Justice Working Papers, Institute for International Law and Justice, NYU School of Law and B Tierney, *The Idea of Natural Rights: Studies on Natural Rights, Natural Law, and Church Law 1150–1625* (Emory University Studies in Law and Religion, Atlanta, 1997) 318–319). Borschberg argues Grotius's knowledge of scholastics is often overrated (see P Borschberg, 'Grotius' Theory of Trans-Oceanic Trade Regulation: Revisiting Mare Liberum (1609)' (2006) International Law and Justice Working Papers, NYU School of Law). Tuck considers there to be a much sharper division between the two traditions (see R Tuck, *The Rights of War and Peace* (Oxford University Press, Oxford, 1999)).

5 See Tuck, ibid, chapter 7 and R Pound, 'Grotius and the Science of Law' (1925) 19 *AJIL* 685.

6 For example, Jeremy Bentham's *Principles of International Law* were written around this time (available from the UCL Bentham Project, edited by Gunhild Hoogensen).

analogous to pre-Kuhnian ideas about the history of physics; so that. . . . Vitoria, Ayala, Beli and Gentili were all trying to "clarify" some inchoate principles of international law'.[7] Such works were thereby received in a teleological sense as being stones on a path to the modern concept of international law. By way of example, JB Coleman Phillipson's introduction to Gentili's *De jure belli* writes that Gentili was the 'first great writer on *modern* international law, the first clearly to define its subject-matter and to treat it in the way which is on the whole consonant to the conception and practice of our own time'.[8] While this ascription may, for many, better belong to the Spanish neo-scholastics or Grotius,[9] he continues that Gentili has already set out the 'the proper method of international law: namely, the examination of actual phenomena, of concrete facts, and then, by a process of induction, the inferring therefrom of general rules, which, however, were still subject to subsequent modification or even cancellation in the light of newly discovered facts'.[10] This is widely considered to be a misconceived reception of his and Grotius's contribution.

The way in which Scott received the works of the great writers on international law is not now taken seriously. Instead, leading commentators like Randall Lesaffer, Richard Tuck, Ross Harrison, Hedley Bull, Benedict Kingsbury and Benjamin Straumann have all identified that Gentili's and Grotius's target was the rise of moral scepticism in the late sixteenth century, found in the work of, for example, Montaigne, Charron and, fundamentally, Machiavelli. Also, and as just mentioned, each was attempting to defend natural law as a way of filling the authoritative void left by the demise of the Holy Roman Empire and the rise of the autonomous sovereign state. Kant, writing nearly two hundred years later, may be better classified as being in a different historical period.[11] But according to John Rawls, it is the case that he was responding to the exact same problem in his moral and legal philosophy as that faced by Gentili and Grotius, although his target was instead David Hume.

Without going into detail, the sceptical position just mentioned comes in a variety of forms; laws were entirely conventional; natural law was merely a reflection of long-standing custom; or, morality was merely a reflection of self-interest or 'passions'. Therefore, natural law was a mirage or a delusion which is better explained in other, more mundane, ways. Gentili, Grotius and Kant were all responding to these forms of scepticism, which rejected the existence of universal and apodictic moral norms which governed both individual and state action. While there are many international lawyers who find inspiration in the work of Gentili, Grotius and Kant, the teleological view suggested by Scott obscures the precise focus and contributions of these philosophers.

---

7 Ibid, 11–12. This view is also taken by del Vecchio (see D del Vecchio, 'The Posthumous Fate of Alberico Gentili' (1956) 50 *AJIL* 664, 666). More generally, see Haggenmacher (note 4, above, 133) and Panizza (note 4, above).

8 A Gentili, *De Jure Belli* (1588–1589, revised edn, 1598) (*JB*), 18a. More generally, see JB Scott, *Law, the State and the International Community* (Columbia University Press, New York, 1939) chapters 25 and 31.

9 See Lessafer (note 3 above) and B Kingsbury and A Roberts, 'Introduction' in Bull, Kingsbury and Roberts (eds) (note 4 above).

10 *JB*, 19a.

11 Lessaffer (note 3, above, 106).

This said, there is a fundamental difference between the approach taken by Gentili and Grotius, on the one hand, and Kant, on the other, and I will consider this in what follows. Examination of this difference reveals a fundamental shift in the way in which legal theorists understood the relationship between international law and morality. To explain, the response to scepticism advanced by Gentili and Grotius is, in the main, a just war theory. While Kant does advance a just war theory of sorts, this is not his central preoccupation. Rather, he wants to show how the law of nations, properly conceived, is a system of willing which can give rise to a set of legal norms, which govern states and which can be employed to peaceably, through juridical structures, settle disputes. Thus Kant's view of the law of nations is as a means of securing peace between states, rather than justifying war as Gentili and Grotius thought. Viewed from Kant's perspective, the Gentilian and Grotian just war tradition is not really about the law of nations, correctly understood, at all.[12] Instead it is merely a set of moral principles, unilaterally interpreted and acted upon by states.

For Kant, moral reason requires states to seek peace through a law-making confederation. This fundamental shift in the way in which moral reason is used to ground international legal theory is one that reflects the enormous influence Hobbes and Rousseau had on the development of legal theory in the intervening period from Grotius to Kant. In what follows, I aim to set out this fundamental shift in approach to the way in which morality, law and the law of nations relate to one another through a description and analysis of the writings of Gentili, Grotius and Kant. My focus is on how each sought to ground civil (or state) law and the law of nations in natural law and thus how they attempted to reply to scepticism. Their contribution to hot contemporary debates on freedom of the seas or the treatment of non-Christian peoples will only be mentioned to the extent that it is relevant to my explanation of my central claims.

3.3 ALBERICO GENTILI

Alberico Gentili was born in 1552 in Gineso, Northern Italy, and came to England in 1580 to escape persecution. He was appointed Regius Professor of Law at the University of Oxford in 1587 and probably died in 1608. He produced three works which are of direct relevance to international lawyers: *De legationibus* (*DL*, *On Embassies*, 1585) which concerned diplomatic law; *De jure belli* (*JB*, *On the Laws of War*, first published in 1588–1589 with a revised edition appearing in 1598) which concerned the laws of war; and *Hispanicae advocationis* (*HA*, *The Pleas of a Spanish Advocate*, 1613 and published posthumously) which is a collection of legal opinions compiled from his practice as an advocate of the Government of Spain in England. English translations of these works are readily found in various volumes published by the Carnegie Endowment for International Peace. It is accepted that Gentili's work has been superseded in its reception by Grotius. However, recently Gentili's work has been reconsidered as an important influence on Grotius's work. As such, a lively debate has developed on the content and plausibility of Gentili's claims and contribution to the philosophy of the law of nations.[13]

---

12 Ibid, 105.

13 See H Bull, in Bull, Kingsbury and Roberts (note 4, above, 134–138).

3.3.1 Natural law

Gentili defends natural law in two ways. His first argument is that natural law arises as a matter of intuition. He then proceeds to support his argument with reference to state practice and the writings of (primarily) humanist philosophers. This style is similar to that taken by Grotius a few years later as will be seen.

While his approach is clear, Gentili's arguments are often not so. This is especially true of his understanding of the foundation, and content, of natural law and its relationship to the law of nations. This said, there are some passages which, if put together, form a picture of the law of nations which is relatively comprehensible and consistent, even if this picture is revealed by sidelining and ignoring other passages. To begin with he writes that there 'are everywhere certain unwritten laws, not enacted by men (since men could not all assemble in one place, not were they all with one speech), but given to them by God. . . . We have not received them through instruction, but have acquired them at birth; we have gained them, not by training, but by instinct.'[14] This passage distinguishes between laws that come from 'training' and those that come from 'instinct'. Put another way, some laws must be taught and some are intuitive or innate. This distinction corresponds to human law and natural law, respectively.

The use of the word 'instinct' indicates, in modern language, an intuitivist grounding for natural law. This ascription is borne out when he writes 'natural reason is evident of itself and therefore those who rely upon it are content merely to say "This is perfectly clear from nature itself"'.[15] This view is also supported by Phillipson's reading of Gentili's natural law in his introduction to *JB*. Here he writes that Gentili's natural law is rooted in 'the sense of humanity, justice and the best common sense of mankind'.[16] Both Scott's commentary on, and van der Mollen's biography of, Gentili support this view.[17]

This foundation gives rise to a range of substantive obligations which forms a basic framework of principles, or natural laws, which govern human social relationships. Gentili gives a variety of examples: 'to live honourably; not to wrong another; to give every man his due; to protect one's children; to defend oneself against injury; to recognize kinship with all men; to maintain commercial relations'.[18] He then transposes these principles into international relations. So, he writes that it is sometimes necessary to come to the defence of an ally (which corresponds to the natural law to live honourably), to protect individuals in another state from their sovereign (to recognise kinship with all men) and to engage in self-defence (to defend oneself against injury).[19] Natural law, then, applies equally to states as it does to human beings acting individually in international relations. These natural laws, it seems, concern how members of a society should treat

---

14 *JB*, 9–10.

15 *JB*, 10.

16 *JB*, 21a.

17 Scott (note 8, above, 374–375) and G van der Molen, *Alberico Gentili and the Development of International Law* (Leiden, Sijthoff, 2nd edition, 1968, first published in 1937) 202–203.

18 *JB*, 18.

19 Gentili also writes: '. . . for if a sword has been given to a magistrate to protect his citizens against harm, why should he not ward off injury which comes from without, as well as that which exists within?' (*JB*, 28).

each other, rather than being understood as explicit subjective natural rights as found in Grotius's work.[20]

3.3.2 The sovereign state

As mentioned in the introduction, from the mid sixteenth century onwards, neo-scholastic and humanist natural lawyers aimed to provide a normative explanation of the new political and legal institution that is known as the sovereign state. Gentili's concept of the state is hinted at in his definition of an enemy. He writes 'He is an enemy who has a state, a senate, a treasury, united and harmonious citizens, and some basis for a treaty of peace, should matters so shape themselves.'[21] Only sovereign states have these characteristics which are necessary, in the language of modern international law, for *effective governance*. Sovereignty, which arises from having these characteristics, means that the state cannot be constrained by civil or public law. He writes that states '. . . are only supreme and they alone merit the title of public, while all others are inferior and are rated as private individuals. The sovereign has no earthly judge, for one over whom another holds a superior position is not a sovereign.'[22] In the absence of a sovereign authority above the state, the only possible constraint on states can be the law of nations in the form of natural law. So, in their external relations, states must abide by natural law. Moreover, natural law sets some rules which govern how states should treat their own citizens. Controversially for the time, he writes that '. . . kingdoms were not made for kings, but kings for their kingdoms'.[23] Therefore, 'It is not lawful . . . to do to subjects whatever one wishes.'[24] Thus, natural law operates as a set of normative constraints on the actions of states both internally and externally.

3.3.3 The law of nations

Kingsbury argues that 'Gentili does not have a systematic theory of sources of international law'.[25] This is true, but as with his natural law theory, the gist of his argument for international legal norms can be established. It was just shown how natural law gives rise to a specific set of principles which bind states. This is one part of the law of nations. The second part of the law of nations is filled out by custom and treaties. Custom forms part of the law of nations to the extent that it coheres with the following necessary and sufficient conditions: (i) it is a rule found in state practice and (ii) it is consistent with natural law.[26] This does not require, as with our modern understanding of custom, implicit consent by every state bound to it. Throughout *JB* he makes a number of references to

---

20 See pp. 72–74, below.
21 *JB*, 25.
22 *JB*, 15.
23 *JB*, 76.
24 *JB*, 78.
25 B Kingsbury, 'Gentili, Grotius, and the Extra-European World' in HN Scheiber (ed.), *The Law of the Sea* (Kluwer, The Netherlands, 2000) 43.
26 *JB*, 17. *DL* and *HA* can be read as an attempt to describe customary laws which comprise part of the law of nations. For a discussion see van der Molen (note 17, above, 94–112 and 159–196).

the idea that custom is the practice of a majority of, if not all, states. So, the existence of custom[27]

> . . . must not be understood to mean that all nations actually came together at a given time, and that thus the law of nations was established. The writers to whom I have referred to not make any such statement, and it is not necessary to understand the word *omnes* in such a way that when one speaks of the usage of all nations it should be considered to mean absolutely every nation.

Elsewhere he writes:[28]

> It is from the known that we learn the unknown. In fact, as the rule of a state and the making of its laws are in the hands of a majority of its citizens, just so is the rule of the world in the hands of the aggregation of the greater part of the world. Moreover, this is especially true of the unwritten law; for a custom is binding upon all the members of a state and is called the custom of the entire state, even if every citizen has not agreed to it, but happily some have even opposed it.

Gentili does not write much about treaty law. Maybe this is because he understands treaties as straightforwardly binding by virtue of the natural law to adhere to agreements. This seems to be the case when he writes '. . . when we unite with one another in such a fellowship, we invoke nature; when we form a treaty, the law of nations; when we are joined together by common laws, the state; when we have a common religion (the strongest tie of all), we appeal to the hearts of men and the saint who is the fountain head of that union'.[29] So, as natural law requires us to keep our promises, which establishes the ties between us, so it requires states to abide by their treaties.

He does envisage that treaties and custom are normatively inferior to natural law. This reflects the modern concept of *jus cogens*. Using a hypothetical example, he claims:[30]

> The offenders do not wish to lose the profits from that traffic of theirs. The English do not wish anything to be done which threatens their safety. The law of trade is just; but that of maintaining one's safety is more so. The former is a law of nations, the latter a law of nature. Let trade therefore give way to the kingdom, man to nature, money to life. Those are the principles on which legal contests are settled, namely, that one should yield to the worthier, more expedient, and more just law; that the profane should yield to the sacred, the things of the body to those of the spirit, the interests of fortune to those of the person . . .

This said, if the volitional law of nations does not correspond with natural law, it has no binding force. This indicates that there is normative rather than analytical or classificatory relationship between natural law and human law. Volitional law exists by virtue of being willed, but need not be followed. Therefore, it could be said that Gentili offers a weak natural law theory. This is indicated when he writes that 'the law which may transgress [justice] is none the less a law.'[31]

---

27 *JB*, 8.
28 *JB*, 9.
29 *JB*, 72.
30 *JB*, 102.
31 *JB*, 7.

3.3.4 The laws of war

States hold each other to account for violations of the law of nations because of the absence of a global authority. This observation is the basis of Gentili's just war theory: war is an attempt to enforce some aspect of the law of nations. This said, before resorting to force, states normally have an obligation to resort to arbitration. Gentili writes that '[f]or whereas there are two modes of contention, one by argument and the other by force, one should not resort to the latter if it is possible to use the former'.[32] For a state to do so is to go against natural law:[33]

> Why, to be sure, in order that those who avoid this kind of contest by arbitration and resort at once to the other, that is, to force, may understand that they are setting their faces against justice, humanity, and good precedent, and that they are rushing to arms of their own free will, because they are unwilling to submit to any one's verdict. For why should the disputes of private individuals be settled by arbitration and those of sovereigns not be thus decided, when the former are often greater than these public ones, or at any rate much less clear.

But it is important to be clear about Gentili's point concerning the relationship between arbitration and war. Each state may consider itself wronged by the other. Presumably, the law of nations is able to be used to determine which of two states' position has the greater force in law, but often this is unclear in practice. Thus, in any inter-state dispute, there is often a prima facie or plausible claim on both sides that an injury has been suffered. In situations like these, states must submit to arbitration, to judgment and, potentially, be prepared to make reparations. But if one side refuses to arbitrate, or if the arbitration comes to nothing, war is justified. Gentili writes '. . . if anything seems doubtful, and the sovereign does not wish to leave it unsettled and undefined, he will take up arms even for a doubtful matter (although with greater hesitation) if the other party by whom the law is supposed to be violated, refused to submit to peaceful arbitration, or if arbitration does not result in a decision'.[34] War is justified, it would seem, in those circumstances where arbitration cannot solve the dispute. Once resorted to, war operates like a duel by which the rightfulness of either party's claim is ascertained. His approach here is in opposition to, and more sensitive to the realities of, international disputes than the approach taken by neo-scholastics. To regard both sides as right is a logical contradiction.[35]

Unlike for Grotius, Gentili argues that war is something that can only occur between states. He considers that '[w]ar is a just and public contest of arms'.[36] It is public in the sense that it is '. . . not a broil, a fight, the hostility of individuals' and is a conflict between states.[37] He offers many reasons why states are justified in going to war for violation of the law of nations which go beyond the modern laws of war. His classification of various justifications for war is once again not entirely clear, so instead I will offer five examples which illustrate the various possibilities he had in mind.

---

32 *JB*, 15.
33 *JB*, 16.
34 *JB*, 93.
35 See Panizza (note 4, above, section 3).
36 *JB*, 12.
37 *JB*, 12.

First, Gentili accepts that an armed attack is a violation of natural law and that states are justified in using force in self-defence. This includes collective self-defence, which is drawn from the natural law, and which requires each of us to act honourably and so to help one's allies.[38] Anticipatory self-defence is likewise justified but its exact scope is unclear. In support of anticipatory self-defence he writes that 'we ought not to wait for violence to be offered us, if it is safer to meet it half way'.[39] However, it seems that he does not go so far to allow pre-emptive self-defence to apply in situations where opposing states are growing too powerful. The distinction between the two forms of self-defence runs as follows:[40]

> . . . a defence is just which anticipates dangers that are already meditated and prepared, and also those which are not meditated, but are probably and possible. This last word, however, is not to be taken literally, for in that case my statement would be that it is just to resort to a war of this kind as soon as any one becomes too powerful, which I do not maintain.

So, a state is allowed to engage in self-defence against a state which might use force against it in the future but which currently has no plans to do so, but it cannot attack a state which is building up its armies for, at the time, unknown purposes. This seems to draw a very fine distinction between justified and unjustified self-defence. Indeed, Panizza sees Gentili as advocating pre-emptive self-defence against the Turks as well as to maintain a 'balance of power'.[41] If Panizza is right it could be that such actions in self-defence are justified, for Gentili, by the likely probability of a currently unplanned future attack. Alternatively, it may be that the boundary between anticipatory and pre-emptive self-defence is not entirely worked out in *JB*. Either way, it is the case that Gentili adopts a much wider understanding of self-defence than both the neo-scholastic philosophers and Grotius.[42]

Secondly, he considers that it is possible to intervene in the internal affairs of another state if the ruler violates the obligations he has under natural law to respect those whom he governs. We might call this a rudimentary justification for humanitarian intervention. Specifically, this arises from the common ties we have as human beings under natural law, coupled to the obligations that the rulers of states have towards those they govern. The use of force in such circumstances rests upon his distinction between the state and commonwealth. A commonwealth takes on a specific meaning for Gentili:[43]

> . . . a dispute concerns the commonwealth, when the number of subjects who are aroused to war is so great and of such a character, that since they defend themselves by arms, it is necessary to make war against them. For those who have so much power share as it were in the sovereignty; they are public characters and on an equality with the sovereign, just as one sovereign is said to be on an equality with another when he is able to resist the other in an offer of violence, no matter how much greater and more powerful the latter may be.

---

38 *JB*, 73. Here Gentili writes '. . . it is lawful for anyone to aid a neighbour against injury'.
39 *JB*, 61. See also Panizza (note 4, above, section 4).
40 *JB*, 66.
41 Panizza (note 4, above, section 4).
42 Ibid.
43 *JB*, 75.

The commonwealth can have some degree of personality under the law of nations in distinction to the state which governs it. This idea (which is similar to Locke's concept of civil society) is that members of a community can incorporate as a commonwealth independently of the establishment of the sovereign state. Once it is established that the commonwealth has personality independent from the state and can defend itself, Gentili is free to argue that states can assist it 'if subjects are treated cruelly and unjustly'.[44]

Thirdly, offensive wars are justified when the state's existence is threatened. One (rather odd) example of when this is justified is when the Romans went to war because nearby peoples refused to intermarry with them. Furthermore, offensive wars are justified to take control of unused land possessed by another sovereign when there is a need by a people for space ('the seizure of vacant places is regarded as a law of nature').[45]

Fourthly, war is justified when used to punish those states which violate natural law. He writes: 'Look you, if men clearly sin against the laws of nature and of mankind, I believe that any one whosoever may check such men by force of arms.'[46] So, he approves 'of the opinion of those [like some neo-scholastics] who say that the cause of the Spaniards is just when they make war upon the Indians, who practised abominable lewdness even with beasts, and who ate human flesh, slaying men for that purpose. For such sins are contrary to human nature.'[47] Other circumstances where war is justified for this reason are when there is a violation of some 'privilege of nature'.[48] This corresponds to freedom of the high seas and the right to safe passage along rivers and through other states. It also includes freedom of commerce.[49]

Fifthly, there are human reasons for making war which concern the 'violation of some man-made law' found in treaties and custom.[50] One example he gives is where a state refuses to punish its national who has committed a wrong against another state.[51] Here he distinguishes two types of case: (i) actions done under the instructions of the state; and (ii) where there is a failure (or omission) to punish a private individual or to stop that individual committing a wrongful act. In such cases, 'satisfaction' must be made by the offending state, 'otherwise war could be made upon the whole state'.[52]

Gentili does not allow war to be justified on the grounds of religion alone. This should come as no surprise as he was forced to flee the inquisition in Italy. He argues that one cannot use force to make someone alter their beliefs and they are a matter of choice. He writes, though, that the exception to this rule would be where the religion demands acts which are contrary to natural law.[53]

---

44 *JB*, 75.
45 *JB*, 80.
46 *JB*, 122.
47 *JB*, 122.
48 *JB*, 86.
49 *JB*, 89.
50 *JB*, 93.
51 *JB*, 99.
52 *JB*, 100.
53 *JB*, 123. Gentili writes: 'war is lawful against idolators, if idolatry is joined with the slaughter of innocent victims; for the innocent must be protected'.

3.3.5 Conclusion

Gentili explains how certain natural laws can be justified and how they give rise to the law of nations which, in turn, constrains the actions of states both internally and externally. Violations of the law of nations give rise to a wide set of justifications for war. While we may question whether his work is always coherent, and whether his arguments are fully justified, it remains the case that Gentili did attempt to provide a system in which diverse cultures and religions could interact in accordance with shared and common rules and so provide a rudimentary reply to those of a sceptical disposition. Often, his substantive contribution is quite modern and familiar and one might expect his influence on modern international law to be greater than it is. But Gentili's work, as well as that offered by neo-scholastics, was soon overshadowed by Grotius's contribution. As will be seen, though, Grotius owes a considerable intellectual debt to Gentili.[54]

3.4 HUGO GROTIUS

Grotius was born in 1583 to one of the wealthy ruling families in the Dutch city of Delft and he died in Rostock in 1645. His major works are *De Jure Praedae* (*DJP*, *The Rights of Prize and Booty*, 1606, also known as *De Indis*), *Mare Liberum* (*ML*, *The Free Sea*, 1609) and *De Jure Belli ac Pacis* (*DJBP*, *The Rights of War and Peace*, 1625). *DJP* was unpublished until its rediscovery in the papers of his family in 1864. It was translated and published in English in 1950 by Williams and Zeydel through the funding of the Carnegie Endowment for International Peace. Once *DJP* had been discovered, it was realised that *ML* was based upon Chapter XII of the much larger work. His most famous work, *DJBP*, was first published in 1625, with a revised second edition being published in 1631. Recently, the Liberty Fund has republished Jean Barbeyrac's 1738 English translation of the second edition of *DJBP* as well as Richard Hakluyt's translation of *ML*, which was first published sometime between 1609 and 1616.[55]

Grotius approaches the study of natural law, law of nations and everything else in between, in two ways. In *DJBP*, he writes that 'My first Care was, to refer to the Proofs of those Things that belong to the Law of Nature to some such certain Nations, as none can deny, without doing Violence to his Judgment.'[56] His approach is to show that to

---

[54] See Holland (note 3, above) as well as Haggenmacher (note 4, above, 145–156).

[55] *DJBP*, which will be of primary focus here, is a massive work which runs (in the Liberty Fund edition) to 1,740 pages. Stylistically, it is a difficult book to read. Harrison puts well what the content of this book is like, '[i]t is much more a collection of quotations from all sorts of writers and authorities than it is any kind of new, let alone deductive, exposition of natural law. Indeed, it could well be used as a dictionary of quotations with respect to the topics it deals with.' (R. Harrison, Hobbes. *Locke and Confusion's Masterpiece* (Cambridge, Cambridge University Press, 2003)). See also B Kingsbury, (note 25, above, 43). Martin Wight puts the same point eloquently: '[t]rying to pick a path once again through the baroque thickets of Grotius' work, where profound and potent principles lurk in the shade of forgotten arguments, and obsolete examples [lie] like violets beneath gigantic overgrown rhododendrons'. (See M Wight, *Systems of States* (Leicester, Leicester University Press, 1977) 127.)

[56] *DJBP*, 110–111.

reject natural law would contradict man's nature as a reasoning human agent. He then supplements this essentially a priori approach with an a posteriori method. So he introduces vast lists of quotations from (primarily) humanist scholars.

As mentioned above, this writing style is very similar to the approach taken by Gentili.[57] Haggenmacher describes this similarity well. He writes that it is as if Gentili's work is 'transposed into a different key' by Grotius.[58] Fundamentally, though, *DJBP* is a far more comprehensive and systematic work than Gentili's *JB*. This accounts, probably, for the popular reception of Grotius, which far outstrips that of Gentili.

3.4.1 Natural law

Grotius's central claim is that there are various interests, as well as obligations, which each human being owes to one another, which are universal, and are the case as a matter of practical reason. He is widely regarded as the first natural lawyer to offer a conception of subjective (in the sense of being personally held) natural rights. Grotius, according to Harrison, and with some plausibility, offers a rudimentary and thin justification for universal natural or human rights. Grotius's project in *DJBP* is, in part, to refute sceptical views concerning the universality of such rights. This seems clear from the passage in *DJBP* where Grotius writes that he is responding to Carneades's claims that law is conventional and that natural law 'is a matter of opinion'.[59] According to Tuck, in this passage he is implicitly attacking the scepticism of Montaigne and Charron.[60]

Grotius's conception of natural rights is defended in the following way. They arise from a thin form of sociability – of moral obligations – which each of us must rationally accept as binding whether we are governed by a state or not. The starting point from which such obligations are derived comes from our duty to preserve ourselves.[61] He writes: 'And that 'tis the first Duty of every one to preserve himself in his natural State, to seek after those Things which are agreeable to Nature, and to avert those which are repugnant.'[62] But this claim should not be understood as a precursor to a proto-Hobbesian view of practical reason understood in terms of prudence and diffidence as Tuck believes.[63] Rather, each

---

57 See Kingsbury (note 25, above, 48). This point is also made by Del Vecchio (note 7, above, 666).

58 Haggenmacher (note 4, above, 159) and Tierney (note 4, above, 316).

59 *DJBP*, 76–77. Lauterpacht, it should be noted, does not spot this connection when he claims that Grotius does not attempt to respond to scepticism. See H Lauterpacht, 'The Grotian Tradition in International Law' (1946) 23 *BYIL* 1, 33–35. On the reception of Grotius by Wight, Bull and Lauterpacht, see B Kingsbury, 'A Grotian Tradition of Theory and Practice?: Grotius, Law, and Moral Skepticism in the Thought of Hedley Bull' (1997–1998) 17 *Quinnipiac Law Review* 3.

60 See Tuck (note 4, above) and R Tuck, 'Grotius, Carneades and Hobbes' (1983) 4 *Grotiana* 43–67. Tierney is sceptical of Tuck's claim (Tierney, note 4, above, 317–324).

61 This takes greater prominence in *DJP* and the first edition of *DJBP* than in the second edition of *DJBP*.

62 *DJBP*, 180.

63 To describe Grotius as a proto-Hobbesian is more accurately ascribed to the process by which the creation of civil law implies the alienation of natural rights. See below, 74–77.

human agent's self-interest is limited by certain moral obligations to others which arise from their 'reasonable and sociable Nature'.[64] Grotius writes:[65]

> Now amongst the Things peculiar to Man, is his Desire of Society, that is, a certain Inclination to live with those of his own Kind, not in any Manner whatever, but peaceably, and in a Community regulated according to the best of his Understanding; which Disposition the Stoics termed *oikeiosis*. Therefore the Saying, that every Creature is led by Nature to seek its own private Advantage, expressed thus universally, must not be granted.

Oikeiosis, for Grotius, refers to a natural affection that we have for each other and he claims that we are naturally sociable. Thus, it is our nature as social beings which imposes strict limits on our pursuit of self-interest. Specifically, it is unjust to act in ways which violate these natural moral obligations towards others. Beyond this, though, people are free to act in accordance with their own interests. He continues:[66]

> This Sociability, which we have now described in general, or this Care of maintaining Society in a Manner conformable to the Light of human understanding, is the Fountain of Right, properly so called; to which belongs the Abstaining from that which is another's and the Restitution of what we have of another's; or the Profit we have made by it, the Obligation of fulfilling Promises, and Reparation of a Damage done through our own Default, and the Merit of Punishment among Men.

These moral obligations are concerned with corrective justice rather than distributive justice.[67] Specifically, they require us not to harm others and not deprive others of that which is rightfully theirs. But they do not include obligations of charity or virtue. The moral obligations he accepts cash out into three natural laws. The first, the *law of inoffensiveness*, requires us to not harm each other: 'Let no one inflict injury upon his fellows.'[68] The second is the *law of abstinence*. We should not seize the property of others.[69] To do otherwise contradicts human sociability: '. . . if every Man were to seize on the Goods of another, and enrich himself by the Spoils of his Neighbour, human Society and Commerce would necessarily be dissolved'.[70] From this also springs his arguments for freedom of the seas: that is, the idea that there are some things which are unownable and to claim otherwise contradicts man's natural sociability.[71] Thirdly, Grotius thinks that we have a moral obligation to *keep our promises*, and to do otherwise, once again, contradicts the premise which is man's sociable nature. He writes: '. . . the fulfilling of Convents belongs to the Law of Nature (for it was necessary there should be some Means

---

64 *DJBP*, 182. See also B Kingsbury and B Straumann 'The State of Nature versus Commercial Sociability as the Basis of International Law: Reflections on the Roman Foundations and Current Interpretations of the International Political and Legal Thought of Grotius, Hobbes and Pufendorf' in S Beson and J Tasioulas (eds), *The Philosophy of International Law* (Oxford, Oxford University Press, 2010) chapter 1.

65 *DJBP*, 79–81.

66 *DJBP*, 86.

67 *DJBP*, 134 and Tuck (note 4, above, 88–89) and R Tuck, *Natural Rights Theories* (Cambridge University Press, Cambridge, 1979) 60–61.

68 Ibid, 85.

69 See Armitage's introduction to *ML* at xiii. Also see Tuck (note 4, above, 85).

70 *DJBP*, 185.

71 See Borschberg (note 4, above).

of obliging Men among themselves, and we cannot conceive any other more conformable to Nature).'[72]

As mentioned above, these minimal moral obligations we have to each other correspond to a set of natural or human rights. If so, this makes Grotius the first of the natural lawyers to give an account of such rights. Harrison writes:[73]

> These basic natural rights are needed for a basic sociability, which, it will be remembered, applies to all people as such and does not depend upon their being members of the same more particular community. Such basic sociability is needed for being fully human, and these natural rights are the basic human rights (rights that all people have merely by virtue of being human).

This very modern way of putting Grotius's three laws does make considerable sense. For Grotius, the right to not be harmed, for our property not to be interfered with, and to have our agreements kept are all forms of possession over which we have, in a sense, sovereignty. For this reason they are subjectively held natural, or human, rights. As possessions, we are able to alienate, or give away, our rights. If these rights are violated by others without consent, a moral duty to afford some sort of reparation arises. If reparations are not forthcoming, a right to punish emerges. For these reasons, it seems safe to claim that Grotius defends a thin concept of natural rights.[74]

3.4.2 Restitution and punishment

As just mentioned, a right to restitution arises from violation of natural law. If restitution is not forthcoming, a subsequent right to punish arises.

One of the most controversial claims Grotius makes is that actions in pursuance of the right to punish need not come from the individual harmed. Rather, anyone can punish those who violate natural law.[75] He writes in *DJP* that '. . . natural Reason informs us, that a Malefactor may be punished, but not who ought to punish him'.[76] This point is crucial when it comes to his theory of the state and the law of nations.

3.4.3 Civil law and the state

The key to Grotius's justification of the state is the idea that, as possessions, individuals can give away or alienate their natural rights. Members of a community establish the state by contracting with each other to give up certain natural rights to state institutions.[77] For

---

72 *DJBP*, 93.

73 See Harrison (note 55, above, 143) and Tuck's introduction to *DJBP*, 55.

74 On the Roman origins of Grotius's concept of natural rights see B Straumann, 'Is Modern Liberty Ancient? Roman Remedies and Natural Rights in Hugo Grotius's Early Works on Natural Law' (2009) 27 *Law and History Review* 55 and K Haakonssen, 'Hugo Grotius and the History of Political Thought' (1985) 13 *Political Theory* 239. See also B Tierney (note 4, above, chapter 13), R Tuck, *Natural Rights Theories: Their Origin and Development* (Cambridge, Cambridge University Press, 1979) chapter 3 esp 72–74 and A Brett, *Liberty, Right and Nature* (Cambridge, Cambridge University Press, 1997) 204 on the validity of the claim that subjective rights emerged with Grotius.

75 See Tuck's introduction to *DJBP*, xx–xxi and also *DJP*, 91–92.

76 See Tuck's introduction to *DJBP*, xii.

77 Grotius writes that contracts or treaties are an 'Alienation of some Part of our Liberty'. See

this reason, it comes as no surprise that his philosophy is often described as a rudimentary social contractarian argument.[78]

Grotius explains the process of state formation in the following way: '. . . since the fulfilling of Convents belongs to the Law of Nature (for it was necessary there should be some Means of obliging Men among themselves, and we cannot conceive any other more conformable to Nature) from this very Foundation Civil Laws were derived.'[79] Thus, the alienation of natural rights through contract is how the state is established and why civil laws enacted by the state are binding. Primarily, the right which is alienated through this contract, and transferred to state institutions, is the right to punish.[80] This is clear from the following:[81]

> Is it not the power to punish essentially a power that pertains to the state? Not at all! On the contrary, just as every right of the magistrate comes to him from the state, so has the same right come to the state from private individuals; and similarly, the power of the state is the result of collective agreement. . . . Therefore, since no one is able to transfer a thing that he never possessed, it is evident that the right of chastisement was held by private persons before it was held by the state.

Grotius argues that we alienate this right on the grounds of expediency or utility. He writes that it is[82]

> . . . more conducive to the Peace of Mankind, that Differences should be decided by a third Person that is disinterested, than that every Man should be allowed to do himself Justice in his own Cause, wherein the Illusions of Self-Love are much to be apprehended: Equity itself, and natural Reason, advise us to submit to so laudable an Institution.

Through this transfer, the sovereign state gains the authority to resolve disputes through the creation and interpretation of civil law, and has a monopoly on the right to punish those who violate it. Grotius argues that it is natural reason which requires us to alienate our right to punish to the state. Natural reason leads each to the conclusion that the state is better able to secure their natural rights.

At this point a central point of contention arises for those who have studied Grotius's work: if the right to punish can be alienated, can the same be said about other natural rights? Grotius's answer is not entirely satisfactory or clear. It seems that while his inclination is to require that civil law is consistent with the natural law, he is reluctant to allow disobedience in the face of unjust civil laws. This ambivalence leads to two views, each of which reflects the relationships between natural rights and the state adopted by Hobbes and Locke later in the seventeenth century.

DJBP, 704 and A Brett, 'Natural Rights and Civil Community: The Civil Philosophy of Hugo Grotius' (2002) 45 *The Historical Journal* 31 at 42–43.

78 See Straumann (note 74 above, 59ff), P Borschberg, 'Grotius, the Social Contract and Political Resistance' (2006/7) International Law and Justice Working Papers, Institute for International Law and Justice, NYU School of Law and Haakonssen (note 74, above).

79 *DJBP*, 93.

80 See Tuck (note 4, above, 78–79).

81 *DJP*, 91–92.

82 *DJBP*, 241. See Brett (note 77, above, 43).

The Lockean view, which is consistent with the idea that Grotius is a natural lawyer, is that civil law simply expands, specifies and amplifies the content of natural law but cannot be in contradiction with it. One example of this line of argument is found in *ML* where he writes: 'It is no more lawful for kings to transgress these [natural laws] than for the common people to impugn the decrees of senators, senators to resist the edicts of presidents, and viceroys the laws and statutes of their kings, for those very laws of people and all cities flowed from that fountain; thence they received their sanctimony and majesty.'[83] Furthermore, in *DJBP*, he writes: 'if civil Powers command any Thing contrary to the Law of Nature, or the Commands of God, they are not to be obeyed'.[84]

Peter Borschberg's essay on the unpublished *Thesis LVI* (which was written around the time of *ML*) offers a degree of clarity to this interpretation of Grotius's view. In this *Thesis*, Grotius argues that the authority of the state is rooted on two contracts: one which creates the commonwealth and the other which entrusts power to the prince, or state. Resistance by the commonwealth is justified against tyranny, that is, against the prince who violates the trust between him and the people.[85] After making this argument, it seems that Grotius wants to narrow the circumstances where resistance is justified. It is only justified where there are no legal procedures by which the prince can be held to account as well as being a violation of natural law. This suggests that he is almost reluctantly endorsing a sort of proto-Lockean view. However, if this view describes Grotius's account then he is some sort of natural lawyer. It is unclear whether natural law takes a classificatory (as in strong natural law theory) or normative function (in the sense of determining the bindingness of acts of sovereign will). If we take this Lockean interpretation as being correct, I would suspect that Grotius would endorse the latter view.[86]

The Hobbesian view is set out by, amongst others, Ross Harrison. He argues that, for Grotius, the whole process of civil incorporation involves the alienation of natural rights to the state. For Grotius, according to Harrison, it is '[w]ill [that] creates the moral universe'.[87] However, rather than just alienating the right to punish to the state, we are able to alienate potentially *any right* through our consent.[88] Thus, the civil law need not be rooted upon any natural right once it is established. However, we are beholden to abide by civil law because we still have an obligation to keep our promises to others unless others waive that right. Moreover, Grotius is prepared to accept that tacit consent is sufficient to alienate rights. So, while we all have natural pre-political rights, by contracting to form the state, we are *assumed* to have submitted to an alienation of any potential rights. This seems to be what Grotius means when he writes:[89]

---

83 *ML*, 6.

84 *DJBP*, 337.

85 See Borschberg (note 78, above, 57).

86 This seems reflected in *DJBP* (at 523) where, discussing marriage, he writes: 'Not all Things which are contrary to the Law of Nature, are, by the law of Nature, null and void.'

87 See Harrison (note 55 above, 149) and Tierney (note 4, above, 336–337).

88 Tierney (note 4, above, 336–337). Also, see Kingsbury (note 25, above, 50), H. Bull, 'The Importance of Grotius' in Bull, Kingsbury and Roberts (note 4, above, 85) and Tuck (note 4, above, 79–81).

89 *DJBP*, 93.

> For those who had incorporated themselves into any Society, or subjected themselves to any one Man, or Number of Men, had either expressly, or from the Nature of the Thing must be understood to have tacitly promised, that they would submit to whatever either the greater part of the Society, or those on whom the Sovereign Power had been conferred, had ordained.

Grotius's view, on this account, is that whatever the sovereign does to us in violation of natural law, we are taken to have given tacit consent and to have alienated our natural rights. This, Harrison suggests, is similar to Hobbes's conclusions made some years later. Read this way, it should come as no surprise that Rousseau argued that there were strong similarities between Hobbes and Grotius when each attempted to justify the state.[90] If this line is correct, Grotius can be considered some form of proto-positivist.

Textually, there seems to be plausibility in both interpretations. It may be that Grotius is not able to grasp a clear solution to the problem of the relationship between natural rights and civil law. This problem is, after all, one of the most intractable problems in political philosophy but that he was able to see the tension was achievement enough. Another possibility is that Grotius's views changed. Tuck regards Grotius's thought as gradually moving from what I have called a Lockean to a Hobbesian view between the publication of *DJP* and *DJBP*.[91] Textually, I suspect, it would be unwise to press his claim too hard.

3.4.4 The law of nations

It seems that for Grotius states have the same natural rights as individuals. It is by this analogy that he is able to claim that war is a form of punishment for those states which violate natural rights. To explain, in the same way as for natural human agents, natural law establishes a set of narrow natural rights which govern the conduct of states. The content of these natural rights are identical to those held by human agents. So, states have rights to their continued existence, their territory and property, to freedom from impediment on the high seas, and a right to have promises kept. From this final natural right, the agreements which states enter into through their direct and indirect consent are binding as a matter of natural law. Such agreements are a form of human volitional law and are the law of nations.[92] Unlike Gentili, the law of nations is entirely conventional, established by contract, and to be distinguished from the natural law.[93] So, it is from 'Custom and tacit Consent'[94] or explicit treaties that the law of nations arises.[95] So, the

---

90 Rousseau writes about Grotius and Hobbes the following: 'The truth is that their principles are exactly the same: they only differ in their expression. They also differ in their method. Hobbes relies on sophisms, and Grotius on the poets; all the rest is the same.' See Tuck's introduction to *DJBP*, xvi. See also Lauterpacht (note 59, above, 1–2, 5 and 9).

91 Tuck (note 4, above, 63–65).

92 See Kingsbury and Straumann (note 64, above, 42).

93 *DJBP*, 94. See Lauterpacht, note 59, above, 21–22.

94 *DJBP*, 75. Here Grotius writes '. . . as the laws of each State respect the benefit of that State; so amongst all or most States there might be, and in Fact there are, some Laws agreed on by common Consent, which respect the Advantage not of one Body in particular, but of all in general. And this is what is called the Law of Nations, when used in Distinction to the Law of Nature.'

95 van Vollenhoven correctly comments on the lack of detail in Grotius's work concerning the law of treaties in what is otherwise a fairly idiosyncratic article on Grotius's reception (C van

positive law of nations provides a set of norms, rooted in consent, and binding by virtue of natural law, which governs a *society of states*.

3.4.5 Justifications for war

On pages 91–92 of *DJBP*, Grotius writes that the state's right to punish arises from violations of civil law (which subjects have consented to) and natural law. However, foreigners and states who are not subjects, and who have not consented to civil law, cannot be punished under it. He writes:[96]

> . . . the state inflicts punishment for wrongs against itself, not only upon its own subjects but also upon foreigners; yet it derives no power over the latter from civil law, which is binding upon citizens only because they have given their consent; and therefore, the law of nature, or law of nations, is the source from which the state receives the power in question.

It is Grotius's argument, then, that foreigners and foreign states can be punished for violations of natural law (so, the natural laws of inoffensiveness, abstinence and the keeping of promises) but not civil law. Because of its origin in the consent of states, States can also be punished for violations of the law of nations.[97] Together, these two sources of a right to punish give rise to his just war theory. Specifically, Grotius writes that 'War is made against those who cannot be restrained in a judicial Way.'[98] Thus, in a community where there is no alienation of the right to punish to the sovereign state, its members themselves must retain a right to use war as a means of punishing those who violate their rights. This is what happens in international relations.

There are two sides to Grotius's justifications for war. First, war must take a particular form. That is, there are certain rules which govern how war is to be prosecuted. It must be proportionate to the end sought,[99] one's cause cannot be supported by taking from third parties[100] and war must adopt some formalities. So, for example, there must be a declaration of war which is made by an 'express Resolution of the Sovereign'.[101] Secondly, there must be a justification for war. There is some controversy in the literature as to how Grotius saw the function of war as a means of vindicating rights. Kingsbury and Roberts have argued that Grotius, like Gentili, argued that both states in a conflict may sincerely believe that they have right on their side and both consider they are engaged in a just war.

Vollenhoven, 'Grotius and the Study of War' (1925) 19 *AJIL* 1 at 5–6). See also Lauterpacht (note 59, above, 42–43).

[96] *DJBP*, 91–92. See also Tuck (note 4, above, 82).

[97] It has been suggested by Martin Wight that, for Grotius, non-Christian states were merely bound by natural law and only Christian states were bound by the law of nations. Perhaps the better view is that there is likely to be a greater density of positive international laws between Christian states than between Christian and non-Christian states. See B Kingsbury and A Roberts in Bull, Kingsbury and Roberts (eds) (note 4, above, 14).

[98] *DJBP*, 101.

[99] *DJBP*, 1186.

[100] *DJBP*, 1187. See Lauterpacht (above, note 59, 39–40).

[101] *DJBP*, 253. See S Neff, *War and the Law of Nations* (Cambridge, Cambridge University Press, 2005) 98–99 and B Kingsbury and A Roberts, in Bull, Kingsbury and Roberts (eds) (note 4, above, 22).

The outcome of the war vindicates the rights of the victor.[102] Panizza, however, argues that in fact Grotius's view was more like that of the neo-scholastics such as Vitoria (and unlike Gentili) who argued that right can only be held by one side: to claim that both sides have a plausible claim is a logical contradiction.[103] One might suspect that, like Grotius's approach to the relationship between natural law and civil law, his views may not be quite consistent nor set in stone, throughout his writings. Either way, he gives three 'causes' or, rather, justifications, for war. He writes: 'Most Men assign three just Causes of War, Defence, the Recovery of what's our own, and Punishment.'[104] While the right to punish actually corresponds to the right to punish those who violate the law of nations, because such law is rooted on the natural law to keep promises, each of the justifications for war arises from violations of the natural law.

The first justification comes from the law of inoffensiveness. He writes: '. . . this Right of Self-Defence, arises directly and immediately from the Care of our own Preservation, which Nature recommends to every one . . .'.[105] This can include the helping of allies and collective self-defence[106] as well as any other state that is suffering armed attack. He writes: '. . . the most extensive Reason of all for assisting others is that relation that all Mankind stands in to each other; and this alone is sufficient'[107] as a justification for war. While this is a wide right to self-defence, it is not unlimited. He does not permit pre-emptive self-defence to extend to a situation where another state is becoming powerful.[108] By rejecting pre-emptive self-defence, Panizza contends that Grotius is arguing directly against Gentili. If correct, this indicates that Grotius read Gentili as supporting pre-emptive self-defence even if the latter is, as was argued above, somewhat ambivalent in his views.

The second justification comes from the law of abstinence, which requires states to both not interfere with the rights of other states and to afford reparations. Thus, 'From such a fault or Trespass there arises an Obligation by the Law of Nature to make Reparations for the Damage, if any be done.'[109] Thus, if reparations are not forthcoming, war is justified. The third justification for war comes from violations of the law of nations. Such norms are obligatory from the right to keep promises.

The right to punish violations of natural law and the law of nations is not only held by the victim, but is held by any state or non-state actor. As has been seen, the right to punish in Grotius's basic moral system is not solely held by the victim. In principle any state or person (including the Dutch East India Company) can punish those who violate natural law or the law of nations.[110] That the right to punish can be

---

102 See B Kingsbury and A Roberts, ibid, 20–21.

103 Panizza (note 4, above, section 3).

104 *DJBP*, 395.

105 *DJBP*, 397.

106 *DJBP*, 1155.

107 *DJBP*, 1157.

108 *DJBP*, 417. Grotius writes: '. . . I can by no Means approve . . . that by the Law of Nations it is permitted to take up Arms to reduce the growing over of a Prince or State, which if too much augmented, may possibly injure us'. See also Panizza, note 4, above, section 4.

109 *DJBP*, 884.

110 *DJBP*, 1021. However, it seems that punishment would normally be undertaken by sovereign powers. Grotius writes: 'Kings, and those who are invested with a Power equal to that of

held by others other than the victim of a violation of the law of nations is clear from the following:[111]

> . . . the Subject of this Right, that is, the Person to whom the Right of Punishing belongs, is not determined by the Law of Nature. For natural Reason informs us, that a Malefactor may be punished, but not who ought to punish him. It suggests indeed so much, that it is the fittest to be done by a Superior, but yet does not show that to be absolutely necessary.

This said, according to Straumann, the right to punish is only justified when there is a 'grevious'[112] or 'severe'[113] violation of law.[114] This chimes with modern conceptions of obligations *erga omnes*[115] as well as the idea that such obligations arise from 'serious' (i.e. 'gross' and 'systematic') violations of peremptory norms as set out in Article 40 of the ILC Articles on Responsibility of States for Internationally Wrongful Acts (2001).[116]

3.4.6 Conclusion

Grotius shows how his relatively thin understanding of natural rights, which is rooted on the self-interest and natural sociability of human beings, can give rise to a justification for the sovereign state and a conception of the law of nations. He can also use this to explain how civil law and the law of nations come to be binding. Through this approach, he attempts to demonstrate that law is not simply the customs of peoples through time and space, and thus attempts to reply to the sceptic's challenge in his grounding of his law of nations.

3.5 IMMANUEL KANT

Kant was born in Königsberg in Eastern Prussia in 1724, and he died there in 1804. His major works on legal philosophy and the law of nations were written towards the end of his life. They include the essays 'Idee zu einer allgemeinen Geschichte in weltbürgerlicher Absicht' (UH, 'Idea for a Universal History with a Cosmopolitan Intent', 1784), 'Über den Gemeinspruch: Das mag in der Theorie richtig sein, taugt aber nicht für die Praxis' (TP, 'On the Proverb: That May be True in Theory, but it is of no Practical Use', 1793), 'Zum ewigen Frieden' (PP, 'Perpetual Peace', 1795) and the book *Die Metaphysik*

Kings, have a Right to exact Punishments, not only for Injuries committed against themselves, or their Subjects, but likewise, for those which do not particularly concern them, but which are, in any Persons whatsoever, grievous Violations of the Law of Nature and Nations.'

111 *DJBP*, 955.

112 *DJBP*, 1021.

113 Straumann (note 74, above, 10).

114 Indeed, Lauterpacht argues that Grotius defended humanitarian intervention when there was a serious violation of the rights of community by its states. This seems, however, dependent upon how one views Grotius's explanation of the relationship between natural law and civil law. See Lauterpacht (note 59, above, 46–47) and above, 74–77.

115 Ibid, 14.

116 See Kingsbury and Roberts (note 4, above, 40).

der Sitten (*MM*, *The Metaphysics of Morals*, 1797[117]). While there are various readily available translations of all of these works, all of the essays just mentioned are published usefully in a collection edited by Ted Humphrey entitled *Perpetual Peace and Other Essays*.[118] The original German versions of these works are to be found in the 6th and 8th volumes of the Academy edition of Kant's *Gesammelte Schriften*.

As mentioned in the introduction to this chapter, Kant's approach to the law of nations is quite different to, and is critical of, the position taken by Gentili and Grotius. For the humanist natural lawyers the law of nations consists of a set of principles that govern international relations, and which are derived from, or validated by, natural law and refined through state consent. There are two reasons why Kant rejects these older philosophies of international law. First, Kant does not regard their law of nations as being a legal system as there is no system for establishing international civil law as an expression of the general will of states. It is on this point that Kant directly attacks Grotius. He writes that for Grotius, 'nations do not stand under any common external constraints'.[119] Grotius and Gentili would probably have accepted this criticism, but would defend their position on the grounds that there can be no earthly law-making power above the sovereign state and therefore the idea of international civil law makes no sense. Secondly, Kant also criticises Grotius, and those like him, because their project is an attempt to justify war. Their arguments are not an attempt to show that morality requires states to seek peace and governance by international civil law. This is why Grotius is understood by Kant to be an 'irritating comforter'. For Kant, Grotius's laws of war merely dress the aggressive behaviour of various states with the clothing of law: his work is claimed to be only ever cited in support of a war, and states never use his doctrines to justify refraining from war.[120] In order to move on from this criticism, Kant must show how civil law can exist in international relations.

Kant's arguments against Grotius would seem to lead him towards some sort of global or universal sovereign body which is capable of creating international civil law. Kant does not go this far. This is because (i) laws 'invariably lose their impact with the expansion of their domain of governance'; [121] and (ii) a global state will be 'a soulless despotism' which 'finally degenerates into anarchy' 'after it has uprooted the soul of good'.[122] Kant, then, needs to find a way of defending a system of international civil law which does not come with the institutional baggage associated with the sovereign state. Only by providing this argument can he steer a path between international morality and a global sovereign state. His argument is that it is reason that requires states to accept the governance of a non-coercive confederation of republican states.

Two controversies arise from this brief statement of Kant's position. The first is that

---

[117] I Kant, *The Metaphysics of Morals* (Cambridge University Press, Cambridge, 1996, translated by M Gregor).

[118] I Kant, *Perpetual Peace and Other Essays* (Hackett, Cambridge, 1983, edited by T Humphrey).

[119] 8:355. References in the text correspond to the Academy edition of Kant's *Gesammelte Schriften*.

[120] 8:355.

[121] 8:367.

[122] 8:367.

the moral content of law and international law is a matter of some debate for Kant scholars. This controversy is worth considering in detail, simply because many use Kant's work as an inspiration when defending human dignity, or something like it, as a fundamental normative value to which forms of law should be orientated. Second, while most agree that Kant's concept of international law must be institutionalised through some sort of federated or confederated structure, the exact makeup of this institution is contentious. In what follows, these moral and institutional controversies will be considered in turn.

3.5.1 Scepticism

Before moving on to these two controversies, it is important to set out the intentions of Kant's moral and legal philosophies. Both represent attempts to refute the sceptic who considers morality and law to be simply conventional. For this reason, he can be said to be engaged in a project which has a similar inspiration to that of the earlier humanist natural lawyers just considered.

For John Rawls, the target for Kant's moral philosophy was Hume. He probably read translations of Hume, whom he remarked on in the highest regard in a letter to Herder in 1768.[123] Furthermore, in *The Critique of Practical Reason* he refers to Hume as perhaps the 'most ingenious of all the sceptics'.[124] By way of response to Hume, Kant attempts to show that morality is not simply an expression of our 'passions' but rather that agents are capable of self-consciously controlling their behaviour so that it is in accordance with practical reason. His supreme principle of practical reason is the categorical imperative.

The categorical imperative requires us to respect the autonomy of those affected by our actions. This means that we should never treat others as a mere means to our ends: they are ends in themselves. Without going into detail,[125] his argument for the categorical imperative aims to demonstrate that the moral obligations we feel we have towards each other are not 'a chimerical Idea' or a 'mere phantom of the brain' but are rather categorical as a matter of practical reason.[126] He offers two arguments to defend this claim. The first argument is the most familiar and is found in the first two chapters of the *Groundwork on the Metaphysics of Morals*.[127] Here he argues that the categorical imperative can be analytically derived from our common understanding of morality. This, however, cannot answer the sceptic simply because it may be that our common understanding of morality might be false. His second line of argument, which is the transcendental deduction set out in the third chapter of the *Groundwork* as well as in the *Critique of Practical Reason*, is that all 'beings with a will',[128] like human beings, must adopt the categorical imperative on pain of contradicting that they are capable of exercising that will. This is Kant's preferred method of responding to the moral sceptic.

---

123 J Rawls, *Lectures on the History of Moral Philosophy* (Harvard University Press, Cambridge, Mass., 2000) 145.

124 Ibid.

125 For an excellent account of Kant's argument for the categorical imperative see H Allison, *Kant's Theory of Freedom* (Cambridge University Press, Cambridge, 1990).

126 4:445.

127 Ibid.

128 See note 26, above.

Likewise, his legal philosophy attempts to ground a concept of law in practical reason alone. He writes:[129]

> Like the much-cited query 'what is truth?' put to the logician, the question 'what is right?' might well embarrass the jurist if he does not want to lapse into a tautology or, instead of giving a universal solution, refer to what the laws in some country at some time prescribe. He can indeed state what is laid down as right . . ., that is, what the laws in a certain place and at a certain time say or have said. But whether what these laws prescribed is also right, and what the universal criterion is by which one could recognize right as well as wrong . . ., this would remain hidden from him unless he leaves those empirical principles behind for a while and seeks the sources of such judgments in reason alone, so as to establish the basis for any possible giving of positive laws (although positive laws can serve as excellent guides to this). Like the wooden head in Phaedrus's fable, a merely empirical doctrine of right is a head that may be beautiful but unfortunately it has no brain.

Therefore, his legal theory is also an attempt to ground a concept of law which refutes a sceptical account of law.

3.5.2 The relationship between morality and law

It is the case that Kant's concept of law draws on his moral philosophy. However, it is not entirely obvious how. Controversy arises in two ways: it is not clear whether (i) it is moral or prudential reason that requires agents to submit to legal constraint and (ii) the content of law must be in accord with the constraints of morality.

Regarding (i), it is clear that Kant's concept of law draws inspiration from the social contractarian tradition, in particular from Hobbes and Rousseau. As such, Kant attempts to show why each and every human agent must, as a matter practical reason, submit to the rule of law. One might think that because Kant regards practical reason as implying moral reason (via his argument for the categorical imperative), then there must be a moral reason why agents must submit to the governance of law. However, Pogge considers that there are essentially prudential reasons why each of us should submit to law. For Pogge, this is because Kant is attempting to show why governance by law must be willed by those who accept his moral philosophy, and those who do not (but who can be persuaded on the grounds of self-interest). The prudential view will be considered first.

Pogge regards Kant's concept of law as being heavily influenced by Hobbes. This leads him to interpret Kant as advocating essentially long-term self-interest as the motivating factor which requires submission to law. Pogge's reasoning runs as follows:[130]

> When Recht is not instantiated, persons' attempts to act are likely to be obstructed in various and unpredictable ways, and they will often fail to complete the actions they want to perform on account of such obstructions and will frequently not even attempt to do what they want to do from fear of being so obstructed. When Recht is instantiated, the conduct or options of persons are constrained by firm restrictions on their external freedom. These constraints are, however, regular and predictable and give each person a clearly delimited space of options that are secure

---

[129] 6:229–30.

[130] T Pogge, 'Is Kant's *Rechtslehre* a "Comprehensive Liberalism"' in M Timmons (ed.), *Kant's Metaphysics of Morals* (Oxford University Press, Oxford, 2002) 133, 146–7.

> from the obstructing actions of others. Persons' external freedom is enhanced far more by the security that some of their options gain by being protected through an effective legal order than it is reduced by the added obstacles that legal prohibition imposes on their remaining options. Therefore persons tend to benefit, on balance, from the existence of a juridical condition.

Pogge is correct to suggest that the role of law, for Kant, is to delimit and enforce normative spaces in which members of a community can act. But why should each member accept legal constraint? For Pogge, Kant's view is that we must submit to law because we 'tend to benefit, on balance, from the existence of juridical condition'. That is, it is our self-interest which provides the justification for law, rather than the moral obligations we owe towards our fellow community members. While there is no obvious textual evidence in *MM* to support this argument there are parts of Kant's work which do seem to take a Hobbesian view of human psychology and motivation and may then support the tenor of Pogge's claim.

The moral interpretation of Kant's justification for law seems, to me, to be more plausible than the prudential interpretation. The key passage from which the interpretation arises runs as follows:[131]

> It is not experience from which we learn of human beings' maxim of violence and of their malevolent tendency to attack one another before external legislation endowed with powers appears. It is therefore not some fact that makes coercion through public law necessary. On the contrary, however well disposed and law-abiding men might be, it still lies *a priori* in the rational idea of such a condition (one that is not rightful) that before a public lawful condition is established individual human beings, peoples, and states can never be secure against violence from another, since each has its own right to do *what seems right and good to it* and not to be dependent upon another's opinion about this.

Kant argues here that a pre-legal state of nature is a priori not-rightful as even well-meaning people must submit to law. This is because in the absence of legal constraint, each individual does '*what seems right and good to it*'. It is for this reason that he describes the state of nature as a situation of 'violence'. If well-meaning people can be 'violent', this word cannot correspond to our intuitive meaning of the word. Indeed, Kant adopts a technical definition for this word. 'Violence', for Kant, is a characteristic of successful human action in a state of nature in that to succeed in claiming something as a matter of right limits the capacity of others to act. Thus, in a state of nature, any claim to have a right to own something, or any right to act in general, is always an unsubstantiated assertion. He writes that in the state of nature, '[b]y my unilateral choice I cannot bind another to refrain from using a thing, an obligation he would not otherwise have'.[132]

The state of nature is, for this reason, a priori not-rightful. Thus, it is not-rightful

---

131 6:312. Tuck thinks that this quotation reflects the Hobbesian, prudential, interpretation of Kant's justification for law. Hobbes, I would contend, saw diffidence as a psychological characteristic of those in a state of nature faced with the judgments and actions of others which conflicts with theirs. This, then, grounded his argument for the state. It is my view that Kant does not need this psychological characteristic to drive his argument for law. That is, the state of nature is not a community in which each member is diffident, wary, and mutually distrusting. Rather, for Kant, it is one where a priori rights cannot be secured. See Tuck (note 4 above, 208).

132 6:261.

independent of any subjective judgment made about how those in the state of nature view their lot. It is also not-rightful independent of any comparison made by legal subjects about the moral validity of the content of legal norms they are asked to comply with, or the instrumental benefits of living under a system of law. That the state of nature is a priori not-rightful is made clear by Kant when he writes that it is by a 'categorical imperative' that governance by law is 'obligatory for us to strive after'.[133] This moral imperative is the product of our recognition that our actions violate the rights of others. Thus, contrary to Pogges's view, which requires the balancing of various interests, it is our moral recognition of the not-rightfulness of the state of nature *qua* system of willing which leads individuals to accept the governance of law. Law, for Kant, is a form of collective willing, and is, in this sense, different from the system of unilateral willing found in the state of nature. It is an expression of the omnilateral will of 'all the wills of a community together'[134] and is institutionalised through the well-known executive, legislative and judicial institutional forms which comprise the sovereign state.[135] This is the moral interpretation of Kant's justification for law. It fits better, I have argued, with the text of Kant's work, and integrates his moral and legal philosophy in the justification for law.[136]

The second point of controversy concerns the moral content of law. That is, the extent to which the categorical imperative should inform the content of legal norms. Pogge, in a manner consistent with his prudential argument for law, considers that Kant regards the content of law as conventional. For Kant, he argues, law[137]

> . . . is instantiated when persons coexist under an effective legal order that delimits and sustains mutually secure domains of external freedom . . . All that is required for such a condition is that there be an effective body of public standing laws that constrains each person's freedom in predictable ways and thereby predictably delimits and secures each person's constrained external freedom.

Therefore:[138]

> [a] person's external freedom is *secure*, then, in so far as possible obstructing actions by others are themselves obstructed. The security of a person's external freedom thus requires that the external freedom of others (to obstruct her external freedom) be constrained. Therefore, a plurality of persons can have security of their external freedom only if and in so far as the external freedom of each is constrained so as to be consistent with the constrained external freedom of all others.

---

133 6:318.

134 6:259. This is from Hastie's translation. See I Kant, *The Philosophy of Law: an Exposition of the Fundamental Principles of Jurisprudence as the Science of Right* (Clark, Edinburgh, 1887, W Hastie (trans)) at 84.

135 A Ripstein, *Force and Freedom: Kant's Legal and Political Philosophy* (Harvard University Press, Cambridge, Mass., 2009) chapters 7–9.

136 See P Capps, *Human Dignity and the Foundations of International Law* (Hart Publishing, Oxford, 2009) ch 7 and P Capps and J Rivers, 'Kant's Concept of International Law' (2010) 16 *Legal Theory* 229–257.

137 Pogge (note 130, above, 139).

138 Ibid, 137.

Pogge claims that law, for Kant, 'may be instantiated in many different ways, only some of which involve equality under the law'.[139] Therefore, '[a]ll that is required for such a condition is that there be an effective body of public standing laws that constrains each person's freedom in predictable ways and thereby predictably delimits and secures each person's constrained external freedom'.[140] Similarly, Wood argues that, for Kant, there is no moral incentive for complying with laws.[141] Rather: '[i]t requires only a system of external legislation, backed by coercive sanctions sufficient to guarantee that [legal] rights will not be infringed'.[142] Waldron also interprets Kant in this way.[143] So, on these interpretations, legal norms must simply establish for each legal subject a domain of external freedom. Such norms set out the legal limits of action for legal subjects but their content is not guided by the constraints of the categorical imperative. Kant is, on this reading, a kind of legal positivist.

Höffe does not accept this view. Rather, he sees Kant as a natural lawyer of some sort. He writes: 'In sharp contrast to strict legal positivism', which must refer to an approach like that just set out, '. . . Kant commits positive law to obligations that he in some places describes as the laws of freedom, and "laws of pure practical reason"'.[144] Furthermore, he writes that Kant's argument is to show that in '. . . a positive legal order, in particular, its authorisation to use coercion, must have a moral underpinning'.[145] Having said this, it is unclear whether Höffe sees Kant as a weak or strong natural lawyer.[146] But either way, for Kant, the moral content of law corresponds to a relatively thin set of human rights.[147]

The plausibility of these two interpretations cannot be considered in detail here. This said, one comment which can be made is that the positivist interpretation seems to lead to a fundamental tension in Kant's practical philosophy. To explain briefly, Kant thinks that morality is explicable, and therefore agents are able to assess the moral quality of legal norms. However, we also have a moral obligation to submit to the governance of law. Therefore, if the moral content of law is conventional, Kant must show us why we have an obligation to obey unjust laws. If Kant's argument is as Pogge believes it is, then he must show why it is in our self-interest to act in accordance with laws which violate morality. If the moral argument for law (if not its content) is Kant's argument, then he must show why we must subsume the obligation to act in accordance with morality to our moral obligation to obey unjust laws.

Notably, Kant does not attempt to make either argument. Of course, this does not mean that the natural law argument is correct, and it could mean that Kant did not see the sort of problem just set out. However, we should interpret Kant charitably, and if so, we should presume that Kant meant the content of law to be structured by morality. This

---

139 Ibid, 138.
140 Ibid, 139.
141 A Wood, 'The Final Form of Kant's Practical Philosophy' in Timmons (note 130, above) 1.
142 Ibid, 8.
143 J Waldron, 'Kant's Legal Positivism' (1996) 109 *Harvard Law Review* 1535.
144 O Höffe, *Kant's Cosmopolitan Theory of Law and Peace* (Cambridge University Press, Cambridge, 2006, A Newton (trans)) 82.
145 Ibid.
146 Ibid, 83.
147 Ibid, 112.

might be put as implying that when human agents will law, they will a specific form of law administered by institutions which are capable of articulating and defending the morally relevant interests of legal subjects. If one takes this line, the arguments in the latter parts of *MM*, which defend democratic rights, legal equality and so on, make more sense. It also, in passing, makes Kant much closer to Rousseau than Hobbes.[148]

3.5.3 The law of nations as a non-coercive confederation of republican states

Kant's concept of international law seems to be based upon a similar justification to the moral justification for law just set out. But while this argument ends with a justification for the state, he argues that the law of nations should adopt a different and distinctive institutional form.

That the law of nations is a system of omnilateral willing and civil law seems clear when he writes in a note in *Perpetual Peace* that '[a]ll men who can mutually influence one another must accept some civil constitution'.[149] This is elaborated on when he writes:[150]

> nations . . . [and] peoples can be regarded as single individuals who injure one another through their close proximity while living in the state of nature (i.e., independently of external laws). For the sake of its own security, each nation can and should demand that the others enter into a contract resembling the civil one and guaranteeing the rights of each.

'Injury' in this quotation means the same as 'violence' in his general legal theory: it is the result of the 'close proximity' of states to each other. He writes, 'if even only one of these [nations] had only physical influence on another, they would be in a state of nature, and consequently they would be bound together in a state of war'.[151] Understood in the context of his general legal theory, 'injury' is the result of any successful state action in international relations rather than the result of the aggressive acts of states. The emphasis on 'security' in the quotation above should not be misunderstood: it refers, I would argue, more to the need to secure a stable framework of interaction than to afford protection from the attack from others.

Kant then argues that the state of nature in international relations (or the state of war) is immoral. This is found in his version of a just war theory. In *MM*, Kant argues that there are certain moral obligations on states which govern when and how they can use force against one other in the state of war. For Kant, these moral obligations cash out into a series of maxims whereby states can only go to war with the consent of those they govern, can only go to war when they have been wronged by another state, cannot use spies or 'poisoners', and so on.[152] Kant's just war theory is similar, in a way, to Gentili's and Grotius's just war theories.[153] This can presumably be added to, to provide a full list of moral obligations states have to one another. However, where Kant fundamentally differs from these humanist natural lawyers is that he thinks that morality requires all

---

148 See M Simpson, *Rousseau's Theory of Freedom* (Continuum, London, 2006).
149 8:348n.
150 8:354.
151 8:348.
152 6:345.
153 6:436.

states to leave the possibility of peace open because to do otherwise would 'reveal . . . a maxim by which, if it were made a universal rule, any condition of peace among nations would be impossible and, instead, a state of nature would be perpetuated'.[154]

The final moral obligation seems to imply that to deny peace through law when using force constitutes a contradiction in the 'will' of a state. Thus, a legal justification for war is a contradiction in terms. This idea of a contradiction in the 'will' is one way in which Kant thinks about the application of the categorical imperative.[155] But how does such a contradiction arise? One answer which Kant gives is that such a maxim would, if universalised, imply a denial that any state could achieve its purposes or that it could *conclusively* acquire things which are useful to the community it governs. The state of nature, then, as a system of willing, is one in which no state can have a conclusive right to achieve its purposes or to hold property. Everything is contingent and rooted on a balance of power. Thus, like his general legal theory, there is a moral obligation on states to leave the state of war and enter a civil condition. Kant is unequivocal on this point: '[s]ince a state of nature among nations, like a state of nature among individual human beings, is a condition that one ought to leave in order to enter a lawful condition, before this happens any rights of nations, and anything external that is mine or yours which states can acquire or retain by war, are merely *provisional*'.[156] The civil condition, which states must seek, is one in which states must 'stand under common external constraints'[157] which are 'independent, universally valid laws that restrict the freedom of everyone'.[158] Thus Kant claims that it is by a moral imperative that states must submit to the civil condition and governance by an omnilateral will. This matches the moral justification for law found in his general legal theory.

Turning now to Kant's view of the institutional form of the international legal order, it seems that the prototypical institutional form of law is the sovereign state. He writes that, 'Every state contains three authorities within it, that is, the general united will consists of three persons . . .: the sovereign authority (sovereignty) in the person of the legislator; the executive authority in the person of the ruler (in conformity to law); and the judicial authority (to award to each what is his in accordance with the law) in the person of the judge . . .'.[159] However, it has already been shown that Kant considers a global state as impermissible. If Kant wants to reject a global sovereign state, how can the law of nations be institutionalised? How can the state of war be transcended?

In order to explain Kant's position, it is useful to define a few terms and draw some distinctions. The omnilateral will is understood as the judgment of 'all the wills of a community together'[160] and is autonomous from the individuated subjective wills of those that comprise a community. It is, in other words, a different form of willing. Establishing an omnilateral will, in the form of a set of common standards, allows each member of a community to determine what they are legally entitled to. However, as the quote above

---

154 6:349.
155 4:446–447.
156 6:350.
157 8:355.
158 8:356–7.
159 6:313.
160 6:259.

suggests, the omnilateral will must be institutionalised somehow, and this, for Kant normally takes the form of the sovereign state.

Those who follow Kant's reasoning to this point diverge when it comes to the institutional structure of the international legal order. Some, like Archibugi, have argued that Kant's international theory offers a justification for distinctive institutions like a cosmopolitan legislature, a suprastate enforcement agency, or a world court with compulsory jurisdiction.[161] There is little or no textual evidence in Kant's work to support this sort of claim, even though institutional claims like these are sometimes considered Kantian.[162]

Kant actually proposes a range of possibilities which can be split into two groups. The first is a group of institutions which resemble a globalised version of the state. He describes a federated state of peoples (*Völkerstaat*). This is an international legal order which resembles a federated model such as that found in the (at the time of writing) fledgling United States of America. This federation would have a permanent constitution[163] alongside some state-like federated structures at the international level. It also would have some sort of executive institution, distinct from member states, which could enforce the law. Federal institutions would also be legally competent to regulate directly individuals within states. He also mentions a world republic or cosmopolitan commonwealth. This is where states are subsumed into a form of unitary government which has a 'single head'[164] and which must necessarily negate international relations.[165] Another possibility is a universal monarchy.[166] According to Byrd and Hruschka this is understood to mean a single world state where there is 'only *one* source, only *one* origin of state power'.[167] Both a world republic and a universal monarchy reflect a globalised version of a unitary sovereign state, but are different forms of it. Presumably, the world republic is distinguished from the universal monarchy by virtue of having representative government.

A different institutional form which Kant suggests is a non-coercive confederation of states. This is not like a global form of sovereign state. In a confederation there are no centralised governmental institutions and no executive power to enforce international law against those states which violate it. States are free to join or leave the confederation. They have plenary jurisdiction and the activities of individuals within states cannot be directly regulated by the confederation. The omnilateral will is given institutional expression through the collective willing of states and states collectively undertake the administrative functions of international legal order.

---

161 D Archibugi, 'Models of International Organisation in Perpetual Peace Projects' (1992) 19 *Review of International Studies* 295.

162 Ripstein's view (above note 135 at 173–174 and 225–230) is that Kant did not complete his argument for global state institutions. However, he accepts that global institutions might look quite different to the sovereign state given the differences between states and individual human agents.

163 6:351.

164 8:311.

165 8:354.

166 8:367.

167 See 8:367. BS Byrd and J Hruschka, 'From the State of Nature to the Juridical State of States' (2008) 27 *Law and Philosophy* 599, 628.

Most modern interpreters suggest that Kant preferred a 'federal state of peoples'.[168] When he rejects a world state, it is the unitary world state described by the world republic or universal monarchy that he is rejecting. In the passages where he appears to accept a confederation he does so as the lesser evil in the hope of better times to come. But this interpretation is difficult to support given a careful reading of his writings.

To explain, Kant argues in favour of a 'universal association of states' which he elsewhere calls a league, congress or federation. Crucially, though, this is not like the federation upon which government of the United States of America is constituted and he directly rejects this form of government.[169] This is why those who interpret Kant as having argued for a federated law of peoples are mistaken. Instead, this association is non-coercive and does not have a centralised executive coercive power. The key passage runs as follows:[170]

> Only in a *universal association of states* (analogous to that by which a people becomes a state) can rights come to hold *conclusively* and a true *condition of peace come about* . . . Such *an association* of several states to preserve peace can be called a *permanent congress of states*, which each neighbouring state is at liberty to join . . . a congress is here understood only as a voluntary coalition of different states which can be *dissolved* at any time, not a federation (like that of the American states) which is based on a constitution and can therefore not be dissolved. – Only by such a congress can the idea of a public right of nations be realized, one to be established for deciding their disputes in a civil way, as if by a lawsuit, rather than in a barbaric way (the way of savages), namely by war.

There is no obvious way of knowing how Kant understood the federated system of the fledgling United States, but it seems that he explicitly rejects here the federal state of peoples which is implied by it. To support this view, he also writes that 'A league of nations in accordance with the idea of an original social contract is necessary, not in order to meddle in one another's internal dissentions but to protect against attacks from without.'[171] So, Kant rejects the idea that the law of nations should interfere with the plenary jurisdiction of states or directly regulate the affairs, or protect the rights, of individuals. He also accepts the centrality of self-defence to the league. More importantly, he refuses to accept the idea that the international legal order should have an executive (and coercive) power like that possessed by states. He writes that 'this league does not seek any power of the sort possessed by nations'.[172] Kant seems to argue in favour of a confederacy and not a federation.

For the confederation to work, Kant claims that the members of the confederation must be republican states. Most commentators consider Kant's argument to be pragmatic,[173] but it seems to be conceptually necessary as well. Kant argues that there are

---

[168] See P Kleingeld, 'Kant's Theory of Peace' in P Guyer (ed.) *Cambridge Companion to Kant and Modern Philosophy* (Cambridge, Cambridge University Press, 2006) 477 and BS Byrd and J Hruschka (above, note 167).

[169] 6:350.

[170] Ibid.

[171] 6:344–345.

[172] 8:356.

[173] Probably the most significant contribution on this point is MW Doyle, 'Kant, Liberal Legacies, and Foreign Affairs' (1983) 12 *Philosophy and Public Affairs* 205 and 'Kant, Liberal Legacies, and Foreign Affairs, Part 2' (1983) 12 *Philosophy and Public Affairs* 323.

two moral obligations placed on states: that they are required to alter their constitution so that it is republican and that they have a moral obligation to leave the state of nature in international relations and enter a state of governance by law. Kant seems to claim that officials in republican states are collectively mature enough to recognise, and act in accordance with, the categorical moral obligation which bears on them to enter their state into a civil condition with others in international relations and accept the external moral obligation to comply with the law of nations.[174] Republican states accept that they have a duty to accept the governance of law and need not be forced to comply with it by the acts of an executive power which characterises federal legal orders.[175] Presumably, without republicanism, the law of nations must adopt a stronger institutional form, like a federated state of peoples. This is probably, for Kant, too close to a global sovereign state and he therefore rejects it as impractical and potentially unjust.

Kant offers some evidence about how the confederation is able to create and interpret international legal norms without the need for state-like institutions. He sees republican states as playing a key institutional role in the administration of the international legal order. For example, in *Universal History*, Kant describes the confederation as an amphictyonic treaty which is designed to result in commonly agreed positive laws reflecting a unified will and power on the part of nations.[176] The volition and agreement of states, then, seems to be integral to the creation of a system of positive international legal norms and suggests that Kant is arguing for some sort of interstate system. In these passages Kant hints that the omnilateral will, which is characteristic of any form of law, is institutionalised through the confederation of states rather than a fully federated institutional system.[177]

3.6 CONCLUSION

The purpose of this chapter is to set out the contributions made by Gentili, Grotius and Kant to the philosophy of international law as well as to make two claims about their contributions. First, it is plausible to interpret all of these philosophers as offering a

---

174 8:355–356. On this point, see A Perreau-Saussine, 'Immanuel Kant on International Law' in S Besson and J Tasioulas (eds), *The Philosophy of International Law* (Oxford University Press, Oxford, 2010).

175 This view is strongly reflected in Rawls's view in *The Law of Peoples* that for ideal theory, there is no need for strong coercive forms of global governance. See J Rawls, *The Law of Peoples* (Harvard University Press, Cambridge, Mass., 2001) 37.

176 8:24 and also 6:345.

177 Kant does suggest some distinctive global or suprastate institutions which more resemble the institutions associated with the sovereign state. One clear example is found in his support for an international forum in which states can discuss and resolve their disputes. He refers to the congress of the States General in The Hague as a good example of the sort of congress he thinks plausible. While the *Stadtholder* of the States General did have considerable executive power to raise armies, enter into treaties and levy taxes, we should note that Kant seems to be referring to the *congress* of the States General rather than the set of more extensive legal institutions of which the congress formed a part. (8:350). There is a difference between a congress in which states can come to agreements and thrash out their problems and a global legislature which seems stronger than his idea of a congress.

theory of natural law as a set of moral principles, rights or duties. As such, each responds to popular sceptical positions advanced at the time they were writing. However, the relationship between natural law and state or civil law raises considerable controversy and this has been explored. It seems that Gentili is most clearly a natural lawyer in that moral constraints limit the substantive scope of law. However, for Grotius and Kant, the extent to which the state is constrained by morality is controversial and not entirely settled. Secondly and with regard to international law, for Gentili and Grotius the absence of a sovereign power above the state means that natural law is pre-eminent and used to justify a just war theory. For Kant, this cannot be a form of law and is simply the articulation of moral principles which justify the aggressive activities of states. Kant argues, in my view, that natural law, as he conceives it, requires states to seek peace and governance through a system of 'external' or civil laws administered, at least in part, through the collective actions of states. That is, the law of nations, for Kant, is a system of collective willing, not a set of unilaterally interpreted moral maxims. Kant shows that morality requires states to transcend a state of war, and move to a system of law which can guarantee the peaceful resolution of disputes between states. This is a key difference between the early natural lawyers who have written on international law – such as Gentili and Grotius – and Kant, writing in the final years of the eighteenth century. I consider the time between these three theorists marks a fundamental theoretical shift in the way we think about international law. And this is the case whether or not Gentili, Grotius or Kant is correctly described as a natural lawyer.

4 The origins of consensual positivism – Pufendorf, Wolff and Vattel

Alexander Orakhelashvili

4.1 THE RELEVANCE OF PUFENDORF, WOLFF AND VATTEL

This chapter will focus on three major thinkers to whose scholarly contribution consensual positivism as a doctrine owes its existence: Samuel Pufendorf (1632–1694), Christian Wolff (1679–1754) and Emer de Vattel (1714–1767). It was the discourse led by these authors, in the context of which the crucial relevance of the consensual imperative for international law became obvious, much as not all of them can be described as consensual positivists proper. It is intended here to focus on principal points of analysis these authors made in relation to nature, sources and operation of international law; to demonstrate the influence of these authors on the current state of the international legal system and try to delimit, in relation to their doctrines, the doctrinal postulation of particular legal principles from the discernment of the actual state and essence of international law.

Pufendorf, Wolff and Vattel conducted their scholarly analysis in the context where Hugo Grotius had already made his major contributions to the scholarship of international law. As explained, Grotius secularised natural law by divorcing it from moral theology and placing it on a secular basis.[1] Pufendorf, it is said, was to Grotius what the system-raiser is to the inventor.[2] It is also suggested that Vattel was arguably the first man to join in a single system the concepts of natural society of nations and of nations at full liberty. This is where the difference between Wolff and Vattel lies. As explained, Vattel 'consciously creates a system in which he emphasises the natural law element of the law of nations more than had Grotius, and the liberty of nations as part of the natural law more than did Wolff'. The idea of natural law as an ethical measure of State action had before been advanced by Vitoria and Grotius, while Hobbes had been emphasising the natural freedom of States, and opposed any inherent criteria of judging the action of States as right or wrong.[3] Vattel has used the sovereignty theory of the State to disprove the possibility of the natural society among States.[4]

Wolff differed from Pufendorf in that while the latter thought that the law of nature is identical with the law of nations, the former would not equate the two. Pufendorf considered that only natural law can bind States; he recognised the system of legal regulation

---

[1] A-H Chroust, 'A Note on Samuel Pufendorf', 1 *Vanderbilt LR* (1947–48), 1.

[2] C Phillipson, 'Samuel Pufendorf', 12 *Journal of the Society of Comparative Legislation* (1912), 233 at 241.

[3] FS Ruddy, 'Vattel's Concept of International Law', 4 *Texas ILF* (1968), 383, 387.

[4] P Allott, 'International Law and International Revolution: Re-conceiving the World', in D Freestone, S Subedi and S Davidson (eds), *Contemporary Issues in International Law – A Collection of the Josephine Onoh Memorial Lectures* (2002), 77 at 93.

beyond natural law, yet denied it legal status. Wolff, on the other hand, accepted the existence of the voluntary law of nations whereby the reach of international law could extend beyond natural law.[5] Thus Pufendorf's reasoning fits better with that of Hobbes and Austin who doubted if there could be positive international law, while Wolff and Vattel developed doctrinal foundations for international law as we know it today. Hobbes has been advancing the idea of self-preservation of States as their absolute right. Wolff and Vattel, as we shall see, have incorporated the right of States to preserve and perfect themselves into their concepts of a law-governed international society, which Wolff has even described as the supreme State. The pattern of international legal thinking developed by Wolff and Vattel comes to terms with consent and agreement being the basis of the bulk of international law, but not its sole basis. Validity and legitimacy of consensually established rules derives from factors other than State agreement.

Assessments of Vattel's treatment of the sources of international law are diverse. It is suggested that Vattel intimated that his version of natural law would be found more persuasive because he drew from the sources of recognised practices and not from nature authoritatively represented as the one and only source of law. His work has indeed been treated as an authoritative rendition of State practices and earned Vattel a measure of authority that Wolff did not enjoy. 'Indeed, for the remainder of the century, no one's authority exceeded Vattel's, especially in the newly independent United States.'[6] But there is also a different understanding of Vattel's credo. According to Fenwick, Vattel's principle is stated in distancing his approach from the practice of nations and takes his stand upon the theoretical basis of the law of nature. It matters not whether States have as a point of fact actually observed such and such rules in their dealings with one another. The great determining principle in international conduct is the conformity of a given act to the abstract law of nature. Thus instead of first ascertaining the actual practice of nations' principles upon a given subject and then criticising that practice in the light of recognised principles of moral conduct, Vattel is satisfied with stating the abstract principle, and he often leaves us in doubt as to whether the principle was recognised by states at that day and, if so recognised, whether it was generally applied in their mutual intercourse.[7] If anything, this proves that the origins of consensual positivism involved little opposition to, still less denial of, natural law.

4.2 NATURAL LAW AND POSITIVE LAW

The natural law reasoning, a major object of study of all these three scholars, appeals to the categories of *jus gentium*, divine law and legal systems of different States in different historical periods. It therefore often involves a generalisation of legal reasoning, accepted or tolerated in a particular society at the particular point of time and recorded by a particular source or authority. Wolff, Vattel and Pufendorf wrote at the time when

---

5 Ruddy, 384–386.

6 N Onuf, 'Civitas Maxima: Wolff, Vattel and the Fate of Republicanism', 88 *AJIL* (1994), 280 at 299.

7 CG Fenwick, 'The Authority of Vattel', 8 *American Political Science Review* (1914), 375 at 377.

the natural law tradition was strong and positive international law was not supported by a rich framework of practice and normative instruments as it is now. Hence their reasoning, and their approach to positive law, was dependent on the foundations and principles of natural law. One implication of this is that the teachings of Wolff and Vattel demonstrate that positivism does not discard the relevance of natural law. The use of natural law arguments may be required to explain positive legal institutions and place them in a systemic context, or to identify the effects and consequences that the operation of those institutions produces.

Wolff suggested the notion of 'the necessary law of nations which consists in the law of nature applied to nations'. The law of nature is immutable and hence 'the necessary law of nations also is absolutely immutable'. Consequently, 'neither can any nation free itself nor can any nation free another from it'.[8] This natural law of nations is, according to Vattel, '*necessary*, because Nations are absolutely bound to observe it'. The necessary law of nations 'is not subject to change'. 'Nations cannot alter it by agreement, nor individually or mutually release themselves from it.'[9]

It is clear that Wolff and Vattel effectively submit that the immutable norms of the law of nature admit of no derogation. This also implies that the 'positive law of nations which takes its origin from the will of nations' and consists of stipulative and customary law,[10] is subject to the immutable law of nature. Vattel expressly maintains this position by submitting that:

> It is by the application of this principle that a distinction can be made between lawful and unlawful treaties or conventions and between customs which are innocent and reasonable and those which are unjust and deserving of condemnation.
>
> Things which are just in themselves and permitted by the necessary Law of Nations may form the subject of an agreement by Nations or may be given sacredness and force through force and custom. Indifferent affairs may be settled either by treaty, if Nations so please, or by the introduction of some suitable custom or usage. But all treaties and customs contrary to the dictates of the necessary law of nations are unlawful.[11]

Scholars are not entirely agreed whether there is a positive law of nations. Some hold that the law of nature is the same thing as the law of nations. Pufendorf fully subscribes to this statement, as he does not 'feel that there is any other voluntary or positive law of nations which has the force of a law, properly so called, such as binds nations as if it proceeded from a superior'. The law of nations is instead defined as proceeding 'from considerations of our requirements which are helped most of all by sociable attitude; for we deny the existence of any law of nations arising from a superior'.[12] Thus sociability is seen as an alternative legitimising factor in the absence of a government.

---

[8] Wolff, 'The Law of Nations Treated according to a Scientific Method', in JB Scott (ed.), *Classics of International Law* (Oxford 1934), 10.

[9] Vattel, 'The Law of Nations or the Principles of Natural Law applied to the Conduct and to the Affairs of Nations and of Sovereigns' in JB Scott (ed.), *Classics of International Law* (Washington 1916), 4 (emphasis original).

[10] Wolff, 18–19.

[11] Vattel, 4–5.

[12] S von Pufendorf, 'The Law of Nature and Nations', in JB Scott (ed.), *Classics of International Law* (Oxford 1934), 226.

Pufendorf disagrees with Hobbes that the law of nature is not proper law because it is not commanded by a sovereign. It is not an invariable requirement of the essence of law that it be spoken, or that it be made known to subjects by words formed into a speech; it can also relate to the superior's inner dictate of the mind or to the nature of business undertaken. A method of promulgating law has no bearing upon its real nature.[13]

Pufendorf distinguishes between international law proper and rules or usages having international dimension yet falling short of commanding the quality of law binding on States, drawing on the description of the law of nations by Roman Jurisconsults as *jus gentium*, a private law institution common to different nations. Such institutions can, however, be changed by any State without consulting others. The law of nations can also be those customs which nations use in relation to each other by reference to a tacit agreement, such as the rules of warfare. However, Pufendorf does not define this as the law proper. States can observe these if they can see an advantage, for instance facing a less cruel enemy in war. Otherwise, by breaching the rules of warfare, States will involve themselves not in an illegality but merely in a kind of ungentlemanliness. 'But he who proceeds to violent and unjust wars follows, it may be, such observances carefully, so as to play the scoundrel with some appearance of right. Since, however, these reasons are not general, they cannot constitute any universal law and such as binds the people.'[14] Law is therefore what binds the State, from what the State cannot absolve itself on its own.

Vattel's natural law is not the same as natural law applied to individuals, but the one suited to the nature of inter-State relations.[15] Vattel sees Grotius as basing the law of nations on the common consent of States and thus distinguishing it from natural law in a broader sense, as emphasising the relevance of universal consent against that of natural reason.[16]

Vattel emphasises the universality of international law, specifying that 'The natural law is the sole rule of the treaties of Nations; religious differences are entirely foreign to them.' Common welfare of nations requires that 'they be able to treat with one another and to rely upon one another in so doing'. But then, 'any religious doctrines which should run counter to the natural law in this matter would deserve to be rejected; . . . if the principles of a religion were of such a character as to call for the use of violence in establishing that religion, and for the oppression of those who do not receive it, the natural law forbids a Nation to support that religion.'[17] Therefore, Vattel's natural law refers to universally acceptable standards binding all nations, and justifies banning a religion or ideology only when it contradicts the operation of the system of international law, as opposed to lesser degrees of objectionability such as the low degree of political acceptability. This essentially differs from using natural law reasoning for conferring an enhanced legitimacy to a particular religion or ideology. Conversely, Vattel's disapproval of calls 'for the use of violence in establishing that religion' resembles justifying use of force for ideological

---

13 Pufendorf, 219.

14 Pufendorf, 227–228.

15 E de Vattel, 'The Law of Nations or the Principles of Natural Law applied to the Conduct and to the Affairs of Nations and of Sovereigns', in JB Scott (ed.), *Classics of International Law* (Washington 1916), 3a.

16 Vattel, 4a.

17 Vattel, 162.

purposes, such as humanitarian or pro-democratic intervention to establish a particular form of government in the relevant country.

Wolff considers that nature herself has established society among all nations and binds States to preserve this society. This obligation is necessary and immutable. 'Therefore society, which nature has established among individuals, still exists among nations and consequently, after States have been established in accordance with the law of nature.' The purpose of this society is to promote public good by combined powers.[18] All nations are thus understood to have come together into a State whose members are individual States. This is called the supreme State. Wolff specifies that Grotius was aware of this supreme State as the basis of the law of nations, but criticises him for not deriving from it the voluntary law of nations 'as he could and ought to have done'.[19]

In the supreme State nations as a whole have a right to coerce individual nations, if they should be unwilling to perform their obligations. Some sovereignty over individual nations belongs to nations as a whole. But Wolff then promptly adds that 'nothing at all results from this, except those things which all willingly recognise as in accordance with the law of nations, or what it is really understood they ought to recognise'. The supreme State has a democratic form of government since nations are equal and not subject to each other. The sovereignty is thus reserved to the nations as a whole. The supreme State is ruled by a fictitious ruler which adopts legal rules and adapts natural or necessary law to the needs of that State.[20]

Wolff's sovereignty conception merely emphasises that States – out of considerations beneficial to all of them – are naturally deemed to be part of the legal community which sets rules of conduct for those States and at times provides for enforcement of those rules; this does not envisage a new international sovereign government. Wolff merely tries to re-invent a decentralised society of sovereign States to inform its concept by relevant moral, social and ethical considerations. In other words, Wolff's supreme State is still a decentralised legal community, but one with an ethical and communitarian purpose.

Vattel's reasoning is conceptually different from that of Wolff in that for Vattel civil society is there to complement the natural State and remedy its imperfections. The civil State is thus qualitatively different from the natural State. From this perspective, Wolff's natural society would only exist fictitiously, and Wolff has not ascribed to it a great practical importance either. According to Vattel, civil society is established when men see that natural laws are not voluntarily observed, and have recourse to political association 'as the one remedy against the degeneracy of the majority' and of protecting the good and restraining the wicked. Natural law approves this. But 'there is by no means the same necessity for a civil society among Nations as among individuals'. For,

> individuals are so constituted that they could accomplish but little by themselves and could scarcely get on without the assistance of civil society and its laws. But as soon as a sufficient number have united under a government, they are able to provide for most of their needs, and they find the help of other political societies not so necessary to them as the State itself is to individuals.

---

18 C Wolff, 'The Law of Nations Treated according to a Scientific Method', in JB Scott (ed.), *Classics of International Law* (Oxford 1934), 11.

19 Wolff, 12–13.

20 Wolff, 14–17.

While societies have strong need, indeed obligation, for mutual communication, such intercourse can be sufficiently regulated by the existing natural law.[21] All this demonstrates that the distinction between Wolff's and Vattel's teachings may not be as great as it could be imagined.

This can also be illustrated by the similarity of the two thinkers' approach to the rights and duties of States in relation to importation of foreign goods into a State territory. While Wolff considers that as part of the supreme State nations ought to perfect themselves and thus import foreign goods if needed for that purpose, he also specifies that

> no nation has the right to sell its goods to another nation without its consent, if any nation is not willing that certain foreign goods be brought into its territory, it does no wrong to the nation from which they come, consequently if the bringing in of foreign goods and their sale is prohibited, there are no just complaints by foreigners concerning this prohibition.[22]

Vattel's views on this question are identical and this similarity does not appear to be prejudiced by general conceptual differences between the two writers. Wolff emphasises the natural duty of perfecting nations for the sake of advancing the aims of the supreme State. Yet once it comes to specific rights and obligations, Wolff instantly adopts a consensual view. Furthermore, in a rather State-centric way, Wolff suggests that 'it depends upon the will of any nation whether it desires to engage in commerce with another nation or not, and upon what condition it desires to engage in it'.[23] A perfect right of external commerce can only be acquired through an agreement and can only be a stipulative right, 'since nations are naturally free'.[24]

While Grotius regards the law of embassies as part of the voluntary law of nations, Puffendorf emphasises their necessity as a matter of natural law to enable them to negotiate and preserve agreements which the law of nature commands men to embrace by all honourable means.[25] Thus positive law of nations does not exist, but sources of voluntary law do exist; according to Pufendorf, these are sources of a lesser legitimacy than natural law, and are actually meant to implement the dictates of natural law. But what strikes in Pufendorf's reasoning is that even the denial of positive law of nations does not lead to the denial of the sources of positive law; it only leads to a re-classification and re-appraisal of their basis and relevance.

Pufendorf envisages the relativity of the binding force of positive law. Natural law is better than agreed law. Thus 'if any custom is based upon the natural law, without doubt far more is done to give it dignity than if its origin is based upon the simple agreement of States'. Agreed law is relative, as 'any one can free himself from such obligations [based on a tacit agreement], if he expressly declares that he is not willing to be bound by them, and that he will not complain should others also not observe them towards him'. Many such observances have arguably become obsolete.[26]

---

21 Vattel, 9a–10a; after this Vattel points out that the modification of the strictness of natural law follows from natural liberty.

22 Wolff, 38–39.

23 Wolff, 43.

24 Wolff, 43–44.

25 Pufendorf, 228.

26 Pufendorf, 228.

Natural law is also seen by Pufendorf as verifying and controlling the permissible content of positive law. The binding force of civil obligations, that is positive law, is conditional on not having an object repugnant to natural law.[27] A disobedience to civil law or divine law is an evil; but when civil law contradicts divine law, its disobedience will cease to be an evil.[28]

Wolff follows Grotius in asserting that the voluntary law of nations derives from the concept of the supreme State, considered to have been laid down by its fictitious ruler and so to have proceeded from the will of nations. The voluntary law of nations is thus equivalent to the civil law and is consequently derived in the same manner from the necessary law of nations. Stipulative law of nations arises from stipulations entered into between different nations. These are pacts and bind States only in so far they have consented to them, and only as between such States as have consented. Hence stipulative law is not universal but particular. Customary law likewise rests on State consent and is particular, not universal. All these three categories constitute positive law. Voluntary law of nations rests on presumed consent, stipulative law on express consent, and customary law on tacit consent. All these three categories have, according to Wolff, to be distinguished from natural law.[29]

Wolff defines his method of teaching the law of nations to teach the necessary law of nations not in isolation from voluntary, stipulative and customary law, and adds that these categories have not been distinguished from it with sufficient care by Grotius. Natural law can change to, or be complemented by, the voluntary, stipulative and customary law.[30] Natural and necessary law cannot apply to the society of nations in all its strictness and thus changes to it are necessary as required by the idea of *civitas maxima*. Vattel contradicts by suggesting that all changes which must be made in the strictness of natural law through the voluntary law of nations 'may all be deduced from the natural liberty of nations, from considerations of their common welfare, from the nature of their mutual intercourse, from their reciprocal duties, and from the distinction between *internal* and *external*, *perfect* and *imperfect* rights'.[31] Thus consensual voluntary law seems to reflect the natural necessities. But this leaves open the question that if voluntary law is created to reflect what is anyway required by or reflects reciprocal duties of States, natural liberty of nations or common welfare, what, then, is the independent relevance of the consensual imperative?

Vattel acknowledges that the difference between his approach and that of Wolff is rather relative and adds that 'terms count for little'.[32] Necessary and voluntary law of nations have both been established by nature, but 'each in its own way'. The former is a sacred law to be respected by all sovereigns, the latter consists of rules of conduct which sovereigns accept out of considerations of common good. Necessary law is derived immediately from nature and recommends sovereigns to accept voluntary law. 'This double law, based upon fixed and permanent principles, is susceptible of demonstration.'

---

27 Pufendorf, 386.
28 Pufendorf, 435.
29 Wolff, 17–19.
30 Wolff, 19.
31 Vattel, 10a (emphasis original).
32 Vattel, 11a.

Arbitrary law derives from the consent of States expressed in compacts, promises and treaties, or through tacit consent. Both treaty and custom are part of special and consensual law binding States which consent to it. Their binding force derives from natural law which demands that nations keep their express and tacit compacts. 'The natural law should likewise regulate the conduct of States with respect to the treaties they conclude and the customs they adopt.'[33] Therefore the basis for the binding force of treaty obligations is not consensual. Substantive international law is created by States but the ways they create that law does not derive from their consent. No positivist account of international law can remain isolated from the extra-positivist foundation of it, whether expressly denoted as natural law or not.

Nations and their rulers are, according to Wolff, 'bound by nature' to observe and not violate their stipulations. That is so, as 'things which have been proved in the law of nature concerning stipulations and promises are true concerning treaties also which are made by sovereign powers'.[34] The natural law basis for the binding force of positive consensual law is thus identified, and this is a crucial aspect where Wolff's approach differs from that of Pufendorf. Natural and positive law are not mutually inimical, but the former provides for the basis which the latter's legitimacy is derived from.

Pufendorf nevertheless succumbs to systemic dictates of consensual positivism and accepts the inevitable relevance that consensual treaties have in international law. Principles of reason, Pufendorf concedes, are not completely feasible because they can never lay firm restraint upon the spirit of men and the latter can turn to consulting their own advantage in some other way. For dictates of reason to be endowed with authority, they have to be turned into the law; such authority can only arise by means of pacts. Observance of human reasons enjoined by the force of laws would have no greater force than do positive laws.[35] Thus Pufendorf accepts that law actually gives shared legitimacy to dictates of reason, without which it can only be a unilaterally advanced policy which is neither properly defined nor obliges anyone to stand by it in a consistent manner.

Pufendorf makes a similar general point on the legitimacy of law: legal obligations exert greater force 'in that because of them there arises an intrinsic necessity to do something from which our inclinations and desires alone would shrink'.[36] In other words, once we move into the field of law, the relevance of our own appreciation of what is best to do decreases in relevance.

According to Wolff, if treaties are made concerning a thing which is due by nature, they transform an imperfect right under natural law to a perfect right, and 'it may be possible to demand what beforehand might only be asked for'. A natural obligation is complemented by a positive obligation, which then transforms a matter of liberty into that of necessity. For instance, nations are imperfectly bound under natural law to engage in commerce with each other, but perfectly under treaties to do so.[37] Thus natural law under this perception is merely a general guidance or deduction from the common under-

33 Vattel, 11a.
34 Wolff, 194.
35 Pufendorf, 217.
36 Pufendorf, 436.
37 Wolff, 200.

standing of common interests and the nature of international society, not law regulating specific matters.

Consensual stipulations give rise to perfect rights, because the promisor binds himself absolutely to the promisee. The promisee now 'can demand it and need no longer beg for it'. Advantages conferred by the treaty can be set at nought if presumptuous power violates it.[38]

It is allowable, Wolff suggests, to add things by treaty, those which have not been determined by natural law, to natural law principles reflected in a treaty. This mainly concerns conditions on which things determined by natural law operate. 'Since the law of nature controls all human acts, it is not to be doubted that it also controls acts as regards things to be added in treaties made concerning that which by nature is already due by way of duty', in relation to particular circumstances and particular contracting parties.[39] Here the law of nature again becomes mandatory law that controls the content of positive law.

Vattel's treatment of positivism is illustrated by his treatment of the law of the sea. It is clear that when Vattel wrote there was no instrument of positive law specifying that access to the high seas is free to all States, and Grotius had earlier explained the freedom of the high seas by reference to natural law. Vattel proceeds to explain freedom of the high seas by advancing a natural law argument: 'nature does not give men the right to appropriate things the use of which is innocent and the supply inexhaustible and sufficient for all'. Thus no nation has the right to exclude another from the enjoyment of high sea freedoms.[40] The next stage of analysis is positivist: Vattel specifies that as every nation is free to renounce a legal right, a nation may acquire through a treaty exclusive rights of navigation and fishing which other nations would renounce in its favour.[41]

The initial explanation of the nature of territorial sea is also naturalist. Vattel specifies that States can appropriate what would produce dangers to their security if left unappropriated. It matters for the security of States that there should be no general liberty to approach their possessions with warships so near as to hinder the passage of trading vessels and disturb navigation. This explains why the passage of foreign ships into such a marginal sea-belt can be only innocent and not purpose-bound.[42] However, once it comes to determining the external limit of territorial sea, Vattel no longer feels content with the use of natural law arguments and specifies that 'precise determination could only be based upon a general consent of nations, which it would be difficult to prove'. Although the initial justification of rights would be based on security needs of a State and its ability to enforce the claimed entitlement, 'in order to put so extensive a right on a sound basis, it must be clearly shown that all [the relevant] powers have given their express or implied consent'.[43] Likewise, the owner of an international strait cannot refuse passage to other nations; doing so would deprive other nations of the advantage granted to them by nature. But then, in a positivist spirit, Vattel specifies that the care of its own

---

38 Wolff, 194–195; the point is also confirmed by Vattel, 163.
39 Wolff, 201.
40 Vattel, 106.
41 Vattel, 107.
42 Vattel, 107–108.
43 Vattel, 108.

safety authorises the nation owning the strait to use precautions and exact formalities, 'commonly regulated by the custom of nations'.[44]

This is precisely the uniqueness of Vattel's legal reasoning: separating the rationale and interest behind legal rules and rights from the legal basis of those rights, namely consent and agreement between States, much as the use of these two factors in Vattel's writings may be interdependent.

4.3 THE NATURE, BINDING FORCE, AND OPERATION OF TREATIES

Pufendorf derives the necessity of having agreements in the inter-State society from the needs related to the human nature. While there are duties States owe to each other in the name of humanity, there are multiple things one cannot expect others to do unless there is a specific obligation to that effect, or unless the one who does it will receive something in return. Pufendorf also refers to the lack of an international government that would cover the entire international society – 'in view of the finite power of man being unable to extend itself to all persons at the same time and with the same force'.[45] Thereby Pufendorf anticipates the *lex specialis* principle, in the sense that 'agreements, especially express agreements, lay upon us an obligation which nature did not otherwise enjoin'.[46] But the obligation is made more binding if a man gives his own free consent to what nature had commanded.[47]

Congenital obligations are those that accrue to men because they are living beings endowed with reason. Adventitious obligations are those which bind men by virtue of some antecedent human deed, with their express or presumed consent.[48] Adventitious obligations arise from an act, either unilateral, which is a gratuitious promise, or bilateral, which is a pact.[49] Pufendorf elaborates upon the ways of giving consent, specifying that 'although consent is usually expressed by signs, such as speaking, writing and nodding, it sometimes happens that it is inferred, without such signs, from the nature of the business and other circumstances. Just as sometimes the absence of signs, or silence, when viewed in certain circumstances, is equivalent to a sign of consent'. Such consent gives rise to tacit pacts.[50] Some congenital obligations, owed by men to God or to other men as such are perpetual and cannot be terminated 'so long as any part of mankind exists'.[51] However, these perpetual duties can be suspended at the time of war when 'hostilities take the place of duties of humanity' and States become entitled to maintain their safety even to the other's hurt.[52]

---

44 Vattel, 109.

45 Pufendorf, *The Law of Nature and Nations*, in JB Scott (ed.), *Classics of International Law* (Oxford 1934), Book III, Chapter IV, 379.

46 Pufendorf, 381.

47 Pufendorf, 400.

48 Pufendorf, 381; see also id., 384, on distinction between natural and civil obligations along similar lines.

49 Pufendorf, 390.

50 Pufendorf, 402.

51 Pufendorf, 387.

52 Pufendorf, 387.

According to Wolff, tacit consent is true consent, similar to consent provided expressly. Both instances give rise to a stipulation and both are sacred.[53] But Wolff does not elaborate on standards to identify whether and how tacit consent has been given. However, it is specified that 'customary law of nations has been introduced by long usage and is observed as law'. It rests on tacit but real consent of nations, and its effect is equivalent to that of stipulative law.[54]

Pufendorf envisages a mutually interdependent role of conventional and natural law, not in terms of determining each other's content but of one determining the legitimacy of another. More specifically,

> what is not or cannot be secured by charity, is secured by agreements, while in cases where agreements are not possible, charity offers its services. And although the nature and kind of agreements entered into by individual men depend on each man's judgment, yet the law of nature commands, in a general way and indefinitely, that men enter into agreements of some kind or other, since without them social relations and peace between men cannot be preserved. . . . Now whenever men enter into any agreements, the social nature of man requires that they must be faithfully observed. For if an agreement lacks this guarantee, much of the largest part of the advantage which accrues to mankind from the mutual interchange of duties would be lost. . . . Furthermore, if it were not necessary to keep promises, it would be in no way possible with any confidence to base one's calculations on the assistance of other men.[55]

There is thus no justification in seeing naturalism and positivism as inimical to each other. The reason behind natural law actually requires the existence and observance of positive law. Natural law can thus be seen as providing a 'Grundnorm' for the validity of positive law.

Pufendorf suggests that promises and pacts regularly limit our liberty and place burdens on us; hence no pertinent reason can be advanced whereby a man can be prevented from complaining that an obligation is burdensome after having assumed it.[56] This anticipates the treatment of the nature of treaty obligations in the Permanent Court's Judgment in the *Wimbledon* case.[57]

Wolff divides stipulations into treaties, which are reciprocally entered into for ever or for a considerable time, and compacts, which contain temporary promises or those not to be repeated.[58] A compact whose object is temporary and is fulfilled by a single act, not by a continuous performance of acts, is called an agreement, convention or arrangement. When the act in question is executed so is the compact. Treaties, on the other hand, are in force as long as they last in the legal sense.[59] According to Vattel, a treaty entered into for a limited period of time can be renewed by express or tacit consent of parties. 'The presumption of the tacit renewal of a treaty can only be based upon acts of such a character

---

[53] Wolff, 284–285.

[54] Wolff, 285–286.

[55] Pufendorf, 380.

[56] Pufendorf, 402.

[57] *SS Wimbledon*, Judgment of 17 August 1923, *PCIJ Series A*, No. 1, 15.

[58] Wolff, 191; sovereigns can also make private stipulations with each other, which would not be treaties.

[59] Vattel, 160.

that they would not have been performed except in virtue of the treaty.'[60] This seems to involve a high threshold of proof to infer tacit consent.

Puffendorf's typology of international obligations specifies that mutual obligations are such as correspond with one another in such a way that one entity undertakes an obligation in return for an obligation undertaken by another entity towards it. Obligations can be perfectly mutual or imperfectly mutual. These latter involve imposing an obligation on one entity in return for an obligation of another entity which is of a different kind or not so efficacious. Examples can be provided by obligations between States and citizens, which consist in a gratuitous promise and its fulfilment.[61] Pufendorf thus anticipates the non-reciprocal nature of human rights obligations undertaken towards individuals, not on a State-to-State plane.[62]

Pufendorf also develops a 'realistic' understanding of treaties by emphasising the paramount relevance of reciprocity. A person should not place too great a confidence in a covenant unless he sees the advantage accrued under it to another party so that a breach of it will cause it more misfortune than its fulfilment. Also, a weaker party should make sure that the stronger party meets its obligations first because if the weaker one does so first it may happen that it may be deceived. Another anticipation of a political realism argument is that it is imprudent to jeopardise one's safety by fulfilling the pact in a way that weakens one in the hope that later one will be aided.[63] As little reliance can be placed on natural obligations of political entities, Vattel specifies that 'the more prudent nations seek to obtain through treaties that help and those benefits which would be secured to them by the natural law were that law not rendered ineffective by the mischievous designs of dishonest statesmen'.[64] This is a rational judgment on the utility of a positivist approach to international obligations. Treaties are required by the rational evaluation by States of their own interests and become a means to safeguard those interests.

4.4 THE INTERPRETATION OF TREATIES

All three thinkers have, as we have seen, devoted great efforts to demonstrating the basis and need for the binding force of international agreements. Such binding force would, however, be illusory unless international law provided a coherent legal framework to ascertain the meaning of treaty obligations. The sanctity of treaties cannot be secured if disagreements as to their meaning cannot be resolved according to a consistent and predictable legal framework.

It is therefore obvious that Pufendorf, Wolff and Vattel have made major efforts to ascertain the nature and rationale of treaty interpretation. Pufendorf regards it necessary to have a definite set of rules through which the true sense of laws and pacts is arrived at.[65]

---

60 Vattel, 176; treaties can also be terminated through mutual consent of parties, id., 179.
61 Pufendorf, 388–389.
62 See on this, A Orakhelashvili, *Peremptory Norms* (Oxford 2006), Chapter 4.
63 Pufendorf, 415.
64 Vattel, 160.
65 Pufendorf, 793–794, then suggesting that international obligations would be voided if they auto-interpreted and expressing the same principle as Wolff that contracting parties can compel

The necessity of interpretation framework explained in terms of the imperatives attendant to the consensual basis of international law:

> even though we should hold that the first languages were directly breathed into men, yet any man had his own faculty to speak, and could use it as he pleased, in applying certain words to certain things; and that faculty could not have come into use had there not been an agreement among men, that every man would use them in a uniform way and express the same things with the same words. For since a man in a state of natural liberty does not hold his faculties subordinate to another man, but may use them according to his own judgment, another would have no right to demand that I should use them in this way and no other, in order that he may thereby be able to judge the meaning of my mind, unless there were some pact between us on the matter. The force of this pact extends no farther than to produce a probable certainty as to another's thoughts, not an infallible one, since men are skilful in dissimulation and deceit.'[66]

However, the agreed content of international law cannot make sense or serve any purpose if there could legitimately be room for disagreement on the meaning of words through which that very content of international law is agreed upon and there is no way of attributing objective or verifiable meaning to what agreements purport to agree upon. Pufendorf observes that

> since the mutual exchange of duties among men could not be exercised unless every one could be certain of the will of men, and since human nature could not make this possible in any other way than by signs open to the perception of the senses, it followed that their use had to be sanctioned and protected by a special agreement, so that each man might be certain of what he could demand of another.[67]

It is not clear whether Pufendorf requires agreement on the meaning of words and if so, whether requiring such additional agreement would not undermine the meaning and binding force of the entire treaty.[68] Pufendorf attempts drawing distinction between the 'proper' and 'accepted' meaning of words and their 'intrinsic force'. The customary meaning of words has to be used just as money is used in exchange, having the public stamp.[69] But the examples Pufendorf records from the ancient and medieval history of Greece, India and Iran actually confirm that his reliance on customary as opposed to intrinsic meaning of words relates to the need to ensure the implementation of treaties in good faith, as opposed to insisting on literal meaning to make treaties actually ineffective.

---

each other to what the right interpretation suggests. 'Otherwise the matter would serve no end and have no result.'

66 Pufendorf, 465–466.

67 Pufendorf, 466; Pufendorf in fact refers to such meaning of words as is accepted in the particular context of the conclusion of an agreement, id., 466–467.

68 See on this, A Orakhelashvili, *Interpretation* (Oxford 2008), Chapter 10.

69 Pufendorf, 794–795 (also including historical examples, such as a promise of Boeotians to deliver a town to Spartans which was indeed delivered after it had been razed; the promise by an Ottoman Sultan to spare the head of a particular man, having then had cut him in two; Tamerlan's promise not to shed the blood of inhabitants of the city should it surrender and then having buried them alive; or the refusal by the Persian king to extradite a fugitive petty king of India to the king of India by putting him in a basket, hanging him on a tree and then insisting that he was actually not on his soil).

This fits with modern canons of interpretation, placing the text with context, object and purpose, and the requirements of effective interpretation.

According to Wolff, a manifestly false interpretation of treaties is utterly opposed to the sanctity of good faith. Nothing else is thereby aimed at 'than that he should break faith who wishes to seem to observe treaties'. Likewise, if one with a similar purpose expresses his intention badly, that is, through unclear and ambiguous words, so that the opportunity of false interpretation later on is created if that will be seen to his advantage, also offends good faith.[70] Similarly, Wolff disapproves the auto-interpretation by States of their treaty obligations, specifying that 'no one can be an interpreter of his own words in stipulations, nor is the promise allowed to interpret the words of the promisor in the sense in which he wishes them to be understood, but has the right to compel the promisor to do that which a proper interpretation warrants, that is, that interpretation which is made through the rules of interpretation'. He who rejects the interpretation pursuant to the respective rules, does the other party an injury.[71]

Wolff further articulates the thesis of effective interpretation.[72] If one nation expressly grants to another some right of transitory acts in its territory, 'the grantor is understood to have promised all things which are necessarily required for the use of this right, since the right would be granted to no purpose unless at the same time those things were granted without which it is not possible to use that right'.[73] Furthermore, 'That is understood to have been tacitly agreed upon, without which that in regard to which there has been agreement cannot occur. For every transaction includes all the actions necessary to obtain an effect, something both positive and negative.' Thus, agreement includes not only things it expressly mentions, but also 'all others which are necessary in order that the thing in regard to which there has been an agreement can be accomplished, and consequently those things are understood to have been tacitly agreed upon'. Wolff draws on the argument of Grotius that certain things belong by nature to the relevant act and must be deemed to have been tacitly agreed upon. For instance, there is indemnity due for the breach of every agreement, as without this condition agreements cannot exist. Another example is the duty of the State that offers its territory for holding an international conference to ensure the security of participants. As for the standard and reasoning required for identifying implied conditions in treaties, Wolff observes the following: 'But those things are rightly said to belong by nature to a certain act, which can be derived from it by way of demonstration; for those things belong to a thing which are derived from the idea of it by direct reasoning.'[74] This is a very important observation and draws on the necessity of the implied 'belonging' for the operation of the principal stipulation. This reasoning then opens the way for explaining the widespread use in international law of the doctrine of implied rights, powers and conditions as a matter of treaty interpretation, whether in relation to States or to international organisations.

---

70 Wolff, 283–284.

71 Wolff, 193.

72 For the modern relevance of this principle, its development and implications, see A Orakhelashvili, *Interpretation* (Oxford 2008), Chapter 11.

73 Wolff, 284.

74 Wolff, 286–287.

Pufendorf has also anticipated the principle of effectiveness as a matter of treaty interpretation:

> when the principal pact has been made with express consent, a tacit pact is understood from the nature of the business to be added to it, and flow from it. Just as it has long been recognised that some tacit exceptions and conditions are to be understood in pacts. And yet these should not be allowed more freely than the general character of human transactions will bear, lest they render pacts too slippery and uncertain.[75]

Vattel's approach to treaty interpretation is most important as it demonstrates the indispensable link between consensual positivism, which reinforces the binding force of treaties, and the moral and ethical aspects of international relations. Vattel considered treaties as a means of adjusting the pretensions of States, and the establishment of fixed rules of conduct under treaties must lead to ascertaining what they are entitled to expect.[76] Giving predominant importance to the need for securing faith and trust through treaties, Vattel observed that the principle of good faith is infringed when treaties are intentionally drafted in equivocal terms and ambiguous expressions are introduced 'to look for opportunities of quibbling, to outwit those with whom we are dealing, and outdo them in cunning and duplicity'. Hence, the interpretative principles are very important in preserving the faith embodied in treaties: 'a clearly false interpretation as contrary to good faith as anything could be imagined to be'.[77]

Consistent with this priority, Vattel considered it 'necessary to lay down rules founded upon reason, and authorized by the natural law and adapted to throw light upon what is obscure, decide what is uncertain, and frustrate the designs of one who enters into the contract in bad faith'.[78] These rules are meant 'to discover not only what one of the parties had the intention of promising, but also what the other reasonably and in good faith believed was being promised to him – what was sufficiently expressed to him and on which his acceptance was based'. Consequently, treaties must be interpreted by 'fixed rules'. Otherwise, 'no agreement can be safely relied upon'.[79] This view of Vattel prioritises the need to construe legal instruments as clear and straightforward, and contradicts the subsequently developed views of so-called deliberate ambiguity. Vattel's textual view is clearly motivated by his priority to safeguard legitimate expectations parties have in treaty obligations:

> The first general rule of interpretation is that it is not permissible to interpret what has no need of interpretation. When a deed is worded in clear and precise terms, when its meaning is evident and leads to no absurdity, there is no ground for refusing to accept the meaning which the deed naturally presents. To have recourse to conjectures in order to restrict or extend its meaning is to attempt to elude it. Once allow so dangerous a practice and there is no deed which it will not render ineffectual. However clearly the provisions of an act be worded, however definite and

---

75 Pufendorf, 402.

76 Vattel, 'The Law of Nations or the Principles of Natural Law applied to the Conduct and to the Affairs of Nations and of Sovereigns' in JB Scott (ed.), *Classics of International Law* (Washington 1916), 188.

77 Ibid., 191.

78 Ibid., 199.

79 Ibid., 200–201.

> precise its terms, all will be of no avail, if it be permissible to argue from extraneous sources that the deed is not to be taken in the sense which it naturally bears.

In addition, Vattel has in fact anticipated the principle of effectiveness in the interpretation of treaties and advocated giving to treaty clauses the full effect following from their content: 'If he who could and should have explained himself clearly and fully has not done it, so much the worse for him; he can not afterwards be admitted to prove restrictions which he has not admitted.'[80] Vattel pleads for objective standards of treaty interpretation: parties cannot be allowed to interpret the treaty according to their fancy and thus render treaty obligations illusory.[81]

4.5 VALIDITY OF TREATIES, CONFLICT BETWEEN TREATIES, VIOLATION OF TREATIES

Pufendorf specifies that the object of a pact must be such whose fulfilment lies within our faculty. A thing illegal in itself cannot be made an object of an agreement. When law forbids an action, it takes away the power of undertaking it. Promising something that is unlawful is wrongful; actually performing it is twice more so. From the fact that legal obligations cannot be assumed in relation to unlawful things, it follows that acts undertaken contrary to law lack validity. However, Pufendorf also admits what today is referred to as a relative invalidity. Sometimes an illegal act is itself a greater misconduct than it would follow from its effects, and the inconveniences from reversing the original act can outweigh those in the act itself. Hence the original act can be invalidated while its consequences would not be affected.[82]

Vattel observes that a treaty is not invalidated if it is disadvantageous to one of the parties; if treaties could be revoked on that basis there would be no stability for the law of nations. Peace and welfare of nations require that the validity of treaties should not be open to attack on such vague and dangerous grounds. States are supposed to weigh up matters carefully before they enter into a treaty.[83] This is yet another rational justification of continuous validity of positive law in the face of objections based on politics. However,

> If a simple injury or some disadvantage does not suffice to render a treaty invalid, the rule does not hold where the results of the treaty are such as to bring about the ruin of the nation. . . . for no ruler has the power to bind himself to do things which could bring about the ruin of the State when the sovereignty has been conferred upon him for his welfare.[84]

Similarly, on the basis of lack of power to contract, a treaty entered into for an unjust or dishonest purpose is absolutely void, as no one can bind himself to do acts contrary to natural law. Thus, an offensive alliance entered into for the purpose of plundering a

---

80 Ibid., 199.
81 Ibid., 200.
82 Pufendorf, 436.
83 Vattel, 161.
84 Vattel, 161.

nation which has done no injury to the parties can and should be broken.[85] But what standard applies to determining that? Is it a subjective ethical standard or a more objective public policy standard? All that depends on the standards for identifying natural law the way the three authors elaborate upon. Both Vattel, and Wolff recognise the role of natural immutable law in setting limits to the validity of positive law.

Wolff specifies that 'It is not allowable to enter into treaties contrary to treaties already contracted with another nation.' This would involve promising things that may not be performed. Both treaties cannot be performed at the same time, and thus the latter promise 'must be violated'. For the later treaty cannot be entered into without the intention to violate the former treaty. Therefore later treaties conflicting with earlier ones are invalid by the law of nature.[86] Vattel also seconds that the latter treaty is void. But this 'voidness' is explained only as the faculty of the wronged party to denounce the latter treaty, but equally as the right to leave it in force on all points that do not conflict with the former treaty.

Vattel elaborates upon the reciprocal nature of treaties and the pattern of bilateralism in the law of treaties, observing that

> there is nothing to prevent a sovereign from entering into agreements of a like nature with two or more Nations if he is in position to fulfil them at the same time with respect to all contracting parties. For example, a treaty of commerce with one Nation does not interfere with similar treaties being made with other nations unless the first treaty contains a promise that the same advantages will not be granted to others.[87]

If a State has promised military assistance to more than one State and both of them need it at one time, the priority of their treaty rights should depend, among other things, on the justice of the cause of war. Otherwise the treaty would be deemed as contracting into an alliance for an unjust cause, which is not permissible.[88]

Vattel suggests that treaties contain promises that are perfect and correlative. If one of the allies fails to carry out his engagements, the other may compel him to fulfil them. But he will sometimes find it more expedient to cancel his own promises and undoubtedly has a right to do so, since his promises were made only on condition that the ally should carry out its own stipulations. Vattel also refers to a doctrinal view that if either of the allies violates one article of the treaty, the other has not immediately the right to annul the entire treaty, but only the relevant article in question. Vattel adds that a treaty is one single whole; even if different articles of it are allegedly mutually independent, they are still bound by common relation, as States agree to certain treaty provisions less beneficial to them in exchange for others that are more beneficial. Grotius has specified that each article of a treaty carries with it a condition, by the non-performance of which the treaty is voided; however, clauses to the contrary are often inserted to preserve the stability of treaties.[89]

The intrinsic force of pacts is not only stating obligations but also implying that in the

---

85 Vattel, 162.
86 Wolff, 196; see also Vattel, 163.
87 Vattel, 163.
88 Vattel, 163.
89 Vattel, 177–178.

case of non-compliance with obligations the aggrieved party can undertake measures to compel the promisor to comply. This right does not have to be included in the treaty expressly. There is no need to have a second pact on the issue of compliance 'when it is no more difficult to break ten than it is to break one'.[90] Reciprocity, together with the option of reciprocal non-compliance with treaties in the case of their violation, is thus an inherent implication of the *pacta sunt servanda* principle.

4.6 CONCLUSION

All three authors have acknowledged the inevitable importance of consent and agreement in creating international law and conferring binding force to it. However, none of the three authors has consistently addressed and clarified the issue of how specific principles of natural law should be identified in a way that is free of ideological inputs. Wolff and Vattel, and to some extent Pufendorf, have compensated for that shortcoming by allocating to natural law the role that can be duly overtaken by positive law, either through its application to facts together with natural law, or overriding natural law as a matter of *lex specialis*. In addition, Vattel's unique contribution to the scholarship of international law is his demonstration that natural law, the idea of international law, the consensual imperative and the State-centred nature of international law are not only mutually compatible, but also mutually interdependent.

---

[90] Pufendorf, 434–435.

5 The transformation of international law in the 19th century

Amnon Lev[1]

Die Wissenschaft des Völkerrechts erschien überhaupt zu früh auf dem literärischen Schauplatze. Sie fand noch kein brauchbares Material zu einer tüchtigen theoretischen Verarbeitung vor und musste sich notwendig zu subjectiven Theorien und allgemeinen Abstractionen wenden, um ihren Bau aufrichten zu können.

Kaltenborn von Stachau, *Kritik des Völkerrechts* (1847)

Ein Gespenst geht um in Europa – das Gespenst des Kommunismus. Alle Mächte des alten Europa haben sich zu einer heiligen Hetzjagd gegen dies Gespenst verbündet, der Papst und der Zar, Metternich und Guizot, französische Radikale und deutsche Polizisten . . . Es ist hohe Zeit, daß die Kommunisten ihre Anschauungsweise, ihre Zwecke, ihre Tendenzen vor der ganzen Welt offen darlegen und den Märchen vom Gespenst des Kommunismus ein Manifest der Partei entgegenstellen.

Marx and Engels, *Manifest der kommunistischen Partei* (1848)

In recent years, international law has come to realize the importance of its history. In what has been described as a historiographical turn, the theory of international law has immersed itself in its past to better understand its present.[2] The turn to history, which it is the great merit of Martti Koskenniemi to have spearheaded, has essentially been a turn to the 19th century. It is in this century that he locates the point of origin of the discipline of international law and it is here that he and, following him, much of recent legal historiography has looked to find the motive forces that have driven the evolution of international law. On the account that Koskenniemi gives, the 19th century is a time of struggle in which liberal internationalism fought to assert itself against the unholy alliance of reactionary conservatism and an Enlightenment rationalism which, while universal in ambition, remained tied to the state. Only in the eighth decade of the 19th century does the liberal disenchantment with the state, exacerbated by the carnage unleashed in the Franco-Prussian war of 1870–1871, grow so acute as to give rise to an awareness of the need for a discipline of international law, liberated from the traditional auxiliary disciplines of government: philosophy, diplomacy and public law. It is this awareness that manifests itself in the city of Ghent on what Koskenniemi takes to be the birth of the discipline of international law, the opening session of the *Institut de droit international* from 8 to 11 September 1873.

This account would seem to have much to commend it. After all, what better sign

[1] All translations are by the author of this article, except where otherwise indicated.

[2] Galindo, George Rodrigo, 'Martti Koskenniemi and the Historiographical Turn in International Law'.

that we have entered into the realm of *legal* history than the foundation of an institute and a journal, both dedicated to the study of international law, both the first of their kind? However, if we look beyond these academic manifestations, the line of separation that Koskenniemi proposes raises a number of questions, the most important of which concerns the relationship of this legal history to that which Koskenniemi, by his demarcation, has relegated into the dimension of pre-history, pre-legal history. How does this pre-history, the first half of the 19th century, of which Koskenniemi tells us that it is not difficult to see why it could not have given rise to a professional discipline of international law,[3] link up with history proper? Is the pre-history of the Ghent meeting just inert matter that the motive forces of liberal internationalism have to overcome to constitute a proper, a scientific, discourse on the rules of state interaction? One might object that such questions bespeak a lack of good faith; that historical beginnings are never absolute and while they are easily deconstructed, this does not take away from their explanatory force. But, as I hope to demonstrate, taking Koskenniemi to task for proposing a historical demarcation of international law is more than a clever, if dubious, rhetorical ploy. To understand the course that international legal theory takes, we must inquire how it gathered the momentum which is then manifested in academic institutions. I shall argue that if a scientific discourse on the rules of state interaction becomes possible in the second half of the 19th century, if its history can be written as the inventory of positions within the field of international legal theory, it is only because the conception of the interstate sphere has changed in Europe. Prior to the French Revolution, the interstate sphere is understood as a dimension of opposition, the opposition between sovereign powers. Opposition is endemic to the interstate sphere, because no power on earth exists that could adjudicate between sovereigns. This conception changes in the course of the 19th century. Despite the continued absence of an international judge, a conception of the interstate sphere gains ground, according to which a state is not, by virtue of its sovereignty, in opposition to other states. The state is a member of a cultural community, the community of European states, and within this domain, communion prevails over opposition; relations between member states no longer need involve subjection and domination. As we shall see, this absence of domination, or rather, the notion of this absence makes it possible to articulate norms of conduct, to which the state can subject itself, while maintaining its sovereignty, because these norms do not reflect a particular position of power; they reflect the will of all. What organizes and emerges from this theoretical communion of states is the possibility of legal construction of the interstate sphere. This possibility constitutes – so I shall argue – the legacy of the 19th century to international law. It is the pivot in the transition between two systems of state interaction which shall deliver us into the 20th century: the transition from the classic state system to the system of international law. What I am treating is thus an aspect of the coming into being of political modernity. To pre-empt the sentiment that my subject matter is of historical interest only; that it has no bearing on our present situation, we would do well to reflect on the nature of the systems of international law which arose out of the 19th century. The possibility of a legal construction of the interstate sphere may have entered into the fabric of the modern world, but its translation into legal structure remains subject to the play of forces

[3] Koskenniemi, Martti, *The Gentle Civilizer of Nations*, p. 35.

between sovereign states. Only if we determine the motive forces which drew the states together in a system of international law, can we come to understand the directions that this essentially open-ended translation is likely to take in years to come.

5.1 FROM STATE SYSTEM TO THE SYSTEM OF INTERNATIONAL LAW

The above considerations are not without importance for my analysis of the transformation of international law. We should not expect to find changes, at least significant changes, at the level of legal structure. This is confirmed if we consider the reception within the theory of international law of the crisis which prompted the movement beyond the state system: the French Revolution, this magnificent sunrise in the history of mankind, as Hegel described it. However, to international law, the French Revolution was anything but a sunrise; in fact, it meant lights out. In 1803, at the close of the only peaceful period between 1789 and 1815, as Gérard de Rayneval published his treatise on the institutions of the law of nature and of peoples, he prefaced his work by an appraisal of the difficulty of the task that he had set himself, namely to treat of the law of peoples:

> I have not hid from myself that, for some 12 years, the matter of which I shall treat has been closed [*une matière epuisée*], especially in France. However, as I considered the never-ending fluctuations of opinions on what principles should be adopted, the misuse that has been made of those opinions, the erroneous views which have successively been introduced into them, the reprehensible actions to which they have given rise and the dangers to which they have exposed France and Europe . . ., I thought that one might again speak of mores, of morality, religion, honour, justice, humanity, of the duties as well as the rights of peoples . . .[4]

Even if we must make allowances for the literary genre that is the preface, the text of de Rayneval bears testimony to the devastating effect that the conflict between France and the coalitions of European powers had on the practice of international law. The renaissance of international law is still too much of an open question for him to consider the effects of its suspension. But as the dust settled, as order returned across the European continent, legal theory could, with the clarity of hindsight, look back on the events which had followed in the wake of the Revolution and attempt to decipher their meaning. From the perspective of legal theory, it is evident that the reaction against the revolutionary endeavour was a necessary precondition of the re-establishment of international law. As Carl Kaltenborn von Stachau indicates in his critique of international law, written in 1847, the restoration of international law was rendered possible by the reaction against the revolutionary endeavour and the return of the ancient order:

> It was only with the determinations [*Satzungen*] made at the Vienna Congress in 1815 and, in its wake, the acts of the so-called Holy Alliance . . . that the venerable foundations of the modern co-existence [*Völkerrechtsleben*] of Christian states were consolidated again, leading to an unprecedented growth in the practice of positive international law. Only then was the belief of science in the importance of a doctrine of positive international law restored and science found

---

4 Rayneval, Gérard de, *Institutions du Droit de la Nature et des Gens*, preface, pp. ii–iii.

> within itself the strength and the calling to open up a new age in the international doctrine of law . . . This revolution in the positive doctrine of international law therefore grows out of a new configuration and consolidation of international life itself.[5]

Seen in retrospect, the suspension and subsequent restoration of international legal practice thus stand out as the defining moment of the Revolution and its aftermath. However, if we attempt to look beyond changes in state practice, if we attempt to identify the changes that the political events caused within the system of international law, a certain perplexity makes itself felt.[6] Kaltenborn von Stachau does not offer any indications, and the earlier accounts of the development of international law are hardly more conclusive. In 1821, as Johann Ludwig Klüber, the pre-eminent theorist of international law of the 19th century, considers the impact of the political upheaval on the system of international law, he withholds final judgement on the state of international law: 'The shocks which the European states have suffered over the last quarter of a century shall most likely [*höchstwarscheinlich*] result in a number of changes or modifications to the principles of positive international law. It was thought, erroneously, that this would be settled at the Vienna Congress.'[7] The tentative nature of Klüber's appraisal of the current state of international law reflects a discrepancy between his politico-historical intuition and his analysis of the state system. The enormity of the political events which had taken place in Europe is such that Klüber cannot but conclude that changes to the system of international law must necessarily occur, but crucially, there is no attempt at a legal qualification of the changes. Klüber cannot indicate their nature nor is he certain that they will occur; he can only opine that it is 'most likely'. This inability to engage in a legal qualification of the events of political history reappears three decades later in another preface, the 1858 preface by Charles Vergé to the second French edition of Georg Friedrich von Marten's *Précis du Droit des Gens Moderne de l'Europe* of 1788. The preface is entitled 'Le Droit des Gens avant et depuis 1789' – the law of peoples before and after 1789. The title implies that the French Revolution serves as the line of demarcation in the historical development of international law, as the threshold between two epochs. But as we read Vergé's text, no attempt is made to indicate the nature of such an epochal transition. In the account that Vergé gives, the history of international law is unbroken. Its trajectory is that of an inexorable movement from the primitive, instinctive Greco-Roman law of peoples to the modern, civilized system of international law. International law is an aspect of the overarching history of human civilization, the motive force of which is the perfection of human nature and society through culture.[8] In this history of the advent of civilization, the interest of the year 1789 is only local; it simply marks the point of suspension of international law,

---

5 Kaltenborn von Stachau, Carl, *Kritik des Völkerrechts*, p. 170.

6 This perplexity is reflected in the appraisal of Wilhelm Grewe of the impact of the French Revolution on the system of international law. As he puts it, the French Revolution inaugurated a 'peculiar' transitional period, because while it was powerless to institute a new system of international law, the forces which it unleashed removed the foundations of the notion of a community of states which had kept in place the traditional state system (Grewe, Wilhelm G., *Epochen der Völkerrechtsgeschichte*, pp. 485–486). We are not told wherein this transformation consisted or how it took place.

7 Klüber, Johann Ludwig, *Europäisches Völkerrecht*, preface, p. 9.

8 Vergé, Charles, 'Le Droit des Gens avant et depuis 1789', pp. XIV–XV.

the nature of which, however, is not affected by this suspension. To Vergé, the sense of both revolution and reaction are contained within this history of human civilization. Not only are they moments in the same history, but the function which they fulfil within this history is intimately connected. If the revolution is seen as a retrograde movement within the development of international law, it is because the reaction against it did not establish a system of international law that would realize the promise of an ever-closer union of peoples, united by a common culture and a common market.[9]

This singular inability to engage with the events of political history, to give a legal qualification of the changes that these events have wrought to the system, indicates that, while the forces, which the revolution unleashed and which Napoleon subsequently spread across Europe, brought about the suspension of the system of international law, they left intact its basic structures. Events may have demonstrated the system of international law to be out of synchrony with political history – this is Klüber's sense – but this detachment is projected into the future; rather than a flaw in the system of international law, it is seen as an indication of its perfectibility, its capacity to accommodate future change. It might seem that we are excessively concerned with matters that are, admittedly, peripheral to the legal construction of the interstate sphere. If we, nevertheless, insist on the importance of this inability of legal construction to engage with political history, it is because it indicates an essential property of the strengthening of the practice of international law that took place in the wake of the Vienna Congress, giving rise to the system of international law. It indicates that the transition from what Koskenniemi designates as the 'Enlightenment rationalism' of Klüber to the position of Vergé, in whose essay we find a 'striking example' of the new reformist spirit out of which the discipline of international law emerged,[10] was articulated from within the traditional state system. If the epochal transition from this system to the system of international law has proven to be intractable to legal analysis, it may well be because it takes place within the legal construction, beneath its radar, as it were. What changes in this epochal transition are not legal structures, but the sense which they carry.

In order to understand the transformation of international law in the 19th century, we must therefore look beyond the structures of the state system, to the manner in which they are implicated in the legal construction of the interstate sphere. Within this construction, their implication is organized around the isomorphism of the state and the interstate sphere, the fact that the principles which govern the interstate sphere are the very same principles that preside over the institution of the state. This is expressed in the notion, first found in stoic philosophy, that there is no essential difference between the law of peoples and the law of nature; the law of peoples is nothing other than natural law applied not within, but between, different political communities.[11] However, this

---

9 Similarly Oppenheim, Heinrich Bernhard, *System des Völkerrechts*, I, iii, § 9, p.43; § 15, pp.57–58; § 20, pp.70–71.

10 Koskenniemi, Martti, *The Gentle Civilizer of Nations*, pp.21, 27.

11 See Cicero, *De Legibus*, I, vii, 23; xi, 32; xv, 42; xxii–xxiii, 61. This idea appears in the writings of almost all major publicists on the state system, see Burlamaqui, Jean-Jacques, *Principes de Droit de la Nature*, II, vi, 5, p. 188; Pufendorf, Samuel von, *Droit de la nature et des gens*, II, iii, 23, p.239; Vattel, Emer de, *Le droit des gens, ou principes de la loi naturelle*, I, preliminaries, pp.2–3. The sole exception would seem to be Hugo Grotius who holds that the law of nations arises through

isomorphism of the state and the interstate sphere does not entail that the two spheres are of equal importance. The state sphere enjoys a definite primacy; it is within the state sphere that the fundamental principles of social interaction, the principles of morality, are articulated, only to be transposed onto the interstate sphere. Within the state system, the isomorphism of the state and the interstate sphere thus serves an edifying function. If there is no essential difference between the two spheres, the morality that holds within civil society must also hold between civil societies. This primacy of the state sphere can be traced back to the circumstances of the return to Aristotle's political philosophy in the late Middle Ages.[12] This return marks the reversal of the Christian subordination of local political order (*civitas*) to universal order (*regnum*), the political form in which the community of the faithful is organized. This reversal lays down the template for modern natural law in which the construction of society revolves around the foundation of political community, the incessant passage from a state of nature into society, and in which the affirmation of civil authority – of sovereignty – comes about through the demarcation of political community from that which lies outside its horizon. This is the situation which Hobbes describes in the famous chapter XIII of *Leviathan*, stating that even if 'there had never been any time wherein particular men were in a condition of war one against another, yet in all times kings and persons of sovereign authority, because of their independency, are in continual jealousies and in the state and posture of gladiators, having their weapons pointing and their eyes fixed on one another'.[13] As appears from Hobbes' description, the violence which inheres in interstate relations is no less real than the violence which threatens within the commonwealth; in fact, it may be more real. But despite the reality of interstate violence, it does not affect the subject with the urgency of the power of the sovereign to whom he has surrendered his liberty. Seen in this perspective, the isomorphism of the interstate and the state sphere is not relevant, because the aim of natural law is accomplished within the state sphere. It is to the sovereign or state power that natural law seeks to set out boundaries through the articulation of a conception of political community. While the existence of a plurality of nations is an empirical fact, it is only of marginal interest to the reflection on the community that unfolds within the state. Natural law is therefore content to leave the government of the interstate sphere to the sovereign, as it does not pertain to the government of political community; it lies beyond the horizon of a format of thought that is primarily concerned with re-establishing the civic conditions of human existence.[14] This accounts for the disinterest that Hobbes shows the interstate relations. In his first work of political philosophy, the *Elements of*

---

general agreement among the states, whereas the law of nature is derived from the principles of human nature (Grotius, Hugo, *The Rights of War and Peace*, preliminary discourse, pp. 112–113; I, I, xiv, p. 163).

[12] See Lev, Amnon, *Foundations of Power. From Natural Law to Legal Science*, PhD thesis, University of Copenhagen, 2009.

[13] Hobbes, *Leviathan*, I, xiii, 12, p. 78.

[14] Georg Jellinek notes that the sciences of state have, since Plato and almost without exception, adopted this restricted focus, as if the state were the only exemplar of its kind (See Jellinek, Georg, *Die Lehre von den Staatenverbindungen*, p. 92). But while he has uncovered that this implicit identification of state power and internal domination (*Herrschaft*) is at the heart of the idea that international law is a logical impossibility, Jellinek does not consider how this idea nevertheless came to impose itself on constitutional thought, from whence it derived its necessity.

Law, a work of 354 paragraphs, he devotes only one paragraph, the last, to the principles that govern the interaction of states: 'And thus much concerning the elements and general grounds of laws natural and politic. As for the law of nations, it is the same with the law of nature. For that which is the law of nature between man and man, before the constitution of the commonwealth, is the law of nations between sovereign and sovereign, after.'[15]

The jusnaturalist perspective is reflected in the relative disinterest of the early theorists of international law in the means by which the interstate sphere is governed, more specifically, the art of diplomacy. In von Martens's treatise, diplomacy is introduced simply as one of the two means by which states resolve their disputes, the other being war.[16] This definition of the place of diplomacy in government strikes a somewhat singular note: the dealings of states, as von Martens describes them, are not exclusively, nor even primarily, concerned with the resolution of conflicts, whether by diplomatic or by belligerent means. In the first volume, von Martens treats extensively of consular envoys that protect the commercial interests of the sender state, even adjudicating conflicts pertaining thereunto, and in the second volume we find a detailed description of the intricacies of diplomatic protocol that demonstrates that this form of interaction had, by then, developed far beyond a simple therapeutic to avoid the ultimate recourse of war. Von Martens's work contains a number of elements which, taken together, point beyond the minimal definition of international co-existence that he offers by way of introduction. However, these elements are not gathered together; they are kept apart by a conception of legal construction that revolves around the jusnaturalist motif of the articulation of human society, keeping in place the distinction of the internal and the external dimension of state sovereignty. This is reflected in the structure of von Martens's work. The rights of states and nations are considered in the first volume, while diplomacy is considered in the second volume, after the chapter dealing with the rights of the person and the family of the sovereign. In a sense, this distinction between the internal and the external dimension of sovereignty constitutes the pivot in the transformation of international law, the nature of which I am seeking to indicate. While this transformation leaves in place the structures of state sovereignty, it encroaches upon the traditional privilege, according to which the government of the interstate sphere is a reserved sovereign domain, a domain of only marginal interest to the legal construction of society. It destabilizes the demarcation of the state sphere from the interstate sphere in that it opens up the horizon of legal construction, thus exposing the precarious nature of the distinction of the internal and the external dimension of sovereignty. The place, which legal construction accords diplomacy in government, might serve as an indicator of this opening of the horizon of sovereignty, as it registers the process by which the government of the interstate sphere enters into the government of men. Seen in this perspective, it is noteworthy that manuals of the sciences of state record the attempt, during the first two decades of the 19th century, to secrete the elements of the art of political negotiations with a view to constitute diplomacy as a science.[17] By 1821, as Klüber considers the question, diplomacy is no longer

---

15 Hobbes, *Elements of Law*, II, 10, 10, p. 190.

16 Martens, Georg Friedrich von, *Précis du Droit des Gens Moderne de l'Europe*, II, vi, 176, p. 19.

17 Pölitz, Karl H. L., *Grundriß für encykopädische Vorträge über die gesammten Staatswissenschaften*, p. 296.

treated as a sovereign art; rather, it is seen to be in the interest of every state to engage in repeated negotiations with other states, not only with a view to concluding treaties, but also to keep an eye on the development of its own external legal and political relations.[18] Diplomacy is no longer simply a method to resolve disputes, an alternative to war; it is an integral part of government.[19] Crucially, these negotiations or consultations are carried out in the interest of the state, not of the sovereign. As if to drive home the point, Klüber adds that while these negotiations are conducted by virtue of the independence of the state – its sovereignty – the person exercising this sovereignty might be subject to limitations on account of the fundamental constitution (*Grundverfassung*) of the state.[20]

This displacement is the register of a momentous transformation of the nexus of the interstate and the state sphere that kept in place political thought from the 17th century. This transformation is perhaps most evident in the limiting case of state intercourse: war. The forces that the Revolution had unleashed upon Europe offered ample demonstration of the inadequacy of the traditional mode of governing the interstate sphere. We find testimony of this in the work of someone who not only fought in the wars against France, but who also attempted to identify the essence of modern war, as it arose out of this conflict. The world that Carl von Clausewitz describes is the world of *l'Ancien Régime*, the world of the European state system in which war was played as a game between sovereigns; a game in which the stakes did not concern the survival of the political community, just as it did not engage the state beyond the stakes that had been put on the table:

> In European politics, it is conventional for states to make offensive and defensive pacts for mutual support; however, not to the point of adopting the enmity and the interests of one another. Instead, they pledge to each other a force, the size of which – usually very modest – is decided in advance, without any regard to the object of war or the scale of the enemy's belligerent efforts. A state which enters into this sort of alliance does not, on this account, consider itself to be in a proper state of war with the enemy [of its ally] . . . But even where two states make war upon a third, this does not always mean that they look upon this third state as their enemy that they must annihilate, lest he annihilate them. The matter is often dealt with as if it were a business deal; in consideration of the risks which he runs and the gains which he hopes to achieve, each party invests a stake [*eine Aktie*] of 30.000 to 40.000 men, pretending that this is all he stands to lose.[21]

Against this background, the peripheral place of diplomacy in the handbooks of international law makes perfect sense. In a world where the decision to engage in war is not seen to constitute an act of aggression between two nations, but merely as a tactical move on the part of a single player who stands apart from the society that he governs – a move

---

18 Klüber, Johann Ludwig, *Europäisches Volkerrecht*, II, ii, iii, § 166, p. 269.

19 This displacement parallels the historical strengthening of the diplomatic apparatus in Europe with the development of the peacetime conference as the institution of diplomacy. See Hamilton, Keith and Richard Langhorne, *The Practice of Diplomacy*, pp. 79–84, 90–91. On the historical background of this strengthening of diplomacy, see Duchhardt, Heinz, *Balance of Power und Pentarchie*, pp. 322–333.

20 The necessity of these consultations is articulated earlier. See Mably, Gabriel Bonnot de, *Principes de Négociations,* i, p. 11. However, this is born out of the grandiose enterprises concocted by the 'princes', seen to be the reserved domain of the sovereign, and the reason for the building of alliances between sovereigns is that of countering the excess of power in certain states.

21 Clausewitz, Carl von, *Vom Kriege*, 8, 6A, pp. 421–422.

that, moreover, does not commit him to any future course of action – the decision as to what course of action to take is, from the perspective of the legal construction of society, arbitrary. While the skill of the diplomat, the savvy of political counsel, is an essential element of the external exercise of sovereign power, it is not an integral part of the government of men, as it has no impact on the society that unfolds under the protective wings of the sovereign. It is this world of chessboard politics that the spread of the revolution beyond the borders of France disrupts. However, the imperial venture of Napoleon not only disrupts the balance of power between the states of Europe; more importantly, it also points beyond the principle that governed power politics on the continent: the joint exclusion of conflict from political community and its containment within a specific domain – the battlefield – in other words, the distinction of the internal and the external dimension of sovereignty that kept in place the notion of war as the reserved domain of the sovereign.

The most readily apparent cause of this movement away from the traditional form of power politics is the heightened intensity of violence deployed in conflict. As a mode of government of the interstate sphere, the conclusion of transitory alliances proved to be insufficient in the face of the violence that Napoleon unleashed upon Europe. This violence had demonstrated the need for a new form of government of the interstate sphere which revolved around the imperative that a choice be taken. As von Clausewitz tells us, 'in recent times, where extreme danger drove people to adopt a more natural perspective, as *against* Bonaparte, and where limitless violence forced them to, as *with* Bonaparte', the 'conventional' business-like conception of alliance warfare has had to give way to 'the natural conception'.[22] The passage is somewhat convoluted, but the fundamental sense is clear: by his campaign, Napoleon placed the European states before a decision that they could not elude; they must join forces, whether it be *against* or *with* him, join forces they must. The urgency of this decision testifies to the dramatic curtailment of the discretionary power of the sovereign to decide which military strategy to adopt, which alliances to seek and which to seek to be released from. In a time of extreme danger, of limitless violence, war cannot be fought with limited stakes; it must be fought as an all-out war, a modern war. This is the 'natural conception' to which von Clausewitz alludes, but which he does not define. In such a war, the decision as to which side to engage on is urgent, as it does not admit of degrees. One cannot delimit the commitment that the state makes by its decision, neither in time nor in the number of lives sacrificed. This curtailment of the discretionary power of the sovereign is reflected in another aspect of warfare that von Clausewitz does not consider, namely the rules of neutrality. In the course of the last decade of the 18th century, with the spilling over of the French Revolution as the immediate motive, a stricter doctrine of neutrality rapidly gains ground, both within and outside Europe; a doctrine that revolves around the preclusion of benevolent neutrality (*unvollständige Neutralität, neutralité bienveillante*): whereas it was formerly recognized that states could, within the limits of their neutrality, offer non-military aid to one of the

[22] Clausewitz, Carl von, *Vom Kriege*, 8, 6A, pp. 421–422: 'Diese Art den Bündniskrieg zu betrachten war ganz allgemein, und hat nur in der neuesten Zeit, wo die äußerste Gefahr die Gemüter in die natürliche Wege hineintrieb, wie *gegen* Bonaparte, und wo schrankenlose Gewalt sie hinein, wie *mit* Bonaparte, der natürlichen weichen müssen.'

warring parties, for example by granting or refusing safe passage, such aid is now seen as strictly incompatible with the obligation of neutrality and hence as an act of war.[23]

This subtle change amounts to what we might call a structuring of the interstate sphere, the circumscription of discretionary power in its government. It might seem that we are attributing this change to the military prowess of the French army. And indeed, the spread of revolutionary ideals, of the *Code Civil*, owes much to the tactical nous of Napoleon and the efficacy of the French troops. However, it is one of the merits of von Clausewitz's essay that he does not reduce the effects of the French Revolution to the means and tactics of war. In fact, of the elements in the successful spread of the Revolution, the military element is by far the least important; the primary cause is political:

> It is true that the essence and forms of war have also undergone important changes that have brought [the phenomenon of] war closer to its absolute form. However, these changes have not come about, because the French government somehow freed itself from the shackles of politics; on the contrary, they have arisen out of the change in politics that the French Revolution introduced in both France and Europe. This new form of politics could marshal other means and other forces and so rendered possible an intensity of warfare which would otherwise have been unimaginable.[24]

This change in politics to which Clausewitz refers is, of course, the advent of popular rule in France. The violence which drove the nations of Europe into closer community is thus inseparable from a transformation of the French political order. This is of interest to us, as the implication of the French people in the war parallels the encroachment of sovereign privileges at the interstate level. The mass mobilization of the *demos*, of which the revolutionary and imperial wars offer the first significant example in the modern age,[25] prepares the way for the introduction of the people into the government of war. If the mobilization of the people marshals hitherto unseen forces, it is because war is no longer seen to be a private affair of the sovereign in which he is free to invest a stock of men who are, themselves, unconcerned by the conflict. In these wars, the *demos* fights as a nation, not as the King's men. The mobilization of the people thus contributes to the destabilization of the demarcation of the internal and the external dimension of sovereignty. The

---

[23] The adoption of this new doctrine grows out of different historico-political situations in America and Europe. The declaration of neutrality in regard to the European conflict by American president Washington of 22 April 1793 serves to protect American trade interest. See Politis, Nicolas, *La Neutralité et la Paix*, pp. 38, 41–42, 45. On the European continent, the stricter doctrine of neutrality is primarily a result of the movement towards armed neutrality, instigated by Russia to counter English maritime ambitions and in which almost all European states joined. These two lines of evolution, which would converge in the course of the 19th century, both revolve around the relationship of continental Europe to a non-continental power and are both born out of the same fundamental perception: that a country cannot play favourites in an ongoing conflict, while expecting to be left to pursue its other interests regardless of the conflict.

[24] Clausewitz, Carl von, *Vom Kriege*, 8, 6A, p. 434. This is corroborated by Mably's description of pre-revolutionary warfare in Europe where he notes that the European powers are wont to spare each other; that they do not conduct their warfare with a view to harming their opponent; that it is even rare that they direct their war effort towards the goal which they hope to achieve by the peace (*Principes de Négociations*, xv, pp. 138–139).

[25] Bell David A., *The First Total War*, pp. 99, 125, 234; Bond, Brian, *The Pursuit of Victory*, pp. 15–16, 27–28; Reinhard, Wolfgang, *Geschichte der Staatsgewalt*, pp. 359–360.

nexus that a state of war establishes between sovereigns – the primordial nexus that is susceptible to legal qualification – is rendered transparent in the sense that the government of the interstate sphere and the government of men now intertwine; from now on, they factor in each other's government. While sovereignty thus continues to flow from the political community that unfolds within the state, it must henceforth be exercised within the horizon of the plurality of states. The fact that the state does not exist in perfect isolation, that the *universum* of the state is in reality a *multiversum*, is no longer simply of marginal interest to legal construction; instead, it becomes an integral part of the concept of the state. In this sense, the imperial venture of Napoleon announces, indeed it even carries, the system of international law.

The movement from the state system to the system of international law does not, as Koskenniemi seems to imply, happen at a determinate point in history where legal discourse somehow sets itself apart from the auxiliary disciplines of government and constitutes itself as a discipline in its own right. In fact, the attempt to identify such a point of origin blinds us to the nature of the transformation of the practice of international law which took place in the wake of the French Revolution. This transformation arises out of a revolutionary shift in the form of social organization, the effects of which include the downfall of *l'Ancien régime* and, eventually, the advent of mass democracy. The meeting in Ghent in 1873 is but one aspect of this transformation, perhaps not even an aspect of the first order. This is not to deny the importance of the genesis of a scientific discourse on international law. However, we shall fail to grasp the trajectory which this discourse shall take, if, taking Koskenniemi's example, we assume that the movement from the state system to the system of international law is driven by one and the same motive force, namely the spread of economic liberalism. Seen in this perspective, the part of the 19th century that precedes the year 1873 appears simply as the pre-history of *legal* history, or more precisely, as the history of a movement held back until the motive force that drives the development of international law suddenly, as if by miracle, overcomes the inertia of historical matter and the real, the *legal*, history of international law begins. Instead, we must place the advent of the system of international law within a fundamental reconfiguration of the state system,[26] a regrouping of certain of its aspects which, while leaving in place the basic structures of the state system, renders the interstate sphere amenable to legal construction. This is the key to understanding how legal construction could, for a time, unfold in a relative independence from political considerations, not because international law did at any point sever the umbilical cord which tied it to the other auxiliary disciplines of government, as Koskenniemi assumes, but because, in the age which the French Revolution ushered in, these disciplines could no longer define or dominate the field within which sovereign states interacted.

5.2 TRANSLATING THE EQUILIBRIUM INTO LAW

To borrow an expression from Ole Spiermann, we might say that the transition which we are trying to describe is that from the binary opposition either/or, which pits sovereignty

---

[26] The use of the idea of a reconfiguration of a given system to analyse epochal transitions is developed in Blumenberg, Hans, *Die Legitimität der Neuzeit*, see especially pp. 59–61.

and international law against one another, to the union either *and* or, which, while maintaining sovereignty, integrates it in a system of international law. While sovereignty continues to serve its traditional function in legal discourse, it is now seen to flow naturally into a domain in which it was formerly absent, or rather, in which it was formerly present only in opposition to other sovereigns: the interstate sphere. The capacity to act within this sphere, always implied in the doctrine of sovereignty, can now come to the fore as an essential attribute of sovereignty, as the exercise of sovereignty no longer constitutes an obstacle to the legal construction of the interstate sphere. This is not to suggest that the transformation of the nexus of state and sovereignty is, at this time, fully articulated. But this transformation prepares the way for an ever-closer cooperation between states, indeed, renders it inevitable. Of course, the decision that Napoleon forces upon the states of Europe does not, as if by *fiat*, call into existence a fully fledged system of international law. Nonetheless, its symbolic importance cannot be overestimated. Unlike the common practice of commercial dealings between states which could, at least in theory, be seen as an exercise of self-interest, this decision concerns what is undoubtedly the most fundamental layer of sovereignty, the decision to risk the independence of the community by engaging in war. As such, it provides a compelling demonstration that even this, the most exclusive of sovereign domains, is now seen to be subject to the necessity of binding state cooperation. As Spiermann has shown in his work on the rise of the international judiciary, the Permanent Court of International Justice shall fashion these, more or less implicit, state practices into a system that revolves around the idea of the state as an international sovereign, supplementing the notion of the state as a national sovereign.[27]

This perspective of interpretation would seem to invite the criticism that it shows historical action to be an ineluctable movement towards a fixed *telos*, the realization of the structural potential of this nexus of sovereignty and state, stripping human action of its contingent nature. However, if we look more closely at international legal theory after the Vienna Congress, there are unmistakeable signs that a discrepancy has arisen between its basic concepts and the function that it is meant to serve as an auxiliary discipline of government. Perhaps the most revealing sign of this state of tension is the controversy which comes to surround the conventional, yet notoriously vague notion that interstate

---

[27] See Spiermann, Ole, *International Legal Argument in the Permanent Court of International Justice*, pp. 134–209 for an analysis of the seminal cases from the foundational period in the Court's jurisprudence, the period 1922–1924. Equally important for our present purposes is that Spiermann articulates a double structure within which not only the structure of legal argument, but also the subsequent development of international law can be analysed: on the one hand, the international law of co-existence, the object of which is to address the conflicts that arise out of the co-existence of states and which therefore remains bound to the sphere of national sovereignty; on the other hand, the international law of cooperation, which grows out of volitional acts, primarily expressed in treaties, and which revolves around the notion of the state as both an international sovereign and subject (pp. 92–98). To Spiermann, this distinction reflects material differences in that certain questions are seen to be international in nature. The analysis which I shall propose parallels the one offered by Spiermann: that the 19th century sees a significant growth in the international law of cooperation, as expressed in the number of treaties concluded between states, because of a consensus that states can no longer be left to their own devices to deal with the matters that belong within the interstate sphere, whereas the international law of co-existence, in which the basic structures of the state system are defined, is not subject to substantial change.

relations in Europe are organized around a precarious balance of power. The genesis of this notion is a matter of some controversy, but at least since the 16th century, this idea, which revolves around the necessity of maintaining a relatively even distribution of power among the states of Europe, is advanced by publicists as the organizing principle of the community of states.[28] As this distribution precludes the establishment of universal hegemony by one power, all powers – this being the assumption – will find their interests served by perpetuating the system. This is the *raison d'être* of the system of equilibrium; by making the independence of each contingent on the independence of all, the system ensures that states act in concert to counter any imbalance within the system. The question of the actual capacity of containment of this mechanism lies beyond the scope of this present work. My concern is with the function that the idea of a balance of power serves in legal construction. At first glance, there is ample reason to be wary of conferring a legal status on a principle which encourages the use of evil to do good and makes the keeping of the peace contingent upon the perpetuation of armed conflict. Even among the champions of the system of equilibrium, there is a palpable concern that it may not be possible to draw a line of demarcation between a legitimate growth in state power and a 'dangerous excess of power' that would justify countermeasures to uphold the equilibrium.[29] And if we take a step back and consider the structure of the system of equilibrium, we find that this concern is well founded: the problem of the demarcation is insoluble. It is of the essence of the system that countermeasures should be indistinguishable from the measures that they are directed against. Within a system which revolves around the upholding of equilibrium, measures and countermeasures, action and reaction, are indistinguishable, as both are potentially and in equal measure disruptive.[30] As Heinrich Oppenheim put it, the system 'had no absolute principle; it had no fixed goal. Its essence [*eigentliches Wesen*] was that of a never-ending oscillation, a mutual self-suspension [*Selbstaufhebens*], boundless disloyalty in the shifting of alliances, the breaking of treaties . . .'.[31] Within the system, all that exists are competing interests that vie for supremacy.

---

28 Duchhardt, Heinz, *Gleichgewicht der Kräfte, Convenance, Europäisches Konzert*, p. 68.

29 See Heffter, August Wilhelm, *Das Europäische Völkerrecht der Gegenwart*, introduction, § 6, p. 13; Schmalz, Theodore A.H., *Das europäische Völkerrecht*, V, iv, p. 207.

30 This is reflected in the widely divergent readings that the theorists of international law propose of the genesis of the system of equilibrium. While they agree that the idea of a European balance of power is a product of the modern age and that it revolves around the preclusion of universal monarchy in Europe, the pervasive and non-essential nature of the opposition of forces, which threatens the equilibrium, means that all major European powers can be identified as the threat that the system of equilibrium was meant to avert: Heffter, August Wilhelm, *Das Europäische Völkerrecht der Gegenwart*, introduction, § 6, p. 13 (Spanish hegemonial ambition); Martens, Georg Friedrich von, *Précis du Droit des Gens Moderne de l'Europe*, IV, I, 122, pp. 323–334 (the hegemonial ambition of Charles V); Oppenheim, Heinrich Bernhard, *System des Völkerrechts*, I, iii, § 4, p. 30 (the threat to European peace that arose in 1688, as the rule over England and the Netherlands devolved on the same person); Saalfeld, Friedrich, *Grundriß eines Systems des europäischen Völkerrechts*, I, i, i, § 2, pp. 22–23 (the rivalry between the houses of Habsburg and Bourbon); Schmalz, Theodore, *Das europäische Völkerrecht*, V, iv, p. 206 (the expansionism of Louis XIV).

31 Oppenheim, Heinrich Bernhard, *System des Völkerrechts*, I, iii, § 4, p. 32. This is reflected in the considerations of de Mably who, in his study of the strategic dealings of European states, notes that 'in relation to a state of which one is not a natural ally, there is, and can only be, fleeting alliances [*alliances passagères*]' (see Mably, Gabriel Bonnot de, *Principes des Négociations*, x, p. 91).

Once inside the system, we cannot find an Archimedean point, from which we might judge the material finality of an action, the interest that it advances. And while the injunction to preserve the balance of power may justify the use of force in a given situation, there is no guarantee that this justified use of force will not, in turn, aim at an excess of power that will endanger the system. As a criterion of the use of force, the idea of equilibrium cannot – as its advocates acknowledge – separate law from the politics of power.

With the principle of equilibrium, of the balance of power, we would thus seem to have left behind the realm of law. However, within the state system, the system of monadic states, such a demarcation of law and politics is not possible, because the very attempt, by one of the actors of the system, to draw a line between the legitimate and the illegitimate use of power would inevitably call forth an opposition which would suspend the normative validity of this demarcation, transforming it from a legal obligation into a power claim. The institution of a legal regime to structure the exercise of power would inevitably be seen as yet another stratagem in the endeavour to attain or consolidate a position of power. Seen in this perspective, it is evident why the principle of equilibrium, despite its non-essentiality and hence non-legal nature, was in fact indispensable to the legal construction of the interstate sphere. The mechanism of auto-correction, which it articulates, cannot deliver on the promise of law. But by introducing laws of movement, in other words, regularity and order, into a system that does not admit of organization, as it is, in theory, constituted by the free play of forces, the endless opposition of wills, the principle of equilibrium holds out the promise of a rationality which is receptive to legal argument. By adopting the principle of equilibrium, legal theory cannot claim the interstate sphere for law, but it can claim the possibility of law among states. The ambiguity that attaches to legal construction is reflected by von Martens who, while acknowledging the shortcomings of the system, holds that it cannot be 'dismissed as superfluous, condemned as illegitimate or effaced from the law of peoples'.[32] Even as he tells us that the system of equilibrium has served only the interests of those seeking to divide continental Europe – the non-continental and the newly arrived powers – von Martens adopts the principle of equilibrium, conferring on it the status of a legal principle, or almost:

> [Although] none of the powers have laboured in earnest and with consistency to uphold or re-establish this equilibrium, with the exception of Great Britain since the end of the 17th century, or later Prussia, at least most of the European powers even today consider themselves to be entitled [*pouvoir prétendre au droit*] to watch over the upholding of this equilibrium as if it were a principle of the law of peoples [*comme à un principe du droit des nations*].[33]

As the above passage indicates, von Martens seeks, despite or because of his misgivings, to bridge the gap between the strategy and the law of nations, but he cannot

---

This would seem to leave the alliances between natural allies, by which Mably understands powers who cannot, by virtue of the position of their respective domains, do each other harm and who are furthermore united by a common interest, a shared enmity towards a third power (ix, p. 79). However, even the bond which unites natural allies is precarious; it can be overturned by 'accidents . . . in a hundred different ways' (ix, p. 81).

32 Martens, Georg Friedrich von, *Précis du Droit des Gens Moderne de l'Europe*, IV, I, 122, pp. 327–328.

33 Martens, Georg Friedrich von, *Précis du Droit des Gens Moderne de l'Europe*, IV, I, 122, p. 334.

completely integrate the principle of equilibrium into legal construction. While it may not be possible to efface this principle from the law of nations, neither can it be included into this law. The equilibrium is, at most, a quasi-legal principle, because it is and remains the point that separates law from power politics, partaking of the characteristics of both. It opens the possibility of legal construction and, at the same time, it keeps legal construction from moving beyond the mere possibility, as any actual construction of the interstate sphere is inevitably seen to be a hostile action within the ongoing conflict, an attempt to gain a position of dominance. Within the state system, the principle of equilibrium is the *pharmakon* of legal construction, both remedy and poison.[34] The oscillation between law and power reflects the mode of interaction within the state system, the essence of which is expressed in the principle of equilibrium; the 'boundless disloyalty in the shifting of alliances, in the breaking of treaties'. The importance of the change in perception of the principle of equilibrium in international legal theory that occurs in the wake of the reaction against the revolution cannot be overestimated. As I have tried to indicate, this change rests upon a transformation of the conception of the interstate sphere. This transformation is reflected in the judgement which Klüber passes on the system that had grown up around the principle of equilibrium:

> The so-called system of equilibrium . . . has no foundation in international law in the absence of treaties. In contrast to legal equilibrium, the *suum cuique*, this supposed system of political equilibrium rests upon the idea of power and the excess of power. But seeing that [this determination of this idea] must take into account not only the given military power and population [of a state], but also . . . in short, the sum total of its spiritual and physical powers, this so-called system remains, legally and politically speaking, an indeterminate idea [*unbestimmte Idee*].[35]

The most salient aspect of this transformation is what, at first glance, looks to be an outright disqualification of the system of equilibrium. Does Klüber not tell us that the system has no foundation in international law; that, on account of its indeterminacy, it cannot serve as the system of state interaction? This indicates the inroads that law has made into the interstate sphere, now seen as a domain that will be ordered only through legal construction. In this sense, Klüber's appraisal is consistent with the nature of the reconfiguration of the state system which I have analysed above. However, a closer reading of Klüber's text reveals that matters are more complex: the treaty-based system of state interaction, to which Klüber alludes, would also seem to revolve around the purpose which was at the heart of the system of equilibrium and for which the Vienna Congress was convened: the establishment, or re-establishment, of the balance of power between the European powers.[36] The question is thus not whether the system of equilibrium has

---

[34] For the analysis of *pharmakon* as the element out of which conceptual construction arises, see Derrida, Jacques, 'La pharmacie de Platon', especially pp. 156–158, 211: '. . . on ne peut pas dans la pharmacie distinguer le remède du poison, le bien du mal, le vrai du faux, le dedans du dehors, le premier du second, etc. Pensé dans cette reversibilité originale, le *pharmakon* est *le même* précisément parce qu'il n'a pas d'identité' (p. 211).

[35] Klüber, Johann Ludwig, *Europäisches Völkerrecht*, II, i, i, 42, p. 81. Writing at the same time, Schmelzing notes the impossibility of turning the 'well-intentioned and easily constructed' notion of a political equilibrium into a European-wide system: Schmelzing, Julius, *Systematischer Grundriß des Europäischen Völkerrechtes*, introduction, § 19, p. 45 n7.

[36] The preamble of the treaty of alliance signed by Austria, Russia, England and Prussia on

any foundation at all, but whether its foundation is to be found in considerations of power or in treaty law. The principle of equilibrium remains the pivot of the system of international law, to which the Vienna Congress helped to give birth.[37]

To understand the transition from the state system into the system of international law that takes place in the 19th century, we must appreciate it in its full complexity. As I have indicated, this transition rests upon a fundamental transformation of the interstate sphere, now subject to legal construction. Seen in this perspective, it becomes clear why the Vienna Congress, the first attempt at legal construction on a continental scale, commanded the loyalty of both a conservative such as Kaltenborn von Stachau and a liberal such as Vergé. When von Stachau invokes the re-establishment of the venerable foundations of the co-existence of Christian states by the Vienna Congress,[38] this is easily interpreted as an expression of his conservatism, but such a reading would blind us to the singular complicity that the transition into the system of international law created between the opponents of yesteryear, between liberal and conservative theorists of the state system. Whatever misgivings Vergé harbours about the spirit of reaction and revenge which animated the Vienna Congress, they are secondary to the possibility which it had opened up, the possibility of a legal construction of the interstate sphere. As different as the liberal vision of a world of nation states, united by commerce, is from the order that the congress brought to life again, the gateway to this shining future of international law is and remains the present and, as Vergé considers the state of international law in 1858, he finds it to be not much changed; with some modifications, the system that the congress settled upon continued to govern interstate relations in Europe.[39] Against Koskenniemi, it would seem that it was not 'simply anathema' for liberal theorists to accept the international legal system that the members of the Holy Alliance had put into place.[40] In fact, there would seem to be little or no alternative. Consequently, we should not be surprised that the liberal attitude, as expressed by Vergé, was one of reform, not of rejection. The development of international law would have to build on what had been established, if only imperfectly, in Vienna. History would have to remedy those imperfections and, according to Vergé, history was already hard at work; despite 'some useful and felicitous measures which are to be saluted, the Vienna Congress is an example of what these gatherings [of states] were like in the past rather than what they should be like in the future; the Paris Congress of 1856 is the real indication of what they could be like from now on'.[41]

This communion of the conservative and the liberal position around the legal construction of the interstate sphere is an essential aspect of the movement beyond the state system. It entails the relative, never complete, bracketing of traditional lines of political

---

1 March 1814, article 32 of which convokes the Vienna Congress within a time limit of two months, states that the purpose of the campaign against France has been to 'put an end to the misery of Europe and to secure her future peace [*repos*] by the re-establishment of a just equilibrium of Powers' (*Acten des Wiener Congresses* (ed. Klüber), I, i, p. 1).

[37] Similarly Baumgart, Winfried, *Europäisches Konzert und nationale Bewegung*, p. 146.

[38] Kaltenborn von Stachau, Carl, *Kritik des Völkerrechts*, p. 170.

[39] Vergé, Charles, 'Le Droit des Gens avant et depuis 1789', pp. XLV–XLVI.

[40] Koskenniemi, Martti, *The Gentle Civilizer of Nations*, p. 35.

[41] Vergé, Charles, 'Le Droit des Gens avant et depuis 1789', pp. XLIX–L.

opposition, opening up a space for legal construction amid the clash of state interests and policies. But the reality of this movement beyond the state system is only one aspect of the transformation of international law in the 19th century. As we have seen, the legal construction of the interstate sphere continues to revolve around the notion of equilibrium. We would argue, again *pace* Koskenniemi, that international law did not assert itself as a discourse by disregarding considerations of state interests;[42] rather, it translated these considerations into another domain in which they could not be articulated except through law. The appreciation of this continuity is essential to an understanding of the success of international legal construction and, more specifically, of the trajectory that it would follow in the 19th century. It allows us to understand why the states did not, once the military threat had been averted and order restored to the continent, disengage from international legal construction, but continued to use treaty law to advance their interests, consolidating and further developing the system of international law.[43] It also allows us to understand why a question that political thought had left in suspense should now become a matter of concern to international legal theory: the question of the order of the community of states. For legal construction to fulfil its dual objective – the maintenance of equilibrium and the containment of the conflicts that arise out of the co-existence of states – the structure of the system could not be seen to rest exclusively on the balance of forces that prevailed in Europe in 1815. The legal translation of the equilibrium, which Klüber announced, would need to be supplemented by a structure that would allow the detachment of legal construction from the play of forces. The advent of this structure, this supplement to legal construction, is reflected in the notes by the Portuguese statesman and philosopher, Silvestre Pinheiro Ferreira, that are printed in the 1831 and later editions of von Martens's work. Commenting upon von Martens's diagnosis of the necessity of the system of equilibrium, Pinheiro Ferreira remarks that, as

> the allied Powers have laboured with success, since 1813, to establish a more just equilibrium of Powers, peace in Europe shall depend exclusively on the upholding of this equilibrium and of the settlement of titles [*état de possession*] which follows from the treaties of 1814–1819. And since most of the Powers within this part of the globe were a party to those treaties and, on this account, would be entitled to oppose any changes to this settlement . . . there would seem to be a less pressing need to decide whether the system of equilibrium is founded on the principles of natural law or whether it could only be founded through public compacts [*conventions publiques*].[44]

The question of the foundation of the system of equilibrium – treaty law or natural law, treaty law or balance of power – is thus rendered secondary, less acute, by the involvement of most powers 'within this part of the world'.

This is the actual justification of the element of coercion that inheres in any system,

42 Koskenniemi, Martti, *The Gentle Civilizer of Nations*, p. 28.

43 It is a sign of this consolidation and development that the practice of holding regular congresses among the European nations accelerates after the 1848 revolution where the concerts of nations almost became a standing institution, despite – or because – the consensus between the states became harder to find, as their strategic objectives began to diverge. See Doering-Manteuffel, Anselm, *Vom Wiener Kongreß zur Pariser Konferenz*, p. 13.

44 Martens, Georg Friedrich von, *Précis du Droit des Gens Moderne de l'Europe*, IV, I, 121, p. 330.

including the just equilibrium of the Vienna Congress. Pinheiro Ferreira gives what appears to be another justification, namely that the signatory states can oppose any future changes. But while this affords the signatory states the assurance that any future changes will not come about through an excess of power, it does not address and can have no bearing on the question of the justice of the Vienna system itself. The only justification of the institution of the Vienna system that Pinherio Ferreira offers is thus found in numbers. The association of most, if not all, within a community that is both legal and geographical serves as the warrant of the foundation of the equilibrium, of its justice as well as its legal pedigree. This implicit nexus of community and justification is rendered explicit in the idea of a European law of peoples which informs 19th-century international legal theory. As Heffter considers the domain of application of the European law of peoples, he does not structure it around the opposition of legitimate and illegitimate constraint, but around the difference between legitimate constraint and absence of constraint: under the European law of peoples, states engage in mutual administration of justice; they form a legal community, held together by the system of equilibrium that rests upon the commitment of all to prevent the rise of and, if need be to combat, a 'worrying' excess of power in individual members.[45] This element of coercion is altogether absent from the intercourse which the European states entertain with those less fortunate than themselves, the states that are not part of the concert of nations. This intercourse is based on the principle of reciprocity; it is free from constraint (*zwanglos*), conducted only according to 'politics and morality'. In contrast, the element of power has been integrated into the community of European states. This community in fact revolves around the pledge to counter any imbalance of power. In this sense, the European law of peoples is an exact structural parallel to the system of equilibrium. But within the domain that the European law of peoples circumscribes, the use of power is not only justified morally; more importantly, it is translated into law. As the treaty regime is seen to reflect the will of all, power can be articulated as law. As power is not articulated from a position of superiority, it does not reflect an imbalance of power. Of course, this introduction of Europe into the legal construction of the interstate sphere does not change the form or modality of state interaction. Its impact is felt elsewhere: it shifts the point of equilibrium of the state system from the never-ending shifting of alliances within a plurality of states to the demarcation of a moral community from what lies beyond its borders. In other words, it displaces the obstacles to legal construction to the periphery, both of the Concert of Nations and of legal theory.

5.3 CONSTRUCTING A SYSTEM OF INTERNATIONAL LAW

The re-establishment of pre-revolutionary order revolves around the notion of a legal community of European states. Considered as a fact of political history, the existence of this community is self-evident. At the turn of the 19th century, Europe's global predominance is such that it can view itself as the theatre of world history. However, once we

[45] Heffter, August Wilhelm, *Das Europäische Völkerrecht der Gegenwart*, introduction, § 7, p. 19, cf. § 5, p. 9.

attempt to translate this historico-political primacy into legal structure, this self-evidence quickly evaporates. As a form of social organization, the region does not lend itself to constitutional construction. It is caught between the two forms of social organization within which man has historically articulated society: (1) the idea of political community, in which the political and the ethical aspects of human existence have been reconciled in the shared exercise of political rule (the Greek *polis* and the modern state), and (2) the Christian notion of a universal community of the faithful; a community 'in which no attention is paid to any differences in the customs, laws, and institutions . . .'.[46] While the *polis* and the universal community of the faithful are kept in place by a conception of civil community that is all-inclusive, at least within its geographical boundaries, the region presents itself as an aggregate entity, made up of a plurality of independent communities, each governed by a sovereign to whom the subjects owe an exclusive loyalty. Consequently, civil community cannot serve as the immediate foundation of the region, as it does within the *polis* and the universal community of the faithful. Within the region, the affirmation of the unity of civil community – inevitably that of a specific community – cannot but highlight its difference from its would-be partners, endangering the regional unity. The region is without an internal principle of cohesion and on account of its aggregate nature, it can only provide such cohesion through its continuous demarcation from that which lies beyond its borders. Only by demonstrating the existence of a generic difference that separates the inner and the outer[47] can the cohesion of the region be secured without sacrificing the unity of its constituent communities. To contain the opposition of sovereign power within a system, legal construction must propose a demarcation of the European concert of nations that shows it to constitute a specific genus, an order *sui generis*. This accounts for a change in the methodology of international legal theory that can be traced back to the first decades of the 19th century: in contrast to the major 18th-century publicists of European public law who described the treaty practices of the dominant European powers without offering a definition of their object of study,[48] the demarcation of Europe as a family of nations now becomes a necessary preliminary of the theoretical construction of the system of international law.

The endeavour to establish an internal principle of cohesion for the new geopolitical order of Europe was already at work at the Vienna Congress. To counter the political liberalism which the revolution had unleashed upon Europe, the Russian Czar Alexander I advanced a conception of the alliance as a league of Christian states, a state system based on the subjection to the religion of the Saviour, a Holy Alliance.[49] The idea of this

---

[46] Augustine, *City of God*, II, xix, 17, p. 685.

[47] It has been pointed out that the notion of a European international law, a *jus publicum europeum* is a fiction; that it does not designate any structural property of the dealings of states, but serves as the ideological underpinning of international legal theory. See Guggenheim, Paul, 'Das *jus publicum europeum* und Europa', pp. 3–5; Orakhelashvili, Alexander, 'The Idea of European International law', in *passim*, especially pp. 334–337. It is equally true that the fiction of a European legal order is indispensable for the conceptual transition into a system of international law.

[48] See Mably, Gabriel Bonnot de, *Droit public d'Europe, fondé sur les traités* (1789); Moser, Johann Jacob, *Grundsätze des Europäischen Völkerrechts in Kriegszeiten* (1752); Neyron, Pierre-Joseph, *Essai Historique et Politique* (1777); Pufendorf, Samuel von, *An Introduction to the History of the Principal Kingdoms and States of Europe* (1719/1682).

[49] Schaeder, Hildegard, *Autokratie und Heilige Allianz*, pp. 80–81.

community of faith, which is reflected in the invocation of the Holy Trinity in the concluding treaties of the congress, continues to inform international legal theory throughout the 19th century.[50] But this foundation of the European law of peoples in religion is precarious; its domain of application does not correspond to its domain of efficacy. As Alexander Orakhelashvili has shown, 'Europe' had already before its invention as a politico-legal order spread itself beyond these allegedly natural borders; the history of treaty practice shows that European states had always recognized not only non-European, but also non-Christian states as equals.[51] In other words, the European system does not cover the domain of international law. This shortcoming is reflected in the embarrassment with which Klüber attempts to justify the assumption of a European law of peoples through the demonstration of a community of European states of Christian faith. Within this community, so Klüber informs us, there is a 'fairly general' consensus as to the manner in which states are to conduct themselves in their mutual dealings: 'Thus tied together by invisible bonds, the Christian Powers of Europe now look upon each other as members of a moral community to which the only non-Christian state in Europe, the Ottoman Porte, seems to be drawing closer. Even some *extra-European* states, like the United States of North America, have by deed and word expressed their wish to join this community.'[52] The integration of international relations, to which Klüber alludes – a phenomenon that the admission of the Ottoman Empire to the concert of nations at the 1856 Paris Conference rendered official – points to the insufficiency of the religious notion of a European law of peoples that had arisen out of the Vienna Congress. Seen from the perspective of the restoration, the notion of Europe possesses considerable rallying power, but in time, the specific demands of legal construction invariably make themselves felt. While the demarcation of Europe as an order *sui generis* is necessary to keep in place the legal construction of the interstate sphere, the explanatory power of this construction depends on its ability to cover the entirety of its domain. If the material definition of the community of states were seen to exclude states already established as equals, this would detach legal construction from the reality which it is supposed to mirror. This is the point made by Bluntschli in his 1868 textbook on international law: 'By founding international law exclusively on religion, the Holy Alliance of 1815 conflated the difference of religion and law. Being only applicable to peoples of the Christian faith, excluding the non-Christian state from the human global order, the alliance unduly restricts the domain of application of international law.'[53]

The importance of this restriction of the extent of the domain of international law goes well beyond the question of the explanatory power of international legal theory. As we have seen, the translation of the equilibrium of power into law rests upon the coincidence of the formal domain of application of the system of international law and the domain of

---

[50] See, for example, Heffter, August Wilhelm, *Das Europäische Völkerrecht der Gegenwart*, § 7, p. 19; Kaltenborn von Stachau, Carl, *Kritik des Völkerrechts*, p. 170; Klüber, Johann Ludwig, *Europäisches Völkerrecht*, I, ii, § 35, pp. 73–74.

[51] Orakhelashvili, Alexander, 'The Idea of European International law', pp. 330–336.

[52] Klüber, Johann Ludwig, *Europäisches Völkerrecht*, I, ii, § 35, pp. 73–74. Similarly Pölitz, Karl H. L., *Die Staatswissenschaften im Lichte unsrer Zeit*, V, i, introduction, pp. 6–8.

[53] Bluntschli, Johann Kaspar, *Das moderne Völkerrecht der civilisirten Staaten*, II, § 102, pp. 98–99.

its efficacy: the system must apply equally to all states that are included in the material definition of the community of states and, perhaps more importantly, this definition cannot be seen to exclude states that have, for the purposes of treaty law, been acknowledged as equals by members of the concert of nations. The legal nature of the construction of the interstate sphere depends on this coincidence. Consequently, the analytic observation that the Vienna system entails an undue restriction of the domain of international law is indisociable from the assertion that this shortcoming must be remedied through the extension of the system to cover the domain of international law. And indeed, Bluntschli goes on to add that while the five power system that the Vienna Congress had put into place could be seen as the beginning of an organization of Europe – a legal organization – it could not be seen as its end point.

The observation that the Vienna system is not truly universal, that it must be extended to encompass all states whose conduct is governed by the rules of international law, is a sign that the interstate sphere is now seen to be amenable to legal construction; the opposition of forces, which constituted the mode of interaction within the state system and which condemned legal construction to remain a possibility only, has now been translated into legal structure. Against this formalization of the theoretical construction of state interaction that gains ground in the course of the 19th century, the assumption of the immediacy of the ties that unite the European states into a community cannot be maintained. The absolute difference between faithful and heathen that the religious definition of the European concert of nations revolves around cannot account for the reality of international legal relations, the implication of Europe in that which lies beyond her borders. This does not signal the end of demarcation within international legal theory; it signals the transformation of demarcation.[54] The absolute difference between Europe and the world gives way to another concept of difference: a difference of degree within a spectrum of which the European concert of nations is the end point and *telos* toward which the series tends. The title of Bluntschli's work – *The Modern International Law of Civilized Peoples* – introduces the concept that supports this spectrum, namely the concept of civilization. Civilization is the element which unites the European concert of nations with the rest of the world, while at the same time maintaining a difference of degree, a relationship of superiority. The point of entry into the system of international law is seen to constitute the boundary between barbary and civilization, between nature and law. But if the fact of having entered into the system entails that a state has lifted itself out of the state of nature, it is the extent of its involvement in the system which indicates the level of its culture, its share in the common legal culture of the civilized world. In the words of Rivier:

[54] It has been suggested that the notion of the European character of international law is a product of positivism within international legal theory. See Anghie, Antony, *Imperialism, Sovereignty and the Making of International Law*, pp. 54–55. However, the matter would seem to be more complex. Certainly, the notion of a European international law did come into prominence with the triumph of positivism over the hitherto dominant jusnaturalism, as Anghie points out. But the advent of positivism within international legal theory is itself only rendered possible by the introduction of a cultural presupposition – the idea of a European community of nations – which positivism renders explicit and transforms.

In the final analysis, the law of peoples can only exist between and for nations that partake of this common juridical sensibility [*conscience juridique commune*]. Thus, it does not exist between or for nations that have no part in this culture. An abyss separates us from the peoples of inferior races, just like the abyss that separated the Greeks from the barbarians, while a less profound chasm, even a simple trench, which one can and does cross, separates us from the intermediary races, from half-civilized states or states whose civilization differs from ours in some essential aspects. It is thus between nations which share with us a common juridical sensibility that our law of peoples reigns and should be applied, and these are the same nations that we are wont to call civilized, because their civilization is ours.[55]

This idea, perhaps expressed in terms less crude, is found in most, if not all textbooks on international law from the second half of the 19th century: the system of international law embodies the usages of the civilized, that is, European peoples and as a non-European nation integrates into the system, it leaves behind its barbaric, heathen practices and accedes to a higher level of civilization.[56]

The assumption of a cultural community of European nations – which is at the heart of the idea of racial superiority – serves as the pivot of the legal construction of the interstate sphere.[57] It does so by rendering irrelevant the question of the foundation of a system of state interaction. The choice between public compacts or natural law, to which Pinheiro Ferreira refers, reactivates the opposition of international obligation and sovereignty that condemns legal construction to remain a possibility only. The introduction of an already given community into legal construction dissolves this opposition. Within this community, compacts are only declarative of what would, in any event, have come about through the exercise of the natural liberty of the state. Sovereignty is no longer seen to be in opposition to international obligation. The legal framework, within which the state is placed, does not constitute a limitation on its liberty, because it only reflects a naturally given order. It is civilization, second nature, not coercion, which ensures that the plurality of state wills converge upon their shared interests: civilized states freely enact what

55 Rivier, Alphonse, *Principes du Droit des Gens*, I, p. 8.

56 Jellinek, Georg, *Die Lehre von den Staatenverbindungen*, p. 96; Lorimer, James, *The Institutes of the Law of Nations*, I, p. 4; Oppenheim, Lassa, *International Law*, I, pp. 147–149; Phillimore, Robert, *Commentaries upon International Law*, I, xxx, pp. 22–23; Schmelzing, Julius, *Systematischer Grundriß des praktischen Europäischen Völkerrechtes*, introduction, § 3, p. 4n2 (already 1818); Triepel, Heinrich, *Völkerrecht und Landesrecht*, I, § 3, i, p. 27; Westlake, John, *Chapters on the Principles of International Law*, pp. 40, 78; Wheaton, Henry, *Elements of International Law*, pp. 18–19.

57 Koskenniemi notes the prominence of notions of racial superiority in the works of 19th-century international legal theorists, but argues that while the assumption of racial superiority may have been 'practicably inevitable' for these 'men of liberal conscience', it was not a necessary aspect of their scientific methodology. See Koskenniemi, Martti, *The Gentle Civilizer of Nations*, p. 103. It is not clear what the nexus is between this 'practical' inevitability and liberal sensibility just as it is not clear why this 'practical' inevitability would be any less palpable to a non-liberal international legal theorist. Whatever the importance of liberalism in the advent of international law, the transition from the state system to the system of international law is characterized by the, at least partial, dislocation of the political context in which liberalism and conservatism are structural opposites. It would thus seem that the inevitability of the assumption of racial superiority should be attributed not to the liberal sensibilities of the international legal theorists – which not all of them shared – but instead to the project of constructing a legal system of state interaction, which they did share.

law enjoins.[58] The assumption of this natural community, uniting the European states, not only keeps in place the legal construction of the interstate sphere; it also keeps in place the primacy of Europe within the system of international law.[59] Thus, the primacy of Europe does not contradict the rule of law; it is the expression of legal commitment. It does not reflect an excess of power; it reflects the extent of obligation. In the words of Robert Phillimore, the obligations of international law apply with 'greater precision, distinctness, and accuracy' to the community of Christian states out of which international law grew.[60] Within this demarcation, which takes place at the periphery of both Europe and of international legal theory, a legal construction of the interstate sphere is possible and it is out of this construction that the system of international law shall emerge. Again, what separates this system from the classic state system is, in the final analysis, only a possibility, of which we have located the genesis in the aftermath of the French Revolution: the opening up of the horizon of sovereignty with the attendant destabilization, even disappearance, of the demarcation of the state sphere and the interstate sphere. We see how legal construction articulates itself around this possibility if we compare the works of two theorists who, even if contemporaries, were placed on either side of the divide that separates the state system from the system of international law: Adolf Lasson and Georg Jellinek. The work of the former transports us back before the transformation of state interaction that we have analysed; back into a world where states act and interact to further their strategic interests, unbound by legal or moral constraints; a world

---

58 This assumption is nowhere more evident than in the work of he who might be considered the father of positivism within international legal theory, Carl Bergbohm. While Bergbohm rejects the notion of a state system (*Staatsverträge und Gesetze als Quellen des Völkerrechts*, p. 85n1) and banishes political ideas and moral maxims from international legal theory (pp. 7–8), his theory rests upon the idea that civilization serves to unify state interaction. The 'real civilized states' are the bearers of international law (p. 110), and it is this cultural community that mediates between the demands of co-existence and those of the preservation and exercise of national power: 'Guided as they are by a deeper insight than the politically undeveloped peoples that are wont to follow their instincts blindly, the states of European culture certainly also seek to further their interest, but an interest that is properly understood; one that conditions and entrenches the endeavour to secure their existence and the free unfolding of all the powers of the nation' (p. 3).

59 In his account of the decline of European public law, Carl Schmitt simply assumes this nexus of cultural demarcation and legal regime; he takes for granted the existence of a binding system which governed interstate relations in Europe from the 1713 Utrecht Peace until the end of the 19th century (see Schmitt, Carl, *Der Nomos der Erde*, p. 160). By not considering the circumstances in which the notion of Europe was introduced into legal doctrine, Schmitt makes himself blind to the historical articulation of the nexus between the domain of application of a European law of peoples and its domain of efficacy. He does not see that the universalization of a European law of peoples, which he reduces to a 'psychological' function of the world view of the European diplomats and jurists of the time (p. 204), obeys the logic of containment that governed the system of equilibrium, only within an expanding domain. His diagnosis of the decline of the *jus publicum Europaeum* through its universalization begs the question. Though he denies it vehemently, the universalization of the European law of peoples would seem to grow out of the notion of Europe which is at the heart of his work. Indeed, he acknowledges that America – the *hegemon* of the undifferentiated, global legal order that replaced the European order – could claim, morally and culturally, to be the incarnation of 'the free, genuine and real Europe' (p. 262).

60 Phillimore, Robert, *Commentaries upon International Law*, I, xxx, p. 23.

in which nothing but the fear of another power could induce a state to caution.[61] It is almost superfluous to tell us, as Lasson does, that international law is law in name only. In contrast, Jellinek's works on international law are meant as contributions to its legal construction – the subtitle of his 1880 treatise on the legal nature of state compacts – and he confidently tells us that in the present state of public juridical awareness, we are justified in holding that international law should be construed as a purely juridical science.[62] At a first glance, everything would thus seem to oppose the two. But if we look beyond the all-too-obvious differences, a closer reading reveals a remarkable structural similarity. Perhaps most importantly, both understand the relation of state law to international law to be one of a difference, not in kind, but of the degree of moral support which shores up the legal order. In the words of Georg Jellinek:

> The major difference between state law and international law, which leads people to consider the former as a more solid and well-founded form of law, consists in the fact that the *moral* guarantees of state law are stronger than those of international law. The feeling, on the part of state power [*Staatsgewalt*], of being bound by the rules that it has set down for itself is stronger in relation to the tasks that the state has to fulfil in relation to its people than in relation to other states. Once the ethical sensibility of peoples has reached the level required for unconditional respect for international obligations, then the guarantees that attach to international law shall be no different from those that protect the state law of civilized peoples.[63]

The tone of Lasson's text is different, but the structure is the same: the essential difference between international law and state law lies not in any structural property of either order, but in our perception of the possibility of resolving conflicts within their respective domains. Within the state, the perception of conflict has been replaced by a feeling of community. Between states, the perception of conflict still reigns. However, with the growing awareness of the community of interests that unites the states, the states could, so Lasson tells us, leave the state of nature, just as the individuals have done within the state.[64] It is thus through a change in perception, rather than through structural change, that international law can be brought forward, and while Lasson dismisses the notion that it could ever be perfected to the point where interstate relations could be settled morally or legally, he goes on to adopt much of the programme of legal internationalism: education of states as to their interests, their enlightened self-interest, could give rise to relations of reciprocity and honesty which would lead to the development of international law and to an unfailing respect for its observation.[65] Lasson goes so far as to envisage the codification of the principles of international law, demonstrating that the system of equilibrium, which he presents as the only alternative to universal monarchy, is not fundamentally different from Jellinek's legal construction.

The point at which the system of international law departs from the state system concerns the will. At a first glance, the structural parallel continues. The will is the fundamental principle of both systems: the state is bound only by its own will; there is nothing

---

[61] Lasson, Adolf, *Princip und Zukunft des Völkerrechts*, II, pp. 28–29; iii, p. 35.
[62] Jellinek, Georg, *Die Lehre von den Staatenverbindungen*, p. 9.
[63] Jellinek, Georg, *Die rechtliche Natur der Staatenverträge*, p. 37.
[64] Lasson, Adolf, *Princip und Zukunft des Völkerrechts*, III, pp. 32–33; V, pp. 42, 46–47.
[65] Lasson, Adolf, *Princip und Zukunft des Völkerrechts*, IX, p. 85.

beyond or above the will of the state.[66] The difference only appears once we consider the horizon within which the will of the state is placed. Lasson insists on the distinction between the external and the internal matrix of state action (*Thätigkeitsform des Staates*),[67] the distinction between the internal and the external dimension of sovereignty which defined the classic state system. At times his insistence on this distinction appears as an article of faith, rather than as a descriptive category. The denial of the legal nature of international law would seem to grow out of refusal to countenance the possibility of change to the system, simply because change implies change: '. . . as if the principle governing the relations of states could ever be different than it has been from the beginning of time until this very day'.[68] In contrast, Jellinek's construction of international law revolves around the implosion of the demarcation of the state and the interstate sphere which I sketched out above. The internal and the external dimension of state sovereignty now coincide to the point where the juridical construction of international law can be measured with the yardstick of state law:

> [We must show] that it is possible for the state to give directives that bind its own will. And this demonstration must be carried out in relation to that which is undoubtedly law. We must show that the internal law of the state contains a reflexive moment; that rules of law exist, of which the legal nature is beyond question; rules which emanate from the state and bind it. If this demonstration is successful, we have found the juridical foundation of international law. If not, then a construction of international law on the basis of the concept of law, which is contained in the internal law of the state, is not possible.[69]

The foundation of legal construction, all forms of legal construction, is thus found in the capacity of the state to command its own will, the self-determination and self-limitation of the state. On the terms posed by Jellinek, this foundation is self-evident, as the capacity to contract obligation is a constitutive characteristic of statehood. As is evident from the passage cited above, the action whereby a state constitutes and subordinates itself to a national legal order is a perfect parallel to the action whereby it contracts obligations in relation to another state. Denying its capacity to do either would entail the disqualification not only of the legal nature of international law, but of public law as such. The state would cease to exist as a legal entity. This explains the assertion by Jellinek that a state that does not acknowledge the system of international law would thereby pronounce its own death sentence; like the ideal of the stoic sage who exists in complete autarchy, liberated from all bonds to others, such a state is inconceivable.[70] It is this integration of the internal and external dimension of state action into the same reflexive moment that enables Jellinek to maintain both the primacy and the unitary nature of state will; to conceive of the state as an autonomous entity, while holding it to the obligations that it has contracted in relation to other states.

---

66 Thus, both Lasson and Jellinek hold that all state actions are premised on the clause *rebus sic stantibus*. See Jellinek, Georg, *Die Lehre von den Staatenverbindungen*, p. 102; Lasson, Adolf, *Princip und Zukunft des Völkerrechts*, VI, p. 62.

67 Lasson, Adolf, *Princip und Zukunft des Völkerrechts*, II, p. 15.

68 Lasson, Adolf, *Princip und Zukunft des Völkerrechts*, IX, p. 84.

69 Jellinek, Georg, *Die Lehre von den Staatenverbindungen*, pp. 6–7.

70 Jellinek, Georg, *Die Lehre von den Staatenverbindungen*, pp. 94–95.

The importance of this integration for legal construction is obvious. However, it comes at a price: the blindness to power. The integration rests upon a narrowing of the focus of construction to the reflexive moment in the constitution of the legal personality of the state, its capacity to contract obligations. This narrowing of focus keeps in place the possibility of a legal construction of international law as the emergence of a common will out of the meeting of separate wills; it excludes from view the modality of interaction, the contest of power that defines the interaction and of which the legal obligation is only the trace. The interaction is seen simply as the point of intersection between two subjects, the subjective constitution of which demands the presence of another, capable of mirroring the obligation which the state has contracted, essentially in relation to itself. Seen in the perspective which Jellinek develops, the interaction of states is nothing more than the event, in which one subject fulfils a structural function in the (ongoing) constitution of another subject. The interacting states are, in this respect, completely equal, irrespective of their strength, which, the state being the exclusive object of its act of self-limitation and self-determination, does not enter into the interaction, at least on its legal construction. Seen in this perspective, the interstate sphere is a completely level playing field. In fact, it is structured through this equality. And indeed, Jellinek not only affirms that all states are equally sovereign, no matter what their size or political importance may be, but also that the equality of states constitutes the first and fundamental principle of international law.[71] Consequently, he banishes from international law all considerations of power, of the differences of power among states; in a juridical perspective, such considerations are 'wholly irrelevant'.[72] It is in this light that we must understand – and only in this light that we can understand – his assertion that a state may 'abdicate the exercise of all rights of suzerainty without, on this account, ceasing to be sovereign'.[73]

Jellinek is, of course, not blind to the existence of political domination and dependence

---

[71] Jellinek, Georg, *Die Lehre von den Staatenverbindungen*, p. 21. Jellinek tempers this by noting that some states are accorded ceremonial priority as a part of diplomatic protocol. What appears as a matter of diplomatic protocol is, in reality, an indication of the profound transformation of international law which I have attempted to describe. The system of preseance, to which Jellinek alludes, is a remnant of the Vienna Congress. It is all that remains of a larger proposal made at the Congress to divide the European nations into three categories, the first comprising the major European kingdoms. The proposal was introduced by France, in line with her strategy of reintroducing herself into the circle of dominant powers in Europe by disrupting the alliances that had been formed against Bonaparte. The fact that the proposal was approved by the majority of the eight-nation commission testifies to the distance which separates the world of the Vienna Congress from a world in which the equality of states is axiomatic, a precondition even of legal construction. Of the five major powers in the commission (Austria, France, Great Britain, Prussia and Russia) only the British representative, Lord Castlereagh, expressed any doubts as to the foundation of classification, but indicated his willingness to abide by the decision of the majority (see *Uebersicht der diplomatischen Verhandlungen des wiener Congresses* (ed. Klüber), II, pp. 167–168). If the commission did not, in the final analysis, deliver on its mandate, but elected to restrict its focus to the question of preseance among the emissaries of the crowned heads of Europe, it is because – so Klüber tells us – agreement could not be reached on the place of the great republics within this tripartite classification. Is this a premonition of the coming democratic age in which the very thought of an internal hierarchical classification between states would soon become inconceivable?

[72] Jellinek, Georg, *Die Lehre von den Staatenverbindungen*, p. 22.

[73] Jellinek, Georg, *Die Lehre von den Staatenverbindungen*, p. 53.

in the relations between states. Among the relations that he studies, some are institutionalized forms of political dependence (treaty-based occupation, protectorate). However, the element of domination is carefully placed outside of the domain of international law. In his classification of the types of state relations, Jellinek distinguishes between two forms: relations of coordination, which fall within the domain of international law, and relations of subordination, which fall within the domain of state law.[74] International law is thus a domain of coordination between autonomous agents who suffer no outside pressure, while the element of domination and coercion is relegated to, and contained within, the inner recesses of the state. This is the format of Jellinek's construction of international law. Thus, the possibility of a construction of the interstate sphere, which emerged in the aftermath of the French Revolution, is articulated into a system in which the sovereignty of the state is conserved and embedded in a community of states. Jellinek's construction represents a mediation of the universal and the singular; a position which occupies a precarious middle ground between the universality of a world state and the singularity of the state. The position, which Jellinek develops, consummates the aspirations of international legal theory of the 19th century. And at the same time, it opens the horizon of the international legal theory of the 20th century. The terms of the opposition between dualism (Heinrich Triepel) and monism (Hans Kelsen) around which international legal theory develops during the first decades of the 20th century are articulated from the vantage point of Jellinek's construction. At first glance, this may not seem evident. The strict dualism that Triepel introduces between the regimes of international law and state law, the impossibility that they could ever regulate the same matters,[75] certainly strikes a different note from Jellinek's integration of the dimensions in which the state projects its power, as does the theory of the general will of states with which Triepel seeks to replace Jellinek's notion of auto-obligation. The critique by Triepel of this notion also turns on the excessive monism, or rather, the absence of plurality, in Jellinek's theory: Triepel acknowledges auto-obligation as an ethical principle, but he dismisses the notion that a legal obligation to others could arise out of a command, which a subject directs to himself, as a 'logical nonsense'.[76] In its stead, Triepel proposes the theory of the general will, a will which arises as the product of the union of a plurality of state wills and which expresses the communion of states in an international community. However, a closer reading reveals that the plurality of Triepel's theory is merely apparent. If we consider the elements in his construction, we find that it remains within the format which Jellinek articulated. Legally, the agreement (*Vereinbarung*) is distinguished from the treaty (*Vertrag*) by marking the union of identical wills (which is why it can serve to found a system of international law). Whereas the treaty serves contrary interests and hence does not transcend the realm of opposition, of state liberty, the agreement fulfils 'shared or identical' interests.[77] Whatever the state encounters as it projects its power into the interstate sphere, its properly legal reflection is that of identity. The fundamental dimension of the system of international law is one of monism. If Jellinek's construction

---

[74] Jellinek, Georg, *Die Lehre von den Staatenverbindungen*, p. 58.
[75] Triepel, Heinrich, *Völkerrecht und Landesrecht*, I, § 2, ii, pp. 19, 23.
[76] Triepel, Heinrich, *Völkerrecht und Landesrecht*, I, § 4, p. 77.
[77] Triepel, Heinrich, *Völkerrecht und Landesrecht*, I, § 3, iv, pp. 51–52.

fails to move beyond the subjectivity of the state, thus obliterating plurality, the state is immediately identified as the bearer of a general will in Triepel's construction.[78] Here, as in Jellinek's theory, the only aspect under which the state is seen is that of the identity between its sovereignty and its status as a subject of international obligations. Seen in this perspective, Triepel's distinction between international law and state law takes on a different complexion: within the state system, the affirmation of the distinction of inner and outer entailed the preclusion of the legal construction of the interstate sphere; the re-affirmation of this distinction by Triepel would seem to be a means to avoid drawing an inconvenient, but seemingly inevitable conclusion: that sovereignty has been completely absorbed into the system of international law. The ambivalence that attaches to Triepel's position is reflected in the image that closes his work: the image of international law as a field marshal who depends on his subordinates, the sovereigns, to issue commands to give effect to his orders.[79] This distribution of labour is kept in place by the distinction of inner and outer, by the impossibility that international law and state law could ever regulate the same matters. But this distinction is not thought from within sovereignty, as the affirmation of the primacy of political community over universal order; it is thought from the vantage point of the system of international law, from where the national sovereigns are seen as subordinate. Indeed, if it were not for the assumption of impossibility, which shores up the distinction of inner and outer, Triepel's field marshal would not need to depend on subordinates to have his bidding done. In this image, we find the structures of Hans Kelsen's monism, the assumption of a global legal order in which the state is sovereign only by delegation[80] and in which the fact of its sovereignty does not warrant the assumption that it could ever, at any moment, exist apart from the system of international law.[81] The ambition of tracing the emergence of the system of international law out of the state system commits us to following the triumphant – and highly problematic – return of international law into the sphere of the subjectivity of the state. I leave that for a later attempt at writing a history, one of the possible histories, of the transformations of the nexus of the universal and the singular.

5.4 THE FUTURE OF THE 19TH CENTURY

In a sense, the ultimate test of a dialectical exposition of history is that it has rendered superfluous the statement of its conclusions that the exposition has served both as a development and a demonstration of the causes that allow us to understand the passage of time as a transition between a point of departure and a point of destination. It has been my ambition to show that the emergence of the system of international law is a

---

[78] As Jellinek points out, Triepel thus presupposes what he needs to prove, namely the existence of an international legal community, a community within which the convergence of a plurality of state wills on a common rule is not factual and contingent, but the reflection of an obligation. See Jellinek, Georg, *Allgemeine Staatslehre*, II, xi, p. 339 n1.

[79] Triepel, Heinrich, *Völkerrecht und Landesrecht*, III, § 10, ii, p. 271.

[80] Kelsen, Hans, *Das Problem der Souveränität*, § 21, p. 86; § 54, p. 267; *Reine Rechtslehre*, § 30, p. 71; § 49, p. 148.

[81] Kelsen, Hans, *Das Problem der Souveränität*, pp. 182, 187.

movement within the state system; a transformation or reconfiguration of the system which, by creating new constellations of elements contained within the system, opened up other avenues for the motive forces that drive the legal construction of the interstate sphere. Seen in this light, the system of international law appears as a richer articulation of the state system. However, we cannot dispense with the reflection on the conclusions which are to be drawn from this attempt at an integration of the 19th century, the entire 19th century, into a history of international law. What uses can we hope to make of this century in the attempt to determine the nature of the restraints on state power which, in the absence of a praetor, would have to grow out of its exercise? At first glance, the verdict is negative. The integration of the 19th century into the history of the coming into being of the system of international law has – it would seem – shown that this history is one of the loss of ability of legal construction to render intelligible the articulation of power in the interaction of states. Did not the exclusion of the consideration of power prove to be a precondition of the legal construction of the interstate sphere? Worse still: in a paradoxical turn of events, legal construction, driven by the ambition of shackling the violence between states, has left the system of international law at the mercy of the most extreme exercise of state power: war. Jellinek, whose construction of international law succeeds precisely because he consecrates the existing forms of political dependence in law, is, for that very reason, compelled to rely on the phenomenon of war to introduce new progressive ideas that might redress the injustices of the present political order. The doctrine of state, which complements his construction of international law, rests upon the necessity of war: every new idea, every progressive ideal – the advent of constitutionalism, the liberation of the American slaves – has entered the realm of historical reality through war.[82] The account of the coming into being of international law thus indicates that international law has somehow taken itself out of competition. These considerations parallel Koskenniemi's diagnosis of the decline of international law after the Second World War, as the multidisciplinary approach of international relations came to replace international law in the American government of the interstate sphere, thus marking a disciplinary, but also, perhaps more importantly, a geopolitical transition from Europe to America. The academic and political marginalization of the European conception of international law, which mirrors the geopolitical marginalization of Europe in the global hegemony of the US, is reflected in the account that Koskenniemi gives of the aporetic situation in which Hans Morgenthau found himself in the wake of the 1965 US invasion of the Dominican Republic. The functionalism, of which Morgenthau had made himself the champion, not only precluded him from branding the invasion as illegal, since this would entail a retreat to the formalism of the interwar years, it also precluded him from giving legal form to his opposition to the new *Pax Americana.* His predicament was that he could find no means of safeguarding the pluralism of the system of international law – and hence its autonomy from American imperialism – within his traditionalist conception of international law:

[82] Jellinek, Georg, *Allgemeine Staatslehre*, II, xi, p. 340; 'Die Zukunft des Krieges', pp. 538–539. This marks another point where the system of equilibrium of Lasson mirrors the construction of Jellinek. If Lasson refuses to acknowledge that state relations are of a legal nature, it is because this would entail the absolute consecration of the given historical state, the legitimist order which arose out of the Vienna Congress (Lasson, Adolf, *Princip und Zukunft des Völkerrechts*, II, p. 27). And, as Lasson goes on to ask, are the existing state configurations so perfect that they cannot be changed?

'There was nothing left for him as a (European) lawyer but to retreat to the position of the outsider. Imperialism was a political, not a legal matter.'[83]

Even if we accept, for argument's sake, that Morgenthau might be considered as the carrier of all three major European traditions of international law that Koskenniemi considers in his book, one might wonder if Koskenniemi has not fallen victim to what is a remnant, perhaps the last, of the idea of a European law of peoples: the belief that a geopolitical shift from Europe would mean the end of international law as such. But if it makes sense at all to write the history of international law as anything other than the compilation of certain documents that we classify as legal by convention, if it makes sense to claim that legal force has a specific history, it is because legal order articulates itself around the nexus of its domain of application and the domain of its efficacy; a nexus which, in the case of the international legal order, does not have the solidity that made the nation the carrier of political community in the modern age. The dethroning of Europe as the centre of the universe has changed the face of international law, but this transformation, which – as we have seen – grows out of the state system, may open windows for legal construction. That Europe, seen from the vantage point of America, has withdrawn from the 'sacred space of sovereignty' and into that of morality and law,[84] may have staked out a domain of legal construction within the order of international law. The coming future of international law may lie in the advent of regional legal orders, of domains of hegemony which Carl Schmitt, under very different historical and political circumstances, predicted in 1941,[85] and which a recent decision from the European Court of Justice seems to admit.[86] In the present circumstances, the choice between the universality and the efficacy of international law may be unpleasant. One might take comfort from the history of the 19th century which, if anything, proves the resourcefulness of the European mind in the invention of fictions which relieve us of a freedom most unwelcome by making what is a fact of geography appear to be a destiny.

---

83 Koskenniemi, Martti, *The Gentle Civilizer of Nations*, p. 482.

84 Kahn, Paul W., *Sacred Violence: Torture, Terror, and Sovereignty*, p. 40.

85 Schmitt, Carl, *Völkerrechtliche Großraumordnung*, pp. 55–63.

86 *Kadi and Al Barakaat International Foundation vs. Council and Commission* (Combined cases C-402/05P and C-415/05P), par. 285. Asked to pronounce upon a resolution of the UN Security Council which imposed measures to freeze the funds of the Afghan Taliban, the European Court of Justice, in a judgment of 3 September 2008, reviewed the resolution for its compliance with the fundamental rights of the EC Charter. As a result of this review, the Court declined to give the resolution effect within the community, as community law was better placed to offer protection. In doing so, it elevated the community legal order above the constitutional document of the international legal order, the UN Charter, article 103 of which states that, in the event of a conflict between the obligations of the member states of the UN under the said charter and their obligations under any other international agreement, the UN Charter shall take precedence. At present, we may paper over the cracks in the international legal order by the piecemeal harmonization of legal documents and systems, but it remains to be seen how the relationship of the European legal order to the order of international law develops, as community law expands to include further domains of political and social life, further widening the domain in which European law is better placed to offer protection.

BIBLIOGRAPHY

Anghie, Antony, *Imperialism, Sovereignty and the Making of International Law*, Cambridge University Press, 2004.

Augustine, *The City of God against the Pagans* (edited and translated by R.W. Dyson), Cambridge University Press, 1998.

Baumgart, Winfried, *Europäisches Konzert und nationale Bewegung. Internationale Beziehungen 1830–1878*, Ferdinand Schöningh, 1999.

Bell, David A., *The First Total War. Napoleon's Europe and the Birth of Modern Warfare*, Bloomsbury Publishing, 2007.

Bergbohm, Carl, *Staatsverträge und Gesetze als Quellen des Völkerrechts*, Verlag von C. Mattiesen, 1877.

Blumenberg, Hans, *Die Legitimität der Neuzeit*, Suhrkamp Verlag, 1966.

Bluntschli, Johann Kaspar, *Das moderne Völkerrecht der civilisirten Staaten als Rechtsbuch dargestellt*, Verlag der J. H. Beck'schen Buchhandlung, 1886.

Bond, Brian, *The Pursuit of Victory from Napoleon to Saddam Hussein*, Oxford University Press, 1996.

Burlamaqui, Jean-Jacques, *Principes de Droit de la Nature*, Janet et Cotelle Librairies, 1821 (1774).

Cicero, *De Legibus* in Blatt, Franz, Thure Hastrup and Per Krarup (eds), *Ciceros Filosofiske Skrifter*, I-V, G. E. C. Gads Forlag, 1969–1972.

Clausewitz, Carl von, *Vom Kriege*, Insel Verlag, 2005 (1832/1834).

Derrida, Jacques, 'La pharmacie du Platon' in *La dissémination*, Éditions du Seuil, 1972.

Doering-Manteuffel, Anselm, *Vom Wiener Kongreß zur Pariser Konferenz. England, die deutsche Frage und das Mächtesystem 1815–1856*, Vanderhoeck & Ruprecht, 1991.

Duchhardt, Heinz, *Gleichgewicht der Kräfte, Convenance, Europäisches Konzert*, Wissenschaftliche Buchgesellschaft, 1976.

Duchhardt, Heinz, *Balance of Power und Pentarchie. Internationale Beziehungen 1700–1785*, Ferdinand Schöningh, 1997.

Galindo, George Rodrigo, 'Martti Koskenniemi and the Historiographical Turn in International Law', *European Journal of International Law*, 2005, 16/3.

Grewe, Wilhelm G., *Epochen der Völkerrechtsgeschichte*, Nomos Verlagsgesellschaft, 1984.

Grotius, Hugo, *The Rights of War and Peace*, I–III (ed. Richard Tuck), Liberty Fund, 2005 (1625).

Guggenheim, Paul, 'Das jus publicum europeum and Europa', 3 *Jahrbuch des Öffentlichen Rechts der Gegenwart* (1954) 1.

Hamilton, Keith and Richard Langhorne, *The Practice of Diplomacy. Its evolution, theory and administration*, Routledge, 1995.

Heffter, August Wilhelm, *Das Europäische Völkerrecht der Gegenwart auf den bisherigen Grundlagen*, Verlag von H.W. Müller, 1882 (1844).

Hobbes, Thomas, *Elements of Law Natural & Politic* (ed. Ferdinand Tönnies), Frank Cass & Co. Ltd., 1969 (1640).

Hobbes, Thomas, *Leviathan* (ed. Edwin Curley), Hackett Publishing Company, 1994 (1651).

Jellinek, Georg, *Die rechtliche Natur der Staatenverträge. Ein Beitrag zur juristischen Construction des Völkerrechts*, Alfred Hölder, 1880.

Jellinek, Georg, *Die Lehre von den Staatenverbindungen*, Alfred Hölder, 1882.

Jellinek, Georg, *Allgemeine Staatslehre*, vol. I: *Das Recht des modernen Staates*, Verlag von O. Häring, 1900.

Jellinek, Georg, 'Die Zukunft des Krieges' in Jellinek, Walter (ed.), *Georg Jellinek. Ausgewählte Schriften und Reden*, Verlag von O. Häring, 1911.

Kahn, Paul W., *Sacred Violence: Torture, Terror, and Sovereignty*, University of Michigan Press, 2008.

Kaltenborn von Stachau, Carl, *Kritik des Völkerrechts nach dem jetzigen Standpunkte der Wissenschaft*, Verlag von Gustav Mayer, 1847.

Kelsen, Hans, *Das Problem der Souveränität und die Theorie des Völkerrechts. Beitrag zu einer reinen Rechtslehre*, Scientia Verlag, 1981 (J. C. B. Mohr, 1920).

Kelsen, Hans, *Reine Rechtslehre. Einleitung in die Rechtswissenschaftliche Problematik*, Scientia Verlag, 1994 (Österreichischen Staatsdruckerei, 1934).

Klüber, Johann Ludwig (ed.), *Acten des Wiener Congresses*, I–IX, Johann Jacob Palm & Ernst Enke, 1815–1835.

Klüber, Johann Ludwig (ed.), *Uebersicht der diplomatischen Verhandlungen des wiener Congresses überhaupt, und insonderheit über wichtige Angelegenheiten des teutschen Bundes*, Andreäische Buchhandlung, 1816.

Klüber, Johann Ludwig, *Europäisches Völkerrecht*, J. G. Cotta'schen Buchhandlung, 1821 (French edition, 1819).

Koskenniemi, Martti, *The Gentle Civilizer of Nations. The Rise and Fall of International Law 1870–1960*, Cambridge University Press, 2002.

Lasson, Adolf, *Princip und Zukunft des Völkerrechts*, Verlag von Wilhelm Hertz, 1871.

Lorimer, James, *The Institutes of the Laws of Nations. A Treatise on the Jural Relations between Separate Political Communities*, William Blackwood & Sons, 1883.
Mably, Gabriel Bonnot de, *Œuvres Completes de l'Abbé de Mably, V: Principes de Négociations, pour servir d'introduction au droit public d'Europe, fondé sur les traités*, 1789.
Mably, Gabriel Bonnot de, *Œuvres Completes de l'Abbé de Mably, V: Droit public d'Europe, fondé sur les traités*, 1789.
Martens, Georg Friedrich de, *Précis du Droit des Gens Moderne de l'Europe*, I–II, Elibron Classics, 2005 (reprint of the edition published by Guillamin et Cie, 1858 (originally published in 1788)).
Moser, Johann Jacob, *Grundsätze des Europäischen Völkerrechts in Kriegszeiten*, Verlag Johann Georg Cotta, 1752.
Neyron, Pierre-Joseph, *Essai Historique et Politique sur les Garanties et en général sur les Méthodes Diverses des Anciens et des Nations Modernes d'assurer les Traités Publiques*, Jean Chretien Dieterich, 1777.
Oppenheim, Heinrich Bernhard, *System des Völkerrechts*, Literarische Anstalt (J. Rütten), 1845.
Oppenheim, Lassa F. L., *International Law: A Treatise*, Longman, Green & Co., 1905.
Orakhelashvili, Alexander, 'The Idea of European International Law', *European Journal of International Law*, 2006, 17/2.
Phillimore, Robert, *Commentaries upon International Law*, Butterworths, 1879 (third edition).
Politis, Nicolas, *La Neutralité et la Paix*, Librairie Hachette, 1935.
Pölitz, Karl Heinrich Ludwig, *Die Staatswissenschaften im Lichte unsrer Zeit*, volume V, J. G. Hinrichsche Buchhandlung, 1824.
Pölitz, Karl Heinrich Ludwig, *Grundriß für encykopädische Vorträge über die gesammten Staatswissenschaften*, J. G. Hinrichsche Buchhandlung, 1825.
Pufendorf, Samuel von, *An Introduction to the History of the Principal Kingdoms and States of Europe*, printed for B. Took at the Middle Temple-Gate, Dan. Midwinter in the Three Crowns in St. Paul's Church-Yard and, T. Ward in Temple Lane, 1719 (German original published in 1682).
Pufendorf, Samuel, *Les Droits de la Nature et des Gens ou Systeme General des Principes les plus importants de la Morale, de la Jurisprudence et de la Politique* (ed. Jean Barbeyrac), Jean Nours, 1740 (1672).
Rayneval, Gérard de, *Institutions du Droit de la Nature et des Gens*, Leblanc Imprimeur-Libraire, 1803.
Reinhard, Wolfgang, *Geschichte der Staatsgewalt. Eine vergleichende Verfassungsgeschichte Europas von den Anfängen bis zur Gegenwart*, C. H. Beck, 2002 (1999).
Rivier, Alphonse, *Principes du Droit des Gens*, I, Arthur Rousseau, 1896.
Saalfeld, Friedrich, *Grundriß eines Systems des europäischen Völkerrechts zum Gebrauche akademischer Vorlesungen*, Johann Friedrich Röwer, 1809.
Schaeder, Hildegard, *Autokratie und Heilige Allianz*, Wissenschaftliche Buchgesellschaft, 1963 (1937).
Schmalz, Theodore Anton Heinrich, *Das europäische Völkerrecht in acht Büchern*, Duncker & Humblot, 1817.
Schmelzing, Julius, *Systematischer Grundriß des Europäischen Völkerrechtes. Für akademische Vorlesungen und Selbst-Unterricht*, Verlag der Hof-, Burg- und Kunsthandlung, 1818.
Schmitt, Carl, *Völkerrechtliche Großraumordnung mit Interventionsverbot für raumfremde Mächte. Ein Beitrag zum Reichsbegriff im Völkerrecht*, Duncker & Humblot, 1991 (Deutschen Rechtsverlag, 1941).
Schmitt, Carl, *Der Nomos der Erde im Völkerrecht des Jus Publicum Europaeum*, Duncker & Humblot, 1997 (1950).
Spiermann, Ole, *International Legal Argument in the Permanent Court of International Justice. The Rise of the International Judiciary*, Cambridge University Press, 2005.
Triepel, Heinrich, *Völkerrecht und Landesrecht*, Verlag von J. C. B. Mohr (Paul Siebeck), 1899.
Vattel, Emer de, *Le droit des gens, ou principes de la loi naturelle, appliqués à la conduite et aux affaires des nations et des souverains* (1758).
Vergé, Charles, 'Le Droit des Gens avant et depuis 1789' (1858) in Martens, Georg Friedrich de, *op. cit.*
Westlake, John, *Chapters on the Principles of International Law*, Cambridge University Press, 1894.
Wheaton, Henry, *Elements of International Law*, Oxford University Press, 1936 (1866).

6 Hans Kelsen's place in international legal theory

Jörg Kammerhofer

6.1 THE PURE THEORY OF LAW *AUJOURD'HUI*

Hans Kelsen and the Pure Theory of Law (*Reine Rechtslehre*) he founded has recently been subject to a revival, even in Anglo-Saxon countries traditionally critical of that approach. Legal scholars seemingly tired of their discipline being colonised by other areas of knowledge such as sociology, ethics or economics now once again seek to focus on the proper core of legal scholarship – to find out what the law itself says. In international law, this revival is much less marked,[1] perhaps because international legal scholarship is a discipline even more steeped in pragmatism than many domestic traditions.

This chapter is an attempt to carry the spirit of the Kelsen revival to the international realm. It seeks to apply the Pure Theory of Law to some of the current problems of international law and thus to endow that theory with a new usefulness that Kelsen is not usually accorded by current international legal scholarship. Another goal of this chapter is to get away from a gut-reaction against Kelsen and to avoid the stigma that is associated with his name in legal theory. This can be achieved by re-engaging with the Pure Theory without placing undue emphasis on polemic defence or attack and by thoroughly 'modernising' the topics discussed. This chapter aims to convince on the merits in order to get colleagues to engage with the Pure Theory of Law more broadly and to apply it to problems of international law.

Hence, the method and purview of the present chapter will be restricted in two ways. First, the following will not be an exercise in intellectual history. The 'historical Kelsen' – Kelsen's person and *vita* – as well as the intellectual context in which Kelsen's works were written will not be the focus here. Rather, the Pure Theory of Law will be applied a-contextually and a-historically to problems of practice. Second and connectedly, this contribution will not focus on the concerns Kelsen had and topics Kelsen treated when he wrote on international law from the mid-1920s to the 1950s. It will emphatically not focus on reconstructing Hans Kelsen's historical arguments and will not provide a synopsis of the major writings on international law.[2] Some of the topics that formed the core of Kelsen's writings on international law, such as the legal nature of international law or the relationship of municipal law to international law are not at the centre of today's scholarly debates anymore. An extended discussion of these topics commensurate with a faithful portrayal of Hans Kelsen's writings would probably contribute to, rather than help dispel, the stigma associated with the name 'Hans Kelsen'. Moreover, a discussion

[1] Though cf. the sympathetic moves shown in: Martti Koskenniemi., *The gentle civilizer of nations. The rise and fall of international law, 1870–1960* (2002).

[2] Others have done so much more thoroughly than is possible in this format: Alfred Rub, *Hans Kelsens Völkerrechtslehre. Versuch einer Würdigung* (1995); Jochen von Bernstorff, *Der Glaube an das universale Recht. Zur Völkerrechtstheorie Hans Kelsens und seiner Schüler* (2001).

of some current topics of relevance in international legal theory – such as the notion of conflict of norms in the ILC's work on fragmentation (Section 6.2.3) – cannot be taken from Kelsen's works on international law, simply because he did not write on these issues. In these cases, the *general* legal theory of the Pure Theory of Law must be reapplied to the international legal problems of today and adapted or modified here or there.

Therefore, the focus will lie in how the Pure Theory of Law – as a theoretical approach connected with, but not restricted to, Hans Kelsen's writings – can be used for today's theoretical challenges. It is here that the Pure Theory shines and can show new ways out of *problematiques* or at least shows the legal core of a problem more clearly than other theoretical approaches. A chapter of a research handbook on international legal theory portraying a particular approach cannot, however, proceed to apply that approach without a brief overview of the jurisprudential foundation. This is the first step, to be covered in the rest of Section 6.1 – the normativist-positivist approach to legal scholarship that could be described as 'legal common sense' (Section 6.1.1), based ultimately on an ethos of legal 'scientificality'. This is the notion that legal scholarship, in order to be able to faithfully portray its object (the law), ought to conform to the rigorous standards of scientific research, even though it cannot be classified as empirical science (Section 6.1.2).

6.1.1 A Legal Common Sense Beyond Eclecticism

The two core tenets of the Pure Theory of Law can be described as (1) the essential and categorical duality of Is and Ought and (2) the notion of scientific rigour in legal scholarship. As such, they are connected and cannot be separated without stepping beyond the Pure Theory's limits. This may sound stark and restrictive – and may well be the cause for much of the misunderstanding and mistrust that many traditional international lawyers have shown vis-à-vis Kelsen's writings – but it is submitted that the Pure Theory can be interpreted as a form of 'legal common sense'. Why is that so? Because it can only be commonsensical to want to know what is the law on any given subject without falsifying one's outcome by indulging in political or moral wishful thinking. The Pure Theory of Law seeks to combine positivist faithfulness to the law in force with the restriction of legal reasoning to legal arguments, which involves excluding non-legal arguments in legal scholarship. It is, after all, good common sense to expect to talk about the law when one sets out to talk about the law; it is the best compromise between extremes of practice and theory. The notion of purity, however, has no moral overtones for Kelsen; it is not the law, but the scholarship that ought to be pure. Purity means to enable a science of norms. 'It calls itself a "pure" theory of law, because it describes only the law and attempts to eliminate from this object of cognition everything that is not strictly law'.[3]

Only a theory that categorically distinguishes between Is and Ought can cognise norms. Only presupposing the Is–Ought dichotomy allows us to perceive 'norms' (Ought) in

[3] 'Wenn sie sich as eine "reine" Lehre vom Recht bezeichnet, so darum, weil sie nur eine auf das Recht gerichtete Erkenntnis sicherstellen und weil sie aus dieser Erkenntnis alles ausscheiden möchte, was nicht zu dem exakt als Recht bestimmten Gegenstande gehört.' Hans Kelsen, *Reine Rechtslehre* (2nd edn. 1960) 1.

the first place. In a science of norms, the ideal of purity requires the categorical and fundamental dichotomy of Is and Ought (*Sein* and *Sollen*); the dichotomy is the basis of the Pure Theory of Law.[4] Ought is the form that ideals take. Without the possibility of Ought no ideals could be perceived or could exist. The Ought is prescription. 'You *ought* to do something' is a categorically different sentence from 'you are doing something'. In order to make 'the ideal' a possible category of thought, it has to be divorced from 'the real'. Confounding Is and Ought reduces ideals to reality: *ens et bonum convertuntur*. With it, the possibility of norm and reality diverging and of an ideal as placing a non-real requirement vanishes. The Ought is norms and norms are the claim to be observed. Most norms postulate a claim that human behaviour conform to its terms.[5] When F orders G to stand up, the norm F creates postulates the claim that G act accordingly, which does no more, but also no less, than to create an Ought – G *ought* to stand up. A norm is also no more than a *claim* to be observed. And this claim equals the norm's 'existence' and its bindingness. If this claim (the Ought) exists, the norm exists in the realm of the ideals, is valid and is binding. There is no need for further validation, no need for moral legitimacy or 'ennoblement'.

The programme of purity as the dichotomy of Is and Ought leads Kelsen to criticise the two mainstream legal philosophies of his time. This 'two-front-war'[6] against both natural law and traditional positivism, is a polemic against what he perceived as a 'syncretism of method'.[7] The syncretism consists in the confusion of description and prescription and of empirical and normative scholarship. The Pure Theory is the only theory not caught up in Koskenniemi's pendulum between descending and ascending patterns of justification, the 'constant movement from emphasizing concreteness to emphasizing normativity and vice–versa'.[8]

First, he saw the idea of a system of natural law as not being able to work in the way its creators intended. Scholars who propound natural law theories presuppose the possibility of absolute values. Absolute norms are imagined to be hierarchically higher than all positive law. Whether it be 'the nature of man', God or reason, some instance or fact that transcends human will creates norms of natural law that are claimed to be hierarchically higher than, and to derogate from, positive law.[9] Kelsen shows that such

---

4 Kelsen, 'Was ist die Reine Rechtslehre?', in: *Demokratie und Rechtsstaat. Festschrift für Zaccharia Giacometti* (1953) 143–161, reprinted in: Hans Klecatsky, René Marcić, Herbert Schambeck (eds), *Die Wiener rechtstheoretische Schule. Ausgewählte Schriften von Hans Kelsen, Adolf Julius Merkl, Alfred Verdross* (1968) 611–629 at 614.

5 Kelsen identifies four norm-functions: (1) obligation/prohibition, (2) permission, (3) empowerment (to create norms) and (4) derogation (Hans Kelsen, *Allgemeine Theorie der Normen* (1979) 76–92). Only the first two refer to human behaviour with a 'claim to be observed'. The latter two refer to acts of will (3) and other norms (3 and 4); they cannot be obeyed or disobeyed.

6 Horst Dreier, *Rechtslehre, Staatssoziologie und Demokratietheorie bei Hans Kelsen* (1990); Horst Dreier, 'Rechtsdeutung zwischen Normativierung der Natur und Naturalisierung des Normativen am Beispiel von Kelsens Rechtsbegriff', in: Clemens Jabloner, Friedrich Stadler (eds), *Beziehungen zwischen dem Wiener Kreis und der Hans Kelsen-Schule* (2001) 291–305 at 298.

7 Hans Kelsen, *Reine Rechtslehre. Einleitung in die rechtswissenschaftliche Problematik* (1934) 2.

8 Martti Koskenniemi, *From apology to utopia. The structure of international legal argument* (1989) 46.

9 Johannes Messner, *Das Naturrecht. Handbuch der Gesellschaftsethik, Staatsethik und Wirtschaftsethik* (1950) 212. Alfred Verdross, one of Kelsen's earliest students, later espoused a

an absolute value cannot exist and that all attempts to found such a value are bound to fail. Kelsen does not deny the idea of values; quite the contrary, he focuses our attention on the Ought. There is no such thing as 'absolute' value,[10] because one can postulate an immoral norm, such as: 'You ought to commit genocide.' More importantly, however, all values are relative, because the Ought is only a claim to be observed, all oughts are a priori equal. Natural law can be seen as an 'ethical-political' standard[11] for positive law, but that does not produce a change in positive law. The noblest ideal is only one claim amongst others. In its form and 'existence' it does not differ from other norms. There simply is no basis for deciding amongst claims, because any basis that we may imagine for deciding can only be another norm, thus: yet another claim!

Second, he turns on traditional positivism. It would typically accept as law those norms which are created by 'the state'.[12] If pressed, the proponents of that view would likely argue that 'the state' is nothing more than the most effective, the most powerful force. Alternatively, certain streams of positivist theory argue that the psychological fact of acceptance is the supra-positive fact creating norms. In response Kelsen points out that the anthropomorphic view of the state is an absolutisation reminiscent of natural law. The notion of state sovereignty is false, because from a legal view the state is the legal order itself. Also, if the fact of acceptance is necessarily the basis of validity of a constitution, this means presupposing just the same type of absolute and external standard as natural law does. Just as natural law, the essential duality of Is and Ought is breached. Traditional positivism can found law's validity as little as natural law theory can. Both confound Is and Ought and seek to reduce one to the other.

The Pure Theory's answer combines the positivity of law – the actual occurrence of acts of will – with the normativity of law (its Oughtness, its nature as an ideal). We simply do not ask the ultimate question, because the validity of norms is put on an 'as if' basis.[13] The ultimate 'norm' of any normative order is the basic norm (*Grundnorm*).[14] The basic norm is merely the condition for the possibility of the cognition of Ought. It is the Is–Ought dichotomy concretised as the transcendental-logical presupposition that allows the cognition of a given normative order.[15] We simply argue as if the normative order were valid: if F orders G to stand up, F's order is valid *if* we argue that it has a basic

---

neo-Aristotelian/neo-Thomassian theory of natural law, but he is among few proponents of natural law theory that do not espouse derogatory powers for natural law vis-à-vis positive law, e.g. Alfred Verdross, *Abendländische Rechtsphilosophie. Ihre Grundlagen und Hauptprobleme in geschichtlicher Schau* (1958) 246–248.

[10] Matthias Jestaedt, 'Der Rechts- und Demokratietheoretiker Hans Kelsen – Eine Einführung', in: Matthias Jestaedt, Oliver Lepsius (eds), *Hans Kelsen. Verteidigung der Demokratie. Abhandlungen zur Demokratietheorie* (2006) vii–xxix at xvi–xvii; Kelsen (1934) *supra* note 7 at 21; Hans Kelsen, *General theory of law and state* (1945) 393–395; Hans Kelsen, 'Die Grundlagen der Naturrechtslehre', 13 *Österreichische Zeitschrift für öffentliches Recht* (1963) 1–37, reprinted in: Hans Klecatsky, René Marcić, Herbert Schambeck (eds), *Die Wiener rechtstheoretische Schule. Ausgewählte Schriften von Hans Kelsen, Adolf Julius Merkl, Alfred Verdross* (1968) 869–912.

[11] Kelsen (1960) *supra* note 3 at 224.

[12] Bernstorff (2001) *supra* note 2 at 24–26.

[13] Kelsen (1979) *supra* note 5 at 206–207.

[14] Kelsen (1960) *supra* note 3 at 196–204.

[15] Kelsen (1960) *supra* note 3 at 204–209; Kelsen (1934) *supra* note 7 at 21–24; Kelsen (1945) *supra* note 10.

norm, for example: 'follow F's orders'. This is no absolute basis, this is a hypothetical (epistemological)[16] basis only; the basic norm is neither a norm properly speaking, nor properly of the normative order.

6.1.2 The Ethos of Scientific Scholarship

The Pure Theory of Law as scientific theory is based on a number of axioms. These can be explained historically, but cannot be justified logically – as axioms their foundation is neither rational nor empirical. The following is a selection of some of these axioms given as a series of dogmatic statements which can be found in Kelsen's work. They *inter alia* serve to position the Pure Theory vis-à-vis post-modernist approaches which are antagonists of the scientific approach to law. These approaches – sometimes loosely classified as the Critical Legal School – construct an alternative view of what academic lawyers do, one which does without the notion of science and is antithetical to, and a critique of, the Enlightenment and breaks with its scientific project.

– *Science means finding 'the truth'*[17] (the word being used in an appropriate sense).[18] The method of finding the truth is perception (or cognition: *Erkenntnis*).[19] 'Truth' used in this sense means the correspondence both of the world in existence with cognition of nature[20] and the correspondence of the valid legal norm with legal cognition. However, the validity of a norm is not 'truth' – nor is nature's existence.[21]

– *Even if 'truth' is a problematic concept or if reality is difficult or even impossible to cognise we must strive for its cognition.* As a modernist, Kelsen does not abandon the quest for truth just because that quest turns out to be problematic. A modernist's response to realising that scientific cognition may be influenced or biased by cultural, ideological, psychological or class factors is *not* to abandon the search for objectivity in cognition.[22] In this modernist sense it is not a series of necessary conditions that determine whether

---

[16] Kelsen (1960) *supra* note 3 at 224.

[17] This (deepest) philosophical axiom cannot be found *verbatim* in Kelsen's writings, but he seems to proceed from this assumption. Vide: 'Horst Dreier, Hans Kelsens Wissenschaftsprogramm', in: Helmuth Schulze-Fielitz (ed.), *Staatsrechtslehre als Wissenschaft* (2007) 81–114; Franz W. Jerusalem, *Kritik der Rechtswissenschaft* (1948) 59; Max Weber, 'Wissenschaft als Beruf' (unpublished, 1919), in: Johannes Winckelmann (ed.) *Gesammelte Aufsätze zur Wissenschaftslehre von Max Weber* (3rd edn. 1968) 582–613 at 610.

[18] Cf. also the related concept of 'reality' (Hans Kelsen, 'Die Rechtswissenschaft als Norm- oder als Kulturwissenschaft. Eine methodenkritische Untersuchung', 40 *Jahrbuch für Gesetzgebung, Verwaltung und Volkswirtschaft im Deutschen Reiche* (1916) 1181–1239, reprinted in: Hans Klecatsky, René Marcić, Herbert Schambeck (eds), *Die Wiener rechtstheoretische Schule. Ausgewählte Schriften von Hans Kelsen, Adolf Julius Merkl, Alfred Verdross* (1968) 37–93 at 41).

[19] Kelsen (1916) *supra* note 18 at 38–39.

[20] Immanuel *Kant, Kritik der reinen Vernunft* (1781, 1787) A 58, B 82.

[21] Kelsen (1979) *supra* note 5 at 143–144, 287.

[22] Compare Max Weber's parallel modernist programme where he develops similar thoughts: Max Weber, 'Die "Objektivität" sozialwissenschaftlicher und sozialpolitischer Erkenntnis', 19 *Archiv für Sozialwissenschaft und Sozialpolitik* (1904) 22–87 at 27; Max Weber, 'Der Sinn der "Wertfreiheit" der soziologischen und ökonomischen Wissenschaften', 7 *Logos* (1918) 40–88; Weber (1919) *supra* note 17 at 600–603.

an inquiry qualifies as 'science', but quasi-ethical norms scholars ought to strive to fulfil for work to be counted as 'production of knowledge'.[23]

– *The goal of a legal science is to cognise the law.*[24] Scholars choose their own object of cognition; hence the choice of cognising *law* is arbitrary. The consequences for the method of cognition begin with the notion that law is a form of norms, i.e. that law is an 'ought'.[25] For Kelsen, the possibility of norms, expressed as the Is–Ought dichotomy, is independent of a nominalist 'definition of law' and has an essentialist core.[26]

– *Norms are a distinct concept, a specific form of existence and can be cognised.* From a general-philosophical point of view, to be able to conceptualise 'ought' requires a modicum of Idealism.[27] Only if we believe that an ideal can form a 'reality' in some sense, rather than trying to reduce 'the world' to brute reality, can we do legal science. In this specific sense we have to believe in the possibility of truth, objectivity and inter-subjectivity, because without this belief, 'law', 'norms' and 'Ought' cannot be constructed or be portrayed. This concept is fundamental for the development of Kelsen's programme and the main reason for his opposition to other theories.

6.2 THE PROBLEMS OF THE MODERN CONSTITUTION OF INTERNATIONAL LAW

Perhaps the most salutary feature of the Pure Theory of Law for the analysis of international law is its ordering function. The hierarchical model Kelsen uses to explain the inter-relationship of norms (the *Stufenbau*) can be used to great advantage in bringing order to the somewhat muddled positions the doctrine of international law holds both on the sources of law and on the mechanics of norm-relationships. Hence, the following will be an exposition of international law's 'constitution' in a specific sense: the highest echelons of a positive legal order, what Kelsen termed 'constitution in the material sense'.[28] In this sense, the sources of international law are the foundation of the international legal order (Section 6.2.1) and the rules and mechanisms of other norm-relationships serve as the operating principles of international law (Section 6.2.3). It will be accompanied by a look at a recent debate in scholarship where the Pure Theory can help to debunk myths.

---

23 Cf. Aulis Aarnio, *Denkweisen der Rechtswissenschaft. Einführung in die Theorie der rechtswissenschaftlichen Forschung* (1979) 6; Julius Binder, *Philosophie des Rechts* (1925) 839.

24 Julius Binder, 'Der Wissenschaftscharakter der Rechtswissenschaft', 25 *Kant-Studien* (1920) 321–365 at 340; Hans Kelsen, *Das Problem der Souveränität und die Theorie des Völkerrechts. Beitrag zu einer reinen Rechtslehre* (1920) iv; Kelsen (1960) *supra* note 3 at iii–iv, 72–78; Franz Weyr, 'Rechtsphilosophie und Rechtswissenschaft', 2 *Zeitschrift für öffentliches Recht* (1922) 671–682 at 672, 678.

25 Kelsen (1960) *supra* note 3 at iii.

26 This duality of the essence of law as norms (as Ought) and the quasi-contingent definition of law as coercive ordering of human behaviour will be discussed in Section 6.3.

27 Hans Kelsen, *Hauptprobleme der Staatsrechtslehre entwickelt aus der Lehre vom Rechtssatze* (1911) vi.

28 Kelsen (1960) *supra* note 3 at 228; Rudolf Aladár Métall, 'Skizzen zu einer Systematik der völkerrechtlichen Quellenlehre', 11 *Zeitschrift für öffentliches Recht* (1931) 416–428 at 421.

6.2.1 The Constitution as Foundation of the International Legal Order

The notion of 'sources' is a relativistic concept. Sources are empowering norms[29] authorising humans to create norms.[30] An empowering norm's function is to identify the norms created under it and *therefore* belonging to it: 'A norm belongs to a legal order only because it is created under the terms of another norm of the same order.'[31] In a sense, the Pure Theory is nothing but a theory of sources,[32] for its construction of normative orders depends upon the authorisation to create norms. The concept of sources espoused by the Pure Theory is that of sources as meta-norms on norm-creation. The validity-relationship established between the 'source' and law created under it creates a hierarchy between the two norms, even in international law.[33] They are norms because the source establishes membership in the normative order and it has to belong to that order, i.e. itself be a norm of that order.[34] The process is 'norm-creation', because the source-norms allow the creation of other norms of that normative order.

The concept of the *Stufenbau* is in many ways one of the most important contributions of the normativist-positivist legal theory of the Vienna School of Jurisprudence.[35] While the dichotomy of Is and Ought (and with it the *Grundnorm*) forms the foundation of the Pure Theory as a whole, hierarchical ordering as a concept is a direct consequence of that theory.[36] If a norm's validity can only be based on another norm,[37] then a connection between norms is established, one based on one norm's validity being dependent upon another norm. The question 'Why ought I to obey this statute?' is answered by reference to the norm that has authorised its creation. The 'higher' law empowers law-creation; that empowerment is the reason the resultant law is valid.[38] Creation establishes a 'hierarchy of legal conditionality'. If, and only if, all conditions imposed by the meta-law on law creation[39] are met, can the norm created be cognised as a norm of the normative order

---

[29] Kelsen (1979) *supra* note 5 at 82–84.

[30] Hans Kelsen, *Principles of international law* (1952) 303.

[31] 'Eine Norm gehört zu einer Rechtsordnung nur, weil sie gemäß der Bestimmung einer anderen Norm dieser Ordnung gesetzt ist.' Kelsen (1960) *supra* note 3 at 239; Kelsen (1979) *supra* note 5 at 247 (N 45); Alfred Verdross, *Die Verfassung der Völkerrechtsgemeinschaft* (1926) 21; Torsten Gihl, 'The legal character and sources of international law', 1 *Scandinavian Studies in Law* (1957) 51–92 at 72.

[32] Valentin Petev, 'Rechtsquellenlehre und Reine Rechtslehre', in: Werner Kawietz, Helmut Schelski (eds), *Rechtssystem und gesellschaftliche Basis bei Hans Kelsen* (1984) 273–287 at 273.

[33] Alfred Verdross, *Die Einheit des rechtlichen Weltbildes auf Grundlage der Völkerrechtsverfassung* (1923) 129.

[34] Robert Alexy, 'Hans Kelsens Begriff der Verfassung', in: Stanley L. Paulson, Michael Stolleis (eds), *Hans Kelsen. Staatsrechtslehrer und Rechtstheoretiker des 20. Jahrhunderts* (2005) 333–352 at 341.

[35] András Jakab, 'Probleme der Stufenbaulehre', 91 *Archiv für Rechts- und Sozialphilosophie* (2005) 333–365 at 1; Theo Öhlinger, *Der Stufenbau der Rechtsordnung. Rechtstheoretische und ideologische Aspekte* (1975) 9.

[36] Jürgen Behrend, *Untersuchungen zur Stufenbaulehre Adolf Merkls und Hans Kelsens* (1977) 61.

[37] Kelsen (1960) *supra* note 3 at 196.

[38] Kelsen (1979) *supra* note 5 at 82.

[39] Robert Walter, *Der Aufbau der Rechtsordnung. Eine rechtstheoretische Untersuchung auf Grundlage der Reinen Rechtslehre* (1964) 61.

in question[40] and only then can the norms be ordered in a multitude of spheres between delegating and delegated norms.[41] Only then can both norms be seen as belonging to the same normative order.[42]

Yet because an authorising norm usually authorises the creation of a multitude of norms, and because usually a multitude of norms are created under it, this multitude of norms with a common 'pedigree' belong to the same source, which the Pure Theory might prefer to call a *Rechtsform*.[43] 'The form legal rules take is determined by the rule that created them; the legal rules that were created according to the same rule of [law-] creation have the same form.'[44] While international law necessarily has a *Stufenbau*, here we do not have the problem of a highly complex network,[45] but of the apparent lack of any rules on rule-making. The hierarchy of legal conditionality is a necessary element of all normative orders: every normative order has at least two layers of norms; it has at least the positive norm created and the presumed (quasi-fictional) *Grundnorm*. If 'A' had never issued a norm and would do so now, this norm would only be conceivable as a norm if the *Grundnorm*: 'Follow A's orders' were presupposed.

Imagine a persistent student asking his lecturer, who has just named the sources of international law, where these sources come from. How is it determined, that student might ask, which sources international law has? This is one of the crucial questions of international law. We seem to take international treaty law, customary international law and 'general principles of law' as sources without asking *why* they are part of the normative order 'international law'. The answer of the Pure Theory to this question is as theoretically clear as it is empirically unsatisfying. For this theory of hierarchically ordered normative orders, a 'source of law' is nothing but meta-law on law-creation.[46] If we combine the notion of 'constitution' as the highest echelon of authorising norms in a given normative order (in international law traditionally treaty law and customary law)[47] with the notion of the hierarchy of norms (*Stufenbau*),[48] at least the correct question to ask in response to the one above appears almost automatically: What norm of international law authorises the crea-

---

40 Kelsen (1960) *supra* note 3 at 239.

41 Adolf Julius Merkl, *Die Lehre von der Rechtskraft, entwickelt aus dem Rechtsbegriff. Eine rechtstheoretische Untersuchung* (1923) 286–287; Verdross (1926) *supra* note 31 at 43.

42 Adolf Julius Merkl, 'Prolegomena einer Theorie des rechtlichen Stufenbaues', in: Alfred Verdross (ed.), *Geselschaft, Staat und Recht. Festschrift für Hans Kelsen zum 50. Geburtstag* (1931) 252–294, reprinted in: Hans Klecatsky, René Marcić, Herbert Schambeck (eds), *Die Wiener rechtstheoretische Schule. Ausgewählte Schriften von Hans Kelsen, Adolf Julius Merkl, Alfred Verdross* (1968) 1311–1361 at 1336.

43 Merkl (1931) *supra* note 42 at 1331.

44 'Der Bestimmungsgrund für die Form der Rechtsvorschriften ist ihre Erzeugungsregel; die gleiche Form haben jene Rechtsvorschriften, die nach der gleichen Erzeugungsregel geschaffen wurden.' Walter (1964) *supra* note 39 at 55 (emphasis removed).

45 Öhlinger (1975) *supra* note 35 at 17.

46 Kelsen (1952) *supra* note 30 at 303; Kelsen (1960) *supra* note 3 at 238–239; Petev (1984) *supra* note 32 at 273.

47 Josef L. Kunz, 'The "Vienna School" and international law', 11 *New York University Law Quarterly Review* (1934) 370–421 at 412.

48 Verdross (1923) *supra* note 33 at 129.

tion of the norms that authorise the creation of (for example) customary international law?[49]

According to the Pure Theory of Law we must find positive norms of international law that create source-law (such as the law on custom-creation).[50] How we are to proceed depends upon the answer we can give and either we find a positive norm authorising source-creation, or we do not. This is a prime example of the self-chosen limits of the Pure Theory: positivist international lawyers will have to do research on the positive-legal bases of the sources and in no case should they assume content. They cannot, for example, simply take Article 38 ICJ Statute as an authoritative statement of the sources[51] simply because it is generally accepted as such. In no case can wishful thinking – natural law superstructure – supplant positive norms.

One example of such a tactic can be found in many writings of the current debate on 'constitutionalism' in European and international law.[52] Here, the term 'constitution' is transformed from a structural principle or hierarchical ordering of legal norms according to their pedigree to a specific legal order with specific (and fixed) content, such as parliamentary-type institutions or specific individual rights. The Constitutionalists thus espouse a modern form of natural law theory, hidden under positivist rhetoric. In effect, the personal politico-moral value preferences of these scholars are thus 'objectivised' and an external norm is espoused to the detriment of the positive law in force. Here, the Pure Theory of Law can help in debunking the myths through its emphasis on the analysis of positive law. If a scholar's idea – or even the prevalent opinion – of what constitutional norms should have as their content conflicts with the positive legal regulation, the Pure Theory helps us realise that the positive law is the positive law. No amount of presupposition of 'necessary constitutional functions'[53] will magic elements of (domestic) constitutional law – such as a mandatory protection of individual rights – into being for international law *if positive international law* does not support it. Here, Kelsenian theory clarifies the issue: scholarly opinion camouflaging as 'absolute values' does not make, change or destroy positive law.[54]

---

49 Rub (1995) *supra* note 2 at 312–313.

50 Verdross (1926) *supra* note 31 at 43.

51 R.S. Pathak, 'The general theory of the sources of contemporary international law', 19 *Indian Journal of International Law* (1979) 483–495 at 484; Gennady M. Danilenko, 'The theory of international customary law', 31 *German Yearbook of International Law* (1988) 9–47 at 17; Rudolf Bernhardt, 'Ungeschriebenes Völkerrecht', 36 *Zeitschrift für ausländisches öffentliches Recht und Völkerrecht* (1976) 50–76 at 64; Jonathan Charney, 'International lawmaking – article 38 of the ICJ statute reconsidered', in: Jost Delbrück (ed.), *New trends in international lawmaking – international 'legislation' in the public interest* (1997) 171–191 at 174; Hugh Thirlway, *International Customary Law and Codification* (1972) 36.

52 E.g. Armin von Bogdandy, 'Constitutionalism in international law. Comment on a proposal from Germany', 47 *Harvard International Law Journal* (2006) 223–242; Bardo Fassbender, *The United Nations Charter as the constitution of the international community* (2009); Theodor Schilling, 'On the constitutionalization of general international law', *Global Law Working Paper* 05/05 (2005); Verdross (1926) *supra* note 31; Erika de Wet, 'The international constitutional order', 55 *International and Comparative Law Quarterly* (2006) 51–76.

53 Paraphrasing Daniel Halberstam, Christoph Möllers, 'The German Constitutional Court says "*Ja zu Deutschland!*"', 10 *German Law Journal* (2009) Number 8 ('Necessary State Functions').

54 For a closer analysis of the debate on constitutionalisation using the Kelsenian approach see

6.2.2 Possible Architectures of the Sources of International Law

In the light of the difficulties to be expected in finding positive norms on source-creation, perhaps the best way to proceed is to ask how the sources of international law could be, or have been, arranged. The 'hierarchy of legal conditionality' (Section 6.2.1) determines the relationship of the meta-norms of international law-creation to each other. Three options are possible:

(1) One source of international law is supreme and the other sources are derived from it. The supreme source authorises the creation of subordinate source(s). The early Kelsen of *Das Problem der Souveränität* (1920)[55] set treaty law as supreme. *Pacta sunt servanda* is at once the basis for treaties and custom, because one is an express conclusion of a convention and the other is construed as a *pactum tacitum*.[56] In *Principles of International Law* (1952) Kelsen postulates that customary international law is the highest source with the *Grundnorm*: 'The states ought to behave as they have customarily behaved.'[57] '*Pacta sunt servanda*' is merely a norm of customary international law.[58] Alfred Verdross – an early student of Kelsen – at one point holds that general principles of law are the fount of all other sources. 'International law's *Grundnorm* would roughly have this content: Sovereign and partially sovereign legal communities ought to behave in their inter-relationships according to the general principles of law'.[59]

(2) Another possibility is an explicit 'constitution of international law' or a 'historically first constitution' as a meta-meta *stratum* whose task would be authorising the creation of sources. Thus, while 'international treaty law' and customary international law would be 'two separate branches of law'[60] of equal standing, they would be connected by a superstructure of meta-meta-laws which regulates the relationship of sources. That special supra-law would have to be composed of positive norms, but it is doubtful whether such positive norms exist.

(3) The 'default theory' would be that the three main formal sources are not hierarchi-

---

Jörg Kammerhofer, 'Constitutionalism and the myth of practical reason: Kelsenian responses to methodological confusion' 23 *Leiden Journal of International Law* (2010) 723–740.

55 Kelsen (1920) *supra* note 24 at 217, 262, 284; cf. Rub (1995) *supra* note 2 at 313; Verdross (1926) *supra* note 31 at 29.

56 Verdross (1926) *supra* note 31 at 43–44.

57 Kelsen (1952) *supra* note 30 at 418; Kelsen (1960) *supra* note 3 at 222, 324–325; Métall (1931) *supra* note 28 at 425.

58 Kelsen (1952) *supra* note 30 at 314, 417; Kunz (1934) *supra* note 47 at 403; Michel Virally, 'The sources of international law', in: Max Sørensen (ed.), *Manual of public international law* (1968) 116–174 at 128; Rub (1995) *supra* note 2 at 314.

59 'Die völkerrechtliche Grundnorm würde also etwa folgenden Inhalt haben: Souveräne und teilsouveräne Rechtsgemeinschaften verhaltet Euch in Eueren gegenseitigen Beziehungen nach den allgemeinen Rechtsgrundsätzen', Alfred Verdross, 'Die allgemeinen Rechtsgrundsätze als Völkerrechtsquelle. Zugleich ein Beitrag zum Problem der Grundnorm des positiven Völkerrechts', in: Alfred Verdross (ed.), *Gesellschaft, Staat und Recht. Untersuchungen zur reinen Rechtslehre. Festschrift Hans Kelsen zum 50. Geburtstage gewidmet* (1931) 354–365 at 362.

60 Grigory Tunkin, 'Is general international law customary law only?', 4 *European Journal of International Law* (1993) 534–541.

cally ordered[61] and are not normatively connected.[62] This would mean that both '*pacta sunt servanda*' and '*consuetudines sunt servanda*' are examples of a *Grundnorm*. If no constitution which binds the two types of norms can be proven to be positive law, it is possible that no connection between them exists. Both types of law may be part of international law, but may only be empirically classified as such. Without such an overarching constitution, the sources currently recognised might be different legal systems altogether.[63] The difference is between a normative link – one normative system and only empirical unity – and an empirical communality – a multitude of normative systems and one defining empirical community. This might well be the consequence of the current mainstream of international legal scholarship that sees the sources as equal.[64]

6.2.3 The constitution in operation: conflict of norms

The conflict of norms, rules or 'regimes' is an area of theoretical reflection which is highly relevant for international law and which has become topical since the International Law Commission (ILC) took to discussing fragmentation of international law in 2002.[65] It is here, where norms 'clash', that the Pure Theory of Law can be used to great advantage. The questions of the inter-relationship of norms are international law's constitution in operation; this is an area where the normativist-positivist approach of the Pure Theory works best. The issues of norm-conflict, which are complex in themselves, could be called part of the 'low-theory' world of describing the workings of legal orders and would not be part of the 'high-theory' world of political or moral philosophising about the goal, sense and faults of law. As mentioned, the Pure Theory of Law – as a common-sense approach – is strong on these issues and seeks to connect legal theory with legal doctrine. It is therefore an eminently more operationalisable approach than many others (including legal pragmatism), but is also eminently more dangerous to a pragmatic anti-intellectualism envisaged in the 'tool-box approach' of many legal practitioners to the problems of norm conflict.

---

61 There are cases where a subordination is obvious. Not every manifestation of norms is completely autonomous. Security Council Resolutions derive their validity from the United Nations Charter, so do International Court of Justice judgments.

62 Kelsen (1920) *supra* note 24 at 106–107.

63 This theory raises interesting problems of the succession of treaties by customary law and *vice versa*.

64 E.g. Maarten Bos, 'The recognized manifestations of international law. A new theory of "sources"', 20 *German Yearbook of International Law* (1977) 9–76 at 73–74; Gihl (1957) *supra* note 31 at 75.

65 The ILC spent four years (2002–2006) considering the topic. Stemming from an initiative by Gerhard Hafner in 2000, the Commission established a study group two years later, then chaired by Bruno Simma. Martti Koskenniemi took over a year later and under his chairmanship the project entered its 'operative phase' and was brought to a conclusion at the ILC's 58th session in 2006, with a final report of the study group (Martti Koskenniemi, 'Fragmentation of international law: Difficulties arising from the diversification and expansion of international law. Report of the study group of the International Law Commission', in: International Law Commission, Documents of its fifty-eighth session, A/CN.4/L.682 (2006)) and a chapter in the Commission's report to the General Assembly (International Law Commission, Report on the work of its fifty-eighth session (1 May to 9 June and 3 July to 11 August 2006) (A/61/10) (2006) 400–423).

This approach was visible also in the ILC study group report on fragmentation and makes this topic and this report ideal for the present purposes. The Study Group provides an account of a number of techniques (tools) that can be used to avoid or mitigate the negative effects of fragmentation and to ensure a measure of coherence in international law, including the classical *lex specialis* and *lex posterior* maxims, international law's own hierarchies of norms as well as systemic integration of external norms by way of interpretation.

The contrast between the Pure Theory and the ILC provides us with an overview of a significant and important part of Kelsen's theoretical construct, i.e. the consequences of the legal hierarchy founded on the Is–Ought distinction. Contrasting traditional scholarship and the Pure Theory in this manner can also demonstrate the continuing significance of the Kelsenian approach. Kelsen did not write on fragmentation of international law, yet a re-reading and re-application of the legal theoretical writings of the Vienna School is highly beneficial and clarifies the issue in a manner traditional scholarship cannot. In the following, two examples of typical tools used by the Study Group showing a lack of critical examination of the positive legal and theoretical basis and demonstrating the main features of the more consistent theoretical approach adopted by the Pure Theory of Law will be taken. The case studies concern the *lex posterior* maxim as an example of the traditional mechanisms for conflict resolution (Section 6.2.3.1) and Article 103 UN Charter, demonstrating the rediscovered uses for hierarchy in international law (Section 6.2.3.2). This type of hierarchy is contrasted with Kelsen's second hierarchy of derogation, the real *lex superior* maxim (Section 6.2.3.3).

6.2.3.1 The lex posterior maxim

The maxim *lex posterior derogat legi priori* is an answer to the question whether norms change over time.[66] However, the reverse is being argued: 'As with any law, [international law] *may change over time*. . . . As a result, any later norm can, in principle, overrule an earlier one'.[67] This confusion of the concepts of change, derogation and the *lex posterior* maxim[68] leads to the apocryphal status of the latter in international law, and to the 'argument by necessity' for its existence, in legal theory.

The first argument is the claim that derogation and change (whether by way of the 'primacy' of the later norm or not) is connected to formal logic. This is a highly complicated claim and the literature on deontic logic – led by the Pure Theory and analytic philosophers – is so vast[69] that the following discussion will have to be severely limited

---

[66] Wladyslaw Czapliński and Gennady M. Danilenkow, 'Conflict of norms in international law', 21 *Netherlands Yearbook of International Law* (1990) 3–42 at 19.

[67] Joost Pauwelyn, *Conflict of norms in international law. How WTO law relates to other rules of international law* (2003) at 14.

[68] Wolfram Karl, *Vertrag und spätere Praxis im Völkerrecht* (1983) at 59.

[69] For intramural deontic debates on the Pure Theory of Law see: Kelsen (1960), *supra* note 3 at 26–27, 76–77, 209–212, 271–282; Kelsen (1979), *supra* note 5 at 84–92, 99–103, 166–179, 266–267; Adolf Julius Merkl, 'Die Rechtseinheit des österreichischen Staates. Eine staatsrechtliche Untersuchung auf Grund der Lehre von der lex posterior', 37 *Archiv des öffentlichen Rechts* (1918) 56–121, reprinted in: Hans Klecatsky, René Marcić, Herbert Schambeck (eds), *Die Wiener rechtstheoretische Schule. Ausgewählte Schriften von Hans Kelsen, Adolf Julius Merkl, Alfred Verdross* (1968) 1115–1165; Merkl (1923) *supra* note 41 at 228–244; Stanley L. Paulson, 'Zum Problem der

in scope. Three interlocking questions need to be answered in the affirmative in order to establish a logical basis for the *lex posterior* maxim.

(a) Can norms in some fashion be called 'true' and 'false' or otherwise be brought into the framework of formal logic? Hans Kelsen changed his position on this point after 1960. The more he questioned the soundness of the role of logic in certain legal 'operations', the less convinced he became of logical automatisms in the face of positive-legal norm-creation and destruction. His scepticism seems well-founded: ascribing truth-values seems a necessary condition for '[r]elations of condition and of logical consequence'.[70] Direct claims that a norm could be 'true' or 'false' are exceedingly rare, but there have been various attempts to make an indirect connection between norms or their properties and a bivalent logical system. For example, the truth of a statement is equated with the validity of a norm. This does not work for two reasons. A positive norm is the meaning or sense (*Sinn*) of an act of will, not of an act of thought. Positive norms are not created by merely *thinking* them or by thinking what they entail.[71] The other reason is that validity is not a property of a norm; it is norms' specific form of existence.[72] A non-valid norm simply does not exist.[73]

Another approach seeks to adapt certain aspects of analytic-linguistic philosophy to normative theory in order to create a deontic logic. John Searle's concept of 'speech act'[74] is key in the attempt to reduce norms to utterances, i.e.linguistic facts.[75] The terms

---

Normenkonflikte', 66 *Archiv für Rechts- und Sozialphilosophie* (1980) 487–506; Stanley L. Paulson, 'On the status of the *lex posterior* derogating rule', in: Richard Tur and William Twining (eds), *Essays on Kelsen* (1986) 229–247; Ewald Wiederin, 'Was ist und welche Konsequenzen hat ein Normkonflikt?', 21 *Rechtstheorie* (1990) 311–333 at 328–329.

For analytic (linguistic) jurisprudence see e.g. Carlos E. Alchourrón and Eugenio Bulygin, 'The expressive conception of norms', in: Risto Hilpinen (ed.), *New studies in deontic logic* (1981) 95–124, reprinted in: Stanley L. Paulson and Bonnie Litschewski Paulson (eds), *Normativity and norms. Critical perspectives on Kelsenian themes* (1998) 383–410; Eugenio Bulygin, 'Norms and logic. Kelsen and Weinberger on the ontology of norms', 4 *Law and Philosophy* (1985) 145–163; Bruno Celano, 'Norm conflicts: Kelsen's view in the late period and a rejoinder', in: Stanley L. Paulson and Bonnie Litschewski Paulson (eds), *Normativity and norms. Critical perspectives on Kelsenian themes* (1998) 343–361; Ota Weinberger, 'The expressive conception of norms: An impasse for the logic of norms', 4 *Law and Philosophy* (1985) 165–198, reprinted in: Stanley L. Paulson and Bonnie Litschewski Paulson (eds), *Normativity and norms. Critical perspectives on Kelsenian themes* (1998) 411–432; Georg Henrik von Wright, *An essay in deontic logic and the general theory of action* (1968).

70 Georg Henrik von Wright, 'Is and Ought', in: Eugenio Bulygin *et al.* (eds), *Man, law and modern forms of life* (1985) 263–281, reprinted in: Stanley L. Paulson and Bonnie Litschewski Paulson (eds), *Normativity and norms. Critical perspectives on Kelsenian themes* (1998) 365–382 at 367.

71 Kelsen (1979) *supra* note 5 at 166.

72 Kelsen (1979) *supra* note 5 at 22, 136–138; Lothar Philipps, 'Normentheorie', in: Arthur Kaufmann, Winfried Hassemer, Ulfrid Neumann (eds), *Einführung in Rechtsphilosophie und Rechtstheorie der Gegenwart* (7th edn. 2004) 320–332 at 328–329.

73 Kelsen (1979), *supra* note 5 at 139; Amedeo G. Conte, 'Hans Kelsen's deontics', in: Stanley L. Paulson and Bonnie Litschewski Paulson (eds), *Normativity and norms. Critical perspectives on Kelsenian themes* (1998) 331–341.

74 John R. Searle, *Speech acts. An essay in the philosophy of language* (1969).

75 Searle explicitly claims to derive Ought from Is: Searle (1969) *supra* note 74 at 175–198.

'prescriptive sentence'[76] or 'ought-sentence'[77] all refer to the same reduction. Some of the proponents seem to implicitly ascribe a post-analytic-turn philosophy to Kelsen's writings and claim that he espouses this sort of reduction himself. Yet even if norms were reducible to linguistic utterances, an argument that they are subject to logic could only be made by negating the Is–Ought dichotomy. To call Kelsen a post-analytic philosopher is incorrect and he disavows any connection: 'It needs to be stressed that the act of will, whose sense is a norm, *needs to be distinguished from the speech-act*, in which the sense of an act of will *is expressed*.'[78] In the end, analytic philosophy cannot found a normative science, since its commingling of Is and Ought means that it cannot conceive of norms properly speaking.

(b) Does the application of the principle of contradiction[79] extend directly or indirectly to the inter-relationship of norms and does a contradiction cause derogation of positive norms? Despite their spirited fight for an assimilation of norm-conflicts to logical contradictions, analytic-linguistic legal theorists are unanimous in their acceptance that the application of logic does not touch the conflicting norms' validity.[80] The problem is that norms are 'existent' (valid) or they are not, and their existence is determined by the meta-norm on norm-creation (the source law) plus an act of will, rather than only the norms' relationship to each other. Statements about the norms existence do not influence a norm's existence. Only if a norm is valid is such a statement true and statements on two conflicting norms are necessarily both true, because they refer to two different objects.[81] This is a beneficial outcome of Kelsen's post-1960 'logical turn'. Thus, a logical basis for the *lex posterior* maxim could be said to have been defeated at this point.

(c) Yet, does the later norm still derogate from the former? If a legislator has created acts that are contradictory over time, traditional scholarship asks how else we could ensure unity and how law can change over time if not by privileging *lex posterior* over *lex prior*? As against this, one could *ex hypothesi* even make a better case for the *prior* norm, because – as Adolf Merkl, Kelsen's first student and close colleague argues – 'the earlier law has been enacted according to the constitution and . . . it has therefore . . . taken a specific place in the legal system and thus taken the place of any contrary legal content,'[82] specifically of later law. Given that one could thus argue in favour of either

---

76 Conte (1998) *supra* note 73 at 330. Implied: Koskenniemi (2006) *supra* note 65 at 60–61 (para 111).

77 Riccardo Guastini, 'Normativism and the normative theory of legal science: Some epistemological problems', in: Stanley L. Paulson and Bonnie Litschewski Paulson (eds), *Normativity and norms. Critical perspectives on Kelsenian themes* (1998) 317–330 at 319.

78 '[Es] ist zu beachten, daß der Willensakt, dessen Sinn eine Norm ist, *von dem Sprech-Akt unterschieden werden muß*, in dem der Sinn des Willenaktes *ausgedrückt wird*.' Kelsen (1979) *supra* note 5 at 131 (emphasis added).

79 The principle of contradiction (*principium contradictionis*) states that contradictory statements (e.g. 'A' and 'non-A') cannot both be true at the same time; in other words: 'A is not not-A.'

80 Alchourrón and Bulygin (1981) *supra* note 69 at 403; Bulygin (1985) *supra* note 69 at 154; Celano (1998) *supra* note 69 at 351; Conte (1998) *supra* note 73 at 333, 339; Guastini (1998) *supra* note 77 at 329; Weinberger (1985) *supra* note 69 at 427. For international law: Karl (1983) *supra* note 68 at 61–66.

81 Conte (1998) *supra* note 73 at 333.

82 'Das frühere Gesetz verfassungsmäßig zustande gekommen ist, daß somit dadurch eine

prior or later law, giving preference to one or the other seems spurious. Even more so, it is a *petitio principii* to say that a later norm derogates a prior norm because it is later. In order to do so we have to presuppose derogating power to later norms and where should that presupposition come from?

For the Pure Theory of Law, a change of law is merely an abbreviation for the addition of new norms to a normative system[83] with a possible derogation of old norms. An authorisation to create norms, however, does not automatically incorporate an authorisation to derogate from norms. 'Not everyone who has created something can also undo it.'[84] The normative basis for creation is hierarchically higher, while a norm created by the organ thus authorised is on the same hierarchical level as all other norms created, whether it purports to derogate or not. This line of thought, however, presupposes a position on *lex superior* (cf. Section 6.2.3.3).

Ascribing primacy to the later treaty because it is the current expression of the consent of the parties, for example, is merely shifting the problem to another level – why should the later expression of consent prevail if earlier consent was able to create a treaty? There is no logical necessity for the *lex posterior* maxim or for any sort of 'automatic' derogation based only on logical rules. Logic neither creates nor destroys law. Only when law is fictional, not positive, thought-product, not sense of an act of will, can logic actually create and destroy.[85]

Second, might the *lex posterior* maxim work if it were a positive norm of international law? A diligent critique shows that in such a fragmented normative order as 'international law', even positive regulation is limited in its effect. A norm with the content '*lex posterior derogat legi priori*' would most likely be a customary or treaty norm or a general principle of law.

Customary international law. Several problems arise in this connection. (i) Customary law is based on usage (customs). Customary norms receive their content from the repetition of similar behaviour. State practice, e.g. the repeated passage of ships through straits, becomes the norm's content and the *opinio iuris* delivers its normativity, i.e. that ships *may* pass. Hence, customary law can only have such content that can be classified as accumulated factual behaviour. While, thus, customary law cannot refer to the ideal level of other norms, derogating norms do so because they establish a 'non-ought'. The content 'earlier norms are repealed, if . . .' cannot form a pattern of factual behaviour in the real world. (ii) The *lex posterior* maxim has the same hierarchical status as other customary international law and a norm claiming observance conflicts with another norm claiming to derogate from it. However, derogation of norms is not dependent upon conflict and conflict does not determine whether one norm derogates from another. The validities of

---

bestimmte Stelle im Rechtssystem . . . eingenommen und damit ferner jedem widersprechenden Rechtsinhalte den Platz genommen hat.' Merkl (1918), *supra* note 69 at 1133.

83 Merkl (1923) *supra* note 41 at 233.

84 'Nicht jeder, der etwas geschaffen hat, kann es wieder ungeschehen machen.' Merkl (1918) *supra* note 69 at 1132; contra: Rainer Lippold, *Recht und Ordnung. Statik und Dynamik der Rechtsordnung* (2000) 405–407; cf. also Erich Vranes, '*Lex Superior, Lex Specialis, Lex Posterior* – Zur Rechtsnatur der "Konfliktlösungsregeln"', 65 *Zeitschrift für ausländisches öffentliches Recht und Völkerrecht* (2005) 391–405 at 397.

85 Kelsen (1979) *supra* note 5 at 202–203.

two norms might clash, but the outcome of the clash is not decided by the content of the two norms. (iii) When the customary *lex posterior* norm is faced with a treaty norm, it seeks to impinge upon a different source of international law.[86] The norms of one source of international law cannot simply derogate from the norms of another,[87] because a source of law creates norms belonging only to its own source. 'Derogation can only occur within one and the same normative order.'[88]

Treaty law and general principles of law. In the case of Articles 30, 39 and 58 of the Vienna Convention on the Law of Treaties 1969 (VCLT),[89] the inter-source hierarchical problems would persist. Only if the enunciation of the maxim *pacta sunt servanda* in Article 26 means that treaties falling under the VCLT derive their validity from the Vienna Convention, which was probably not intended for Article 26, would the VCLT be a meta-law on treaty making. This means that the question is moved to the *lex superior* maxim, which will be discussed in Section 6.2.3.3. Inter-source problems would equally apply to a general principle of law. In addition, one would have to contend with grave theoretical doubts as to the very possibility of general principles as *positive* international law aside from the narrow ambit of Article 38(1)(c) of the Statute of the International Court of Justice. How can a comparison of scientific abstractions from diverse legal systems in any shape be 'willed' as part of international law? Verdross argues that this source is, in effect, a natural law construction,[90] a result borne out by the discussion in 1920 of the Advisory Committee of Jurists on the point.[91] Their 'positivisation' in Article 38(1)(c) ICJ Statute is relevant only for the Court. Kelsen argues that they 'are norms which become international law applicable before the International Court of Justice, because Article 38(1)(c) authorises the International Court of Justice to apply them.'[92]

6.2.3.2 Article 103 UN Charter and international law's hierarchies

The case for *sui generis* 'hierarchies' in international law can be defeated by taking Article 103 UN Charter as an example. There is no doubt that it is an obligation binding upon the member states of the United Nations, but what makes the Charter a 'higher' norm? Article 103 does not specify exactly what happens to the non-Charter obligations[93] and it does not say whether the validity of the other norm is ended, except that it shall 'prevail'.[94]

---

86 Jörg Kammerhofer, 'Uncertainty in the formal sources of international law: Customary international law and some of its problems', 15 *European Journal of International Law* (2004) 523–553 at 549–550.

87 Karl (1983) *supra* note 68 at 109.

88 'Derogation kann nur innerhalb ein und derselben normativen Ordnung erfolgen.' Kelsen (1979) *supra* note 5 at 102.

89 Koskenniemi (2006) *supra* note 65 at 128–134 (paras 251–266).

90 Alfred Verdross, *Völkerrecht* (3rd edn. 1955) 11–12, 22–23.

91 Permanent Court of International Justice, Advisory Committee of Jurists, *Procès-verbaux of the proceedings of the Committee June 16th–July 24th 1920 with Annexes* (1920) 293–338, 584.

92 'Normen . . ., die dadurch von dem Internationalen Gerichtshof anzuwendendes Völkerrecht werden, daß Art. 38 § 1c den Internationalen Gerichtshof ermächtigt, sie anzuwenden.' Kelsen (1979) *supra* note 5 at 99.

93 Rudolf Bernhardt, 'Article 103', in: Bruno Simma (ed.), *The Charter of the United Nations. A commentary* (2nd edn. 2002) 1292–1302 at 1295 (RN 6).

94 Re-emphasised by the Court: *Military and Paramilitary Activities in and against Nicaragua (Nicaragua* v. *United States of America)*, Jurisdiction and Admissibility, Judgment of 26 November

This could also mean that international lawyers ought to pragmatically ignore the non-Charter norm. Some writers such as Rudolf Bernhardt argue that in some cases the non-Charter norm is either void *ab initio* or voided:[95] 'World peace itself may depend on respect for the higher rank and binding force of the Charter as emphasized by Art. 103.'[96] However, norms' 'bindingness' equals their existence and because existence is not gradual, there can be no *higher* binding force: all 'ought' is *a priori* equal. The Charter may be the most important treaty valid today, but its moral and political importance does not mean that it has the status of a superior norm (understood as derogatory power) vis-à-vis other treaties. There still is a conflict between two treaties and even if one of them claims to 'prevail' over the other that does not mean that it actually does.

Concepts of hierarchy such as this are not based upon validity-dependence by law-creation. Article 103's claim to superiority faces the same problems as other such claims. We will next turn to the question whether an expanded concept of Merkl's and Kelsen's *Stufenbau* fares better and whether norm-conflict vanishes before a 'truly' superior norm.[97]

6.2.3.3 The other hierarchy of norms: deference to really superior law?

There is another hierarchy of norms in the Pure Theory (in addition to the one presented in Section 6.2.1), developed by Merkl, but not explicitly distinguished by Kelsen:[98] the hierarchy of derogation (*Stufenbau nach der derogatorischen Kraft*).[99] This concept has the potential to help embattled international legal scholars seeking conflict-resolution devices, since norm-conflicts can only be solved by derogation. When can norms *validly* derogate, which norms have what sort of derogatory force? However, while the first type of hierarchy is a necessary element of all normative orders, the second type of hierarchy is not necessary. Derogation never is a logical operation and must be a feature of positive regulation.[100] In particular, we must enter the vicious circle of claiming 'if a hierarchy is created by derogation, the higher norm will derogate the lower norm, thus any derogating norm is higher and any norm that claims to derogate derogates', proving no more than that the hierarchy of derogation comes from derogation, while the derogating force comes from hierarchy.[101] Thus, we must tackle the question whether the hierarchy of legal conditionality can be the foundation for the hierarchy of derogation. At first glance, this option seems natural, for why should not the type of norm that has created the norm in question determine when it should end? 'If there is hierarchically higher and lower law in a legal order, the *lex inferior* has in principle to yield to the *lex superior*, if the structure of the legal order is not to be led *ad absurdum*.'[102]

Against this, Merkl argues that the two hierarchies may diverge significantly, for a

---

1984, ICJ Reports (1984) 392 at 440; *Questions of Interpretation and Application of the 1971 Montreal Convention arising from the Aerial Incident at Lockerbie (Libyan Arab Jamahiriya* v. *United Kingdom)*, Preliminary Objections, Judgment of 27 February 1998, ICJ Reports (1998) 9 at 31.

95 Bernhardt (2002) *supra* note 93 at 1297 (RN 15).

96 Bernhardt (2002) *supra* note 93 at 1302 (RN 37).

97 Kelsen (1979) *supra* note 5 at 178–179.

98 Behrend (1977) *supra* note 36 at 42.

99 Walter (1964) *supra* note 39 at 55.

100 Behrend (1977) *supra* note 36 at 36–38.

101 Theodor Schilling, *Rang und Geltung von Normen in gestuften Rechtsordnungen* (1994) 400.

102 'Soweit es in der Rechtsordnung höherrangiges und niederrangiges Recht gibt, muss die

norm being called 'higher' than another does not automatically mean that it is higher in every respect.[103] It may not be the case that equal origin determines equal rank, for Merkl believes that one cannot conclude solely from the fact that a constitution provides a multitude of authorising norms for e.g. statutes and administrative orders that they are of equal rank.[104] Merkl's scepticism is shared by Theo Öhlinger. The law on law-creation (*Erzeugungsregel*) can only create a norm that purports to derogate, but does not tell us whether the derogating norm is in a position to actually derogate. 'But *this relationship* between derogating and derogable norm is what matters for the hierarchy of derogation.'[105] A connection between the conditions of law-creation and derogation cannot be a logical necessity.[106]

However, this abstract question does cause concrete problems when we seek to apply the Pure Theory's notion of *lex superior* as a second hierarchy to norm-conflict resolution. We must determine under which conditions a norm designated as 'higher' actually derogates from a 'lower' norm. The three possible categories of *lex superior–lex inferior* conflict-situations that follow from an application of the Pure Theory of Law will briefly be presented and discussed. The problems uncovered, however, might be systemic and a matter of the very nature of positive normative orders.

(1) A substantive norm may conflict with a 'higher' norm of the same legal order, e.g. where a statute prescribes 'you must do *A*' while the constitution prescribes 'you may not do *A*'. This is a conflict of observability, where the norms do not impinge upon one another, but where a subject of law may be factually unable to act in accordance with both norms. In this case, the problem lies in defining which norm is higher and which is lower in the hierarchy of norms. Since super-ordination cannot be based on mere claims (a norm's claim to be superior to another), what other criteria can validly be used to establish superiority? Even within a normative order, a norm may not be directly connected to another, for example between a norm of the constitution and a statute created under another norm of the constitution authorising the creation of statutes by parliament. While we might be tempted to conclude that the former is higher than the latter, all norms' inherent equal claim to be observed precludes this. Only the direct relationship of validity-dependence ('creation') establishes a hierarchy.[107] The lower norm depends only upon its 'source-law', not upon other, indirectly higher norms[108] and hence 'a rule is only erroneous with respect to the rules which are directly conditional for its validity.'[109] Unless the 'higher' norm can be interpreted as part of the conditions for law-creation of the lower norm, it is not *lex superior* in our sense.

(2) A norm may conflict with a 'higher' norm of the same order expressly derogating

---

lex inferior im Grundsatz der *lex superior* weichen, wenn nicht die Struktur der Rechtsordnung *ad absurdum* geführt werden soll.' Vranes (2005) *supra* note 84 at 397–398.

[103] Merkl (1931) *supra* note 42 at 1342.

[104] Merkl (1931) *supra* note 42 at 1340–1341.

[105] 'Auf *diese Relation* zwischen derogierender und derogierbarer Norm kommt es aber im Stufenbau nach der derogatorischen Kraft an.' Öhlinger (1975) *supra* note 35 at 23.

[106] Öhlinger (1975) *supra* note 35 at 25–26; Merkl (1923) *supra* note 41 at 299.

[107] Schilling (1994) *supra* note 101 at 402.

[108] Kelsen (1960) *supra* note 3 at 212; Kelsen (1979) *supra* note 5 at 207.

[109] 'die Fehlerhaftigkeit einer Rechtsvorschrift besteht immer nur Hinblick auf die direkt bedingende Regelung.' Lippold (2000) *supra* note 84 at 390 (emphasis removed).

from it, e.g. where a constitutional norm prescribes 'The statute *X* is herewith repealed.' This is a conflict of ideals where an Ought is impinged upon by a non-Ought, i.e. a derogation. Here, the situation is more complicated than in (1). Again, we cannot simply take derogating norms at their word and admit successful derogation of *any* norms that claim to do so. In addition to the problem of not being able to count as higher a norm outside the conditions for law-creation of the lower norm, we are still left with uncertainty as to the derogatory force of derogating norms. To claim that higher norms derogate from lower norms because they are higher is an empty tautology.

(3) The most complex case is where a norm does not fulfil all the conditions of the meta-law on law-making, e.g. where a statute is not passed with the correct majority present and voting. This is the question of the error in law-making. The easy answer is that the norm simply does not exist. No derogation is necessary, because no norm was created in the first place.[110] In light of the intensive scholarly discussion in 19th-century German public law, the Pure Theory problematised this aspect of norm-conflicts with respect to erroneous acts in positive legal orders and created the theories of the *Fehlerkalkül* and the 'tacit alternative clause' to accommodate the unique characteristics of norms, on the one hand, and of positive enactment, on the other hand. These are two crucial, often misunderstood and complex elements of the Pure Theory of Law.[111] While a discussion of these is neither possible nor necessary here, we will discuss the outcome of this type of conflict. What happens if a court judgment delivers a 'wrong' verdict or if the Security Council orders Chapter VII action because it believes that a situation constitutes a 'threat to the peace', even though there 'really' is no such threat (Section 6.3)? There are only three possible solutions to an 'unlawful' final decision: First, the norms are valid, but annullable, which would make the decision anything but final. Second, they are void *ab initio*, which is unascertainable without specifying someone to ascertain voidness, which would not make the decision final either. The only option left is that they are fully valid and not subject to appeal. In this case 'we have to find legal rules in which the validity of these "unlawful" final decisions is grounded'.[112]

Even within the most obvious case of a norm-conflict being 'resolved' *ex ante*, the Pure Theory of Law has to face a problem that becomes a paradox: on the one hand, the duality of Is and Ought demands of us to found norms' validity only in norms. Norm-creation is a founding exercise: without a basis in norms, alleged norms cannot be norms. *The normativity of normative systems demands a strict foundation in norms.* On the other hand, an authorised organ is authorised to decide and its decision is a decision. If the Security Council says there is a threat to the peace, there is a threat to the peace because it and no one else is authorised by law to make *that* decision.[113] The act of will is a necessary condition for the creation of a positive norm. Creation is constitutive, whether or not it conforms to conditions of law-creation. *The positivity of norms gives positive acts of will creative powers.* This is the paradox of positive normative orders: a truly superior norm endangers positivity, while a truly positive norm endangers the unity of the normative

---

110 Merkl (1923) *supra* note 41 at 286–287.

111 The following discussion draws heavily on: Christoph Kletzer, 'Kelsen's development of the *Fehlerkalkül*-Theory', 18 *Ratio Juris* (2005) 46–63.

112 Kletzer (2005) *supra* note 111 at 52.

113 Kelsen (1960) *supra* note 3 at 274.

order. It is not a paradox of the Pure Theory, but Kelsen brings to light what other theories manage to hide behind pragmatism.

The present author's take on the paradox is that any act of will purporting to create a norm necessarily creates a norm, whether or not it fulfils the creation-conditions of the normative order in question. If it fulfils these conditions it is a norm of that normative order, if not, it belongs to its own normative order (consisting of it and its *Grundnorm*). There may be a hint of this solution in Kelsen's writings, for when he tells us that a norm not determined by a higher norm 'cannot be valid as a norm *enacted within the legal order*'[114] he distinguishes between a norm's validity and its membership in a given normative order. However, this means that the connection between norms in a normative order becomes weak, if norms start to exist with an act of will irrespective of the empowering norm, which, in turn, is reduced to becoming the lower norm's membership criterion. It seems that at least the conflict between a law and its meta-norm on law-creation is resolved or avoided by simply not recognising 'faulty' norms as norms of the normative order in question. This, however, comes at the price of endangering the unity of the legal order (a point also briefly raised in Section 6.2.2).

The three 'traditional resolving devices' most commonly used in doctrine have fared extremely weakly, for they have no basis in logic and the problems start to mount if we assume them to be part of positive law. Only the relationship of a norm to its own 'mother', to its source-norm is special; like a real mother, it gives birth to a norm, without it, a norm of that normative system does not come to life.

6.3 CHAPTER VII OF THE UN CHARTER AND SECURITY COUNCIL ACTION

The following is a discussion of elements of the Pure Theory's construction of Chapter VII of the UN Charter. Choosing this topic felicitously unites three elements identified at the outset as meriting special attention in a portrayal of the Vienna School of Jurisprudence's theory of international law. First, it gives a good example of the continued relevance of its theoretical model for a current debate of international legal doctrine. Second, it also shows an important part of international law's constitution in operation, in particular the notion of 'erroneous' decisions of final-instance organs identified in Section 6.2.3.3 vis-à-vis the Security Council's powers under Chapter VII. Third, it provides arguments for de-personalising the treatment of a theoretical approach. Kelsen's own writings retain their usefulness but are concerned with notions which are regarded as 'outdated' nowadays and which are best seen through a re-application of the Pure Theory of Law's general theory rather than discussed by reference to Kelsen's own *The Law of the United Nations* (1950)[115] or similar specific pieces.

(1) Kelsen himself constructs Chapter VII in light of two theoretical concepts: the

[114] 'kann nicht als eine *innerhalb der Rechtsordnung gesetzte* Norm gelten': Kelsen (1960) *supra* note 3 at 241 (emphasis added).

[115] Hans Kelsen, *The law of the United Nations. A critical analysis of its fundamental problems* (1950).

coercive order paradigm (*Zwangsnormpostulat*) and a reformulated *bellum iustum* doctrine. The coercive order paradigm is Kelsen's answer to the question of what distinguishes legal orders from other kinds of normative orders. '[A] feature common to societal orders designated as law is that they are coercive orders in the sense that they react to anti-social "facts", especially to such human behaviour, by [prescribing] an evil',[116] i.e. *sanctions*. Thus, coercion *prescribed* as reaction against certain behaviour is the distinguishing feature of law. Kelsen saw the application of the coercive order paradigm to international law as rooted in a simplified and secularised version of the *bellum iustum* doctrine:[117] 'Without the so-called principle of "bellum iustum" there is no international law'.[118] If there is a total prohibition on the use of force which includes the possibility of justifying forcible actions as sanctions, international law truly is law.[119]

Kelsen sees the *bellum iustum* principle embodied in Chapter VII, yet in *The Law of the United Nations* he gives two alternative interpretations of its provisions.[120] In the first interpretation the enforcement measures under the Charter cannot be characterised as 'sanctions', because they are not necessarily a reaction against a state violating the Charter. The 'threat to the peace, breach of the peace, or act of aggression' clause in Article 39 is not a prohibition and the Security Council may determine that situations constitute a threat to the peace and it might also order measures against a state not having violated its obligations under Article 39. The Council is also not obligated to initiate enforcement measures against a state which has used force.[121] Kelsen argues: 'The enforcement actions taken under Article 39 are purely political measures, that is to say, measures which the Security Council may apply at its discretion for the purpose to maintain or restore international peace.'[122]

Under the other interpretation of the Charter, 'enforcement actions determined by Articles 39, 41 and 42 must be interpreted as sanctions'.[123] Transposing the *bellum iustum* doctrine to the UN Charter regime, measures under Article 41 play the role of reprisals while enforcement under Article 42 fulfils the function of war.[124] However, in pre-Charter law, reprisals could involve the use of force, while countermeasures may no longer do so. With the exception of an element of self-help, i.e. of decentralised enforcement in the provisions allowing for self-defence in Article 51,[125] the enforcement of Charter law

---

116 'Ein . . . den als Recht bezeichneten Gesellschaftsordnungen gemeinsames Merkmal ist, daß sie Zwangsordnungen in dem Sinne sind, daß sie auf bestimmte für unerwünscht, weil sozial schädlich angesehene Umstände, insbesondere auf menschliches Verhalten dieser Art, mit einem Zwangsakt, das heißt mit einem Übel . . . reagieren': Kelsen (1960) *supra* note 3 at 34.

117 Danilo Zolo, 'Hans Kelsen: international peace through international law', 9 *European Journal of International Law* (1998) 306–324 at 312.

118 'Ohne den sogenannten Grundsatz des "bellum iustum" gibt es kein Völkerrecht': Hans Kelsen, 'Völkerrechtliche Verträge zu Lasten Dritter', 14 *Prager Juristische Zeitschrift* (1934) column 419–431 at 427.

119 Kelsen (1952) *supra* note 30 at 58; Rub (1995) *supra* note 2 at 230.

120 Kelsen (1950) *supra* note 115 at 727–737.

121 Kelsen (1950) *supra* note 115 at 727–731, 734.

122 Kelsen (1950) *supra* note 115 at 732–733.

123 Kelsen (1950) *supra* note 115 at 735.

124 Kelsen (1952) *supra* note 30 at 46–47.

125 Kelsen (1952) *supra* note 30 at 60. It is questionable whether self-defence as it is shaped today is a measure of law enforcement, rather than of mere repulsion of an act irrespective of its legality.

is centralised.[126] While Kelsen insists that Article 41 measures can only be interpreted as sanctions, because 'reprisals are permissible only against a violation of international law',[127] the nature of Article 42 measures are disputed. If 'threats to the peace', 'breaches of the peace' and 'acts of aggression' are indeed prohibited, the (tenuous) connection is that the term 'in any manner inconsistent with the Purposes of the United Nations' in Article 2(4) refers to the phrase 'to take effective collective measures for the prevention and removal of threats to the peace, and for the suppression of acts of aggression or other breaches of the peace' in Article 1(1), which again refers to the clause in Article 39.[128] He further concludes that if force is prohibited unless it constitutes a collective response (measures under Article 41 and 42), then Article 39 becomes – via Articles 1(1) and 2(4) – a prohibition: it prohibits threats to the peace, breaches of the peace, or acts of aggression by authorising sanctions under Articles 41 and 42.[129]

Yet, the present author argues that the first interpretation of Chapter VII – eliminating sanctions – fits the system of the Charter better. It is also submitted that eliminating the coercive order paradigm from the interpretation of the Charter is more in keeping with the Pure Theory of Law's basic assumptions about the nature of law and norms. The following, therefore, will briefly reason why the elimination of that paradigm is beneficial, will reiterate some salient features of Chapter VII and will finally connect this argument to the powers of the Security Council to create individual norms.

Does the *bellum iustum* doctrine fit the UN Charter? Kelsen demonstrates that while the doctrine is not a logical necessity, the Charter can be seen in this light.[130] However, the argument here is that the two paradigms can be eliminated from the interpretation of the Charter's terms. As mentioned above, Kelsen introduced the coercive order paradigm to provide for a defining feature for legal orders vis-à-vis moral, political or other types of normative order. However, there is a crucial distinction to be made between two types of classification, i.e. between the differentiation of various 'types' of normative systems and the delimitation of norms vis-à-vis things existing in reality (the Is–Ought dichotomy discussed in Section 6.1.1). The question of the uniqueness of *legal* norms is an empirical description. This differentiation does not 'un-make' a norm, whereas the decision whether a given 'idea' is a norm impinges upon its 'existence' as validity. In other words: there are norms in existence which fail the test of being legal norms, but there can be no non-binding norm. Also, the empirical closeness of various legal orders may not in fact be as great as is commonly assumed: the coercive elements of different orders, for example, are shaped differently and the importance of the coercive element varies broadly. Thus, law's classification is a matter for sociological methodology and to make law dependent on its coercive elements means making it

---

Cf. Jörg Kammerhofer, 'Uncertainties of the law on self-defence in the United Nations Charter', 35 *Netherlands Yearbook of International Law* 2004 (2005) 143–204 for an overview.

126 Kelsen (1950) *supra* note 115 at 726.

127 Kelsen (1950) *supra* note 115 at 735.

128 Kelsen (1950) *supra* note 115 at 726.

129 Kelsen (1950) *supra* note 115 at 736 (emphasis added).

130 See John H. Herz, 'The Pure Theory of Law revisited: Hans Kelsen's doctrine of international law in the nuclear age', in: Salo Engel (ed.), *Law, state and international legal order. Essays in honor of Hans Kelsen* (1964) 107–118 at 109–111. Cf. Rub (1995) *supra* note 2 at 269.

dependent on facts. This would violate Kelsen's own dichotomy of Is and Ought and it is thus best omitted.

Therefore, a reconceived Chapter VII does not conform to the *bellum iustum* doctrine. 'Coercive actions' by the Security Council need not exclusively be directed at member states violating their obligations under the Charter[131] and are thus not necessarily *a response to a wrong*. Article 39 is not formulated as a prohibition and Security Council action is not directed specifically against acts fulfilling the terms of the clause in that article, or even to redress Article 39's 'violation'.[132] The Council's freedom to find concrete occasions for enforcement also undermines the application of a strict concept of law-enforcement.[133] The measures under Article 41 and 42 cannot be seen as sanctions in the Kelsenian sense of the word.[134] The Charter's Preamble and Article 1(1) make quite clear that the goal of the Charter VII mechanism is not to enforce the law, but to maintain international peace and minimise the use of force.

(2) What if the Security Council 'exceeds its powers' – in Kelsenian terms: does not conform to all the conditions laid down for norm-creation? This is an application of the special case of norm-conflict discussed in Section 6.2.3.3 where a norm 'conflicts' with the norm that authorises (is the legal condition for) its creation. While entering into an in-depth discussion of the terms of the Charter, of *ultra vires* action and judicial review are beyond the purview of this chapter, a very brief overview of some *theoretical* issues may illustrate how the Pure Theory of Law may shed some light on how this approach may help clarify these.

The conditions under which the Council may create norms binding for the member states – the meta-law of law-creation – are laid down in several articles specifying the 'powers' of the Council (Chapter VII will be used as an example). Article 24(2) specifies two conditions for norm-creation for the maintenance of international peace and security: first, the Council has to act in accordance with the Purposes and Principles (Articles 1–2)[135] in creating norms and second, it limits the Council to the specific powers granted in (*inter alia*) Chapter VII.[136] In that chapter, Article 39 provides a further limitation by requiring a finding of a 'threat to the peace, breach of the peace, or act of aggression' by the Council and a restriction to either non-forcible measures under Article 41 (which may include positive obligations, prohibitions or permissions vis-à-vis member states) or to except forcible action by the Organisation or its members under Article 42 from the prohibition of the use of force. In addition, other institutional and procedural norms for the operation of the Council apply (e.g. Article 27 for the voting majorities). These powers are very wide, for each of the limitations is couched in very vague language.

Yet despite the Council's wide remit, it is possible for the conditions not to be fulfilled completely by the Council in purporting to create a resolution binding on the member states. Relatively clear examples – differing from others only by degree, not in kind – would be the violation of the majority requirement, e.g. if one of the permanent members

---

131 Kelsen (1950) supra note 115 at 725.
132 Kelsen (1950) *supra* note 115 at 726.
133 Kelsen (1950) *supra* note 115 at 729.
134 Kelsen (1950) *supra* note 115 at 733.
135 Kelsen (1950) *supra* note 115 at 282, 287–288.
136 Kelsen (1950) *supra* note 115 at 287–291.

were not to cast a 'concurring' vote (Article 27(3)) or if a measure under Articles 41–42 were not preceded by a finding under Article 39. If the Council does not fulfil *all* conditions for norm-creation, the case discussed above entails: no norm is created. There can be no doctrine of 'valid, but voidable' norms for the Council, because there is no *Fehlerkalül*, which would allow for the validity, but derogability of norms only fulfilling some conditions for law-creation. Thus, since all conditions are separately necessary and cumulatively sufficient for norm-creation, even the most insignificant violation results in the failure to create a norm. An unlawful Security Council resolution simply does not exist.

Because the Security Council's resolutions are not subject to a process of derogation and since the International Court of Justice's powers – whatever its precise remit for 'authoritative' ascertainment[137] – do not include the right to derogate (i.e. destroy) a Council resolution, the situation is unclear (as it is for any final organ, cf. Section 6.2.3.3). In the realm of norms, the resolution as norm is valid or is not. It is valid only if the concretisation of the conditions for law-creation chosen by the Council is a possible meaning of that meta-law; it is not if the Council has chosen a meaning that is not covered by the meta-law. To give a concrete example: arguably, the term 'concurring votes' of the permanent members in Article 27(3) can only mean a positive response (a 'yes' vote), not an abstention, because silence does not equal consent. If that is the limit of the possible meanings of that term in Article 27(3) – and, admittedly, it is not even clear what the possible meanings of that term are – no putative resolutions passed with abstentions by permanent members have actually become norms. Yet, as can easily be seen under the Pure Theory's sharp analytical gaze, the problem lies more in our capacity to cognise, i.e. with epistemics. This makes for great *factual* uncertainty and for the *factually* unlimited nature of limits for Council action, as can be seen from the Council's expansive use of the term 'threat to the peace'. Legally speaking, there are restrictions though. If a situation is not a 'threat to the peace, breach of the peace, or act of aggression', it is not. The Pure Theory of Law, however, clarifies the nature of the limits of the Council's powers, of the consequences of *ultra vires* action and identifies perceptibility as the true problem in this respect.

6.4 EVALUATION

The Pure Theory of Law deserves to be more widely know among international lawyers. More importantly, it deserves to be more widely applied to concrete problems of international law. Its 'common legal sense' approach provides a connection of concrete problems of doctrine to its theoretical dimension, more so, it is submitted, than any other theory, because the Pure Theory alone focuses on the *legal* core of these problems. It is thus the ideal theory for those concerned with positive international law, rather than with political ideals.

The Pure Theory's greatest advantage lies in the dual tracks of deconstruction and construction. While many other theories are either proficient at criticising elements of

[137] Unfortunately, a discussion of the Court's potential remit for judicial review cannot be included here.

law from a particular ideology or at constructing an uncritical edifice of law, Kelsen's 'critical' positivism combines both elements – and does so admirably well. In showing no tolerance for the pragmatic fudging of the positive law whenever the strict application of law would not lead to the desired outcome, in uncovering hidden politico-moral elements in scholarship as external to the law in force, and in pointing out the 'real' legal-theoretical dimension behind ostensibly uncomplicated dogmatic arguments, it deconstructs the notion of a clear and pragmatically usable international law. In developing the notion of normative orders based on the dichotomy of Is and Ought, of reality and norm, in hierarchically ordering norms by virtue of the norm-creation relationship and thus constructing a constitution of international law based on points of law rather than perceived necessities of content or in reducing the problems of erroneous law-creation to its legal core, it constructs a scholarship of law based only on the law and clarifies the legal issues and legal problems where they exist and shows many other 'problems' to be caused by extra-legal factors and thus to be void. In this light it is to be hoped that the Kelsen revival mentioned at the beginning of this chapter will strengthen and extend to international legal scholarship.

7 'The holiness of the heart's affection':[1] Philip Allott's theory of Social Idealism

Iain Scobbie

7.1 SETTING THE SCENE

Philip Allott has summarised the aim of his theory of Social Idealism in a pithy aphorism:

> To change fundamentally the social organisation of the world by changing fundamentally the ideas that support the social organisation of the world.[2]

The key features of Allott's Social Idealism are:

> a belief in the capacity of the human mind to transcend itself in thought, to take power over the human future, to choose the human future, to make the human future conform to our ideals, to our best ideas of what we are and what we might be.[3]

As he has repeatedly stated, he seeks 'a revolution in the mind, not in the streets'. This is a recurring slogan in his writings. These comprise his monograph *Eunomia*,[4] numerous

---

[1] From John Keats's letter to Benjamin Bailey dated 22 November 1817: this phrase formed part of the epigraph to Tom Franck's presentation at the celebratory meeting marking Philip Allott's retirement from the University of Cambridge in May 2004, see Franck TM, *The fervent imagination and the school of hard knocks*, 16 European Journal of International Law 343 (2005). The papers presented at this meeting, and an edited transcript of the proceedings, have been published as *Philip Allott's 'Eunomia' and 'The health of nations', Thinking another world: 'This cannot be how the world was meant to be'*, 16 European Journal of International Law 255 (2005) [hereinafter *Thinking another world*]. Apart from Professor Franck's essay, the other contributions to this symposium are Higgins R, *Final remarks*, ibid 347; Knop K, *Eunomia is a woman: Philip Allott and feminism*, ibid 315; Koskenniemi M, *International law as therapy: reading 'The health of nations'*, ibid 329 [hereinafter *International law as therapy*]; and Scobbie I, *Slouching towards the Holy City: some weeds for Philip Allott*, ibid 299 [hereinafter *Slouching towards the Holy City*]. Thanks are due to Philip Allott for copies of unpublished papers; to Jason Beckett, Sarah Hibbin and Alon Margalit for their comments on successive drafts of this chapter; and to Alexander Orakhelashvili for his patience: all deficiencies of content and expression remain mine. This is in fond memory of Tom Franck.

[2] Allott P, *Changing the world*, Fellows Research Talks, Trinity College, Cambridge, 11 March 2009 (unpublished).

[3] Allott P, *The health of nations: society and law beyond the State* (Cambridge University Press, Cambridge, 2002) x [hereinafter *Health of nations*].

[4] *Eunomia: new order for a new world* (Oxford University Press, Oxford, 1990, reprinted 2001) [hereinafter *Eunomia*]. The text of the reprint usefully retains the pagination of the first edition, but is augmented by a lengthy new preface (vii–xl) which summarises the core ideas of Allott's thought and replies to the principal criticisms made to *Eunomia* on its first appearance. The preface constitutes both a restatement and defence of Allott's vision. All subsequent references to *Eunomia* which are expressed in roman numerals refer to the preface to the 2001 reprint.

essays, the most significant of which are collected in *The health of nations* and *Towards the international rule of law*,[5] and two witty subversive novels, *Invisible power* and *Invisible power 2*.[6] The core of Allott's analysis of the international system as it currently exists, and as it has existed for centuries, is that it 'is a form of madness. Not metaphorically or rhetorically, but literally – a mental disease that is self-harming, self-destroying, and may terminate human civilisation.'[7] All is not yet lost, however. Allott claims that there have been five enlightenments in the cultural history of Western Europe since the end of the Roman Empire in the West, each of which has occurred every three centuries, namely: western monasticism in the sixth century, exemplified in the Rule of St Benedict; the Carolingian renaissance of the ninth century, which was centred on the court of Charlemagne; the twelfth-century renaissance based in the University of Paris; that of the fifteenth century which arose in Italy; and the eighteenth-century Enlightenment.[8] Accordingly, should we expect another in the twenty-first century?[9] This cannot be guaranteed. Allott is sceptical of the explanatory power of historicist explanation, although he concedes that: 'historical determinism and astrology will remain popular as long as people need the consoling idea that the future is not wholly unknowable and not wholly in our unreliable hands'.[10] On the other hand, Allott rails against a defeatism which sees the contemporary order of things as inevitable and natural as he is convinced of the transcendent possibilities of the human mind to make new the reality of social and international relations. This is, moreover, a moral necessity: 'how can any morally sensitive person, knowing what happened in the twentieth century and seeing the prospects of the twenty-first century, fail to recognise a heavy burden of moral responsibility to do whatever can be done to improve human reality?'.[11] Humankind may have unreliable hands, but not impotent minds.

Philip Allott's work is complex and challenging in both its substantive content and its mode of expression. It sets out a general (social) philosophy in which law plays an important role, rather than a philosophy of law as such. It is not a narrow pragmatic legal philosophy which aims to improve the functioning of law, nor a heuristic one in the sense that it seeks to provide better or optimal solutions to specific problems.[12] It simply does not fall within recognised categories of theoretical schools of legal philosophy. For instance, it is not an analytical positivist account of the structure of international law.[13] Nor, for that matter, is it 'critical' in the contemporary sense of the broad church which is labelled 'Critical Legal Studies',[14] although it is undoubtedly a work of critical social philosophy. The breadth of Allott's vision, and his idealism, distinguishes his work from

---

5 *Towards the international rule of law: essays in integrated constitutional theory* (Cameron May, London, 2005) [hereinafter *International rule of law*].

6 *Invisible power: a philosophical adventure story* (Xlibris, 2005) [hereinafter *Invisible power 1*] and *Invisible power 2: a metaphysical adventure story* (Xlibris, 2008) [hereinafter *Invisible power 2*].

7 Allott, *Changing the world*, above n. 2.

8 *Health of nations*, 79, ¶3.18 n. 15.

9 See *Health of nations*, chapter 5, 'New enlightenment: the public mind of all-humanity'.

10 See *Health of nations*, chapter 11, 'International law and the idea of history', especially at 331–335, ¶11.34–11.39: quotation at 335, ¶11.39.

11 *Health of nations*, 33, ¶1.62.

12 See *Health of nations*, 45–46, ¶2.23–2.24 and, generally, chapter 2, 'The phenomenon of law'.

13 See *Health of nations*, 47–54, ¶2.27–2.39.

14 See *Health of nations*, 54–55, ¶2.40–2.42.

its peers. It does not examine international law in isolation but rather integrates it within a framework of more fundamental, if not foundational, philosophical issues such as epistemology and the psychology of action. In doing so Allott aims to provide a universal theory, 'offering theoretical explanations which are not merely explanations valid for a given society at a given time'.[15]

Allott's work sets out his vision of *eunomia*, of good social order, which seeks to 're-imagine the human world by proposing a new ideal of international society, the society of all-humanity, the society of all societies'.[16] Associated with this is his *eutopian* project which 'includes the task of reconceiving the way in which we form our ideas, our values, and our purposes'.[17] Allott notes that after the *eunomian* and *eutopian* projects, there remains the *eusophian* project which aims at reconceiving the universal, namely, religion. There are hints of this in Allott's work, but although it is not developed in detail,[18] some commentators have noted its presence.[19]

This introduction to Allott's philosophy of Social Idealism adopts the following structure. The next section discusses the style of his work, and introduces some of his principal recurring themes, and then a brief account is given of one of his key concepts – the idea of the ideal. Following this, Allott's account of the role of the human mind to structure social reality, and its power to restructure that reality, is summarised. An account is then given of his criticism of the existing international order which he blames on the influence of Vattel and castigates as privileging the interests of States or ruling elites over those of humanity as a whole. His antidote to this state of affairs, which lies in the implementation of Social Idealism and indeed the moral imperative to do so, is then examined, along with the role and importance of law in this process. The final section considers some criticisms of Allott's theory.

---

15 *Eunomia*, 192, ¶13.37.

16 See, eg, *Eunomia*, xxvi–xxvii (quotation at xxvi), and also *Health of Nations*, 152–153, ¶5.60–5.61.

17 See *Health of nations*, 153–157, ¶5.63–5.73, quotation at 154, ¶5.64; see also 156, ¶5.70, n. 30.

18 While religion is touched on in *Eunomia* (94–96, ¶6.18–6.23) and *Health of nations* (see 267–268, ¶9.10–9.13 and 354–357, ¶12.33–12.38), the most sustained exposition of this aspect of Allott's thought appears to be in an as yet unpublished paper he presented to the Cambridge University Catholic Graduate Society on 2 November 2009, *The revolutionary potentiality of Catholic Christianity*. In this he drew a 'radical distinction' between Catholic Christianity and the Roman Catholic Church: 'Catholic Christianity is a wonderful thing, *a source of joy and hope*. The Roman Church is a *problem*' (¶39). In this paper Allott called for a coalition of 'all those people who are still able to recognise intellectually the *trancendental dimension* within human existence, whether or not they profess any particular religion' (¶116) in order to reach a new 'understanding of the structural dimensions of human existence' (¶140). This is not a narrowly Christian enterprise, but one which acknowledges that other transcendental religions 'are on the right side in proclaiming a layer of reality and value transcending the harsh reality of the everyday world, and, particularly, the world of the 21st century' (¶124).

19 See, for example, the comments by Sands, Allott, Knop, Franck and Tasioulas in *Thinking another world*, above n. 1, at 267–268, 270 and 286–287.

7.2 READING, AND RE-READING, PHILIP ALLOTT

On reading Philip Allott, one is immediately struck by his unusual style of writing. It is dense, repetitive, and can be hypnotic. There are few simple declarative or propositional sentences. It can be rather daunting to understand, or even to read, until one gets used to it – 'the prose flows and unsettles and flusters and finally threatens to overwhelm: blink, and you might miss it'.[20] Allott's style has attracted comment,[21] but it is an intentional feature of his work:

> As to the style question, the esoteric style, I agree that it is literature one is trying to write. I can't see what the point of academic writing is. But literature is performative in character. The act of doing it is its content . . . The influential books in the world have not been concerned with academic debates. They have been performative events invoking the imagination of the reader to join in.[22]

This idea of philosophy as literature might explain, in whole or in part, Allott's novels, but a paradox is that *Invisible power 1* and *Invisible power 2* both contain extensive references and explanatory notes while *Eunomia*, nakedly, does not.

Eunomia is an unusual book if we consider that it is aimed at an academic audience. It breaks all the rules of academic protocol. It contains neither footnotes, nor bibliography, nor the exegesis of other theories. As Allott states, 'the book does not seek to be taken up into the academic mill of reinterpretations of previous interpretations of thought about social and legal philosophy . . . [I]t contains a theory; it is not a book about theory.'[23] It accordingly contains few express references to other theorists, apart from Vattel. Significantly, the few passing references that are made – to Vitoria, Suarez, Hobbes and Grotius – are contained in the introductory paragraph to Allott's repudiation of the Vattellian conception of international relations.[24] Allott considers that Vattel's influence is a key determinant of the structure of the contemporary world: this is a recurring theme in his work.

MacDonald argues that in *Eunomia*, although Allott can be seen to draw on established philosophical theories, for instance on Hegelian dialectics, because he neither acknowledges them nor refers to works in which they receive a more elaborate formulation and analysis, this shields his argument from criticism – it 'makes the task of criticism both more difficult and less urgent'.[25] Further, he claims that the reader may also be unsettled by Allott's 'relentless creation of new, and problematisation of old, vocabulary throughout the course of his work'. This modulation of meaning combines with the apparent isolation

---

20 MacDonald E, *The rhetoric of Eunomia*, IILJ Working Paper 2008/1 (History and Theory of International Law Series, Institute for International Law and Justice, New York University School of Law, 2008), <www.iilj.org/publications/documents/2008-1.HT.MacDonald.pdf>, 25.

21 See in particular Koskenniemi, *International law as therapy*, above n.1; and MacDonald, *The rhetoric of Eunomia*, above n. 20.

22 Allott, *Thinking another world*, above n. 1, 271.

23 *Eunomia*, l–li.

24 See *Eunomia*, 242–249, ¶13.104–13.107: the 'Rousseau-Kant tradition' is mentioned in ¶13.107 without further explanation, and in opposition to the Vattel tradition.

25 MacDonald, *The rhetoric of Eunomia*, above n. 20, 23.

from academic tradition to deny the reader opportunities to anchor Allott's argument to existing bodies of thought: 'it is easy to feel entirely cast adrift at any number of points'.[26]

The problems that might arise from the absence of reference in *Eunomia* are ameliorated in Allott's later work where he reveals foundational influences drawn from Kant, Marx, Freud, Wittgenstein and, to some extent, Darwin.[27] Nevertheless, the self-enclosed nature of *Eunomia* can be justified by its declared programme that it exists as a theory-in-itself, and is not a book about theory or a re-interpretation of existing theory. Similarly, as we shall see, the modulation of meaning through definition and redefinition that runs rampant throughout Allott's work can be seen as a conscious rhetorical technique aimed at thickening the meaning of the terms used. It is only unsettling in the sense that it calls upon the reader to question and reflect upon his understanding of the text. Allott seldom surrenders his meaning in a single reading: he demands that 'the imagination of the reader . . . join in'.

Although Allott's later work is more candid regarding his intellectual influences, and engages overtly with other writers, nevertheless Koskenniemi's observation remains true that it is difficult 'to situate the work by reference to any academic tradition'.[28] He further observes that this can lead to distrust on the part of the reader:

> it is exceptionally hard to make out how one should react to what on the surface appears as a devastating criticism of the way societies are. This may of course be an aspect of the reader's uncertainty. Suspicious of a text that does not declare its party affiliation on the first page, the reader is invited to perform an exceptionally difficult feat. Decide yourself![29]

Reading (and re-reading) Allott is an exegetical act, and 'like the great writers of the 16th century, the theologians, he numbers his paragraphs'.[30] Koskenniemi observes that this 'suggests that each idea is precisely where it should be. That the world as ideas can be faithfully organised as a totality of paragraphs, divided and subdivided in groups . . . If Philip writes that there are "eight systematic implications of [such] an idea of the social function of law in general", then eight there are, no more and no less . . .'[31] This technique can therefore be seen as having a rhetorically persuasive function that goes beyond the mere structural organisation of the material. It gives the impression of inevitability in the progress of the immediate argument, and of its place in the thesis as a whole.

The appeal to inevitability is bolstered by another aspect of Allott's style, namely, the characterisation of key propositions as self-evident. MacDonald comments that this means that these claims are only as good as their inherent persuasive ability,[32] while

---

26 MacDonald, *The rhetoric of Eunomia*, above n. 20, 25–26.

27 For terse acknowledgements of these influences, see, eg, *Health of nations*, 33, ¶1.64, 98–99, ¶4.2–4.3, 145, ¶5.42, 146–168, ¶5.47–5.49, and 322, ¶11.14.

28 Koskenniemi, *International law as therapy*, above n. 1, 329.

29 Koskenniemi, *International law as therapy*, above n. 1, 330.

30 Anghie, *Thinking another world*, above n. 1, 277. Apart from the novels, the exceptions to this are the preface to the 2001 reprint of *Eunomia* and the essays contained in *International rule of law* which are grouped thematically without sequential numbering.

31 Koskenniemi, *International law as therapy*, above n. 1, 333, note omitted, see also MacDonald, *The rhetoric of Eunomia*, above n. 20, 23.

32 MacDonald, *The rhetoric of Eunomia*, above n. 20, 5.

Koskenniemi sees it as an exclusionary device[33] central to the construction of Allott's authorial voice, which he terms an *effet d'histoire*, 'an effect as if history itself were speaking in his writing', which does not present an argument but which conveys perennial truths. The impression arising from this authorial voice is that 'something larger is being conveyed than mere authorial meanings, that the text itself is part of the stream of historical narrative within which it invites the reader: this was written by reality herself, and not in a disinterested manner but in order to make a normative point'.[34] The dimensions of history – history as individual and collective memory, history as the influence of the past in the present, history as the projection of the past through the present into the future – are a constant presence in Allott's writing. History is multifaceted in its significance and in the consequences it has had, has now, and might have for human society. It is not an overstatement to state that, for Allott, individual and societal attitudes to, and awareness of, history and historical forces are crucial factors in the process which will determine whether humankind flourishes or withers.

Like history, language plays a central role in Allott's work. Language constructs the world – 'The human world is a world of words.' Language is a necessary component of social reality because it allows for communication: 'Connecting the personal mind, where we speak to ourselves in isolation, to the interpersonal and social minds, and by integrating the personal and social minds with the spiritual mind, language has made the human species what it is for-itself and what the universe of all-that-is is for us human beings'.[35] Nevertheless, there are limitations on our capacity to communicate which thus constrain the possibilities of constructing social reality – 'In becoming conscious of language as a non-transparent, non-neutral, reflexive medium, we are able also to see better the role which *truth* and *value* play as ultimate structural axes in the making of human reality.'[36]

Allott's work consciously plays on the limitations of language, and in particular its imprecision.[37] Language is not univocal: each word carries a range of meaning. Language is accordingly inherently ambiguous. The Polish-Belgian rhetorical theorist Chaïm Perelman illustrated the non-univocity of language using the notion of apparent tautology such as 'boys will be boys' or 'business is business'. To give these intelligible meaning, different interpretations must be given to the repeated terms, whereas in formal logical systems propositions such as these would be meaningless because of the systemic requirement of the principle of identity which requires that terms be univocal: let $x = x$ conveys no information, apart from the postulate that x is, indeed, x.[38] Allott exploits the

---

33 Koskenniemi, *International law as therapy*, above n. 1, 335.

34 Koskenniemi, *International law as therapy*, above n. 1, 332–333, quotations at 333: see also MacDonald, *The rhetoric of Eunomia*, above n. 20, 28–30.

35 *Health of nations*, 78–79, ¶3.16–3.17.

36 *Health of nations*, 147, ¶5.49: see also 7, ¶1.11.

37 On the consequences of the imprecision of natural language for law, see *Health of nations*, 296–297, ¶10.16.

38 See, for instance, Perelman Ch and Olbrechts-Tyteca L, *The new rhetoric: a treatise on argumentation* (University of Notre Dame Press, Notre Dame, 1969: translation of *La nouvelle rhétorique: traité de l'argumentation*, Presses Universitaires de France, 1958) 216–218 and §51, 442–443, §94; Perelman Ch, *Logique juridique: nouvelle rhétorique* (Dalloz, Paris, 1976) 114–116, ¶56bis; and also his *Justice, law and argument: essays on moral and legal reasoning* (Reidel, Dordrecht, 1980) 97 and 126.

equivocal nature of natural language, the multiple meanings of words, through the use of repetition which relies on subtle shifts in the meaning of the terms employed. This, in turn, extends the definition of these terms and is an aspect of the 'relentless creation of new, and problematisation of old, vocabulary' to which MacDonald refers.[39] The result is a style of writing which can be rather hypnotic and, as Koskenniemi notes, a rhythm arises from the syntax and repetition Allott deploys.[40] For example, consider the following passage:

> A society does not have a constitution. A society is a constituting, an unceasing process of self-creating. A society constitutes itself simultaneously in three dimensions – as ideas, as practice, and as law. Each society, including the international society of all-humanity, the society of all societies, is a unique but ever-changing product of its threefold self-constituting. In its *ideal* constitution, a society presents its becoming to itself as actuality and potentiality, forming a *reality-for-itself* which includes its *history*; its self-explanatory *theories* and its *ideals*. In its *real* constitution, the willing and acting of individual human beings is socialised as they exercise *social power* in the course of their personal self-constituting. In its *legal* constitution, social power is given the form of *legal power*, so that the willing and acting of individual human beings may serve the *common interest* of society in its self-constituting.[41]

The key term in this paragraph is obviously 'constitution', but consider how its meaning mutates. The first use seems counter-intuitive: to say that a society does not have a constitution seems odd, as one could argue that most societies are governed by reference to some foundational legal document(s), in other words, by a constitution. But, as the second sentence makes clear, this is not the meaning the term is initially intended to bear, nor is it its primary meaning. A more corporeal understanding is intended: a constitution in the sense of the structure and functioning of the body politic, but there is no uniform template – each society has to fashion its own. This act of self-creation (of self-constitution) has three aspects, and is never finished because the *ideal* constitution is essentially aspirational as it guides the future development of the society. The *real* constitution lies in the daily life of the individuals who compose the given society, the aggregation and integration of the activities they undertake in the pursuit of their own ends. Only the third aspect, the *legal* constitution, approximates to the lawyer's common understanding of 'constitution'.

7.3 THREES AND TWOS – AND TOWARDS THE IDEAL

It is worth pointing out a further rhetorical feature of this passage which is common in Allott's work. He often splits a concept or a general term into three parts – a triad. This has a resemblance to the rhetorical 'rule of three' which is often employed in political discourse as well as in literature:[42] in classical rhetoric, this is termed a tricolon. This may be a chance phenomenon in Allott's writing style rather than a conscious choice, as not all concepts are split into triads. For example, he argues that there are four levels of reality

---

39 See MacDonald, *The rhetoric of Eunomia*, above n. 20, 25–26.

40 See Koskenniemi, *International law as therapy*, above n. 1, 331–332.

41 *Health of nations*, 79–80, ¶3.19: emphasis in original, note omitted.

42 On the rule of three in contemporary political discourse, see Atkinson M, *Our masters' voices: the language and body language of politics* (Routledge, London, 1984).

of the human world: the so-called *real reality* which comprises 'the world of power, war, murder, diplomacy, marriage, procreation, society, law'; *philosophical reality*, which is the world made by the mind and the mental construction of concepts – 'good is good, and evil is evil because thinking makes them so'; *psychological reality*, which lies in interpersonal relationships and 'normal and abnormal states of mind'; and *imaginary reality* 'where the world's a stage and we make reality out of dreams and the imaginative power of language, where everything is possible'.[43]

In contrast, Allott is much more explicit in his reliance on the use of contrasting or opposing pairs in the construction of his argument.[44] He sees this duality as a natural, and possibly biological, propensity of the human mind which in philosophy is expressed in dialectical thought:

> What may be an aspect of the physiology of the human brain, which has determined the functioning of the human mind, and which has been reproduced in the structure of human language through the long process of socialising, has given to human reality a peculiarly *dualistic* structure – life and death, being and nothing, appearance and reality, essence and existence, mind and matter, good and evil, pleasure and pain, true and false, the past and the future, the actual and the potential.[45]

Of these contrasting pairs, the most important for the realisation of *eunomia* is that of 'the actual and the potential' which has 'allowed us to make human reality into a moral order in which the actual can pass judgement upon itself by reference to its better potentiality, which is the ideal'.[46] The never-ending quest for the ideal, the pursuit of the aspirational, is the central message of Allott's philosophy of Social Idealism. This encompasses a set of interlocking propositions, namely: a belief in the reality of the human mind; that the human mind is capable of reconstructing reality in the form of ideas; that the human mind is capable to share consciousness not only in interpersonal relations but also in society, which he sees as an organised sharing of consciousness; and that the human mind can determine individual and social human behaviour in terms of ideals.[47]

The potential for human self-creation, and thus the self-constituting of human societies, accordingly, lies in the ideal. This occurs when the mind evaluates the present by reference to a possible imagined future state of affairs which it thinks is better. Quite simply, the human mind has the power to form the future by imagining what that future should be, and then to use reason to implement this idea. Ideas, however, are not self-executing as consciousness only 'enables us to present possibilities to ourselves before we take action'.[48] Action depends on choice, on an act of will, whose exercise depends on values to serve 'as a ground for choosing between possibilities'.[49] Among 'the ideas which help constitute a society are ideas of a particular kind', namely ideals:

---

[43] *Invisible power 1*, 128.
[44] For a general discussion of this technique, see Perelman and Olbrechts-Tyteca, *The new rhetoric*, above n. 38, chapter 4.
[45] *Health of nations*, 82–83, ¶3.25.
[46] *Health of nations*, 83, ¶3.26.
[47] *Invisible power 1*, 140.
[48] *Eunomia*, 40–41, ¶3.8.
[49] *Eunomia*, 48, ¶3.27.

> Our ideals allow us to say what is wrong with our world and to imagine ways in which it could be better, and they inspire us to want to make a better world . . . A society which did not contain the idea of the ideal would be, at best, a static society or, more probably, a self-destroying society. It is for this reason that we look anxiously and hopefully for any signs of the idealizing of international society, a society whose long pre-history . . . has been filled with the follies and the evils perpetrated by holders of public power.[50]

Progress towards this better future is dependent upon a moral choice: the decision to take action to realise this concept of the ideal.[51] The parameters of the ideal are determined by human imagination as it contemplates the present, but the re-imagination of the actual state of affairs is a constant process which lies in the 'dialectical *negation* of the actual which nevertheless affirms a *potentiality* of the actual. The ideal is the perfectability of the actual.'[52]

This process could be mundane: it could simply be the realisation that a specific problem exists which needs to be addressed, and the consequent formulation of a proposed solution. While this piecemeal approach surely is implicated in the realisation of the ideal, in Allott's work, the principal emphasis is much more ambitious than a mere incremental tinkering with social conditions, presented in the guise of discrete particular issues. He aims to transcend and transform existing social structures – 'To change fundamentally the social organisation of the world by changing fundamentally the ideas that support the social organisation of the world'.[53]

7.4 THINKING, AND RETHINKING, THE WORLD

Accordingly, at the heart of Allott's project lies an ultimate conviction in the power of ideas both to structure and to change – to restructure – the world: 'We make the human world, including human institutions, through the power of the human mind. What we have made by thinking we can make new by new thinking.'[54] Societies create themselves on the basis of ideas – 'Each human society is an infinitely complex and dynamic structure of ideas. The health of a society, its degree of well-being, is determined by the ideas which take actual effect in the process of its day-to-day self-constituting as a society. To reform or redeem a society is to change those determining ideas. Our quality of life is a function of the quality of our ideas.'[55] Human consciousness accordingly provides the template for human reality and thus human action.

Allott employs a wide notion of 'society' which encompasses human groups which range from the family through the State to the 'international society of the whole human race' – 'the society of all societies'. The feature common to all is that they are ultimately constituted through the operation of the human mind. The public mind of a society (or social consciousness) operates in ways akin to that of individuals, but also in ways

---

50 *Eunomia,* xxii.
51 *Health of nations*, 81, ¶3.22.
52 *Health of nations*, 156, ¶5.70.
53 *Changing the world*, above n. 2.
54 *Eunomia*, xxvii.
55 *Health of nations*, x.

peculiar to itself.[56] A significant difference, for example, is that a society's public mind, while resulting from the product of 'particular human minds at particular moments in time', persists through time and provides the environment in which not only that society's self-consciousness is formed and mutates but also provides the environment in which the minds of society-members are formed:[57] 'Societies live within the theories they make. A society generates a theory-filled reality which shapes its willed action which, in turn, shapes its actual everyday living.'[58] National self-consciousness, and specifically national identity, is constituted through received historical narratives and ideas of tradition and values which are transmitted down through generations – 'We are as we are because we have been as we were.' It is also constructed in opposition to others – 'We are who we are because, fortunately, we are not as other peoples are.' This might, in turn, impact on the personal identity of individuals – 'I am as I am because we are who we are.'[59]

National identity is, however, only one aspect of the broad social public mind or societal self-consciousness: 'The "end of ideology" was a thing people hoped for in the twentieth century. By "ideology" they meant the social enforcement of big ideas. But one thing we have learned is that you cannot escape ideology. All societies enforce big ideas.'[60] Society's ideas are, moreover, idea-forces as they are ideas which have the power to control human lives:[61]

> The monopolising of a society's mental power is as much a threat to its freedom as the monopolising of its political or economic power. A failure in the creative energy of a society's mental production, a decline in the value of its gross mental product, is likely to be a symptom, sometimes even a cause, of that society's general decay.[62]

To counter this danger the solution lies within the mind: 'the only power over power is the power of ideas'.[63]

Allott's social idealist theory aims at realising for humanity 'the natural human purpose of survival and prospering'.[64] This is rooted in 'the wonderful capacity of human consciousness to make the future other than it has been . . . to choose its future from all the possibilities which imagination can conceive and which reason can order'.[65] This requires humanity 'to take possession of the waste-land of international society in the name of the people and in the name of justice'[66] as, in the contemporary situation of 'a semi-social international society, all the world is the Wild West'.[67] Allott adheres to the fundamental belief that:

---

56 See *Health of nations*, 72–74, ¶3.6–3.9: see also *Catholic Christianity*, above n. 18, ¶147–150.

57 *Health of nations*, 76–77, ¶3.14, and see chapter 14, *The nation as mind politic: the making of the public mind.*

58 *Eunomia*, 38, ¶2.64.

59 *Health of nations*, 109–110, ¶4.27–4.31: but see 109–121, ¶4.27–4.55.

60 *Health of nations*, 136, ¶5.15.

61 *Health of nations*, 63, ¶2.64.

62 *Health of nations*, 9, ¶1,16.

63 Allott, *Changing the world*, above n. 2.

64 *Eunomia*, 387, ¶18.30.

65 *Eunomia*, 265, ¶15.13.

66 *Eunomia*, 254, ¶14.1.

67 *Eunomia*, 383, ¶18.21.

> international society has the ultimate capacity to enable all societies to promote the ever-increasing well-being of themselves and their members, the ultimate responsibility to prevent societies from doing harm to themselves and to other societies. It is in international society that humanity's capacity to harm itself can achieve its most spectacular effects. And it is in international society that the ever-increasing well-being of the whole human race can, must, and will be promoted.[68]

At the root of Allott's explanation is the notion of consciousness, the active power of the human mind to determine the course of human affairs – 'In forming our ideas we form our reality. In forming our reality we form our consciousness. In forming our consciousness we form ourselves.'[69] This notion has obvious affinities with the Marxist theory of ideology, but Allott's version is neither determinist nor limited to manipulations of the economic base/superstructure relationship. For Allott, consciousness can critique and transcend social circumstances, but the implementation of that critique is a matter of choice rather than historical determinism. This seems to be more redolent of Kant's argument that theory guides practice[70] than Marx.

On the other hand, like many Marxist theorists, Allott places a premium on the role of the intellectual in effecting social change – 'We can't wait for the Workers of the World to Unite. We, the ruling class, must do the revolutionary job ourselves.'[71] He describes himself as 'a High Tory Bolshevik',[72] as a 'conservative revolutionary is much like a socialist revolutionary. The one wants a new order of things formed from perfecting the best of the old order. The other wants a new order of things formed from the destruction of the worst of the old order.' The High Tory Bolshevik is 'a revolutionary of both kinds – passionate lover of the best of the old, passionate hater of the worst of the old'.[73] Despite its revolutionary connotations, Allott's theory is nevertheless professedly an elite theory, or a theory for elites:

> To change human consciousness is to change human reality. To change human reality is to change the course of human history. It follows that, if it is our purpose to make a new human reality, we must find a way to stimulate the self-consciousness, the sense of social responsibility, the moral awareness, and the intellectual creativity of the ruling class . . . and, especially, of those who hold responsible positions in the mental service-industries – religion, politics, administration, commerce, the law, mathematics and the natural sciences, literature and the fine arts, the media of information and entertainment. It is they whose responsibility is not merely

---

[68] *Eunomia*, 180, ¶12.5.

[69] *Eunomia*, 28, ¶2.37.

[70] Kant I, *On the common saying: 'This may be true in theory, but it does not apply in practice'* (1793), in Reiss H (ed.), *Kant's political writings* (Cambridge University Press, Cambridge, 1970) 61: translated by Nisbet HB.

[71] Allott, *Changing the world*, above n. 2.

[72] Robert Jennings, former President of the International Court of Justice, either described Allott as a 'Tory revolutionary' (see Allott, *Thinking another world*, above n. 1, 271) or as a 'Tory Bolshevik' (see Allott, *Changing the world*, above n. 2) – although Allott noted there that this description was only 'True in parts. "High Tory Bolshevik" would be better.' See also Kennedy D, *Remarks for the 'New governance workshop', Harvard Law School, February 25–26, 2005*, <www.law.harvard.edu/faculty/dkennedy/speeches/Remarks.pdf> 2: 'My Cambridge friend Philip Allott – who styles himself a Bolshevik Tory – likes to say we are living in "pre-revolutionary times".'

[73] *Invisible power 1*, 48: I thank Philip Allott for pointing out this descriptor.

> to imagine a new human reality but also to transform the human world as it is into the human world as it will be.[74]

Allott's avowed aim is manifestly revolutionary. History is replete with examples of change, where societies have adopted new methods not only in the distribution and exercise of social power (that is, in their *real* constitution), but also in their *ideal* constitution which embodies their ethos and ambition and thus is their repository of societal values. These revolutionary changes start as revolutions in the mind, made manifest in 'moments of human self-enlightenment which transform the potentiality and actuality of those societies'. Allott thinks that international society is capable of a similar act of revolutionary self-renovation and that there is 'every reason, derived from the lamentable history of its own self-constituting, why it should find a new potentiality for human self-creating at the level of all-humanity, the self-evolving of the human species, a revolution in the human species-mind':[75]

> there are remarkable precedents for humanity's self-civilising – the abolition of judicial torture, of maiming as a legal penalty, of burning at the stake, of public executions, of the slave trade, of slavery, of apartheid, of capital punishment. All of those practices had seemed natural and inevitable to very many people for a very long time. But some people, at a particular moment, began to say: 'No. Humanity's humanity must not be equated with what humanity customarily does.' And eventually the abolitionists won, and human behaviour was changed.[76]

But why does Allott see a need for a revolution in international affairs?

7.5 'THIS CANNOT BE HOW THE WORLD WAS MEANT TO BE'[77]

Allott squarely blames the failings, if not the criminality, of international society on the influence of Vattel:[78]

---

[74] *Health of nations*, 4–5, ¶1.3: see also Allott, *Thinking another world*, above n. 1, 271 – 'Thinking, as Adam Ferguson suggested [in *An essay on the history of civil society* (1767), §II.1], has become a sort of specialised activity of a few people' (note omitted). To give Allott his due, however, he then comments 'We have to recover the idea that thinking people are not a special caste, that thinking is not a special craft, but part of the very fabric of existence.' Nonetheless, in *Invisible power 2*, one character comments 'The minds of the masses are not their own. They are mind-slaves held in the iron cages made by mind-masters who corrupt and dehumanise them with a diet of junk education, junk politics, junk religion, junk information, junk entertainment, junk ideas.' The antidote to this, at least in the novel, is the Movement of Thinking Humans – see *Invisible power 2*, chapter 19: quotation at 119.

[75] *Health of nations*, 81, ¶3.21.

[76] *International rule of law*, 401.

[77] At his retirement conference on 28 May 2004, Allott noted that the next day was the 551st anniversary of the Sack of Constantinople on 29 May 1453. This date is generally regarded as marking the start of the Italian renaissance because many scholars then moved from Constantinople to Italy. 29 May 1953 was Allott's 16th birthday,'and when you are at that age you think such things are significant'. On his birthday, he experienced an epiphany – 'I remember saying, and I wrote on a piece of paper: "this is not how the world was meant to be". That became the project of my life, that sentence: what I have done since derives from that moment of enlightenment' – Allott, *Thinking another world*, above n. 1, 260.

[78] Emmerich de Vattel (1714–1767) was a Swiss-born diplomat whose major work, *Droit des gens: ou, principes de la loi naturelle appliqués à la conduite et aux affaires des nations et des*

> The eventually dominant Vattel tradition is not merely a tradition of international law. It implies a pure theory of the whole nature of international society and hence of the whole nature of the human social condition; and it generates practical theories[79] which rule the lives of all societies, of the whole human race. It is nothing but mere words, mere ideas, mere theory, mere values – and yet war and peace, human happiness and human misery, human wealth and human want, human lives and human life have depended on them for two centuries and more. [80]

Allott argues that the Vattellian conception of international relations supplied the philosophical foundations of 'international unsociety', a world governed by and tailored to the interests of States, or perhaps more accurately to the interests of ruling national elites (which he terms the *hofmafia*),[81] rather than to the interests of humanity as a whole. Just as the State is not coextensive with the national society, international unsociety, where States dominate, is markedly less representative of humanity.

Vattel's *Droit des gens* 'was on the desk of every diplomat for a century or more. It was a book which formed the minds of those who formed international reality, the international reality which is still our reality today.'[82] Although Vattel conceded that there was a universal society of humanity governed by the law of nature, he claimed that this changed with the emergence of States and consequently 'the ancient idea of a natural society of all human beings [was] simply side-lined in international social consciousness'.[83] Allott identifies the following as the crucial passage in *Droit des gens*:

> [W]hen men have agreed to act in common, and have given up their rights and submitted their will to the whole body as far as concerns the common good, it devolves thenceforth upon that body, the State [*l'Etat*], and upon its rulers, to fulfil the duties of humanity towards outsiders in all matters in which individuals are no longer at liberty to act and it peculiarly rests with the State to fulfil these duties towards other States.[84]

Allott claims that Vattel 'made the myth of the state of nature into the metaphysics of the law of nations',[85] and thus used the theory of State sovereignty to reject the possibility of a natural society among States.[86]

---

souverains (*The law of nations, or the principles of natural law applied to the conduct and to the affairs of nations and of sovereigns*) was published in 1758.

[79] Allott's distinction between practical and pure theories is that a practical theory is society's way of explaining to itself or justifying the actions it takes, the choices it makes, and its social arrangements. A pure theory lies behind the practical theory as it is the way it explains its practical theory, for example, a theocracy would explain itself in terms of the religion to which it adheres. Allott classifies *Eunomia* as an essay in pure theory, while *Health of nations* is an account of a practical theory which implements that pure theory. See *Eunomia*, 31–38, ¶2.49–2.64, and *Health of nations*, x–xi, 80–81, ¶3.20, and 344–346, ¶12.6–12.7.

[80] *Eunomia*, 243, ¶13.105.

[81] See *Health of nations*, chapter 13, *International law and the international hofmafia*: and also *International rule of law*, chapter 8, *The emerging international aristocracy*. The term *hofmafia* is drawn from the diplomatic machinations of royal and aristocratic courts and translates as 'court-mafia' (see *Health of nations*, 384, ¶13.9), *diplo-mafia* is a term which perhaps has a more contemporary resonance, and was used by Allott in *Thinking another world*, above n. 1, 296.

[82] *Health of nations*, 416, ¶14.45.

[83] *Health of nations*, 329, ¶11.29.

[84] Quoted *Health of nations*, 413–414, ¶14.42.

[85] *Health of nations*, 58, ¶2.47.

[86] *Health of nations*, 415–416, ¶14.44.

This 'strange idea' of the state of nature had been instrumental in the transformation of some societies in the seventeenth and eighteenth centuries – 'Epistemically dubious, historical only in form and suspiciously convenient in its content, the idea of the state of nature made possible the creation-myth of social contract theory, a theory about the origin of human society in general.' This theory was practically useful at that time because it met the needs of a 'deep-structural social transformation' as 'the displacement of social power in favour of a newly dominant social class needed a displacement of old theories about the source of ultimate social authority – whether God, the King or tradition'. It was not, however, applied in international relations as domestic power elites decided that there was no need to extend this changed nature of social relationships to the international sphere – 'an old-regime ruling-class managed to retain its dominance over international social consciousness, long after it had lost dominance over social consciousness within some national societies'.[87] Thus international unsociety remained 'a constitution-free zone', 'a form of co-existence which was clearly not a society, with only the most crude of organising systems (diplomacy, war)':

> And international unsociety was evidently a morality-free zone, in which moral discourse had only a marginal rhetorical or tactical function, and the only recognised ethical imperative was a self-judging machiavellian princely virtue. For the controllers of the national public realms and their apologists, an international public realm without law or justice seemed to be a state of nature of the most exciting kind, in which the survival of the fittest is decided by an intoxicating mixture of urbane diplomacy and mass murder.[88]

This was the inevitable outcome of the reception of Vattellian thought which came to structure the practice of international affairs as a result of the Congress of Vienna (1815) – 'the last great party of the old order dancing on its own grave':[89]

> It is a reality which was welcome to the ruling classes of western Europe, the classes who still had most control over social reality-forming, including the self-conceiving of society in theory and including reality forming far beyond the territorial limits of western Europe. It was most welcome of all to the political and administrative sections of those ruling classes, who could speak to each other and compete with each other across frontiers, safe in the fastnesses of their self-contained internal-external state-systems.[90]

The Vattellian tradition, precisely because of its emphasis on the State as the primary actor and bearer of values in international relations is an anathema to Allott.

> The state (public realm under the authority of a government) having developed as a way of internally organizing a certain sort of society . . . came to be conceived also as the external manifestation of the given societies. The state was turned inside out, like a glove. The governments of the statally organizing societies recognize in each other that which is state, not that which is society.[91]

---

87 *Health of nations*, 328–330, ¶11.27–11.29.
88 *Health of nations*, 295, ¶10.11.
89 *Health of nations*, 382, ¶13.5.
90 *Eunomia*, 248–249, ¶13.106.
91 *Eunomia*, 243, ¶13.105(1).

This tradition has generated a wrong consciousness, a fundamental misconception about what matters. For Allott, what matters is humanity rather than a collection of States, and the pursuit of States' interests has all too often harmed humans:

> The holders of public-realm power, kings and public officials, could identify their self-interest with the public interest of the One they so nobly served, and could, by force or mind-manipulation, induce the people to suppose that it was their patriotic and moral duty to kill and be killed by their neighbours on behalf of their own so-called commonwealths.[92]

Perhaps cynically, but definitely wryly, Allott recounts 'a lesson which is as old as human society. The only constant in human social history is the ruthless self-protecting of social privilege. The only human right which is universally enforced is the right of the rich to get richer.'[93]

The problem, however, lies not so much with the State as such, but with governing elites.[94] The State has an important role to play in facilitating the inter-play and reconciliation of individuals, social organisation and the common interest. The Vattelian tradition, however, conceives the State as an organ of public power which is both hierarchically superior to and in competition with (if not opposition to) other *loci* of public power and private interest. The State is thus divorced from the society to which it gives formal expression, and the effects of this are intensified in international relations.[95] As Tasioulas has noted, while it may be argued that international law should be responsive to the interests of humans, the best way of serving these interests might be through norms which are predominantly addressed to States.[96]

Nevertheless, the conduct of international affairs through State-centred mechanisms had the result that sovereignty, which projects 'an authority-based view of society', became the structural premise of international affairs. This: 'tend[s] to make all society seem to be essentially a system of authority, and . . . to make societies incorporating systems of authority seem to be the most significant forms of society, at the expense of all other forms of society, including non-patriarchal families, at one extreme, and international society, at the other'.[97] The consequence is that this State-centred international system alienates people from international law which 'seems to be the business of a foreign realm, another world, in which they play no personal part.'[98] It is something, at best, imposed upon them and not something in which they participate, nor forge through the force of their consciousness. Thus the dominant perception has arisen that domestic and international affairs are 'intrinsically and radically separate'[99] as citizens

---

92 *Health of nations*, 89, ¶3.41.

93 *Health of nations*, 92, ¶3.46.

94 Making a fetish of the State is a criticism Allott made of my earlier attempt to give an account of his theory in *Slouching towards the Holy City* – see Allott, *Thinking another world*, above n. 1, 264 – 'I have not joined the end-of-sovereignty movement. Everyone knows that the state is going to go on in some sense.'

95 See Allott, *Thinking another world*, above n. 1, 264.

96 Tasioulas, *Thinking another world*, above n. 1, 262.

97 *Eunomia*, 200, ¶12.54.

98 *Eunomia*, 298–299, ¶16.8.

99 *Eunomia*, 243, ¶13.105(1).

can only participate in international affairs through the mediation of their governments. International law has not been integrated into the social process of humanity and is 'doomed to be what it has been – marginal, residual, and intermittent'.[100] As things stand, 'international law is left speaking to governments the words that governments want to hear'[101] and remains marginal in the international system: 'International law has been neither very threatening nor very useful to the politicians and the diplomats.'[102] This is not the way things should be, as law is a core institution of society, 'an integral part of the whole activity of consciousness, individual and social'.[103] In current circumstances, this alienated international law cannot play its proper part in the realization of *eunomia* – 'the good order of a self-ordering society'.

International unsociety has chosen 'to regard itself as the state externalized, undemocratized, and unsocialized'.[104] The purposes pursued in the world of States are those of States: 'purposes related to the survival and prospering of each of those state-societies rather than the survival and prospering of an international society of the whole human race'.[105] Morality has thus become discontinuous between the domestic and international spheres,[106] and governments are able to act internationally free from the moral restraints that constrain them in domestic affairs, 'murdering human beings by the million in wars, tolerating oppression and starvation and disease and poverty, human cruelty and suffering, human misery and human indignity':[107] 'we have witnessed countless examples of realities, both religious and political, whose inner perspective was absolute moral certainty and whose outer expression was morally outrageous behaviour'.[108] Despite the exclusion of wider humanity from the consciousness and thus the conduct of international relations, despite the dissociation of the national and the international, despite the self-serving immorality of ruling elites, humanity is somehow strangely resilient:

> It is remarkable that the human species has managed to survive for almost 250 years in the grip of the bizarre Vattelian legal world-view. In the twentieth century, the crazy idea that the human race might not survive was treated as a suitable topic for rational discussion and rational decision-making. People who are otherwise sane and sensible could talk about Mutually Assured Destruction and the End of Civilisation. People who are otherwise sane and sensible could make and manage total war, wars with no necessary geographical limit, no effective limit to the methods of death and destruction, no limit to the suffering to be endured by powerless and blameless human beings. In the twentieth century, people who are otherwise decent and caring could regard it as regrettable, but natural that countless millions of human beings should live in conditions of life which are a permanent insult to their humanity, or in chaotic societies dignified by the name of 'state', or in subjection to criminal conspiracies dignified by the name of 'government'.[109]

---

[100] *Eunomia*, 304, ¶16.17.
[101] *Eunomia*, 296, ¶16.1.
[102] *Eunomia*, 297, ¶16.3.
[103] *Eunomia*, 171, ¶11.12.
[104] *Eunomia*, 240, ¶13.98.
[105] *Eunomia*, 247, ¶13.105(13).
[106] *Eunomia*, 244, ¶13.105(6).
[107] *Eunomia*, 248, ¶13.105(16).
[108] *Health of nations*, 28, ¶1.51.
[109] *Health of nations*, 56–57, ¶2.44.

7.6 FROM LAKE GENEVA TO THE FINLAND STATION[110]

How does Allott, the self-identifying 'High Tory Bolshevik', propose that this situation should be remedied? How can we reform the situation in which we find ourselves, where we live in: 'a world [only] fit for governments . . . an unsociety ruled by a collective of self-conceived sovereigns whose authority is derived neither from the totality of international society nor from the people but from the inter-mediating state-systems'?[111] How can *eunomia* be realised?

The reconstruction and amelioration of the international system is, for Allott, a moral imperative as 'international society has produced a diseased social reality, a pyschopathic condition which threatens the survival of the human species'.[112] This state of affairs has come about because of the duality of human societies where international society is in practice isolated from national social systems; in the realm of ideas international and national realities are separate; and the development of international law has been isolated and insulated from developments in national legal systems.[113] National societies – States – have turned inward, preoccupied with their own interests which they selfishly pursue, unduly disregarding those of the universal society of all-humanity. A governing standard of accountability which may appraise States' conduct is absent:

> Society produces its own idea of *evil* as it condemns *sin* and punishes *crime* . . . But, if society is to be the judge of evil, who is to be the judge of society? In the light of our experience of the long and tempestuous twentieth century, it is this question which has become the crux of a new form of the problem of evil.[114]

There is a disjunction between the moral values that govern domestic and international relations, which unshackle governmental behaviour externally in a way that could not be contemplated internally. The governing elites of States have used

> the language of law to dignify, as right and duty, the self-seeking of those who could continue to behave externally as if they were *ancien régime* monarchs, more or less free from the tiresome requirements of political or moral accountability, free from the burden of any form of self-justification beyond the anti-morality of *reason of state*.[115]

This is an anathema to Allott who claims that for human individuals and human societies, there is only one moral order – 'The moral order does not contain political frontiers.'[116] In consequence, Allott wonders:

---

110 At times, Allott rails against 'the fantasy-forms of popular culture' (see, eg, *Health of nations*, 14, ¶1.24): while this sub-heading might make one think of Lenin, and therefore Bolshevism, it is also a line in the lyric of the Pet Shop Boys' song *West End girls*, just as the earlier phrase *Let x = x* was taken from Laurie Anderson's song of the same name, and although some might argue that Laurie Anderson is hardly popular, she should be.

111 *Eunomia*, 249, ¶13.109.

112 *Health of nations*, 88, ¶3.38.

113 *Health of nations*, 88–89, ¶3.39.

114 *Health of nations*, 63, ¶2.64.

115 *Health of nations*, 90, ¶3.43.

116 *Health of nations*, 90, ¶3.42: see also 69, ¶2.79 and 95, ¶3.53.

> how can any morally sensitive person, knowing what happened in the twentieth century and seeing the prospects of the twenty-first century, fail to recognise a heavy burden of moral responsibility to do whatever can be done to improve human reality? Must we deny our feelings of righteous *anger* at the social evil that plagues the human world, of *pity* for the immeasurable suffering caused by the acts and omissions of holders of public power, of invincible *hope* that a better human world is possible?[117]

Societies, like individuals, know good but do evil, but how can individuals take power over the power of society to do evil? If we believe that the power of the human mind cannot transcend the existing social systems it created, this accords these systems 'a moral omnipotence' which results in 'a form of human self-dehumanising'.[118] Social systems, and the conditions they have created, must be transcended by the power of the human mind.

The notion of the ideal allows us to transform societies, and we have a moral duty to make a better human future.[119] Because individual consciousness creates national consciousness, we have a moral responsibility for the content of that national consciousness,[120] and the role of the ideal is to evaluate the current conditions to determine a better future. The bridge between the past and the future lies in the present, which thus is pivotal in influencing the move from the actual to the potential. Living in the present entails responsibility – 'the permanent and inescapable burden of choosing the future, of choosing what to do next'.[121] For individuals and societies, the passage of time is a process of becoming but it is also a process of choosing to become. Humans are moral beings because we cannot avoid the charge of choosing, of deciding how to act. We have a moral responsibility regarding the future, and how it is to be shaped.[122] We cannot, however, be sure that a chosen projected future will come in to being: 'We can make the future but we cannot determine it. What will be will be what we do, but not only what we do. The future will also be made by the willing and acting of other human beings and other human societies.'[123] When public interest permits no other course of action, governments and officials will continue to do evil – 'To do evil is to do good, if that is their professional duty, as they understand their duty' – and their self-justification of the course of conduct adopted will become increasingly more sophisticated as challenges become more sophisticated. 'Legalism breeds legalism. Legalism does not, and cannot, redeem.'[124] The disorder of an evil social order can only be overcome by a higher moral order – 'The actual is made better only by the power of negation which is present in our knowledge of the good.'[125]

In this process of re-envisioning society, law – but not legalism – plays a key role. Legalism is a perversion of the law, and Allott sees it as an unfortunate and persistent feature of the current international unsociety of States:

117 *Health of nations*, 33, ¶1.62.
118 *Health of nations*, 64, ¶2.65.
119 *Health of nations*, 96, ¶3.54.
120 *Health of nations*, 115–116, ¶4.44.
121 *Health of nations*, 72, ¶3.4.
122 *Health of nations*, 133, ¶5.3.
123 *Health of nations*, 71, ¶3.2: see 71, ¶3.1–3.3.
124 *Health of nations*, 68, ¶2.76.
125 *Health of nations*, 68, ¶2.77.

> Legal festishism and legal scepticism are rife, not least among governments which have traditionally supported, and profited from, the Rule of Law. They are two faces of a legal cynicism which, as the occasion demands, either overvalues or undervalues law. It is interesting to compare and contrast two forms of behaviour: strong support for the massive legal edifice of the World Trade Organisation and perverse interpretations of the Geneva Conventions or the Torture Convention.[126]

In contrast to legalism, law is the optic for the realisation of the ideal and of the common interest. Allott argues that 'a society constitutes itself simultaneously in three dimensions – as ideas, as practice, and as law',[127] but, in this process of self-constitution, law transforms ideas into practice while ensuring both social continuity and change. Law is not only a means of social restraint but also the most reliable means of social liberation, as by distributing social power in the form of legal power, it sets out the legal limits of social power. Law also embodies societal values whose function is to control the substantive and procedural content of law:[128]

> Law, including international law, has a threefold social function. Law carries the structures and systems of society through time. Law inserts the common interest of society into the behaviour of society-members. Law establishes possible futures for society, in accordance with society's theories, values and purposes.
> Law is a presence of the social past. Law is an organising of the social present. Law is a conditioning of the social future.[129]

Law is not a system of legal rules but one of legal relationships which creates a parallel legal reality 'in which every possible aspect of social reality has a second significance, in which language has a legal meaning, persons have a legal status, natural and human events have a legal character'.[130] This rather dense account of the role and importance of law needs to be unpacked.

In Allott's theory, law is the intermediary between power and ideas: it is the mechanism by which ideas are given substance in the lives of societies – 'In the making of the human world, nothing has been more important than what we call *law*'.[131] In particular, law is the principal mechanism through which Allott's notion of the ideal may be put into practical effect because law is a social institution which subsists through time. This allows societies to carry structures and systems from the past through the present to the future:

> Law defeats the passage of time by retaining choices made in a society's past, in a form – the law – which can take effect in a society's future. The law which is retained from society's past takes effect in society's present, as the law is interpreted and applied in the light of actual circumstances, and so helps to make society's future. The law carries the past through the present into the future. The law offers to society stability in the midst of ceaseless change, and change-

126 *International rule of law*, 389–399.
127 *Health of nations*, 79, ¶3.19.
128 *Health of nations*, 150, ¶5.54.
129 *Health of nations*, 290, ¶10.1–10.2: see also chapter 11, *International law and the idea of history* for an extended account of law as the link between past, present and future.
130 *Health of nations*, 296, ¶10.15–10.16.
131 See, eg, *Health of nations*, 134, ¶5.6.

> from-stability as new human circumstances demand new human choices . . . Law is a wonderful, and insufficiently appreciated, human invention.[132]

Law provides a platform in which critical evaluations of existing arrangements may be embodied in authoritative form in order to pursue and effectuate a situation which is perceived to be better. It may be recalled that Allott refers to the ideal as 'the perfectability of the actual' which can be expressed in terms of truth and value. As such, the ideal can become the governing principle of individual and social action:

> at every level of social organisation from the village to the international society of all-humanity. The ideal can determine the way in which we understand our potentiality for self-perfecting. It can then condition our choice among our potentialities, the potentialities which we choose to actualise, as individuals and societies. The ideal is the efficient secret of human self-perfecting.[133]

Law is the incarnation of society's dynamic pursuit of the ideal – 'the most efficient instrument for the actualising of the ideal'[134] – and thus its pursuit of morality: 'The idea of the ideal makes possible a morality of society. It makes possible the idea that society's systems, including the legal system, can have a moral purpose at the systematic level.'[135]

Further, the existence of law as a social institution enables society to insert the common interest into individuals' acts and to secure its realisation. Allott's idea of the common interest is in essence formal. It is not a morally loaded notion of some substantive predetermined common good:

> Common interest is a society's self-interest, a self-interest which may conflict with the self-interest of society-members in their capacity as individual human beings, but which is in their interest in their capacity as society-members. Common interest is not merely an aggregation of particular interests. It is formed at the intersection between the ideal and the real, as society responds to its current and potential situation in the light of its continuing theories, values and purposes. It is an idea of society's enlightened self-interest formed in a society's public mind.[136]

Law provides an authoritative determination from the competing versions of what the common interest should be by giving substance to the outcome of the deliberations of the political process.[137] Allott conceives politics broadly. He sees it as the process by which a society's values and purposes are identified and eventually resolved through the struggle which determines which will be embodied in law:[138] 'The exercise of public-realm power, especially the making of law, is a sustained effort to resolve the struggle of politics into an act which defines and enacts the common interest of society and transcends particular interests . . . all law-making is a by-product of politics.'[139]

---

132 *Health of nations*, 134, ¶5.7.
133 *Health of nations*, 156, ¶5.70: terminal note omitted.
134 *Health of nations*, 84, ¶3.29–3.30: quotation at ¶3.30.
135 *Health of nations*, 294, ¶10.10.
136 *Health of nations*, 295, ¶10.13.
137 *Health of nations*, 86, ¶3.35.
138 *Health of nations*, 153, ¶5.63.
139 *Health of nations*, 309, ¶10.48: comma omitted in the final phrase.

Allott, however, cautions that the effective socialisation of the international system requires that it develops an appropriate political process which allows it to determine its own values and purposes.[140] His vision is of a form of international law which realises the 'common interest of international society, the society of all societies' which embodies 'the self-constituting of all-humanity through law'.[141] But 'a legal system cannot be better than the social consciousness that it enacts',[142] and a perverted social consciousness can result in law that promotes social evil rather than the common interest. This can be done in one or more of four ways: by permitting conduct which should be prohibited; by using categories which are in themselves evil (for instance, just war theory); by turning complex human judgements into legalistic disputations; or by making an evil *status quo* resistant to a good status *ad quem.*[143] As evidence of this, the pernicious influence of the social consciousness arising from the Vattellian international system, and the discontinuity this has engendered between national and international notions of morality, culminated during the twentieth century in:

> war, genocide, oppression, exploitation and the physical and mental degradation of human beings on an unprecedented scale, all in the name of ideas. All this in a century in which fantasy-forms, new mythologies, came to be the dominant form in which the ruling classes, political and economic, communicate with the people. A godless world is, once again, full of gods, to echo Thales, the pre-Socratic philosopher. Max Weber said that the old gods, with their magic taken away, rise up from their graves, in the form of impersonal forces.[144]

Law is a core institution of society, 'an integral part of the whole activity of consciousness, individual and social',[145] but in current circumstances, as international law is alienated from all-humanity's consciousness, it cannot play its proper part in the realization of *eunomia* – 'the good order of a self-ordering society' – as 'The governments of states, acting in relation to each other, are at an infantile stage of moral development':[146]

> Somehow, in the new century and the new millennium, humanity has to find the courage to believe in its own self-transforming potentiality, its unlimited capacity for self-evolving and self-perfecting. Humanity is its own re-creator. We are what we think . . . It is a call to a human revolution, a revolution not in the streets but in the human mind.[147]

7.7 ORIGINAL SIN AND THE BANALITY OF EVIL

If Allott's inclusive international society were to be realised, international law would become a matter directly within individual consciousness. Accordingly, individuals (ultimately) rather than the State would determine and thus be responsible for the substantive

140 *Health of nations*, 153, ¶5.63.
141 *Health of nations*, 297, ¶10.18.
142 *Health of nations*, 313, ¶10.60.
143 *International rule of law*, 393: on Allott's excoriation of just war theory, see 394–396.
144 *Health of nations*, 26, ¶1.49: note omitted.
145 *Eunomia*, 171, ¶11.12.
146 *Health of nations*, 68, ¶2.78.
147 *Health of nations*, 157, ¶5.73.

content of international law. With that responsibility, Allott's hope is that morality would no longer be discontinuous between domestic and international society.

But is this too much to hope for? Does Allott's theory present us with a vision or merely a vain illusion? Can it provide a blueprint for a better future capable of practical implementation, or is it condemned to be a speculative chart of an unrealisable path to a non-existent Shangri-la? It could be argued that it all depends. Allott has, indeed, been accused of being a hopeless idealist, consciously adrift in a dream of utopia. But what does his theory offer? For Allott, law as a social technique is 'a more or less empty framework capable of taking more or less any substantive content'.[148] He is not programmatic about how that technique is to be used, although hopes that it should be used for the good. Nor, for that matter, does he specify the end to be sought, apart from his constant plea for the amelioration of the human condition. There is no determinate end-point identified in Allott's theory because the process of becoming is never-ending because it is the aspirational in pursuit of the ideal:

> In the Western philosophical tradition, originating in the philosophy of ancient Greece, it was very soon accepted that there could be no one answer, let alone one final answer. On the contrary, the clash of opposing solutions to the problem itself became the means of powerfully enriching the substance of human self-contemplating . . . The dialectic of idealism and realism, and of the countless intermediate positions, continues to the present day.[149]

And no doubt the dialectic projects into the human future.

Koskenniemi argues that Allott's work embodies the politics of conservative revolution, and continues a tradition which has sought 'new ways to articulate the basis for a universal law',[150] which is perhaps appropriate for a High Tory Bolshevik, but he also notes the absence of substantive political theory:

> After the 'Nations' have been restored to their 'Health' through the therapeutic effects of everyone finally seeing the truth, all the rest (what rest?) will either happen automatically or will be left for the projects that enlightened human beings will now be able to agree upon in their (now enlightened) political process.[151]

David Kennedy has made a similar observation: 'We have always thought politics was everywhere and what we needed was law; Philip was, I think, the first to say clearly that we have got law everywhere, and how did we come to be so governed with so little politics.'[152] I think that Allott would not disagree with these assessments as, after all, he counsels that the international system needs to develop a political process that would allow it to determine its own values and purposes;[153] politics determines what will become embodied in law; and law is 'the most efficient instrument for the actualising of the ideal'.[154] Allott's work sets out a vision of difference, of how the world could be

---

148 *Health of nations*, 52, ¶2.36.
149 *Health of nations*, 74, ¶3.10: terminal note omitted.
150 Koskenniemi, *International law as therapy*, above n. 1, 335–341: quotation at 340.
151 Koskenniemi, *International law as therapy*, above n. 1, 337.
152 Kennedy, *Thinking another world*, above n. 1, 272.
153 *Health of nations*, 153, ¶5.63.
154 *Health of nations*, 84, ¶3.30.

if 'the bizarre Vattelian legal world-view'[155] were discarded, but it does not detail the precepts that should be implemented to achieve that vision. The probability is that this vision can never be realised, but is rather an ideal, an aspiration, to which humanity should strive:

> [There is] no action-programme, no enforceable orthodoxy . . . only a foundational belief – in the power of the mind to make and re-make reality. And . . . a foundational value – the value of value. Our revolutionary programme is the revaluation of values through the revaluing of the idea of value. The only power over power is the power of ideas. The only power over bad ideas is better ideas. Our revolution is a revolution in the mind, not in the streets.[156]

Accordingly, Allott's vision of *eunomia* is undoubtedly idealist, which some have criticised. He correctly rejects this criticism as unfounded: ideas are the basis for the understanding, structuring and restructuring of the world. This is apparent in any society as politics, the claims made about the way in which that society should develop, is manifestly the clash of ideas.[157]

Less easy to shrug off is the criticism of utopianism.[158] Allott assumes that a fully socialised international society will be benevolent and eschew conflict, which he thinks arises from the competing interests of States. Allott roundly denies that the criticism of utopianism has any force: 'In response to this criticism, it is surely only necessary to say that our experience of the revolutionary transformation of national societies has been that the past conditions the future but that it does not finally and inescapably determine it. We have shown that we can think ourselves out of the social jungle.'[159] This riposte fails to convince; the possibility of escape from any jungle is mere speculation. It would perhaps have been better, more grounded in his own argument, had Allott adverted to the role of the ideal as the driving force of social reconstruction because it impels the emergence of a new consciousness which, through the contest of politics, may become consolidated in law. Allott could have underlined that the ideal is based firmly in reality – 'the power of the ideal stems from the fact that the idea of the better contains both the idea of the possible and the idea of the desirable. It generates a powerful attractive force inclining us to seek to actualise it.'[160] The ideal, the idea of the possible, informs politics; politics, as Bismarck is supposed to have said, is the art of the possible; and the possible is the antithesis of the utopian.

This line of thought is probably too glib an argument for Allott, who would see Bismarck's aphorism simply as an approval of the pursuit of pragmatism in political

---

155 *Health of nations*, 56, ¶2.44.

156 *Invisible power 2*, 126.

157 See *Eunomia*, xxxi.

158 Strictly, Allott would categorise his vision as *eutopian*, rather than *utopian* as the 'word *eutopia* (good place) is used . . . in preference to the word *utopia* (no place), another invented word using Greek roots, to emphasise that the nature of the New Enlightenment challenge is to find and to enact the new ideals of a new human mind-world, rather than, as in Thomas More's *Utopia* (1516), to criticise the actual by reference to an imaginary alternative which, in More's own pessimistic words . . . he wished rather than expected to see realised' – *Health of nations*, 132 at 156, ¶5.70, n. 30.

159 *Eunomia*, xxxii.

160 *Health of nations*, 83, ¶3.27.

affairs. In its everyday sense, pragmatism, the 'art of the possible', evaluates the utility of ideas and actions in terms of their potential practical impact. Philosophical accounts of pragmatism, especially those which are grouped loosely into the American school of pragmatism (which, perhaps paradoxically, sees itself as post-philosophical), hold to the view that ideas of truth and value are merely by-products of existing social processes which they cannot transcend.[161] This is an anathema to an idealist philosopher such as Allott, the essence of whose work is to stress the possibility that we may transcend existing conditions and arrangements through the pursuit of the ideal – the new social consciousness which will transform the actual.

For Allott, the criticism that his philosophy is utopian is simply beside the point. Social philosophies in themselves do not cause fundamental social transformation, although they may be employed in debates about possible social futures. When social conditions conspire to cause fundamental social transformation, existing social philosophies provide models to help interpret, manage and guide that process: 'Ideas are changed when the reality of the streets demands new ideas, and when there are ideas – good ideas and evil ideas – ready and waiting to form a new reality.'[162] This is the principal practical function of Allott's philosophy of Social Idealism. It may be used as a focus of debate about possible global futures, which subsequently could function as an ideal model in the unfolding process of the fundamental transformation of global society, should this happen. Allott not only thinks that it must, but that it will: he is of the opinion that globalisation seems to contain the critical mass of economic, political and social factors that will demand fundamental global change.[163]

Having said that, Allott's presupposition that humanity would develop a more just, loving and peaceful consciousness and choose to implement this in its social reality is difficult to accept without some hesitation. His argument is predicated on the belief that bad or wicked choices have been made which have caused human misery. It might be that Allott does not believe in the possibility of 'pure' evil, of wicked acts done in and for themselves, as forming part of the individual human condition. Indeed, he does seem to be rather agnostic about this possibility:

> I am not suggesting that people are good or evil naturally. I believe that it is part of what I call the constituting of societies that people also get constituted in the societies they constitute: all I want to put into the equation is the possibility of good in the self-constituting of peoples and the self-constituting of societies, because one of my main themes is that consciousness flows from such processes. This is a natural process in the self-constituting of societies: they have a capacity for self-improvement, but they have terrible evil capacities as well, and I believe that consciousness flows between the two, the private mind and the public mind, and either they corrupt each other or improve each other, just depending on what happens. One wants to put into the equation the possibility of improvement against the despair of the modern world, which is that systems will determine the good life. And if the systems do not contain the possibility of the good they will produce the bad life.[164]

---

161 See *Invisible power 2*, 147–148 and 313–314.
162 *Invisible power 2*, 126.
163 Allott, personal communication to author, 19 April 2010.
164 Allott, *Thinking another world*, above n. 1, 295.

Accordingly, for Allott, evil seems to be simply a contingent possibility, the product of a corrupted consciousness arising from

> the evil done by human beings in their official capacity and in what they believe to be the public interest – killing people, exploiting and oppressing people, individually and by the million, in the name of what they believe to be good ideas – with their good idea of the public interest sometimes conveniently coinciding with their idea of their private interest.

Essentially this is a form of public rather than private evil, which Allott terms 'social evil', and which at times may not be morally attributable to individuals as it is 'social-systematic evil, evil generated systematically by social systems', such as the asocial conduct of international affairs.[165]

Consequently, it seems that Allott does not consider evil to be a necessary part of the human condition, and that it may be banished through the transformation of human consciousness in the strive for *eunomia* – 'things could become better, very much better – as they have in many national societies – if we are clever enough and if we allow ourselves to be led by the potentiality of self-perfecting inherent in individual and social behaviour'.[166] This belief, nevertheless, appears to be more an act of faith than a demonstrable proposition. As St Augustine argued in *The City of God*, man's free will may be exercised perversely, to attain evil or sinful ends:

> Accordingly God, as it is written, made man upright, and consequently with a good will. For if he had not had a good will, he could not have been upright. The good will, then, is the work of God; for God created him with it. But the first evil will, which preceded all man's evil acts, was rather a kind of falling away from the work of God to its own works than any positive work. And therefore the acts resulting were evil, not having God, but the will itself for their end; so that the will or the man himself, so far as his will is bad, was as it were the evil tree bringing forth evil fruit.[167]

But need one consciously do evil to be evil, or be evil to do evil consciously? What are the implications of everyday and commonplace individual evil for Allott's world-view?

In Allott's theory, consciousness is formed by elites and, when this is fed into the social system, it is adopted or followed by the less-elite: in the latter's conception of social action, in their expression of the social good, they only follow orders. In her report of the *Eichmann* trial,[168] Hannah Arendt coined the phrase the 'banality of evil' to express this phenomenon:

---

165 *Health of nations*, 138, ¶5.21: see also 93, ¶3.48.

166 Allott, personal communication to author, 19 April 2010.

167 St Augustine, *The City of God* (c.413–426), Book XIV, chapter 11; see Book V, chapters 9–10 and Book XIV generally. An online edition is available at <www.newadvent.org/fathers/1201.htm>.

168 Otto Adolf Eichmann (1906–1962) was an SS Obersturmbannführer who was responsible for the logistics of the mass deportation of Jews to ghettos and extermination camps in German-occupied Eastern Europe during World War Two. He was tried in 1961 in Israel, charged on various counts, including crimes against humanity and crimes against the Jewish people, under the 1950 Nazi and Nazi Collaborators (Punishment) Law; found guilty; and executed. For an account of the trial and its impact on Israeli society, see Yablonka H, *The State of Israel vs Adolf Eichmann* (Schocken, New York, 2004).

> when I speak of the banality of evil, I do so only on the strictly factual level, pointing to a phenomenon which stared one in the face at the trial. Eichmann was not Iago and not Macbeth, and nothing would have been further from his mind than to determine with Richard III 'to be a villain'. Except for an extraordinary diligence in looking out for his personal advancement, he had no motives at all. And this diligence was in no way criminal; he certainly would never have murdered his superior in order to inherit his post. He *merely*, to put the matter colloquially, *never realized what he was doing.*[169]

This seems common to all individual 'crimes of obedience',[170] although we must bear in mind that Allott sees social evil as comprehending more than conduct which is criminal, whether in the domestic or international spheres. Indeed, Allott is hostile to the very idea of international criminal law – 'Feeble old men and their seedy subordinates shuffle into the court-room, shrunken figures bearing no physical relationship to the physical scale of the suffering for which they are responsible . . . The causes and the effects of extreme social evil remain, its human price, but our moral outrage is clouded by the charade of judicial retribution.'[171]

But if the consciousness of the less-elite is formed by the social forces put into play by the elite, does Allott demand too much of the latter in renewing consciousness and thus society? He appears to assume, or demand, that they will demonstrate a degree of scepticism and critically reflect upon ideas and values which they hold dear. Some might not wish, or be afraid, to do this: for example, those committed to a strict religious perspective might not consider questioning of their beliefs or the resulting social consequences because it is sinful or forbidden to do so. How can people transcend ideas, whether religious, political, or of whatever stamp, which are constitutive of their identity, fundamental to their understanding of who they are? The problem is the idealism demanded of the idealist: Allott seems to demand a dynamic fluidity of being which is perpetual in its process of becoming.

Allott also perhaps fails to give due weight to the possibility that social evil may emerge from idealistic or even (e)utopian intentions as the unintended consequence of intended action. The 1917 Russian revolution, and subsequent Stalinist terror, is perhaps an example of a politically structured reality 'whose inner perspective was absolute moral certainty and whose outer expression was morally outrageous behaviour'.[172] Nevertheless, this society was infused and impelled by idealism. The search for a world transformed for the better was inherent in popular support for the Stalinist agenda:

---

[169] Arendt H, *Eichmann in Jerusalem: a report on the banality of evil* (1963): extracted in Baehr P (ed.), *The portable Hannah Arendt* (Penguin, London, 2000) 313 at 379: see also her *'A daughter of our people': a response to Gershom Scholem*, ibid, 391 at 396.

[170] See Kelman HC and Hamilton VL, *Crimes of obedience: toward a social psychology of authority and responsibility* (Yale University Press, New Haven, 1989); and also Nollkaemper A and van der Wilt H (eds), *System criminality in international law* (Cambridge University Press, Cambridge, 2009).

[171] *Health of nations*, 67, ¶2.75: terminal note omitted. See also 67–68, ¶2.74–2.78 (more generally 62–69, ¶2.61–2.79), and 138, ¶5.22; and *International rule of law* chapter 11, *Law and war – a sinister partnership*, especially at 396 *et seq.*

[172] *Health of nations*, 28, ¶1.51.

> This was an age of utopianism. Political leaders had utopian visions, and so did many citizens, especially the younger generation. The spirit is hard to capture in an age of skepticism, since utopianism, like revolution, is so unreasonable. How could anyone have seriously believed in a radiant future, totally different from the miserable past and the chaotic present? The problem of understanding is all the greater because of the distance between the utopian vision and Soviet reality. It is tempting to dismiss the vision as simply deception and camouflage, especially since the utopian rhetoric actually did serve those purposes, among others, for the Soviet regime. But the vision . . . was [not only] a part of Stalinism, and an important one at that, but it was also a part of everyone's everyday experience in the 1930s. A Soviet citizen might believe or disbelieve in a radiant future, but could not be ignorant that one was promised.[173]

Allott sees totalitarianism, whether of left or right, as deploying 'the power of the mind-filling institutional authority of the state-system'.[174] Within such a system, the question must arise of how dissent, an alternative consciousness, can take root and become the social consciousness necessary to effect change? As he notes:

> By the end of the twentieth century, we . . . found ourselves living in societies in which reality is, for the individual society-member, a heteronomy, societies so complex that we can no longer identify the processes by which social reality is formed, societies in which the public mind contains, in a turmoil of mutual conditioning, the despotism of rationalistic bureaucracy, the anarchic order of extra-parliamentary politics, the imperious order of the market-place, and the fantasy-forms of popular culture.[175]

Yet, as history has shown, even totalitarian societies fade and fall away. Allott is perhaps not candid enough on how this process can and does occur as a matter of practical rather than pure theory, and this also appears to be true for his exhortations regarding the reconnection of morality with action in the international system.

Allott does not see hope for change in the organisation and conduct of existing international unsociety lying in the emergence of 'international civil society', and argues that this notion must be treated with caution. The contemporary understanding of civil society Allott traces to Hegel, which contrasts civil society with the public power of the State. This contradicts orthodox views of liberal democracy which require people to govern themselves through representative institutions. Accordingly:

> To introduce into international society the idea that governments and intergovernmental organization simply co-exist with a random collection ('civil society') of self-appointed and self-legitimating, more or less institutionalized, representations of individual interests, special interests, and public interests is to condemn international society to be a pre-revolutionary or counter-revolutionary system, as seen from the point of view of at least one orthodox theory of liberal democracy.[176]

There is some merit in this position. Apart from the democratic complications posed by non-governmental organisations, these need not be benign: organised criminal fraternities do not pursue socially benevolent ends.

On the other hand, there is some evidence that civil society, particularly in the guise of

---

173 Fitzpatrick S, *Everyday Stalinism. Ordinary life in extraordinary times: Soviet Russia in the 1930s* (Oxford University Press, New York, 1999) 67.

174 *Health of nations*, 127, ¶4.77.

175 *Health of nations*, 14, ¶1.24.

176 *Eunomia*, xxi.

non-governmental human rights bodies, is attempting to mend the radical discontinuity Allott perceives to exist between the domestic and international spheres by trying project morality – or at least legality – into the affairs of States. It is an effort to oppose social evil by taking advantage of established legal structures, and perhaps also the indeterminacy of law: 'the abstract content of a legal relation necessarily allows for a wide range of interpretations when the question arises of its application to actual persons and situations, interpretations which may alter with the identity of the interpreter and as a function of the time and context in which the interpretation occurs'.[177] This strategy is sometimes known as 'lawfare', where non-State actors attempt to make States and State officials live up to their obligations imposed by international law. A US military lawyer, Charles Dunlap, coined this term initially to describe the way that law has been deployed as a weapon during conflict by, for instance, those seeking to gain a moral or propaganda advantage by claiming that war crimes have been committed by a stronger adversary.[178] The notion has since been extended, and can be summarised as the employment of the power of legal accountability, generally by a non-State actor such as a non-governmental organisation, against official State action.[179] It may be seen as a strategy of resistance to the political desires of States, but can only be a piecemeal quest towards the ideal of ending impunity, by bringing home to perpetrators the responsibility they bear for the social evil they commit, or of which they are the passive instruments. These efforts might also have the consequence, whether intended or not, of changing the consciousness of the societies and individuals involved by exposing their misdeeds.

Lawfare cannot, however, remedy comprehensively the ills of the world. This requires a radical root-and-branch reshaping of societies and the international society of all societies. While Allott may not hold all the answers as to how this is to be done, his work points the way to renewal. Contemporary arrangements are not immutable, and change is always possible. We exist in a state of flux:

> The present is the presence of the past . . . all our social institutions are inheritances, each the particular product of a particular succession of events which occurred within the general history of human socialising, and in one or more of its particular sub-histories . . . both the capacities and the limitations of our social institutions, social good and social evil, are by-products and side-effects of that history and those histories. Above all . . . all our ideas have been historically produced – our ideas of God and gods, our ideas of nation and gender and race, our ideas of the true and the good and the beautiful, our ideas of society and law, our ideas of international society and international law, our ideas about our own humanity, our ideas about the past and the future, our ideas about ideas. All of them might have been otherwise. All of them are not otherwise. Social consciousness forms itself organically, by accretion and transformation. New ideas grow in the compost of old ideas.[180]

The revolution, as we have been told, starts in our minds.

---

177 *Health of nations*, 296–297, ¶10.16.

178 See Dunlap CJ, *Law and military interventions: preserving humanitarian values in 21st century conflicts*, <www.duke.edu/~pfeaver/dunlap.pdf> (2001); and his *Lawfare amid warfare*, Washington Times, 3 August 2007, <www.washingtontimes.com/news/2007/aug/03/lawfare-amid-warfare/>.

179 Herzberg A, *NGO 'lawfare': exploitation of courts in the Arab-Israeli conflict* (Jerusalem, NGO Monitor, 2008), available at <www.ngo-monitor.org/data/images/File/lawfare-monograph.pdf>.

180 *Health of nations*, 350–351, ¶12.22.

PART II

THEMATIC ASPECTS OF INTERNATIONAL LEGAL THEORY

8 International human rights law theory

Frédéric Mégret

International human rights theory is a broad term that describes a variety of foundational and conceptual dilemmas which scholars and practitioners of international human rights engage with. These raise fundamental issues about the nature, purpose, transformation and direction of human rights on the global level. International human rights theory is not human rights 'in theory', a sort of utopian blueprint of what might be, but the *theory of* international human rights as the set of assumptions and general understandings that comprehensively structure the project's very daily operation.

International human rights law can be analysed here as the partly deliberate, partly accidental fusion of three ideas: international (an environment, a political set up, an idea), human rights (an ideological project), and law (a tool and a project). The resulting dilemmas are therefore simultaneously *human rights*, *international*, and *legal* dilemmas. Human rights raise issues of the foundation, nature, and content of right; their transplantation in the international arena raises issues about what it means for human rights to become international and for the international to become more dominated by the idea of rights; and the process of legalization of human rights internationally then creates challenges for both human rights (which may suffer distortions) and international law (which may come under challenge). In practice these dilemmas are often difficult to disentangle. This chapter merely aims to give a short overview of the sort of problems they create for those interested in developing a theory of international human rights law.

More perhaps than general public international law, international human rights law has from its inception and increasingly with time become a locus of disciplinary fusion: partly domestic, partly legal; partly legal yet in very crucial ways moral and political.[1] 'International human rights' as an object of study has contributed to blur many lines, so that today 'human rights studies' are typically a fusion of many approaches.[2] The insights of the social sciences, history, sociology, and economics have all contributed tremendously to a study that is often impoverished when it is exclusively envisaged as a legal byproduct.[3] This does not necessarily detract from the distinctiveness of international human rights law as a legal project, but it does raise central questions for international human rights lawyers: how distinct is that law from the values it embodies? How distinct, in turn, are human rights from the international law that has been one of the principal vehicles of their universalization?

This chapter is a broad overview of international human rights theory research. As such,

[1] M. Freeman, *Human Rights: An Interdisciplinary Approach* (2002); H. J. Steiner, P. Alston and R. Goodman, *International human rights in context: law, politics, morals: text and materials* (2008).

[2] As illustrated, for example, by the discipline's (or the object's) flagship journal, *Human Rights Quarterly*.

[3] T. Landman, *Studying human rights* (2006).

it will be more literature review than systematic substantive engagement with the arguments that have been made over time about the theory of international human rights. However, it is hoped that, in exploring the agendas of scholars and thinkers, some sense of where the discipline's core dilemmas lie will emerge. The chapter will envisage, in succession, the theory of human rights, the theory of international human rights, and the theory of international human rights law, although these three levels of analysis are profoundly integrated.

8.1 THE THEORY OF RIGHTS

8.1.1 The Existence, Foundation, and Justification of Human Rights

Much soul searching has gone into the issue of whether rights actually 'exist' in a fundamentally demonstrable way. There has been a feeling that the movement would be on a much firmer footing if it could make a strong case about its intellectual bases. Although this is an issue that could be raised in a strictly domestic context, the internationalization of rights has made it much more sensitive,[4] as the human rights movement came under a variety of attacks urging it to better justify its founding assumptions.

The traditional view is that human rights are based on a strong truth or validity claim. Human rights *exist*, in a strong sense.[5] Religious thinkers (e.g. neo-scholastics such as De Vitoria and Suarez) gave the initial impetus to some ideas about natural law as a ground for at least natural rights,[6] but also human rights;[7] secular natural law theorists believe that rights inhere in human nature or are somehow inherently deducible from it;[8] Enlightenment philosophers believed they could be discovered and justify rights through Reason. Immanuel Kant, for example, is often presented as one of the great human rights thinkers, because of his attempt to deduce universally valid moral principles derived from transcendental considerations.

These strong ontological claims about rights have come under substantial attack, although probably no more so than the Enlightenment project in general and a certain unmitigated faith in the force of Reason. Attacks have come from all kinds of political quarters. Political conservatives, from Burke onwards, for example, have had problems with the idea that rights belong equally to all, preferring a more patrician model. A utilitarian like Jeremy Bentham once described rights as 'nonsense upon stilts'. Marxists were prone to see human rights as little more than a liberal bourgeois ideology.[9] 20th-century totalitarianism has also challenged the foundation of rights.

---

4 J. J. Shestack, 'The Philosophic Foundations of Human Rights', 20 Hum. Rts. Q. 201 (1998); M. Freeman, 'The Philosophical Foundations of Human Rights', 16 Hum. Rts. Q. 491 (1994).

5 P. J. Fitzgerald, 'Do Human Rights Exist – A Reply', 37 Quis Custodiet 132 (1972). David McCarthy, 'Human Rights: Do They Exist – A Reconsideration', 35 Quis Custodiet 60 (1972).

6 R. J. Araujo, 'The Catholic Neo-Scholastic Contribution to Human Rights: The Natural Law Foundation', 1 Ave Maria L. Rev. 159 (2003).

7 J. Maritain, *Les droits de l'homme et la loi naturelle* (1947).

8 R. McInerny, 'Natural Law and Human Rights', 36 American Journal of Jurisprudence 1 (1991).

9 J. Waldron, *'Nonsense upon stilts': Bentham, Burke, and Marx on the rights of man* (1987).

The reaffirmation of rights after the Second World War has coincided with a reassessment of the foundation of rights. To a large extent, lawyers, whether domestic or international, have sought to affirm the existence of rights on the basis of the existence of the law itself – when it happens to support the existence of rights – whether it be through constitutions or international instruments. The problem with a merely positivistic theory of the foundation of rights is that most human rights lawyers like to think that certain rights exist regardless of whether the state has recognized them as such. In other words, domestic and international human rights law is always tempted to reach beyond positive law, especially at times when rights are arguably needed most, namely when a state, for example, refuses to recognize them at all. Moreover, purely positivist justifications of the existence or importance of rights can be quite shallow, as many different actual attitudes to rights might lie behind the bare act of ratifying a human rights treaty.

Today, the foundation of human rights is more often seen to lie in a variety of alternative foundations which one might describe as 'intermediary', i.e. neither entirely metaphysical nor entirely positivist.[10] Rights may not exist in a strong sense, but they are not simply a random political choice and exert some sort of higher claim to our normative commitments. Rights might not exist, in other words, but they can certainly be *justified*. If nothing else, according to one popular interpretation, the late modern claim to rights is based on the historical affirmation, intuitive and empirical as it may be, that rights are necessary if humanity is to avoid a repeat of the Holocaust (or various episodes of systematic rights violations experienced in given society).[11] Alternatively, rights are presented sociologically as a social construct emerging from the need to fight against oppression.[12]

In terms of more distinctly philosophical and speculative discourse, the search for a foundation of rights is marked by work at the intersection between moral and political philosophy. Rights are a moral theory that calls to be translated in a particular political system. Inevitably, the attempt to ground human rights involves difficult exercises about what makes humans human, and how rights can respond to that fundamental intuition. Possible foundations of rights thus include human beings' rationality, their autonomy, their aspiration to happiness, their fundamentally social nature, their inherent freedom, etc. An alternative to looking at what human beings are, is to look at what they *want*. Some utilitarian theorists, in particular, have sought to show how human rights can protect certain values that are in themselves goods that all human beings aspire to. The problem is that we know human beings want very different things, and that utilitarianism tends not to take their autonomy very seriously.[13] The temptation, thus, is to return to a naturalist or Kantian notion of human rights, based on a moral theory about how human beings should treat each other (e.g. as ends rather than means), although how one translates an inter-personal theory of morality into a fundamental political system is

---

[10] J. W. Nickel, *Making sense of human rights* (2007).

[11] D. Levy and N. Sznaider, 'The institutionalization of cosmopolitan morality: the Holocaust and human rights', 3 Journal of Human Rights 143–157 (2004). J. Morsink, 'World War Two and the Universal Declaration', 15 Hum. Rts. Q. 357 (1993).

[12] M. Winston, 'Human Rights as Moral Rebellion and Social Construction', 6 Journal of Human Rights 279–305 (2007).

[13] R. Dworkin, *Taking rights seriously* (1978).

problematic. A certain scepticism has at times emerged that the tension between utilitarian and deontological conceptions of rights can ever be alleviated.[14]

Much thought has also gone into renovating some of the bases of social contract theory in the context of a renewed interest in the notion of justice. For example liberal theories of rights present them as the minimal requirements of being able to live the good life, in a world that has become sceptical of ever fully determining what the good life might be. In other words, liberalism emphasizes a 'thin theory' of the good society, one in which what matters is that individuals be able to self-determine themselves and choose their own ends.[15] Others, expanding on earlier Enlightenment themes, have emphasized that rights are what the members of a particular society agree to, or would agree to under certain conditions (for example, behind a Rawlsian 'veil of ignorance' where participants do not know what their actual condition in society would be).[16] There has been some impatience with Rawls's focus on rights as emerging within particular preconstituted societies and being of limited applicability internationally,[17] and some of the search for foundations is now oriented towards seeing human rights as one of the basic requirements of a global theory of justice.[18] Human rights, it has been argued, should be grounded in a sense of 'social ethics, sustainable by open public reasoning'.[19]

Finally, a whole strand of human rights theory is deeply sceptical of all of the above, and argues that it is the foundational question itself that is *passé*. Postmodern thought, for example, is very sceptical of any notion of objectivity and with the decline of a faith in Reason and truth comes a decline in the belief in rights as fundamentally 'rational' or 'true'. Interestingly, this scepticism does not necessarily lead those who profess it to entirely abandon the language of rights (although some may), and can lead, as with Rorty, to a pragmatic acknowledgment of the fundamentally emotional, faith-based nature of the *belief* in rights.[20] The question today is not to ask naively whether rights exist but, acknowledging fully their constructed and even localized character, to better understand them as an ongoing struggle informed by a mix of faith and politics. This comes perilously close to giving up any claim to human rights specificity, but in some ways the human rights movement was always marked by a form of faith in its core aspiration ('we hold these truths to be self-evident'), so that late modern thinking may rediscover something that was always there in the first place. The value of international human rights may lie in the fact that it is the last 'totalizing Grand Narrative'.[21]

---

[14] H. L. A. Hart, 'Between Utility and Rights', 79 Columbia Law Review 828 (1979).

[15] On the issue of human rights and liberalism generally, see J. Donnelly, 'Human Rights and Western Liberalism', Human Rights in Africa: Cross-Cultural Perspectives 31–55 (1990).

[16] J. Rawls, *A Theory of Justice* (1999).

[17] J. Rawls, *The law of peoples: with, The idea of public reason revisited* (2001).

[18] C. Beitz, 'What Human Rights Mean', 132 Daedalus 36–47 (2003).

[19] A. Sen, 'Elements of a theory of human rights', 32 Philosophy & Public Affairs 315–356 (2004).

[20] R. Rorty, S. Shute and S. Hurley, *On Human Rights: The Oxford Amnesty Lectures 1993* (1993).

[21] J. A. L. Alves, 'The Declaration of Human Rights in Postmodernity', 22 Hum. Rts. Q. 478–500 (2000).

8.1.2 The Universality Question

Closely tied to the foundation question is one of the questions that has been most debated in the last two decades, namely that of human rights' universality. The claim to a certain universality has always featured prominently in the discourse of human rights, although that claim coexisted in practice with substantial degrees of exclusion.[22] One is dealing with a theoretical claim (i.e. that rights are actually universal), which is of course coupled with a strong normative claim (i.e. that, because human rights are universal, they should be universally applied and respected).

Claims about universality are problematically rooted in at least 2,500 years of Western thinking about the reality and possibility of universal concepts of the good, the true, and justice. The internationalization of rights is born from taking seriously the idea of rights' universality, but paradoxically internationalization has also put the question of universality in sharp focus and led to a crisis of claims made about rights.[23] This challenge has taken a variety of forms. As early as 1948, the American Anthropological Association had issued a statement criticizing the concept of universal human rights as being in denial of cultural diversity.[24] Saudi Arabia, in what was to inaugurate a complex relationship between human rights and Islam, was one of the states that abstained at the General Assembly session that adopted the UDHR. Lee Kuan Yu, the Prime Minister of Singapore, has famously insisted that 'Asian values' emphasized a more communal outlook on social life that was at odds with liberal human rights.[25] Human rights have also disrupted a number of traditional or customary practices. Female genital mutilation has notably become something of a *cause célèbre* of the universalism v. relativism debate,[26] as are a number of women's rights issues that clash with certain traditional and religious practices.

International human rights lawyers have responded in a number of ways to these challenges to universality, seeking to salvage what could be salvaged of the claim, and emphasizing the extent to which claims of difference could be overstated, whilst conceding some points about cultural difference.[27] Some are nonetheless typically unrepentant

---

22 A. S. Fraser, 'Becoming Human: The Origins and Developments of Women's Human Rights', 21 Hum. Rts. Q. 853 (1999).

23 C. Brown, 'Universal human rights: A critique', 1 The International Journal of Human Rights 41 (1997).

24 K. Engle, 'From Skepticism to Embrace: Human Rights and the American Anthropological Association from 1947–1999', 23 Hum. Rts. Q. 536 (2001); M. B. Dembour, 'Human rights talk and anthropological ambivalence', Inside and outside the law: Anthropological studies of authority and ambiguity 19–40 (1996).

25 F. Zakaria and L. K. Yew, 'Culture Is Destiny: A Conversation with Lee Kuan Yew', 73 Foreign Affairs 109–126 (1994).

26 H. Lewis, 'Between Irua and Female Genital Mutilation: Feminist Human Rights Discourse and the Cultural Divide', 8 Harv. Hum. Rts. J. 1 (1995); K. Boulware-Miller, 'Female Circumcision: Challenges to the Practice as a Human Rights Violation', 8 Harv. Women's L. J. 155 (1985).

27 See, for example, A. Dundes Renteln, 'The Unanswered Challenge of Relativism and the Consequences for Human Rights', 7 Hum. Rts. Q. 514 (1985); Michael J. Perry, 'Are Human Rights Universal? The Relativist Challenge and Related Matters', 19 Hum. Rts. Q. 461–509 (1997); D. L. Donoho, 'Relativism versus universalism in human rights: The search for meaningful standards', 27 Stan. J. Int'l L. 345 (1990).

about the claim to universality, if only because of the argument that international human rights treaties have been ratified broadly.[28] This can be more than a little formalistic, given the superficiality of some accession processes and the remarkable degree of indifference in which human rights instruments are effectively held by some governments.

More significantly, defenders of at least a certain human rights universality have accused culturalists of reifying and simplifying cultures.[29] The disagreement has been recast as an argument about certain concepts of human rights over others rather than straightforwardly 'against' human rights. Many scholars have called for a greater acknowledgment of the Western origins of human rights.[30] On a more positive note, scholars have sought to re-explore what universality means,[31] or the conditions under which agreement about universality might be reached,[32] the possibility of human rights emerging from inter-subjective consensus rather than any a priori deduction,[33] or to reach some kind of synthesis between the insights of relativism and universalism.[34] They have explored the potential of concepts such as human dignity as having more immediate and intuitive appeal in many cultures than rights talk per se.[35] There has, in addition, been a considerable effort to uncover non-Western origins of rights, and to build bridges between non-Western traditions and human rights (particularly with Islam,[36] African'[37] and Asian values). Some of these attempts will clearly be more convincing than others, and may be slightly self-serving. However, they have also opened up a space for an unprecedented level of dialogue that makes human rights a meeting ground rather than a definitive programme for the 'good society'.

Some have pointed out that the universalist/relativist debate has had the consequence of marginalizing more 'transformative' practices of human rights operating at the

---

[28] F. R. Teson, 'International Human Rights and Cultural Relativism', 25 Virginia Journal of International Law 869 (1984).

[29] O. Bruun and M. Jacobsen, *Human rights and Asian values: contesting national identities and cultural representations in Asia* (2000).

[30] A. Woodiwiss, 'Human rights and the challenge of cosmopolitanism', 19 Theory Culture and Society 139–156 (2002).

[31] J. Donnelly, 'The Relative Universality of Human Rights', 29 Hum. Rts. Q. 281–306 (2007).

[32] C. Taylor, 'Conditions of an unforced consensus on human rights', The Politics of Human Rights 101–19 (1999).

[33] S. Chesterman, 'Human rights as subjectivity: The age of rights and the politics of culture', 27 Millenium: Journal of International Studies 97 (1998).

[34] J. Donnelly, 'Cultural Relativism and Universal Human Rights', 6 Hum. Rts. Q. 400 (1984).

[35] O. Schachter, 'Human dignity as a normative concept', 77 The American Journal of International Law 848–854 (1983).

[36] A. E. Mayer, *Islam and human rights: tradition and politics* (2006); B. Tibi, 'Islamic Law/Shari'a, Human Rights, Universal Morality and International Relations', 16 Hum. Rts. Q. 277–299 (1994); A. A. An-Na'im, *Toward an Islamic reformation: civil liberties, human rights, and international law* (1996); S. Waltz, 'Universal Human Rights: The Contribution of Muslim States', 26 Hum. Rts. Q. 845 (2004).

[37] J. A. M. Cobbah, 'African values and the human rights debate: an African perspective', 9 Hum. Rts. Q. 309–331 (1987); A. A. An-Na'im, A. A. A. Na m and F. M. Deng, *Human rights in Africa: cross-cultural perspectives* (1990); B. Ibhawoh, 'Between Culture and Constitution: Evaluating the Cultural Legitimacy of Human Rights in the African State', 22 Hum. Rts. Q. 838 (2000); R. Thandabantu Nhlapo, 'International Protection of Human Rights and the Family: African Variations on a Common Theme', 3 Int. J. Law Policy Family 1–20 (1989).

margins of mainstream discourse.[38] Of late, the debate has significantly shifted from the foundational issue of whether rights are universal or values relative to a debate on the tension between cosmopolitan liberalism and value pluralism, which is both part of an ongoing debate on the nature of liberalism[39] and the possibility and desirability of a cosmopolitan model.[40]

8.1.3 The Status and Nature of Rights

A very significant part of international human rights theory, both a continuation of and an influence on similar domestic debates, is concerned with what rights actually are. First, issues arise about the status of rights. A strong view is that rights are both pre-legal and legal, that they are in a sense recognized by positive law, but exist independently of it. Needless to say, this view raises significant theoretical and doctrinal tensions.[41] A related view is that rights typically stand quite high up in the hierarchy of norms and have some sort of constitutional or supra-legal status. This claim is typically made both domestically (where it translates into demands for constitutionalization) and internationally (where it is associated with claims that human rights have *jus cogens* and/or *erga omnes* status). Internationally, it has been particularly made in relation to strong assertions of immunity, or in the context of global economic arrangements by those seeking to argue the normative primacy of rights. Human rights appear as good candidates,[42] moreover, to secure a relatively elevated place in the emerging hierarchy of international norms,[43] even as part of some sort of global constitution,[44] an increasingly important theme in international legal theory.

Second, there is much search for an understanding of the nature of rights as focuses of adjudication. Rights typically function as principles rather than rules, which produces particular forms of adjudication. Because rights are often formulated in sweeping and absolute fashion, the idea may emerge that rights are by nature absolute. A legal theorist like Ronald Dworkin has done much to accredit this idea, insisting that rights should be 'taken seriously' and that they should be seen as 'trumps'.[45] This idea, however, has to be taken with a pinch of salt with all but a very few number of rights (e.g. torture). As argued

---

38 D. Otto, 'Rethinking the Universality of Human Rights Law', 29 Columbia Human Rights Law Review 1 (1997).

39 A. Langlois, 'Human Rights and Cosmopolitan Liberalism', 10 Critical Review of International Social and Political Philosophy 29–45 (2007).

40 P. G. Danchin, 'Between Rogues and Liberals: Towards Value Pluralism as a Theory of Freedom of Religion in International Law', All Faculty Publications 633 (2006).

41 L. Henkin, 'International Human Rights as Rights', 1 Cardozo Law Review 425 (1979).

42 D. Shelton, 'Hierarchy of Norms and Human Rights: Of Trumps and Winners', 65 Sask. L. Rev. 301 (2002).

43 D. Shelton, 'Normative hierarchy in international law', American Journal of International Law 291–323 (2006); J. H. H. Weiler and A. L. Paulus, 'The Structure of Change in International Law or Is There a Hierarchy of Norms in International Law?', 8 European Journal of International Law 545 (1997).

44 S. Gardbaum, 'Human Rights as International Constitutional Rights', 19 European Journal of International Law 749 (2008); M. Kumm, 'The Legitimacy of International Law: A Constitutionalist Framework of Analysis', 15 Eur. J. Int. Law 907–931 (2004).

45 R. Dworkin, *Taking rights seriously* (1978).

by Richard Pildes, rights rather 'police the kind of justifications government can act on in different spheres' and are 'means of realizing various common goods'.[46] The existence of general or specific limitation clauses in most international human rights instruments suggests that rights are indeed a starting point, but that their precise extent needs to be ascertained in the light of potentially countervailing and legitimate societal goals.[47]

Third, a number of debates have emerged about the intensity of human rights obligations. The famous tripartite distinction between obligations to 'respect, protect and fulfill' has generated a debate that is very different from general international law's theories of compliance. Particularly the idea of a responsibility to protect poses significant and novel issues of 'indirect horizontal responsibility' for states. This debate on the nature of human rights obligations is, in turn, indissociable from the debate on the identify of human rights duty holders and, in particular, the possibility that a variety of non-state actors have 'horizontal' human rights duties vis-à-vis each other.[48] The degree to which states should rigorously comply with international human rights standards is an important level of debate. In practice, international human rights law has implicitly acknowledged the importance of a fairly broad tolerance for local variation (something worth considering in the context of the debate on cosmopolitanism and value pluralism), and much scholarly research is dedicated to understanding how in practice the abstract tension between universalism and relativism is mediated by regionalization,[49] subsidiarity,[50] and the 'margin of appreciation'.[51]

8.1.4 The Content and Development of Rights

To the extent that human rights is not simply an idea, but a vessel that needs be filled with content, considerable theoretical issues are raised by what count and what do not count as rights. In addition to the doctrinal-descriptive exercise of categorizing rights, for example

---

46 R. H. Pildes, 'Why Rights Are Not Trumps: Social Meanings, Expressive Harms, and Constitutionalism', 27 The Journal of Legal Studies 725–763 (1998).

47 J. Viljanen, *The European Court of Human Rights as a developer of the general doctrines of human rights law: a study of the limitation clauses of the European Convention on Human Rights* (2003).

48 J. H. Knox, 'Horizontal human rights law', 102 Am. J. Int'l L. 1 (2008); I. Leigh, 'Horizontal Rights, the Human Rights Act and Privacy: Lessons from the Commonwealth?', 48 International and Comparative Law Quarterly 57–87 (2008).

49 T. Buergenthal, 'International and Regional Human Rights Law and Institutions: Some Examples of Their Interaction', 12 Tex. Int'l L. J. 321 (1977).

50 P. G. Carozza, 'Subsidiarity as a structural principle of international human rights law', 97 Am. J. Int'l L. 38 (2003).

51 E. Brem, 'The Margin of Appreciation Doctrine in the Case Law of the European Court of Human Rights', 56 Zeitschrift für ausländisches öffentliches Recht und Völkerrecht 240–314 (1996); J. A. Brauch, 'The Margin of Appreciation and the Jurisprudence of the European Court of Human Rights: Threat to the Rule of Law', 11 Columbia Journal of European Law 113 (2004); T. A. O'Donnell, 'The Margin of Appreciation Doctrine: Standards in the Jurisprudence of the European Court of Human Rights', 4 Hum. Rts. Q. 474 (1982); E. Benvenisti, 'Margin of appreciation, consensus, and universal standards', 31 New york university journal of international law and politics 843 (1998); H. C. Yourow, *The margin of appreciation doctrine in the dynamics of European human rights jurisprudence* (1996).

in 'generations',[52] perhaps the most famous debate in that respect has opposed negative, 'freedom from', and 'liberty', 'security' rights, to positive, 'right to', 'entitlement', and 'subsistence' rights. This closely matches the distinction between civil and political rights on the one hand, and economic and social ones on the other. Whilst civil and political rights have in a sense always been associated with the liberal human rights project, there are long lines of both proponents and opponents of economic and social rights with a distinct welfarist dimension.

Critics emphasize that one cannot have a right to something that is a scarce resource; that economic and social rights prejudge the sort of political economic system that states ought to be able to choose; that economic and social rights are too broad and vague to be adjudicated; that they create a culture of dependency; in short, that economic and social rights are in some way or another a 'road to serfdom'.[53] Proponents argue for the fundamental justifiability of rights to certain social goods that are absolutely indispensable to the ability to live a good life, at least within particular societies; they emphasize the artificiality of the distinction between negative and positive rights, as most negative rights in fact require positive measures from the state, and some economic and social goods merely require the state to do nothing to stop people from accessing them.[54] Amarty Sen, in particular, has developed the notion of rights as 'capability', underlining the formalism of negative rights when the minimum 'functionings' are not available (e.g. what is the point of a right to vote if you do not have public transportation to reach the polling booth?).[55]

The response of such bodies as the Committee on Economic and Social Rights of the United Nations has been very supportive of economic and social rights, whilst recognizing that they do occasionally operate in significantly different ways.[56] For example, the idea of 'progressive realization' means that there is an understanding that states that cannot guarantee all economic and social rights here and now, but that they must show that they are 'taking economic and social rights seriously' by setting aside the resources needed to tackle, as a matter of priority, the basic economic needs of their populations.[57] There has been an increasing amount of attention to the international dimensions of economic and social rights, and particularly the issue of the extent of human rights

---

52 K. Vasak, 'Human rights: a thirty-year struggle: the sustained efforts to give force of law to the Universal Declaration of Human Rights', 30 UNESCO Courier 316–25 (1977).

53 C. Sunstein, 'Against positive rights', 2 E. Eur. Const. Rev. 35 (1993); S. Yoshihara, 'The quest for happiness: how the U.N.'s advocacy of economic, social, and cultural rights undermines liberty and opportunity', in *ConUNdrum: the limits of the United Nations and the search for alternatives* (B. D. Schaefer ed., 2009).

54 H. Shue, 'Basic rights', *Contemporary political philosophy: an anthology* (2006); R. Peffer, 'A defense of rights to well-being', 8 Philosophy and Public Affairs 65–87 (1978); T. Pogge, 'Severe poverty as a violation of negative duties', 19 Ethics and International Affairs 55–84 (2005).

55 A. Sen, 'Equality of what?', Contemporary political philosophy: an anthology 476–486 (1998); M. Nussbaum, 'Women and equality: the capabilities approach', 138 Int'l Lab. Rev. 227 (1999).

56 P. Alston and G. Quinn, 'The nature and scope of states parties' obligations under the International Covenant on Economic, Social and Cultural Rights', Hum. Rts. Q. 156–229 (1987).

57 P. Harvey, 'Human Rights and Economic Policy Discourse: Taking Economic and Social Rights Seriously', 33 Columbia Human Rights Law Review 363 (2001).

obligations to alleviate world poverty.[58] Moreover, a very significant strand of research on economic and social rights seek to adapt the concept's basic intuitions to specific rights or clusters of rights.[59] The relationship of civil and political to economic and social rights has also been clarified. The UN typically presents them as 'interrelated, indivisible, and interdependent'. This is a seductive formula, although it may be a little broad for its own good. It has not prevented the emergence of a debate on the possible existence of a hierarchy among human rights.[60]

Another intense area of inquiry deals with so-called 'third generation' or collective, 'solidarity' rights.[61] This is a quite broad category whose existence is relatively settled in international human rights law, even though it is regularly challenged and its legal implications sometimes seem hard to tease out. Among the rights that have been claimed under that heading, three stand out as having been most formally and consistently recognized: the right to self-determination,[62] the right to development,[63] and the rights of minorities.[64] A good emerging contender is the right to a clean environment.[65] Needless to say, the collective nature of these rights raises significant challenges for both human

---

58 T. Pogge, *Freedom from poverty as a human right: who owes what to the very poor?* (2007); T. Pogge, *World poverty and human rights: Cosmopolitan responsibilities and reforms* (2008).

59 M. J. Dennis and D. P. Stewart, 'Justiciability of Economic, Social, and Cultural Rights: Should There Be an International Complaints Mechanism to Adjudicate the Rights to Food, Water, Housing, and Health?', American Journal of International Law 462–515 (2004); A. Eide, A. Oshaug, and W. B. Eide, 'Food Security and the Right to Food in International Law and Development', 1 Transnat'l L. & Contemp. Probs. 415 (1991); P. Alston and K. Tomaševski, *The right to food* (1984); J. H. Spring, *The universal right to education: Justification, definition, and guidelines* (2000); K. Tomasevski, *Education denied, Costs and remedies* (2002); V. A. Leary, 'The right to health in international human rights law', Health and human rights 24–56 (1994); B. C. A. Toebes, *The right to health as a human right in international law* (1999); J. Scanlon, A. Cassar, and N. Nemes, *Water as a human right?* (2004); P. H. Gleick, 'The human right to water', 1 Water Policy 487–503 (1998); S. M. A. Salman and S. A. McInerney-Lankford, *The human right to water: legal and policy dimensions* (2004).

60 T. Koji, 'Emerging hierarchy in international human rights and beyond: from the perspective of non-derogable rights', 12 European Journal of International Law 917 (2001); T. Meron, 'On a Hierarchy of International Human Rights', 80 American Journal of International Law 1–23 (1986).

61 P. Alston, 'A Third Generation of Solidarity Rights: Progressive Development or Obfuscation of International Human Rights Law?', 29 Neth. Int'l L. Rev. 307 (1982); R. N. Kiwanuka, *The Meaning of 'People' in the African Charter on Human and Peoples' Rights* (1988).

62 P. Thornberry, 'Self-determination, minorities, human rights: a review of international instruments', 38 International and Comparative Law Quarterly 867–889 (2008); R. McCorquodale, 'Self-determination: a human rights approach', 43 International and Comparative Law Quarterly 857–885 (2008); H. Hannum, *Autonomy, sovereignty, and self-determination: The accommodation of conflicting rights* (1996).

63 J. Donnelly, 'In Search of the Unicorn: The Jurisprudence and Politics of the Right to Development', 15 California Western International Law Journal 473 (1985); P. Alston, 'Making Space for New Human Rights: the Case of the Right to Development', 1 Harv. Hum. Rts. YB 3 (1988).

64 Y. Dinstein, 'Collective human rights of peoples and minorities', 25 International and Comparative Law Quarterly 102–120 (2008); P. Thornberry, *International law and the rights of minorities* (1993).

65 R. Picolotti and J. D. Taillant, *Linking human rights and the environment* (2003); D. Shelton, 'Human Rights, Environmental Rights, and the Right to Environment', 28 Stan. J. Int'l L. 103 (1991).

rights (tension between collective and individual rights) and international law (tension between collective rights and sovereignty).

One should also point out that an essential dimension of the development of rights, which challenges some of the project's theoretical premises, has been a diversification of its beneficiary subjects. For a time, the main challenge seemed to extend the promise of human rights to all human beings. But increasingly, special instruments have been sought for specific groups or categories within humanity. These claims have been framed as claims for equality, but also claims for a recognition of a certain difference in human rights. After the great anti-discrimination conventions of the 1970s (CERD, CEDAW), for example, more recent treaties fit the description of recognizing claims for at least partially special treatment, whether it be the Convention on the Rights of the Child,[66] the Convention on the Rights of Persons with Disabilities,[67] the Convention on the Rights of Migrant Workers,[68] or the Declaration on the Rights of Indigenous Persons.[69] Finally, it is worth mentioning that the multiplication of international human rights instruments has long raised concerns about their continued quality, and the risk that treaty inflation might dilute the vigour of the norms.[70]

8.2 THE THEORY OF INTERNATIONAL HUMAN RIGHTS

8.2.1 The History of International Human Rights

A part of international human rights theory is concerned with the historical construction and development of international human rights as a project. There has been a significant effort, in particular, to de-Westernize and broaden the historical narrative of human rights by highlighting the diversity of its conceivable origins.[71] Historians have studied the emergence of canonical human rights texts in the Enlightenment, and their diffusion throughout the 19th and 20th centuries. Some attention has been devoted to potential predecessors of the 'international human rights movement' and the argument has often

---

66 E. Verhellen, *Convention on the Rights of the Child* (2000); S. Detrick, *A Commentary on the United Nations Convention on the Rights of the Child* (1999).

67 F. Mégret, 'The Disabilities Convention: Human Rights of Persons with Disabilities or Disability Rights?', 30 Hum. Rts. Q. 494 (2008); M. A. Stein, 'Disability Human Rights', 95 Cal. L. Rev. 75 (2007).

68 R. I. Cholewinski, *Migrant workers in international human rights law: their protection in countries of employment* (1997).

69 S. J. Anaya and R. A. Williams Jr, 'The Protection of Indigenous Peoples' Rights over Lands and Natural Resources under the Inter-American Human Rights System', 14 Harv. Hum. Rts. J. 33 (2001); R. Stavenhagen, 'Indigenous rights: some conceptual problems', Constructing democracy: Human rights, citizenship, and society in Latin America 141–59 (1996); P. Thornberry, *Indigenous peoples and human rights* (2002).

70 P. Alston, 'Conjuring up new human rights: A proposal for quality control', 78 American Journal of International Law 607–621 (1984).

71 P. G. Lauren, *The evolution of international human rights: visions seen* (1998). M. Ishay, *The history of human rights: from ancient times to the globalization era* (2008). E. Engle, 'Universal Human Rights: A Generational History', 12 Annual Survey of International & Comparative Law 219 (2006).

been made that the anti-slavery movement was an interesting rehearsal.[72] A considerable amount of historical research has concentrated on such a foundational moment as the adoption of the Universal Declaration of Human Rights,[73] or the European Convention on Human Rights,[74] or particular institutions in the international human rights edifice.[75] This has in turn encouraged renewed interest in some earlier 20th-century attempts to secure a human rights foothold in international law.[76] This historical work is almost always theoretical in some respect (one might say, genealogical),[77] inscribed as it is in the history of ideas, and therefore indispensable to understand the genesis of international human rights as a particular post-War project.[78] Finally, some scholars have begun writing a contemporary history of international human rights.[79]

This historical study also suggests it is often difficult to distinguish the development of 'international human rights' from the development of 'international law', because the two have in a sense always been intimately related. Grotius was already reflecting on the relative importance of natural law and humanity in a world of consolidating sovereignty, and late-19th century international legal visionaries were liberal cosmopolitans before they were internationalists.[80] This thinking about the status of values, particularly values emphasizing individual and communitarian accomplishment, has always accompanied the great transformative moments of the international system. Indeed, international human rights theory is intimately linked to the history of international legal theory *tout court*, as reflected by a long list of international legal thinkers who have thought deeply about the role of human rights.[81]

---

72 J. J. S. Martinez, 'Anti-Slavery Courts and the Dawn of International Human Rights Law', 117 Yale Law Journal (2007).

73 B. Farrell, 'Habeas Corpus and the Drafting of the Universal Declaration of Human Rights', 11 Journal of the History of International Law 81–101 (2009); S. Waltz, 'Reclaiming and rebuilding the history of the Universal Declaration of Human Rights', 23 Third World Quarterly 437–448 (2002).

74 V. Butkevych, 'The European Convention on Human Rights in the Context of the History of International Law', in *Liber Amicorum Luzius Wildhaber: Human Rights-Strasbourg Views [Droits de l'homme-Regards de Strasbourg]* 177–192.

75 A. J. Hobbins, 'Humphrey and the High Commissioner: The Genesis of the Office of the UN High Commissioner for Human Rights', 3 J. Hist. Int'l L. 38 (2001).

76 J. H. Burgers, 'The Road to San Francisco: The Revival of the Human Rights Idea in the Twentieth Century', 14 Hum. Rts. Q. 447–477 (1992).

77 R. Teitel, 'Human Rights Genealogy', 66 Fordham Law Review 301 (1997).

78 J. von Bernstorff, 'The Changing Fortunes of the Universal Declaration of Human Rights: Genesis and Symbolic Dimensions of the Turn to Rights in International Law', 19 Eur. J. Int. Law 903–924 (2008).

79 K. Cmiel, 'The Recent History of Human Rights', 109 The American Historical Review 117–135 (2004).

80 This is a point that has been made most consistently by Martti Koskenniemi. See, for instance, M. Koskenniemi, 'Hersch Lauterpacht and the Development of International Criminal Law', 2 Journal of International Criminal Justice 810 (2004); M. Koskenniemi, 'Legal Cosmopolitanism: Tom Franck's Messianic World', 35 New York University Journal of International Law and Politics 471 (2002).

81 H. Lauterpacht, 'The Universal Declaration of Human Rights', 25 Brit. YB Int'l L. 354 (1948); M. S. McDougal, H. D. Lasswell, and L. Chen, 'Human Rights and World Public Order: A

8.2.2 International Human Rights, the International Project, and Sovereignty

The project of international human rights is one that is fundamentally different, in its ambition and inspiration, from that of international law. International law was the system that emerged from the Peace of Westphalia to regulate the relationship of equal and sovereign entities. The implicit condition of the Westphalian compact was that whatever happened domestically was beyond the realm of international law. Of all things, international law had nothing (or little) to say on how a sovereign treated its own population. The international system was the locus of organized coexistence, not one dedicated to a cosmopolitan ambition or a common social project. Sovereignty acted as a sort of veil that protected the state from outside scrutiny. The system was, in other terms, more interested in securing order between equals than ensuring justice for all.

In many ways, the global projection of human rights challenges this very stable setup – at least there has always been a certain amount of hubris in the discipline about its potential to radically upset the traditional international legal system.[82] The resurgence of human rights in the post-Cold War era coincides with a reappraisal of some neo-Kantian themes in international law.[83] Human rights has the ambition to 'pierce the sovereign veil' and prescribe, sometimes in minute detail, how sovereigns should behave vis-à-vis their own population. Sovereignty, thus, becomes less an end in itself, than (almost) a form of international delegation of authority that is closely monitored by the 'international community'. International human rights law is therefore potentially part of a fundamental redefinition of what sovereignty means.[84] Sovereignty was the specific form of power that was absolute internally. If sovereignty is no longer that, then it loses much of its analytical trenchant, and becomes one form of power among many. International human rights also fundamentally changes our sense of the relevant political or even moral community. Although no doubt the state remains important, it is ultimately not as important – in the terms of the human rights project – as a broader 'world' or 'global' community of mankind, which was always a prominent feature of jusnaturalist writing about the international.

In *redefining* sovereignty rather than doing away with it,[85] international human rights have the potential to fundamentally change the nature of the international project. It is

---

Framework for Policy-Oriented Inquiry', 63 The American Journal of International Law 237–269 (1969).

[82] Anouncing the end of the Westphalian system is almost a separate genre in the discipline, one that never ceases to find eloquent spokespersons. See for example L. B. Sohn, 'The New International Law: Protection of the Rights of Individuals Rather Than States', 32 Am. UL Rev. 1 (1982).

[83] F. R. Teson, 'The Kantian Theory of International Law', 92 Colum. L. Rev. 53 (1992).

[84] W. M. Reisman, 'Sovereignty and human rights in contemporary international law', 84 The American Journal of International Law 866–876 (1990).

[85] On the normative underpinnings of sovereignty and the fact that the current movement is part of the 'evolving constitution of sovereignty' rather than the complete desuetude of the concept, see J. S. Barkin, 'The evolution of the constitution of sovereignty and the emergence of human rights norms', 27 Millenium: Journal of International Studies 229 (1998); C. Reus-Smit, 'Human rights and the social construction of sovereignty', 27 Review of International Studies 519–538 (2001).

sometimes said of the most enthusiastic international human rights lawyers that they proceed by way of 'domestic analogy', denying the 'international' any irreducible specificity.[86] The goal of the international system is no longer to ensure the coexistence of equals in a system that emphasizes order, but to guarantee that domestic political arrangements are not subverted in ways that fundamentally compromise the rights of persons within a state's jurisdiction. Pushed further, the project can come close to a Kantian horizon of global federalism.

Of course, in practice, this is to a large extent a very tentative move: it may be the implicit ambition of international human rights, but there are powerful forces of resistance.[87] The tension between the world of states and a budding world of human rights is periodically manifested through such flashpoints as the use of force in 'humanitarian intervention'[88] or the issue of immunities.[89] It should be read in the context of strong claims about human rights as increasingly a matter of common concern justifying international action and cooperation.[90] However, the fact that it is not simply a *vue de l'esprit* can be gauged by the profound (even if occasionally problematic) affinity between the supranational ambition to protect human rights and projects of regional integration that seek to profoundly redefine the bounds of community.[91] This is particularly apparent in the Americas but also, especially, the African continent, where the human rights and regionalization projects are a close match. But even the European Court of Human Rights (ECtHR) has described the Convention as a 'constitutional instrument of European public order' and it is well known that the EU is increasingly influenced by that public order.[92]

8.2.3 International Human Rights, State Behaviour, and International Relations

There has long been an interaction between the claims of international human rights law theorists and those of scholars involved in political science, particularly those interested in international state behaviour.[93] At the end of the Cold War, for example, scholarship

---

86 H. Suganami, *The domestic analogy and world order proposals* (1989).

87 For a sophisticated response to the criticism that international law cannot become a law of human rights enforcement, see A. D'Amato, 'The Concept of Human Rights in International Law', 82 Columbia Law Review 1110 (1982).

88 S. M. Makinda, 'Human Rights, Humanitarianism, the Transformation in the Global Community', 7 Global Governance 343 (2001).

89 A. Bianchi, 'Immunity versus human rights: the Pinochet case', 10 European Journal of International Law 237 (1999).

90 C. R. Beitz, *The Idea of Human Rights* (2009).

91 E. De Wet, 'The emergence of international and regional value systems as a manifestation of the emerging international constitutional order', 19 Leiden Journal of International Law 611–632 (2006).

92 P. Alston, M. R. Bustelo, and J. Heenan, *The EU and human rights* (1999); P. Alston and J. H. H. Weiler, 'An "Ever Closer Union" in Need of a Human Rights Policy', 9 European Journal of International Law 658 (1998); A. Von Bogdandy, 'The European Union as a human rights organization? Human rights and the core of the European Union', 37 Common Market Law Review 1307–1338 (2000).

93 R. J. Vincent, *Human Rights and International Relations* (1986); D. P. Forsythe, *Human rights in international relations* (2006).

emerged that emphasized the power of human rights norms in bringing about fundamental change in international politics.[94] Indeed, the dialectics of human rights and power are among the most interesting to understand the development of international relations. Although human rights lawyers typically focus on adjudication and formal law implementation, political scientists can bring a highly useful focus on how human rights are also embedded in logics of power. For example, foreign policy[95] or development conditionality – not to mention so-called 'humanitarian intervention' – are probably today among the most powerful ways in which the human rights project expresses itself or is undermined. These obviously raise issues about the nature of human rights as an international project.

One of the great puzzles for international human rights theory remains why states would want to bind themselves to international human rights obligations in the first place. Traditional realist explanations of states' interests typically minimize the importance of 'ideas' or even 'ideals' in the conduct of international relations, emphasizing instead the key notion of the 'national interest', understood as power (military, economic, political). Human rights are thus seen as an even more improbable way of understanding international relations than international law (about which there has always been significant scepticism from political realists) was. Although some work has been done to fit international human rights norms within realist theory,[96] this almost seems to ask too much of the paradigm. Notwithstanding this, there are several schools of thought that have sought to transcend this apparent paradox by finding ways to reconcile interest and values. Some have complexified the realist paradigm by emphasizing the extent to which, especially in the international politics of today, power also includes diffuse reputational advantages such as, precisely, respecting (or being seen as respecting) human rights. The so-called 'English school' of international relations has always been more sensitive to the role of norms in constructing international society and although some of its key proponents have been sceptical of radical change,[97] some have certainly helped outline the scenarios by which human rights might acquire a more dominant worldwide status. [98]

The rather vast set of thinkers associated with 'liberal' approaches to political science and international relations (IR) have also stressed the need to go beyond realist assumptions. One type of analysis emphasizes the nature of certain political regimes as a fairly accurate predictor of whether states will abide by international human rights standards (even though they may not become bound by them formally). Predictably, these theorists often conclude that liberal democracies tend to respect human rights more, all other things being equal, than states that are neither liberal nor democracies. Arrangements like the ECHR are presented as successful precisely because they were based on pre-existing

---

94 T. Risse-Kappen et al., *The power of human rights: International norms and domestic change* (1999).

95 J. Mertus, *Bait and switch: human rights and US foreign policy* (2008).

96 S. D. Krasner, 'Sovereignty, regimes, and human rights', Regime theory and international relations 139–167 (1993); J. Donnelly, 'International Human Rights: A Regime Analysis', 40 International Organization 599–642 (1986).

97 H. Bull, *The anarchical society* (1977).

98 R. J. Vincent, *Human Rights and International Relations* (1986).

democracies bent on the rule of law and a culture of rights.[99] There may be a gist of truth to this, but it must be recognized that, apart from ample evidence that liberal democracies are very capable of rights violations (e.g. in the context of the war on terror, or vis-à-vis indigenous, religious, or migrant communities, or in tolerating large amounts of significant poverty), this sort of reasoning is also quite dependent on certain fundamental assumptions about what 'complying' with human rights means (see below).

Scholars of the transnational dimension of politics have tended to put more emphasis on the role of norms in international relations,[100] particularly a dimension of 'moral proselytizing' by 'norm entrepreneurs',[101] or the role of transnational activists,[102] including leading human rights NGOs[103] and social movements.[104] Scholars more inclined towards constructivist approaches have emphasized the extent to which ideas such as human rights help construct the world in which we live, including notions of the national interest and sovereignty, rather than simply being shaped by them.[105] Innovative explanations at the intersection between historical research and political strategizing have emphasized the degree to which human rights can be a way for states that have recently emerged from authoritarian histories to protect themselves against a recurrence of such episodes by 'anchoring' their commitment to rights internationally.[106]

International human rights also bring attention to the extent to which IR's traditional concept of the main actors of IR is limited. Non-state actors have steadily become more important in IR, but perhaps nowhere more so than in a field with which they have identified strongly, namely the generation, implementation, and even enforcement of international human rights norms. This phenomenon is visible in such landmark events as the Beijing women's rights conferences, the Ottawa landmines conference, or the adoption of the Statute of the International Criminal Court in Rome. It is also clearly visible in traditionally inter-state fora like the Human Rights Council (formerly Commission) where civil society actors have long sought to have their voice heard. [107]

---

[99] A. Moravcsik, 'Explaining International Human Rights Regimes: Liberal Theory and Western Europe', 1 European Journal of International Relations 157–189 (1995).

[100] K. Sikkink, 'Transnational Politics, International Relations Theory, and Human Rights', 31 Political Science and Politics 517–523 (1998).

[101] C. Powell, 'The Role of Transnational Norm Enterpreneurs in the US War on Terrorism', 5 Theoretical Inquiries in Law 47 (2004).

[102] S. D. Burgerman, 'Mobilizing principles: the role of transnational activists in promoting human rights principles', 20 Hum. Rts. Q. 905–923 (1998).

[103] A. M. Clark, *Diplomacy of conscience: Amnesty International and changing human rights norms* (2001); P. R. Baehr, *Non-Governmental Human Rights Organizations in International Relations* (2009).

[104] N. Stammers, 'Social movements and the social construction of human rights', 21 Hum. Rts. Q. 980 (1999); B. Rajagopal, *International law from below: development, social movements, and Third World resistance* (2003).

[105] D. C. Thomas, *The Helsinki effect: international norms, human rights, and the demise of communism* (2001); Reus-Smit, *supra* note 85.

[106] A. Moravcsik, 'The origins of human rights regimes: Democratic delegation in postwar Europe', 54 International Organization 217–252 (2003).

[107] J. Smith, R. Pagnucco, and G. A. Lopez, 'Globalizing human rights: The work of transnational human rights NGOs in the 1990s', 20 Hum. Rts. Q. 379 (1998).

8.2.4 International Human Rights and Globalization

A significant area of exploration for scholars of international human rights, in addition to the traditional study of international relations, has been the intersection with the phenomenon of globalization.[108] One would tend to think that globalization has been broadly facilitative of the diffusion of human rights as an ideology, and there is probably much truth to this. Seeing the diffusion of ideas about human rights as a byproduct of globalization opens very interesting avenues for research. The typical emphasis has traditionally been on international or *supranational* human rights as a set of norms being channelled from above, in very 'top down' fashion, by the 'international community' first to the state and ultimately to the end beneficiaries of human rights. Globalization studies, on the other hand, tend to emphasize how the phenomenon is reshaping the nature of processes occurring both at the micro-local and at the global level.

A certain aspiration to world government to which the human rights project was partly tied is increasingly being replaced by an emphasis on the very multiple ways in which something as loosely defined as 'global governance' occurs. There are clear legal implications to this research agenda. As opposed to a vision of international law being the driving force behind the spread of human rights, 'globalists' stress the importance of transnational diffusion of norms, of networks of interest, of social movements, of new geographies, and of exchanges between different levels of governance. Scholars such as Sally Engle Merry have emphasized the extent to which the production of international human rights norms is increasingly marked by a very close association between local NGOs, states, and international governance structures.[109]

Yet at the same time, globalization creates strong phenomena of resistance that can militate against the spread of rights. The very erosion of sovereignty, so often seen as a goal for human rights activists, can have powerfully corroding effects on the ability of anyone to guarantee rights.[110] Moreover, globalization creates distinct and relatively new threats to rights, whether economic, political, or technological.[111] Whilst international human rights law traditionally focused on the state and what was happening 'within it', it increasingly has shifted its gaze to more complex phenomena generated by globalization. Among these, three perhaps stand out. First, the importance of the 'extra-territorial'. States are increasingly – although this is a phenomenon that has its roots in the colonial

---

108 A. Brysk, *Globalization and human rights* (2002).

109 S. E. Merry, 'Transnational human rights and local activism: Mapping the middle', 108 American Anthropologist 38 (2006); S. E. Merry, 'Rights talk and the experience of law: Implementing women's human rights to protection from violence', 25 Hum. Rts. Q. 343 (2003); S. E. Merry, 'Human rights and global legal pluralism: reciprocity and disjuncture', in F. von Benda-Beckmann, K. von Benda-Beckmann, and A. Griffiths (eds) *Mobile People, Mobile Law. Expanding Legal Relations in a Contracting World* 215–32 (2005); S. E. Merry, 'Global Human Rights and Local Social Movements in a Legally Plural World', 12 Can. J. L. & Soc. 247 (1997); S. E. Merry, 'Constructing a Global Law – Violence Against Women and the Human Rights System', 28 Law & Soc. inquiry 941 (2003); Zakaria and Yew, above note 25.

110 Louis Henkin, 'That S Word: Sovereignty, and Globalization, and Human Rights, Et Cetera', 68 Fordham Law Review 1 (1999).

111 R. McCorquodale and R. Fairbrother, 'Globalization and human rights', 21 Hum. Rts. Q. 735–766 (1999).

age – projecting their sovereignty outside their territory, raising questions about their human rights responsibilities in far-flung locations.[112] Second, the importance of the 'transnational' dimension for human rights. The transnational is the space that opens up 'in between' and beyond states. It creates significant human rights challenges, whether it be for refugees, migrants, fugitives, or victims of trafficking. Finally, globalization brings attention to a number of specifically global phenomena that might have a considerable impact on rights: the global distribution and circulation of capital and investment, and therefore more generally the importance of the economy; the global degradation of conditions on the planet; the global privacy and freedom implications of a medium such as the Internet.[113]

In this context, international human rights law certainly has the ambition to not simply be a branch of international law regulating state conduct at home but, increasingly, an international regulatory framework bent on orienting globalization in a certain direction – even as globalization threatens to undermine the international legal model on which rights promotion relied so crucially.[114] Human rights in a time of globalization seek to redefine the nature of international political association. This is manifested, for example, in the increasing association between at least certain internationally protected human rights and the idea of international constitutionalization,[115] although it also raises persistent issues about international human rights' democratic deficit.[116] This claim is reinforced by a whole strand of authors who seek to bring attention to the strong association of human rights with self-determination[117] or the idea of (national) democracy,[118] and the attendant risks of 'de-localized' human rights.

8.2.5 Critical Views of International Human Rights

Critical views of international human rights have emerged strongly in the last two decades as a result of the rising fortunes of the movement, but have existed for much longer, and

---

[112] M. J. Dennis, 'Application of Human Rights Treaties Extraterritorially in Times of Armed Conflict and Military Occupation', 99 The American Journal of International Law 119–141 (2005); M. Happold, 'Bankovic v. Belgium and the Territorial Scope of the European Convention on Human Rights', 3 Human Rights Law Review 77–90 (2003); S. I. Skogly and M. Gibney, 'Transnational Human Rights Obligations', 24 Hum. Rts. Q. 781 (2002).

[113] R. A. Falk, *Human rights horizons: the pursuit of justice in a globalizing world* (2000).

[114] T. Evans and J. Hancock, 'Doing something without doing anything: international human rights law and the challenge of globalization', 2 International Journal of Human Rights 1–21 (1998).

[115] An idea already implicit in the designation of the UDHR/ICCPR/ICESCR trio as the 'International bill of rights' as if they formed collectively the backbone of an emerging world polity. See S. Gardbaum, 'Human Rights as International Constitutional Rights', 19 European Journal of International Law 749 (2008).

[116] D. L. Donoho, 'Democratic Legitimacy in Human Rights: The Future of International Decision-Making', 21 Wis. Int'l. L. J. 1 (2003).

[117] R. McCorquodale, 'Self-determination: a human rights approach', 43 International and Comparative Law Quarterly 857–885 (2008).

[118] H. J. Steiner, 'Two Sides of the Same Coin? Democracy and International Human Rights', 41 Israel Law Review 445–476 (2008); J. O. McGinnis and I. Somin, 'Democracy and International Human Rights Law', 84 Notre Dame L. Rev. 1739 (2008).

have had famous proponents (among the more respectable) including Jeremy Bentham and Edmund Burke. They challenge 'mainstream' international human rights theory from a number of angles and come from both the political right[119] and the political left,[120] as well as a variety of conservative,[121] romantic or post-modern backgrounds, prompting some to herald 'the end of human rights'.[122] Human rights have been criticized on a number of grounds. Some have to do with the project itself and, apart from various foundationalist or relativist critiques that have already been alluded to, have tackled rights discourse's excessive individualism and socially-disaggregating effects,[123] or its fundamentally anti-democratic nature,[124] or simply its infatuation with self.[125] Some critiques focus on specific facets of international human rights' deployment and the particular forms this takes. For example, the excessive dominance of legal discourses on international human rights,[126] and the risks that come with overlegalization,[127] have long been a critical concern.

But most critiques operate at a deeper philosophical, jurisprudential, ideological, or political level. Some are critiques of a version of 'human rights in power', in regions where they have become very well entrenched. Their determinacy of rights and the whole notion of human rights adjudication has been challenged as vacuous, or as a way of conducting politics under the cloak of law. Enforcing human rights is presented as endless repetition of the liberal dilemmas that gave rise to them, and always at risk of degenerating into discretionary disserting on the meaning of such notions as 'reasonable' or 'proportional'.[128] Outside the areas where they are dominant, international human rights have been criticized for constituting a thinly veiled attempt to impose a particular Western, liberal project on the rest of the world, and as a process of subtle 'otherization'. For example Makau Mutua has argued that the project is embedded in a 'savages, victims and saviors' metaphor that systematically portrays the periphery as a place in need of

---

119 See, for example, the various human rights chapters in the CATO sponsored *ConUNdrum: The Limits of the United Nations and the Search for Alternatives* (2009).

120 M. Tushnet, 'Essay on rights', 62 Tex. L. Rev. 1363 (1983); W. Brown, *States of injury: Power and freedom in late modernity* (1995); D. Kennedy, 'The critique of rights in critical legal studies', Left Legalism/Left Critique 178–228 (2002).

121 Maurice Cranston, 'Are There Any Human Rights?', 112 Daedalus 1–17 (1983).

122 C. Douzinas, 'The End(s) of Human Rights', 26 Melb. UL Rev. 445 (2002).

123 A. Etzioni, *Rights and the common good: the communitarian perspective* (1995).

124 G. Souillac, *Human rights in crisis: the sacred and the secular in contemporary French thought* (2005).

125 M. Ignatieff, K. A. Appiah, and A. Gutmann, *Human rights as politics and idolatry* (2003).

126 T. Evans, 'International human rights law as power/knowledge', 27 Hum. Rts. Q. 1046 (2005).

127 L. R. Helfer, 'Overlegalizing Human Rights: International Relations Theory and the Commonwealth Caribbean Backlash against Human Rights Regimes', 102 Columbia Law Review 1832 (2002); C. Chinkin, 'International law and human rights', in *Human rights fifty years on: A reappraisal* 105–29 (T. Evans ed., 1998).

128 M. Koskenniemi, 'Olivier Corten, L'utilisation du 'raisonnable' par le juge international: Discours juridique, raison et contradictions', 94 American Journal of International Law 198 (2000); M. Koskenniemi, 'The Pull of the Mainstream', 88 Michigan Law Review, 1946–1962 (1990); M. Koskenniemi, 'The effect of rights on political culture', The EU and Human Rights 99–116 (1999); M. Koskenniemi, 'Occupied Zone: A Zone of Reasonableness?', 41 Isr. L. Rev. 13–677 (2008).

being 'saved' by human rights, in ways that are strongly reminiscent of the 'White man's burden'.[129] Nathaniel Berman has uncovered some of the deep affinities between early human rights movements and colonialism,[130] and Ratna Kapur has emphasized the continuing strength of such legacies.[131] Feminists have critiqued international human rights law's persistent androcentrism,[132] and in turn been criticized by critical race feminists for their Western-centrism.[133] Various strands of critical race theory have challenged the 'whiteness' of the dominant human rights narrative,[134] whilst others have challenged the dominance of an unproblematized human 'subject' of human rights, whether from the perspective of indigenous people,[135] or the gay and lesbian community.[136] Common to these critiques is a vision of human rights as power and as a device that is, in a variety of contexts, a lot more apologetic and legitimating of the status quo than it cares to recognize.[137] David Kennedy, in particular, has long challenged the praxis of human rights lawyering as one rooted in differentials of power and dominance, and at risk of being reductionist.[138]

8.3 THE THEORY OF INTERNATIONAL HUMAN RIGHTS LAW

As human rights challenge the fundamental tenor of the international project, so does international human rights law challenge some fundamental tenets of public international

---

[129] M. Mutua, 'Savages, victims, and saviors: the metaphor of human rights', 42 Harv. Int'l. L. J. 201 (2001); M. Mutua, 'The Ideology of Human Rights', 36 Virginia Journal of International Law 589 (1995); M. Mutua, *Human rights: A political and cultural critique* (2002).

[130] N. Berman, '"The Appeals of the Orient": Colonized Desire and the War of the Riff', in *Gender and Human Rights* (K. Knop ed., 2004).

[131] R. Kapur, 'Human Rights in the 21st Century: Take a Walk on the Dark Side', 28 Sydney Law Review 665 (2006).

[132] C. Romany, 'Women as Aliens: A Feminist Critique of the Public/Private Distinction in International Human Rights Law', 6 Harvard Human Rights Journal 87 (1993).

[133] P. E. Andrews, 'Globalization, Human Rights and Critical Race Feminism: Voices from the Margins', 3 Journal of Gender, Race and Justice 373 (1999); A. K. Wing, 'Critical race feminism and the international human rights of women in Bosnia, Palestine, and South Africa: Issues for LatCrit Theory', The University of Miami Inter-American Law Review 337–360 (1996).

[134] H. Lewis, 'Reflections on Blackcrit Theory: Human Rights', 45 Villanova Law Review 1075 (2000).

[135] R. A. Williams Jr, 'Encounters on the Frontiers of International Human Rights Law: Redefining the Terms of Indigenous Peoples' Survival in the World', Duke L. J. 660 (1990).

[136] D. Sanders, 'Getting Lesbian and Gay Issues on the International Human Rights Agenda', 18 Hum. Rts. Q. 67 (1996).

[137] A. M. Gross, 'Human Proportions: Are Human Rights the Emperor's New Clothes of the International Law of Occupation?', 18 European Journal of International Law 1 (2007); J. H. H. Weiler, 'Human rights, constitutionalism and integration: iconography and fetishism', 3 Int'l LFD Int'l 227 (2001).

[138] D. Kennedy, *The dark sides of virtue: reassessing international humanitarianism* (2004); D. Kennedy, 'International Human Rights Movement: Part of the Problem?', 15 Harv. Hum. Rts. J. 101 (2002); D. Kennedy, 'Spring Break', 63 Tex. L. Rev. 1377 (1984); D. Kennedy, 'Autumn Weekends: An Essay on Law and Everyday Life', in Sarat and Kearns (eds), *Law's Violence* (1993).

law.[139] Human rights as a project could only become 'international' by becoming binding under international law. However, the integration of human rights into public international law creates a complex dialectic. On the one hand, human rights law is constantly tempted to retreat from international law and 'play by its own rules' (or to conquer and dominate international law). Public international law's voluntarism (i.e. the idea that states are bound only by that to which they consent) is in tension with human rights' claimed immanence (the idea that rights exist and are in at least some way enforceable even though they have not been ratified formally). For example, international human rights lawyers may be tempted to revert to the discipline's default position that rights exist independently of positive international law whenever the rules of international law do not allow them to reach certain goals. International human rights law is often the site of unorthodox normative practices, from the point of view of classical international law.[140]

In practice of course this is not very sustainable and so the goal of every self-respecting human rights lawyer and activist in the last 200 years has been to convert rights' naturalist claim into the hard currency of positive law. In that respect the international human rights movement merely tries to replicate the best successes of domestic liberal revolutions that have culminated in the adoption of bills of rights and the like. Human rights therefore need to engage with international law and many international human rights lawyers seek to present themselves as orthodox – if progressist – public international lawyers.[141] As a result of their historical alliance with international law, human rights have become at least formally universalized.

However, tensions arise as a result of this embededness in public international law, a law that was designed originally with a very different purpose in mind than the worldwide promotion of an ideal of the good society. The tensions are between the mythology of human rights as rights inhering in human beings and the reality of human rights as rights that only have much traction if they have become positive law. These tensions can be seen to emerge at the level of sources, status, and even subjects of international human rights norms and to redefine such key notions as enforcement. In the process of seeking to deal with those tensions, human rights continue to have a profound impact on the various strands of doctrinal theorizing about public international law.

8.3.1 The Sources of International Human Rights

A priori, international human rights as a branch of international law should draw on the same sources and in the same way as general international law, namely article 38 of the Statute of the ICJ and its emphasis on custom, treaties, and general principles, complemented by precedents and the writings of the most senior publicists. In some respects, international human rights law very much mimics public international law. For example, international human rights treaties typically come into existence in the same way as ordinary treaties (they are negotiated, drafted, signed, and ratified). Much of the

---

139 M. T. Kamminga and M. Scheinin, *The impact of human rights law on general international law* (2009).

140 M. Koskenniemi, 'The Pull of the Mainstream', *supra* note 128.

141 T. Meron, *Human rights and humanitarian norms as customary law* (1989).

Vienna Convention on the law of treaties is applicable to human rights treaties. Indeed, international human rights has perhaps most clearly converged with public international law in its acquiescence to the idea that the treaty is increasingly the 'gold standard', with custom only a second best.

Without rejecting this, international human rights lawyers have arguably taken considerable liberties with the canons of sources. A good example is customary international law, an old and venerable source of public international law, whose understanding human rights have contributed to renovate or even revolutionize. Human rights lawyers have not been adverse to resorting to customary international law when it serves their purpose, i.e. typically when it allows them to dynamically adapt, even expand, the content of applicable human rights law, or to consider that states are bound by human rights norms even when they have not ratified the relevant treaties.

But customary law does create difficulties for human rights. For example, it is above all indexed on state behaviour and an element of state *practice*. The problem with practice is that human rights are often, unfortunately, honoured in the breach. What is one to make, for example, of the fact that, according to Amnesty International, as many as 70 states regularly practise torture? One may draw some comfort from the fact that none (or very few) of these states actually officially condone torture: most will claim that they do not commit any, in a sort of tribute paid by vice to virtue. In fact, one typical strategy for human rights lawyers has been to foreground *opinio juris* – states' vehement proclamations that they respect human rights and recognize them as such – at the expense of practice, thereby accelerating a process of unorthodox development of custom. States have been taken at their word, rather than held up to their own actual standard of behaviour.

This can be criticized as arbitrary, however, and as coming at a significant risk of compromising international law's theory of custom.[142] Others have emphasized the need to diversify the circle of relevant 'participants' for the purposes of elucidating human rights custom, including non-state actors and inter-governmental organizations.[143] However, the often unacknowledged bottom line is that most human rights lawyers would probably consider torture and many other human rights violations to be illegal regardless of the fact that most states practised them, or indeed even if states affirmed that they did not consider the prohibition on torture to be binding. That is because the source of the prohibition of torture is not really the treaties that say so, even though having the treaties both reinforces the status of the prohibition and creates an ambiguity about its foundation.

Even human rights' concept of treaty law is somewhat at variance with the mainstream of international law. International human rights treaties may superficially look like any other international law treaty (a binding agreement between sovereigns), but they differ in both form and substance. First, their grand proclamative and programmatic aspect suggests that something else is at stake than the ordinary manifestations of voluntarism: it is the voluntarism of recognizing something that is already supposedly there. Second,

---

142 B. Simma and P. Alston, 'The Sources of Human Rights Law: Custom, Jus Cogens, and General Principles', 12 Aust. YBIL 82 (1988).

143 J. J. Paust, 'The Complex Nature, Sources and Evidences of Customary Human Rights', 25 Georgia Journal of International and Comparative Law 147 (1995).

international human rights treaties are perhaps one of the clearest manifestations of 'law-making' or even 'constitutional' treaties, rather than the more 'contractual' model traditionally envisaged by international law.[144] International human rights law has also developed its own theory of interpretation that is at variance with the mainstream of international law, emphasizing *sui generis* tools such as the idea of treaties as 'living instruments' and their teleological and dynamic interpretation,[145] that would be inconceivable with normal international treaties.[146]

Another characteristic of the sources of international human rights law is an increasing focus on 'soft sources' (resolutions – starting with the UDHR, declarations, rather than conventions), and a tendency for the discipline to think of its sources in 'self-contained' terms. This leads to significant trans-judicial dialogue about human rights between constitutional judicatures (which increasingly find, in international human rights law, a common language), but also between different international human rights bodies, judicial or not.[147] However, one might argue that international human rights law is to some extent going even further and that there is a clear departure from, for example, article 38 of the ICJ. For example, there has been a broadening of what counts as a source to include reference to certain societal or communal values.[148] In fact, the movement is also at times transcending the notion of sources altogether, through reliance on certain fundamental values that are so broad to not really qualify as sources at all,[149] and even an affirmation (which is also in some ways a return to human rights' inspiration) that some rights exist for no other reason than the fact that they are believed in or are essential, or are morally and philosophically justified. In other words, international human rights law marks the resurgence of a sort of denaturalized natural law that is an implicit rejection of positivism's 'scientific' theory of sources, although that process is of course never quite explicit.

---

144 M. Craven, 'Legal differentiation and the concept of the human rights treaty in international law', 11 European Journal of International Law 489 (2000).

145 G. Letsas, *A theory of interpretation of the European Convention on Human Rights* (2007).

146 In fact, international human rights courts are criticized whenever they interpret human rights treaties according to traditional international law principles emphasizing restrictive interpretation to protect state voluntarism. A. Orakhelashvili, 'Restrictive Interpretation of Human Rights Treaties in the Recent Jurisprudence of the European Court of Human Rights', 14 European Journal of International Law 529 (2003).

147 A. Clapham, 'Symbiosis in International Human Rights Law: The Ocalan Case and the Evolving Law on the Death Sentence', 1 Journal of International Criminal Justice 475–489 (2003).

148 What is necessary in a 'democratic society' for the purposes of limiting rights, for example, is almost never ascertained by reference to state practice and *opinio juris*, but through an exploration of degrees of convergence within regional systems or even an exercise of speculative deduction from human rights first principles and jurisprudence. The African Convention on human rights is also noteworthy for including a reference to 'African practices' as a regional and domestic standard that would have had no equivalent in classical international law.

149 The Martens clause would be a good example in international humanitarian law. Its reference to 'the laws of humanity and the requirements of the public conscience' seems to act as a pseudo-positive conduit for the introduction of all kinds of considerations about how that particular regime should operate. T. Meron, 'The Martens Clause, Principles of Humanity, and Dictates of Public Conscience', 94 The American Journal of International Law 78–89 (2000); A. Cassese, 'The Martens Clause: half a loaf or simply pie in the sky?', 11 European Journal of International Law 187 (2000).

8.3.2 The Status and Nature of International Human Rights Obligations

In more ways than one, international human rights obligations differ significantly in their status and nature from traditional international legal obligations. First, their beneficiaries are individuals rather than states. Second, they apply primarily domestically where most traditional international legal obligations apply primarily internationally. Third, they are typically considered to have a high axiological validity and, for example, seen as transcending domestic and even other international norms.

A good example of how human rights lawyers have tackled such a potential tension is by forging what is sometimes known as the 'special character' of human rights obligations. Essentially, the idea of the 'special character' is a claim – somewhat circular and never fully substantiated except by appeal to the very notion of rights – that human rights norms operate in significantly, even radically different, ways from normal international legal obligations. This special character is most typically invoked in the context of treaty obligations, but one can make the case that it also has an impact on how obligations emerging from other sources (e.g. custom) should be understood. The idea of the special character has been referred to in the case law of the ICJ,[150] the ECmHR[151] and ECtHR,[152] and the Inter-American Court.[153]

The key intuition is that international human rights treaties are in some ways only treaties in form. Superficially, they resemble an exchange of promises between states, just like any treaty. Yet in reality what is occurring is very distinct and more complicated. What states are really doing is committing to respect the rights of persons within their jurisdiction. That promise is only tangentially made to other states (as reflected, for example, in the marginalization of inter-state procedures in advanced protection systems), and is in significant ways a promise to the beneficiaries of rights (populations), the international community, or even a complex form of 'promise to self' anchored in international commitment. This means that international human rights are less a commitment that is exchanged between equals in exchange for something, and more in the nature of a 'common interest' protected together; they represent less subjective than objective obligations; and they are in nature more unilateral than reciprocal. In other words, although human rights obligations appear under the a priori synallagmatic, and reciprocal form of treaties, this is in tension with their content as norms that are neither synallagmatic nor reciprocal.[154]

The notion of the 'special character' of human rights obligations has been associated with a whole series of remarkable developments in international law that seem to challenge core assumptions about the nature of international legal obligation: the *jus cogens*[155]

---

150 Reservations to the Convention on the Prevention and Punishment of the Crime of Genocide, ICJ Report 1951.

151 ECmHR, *Austria v. Italy*, 1961.

152 ECtHR, *UK v. Ireland*, 1978.

153 IACHR, Advisory opinion, The Effect of Reservations on the Entry Into Force of the American Convention on Human Rights, 1982.

154 This is what Matthew Craven has described as a fundamental tension between 'form' and 'function' in human rights treaties. Craven, *supra* note 144.

155 A. Bianchi, 'Human Rights and the Magic of Jus Cogens', 19 Eur. J. Int. Law 491–508

and *erga omnes*[156] of international human rights obligations; stricter rules in terms of permissible reservations[157] and the consequences of reservations being found incompatible with the object and purpose of a treaty;[158] a regime of quasi-automatic succession to human rights treaties unlike the default regime in international law;[159] an inability to withdraw from substantive[160] and even institutional or jurisdictional international human rights obligations;[161] a rejection of the defence of necessity to justify non-compliance and its replacement by a *sui generis* and embedded regime of derogations in times of national emergency;[162] a rejection of non-compliance as a remedy to non-execution of obligations by another party; a specific regime of enforcement emphasizing supranational scrutiny and individual triggering rather than inter-state disputes.[163]

8.3.3 The Subjects of International Human Rights Obligations

Human rights have also been at the source of much speculation about international law's theory of its legitimate subjects. As is well known, international law traditionally defined the only subjects of international law as being states. To a certain degree, international human rights law bows to this reality, if only because human rights have themselves been deeply marked by the state domestically, and because internationally states are effectively

---

(2008); E. De Wet, 'The Prohibition of Torture as an International Norm of jus cogens and its Implications for National and Customary Law', 15 European Journal of International Law 97 (2004).

156 A. Shapira, 'The Erga Omnes Applicability of Human Rights. Comment on Dinstein – The Erga Omnes Applicability of Human Rights', 30 AVR 22–27 (1992); Y. Dinstein, 'The erga omnes applicability of human rights', 30 Archiv des Völkerrechts (1992); K. Oellers-Frahm, 'Comment: The erga omnes Applicability of Human Rights', 30 Archiv des Völkerrechts, Bd 28–37 (1992).

157 L. Lijnzaad, *Reservations to UN human rights treaties: ratify and ruin?* (1995); E. A. Baylis, 'General Comment 24: Confronting the Problem of Reservations to Human Rights Treaties', 17 Berkeley J. Int'l. L. 277 (1999); W. A. Schabas, 'Reservations to human rights treaties: time for innovation and reform', 32 Can. YB Int'l. L. 39 (1994).

158 Makinda, *supra* note 88.

159 M. T. Kamminga, 'State Succession in Respect of Human Rights Treaties', 7 European Journal of International Law 469–485 (1996).

160 N. P. Concepcion, 'The Legal Implications of Trinidad & Tobago's Withdrawal from the American Convention on Human Rights', 16 Am. U. Int'l L. Rev. 847 (2000); E. Evatt, 'Democratic People's Republic of Korea and the ICCPR: Denunciation as an Exercise of the Right of Self-Defence', 8 AJHR 1 (1999); Ed. Bates, 'Avoiding Legal Obligations Created by Human Rights Treaties', 57 International & Comparative Law Quarterly 751–788 (2008).

161 N. Schiffrin, 'Jamaica Withdraws the Right of Individual Petition Under the International Covenant on Civil and Political Rights', American Journal of International Law 563–568 (1998); M. F. Tinta, 'Individual Human Rights v. State Sovereignty: The Case of Peru's Withdrawal from the Contentious Jurisdiction of the Inter-American Court of Human Rights', 13 Leiden Journal of International Law 985–996 (2004); K. C. Sokol, 'Ivcher Bronstein v. Constitutional Tribunal. Inter-American Court of Human Rights judgment on right of a state to withdraw its acceptance of compulsory jurisdiction', 95 American Journal of International Law 178 (2001).

162 D. McGoldrick, 'The interface between public emergency powers and international law', 2 International Journal of Constitutional Law 380–429 (2004); S. Joseph, 'Human Rights Committee: General Comment 29', 2 Human Rights Law Review 81 (2002).

163 T. Meron, 'Norm Making and Supervision in International Human Rights: Reflections on Institutional Order', 76 American Journal of International Law 754–778 (1982).

among the actors that have most potential to harm human rights (and, correlatively, to fulfil them). However, the international human rights movement has also contributed significantly to the renewal of international law's perception of its rightful subjects through at least two developments emphasizing the status of individuals:[164] first, the idea – once seemingly unattainable –[165] that individuals have standing before international bodies and courts to complain of violations of human rights committed by certain states,[166] and even in many cases to invoke the benefit of human rights treaties before domestic courts;[167] second, the idea that individuals can commit international crimes which, although they may not be the same thing, are often at least implicitly conceived in terms of (massive) human rights violations.[168]

More generally, one could argue that human rights as a project is clearly less committed to the idea of the state's exclusivity as a subject of international law than public international law was. This is partly because there is an occasionally anti-sovereign bias in human rights activism. It is also because international human rights is a priori mostly interested in what social arrangements, domestically or internationally, might negatively affect or maximize human rights, and therefore more agnostic about what the legitimate subjects of ought to be (as opposed to a normative system like public international law which is committed to a particular theory of legitimate subjects as part of its very normative project). If it turns out that multinational corporations,[169] guerilla groups,[170] or intergovernmental organizations[171] have most impact on human rights, a human

---

164 I. Brownlie, 'The Place of the Individual in International Law', 50 Va. L. Rev. 435 (1964); R. Higgins, 'Conceptual thinking about the individual in international law', British Journal of International Studies 1–19 (1978).

165 J. W. Bruegel, 'The Right to Petition an International Authority', 2 The International and Comparative Law Quarterly 542–563 (1953).

166 K. Boyle and H. Hannum, 'Individual Applications under the European Convention on Human Rights and the Concept of Administrative Practice: The Donnelly Case', 68 Am. J. Int'l L. 440 (1974); L. Heffernan, 'A Comparative View of Individual Petition Procedures under the Human Convention on Human Rights and the International Covenant on Civil Political Rights', 19 Hum. Rts. Q. 78 (1997).

167 A. Z. Drzemczewski, *European human rights convention in domestic law: a comparative study* (1998).

168 L. S. Sunga, *Individual responsibility in international law for serious human rights violations* (1992).

169 S. R. Ratner, 'Corporations and human rights: a theory of legal responsibility', 111 Yale L. J. 443 (2001); A. Clapham, *Human rights obligations of non-state actors* (2006); P. Alston, *Non-state actors and human rights* (2005); C. Jochnick, 'Confronting the impunity of non-state actors: new fields for the promotion of human rights', 21 Hum. Rts. Q. 56 (1999); B. Stephens, 'The Amorality of Profit: Transnational Corporations and Human Rights', 20 Berkeley J. Int'l. L. 45 (2002); J. J. Paust, 'Human Rights Responsibilities of Private Corporations', 35 Vand. J. Transnat'l. L. 801 (2002); J. G. Ruggie, 'Business and human rights: The evolving international agenda', American Journal of International Law 819–840 (2007).

170 A. Clapham, 'Human rights obligations of non-state actors in conflict situations', 88 International Review of the Red Cross 491–523 (2007).

171 F. Mégret and F. Hoffmann, 'The UN as a human rights violator? Some reflections on the United Nations' changing human rights responsibilities', 25 Hum. Rts. Q. 314–342 (2003); T. Ahmed and I. de Jesus Butler, 'The European Union and human rights: An international law perspective', 17 European Journal of International Law 771 (2006); A. Reinisch, 'Developing Human Rights and Humanitarian Law Accountability of the Security Council for the Imposition

rights pragmatist will be inclined to think, then these should be subjects of international human rights law (and therefore, at least to a limited extent, of public international law) at least insofar as this will enhance the goals of human rights. This of course raises not just technical but theoretical problems: under what theory should non-state actors have human rights obligations? How might their responsibility relate to that of states? What kind of subjecthood results? International human rights law is beginning to answer these important legal questions.

8.3.4 International Human Rights Law, Implementation, and Domestic Law

No branch of international law has done more to revive theoretical debates about implementation than international human rights law, especially in view of the largely shared view that domestic courts should be at the forefront of human rights enforcement,[172] and that international human rights treaties are of little use if they do not impact domestic law.[173] In international legal theory, of course, states can be found liable directly under international law for violations of human rights. But, apart from the fact that no human rights court may be available to engage that responsibility (and that the ICJ is for most purposes an unlikely forum), even when a human rights court does exist state complaints are the exception, and international remedies always distant, so that domestic courts should be able to provide a first remedy.

The problem is that, for all the individual-orientedness of human rights, there is much resistance to international human rights obligations, particularly treaties, being applicable directly in domestic law. This has been especially noticeable in dualist countries that have, historically, proved to offer most opposition to the domestic incorporation of international human rights obligations.[174] Human rights may appear to some as naturally self-executing treaties, but in countries with a strong tradition of parliamentary sovereignty and possibly no tradition of constitutional rights protection, international ratification without implementation will make prospects of human rights domestic enforcement very unlikely. Dualism has been criticized for creating a situation largely incompatible with the spirit of international human rights obligations: states ratify international human rights treaties, supposedly to protect individuals within their jurisdiction, but these individuals cannot complain of human rights violations under these treaties, which are considered to be only commitments made between states.

This is also in tension with the 'special character' of human rights treaties, and human rights bodies regularly plead for the direct applicability of their norms in domestic law.

---

of Economic Sanctions', American Journal of International Law 851–872 (2001); C. Dommen, 'Raising Human Rights Concerns in the World Trade Organization: Actors, Processes and Possible Strategies', 24 Hum. Rts. Q. 1 (2002); H. V. Morais, 'The Globalization of Human Rights Law and the Role of International Financial Institutions in Promoting Human Rights', 33 George Washington International Law Review 71 (2000).

172 B. Conforti and F. Francioni, *Enforcing international human rights in domestic courts* (1997).

173 C. Heyns and F. Viljoen, 'The impact of the United Nations human rights treaties on the domestic level', 23 Hum. Rts. Q. 483–535 (2001).

174 L. Henkin, 'Implementation and Compliance: Is Dualism Metastasizing', 91 American Society of International Law Proceedings 515 (1997).

Some have spotted a 'creeping monism' in traditionally dualist countries when it comes to human rights, through techniques of interpretative incorporation.[175] In certain regional contexts, particularly that of the Council of Europe, dualism has become gradually unsustainable for states, as it has exposed them to too many findings of being in breach because of the inadequacy of domestic remedies,[176] prompting the adoption of such landmark implementing legislation as the British Human Rights Act.[177] Indeed, whether dualist or monist, the increasingly constitutional force of human rights guarantees and the openness of at least some constitutions to the supra-legislative force of international treaties has made incorporation a much more significant reality than ever.[178]

8.3.5 International Human Rights, Fragmentation, and Other Branches of Public International Law

International human rights law is still classically seen as a branch of public international law, and not an isolated and self-contained regime – despite elements of strong self-reliance.[179] Nonetheless, some of the most interesting theoretical debates on the nature of international human rights law in the past decade have been part of a larger discussion about the fragmentation of international law and the competing pull of other significant and, each in their own way, potentially hegeomonizing branches of international law. For example, considerable attention has been paid to policing/problematizing the frontier between international humanitarian and international human rights law,[180] specifically as a problem of fragmentation.[181] Part of the work in this vein is merely concerned with filling gaps between the two,[182] but some has been more riddled with fundamental value conflicts. Whilst international humanitarian lawyers are prompt to make a claim on

---

175 M. A. Waters, 'Creeping Monism: The Judicial Trend Toward Interpretive Incorporation of Human Rights Treaties', 107 Colum. L. Rev. 628 (2007).

176 A. Z. Drzemczewski, *European human rights convention in domestic law: a comparative study* (1998).

177 I. Leigh and L. Lustgarten, 'Making rights real: the courts, remedies, and the Human Rights Act', 58 The Cambridge Law Journal 509–545 (1999).

178 Y. Shany, 'How Supreme Is the Supreme Law of the Land – Comparative Analysis of the Influence of International Human Rights Treaties upon the Interpretation of Constitutional Texts by Domestic Courts', 31 Brooklyn Journal of International Law 341 (2005); T. Buergenthal, 'Modern Constitutions and Human Rights Treaties', 36 Columbia Journal of Transnational Law 211 (1998).

179 L. Wildhaber, 'The European Convention on Human Rights and International Law', 56 International & Comparative Law Quarterly 217–231 (2007); S. P. Ridruejo and J. Antonio, 'Droit international et droit international des droits de l'homme: unité ou fragmentation?', in *Human Rights, Democracy and the Rule of Law: Liber Amicorum Luzius Wildhaber* (S. Breitenmoser ed., 2007).

180 R. Provost, *International human rights and humanitarian law* (2002).

181 A. Orakhelashvili, 'The Interaction between Human Rights and Humanitarian Law: Fragmentation, Conflict, Parallelism, or Convergence?', 19 European Journal of International Law 161 (2008); A. E. Cassimatis, 'International Humanitarian Law, International Human Rights Law, and Fragmentation of International Law', 56 International and Comparative Law Quarterly 623–639 (2008).

182 A. Eide, A. Rosas, and T. Meron, 'Combating lawlessness in gray zone conflicts through minimum humanitarian standards', American Journal of International Law 215–223 (1995).

behalf of the laws of war as a *lex specialis*,[183] some emphasize the influence of human rights on the laws of war,[184] some would displace international humanitarian law in at least cases of non-international armed conflict,[185] and yet others remain uncomfortable with what seems an excessive toleration for violence and the killing of the innocent.[186] A similar tension arises in the context of the so-called 'war on terror' and opposes those who think that global terrorism should be dealt with primarily under humanitarian or human rights law.[187]

Another very significant fault line has opened between international human rights and international trade law.[188] One scholar in particular, Ernst Ulrich Petersmann, has energetically argued for the integration of human rights in world trade law.[189] This has been met by an equally vigorous series of responses.[190] There has also been much discussion of the intersection of what might be termed international security law (particularly action by the Security Council) and international human rights law;[191] international criminal law, despite being apparently significantly driven by rights concerns,[192] raises periodic issues about how seriously it should take human rights;[193] some have suggested that refugee law be framed more in terms of human rights;[194] development law is increasingly under the influence of human rights 'mainstreaming';[195] significant tensions exist between international labour law as a model of worker protection and rights approaches;[196] and

---

183 K. Anderson, 'Who Owns the Rules of War?', 13 New York Times Magazine (2003).

184 T. Meron, 'The humanization of humanitarian law', 94 The American Journal of International Law 239–278 (2000).

185 W. Abresch, 'A human rights law of internal armed conflict: the European Court of Human Rights in Chechnya', 16 European Journal of International Law 741 (2005).

186 Karima Bennoune, 'Toward a Human Rights Approach to Armed Conflict: Iraq 2003', 11 U.C. Davis Journal of International Law & Policy 171 (2004).

187 R. Ehrenreich Brooks, 'War Everywhere: Rights, National Security Law, and the Law of Armed Conflict in the Age of Terror', 153 University of Pennsylvania Law Review 675 (2004).

188 T. Cottier, 'Trade and Human Rights: a relationship to discover', 5 Journal of International Economic Law 111 (2002).

189 For one in a long series of such articles, see E. U. Petersmann, 'Time for a United Nations "Global Compact" for Integrating Human Rights into the Law of Worldwide Organizations: Lessons from European Integration', 13 European Journal of International Law 621 (2002).

190 R. Howse, 'Human Rights in the WTO: Whose Rights, What Humanity? Comment on Petersmann', 13 EJIL 651–659 (2002); P. Alston, 'Resisting the Merger and Acquisition of Human Rights by Trade Law: A Reply to Petersmann', 13 European Journal of International Law 815 (2002).

191 D. L. Donoho, 'The Role of Human Rights in Global Security Issues: A Normative and Institutional Critique', 14 Mich. J. Int'l. L. 827 (1992); I. Johnstone, 'The UN Security Council, Counterterrorism and Human Rights', in *Counterterrorism: Democracy's Challenge* (A. Bianchi and A. Keller eds, 2008).

192 D. F. Orentlicher, 'Settling accounts: the duty to prosecute human rights violations of a prior regime', 100 Yale L. J. 2537 (1990).

193 S. Zappala, *Human rights in international criminal proceedings* (2003).

194 J. C. Hathaway, 'Reconceiving refugee law as human rights protection', 4 Journal of Refugee Studies 113 (1991).

195 B. I. Hamm, 'A Human Rights Approach to Development', 23 Hum. Rts. Q. 1005 (2001); P. Alston, 'Ships passing in the night: The current state of the human rights and development debate seen through the lens of the Millennium Development Goals', 27 Hum. Rts. Q. 755 (2005).

196 P. Alston, *Labour rights as human rights* (2005).

human rights are presented as one way to instil a sense of urgency about international environmental obligations.[197] In short, international human rights law is at once potentially hegemonic, vigorously challenged by the dominance of other agendas and, quite possibly, harbours the ambition to be in a position to arbitrate value conflicts with all of the above, from the point of view of the best interest of human beings.

8.3.6 International Human Rights and the Notion of Enforcement

As with international law, much scholarship in international human rights is geared towards specifying the conditions under which international human rights law is most likely to be 'enforced'.[198] International human rights lawyers have always been very keen on institutional work, for the obvious reason that human rights that are not implemented are of little interest to those they are supposed to benefit. In this respect, there has often been a perceived considerable gap between proclaimed intentions, the relative success of human rights *discourse*, and the reality of rights.[199] This has led to periodic disenchantment, but also a vigorous search and international legal activism in favour of stronger international human rights mechanisms and occasionally an urge to raise old questions anew.[200]

In this respect, the search for the 'best possible' international human rights institutions is linked to a respectable and ancient study of the reality and prospects of 'International Organization' (the macro-organization of the system itself) and international organizations (the actual mechanisms).[201] It has contributed to the creation and better understanding of a number of quite remarkably *sui generis* mechanisms for international human rights promotion. For example, to a much more considerable degree than classical public international law, international human rights law emphasizes the importance of human rights implementation.[202] This was not so much of an issue for international treaties that were not meant to create particular benefits, let alone rights, for individuals, but it obviously is foremost in the minds of international human rights lawyers. International human rights bodies have also considerably broadened our concept of what might count as enforcement. There has been, and continues to be, considerable interest in what traditional international lawyers might consider remarkably unorthodox ways of enforcing an international legal regime (supervision, reporting, recommendations, codes of conduct).[203]

---

197 W. Sachs, 'Climate change and human rights', 51 Development 332–337 (2008).

198 H. H. Koh, 'How is international human rights law enforced?', 74 Ind. L. J. 1397 (1998).

199 E. M. Hafner-Burton and K. Tsutsui, 'Justice Lost! The Failure of International Human Rights Law To Matter Where Needed Most', 44 Journal of Peace Research 407–425 (2007); E. M. Hafner-Burton and J. Ron, *Can the Human Rights Movement Achieve its Goals?* (2007).

200 R. B. Bilder, 'Rethinking International Human Rights: Some Basic Questions', 1969 Wisconsin Law Review 171 (1969).

201 P. Alston and F. Mégret, *The United Nations and Human Rights* (2010); L. R. Helfer, 'Redesigning the European Court of Human Rights: Embeddedness as a Deep Structural Principle of the European Human Rights Regime', 19 European Journal of International Law 125 (2008).

202 B. Conforti and F. Francioni, *Enforcing international human rights in domestic courts* (1997).

203 D. Donoho, 'Human Rights Enforcement in the Twenty-First Century', 35 Georgia Journal of International and Comparative Law 1 (2006).

The move from lofty rhetoric about rights to talk of their enforcement – especially when enforcement is understood quite literally as the use of force – has historically generated a significant resistance. For many states and scholars, international human rights law, though important, should never trump sovereignty to the point of undermining a fundamental tenet of public international law, namely the non-use of force. For others, the international human rights corpus does not amount to much if states cannot rise up to the occasion of fundamental threats to populations by using force when absolutely necessary and as a last resort. The Kosovo debate, in that respect, has crystallized many anxieties about the current predicament of international law in an age of rights, and strongly given the impression that human rights were part and parcel of logics of dismantlement of the international legal order, or even a new form of imperialism.[204] However, it is not just the use of force that has generated resistance and even the comparatively mild scrutiny of international bodies or transnational human rights litigation[205] have been criticized as illegitimate, often on principled grounds. The remoteness of all things international, the non-democratic character of international institutions, are all aspects that have been drawn upon to seek to limit the growing reach of human rights enforcement.

Moreover, enforcement has been criticized as not happening or at least as not happening the way the mainstream international human law theory sought to portray it. Scholars operating at the intersection of international human rights and international relations, for example, have been willing to ask a number of hard questions about the treaty, which has long been established as the 'gold standard' of the international human rights movement. But how much of a difference do international human rights treaties actually make? Various authors have provocatively argued that treaties have very little influence: they tend to be ratified most readily by states with bad human rights records who typically do not take their human rights obligations seriously, where states that are relatively more scrupulous about human rights and take treaties seriously may decide not to ratify them on narrow technical grounds.[206] This sort of work, which blossomed like a fad during the last decade, raises interesting challenges to international lawyers who might assume a little too readily that treaties must *necessarily* make a difference, although its epistemological stance and empirical data has been questioned.[207]

Scholars of how enforcement actually takes place have sought to go beyond ideological debates about enforcement and to show enforcement to be a much more complex issue theoretically. The idea that treaties probably do not make a difference as such, and certainly not in any narrow command-and-control fashion, was probably always rather obvious. Instead, human rights 'performance' – if there is such a thing – will depend on

---

[204] D. Chandler, *From Kosovo to Kabul and beyond: human rights and international intervention* (2006); A. Orford, *Reading humanitarian intervention: Human rights and the use of force in international law* (2003).

[205] C. A. Bradley and J. L. Goldsmith III, 'The Current Illegitimacy of International Human Rights Litigation', 66 Fordham L. Rev. 319 (1997).

[206] L. Camp Keith, 'The United Nations International Covenant on Civil and Political Rights: Does It Make a Difference in Human Rights Behavior?', 36 Journal of Peace Research 95–118 (1999); O. A. Hathaway, 'Do human rights treaties make a difference?', 111 Yale L. J. 1935 (2001); Hafner-Burton and Tsutsui, *supra* note 199.

[207] R. Goodman and D. Jinks, 'Measuring the effects of human rights treaties', 14 European Journal of International Law 171 (2003).

how treaties operate in conjunction with a set of other factors,[208] or through unexpected and indirect ways such as encouraging civil society.[209] Contra notions that enforcement is mostly a vertical process of 'international community imposition', they have emphasized the horizontal dimension of enforcement, one that allows local and transnational participants in the debate to use 'norm portals' to reform domestic law from within by pointing to its remoteness from 'evolving standards'.[210]

The term 'enforced', in fact, may be part of the problem in that it already betrays an indebtedness to a concept of law as a form of 'command backed by force', a vision that many find outdated and reductionist. One strand of contemporary international human rights theory, inspired by a whole tradition of international law as a socializing process, has thus sought to emphasize not so much force as implementation, not so much orders as influence.[211] The dominant international legal theory on human rights still tends to be very top-down, and interested in what rights are 'from above'. Its concept of human rights norm production is one that emphasizes states and the 'international community'. It focuses on the role of international organizations and courts in implementing human rights.

Curiously, for an idea that otherwise almost idealizes the idea of human agency, it seemingly has little to say at times on how human rights norms are not only received but also produced locally. A new generation of work on human rights has, on the contrary, emphasized a sense of 'human rights from below', of rights evolving through struggles and social movements, rather than through the superstructure of liberal institutions.[212] Others, particularly anthropologists, have emphasized the need to actually go into the field and better understand how rights are absorbed, incorporated and adopted, but also resisted and rejected or reimagined and reinterpreted.[213] Yet others have emphasized new modes of regulations, including soft regulation, as better approximating what human rights law might come to resemble in the future.[214] Legal pluralism is increasingly emerging as a possible paradigm to analyse the coexistence of multiple legal orders conducive to human rights.[215]

---

208 E. Neumayer, 'Do international human rights treaties improve respect for human rights?', 49 Journal of Conflict Resolution 925 (2005); D. Cassel, 'Does international human rights law make a difference?', 2 Chi. J. Int'l. L. 121 (2001).

209 E. M. Hafner-Burton and K. Tsutsui, 'Human Rights in a Globalizing World: The Paradox of Empty Promises', 110 American Journal of Sociology 1373–1411 (2005).

210 M. E. McGuinness, 'Medellin, Norm Portals, and the Horizontal Integration of International Human Rights', 82 Notre Dame Law Review 755 (2006).

211 R. Goodman and D. Jinks, 'How to Influence States: Socialization and International Human Rights Law', 54 Duke Law Journal 621–704 (2004).

212 B. de Sousa Santos and C. A. Rodríguez-Garavito, *Law, politics, and the subaltern in counter-hegemonic globalization*, Law and Globalization from Below (2005); B. Rajagopal, 'Counter-hegemonic International Law: rethinking human rights and development as a Third World strategy', 27 Third World Quarterly 767–783 (2006); B. Rajagopal, 'The International Human Rights Movement Today', 24 Maryland Journal of International Law 56 (2009).

213 M. Goodale and S. E. Merry, *The practice of human rights: tracking law between the global and the local* (2007).

214 D. Kinley and R. Chambers, 'The UN Human Rights Norms for corporations: The private implications of public international law', 6 Human Rights Law Review 447 (2006).

215 F. Mégret, 'International human rights and legal pluralism: a Reseach Agenda', in *Human Rights and Legal Pluralism* (R. Provost and C. Sheppard eds. 2010).

8.4 CONCLUSION

A few words of conclusion are in order on international human rights theory's relationship to the practice of the discipline. International human rights law is seen as a practice, which in many ways it very much is. However, even though some human rights lawyers probably aspire to this, it is very difficult to 'bracket out' the theory of human rights from their application. Much of the international law of human rights is deeply embedded in – indeed, defined by – some of the perennial debates that gave rise to human rights in the first place, and is part of a tricky and ongoing conversation about the nature and development of international law. International human rights theorizing, in this respect, is not a distraction from the serious work of practice, but a way of thinking about what it means to 'do international human rights law' that foregrounds the active role of the human rights practitioner not as a slave to the law, but as an ideally conscious and articulate interpreter of a project in the making.

9 The philosophy of international criminal law

Robert Cryer

9.1 INTRODUCTION

International criminal law is an area that recently has become the subject of significant attention, both by lawyers and philosophers, as well as those working at the interface of the two disciplines. Although, as is often the case, practitioners in the area are somewhat sceptical of such inquiry, jurisprudential considerations have long been an integral, if not always acknowledged, part of international criminal law. This is entirely appropriate; criminal law is an area of study which has traditionally been the subject of philosophical enquiry at the domestic level.[1] Although, as we will see, some are dubious, international criminal law, since its aims are cognate[2] to those that criminal law seeks to achieve at the domestic level, ought to be subject to similar scrutiny. The analogous nature of international and domestic criminal law is underpinned now by the fact that the principle of complementarity, which underpins the relationship between the International Criminal Court and national jurisdictions, emphasises the role of domestic prosecutions in the international regime that responds to such crimes.[3]

Similarly to domestic criminal law, there are various different ways in which philosophy and international criminal law intersect. Some scholars working in the area work on the philosophical foundations of punishment at the international level.[4] Others work on applying doctrinal criminal law theory to international criminal law;[5] still others have attempted to provide philosophical foundations for particular international crimes.[6]

---

[1] See, for example, Andrew Ashworth, *Principles of Criminal Law* (Oxford: OUP, 6th edn., 2009); A.P. Simester and A.T.H. Smith (eds) *Harm and Culpability* (Oxford: OUP, 1996); H.L.A. Hart, *Punishment and Responsibility* (Oxford: OUP, 2nd edn., 2008); George P. Fletcher, *Rethinking Criminal Law* (Boston, Mass.: Little, Brown & Co, 1978).

[2] On the aims and objectives of international criminal law see Robert Cryer, Håkan Friman, Darryl Robinson and Elizabeth Wilmshurst, *An Introduction to International Criminal Law* (Cambridge: CUP, 2nd edn, 2010) Chapter 2.

[3] On complementarity see, e.g. Mohamed el Zeidy, *The Principle of Complementarity in International Criminal Law: Origin, Development and Practice* (The Hague: Brill, 2008); Jann K. Kleffner, *Complementarity in the Rome Statute and National Criminal Jurisdictions* (Oxford: OUP, 2008); Jo Stigen, *The Relationship Between the International Criminal Court and National Jurisdictions: The Principle of Complementarity* (The Hague: Brill, 2008).

[4] See, e.g. Antony Duff, 'Authority and Responsibility in International Criminal Law' in Susanna Besson and John Tasioulas (eds), *The Philosophy of International Law* (Oxford: OUP, 2010) 589.

[5] Notable examples include Kai Ambos *Der Allgemeine Teil des Völkerstrafrechts – Ansätze einer Dogmatisierung* (Berlin: Duncker and Humblot, 2nd edn., 2004), and Gerhard Werle, *Principles of International Criminal Law* (Cambridge: CUP, 2nd edn. 2009).

[6] Perhaps the most important examples of such scholarship include Larry May, *Crimes Against Humanity: A Normative Account* (Cambridge: CUP, 2005); Larry May, *War Crimes and*

There are, of course, others who approach international criminal law scholarship, as international law, with an avowedly theoretical bent.[7] This chapter will attempt to provide a short chronological study of the development of such works and a survey of some of these approaches. However, owing to the breadth of the subject, it cannot be claimed that this is a comprehensive survey of the detailed and rich contributions made to international criminal law by the more philosophically inclined. It ought also to be said at the outset that not all the scholars who are classified under the taxonomy below would necessarily consider themselves exemplars of the tradition they have been taken to represent, or perhaps even related to it. It is also true that a person can reflect more than one philosophical approach in their work.[8] Self-identification, nonetheless, is only one taxonomical approach, and what has been attempted here is to group ideas together as best as possible.

9.2 A BRIEF HISTORY OF THE PHILOSOPHY OF INTERNATIONAL CRIMINAL LAW

9.2.1 1945–1990

International criminal law has been around in some form or other for a considerable period of time. Nonetheless, the modern idea of philosophising about it as a matter of law, rather than morals, can be dated largely to the era beginning with World War I, at least in the English speaking world.[9] It is possible to trace the influence of natural law, and the critiques of it, to the Commission on the Responsibility of the Authors of the War of 1919. The idea of prosecuting violations of the 'laws of humanity', and the rejection of that proposition by the American dissenters from the report, on the basis that such rules were too subjective to admit of criminal liability, could be read in this way. After all, the idea of 'laws of humanity' was probably not a reference to general principles of law per se, but to more nebulous ideas of what 'humanity' required.[10] The American response, that such a suggestion was simply a universalisation of a subjective standard, could easily

Just War (Cambridge: CUP, 2007); Larry May, *Aggression and Crimes Against Peace* (Cambridge: CUP, 2008); Larry May, *Genocide: A Normative Account* (Cambridge: CUP, 2010); David Luban, 'A Theory of Crimes Against Humanity' (2004) 29 *Yale Journal of International Law* 85.

7 For examples, see e.g. Yasmin Q. Naqvi, *Impediments to Exercising Jurisdiction Over International Crimes* (The Hague: T.M.C. Asser Press, 2010), Chapter 1; Helen Silving, 'In re Eichmann: A Dilemma of Law and Morality' (1961) 55 *American Journal of International Law* 307.

8 For further explanation of some of the difficulties that arise here, see Robert Cryer, Tamara Hervey, Bal Sohki-Bulley with Alexandra Bohm, *Research Methodologies in International and EU Law* (Oxford: Hart, 2010).

9 For brief histories see T.L.H. McCormack, 'From Sun-Tzu to the Sixth Committee: The Evolution of an International Criminal Law Regime' in T.L.H. McCormack and Gerry Simpson (eds), *The Law of War Crimes: National and International Approaches* (The Hague: Kluwer, 1997) 31; Robert Cryer, *Prosecuting International Crimes: Selectivity and the International Criminal Law Regime* (Cambridge: CUP, 2005) Chapter 1.

10 On such concepts at the time see Martti Koskenniemi, *The Gentle Civilizer of Nations: The Rise and Fall of International Law* (Cambridge: CUP, 2001).

be seen as a positivist reaction to naturalistic assertions of what 'humanity' wanted or needed. Since the report did not in the end lead to any practical action, it may be to over-read it to draw many conclusions from it, although many of the concerns in the report reflect more modern debates.[11]

That said, the first major, express, engagement of philosophical considerations in modern international criminal law came during World War II. Three of those heavily involved in the Allied plans for the prosecution of Axis international criminality were quite clear about their use of natural law principles in support of this effort. For example, Quincy Wright, who was US Chief Prosecutor Robert Jackson's legal adviser was quite clear that his view positivism was not enough, and that the Nuremberg Charter 'rests on the assumption that the enunciation of principles of justice can be creative, that such principles are a source of law, and that they may generate institutions which can enforce the law'.[12] Similarly, the President of the United Nations War Crimes commission, Lord Wright, could hardly have been clearer about his views on the matter, opining in his introductory chapter to the history of that body, that '[i]nternational law is a product of natural law, that is, it has grown and developed from the workings of the moral impulses and needs of mankind by a sort of instinctive growth, as well as by edicts or decrees or authoritative pronouncements.'[13] Perhaps the most notable naturalist engaged in the preparations for the Nuremberg trial, however, was Sir Hersch Lauterpacht. Lauterpacht was involved in advising the British government (and is probably the person who suggested the term 'crimes against humanity' to Robert Jackson).[14] Lauterpacht's debt to natural law thinking is a matter of record and hardly needs repeating.[15]

It ought not to be thought that naturalism was the sole guiding force,[16] or leading the academic charge at the time, for the most frequent approach to the matter was one firmly based in legal positivism. These included such luminaries as Hans Kelsen,[17] Georg

[11] 'Report of the Commission on the Responsibility of the Authors of the War and on Enforcement of Penalties' (1920) 14 *American Journal of International Law* 95, pp. 113, 134. On its modern resonances see Gerry Simpson, 'Stop Calling it Aggression: War as Crime' (2008) 61 *Current Legal Problems* 191, pp. 208–209.

[12] Quincy Wright, 'Legal Positivism and the Nuremberg Judgment' (1948) 42 *American Journal of International Law* 405, p. 408.

[13] UNWCC, *The History of the UNWCC* (London: HMSO, 1048) p. 8. See also Lord Wright, 'War Crimes under International Law' (1946) 62 LQR 40 and Neil Duxbury 'Lord Wright and Innovative Traditionalism' (2009) 59 *University of Toronto Law Journal* 265.

[14] See generally Martti Koskenniemi, 'Hersch Lauterpacht and the Development of International Criminal Law' (2004) 2 *Journal of International Criminal Justice* 810.

[15] Hersch Lauterpacht, 'The Law of Nations and the Punishment of War Crimes' (1944) 21 *British Yearbook of International Law* 58; Hersch Lauterpacht, 'The Grotian Tradition in International Law' (1946) 23 *British Yearbook of International Law* 1.

[16] The French delegate, Henri Donnedieu de Vabres, was a notable sceptic on a number of grounds, see Ann Tusa and John Tusa, *The Nuremberg Trial* (London: BBC Books, 1995) 456–459.

[17] Hans Kelsen, 'Individual and Collective Liability in International Law: With Particular Regard to the Punishment of War Criminals' (1943) 31 *California Law Review* 530; Andrea Gattini, 'Kelsen's Contribution to International Criminal Law' (2004) 2 *Journal of International Criminal Justice* 795.

Schwarzenberger[18] and Manfred Lachs[19] as well as less remembered figures such as George Manner.[20] Perhaps the most controversial aspect of the approach of some (but by no means all) of the positivists was that international law did not directly apply to individuals in the case of international criminal law, as international law only applied to States.[21] What is interesting about this position is that it is by no means necessarily the case that a positivist reading of the law led to this conclusion even then. The Permanent Court of International Justice, hardly a bastion of the law of nature, had accepted in 1928 that international law could apply to individuals if that was the intention of the creators of the relevant law.[22] This is an early example in the history of the philosophy of international criminal law of the risks of assuming that any tradition is a monolithic structure, with a singular set of beliefs.

Of course, on substance, the position was firmly rejected by the Nuremberg International Military Tribunal's judgment, in its famous pronouncement that

> crimes against international law are committed by men, not abstract entities, and only by punishing individuals who commit such crimes can the provisions of international law be enforced . . . individuals have international duties which transcend the national obligations of obedience imposed by the individual state.[23]

As we will see later there are elements of natural law and positive law in the judgment, and the response to it tended frequently to fall along the positive/natural law divide. Those in the former camp tended to point to technical flaws in the judgment.[24] For example, many German criminal lawyers especially, from a strongly positivist background, found the Nuremberg IMT unsatisfactory from that point of view.[25] Those on the naturalist side of the debate, though, tended to applaud the Trial's contribution to international law, seeing in it a beacon for development in the future.[26]

In Tokyo, it is interesting to note that natural lawyers had a guiding (but not determinative) hand in the prosecution. This is because although they had the Nuremberg Charter 'precedent' to work on, the Chief Prosecutor[27] and his chief juridical assistant

---

18 Georg Schwarzenberger, *International Law and Totalitarian Lawlessness* (London: Jonathan Cape, 1943).

19 Manfred Lachs, *War Crimes: An Attempt to Frame the Issues* (London: Stevens, 1945).

20 George Manner, 'The Legal Nature and Punishment of Criminal Acts of Violence Contrary to the Law of War' (1943) 37 *American Journal of International Law* 407.

21 *Ibid.*

22 *Jurisdiction of the Courts in Danzig* case (1928) PCIJ Series B, No 15, p. 17.

23 Nuremberg IMT: 'Judgment and Sentences' (1947) 41 *American Journal of International Law* 172, p. 221.

24 E.g. Georg Schwarzenberger, 'The Judgment of Nuremberg' (1947) 21 *Tulane Law Review* 329; Hans Kelsen, 'Will the Judgment in the Nuremberg Trial Constitute a Precedent in International Law?' (1947) 1 *International Law Quarterly* 153.

25 Hans Ehard, 'The Nuremberg Trial Against the Major War Criminals and International Law' (1949) 43 *American Journal of International Law* 223; August von Knieriem, *The Nuremberg Trials* trans. Elizabeth B. Schmitt (Chicago: Regnery, 1959).

26 Quincy Wright, 'The Law of the Nuremberg Trial (1947) 41 *American Journal of International Law* 37; F.B. Schick, 'The Nuremberg Trial and the International Law of the Future' (1947) 41 *American Journal of International Law* 770.

27 Unlike in Nuremberg there was only one such prosecutor.

self-identified as strong proponents of the natural law tradition. They argued after the trial that

> the Tokyo and Nuremberg war crimes trials were manifestations of an intellectual and moral revolution . . . they maintain that the international moral order must be regarded as the cause, not the effect, of positive law; that such law does not derive its essence from physical power, and that any attempt to isolate such law from morals is a symptom of judicial schizophrenia caused by separation of the brain of the lawyer from the brain of the human being.[28]

As with many of the naturalist defences of the IMTs, it is interesting to note the extent to which the defenders not only claim that the tribunals were part of a universal, ahistorical set of norms, but also a change in the law. There is more than a hint here of an attempt to have a theoretical cake and to eat it. Nonetheless, the naturalist philosophical approach of the Prosecution affected their argumentation before the trial, and received considerable criticism, as we will discuss. It is notable that in the Tokyo IMT though, unlike in Nuremberg, a number of judges expressly took (conflicting) jurisprudential positions (on which, more later). There was perhaps less commentary on the Tokyo IMT after its judgment was issued, but, again, it tended to be the case that those who were most critical were of a more positivist bent,[29] and its supporters speaking to its future value and naturalist foundations.[30]

In the early post-war era, there were some considerable contributions from philosophers relating to international criminal law, notably, from the natural law school, Gustav Radbruch, who found reason to believe that laws as unjust as those emanating from the Nazi regime were not, strictly speaking, law at all.[31] Perhaps more directly on point, the neo-Kantian/proto-existentialist philosopher Karl Jaspers, before the 1940s were out, came up with a highly sophisticated discussion on the nature of guilt, both of individuals criminally responsible, and members of society.[32] Neither, though, at this point, expressly saw themselves as working within a tradition of international criminal law, although Jaspers was more centrally concerned with the type of questions that are traditionally considered those of international criminal law than Radbruch. Of course, the classic Hart/Fuller debate that occurred in the early 1960s[33] had Nazi laws as their underlying concern, but again, that debate was not directly about international criminal law.

With respect to philosophical engagement with international criminal law, interest waned rather when the Nuremberg and Tokyo IMTs receded into the historical distance,

---

[28] Joseph Berry Keenan and Brendan Francis Brown, *Crimes Against International Law* (Washington DC: Public Affairs Press, 1950) pp. v–vi.

[29] See e.g. Georg Schwarzenberger, 'The Problem of an International Criminal Law' (1950) 3 *Current Legal Problems* 263, p. 291.

[30] Keenan and Brown, *supra* n. 28; B. V.A. Röling, *International Law in an Expanded World* (Amsterdam: Djambtan, 1960) p. 2.

[31] For a sophisticated view on the matter see Stanley L. Paulson, 'Radbruch on Unjust Laws: Competing Earlier and Later Views?' (1995) 15 *Oxford Journal of Legal Studies* 489.

[32] Karl Jaspers, *The Question of German Guilt* trans. E.B. Ashton (New York: The Dial Press, 1947).

[33] See H.L.A. Hart, 'Positivism and the Separation of Law and Morals' (1958) 71 *Harvard Law Review* 593; Lon L. Fuller, 'Positivism and Fidelity to Law – A Reply to Professor Hart' (1958) 71 *Harvard Law Review* 630.

and the project for an International Criminal Court was shelved in the early 1950s. Perhaps the next major engagements between international criminal law and philosophy occurred in the early 1960s, in relation to two major trials. The first of these was the prosecution of Adolf Eichmann, which led the famous reflection on the banality of evil from the existentialist Hannah Arendt.[34] A different innovation occurred with respect to another famous trial, the Frankfurt Auschwitz trial. This trial, which found considerable difficulty reconciling norms of individual responsibility strongly embedded in German criminal law, led German criminal law theoreticians to attempt to conceptualise of forms of responsibility that accurately portray the nature of mass crimes, which later proved influential.[35]

These were relatively isolated examples of interaction between international criminal law and philosophy though. Through the 1970s, there were a few contributions to the literature, such as Jean-Paul Sartre's *On Genocide*,[36] although such contributions tended towards the political rather than philosophical in their approach. Such scholarly works from international lawyers in this period (which ran up into the 1980s) tended to be attempts to induct a basis for international criminal law in the broader sense (i.e. what would include what would now be called transnational criminal law). They were also as often as not exercises in wishful thinking, and not really exercises in philosophy or jurisprudence.[37] There were a few exceptions to this, such as the contributions to the canon from Stanley Paulson and (a little later) David Luban.[38] Outside of these isolated contributions it took other trials in the 1980s to promote further philosophical reflection. In France, this took the form of the trial of Klaus Barbie, which prompted further philosophical reflection on guilt, this time from Alain Finkielkraut. Contrary to Arendt, Finkielkraut took the view that although people may be cogs in a machine, and thus banal, that does not mean that they are not fully worthy of punishment and consideration as morally very wrong (although it might be questioned if Arendt ever went as far as to say that).[39] In Latin America the philosopher-statesperson Carlos Santiago Nino used personal experience, as well as his Kantian/natural law leanings, to not only influence

---

34 Hannah Arendt, *Eichmann in Jerusalem: A Report on the Banality of Evil* (London: Penguin, 1965). Although Arendt's work is now a mainstay of debate, it ought to be remembered that it was highly controversial on its release, see e.g. Jacob Robinson, *And the Crooked Shall Be Made Straight: The Eichmann Trial, the Jewish Catastrophe, and Hannah Arendt's Narrative* (New York: Macmillan, 1965).

35 See Devin O. Pendas, *The Frankfurt Auschwitz Trial, 1963–1965: Genocide, History, and the Limits of the Law* (Cambridge: CUP, 2005); Mark Osiel, 'The Banality of Good: Aligning Incentives Against Mass Atrocity' (2005) 105 *Columbia Law Review* 1751, 1831–1837; Claus Kreß, 'Claus Roxin's Lehre von der Organisationsherrschaft und das Völkerstrafrecht' (2006) *Goltdammers Archiv für Strafrecht* 304.

36 Jean-Paul Sartre, *On Genocide* (Boston: Beacon Press, 1968).

37 See, e.g. Quincy Wright, 'The Scope of International Criminal Law: A Conceptual Framework' (1975) 15 *Virginia Journal of International Law* 561; Robert A. Friedlander, 'The Foundations of International Criminal Law: A Present Day Inquiry' (1983) 15 *Case Western Reserve Journal of International Law* 13.

38 Stanley L. Paulson, 'Classical Legal Positivism at Nuremberg' (1975) 4 *Philosophy and Public Affairs* 132; David Luban, 'The Legacies of Nuremberg' (1987) 54 *Social Research* 779.

39 Alain Finkielkraut, *Remembering in Vain: The Klaus Barbie Trial and Crimes Against Humanity* trans. Roxanne Lapudus (New York: Columbia UP, 1988).

the Argentinean government in the trial of the *junta*, but also to provide a philosophical defence of the approach they took.[40]

9.2.2 1990–the Present

It was during the late 1980s that international criminal law began to resurface as an area of practice and therefore as an area of study, and, unsurprisingly, it is in this period that scholarship from all areas of philosophy also took an upturn. After all, it was more contemporary, and there were developments that could be discussed, even if those developments were used as springboards for discussion of older problems.[41] This was, naturally, catalysed by the creation of the International Criminal Tribunal for former Yugoslavia (ICTY) and the International Criminal Tribunal for Rwanda (1994), then the International Criminal Court (ICC) in 1998.[42] During this period, although there was an upswing in the interest in the theory of international criminal law in some ways, literature was still somewhat sparse on point.[43]

After the drafting of the Rome Statue of the ICC, though, developments occurred apace. Criminal law scholars, in particular, although not only, from Germany, started to publish (in English) on doctrinal (in the German sense) aspects of international crimes.[44] Common law scholars also, from a slightly different perspective, also sought to bring philosophical insights to the substantive aspects of international criminal law.[45] In the (just) post-Rome Statute era, international lawyers of a philosophical mindset were asked expressly in the *American Journal of International Law* to apply their theories (or the theories they professed) to matters of international criminal law as an example of how those theories and methods could be applied to a specific issue in international law.[46]

---

40 Carlos Santiago Nino, *Radical Evil on Trial* (New Haven: Yale UP, 1996).

41 There were also other works that related back more directly to the Holocaust in this period too, see, e.g., Zygmunt Baumann, *Modernity and the Holocaust* (Oxford: Polity, 1989).

42 For an explanation of the developments see William A. Schabas, *The International Criminal Court: A Commentary* (Oxford: OUP, 2010) pp. 1–27.

43 A high-profile and highly controversial contribution to the debate at this time was Alfred P. Rubin's *Ethics and Authority in International Law* (Cambridge: CUP, 1997), which, in something of a Jeremiad aimed at international criminal law, reiterated many of the pre-war positivistic tropes in relation to the application of international law to individuals.

44 See, e.g. Kai Ambos, 'Article 25' in Otto Triffterer (ed.), *Commentary on the Rome Statute of the International Criminal Court: Observer's Notes: Article by Article* (Baden-Baden: Nomos, 1999) 475; Otto Triffterer, 'Causality, A Separate Element of the Doctrine of Superior Responsibility as Expressed in Article 28 of the Rome Statute?' (2002) 15 *Leiden Journal of International Law* 189.

45 May, *supra* n. 6; Robert Cryer, 'Superior Orders and the International Criminal Court' in Richard Burchill, Nigel D. White and Justin Morris (eds), *International Conflict and Security Law: Essays in Memory of Hilaire McCoubrey* (Cambridge: CUP, 2005).

46 Anne-Marie Slaughter and Steven R. Ratner (eds), Symposium on the 'Methods of International Law' (1999) 93 *American Journal of International Law* 291. The symposium was republished, with an additional chapter, as Steven R. Ratner and Anne-Marie Slaughter (eds), *The Methods of International Law* (New York: ASIL/Hein, 2006). The additional chapter reflected an argument over what the relevant canon of approaches to international law was. See e.g. the correspondence at (2000) 94 *American Journal of International Law* 99. At this point, though, some international legal theorists rejected international criminal law entirely: Philip Allott, *The Health of Nations* (Cambridge: CUP, 2005) pp. 62–69.

At roughly the same time legal philosophers, and philosophers more generally, also began to look at international criminal law, or the issues it raised, again. Such work approached the subject from various perspectives. Some legal philosophers looked to the legitimate bases of prosecution at the international level,[47] and others at the aims and objectives of international criminal law, and the extent to which they could be fulfilled by prosecution.[48] Some philosophers also turned directly to the questions that international criminal law raises, although it is not necessarily the case that this turn in the literature has been caused by the increased level of attention to international criminal law by others.[49] Nonetheless, there is now a significant body of literature relating to the philosophy of international criminal law, which this chapter will seek, after this quick chronological survey to convey its major aspects.

9.3 THE MAJOR JURISPRUDENTIAL POSITIONS AND INTERNATIONAL CRIMINAL LAW

9.3.1 Naturalism and Positivism in International Criminal Law: The International Criminal Tribunals

In many ways much (although not all) of the practice of international criminal law by the international criminal tribunals can be seen through the lens of the mutually antagonistic interplay of legal positivism and the strictures of natural law in terms of the applicable law. These theories by no means exhaust the theoretical implications and applications of international criminal law, and other more external theoretical approaches will be returned to later. Still, in part this is because of the nature of the acts which international criminal law has traditionally dealt with, which, insofar as they tend to reflect what Hart might have considered the minimum content of natural law,[50] exist in a liminal point in criminal law.

This is because in spite of a countervailing positivism, with which criminal law has traditionally been associated, not least owing to the influence of the *nullum crimen sine lege* principle,[51] there is a residual concern that whether or not there is a clear prohibition of

---

47 R.A. Duff, *Answering for Crime* (Oxford: Hart, 2007).

48 One example is the work of Mark Drumbl; see, Mark Drumbl, *Atrocity, Punishment and International Law* (Cambridge: CUP, 2007); Mark Drumbl, 'A Hard Look at the Soft Theory of International Criminal Law' in Leila N. Sadat and Michael P. Scharf, *The Theory and Practice of International Criminal Law: Essays in Honor of M. Cherif Bassiouni* (Leiden: Nijhoff, 2008) 1. See, more generally, Larry May and Zachary Hoskins (eds), *International Criminal Law and Philosophy* (Cambridge: CUP, 2009).

49 See, e.g. Arne J. Vetlesen, *Collective Evil and Human Agency* (Cambridge: CUP, 2005); Claudia Card, *Confronting Evil: Terrorism, Torture, Genocide* (Cambridge: CUP, 2010); Charles Griswold, *Forgiveness: A Philosophical Account* (Cambridge: CUP, 2007); Lars Svendson, *A Philosophy of Evil* trans. Kerri A. Pierce (London: Dalkey Archive Press, 2010).

50 H.L.A. Hart, *The Concept of Law* (Oxford: Clarendon, 1961) pp. 193–200.

51 Especially when interpreted, as it is by many civil law scholars, as implying *nullum crimen sine lege scripta*, in spite of the fact that international human rights law does not require this. See generally Cryer, Friman, Robinson and Wilmshurst, *supra* n. 2, pp. 17–21.

such conduct in extant criminal law, there ought to be. There is, as a result, something of a reluctance to insist so severely on the principle of (positive) legality than might otherwise be the case.[52] It is clear, from the practice of the European Court of Human Rights, for example, that many are uncomfortable with undermining any prosecution for international crimes on the basis of the prohibition of retroactive criminal liability in Article 7 of the European Convention on Human Rights.[53]

On the other hand, there are limits to such tolerance, and when the bounds of legality have been stretched too far, commentators are nowadays comfortable in being critical. The difficulty, of course, comes in determining when this limit has, or has not, been passed. For the moment, however, the focus of this chapter is the tension between naturalism and positivism, and how it has played itself out in the international criminal tribunals, and what this tells us about international criminal law.[54]

9.3.1.1 Nuremberg and Tokyo

As was discussed above, in both Nuremberg and Tokyo, there were participants who had a naturalist tinge, and those who had a countervailing positivist approach. The particular issue upon which this fracture can be seen was in relation to the prosecution of crimes against peace. It was by no means clear that positive (treaty or customary) law criminalised aggressive war at the time, and so the positions adopted exist, in some ways, at the awkward intersection of positive and natural law, in particular just war theory.[55]

In Nuremberg, in spite of the influence of the naturalist advisors (who were by no means the only members of the team), the basic thrust of the Prosecution argument was largely positivist, at least in presentation. In other words, the argument was based around the authoritative nature of the Nuremberg Charter, and, as a default position, that international law already criminalised crimes against peace. Even if it did not, the Prosecution argued that the *nullum crimen* principle was not a binding rule of international law, but a 'principle of justice'.

The judgment of the Nuremberg IMT was, in many ways, more positivist than the most stereotypical 19th-century commentator would have likely possibly imagined.[56] After

---

[52] See the excellent piece on point, Beth van Schaack, '*Crimen Sine Lege*: Judicial Lawmaking at the Intersection of Law and Morals' (2008–2009) 97 *Georgetown Law Journal* 119. See e.g. in relation to even Carl Schmitt, Claus Kreß, 'Versailles–Nuremberg–The Hague: Germany and International Criminal Law' (2006) 40 *International Lawyer* 15 p.22.

[53] See David J. Harris, Michael O'Boyle, Ed P. Bates and Carla M. Buckley, *Harris, O'Boyle and Warbrick, Law of the European Convention on Human Rights* (2nd edn., Oxford: OUP, 2009) ch 7; *Jorgić* v *Germany*, Judgment, Application No. 74613/01, 10.12.2007. *Kononov* v *Latvia*, Judgment, Application No/ 36376/04, 17 May 2010. For comment on the earlier decision of the ECHR on point see Judgment, Application 36376/04, 24 July 2008; on the decision see Giulia Pinzauti, 'The European Court of Human Rights' Incidental Application of International Criminal Law and Humanitarian Law: A Critical Discussion of *Kononov v Latvia*' (2008) 6 *Journal of International Criminal Justice* 1043.

[54] See further van Schaack, *supra* n. 52.

[55] See Neil Boister and Robert Cryer, *The Tokyo International Military Tribunal: A Reappraisal* (Oxford: OUP, 2008) pp. 128–134.

[56] Although on the imagined views of commentators of that period see David Kennedy,

all, part of its judgment was that their authority was limited to that which the London Charter expressly granted them, as they said:

> The jurisdiction of the Tribunal is defined in the Agreement and Charter, and the crimes coming within the jurisdiction of the Tribunal, for which there shall be individual responsibility, are set out in Article 6. The law of the Charter is decisive, and binding upon the Tribunal.[57]

In spite of this, the Tribunal was clearly concerned that this might not be enough to overcome the plea that the law imposed by the Charter on the Tribunal was, in fact, *ex post facto*, thus contrary to the *nullum crimen sine lege* principle. Hence they took a more ambivalent, and perhaps naturalistic, approach, by asserting that the *nullum crimen* principle was not actually a binding rule of law, but a non-binding principle of justice, which, as a result, was dismissible if there were a more convincing rule of (natural) justice:

> In the first place, it is to be observed that the maxim nullum crimen sine lege is not a limitation of sovereignty, but is in general a principle of justice. To assert that it is unjust to punish those who in defiance of treaties and assurances have attacked neighbouring states without warning is obviously untrue, for in such circumstances the attacker must know that he is doing wrong, and so far from it being unjust to punish him, it would be unjust if his wrong were allowed to go unpunished.[58]

The idea that an imputed understanding of wrongdoing is, per se, evidence of fair warning, as criminal law tends to require, is problematic.[59] That said, it is not clear that the Tribunal convinced itself on point; it felt obliged to also make its views known, against the backdrop of the apparently binding nature of the Charter and non-binding nature of the *nullum crimen sine lege* principle.[60] As a result, it engaged in a rather unconvincing discussion of a number of unratified treaties and non-binding recommendations, to attempt to ground its interpretation of the 1928 Kellog-Briand Pact (the Pact of Paris) as creating criminal liability in authority rather than reason or natural law.[61] The way the Tribunal phrased itself shows its ambivalent stance on the matter though:

> All these expressions of opinion, and others that could be cited, so solemnly made, reinforce the construction which the Tribunal placed upon the Pact of Paris, that resort to a war of aggression is not merely illegal, but is criminal. The prohibition of aggressive war demanded by the conscience of the world, finds its expression in the series of pacts and treaties to which the Tribunal has just referred.[62]

What can be seen here is the relationship between natural and positive law that can often be seen in international tribunals' judgments; the inspiration is not infrequently natural

---

'International Law and the Nineteenth Century: The History of an Illusion' (1997) 17 *Quinnipiac Law Review* 99.

57 Nuremberg IMT Judgment, p. 216.

58 *Ibid.*, p. 217. See van Schaack, *supra* n. 52, pp. 125–130.

59 A.P. Simester, J.R. Spencer, G.R. Sullivan and G.J. Virgo, *Simester and Sullivan's Criminal Law: Theory and Doctrine* (Oxford: Hart, 4th ed., 2010) pp. 22–26.

60 Nuremberg IMT Judgment, p. 217.

61 *Ibid.*, pp. 218–220.

62 *Ibid.*, p. 220.

law, but the argumentation tends to be framed in a (more or less transparent) positivistic idiom.[63] The Tribunal, having spoken of the justice of prosecuting the defendants, and of the conscience of the world demanding the criminalisation of aggression, turned to an attempt at a positivistic demonstration of the legal position, which looked more like rationalisation than proof.

On other aspects of the judgment, it is interesting that the Tribunal basically followed the Charter, but in some instances, such as in relation to crimes against humanity (which some claim can be defended on the basis of natural law principles – more so than crimes against peace)[64] the defence did not put up much of a fight.

Although often overlooked, the Tokyo IMT was a hotbed of philosophising.[65] The Prosecution, as mentioned above, was inspired in part by natural law. This came through in particular in their attempt to revive just war theory through charges of murder in an unlawful war (which the Tribunal decided were subsumed into crimes against peace), and Joseph Keenan's confident rhetoric, and their view that the definition of aggression could be found in natural law.[66] The Prosecution did, however, also bolster their position with more positivistically inclined arguments, in particular in response to the self-consciously positivist stance of the defence, who were, though, also more than capable of taking on the naturalism of the Prosecution head on.

The judgment of the majority, and the separate and dissenting opinions of the judges, reveal a fascinating clash of legal cultures. The majority, as is well known, essentially chose to adopt the Nuremberg IMT's reasoning.[67] However, this was against the background of the General Assembly having, in 1946, asserted that the Nuremberg Charter and judgment reflected customary international law.[68] As a result, their approach can be considered perhaps more positivist than the Nuremberg judgment. Also, the majority did not seem impressed with the Prosecution's assertion of a universal order covering Japan that was derivable from the law of nature. Instead, they found that Japan was a member of the international community of States by referring, in a truly positivist fashion, to the various treaties that Japan had ratified that were relevant to the indictment.[69]

In the separate and dissenting opinions, though, we see more open naturalism and positivism, sometimes within the same judgment. Perhaps the most consistent judge was Judge Bernard, who openly, and avowedly based his opinion on natural law (and

---

[63] Paulson, *supra* n. 38, goes further, to say that the Nuremberg IMT rejected classical legal positivism, as otherwise it would have been necessary to reject international law. It is not necessary for our purposes to make such a strong claim, as here we are discussing positivism as a method of international law, not whether or not international law can be defended on positivistic grounds. For those who are counting, however, it can, see e.g. Ian Brownlie, *The Rule of Law in International Affairs* (The Hague: Nijhoff, 1998) Chapter 1.

[64] M. Cherif Bassiouni, *Crimes Against Humanity in International Criminal Law* (The Hague: Kluwer, 2nd edn., 1999) chapter 3.

[65] See generally Boister and Cryer, *supra* n. 55, chapter 10.

[66] See *ibid.*, chapter 6.

[67] Tokyo IMT Judgment, reprinted in Neil Boister and Robert Cryer (eds), *Documents on the Tokyo International Military Tribunal* (Oxford: OUP, 2009) pp. 80–81.

[68] Resolution 95(I). The Tokyo IMT's judgment was issued in 1948.

[69] *Ibid.*, pp. 88–110. See Boister and Cryer, *supra* n. 55, pp. 279–80.

was heavily criticised for it).[70] The President, William Webb, similarly showed strong sympathy for naturalism, but (probably in response to criticism from colleagues) soft-played the naturalist influence in the published version of his opinion.[71] Judge Röling, the Dutch Judge, was also somewhat eclectic in his approach. In relation to crimes against, peace, for example, Röling was highly positivist in the sense that he rejected the case that they were an extant crime in 1945.[72] Equally, he was also not averse to speaking of *bellum justum* in his opinion,[73] and later described the trial as part of the formation of the 'natural law of the atomic age'.[74]

The last judge, whose opinion has received the most attention,[75] Judge Pal, although on the surface highly positivist in inclination (on the rejection of crimes against peace and the definition of aggression), is in fact more complex. Although he castigated natural law as 'for many . . . [having] . . . a rich, deep odor of the witches' cauldron',[76] and being changeable according to fashion,[77] to consider him as a pure positivist, as, for example Judith Shklar does,[78] does not do justice to all of his opinion. Pal also adopted an anti-colonial tone, that at times came very close to a naturalistic tone he decried elsewhere.[79] In addition, his judgment on war crimes and sense of empathy with the victims of the Allied bombings are best explained on the basis of the unacknowledged moral basis of his opinion which is more at home in natural law than the idiom he adopted.[80]

9.3.1.2 The ICTY and ICTR

Whilst there has been a great deal written about the next two international tribunals,[81] there has been relatively little written about the legal philosophy underlying them or the

---

70 Dissenting Opinion of the Member from France, reprinted, *ibid.*, 661; for critique see Thomas Baty, *International Law in Twilight* (Tokyo: Maruzen, 1954) p. 188.

71 Separate Opinion of the President, reprinted in Boister and Cryer, *supra* n. 67, 629; see Boister and Cryer, *supra* n. 55, pp. 281–282.

72 Dissenting Opinion of the Member from the Netherlands, reprinted *ibid.*, 679. See generally Robert Cryer, 'Röling in Tokyo: A Dignified Dissenter' (2010) 9 *Journal of International Criminal Justice* 1109.

73 *Ibid.*, p. 701.

74 B.V.A. Röling, *supra* n. 30, p. 2.

75 See e.g. Elizabeth Kopelman, 'Ideology and International Law: The Dissent of the Indian Justice at the Tokyo War Crimes Tribunal' (1990–1991) 23 *New York University Journal of International Law and Politics* 373; T.S. Rama Rao, 'The Dissenting Judgment of Mr Justice Pal at the Tokyo Trial' (1953) 2 *Indian Yearbook of World Affairs* 267; Ashis Nandy, 'The Other Within: The Strange Case of Radhabinodh Pal's Judgment on Culpability' (1992) 23 *New Literary History* 45.

76 Dissenting Opinion of the Member From India, reprinted in Boister and Cryer, *supra* n. 67, p. 872. The reference is to a comment of Lon Fuller's.

77 *Ibid.*, pp. 872–873.

78 Judith Shklar, *Legalism: Law, Morals and Political Trials* (Princeton: Princeton UP, 1986) p. 186.

79 See, e.g. Kopelman, *supra* n. 75, pp. 422–423.

80 See Nandy, *supra* n. 75, p. 59.

81 For a smattering see, e.g., Virginia Morris and Michael P. Scharf, *An Insider's Guide to the International Criminal Tribunal for the Former Yugoslavia* (New York: Transnational, 1995); Virginia Morris and Michael P. Scharf, *The International Criminal Tribunal for Rwanda* (New York: Transnational, 1998); William Schabas, *The UN International Criminal Tribunals: The*

philosophical approach they have adopted.[82] In spite of claims that the creation of the ICTY implied a naturalist approach to the international legal order that was at odds with reality,[83] the United Nations Secretary-General, and the ICTY itself, were careful to base the authority of the Tribunal squarely within the positive international law of the Charter. The Secretary-General, for example, looked at the possibility of other methods for the creation of the ICTY, but placed the legality firmly within the Chapter VII powers of the Security Council, explaining himself on the basis of past practice of the Council.[84] Similarly, the Appeals Chamber of the ICTY, in the seminal *Tadić* decision,[85] engaged in a detailed review of the Security Council's action, placing its legality on this matter squarely within Article 41 of the Charter.

In terms of substantive law, the Secretary-General could be seen to be adopting a strong positivist stance, in particular owing to the *nullum crimen* principle, as he averred that:

> In the view of the Secretary-General, the application of the principle *nullum crimen sine lege* requires that the international tribunal should apply rules of international humanitarian law which are beyond doubt part of customary law so that the problem of adherence of some, but not all States to specific conventions does not arise. This would appear to be particularly important in the context of an international tribunal prosecuting persons responsible for serious violations of international humanitarian law.[86]

This, in fact goes beyond what the *nullum crimen* principle requires, in that treaties can also form the basis of individual responsibility, as the ICTY has (albeit not without considerable debate) found.[87]

The Chambers of the ICTY have interpreted their mandate here quite widely. This is especially the case with respect to war crimes. Article 3 of the ICTY Statute grants the ICTY jurisdiction over violations of the laws and customs of war. Importantly, the list of war crimes is not closed, so the ICTY has interpreted this as a reference to all of the law of armed conflict applicable in former Yugoslavia at the relevant times (other than Grave Breaches of the Geneva Conventions, which are criminalised in Article 2 of the Statute).[88]

Former Yugoslavia, Rwanda and Sierra Leone (Cambridge: CUP, 2006); and the symposia in (2004) 2 *Journal of International Criminal Justice* 353–597 and (2002–2003) 37 *New England Law Review* 865–1080, (1997) 321 *International Review of the Red Cross* 665–732 and (2005) 3 *Journal of International Criminal Justice* 801–1033.

[82] One exception is Alfred Rubin, 'An International Criminal Tribunal for Former Yugoslavia' (1994) 6 *Pace International Law Review* 7. See again, van Schaack, *supra* n. 52.

[83] *Ibid.*

[84] Report of the Secretary-General Pursuant to Paragraph 3 of Security Council Resolution 808 UN Doc. S.25704, paras18–30.

[85] *Prosecutor* v *Tadić*, Decision on Defence Interlocutory Appeal on Jurisdiction, IT-94-1-AR72, 2 October 1995.

[86] Secretary-General's Report, *supra* n. 84, para 34. See Tamás Hoffmann, 'The Gentle Civilizer of Humanitarian Law – Antonio Cassese and the Creation of the Customary Law of Non-International Armed Conflicts' in Carsten Stahn and Larissa van den Herik (eds), *Future Perspectives on International Criminal Justice* (The Hague: TMC Asser Press, 2010) 58, p. 68.

[87] *Tadić, supra* n. 85, para 143; *Prosecutor* v *Kordić and Čerkez*, Judgment, IT-95-14/2-A, 17 December 2004, paras 41–46; *Prosecutor* v *Galić*, Judgment, IT-98-29-A, 30 January 2006, para 85.

[88] *Tadić, supra* n. 85, paras 71–93.

This has granted the ICTY a very broad mandate to determine what those rules were, and whether or not they were customary. Similarly, owing to the fact that the ICTY Statute only contains very brief provisions concerning principles of liability and defences, and the Secretary-General expressed the wish that the gaps be filled in by the Tribunal in its jurisprudence,[89] the ICTY has had a similarly broad role here. Its jurisprudence on these matters at times gives an insight into the underlying legal philosophies that animate the different judges (it must be borne in mind that unlike at the IMTs, there has been a revolving door of judges sitting on the ICTY – although as we will see, sometimes judges have adopted more than one approach). Owing to the fact that there have been so many cases, and so many judges, a caveat ought to be entered at this point: it is not possible to engage with all of the case law; only a selection can be covered here.[90]

Probably the first major case in the ICTY contained some argumentation that can be seen to have philosophical grounding. This is the *Tadić* case,[91] the majority opinion in which is generally accepted to have been the work of then-President of the ICTY Antonio Cassese.[92] The influence of the case on the law of non-international armed conflict has been profound, with some of its more controversial propositions now being considered commonplace, or, at the very least, the starting point of debate. In particular, prior to *Tadić* the question of whether or not international criminal law provided for war criminality in such conflicts was deeply controversial, and the idea that there was customary law on point that was not equivalent to common Article 3 of the Geneva Conventions and certain provisions of Additional Protocol II was almost unthinkable.[93]

It is true that the Chamber rejected a US argument about the applicability of the grave breaches provisions of the Geneva Conventions on the basis that is was 'unsupported by any authority'.[94] There are references to sources doctrine,[95] the intention of the drafters of the Statute,[96] and State (and international organisational) practice,[97] which could give succour to the traditional positivist, but we also have statements such as:

---

[89] ICTY Statute, Article 7, Secretary-General's Report, *supra* n. 84, para 58.

[90] For discussion along analogous lines of a partially different selection of cases, see van Schaack, *supra* n. 52. It might be objected that this chapter concentrates unduly on Cassese's judicial work. Given limitations of space, and the huge influence he had on the early jurisprudence of the ICTY, in its formative period, as well as the clarity of the positions he adopted, it is to be hoped that this limitation is understandable.

[91] *Supra* n. 85.

[92] Theodor Meron, 'Cassese's Tadić and the Law of Non-International Armed Conflicts' in Lal Chand Vohrah *et al* (eds), *Man's Inhumanity to Man: Essays in Honour of Antonio Cassese* (The Hague: Kluwer, 2003) 533.

[93] See, e.g. Anthony Cullen, *The Concept of Non-International Armed Conflict in International Humanitarian Law* (Cambridge: CUP, 2010) Chapter 4; Eve La Haye, *War Crimes in Internal Armed Conflicts* (Cambridge: CUP, 2007) p. 136.

[94] *Tadić supra* n. 85, para 83.

[95] *Ibid.*, para 99, although it is worth bearing in mind that it was a, shall we say, progressive approach.

[96] *Ibid.*, para 88.

[97] *Ibid.*, paras 100–118, 120–124. This aspect of the opinion could be considered part of the modern positivist phase of the judgment, on which see Bruno Simma and Andreas Paulus, 'The Responsibility of Individuals for Human Rights Abuses in Internal Conflicts: A Positivist View' in Ratner and Slaughter (eds), *supra* n. 46, 23.

> the impetuous development and propagation in the international community of human rights doctrines, particularly after the adoption of the Universal Declaration of Human Rights in 1948, has brought about significant changes in international law, notably in the approach to problems besetting the world community. A State-sovereignty-oriented approach has been gradually supplanted by a human-being-oriented approach. Gradually the maxim of Roman law *hominum causa omne jus constitutum est* (all law is created for the benefit of human beings) has gained a firm foothold in the international community as well.[98]

Cassese has himself commented on his theoretical approach to international law, tracing his own intellectual journey from his positivist roots to a more humanitarian-informed approach.[99] As he himself has said, 'I was moved by the old maxim of Roman wisdom: *Hominum causa ome jus constutatum* . . .'[100] This is, of course, hardly the terminology of a positivist, reaching back further, into more naturalistic territory. In fact, quite a lot of *Tadić's* majority opinion, although largely clothed in positivist garb, reads with more than a hint of the law of nature. Although the majority in *Tadić* was careful to attempt to bolster their case with references to relevant (and, at times, less relevant) state practice,[101] Cassese has all but admitted this was cover for 'humanizing' the law applicable to non-international armed conflicts.[102]

Cassese was also content to make arguments reason, (a tenet of secular naturalism) where authority was lacking. This was entirely intentional, as Cassese later said in relation to *Tadić*: 'we were breaking new ground. You go beyond the black letter of the law because you look at the spirit of the law.'[103]

Therefore, straight after the comment cited above, the majority continued to say:

> It follows that in the area of armed conflict the distinction between interstate wars and civil wars is losing its value as far as human beings are concerned. Why protect civilians from belligerent violence, or ban rape, torture or the wanton destruction of hospitals, churches, museums or private property, as well as proscribe weapons causing unnecessary suffering when two sovereign States are engaged in war, and yet refrain from enacting the same bans or providing the same protection when armed violence has erupted 'only' within the territory of a sovereign State? If international law, while of course duly safeguarding the legitimate interests of States, must gradually turn to the protection of human beings, it is only natural that the aforementioned dichotomy should gradually lose its weight.[104]

---

98 *Tadić*, *supra* n. 85, para 97.

99 'Soliloquy' in Antonio Cassese, *The Human Dimension of International Law: Selected Papers* (Oxford: OUP, 2008) lix, pp. lx–lxv.

100 *Ibid.*, p. lxx. See generally Hoffmann, *supra* n. 86.

101 Christopher Greenwood, 'International Humanitarian Law and the *Tadic* Case' (1996) 7 *European Journal of International Law* 265; Colin Warbrick and Peter Rowe, 'The International Criminal Tribunal for Yugoslavia: The Decision of the Appeals Chamber on the Interlocutory Appeal on Jurisdiction in the *Tadić* Case' (1996) 45 *International and Comparative Law Quarterly* 691; Geoffrey R. Watson, 'The Humanitarian Law of the Yugoslavia War Crimes Tribunal: Jurisdiction in *Prosecutor v Tadic*' (1996) 36 *Virginia Journal of International Law* 687, pp. 709–728.

102 Hoffmann, *supra* n. 86, p. 68.

103 'The Judge: Interview with Antonio Cassese' in Heikelina Verrijn Stuart and Marlise Simons, *The Prosecutor and the Judge: Benjamin Ferencz and Antonio Cassese: Interviews and Writings* (Amsterdam: Amsterdam University Press, 2009), 47, p. 53.

104 *Tadić*, *supra* n. 85 para 97. Cassese is proud to have managed to ensure its appearance in the *Tadić* opinion, 'Soliloquy' *supra* n. 99, p. lxi.

A similar approach can be seen elsewhere in *Tadić*, where the majority assert that:

> elementary considerations of humanity and common sense make it preposterous that the use by States of weapons prohibited in armed conflicts between themselves be allowed when States try to put down rebellion by their own nationals on their own territory. What is inhumane, and consequently proscribed, in international wars, cannot but be inhumane and inadmissible in civil strife.[105]

Whilst this may be morally correct, this is quite clearly a statement based upon a naturalistic argument, i.e. one based purely on reason, rather than the traditional sources of international law. This is an implication that is only bolstered by the reference to 'elementary considerations of humanity' whose status in positive international law cannot be considered clear.[106]

Both of the above are open to the purely positivist response that '[i]t is difficult to justify, on grounds of logic, a different regime of criminal responsibility for an act depending solely on whether it was committed during an international or a non-international armed conflict . . . But that is what States did.'[107] This was noted by one of the judges in the case, Judge Li, who asserted, '[t]he Decision on this question is in fact an unwarranted assumption of legislative power which has never been given to this Tribunal by any authority.'[108] It is therefore rather the case that although the presentation of the State practice and the presentation was, again, intended to give the opinion positivist credentials, the underlying inspiration was far more naturalist. The interweaving of naturalist sentiment and positivist proof has proved remarkably successful, in that the majority of what was said in *Tadić* was adopted in the Rome Statute in 1998, and even more in 2010.[109] As Theodor Meron put it, 'Cassese, the judge, is thus the rare person, about whom it can be said that he has been a prophet in his own time.'[110]

Equally, at times, the more naturalistic tone that has been adopted in other cases has proved less convincing to States. The next example of this came in the *Erdemović* case.[111] The issue that arose in this case, as is well known, was the question of whether or not duress existed as a defence to crimes involving killing. The Prosecution, and Judge Li, took the view that post-war case law took the view that it was not.[112] Judges MacDonald,

---

105 *Tadić*, *supra* n. 85, para 119.

106 Although the ICJ has, on occasion, referred to them e.g. *The Corfu Channel Case* (*UK* v *Albania*) (1949) ICJ Rep, p. 22.

107 Rowe, *supra* n. 101, p. 698.

108 *Tadić*, *supra* n. 85, Dissenting Opinion of Judge Li, para 13.

109 See Rome Statute of the International Criminal Court, Article 8(2)(d)(f) and Review Conference, Resolution RC/Res.5 adopted at the 12th plenary meeting, on 10 June 2010.

110 Meron *supra* n. 92, p. 538.

111 *Prosecutor* v *Erdemović*, Judgment, IT-96-22-A, 7 October 1997. See, e.g. Peter Rowe, 'Duress as a Defence to War Crimes After Erdemović: A Laboratory for a Permanent Court?' (1998) 1 *Yearbook of International Humanitarian Law* 210; Claus Kreß, 'Zur Methode der Rechtsfindung im Allgemeinen Teil des Völkerstrafrechts. Die Bewertung von Tötungen im Nötigungsnotstand durch die Rechtsmittelkammer des Internationalen Straftribunals für das ehemalige Jugoslawien im Fall Erdemović' (1999) 111 Zeitschrift für die gesamte Strafrechtswissenschaft 597; Robert Cryer, 'One Appeal, Four Opinions, Two Philosophies and a Remittal' (1998) 2 *Journal of Armed Conflict Law* 193.

112 *Erdemović*, *supra* n. 111, separate Opinion of Judge Li.

Vohrah and Cassese did not agree, taking the view that the relevant case law actually did not decide the position.[113] As a result of this seeming *lacuna*, McDonald and Vohrah (who, in result, formed the majority with Judge Li) took a decidedly anti-positivist, 'policy' approach, which, given that it attempts to derive substantive rules from abstract principle, is more in the deductive/naturalist line of thinking than the inductive, positivist school.[114] As a result, they argued that:

> the law should not be the product or slave of logic or intellectual hair-splitting, but must serve broader normative purposes in light of its social, political and economic role. . . . The purview of the International Tribunal relates to war crimes and crimes against humanity committed in armed conflicts of extreme violence with egregious dimensions. . . . We are concerned that, in relation to the most heinous crimes known to humankind, the principles of law to which we give credence have the appropriate normative effect upon soldiers bearing weapons of destruction and upon the commanders who control them in armed conflict situations. . . . We must bear in mind that we are operating in the realm of international humanitarian law which has, as one of its prime objectives, the protection of the weak and vulnerable in such a situation where their lives and security are endangered.[115]

In doing so, McDonald and Vohrah expressly relied on Rosalyn Higgins's sophisticated approach to the McDougalite, Yale School policy approach.[116] This approach has, rightly, been identified as a form of naturalism, and has been criticised as such.[117]

Cassese, interestingly, this time with a far more positivist bent, retorted sternly that reliance on such an approach was inappropriate, not simply on the basis that the majority essentially merely adopted common-law policy arguments, but that in doing so, they transgressed their role as judges in criminal cases:

> the majority of the Appeals Chamber has embarked upon a detailed investigation of 'practical policy considerations' and has concluded by upholding 'policy considerations' substantially based on English law. I submit that this examination is *extraneous to the task of our Tribunal*. This International Tribunal is called upon ~~to apply inter~~national law, in particular our Statute and principles and rules of international humanitarian law and international criminal law. Our International Tribunal is a court of law; it is bound only by international law. It should therefore refrain from engaging in meta-legal analyses. In addition, it should refrain from relying exclusively on notions, policy considerations or the philosophical underpinnings of common-law countries, while disregarding those of civil-law countries or other systems of law. What is even more important, a policy-oriented approach in the area of criminal law runs contrary to the fundamental customary principle *nullum crimen sine lege*.[118]

---

[113] *Ibid.*, Joint Opinion of Judges McDonald and Vohrah, paras 40–55, Dissenting Opinion of President Cassese, paras 19–46. Judge Stephen agreed with Judge Cassese on the result, but not on the reasoning, but not on grounds that need detain us here.

[114] See e.g. Georg Schwarzenberger, *The Inductive Approach to International Law* (London: Stevens, 1965). For (highly) qualified support of McDonald and Vohrah from another judge at the ICTY see Mohamed Shahabbuddeen, 'Policy Oriented Law in the International Criminal Tribunal for former Yugoslavia' in Vohrah *et al* (eds), *supra* n. 92, 889.

[115] McDonald and Vohrah, *supra* n. 113, para 75.

[116] Rosalyn Higgins, *Problems and Process: International Law and How We Use It* (Oxford: OUP, 1994), cited in McDonald and Vohrah, *ibid.*, para 78.

[117] See, e.g. Neil Duxbury, *Patterns of American Jurisprudence* (Oxford: OUP, 1995) pp. 191–199.

[118] Cassese, *supra* n. 113, para 11.

McDonald and Vohrah replied that it is naïve to say that international law is divorced from policy, and in criminal law, this is the case domestically too.[119] Theirs was not, though, a line of reasoning that appealed to the drafters of the Rome Statute, who took Cassese's view on the substantive issue at bar, that duress as a defence is at least in theory available to all international crimes, including those that involve the killing of innocents.[120]

Erdemović was not the last time that the ICTY (or Professor Cassese) entered into the international legal fray. Almost coterminously with Cassese publishing an article identifying the Martens clause as a major influence on the creation of customary international humanitarian law,[121] the Trial Chamber over which Cassese presided issued its decision in the *Kupreškić* case.[122] In this case, the lawfulness of reprisals against the civilian population was at issue, albeit largely tangential to the major issues before the Tribunal.[123] The Chamber came to the conclusion that such reprisals were unlawful, on the basis of a very controversial reading of a small amount of state practice, bolstered by an interpretation of the Martens clause (tracing the argumentation that appeared in Cassese's piece) and took the view that such reprisals were unlawful. The Martens clause reads (in its 1907 formulation):

> Until a more complete code of the laws of war has been issued, the High Contracting Parties deem it expedient to declare that, in cases not included in the Regulations adopted by them, the inhabitants and the belligerents remain under the protection and the rule of the principles of the law of nations, as they result from the usages established among civilized peoples, from the laws of humanity, and the dictates of the public conscience.[124]

The Trial Chamber in *Kupreškić* interpreted the Martens clause in a way that attempted to introduce natural law into the law here. The Chamber began in a way that seemed to deny any attempt to sneak this in through the back door, denying that the Martens clause meant that principles of humanity or the dictates of the public conscience were sources of international law in themselves.[125] The Chamber went on, though, to assert that the importance of the clause is that it means customary law can form 'under the pressure of the demands of humanity or the dictates of public conscience, even where State practice is scant or inconsistent'.[126] On the basis of this argument, the Chamber argued (in the

---

119 McDonald and Vohrah, *supra* n. 113, para 78.

120 Rome Statute, Article 31(d). See Schabas, *supra* n. 42, p. 490.

121 Antonio Cassese, 'The Martens Clause: Half A Loaf or Simply Pie in the Sky?' (2000) 11 *European Journal of International Law* 193; for a contrary view see Theodor Meron 'The Martens Clause, Principles of Humanity and the Dictates of Public Conscience' (2000) 94 *American Journal of International Law* 78.

122 *Prosecutor* v *Kupreškić et al*, Judgment, IT-95-16-T, 14 January 2000. See generally Christopher Greenwood, 'Belligerent Reprisals in the Jurisprudence of the International Criminal Tribunal for the Former Yugoslavia' in Horst Fischer, Claus Kreß and Sascha Rolf Lüder (eds), *International and National Prosecution of Crimes Under International Law* (Berlin: Verlag Arno Spitz, 2001) 359.

123 This is not unusual, the majority of the seminal discussion in the *Tadić* case was also, as is often overlooked, *obiter*.

124 Hague Convention IV 1907, 9 UKTS (1910) Cd.5030.

125 *Kupreškić*, *supra* n. 122, para 525.

126 *Ibid.*, para 527.

face of significant State practice to the contrary) that owing to the 'pressure' of humanity and the dictates of public conscience, customary law prohibited reprisals against civilians outside of occupied territory.[127]

As Tamás Hoffmann notes, this amounted to 'the equation of morality with custom'.[128] What needs to be added to such comment is that although this may be the case, the argumentation is notionally, or presentationally, positivist. The argument of the Chamber was that custom accepted the position, and, again some State practice was (mis)quoted. It is clear, though, that the underlying ideal of the opinion is naturalist. On the question the Chamber was dealing with, though, that reprisals of the nature discussed in *Kupreskić* are unlawful, the attempt to push the (positive) law has failed. The opinion gathered considerable negative commentary, for example, Fritz Kalshoven chose (in Cassese's *Festschrift)* to note that the decision uses the Martens clause as a '*deus ex machina*', and that it 'may be founded on quicksand'.[129] The Appeals Chamber of the ICTY has now disavowed that position, and reasserted the potential lawfulness of certain reprisals.[130]

The judges at the ICTY have certainly leaned more to natural law/morality in some decisions. As van Schaack has noted, the chambers have at times

> elide[d] the morally wrong and the legally criminal, invoke[d] the natural law tradition found in all natural law. This tradition is particularly cogent in ICL [International Criminal Law] . . ., which has its origins in the belief that the law must conform to a universal transnational morality and conception of justice. Many ICL cases proceed as though a transcendent law exists that has yet to be reduced to positive law but that can be discovered and invoked in criminal proceedings.[131]

On occasion, though, the ICTY has been very rigidly positivistic in its outlook. Probably the most notable example of this was the *Vaslijević* case.[132] In this case, the issue arose of whether or not the defendant could be convicted of the crime of 'violence to life and person', pursuant to the customary concomitant to that phrase in common Article 3(1)(a) of the Geneva Conventions. The Trial Chamber took a very strict view of the matter, not only stating that only customary law could ground criminal liability (which was not only incorrect, but contrary to binding authority at the Tribunal), but that customary law was insufficiently clear to ground liability here, as:

> If customary international law does not provide for a sufficiently precise definition of a crime listed in the Statute, the Trial Chamber would have no choice but to refrain from exercising jurisdiction over it, regardless of the fact that the crime is listed as punishable in the Statute. This is so because . . . anything contained in the statute of the court in excess of customary international law would be a utilisation of power and not of law.[133]

---

127 *Ibid.*, paras 530–1.

128 Hoffmann, *supra* n. 86, p. 76.

129 Fritz Kalshoven, 'Reprisals and the Protection of Civilians: Two Recent decisions of the Yugoslavia Tribunal' in Vohrah *et al* (eds), *supra* n. 92, 481, pp. 403, 504. See further Hoffmann, *supra* n. 86, pp. 76–77.

130 *Prosecutor* v *Martić*, Judgment, IT-95-11-A, 8 October 2008, paras 263–7.

131 Van Schaack *supra* n. 52, p. 157. Some scepticism might be expressed that natural law is present in all international law, but that debate need not (and probably could not) be settled in a chapter with this focus (or in one chapter at all).

132 *Prosecutor* v *Vasiljević*, Judgment, IT-98-32-T, 29 November 2002.

133 *Ibid.*, para 202. Again here we do see a slight difference in the form of positivism adopted in,

As a result of this determination, that customary law was necessary, the Trial Chamber also decided that it would not be permissible to resort to the ICRC *Commentaries* to the Geneva Conventions,[134] because 'as useful as the *Commentaries* to the 1949 Geneva Conventions may be to interpret the Conventions they do not constitute State practice'.[135] Indeed, they rejected a previous interpretation of common Article 3 (as a matter of treaty law) by another Trial Chamber (in the *Blaškić* case)[136] on the basis that the (other) Trial Chamber had not cited State practice to support its contention. The approach of the Trial Chamber in *Vasiljević* was a particularly rigid form of positivism, which, in fact, led the Chamber astray. Professor Cassese was unimpressed, criticising the Chamber for its 'Black letter' (über-positivist) approach.[137]

It might be thought, given the above, that the ICTY has been consistently inconsistent in its approach to the law. However, it must be remembered that for the most part, the ICTY has tended to follow a generally positivist methodology, even where it is rather quick to conclude that a provision is customary. Later cases before the ICTY, in particular, tend to rely heavily on past decisions and the Tribunal's system of precedent rather than reasoning things anew.

Turning to the ICTR, there is comparatively little evidence of philosophy directly affecting the reasoning of the Tribunal. The most likely reason for this is that the vast majority of charges before that Tribunal have been based on the Genocide Convention, and therefore the majority of work that needs to be done is treaty interpretation, rather than interpretation of customary law, which is where, for the most part, the evidence of (at times) implicit theoretical stances can be found. It could be argued that in the *Akayesu* case,[138] the approach of the Trial Chamber, which sought to re-read the *travaux préparatiores* to come to the conclusion that that Convention protected all stable and permanent groups, was, as discussed above, naturalism part-covered by a patina of positivist argumentation (in particular the reference to the *travaux préparatiores*). This decision, however, cannot really be seen as a matter of applied philosophy: sometimes courts just get the law wrong, and their attempts to reconcile their intuitions about what the law is and how it ought to apply to the case before them are merely unconvincing.[139] In reality, the decision was simply based on a misunderstanding of the Convention.

9.3.1.3 The Special Court for Sierra Leone

There has, in general, been little direct philosophical debate in the Special Court for Sierra Leone, although upon occasion there have been hints of it. There are two possible

---

for example, the Nuremberg IMT, which based itself first on the Charter, only then on customary law. This may be owing to the increased influence of the *nullum crimen sine lege* principle.

134 E.g. Jean Pictet, *Commentary: I Geneva Convention* (Geneva: ICRC, 1952).

135 *Ibid.*, n. 549. For critique see Robert Cryer, 'Prosecutor v Vasiljević' in André Klip and Göran Sluiter (eds), *Annotated Leading Cases of the International Tribunals* (Antwerp: Intersentia, 2007) 688, pp. 692–4.

136 *Prosecutor* v *Blaškić*, Judgment, IT-96-14-T, 3 March 2000, para 182.

137 Antonio Cassese, 'Black Letter Lawyering vs Constructive Interpretation: The Vasiljević case' (2004) 2 *Journal of International Criminal Justice* 265.

138 *Prosecutor* v *Akayesu*, Judgment, ICTR-96-4-T, 2 September 1998.

139 See William A. Schabas, *Genocide in International Law: The Crime of Crimes* (Cambridge: CUP, 2nd ed., 2009) chapter 3; Cryer, Friman, Robinson and Wilmshurst, *supra* n. 2, pp. 208–209.

examples. The first is the decision in the Appeals Chamber in the *Norman* Child Soldiers Opinion.[140] In this, the Appeals Chamber provided a very brief review of State practice to come to the conclusion that enlisting or using child soldiers (i.e. under-15s) was a war crime prior to its positive codification in the Rome Statute in 1998.[141] Given that the majority relied in part on the fact that the prohibition reflected 'important values',[142] it could be thought that they were engaging in some naturalistic speculation, and seeking to equate a (somewhat contested) morality with existing law. However, their discussion on point begins from the relevant conventions, to attempt to ground the prohibition in positive law, rather than a more general theory of values or community (in a way not utterly dissimilar to the majority in the Tokyo IMT when discussing whether Japan was a member of the society of civilised States, as discussed above). This decision was subject to a bitter dissent by Judge Robertson, on the basis that:

> It must be acknowledged that like most absolute principles, *nullum crimen* can be highly inconvenient – especially in relation to conduct which is abhorrent or grotesque, but which parliament has not thought to legislate against. Every law student can point to cases where judges have been tempted to circumvent the *nullum crimen* principle to criminalise conduct which they regard as seriously anti-social or immoral, but which have not been outlawed by legislation or by established categories of common-law crimes. This temptation must be firmly resisted by international law judges, with no legislature to correct or improve upon them and with a subject – international criminal law – which came into effective operation as recently as the judgment at Nuremberg in 1946. Here the Prosecution asserts with some insouciance that 'the principle of nullum crimen sine lege is not applied rigidly, particularly where the acts in question are universally regarded as abhorrent and deeply shock the conscience of humanity.' On the contrary, it is precisely when the acts are abhorrent and deeply shocking that the principle of legality must be most stringently applied, to ensure that a defendant is not convicted out of disgust rather than evidence, or of a non-existent crime.[143]

The difference with the majority opinion, here, and perhaps more significantly with the majority in the *Kupreškić* case in the ICTY could hardly be clearer. That said, it cannot be definitively proved whether or not this was a genuine difference of philosophy between the judges (although the prosecution was clearly hinting at a naturalist approach) rather than a judicial debate within a positivist tradition. Admittedly, the line between this and a positivist presentation of a naturalist inspired position is not entirely impermeable, and the sympathies of the majority of the judges were probably on the side of the prosecution on the moral aspects of the case.[144] Still, to say more than that would be entirely speculative.

The same cannot be said for the decision of the Appeals Chamber in the *Fofana and*

---

[140] *Prosecutor* v *Norman*, Decision on Preliminary Motion Based on Lack of Jurisdiction (Child Recruitment), SCSL-2004-14-A, 31 May 2004. Again, it is important to note that these cases occur generally against the background of most of the cases not being so clearly on one side or the other. Only a detailed deconstruction of all the cases could give a definitive discussion on point, but this lies far beyond the remit of this chapter.

[141] *Ibid.*, paras 17–24.

[142] *Ibid.*, paras 28–9.

[143] Dissenting Opinion of Judge Robertson, para 12. See van Schaack, *supra* n. 52, pp. 162–163.

[144] The Defence had previously sought to have Judge Winter removed, on the basis of her prior advocacy of child rights, see *Prosecutor* v *Norman*, Decision on the Preliminary Motion to Recuse

Kondewa case.[145] In this case the defence raised the issue that, in spite of the crimes that were alleged against them, the defendants were the legitimate government, facing rebels who did not pay any heed whatsoever to the law of armed conflict. The idea that the law of armed conflict only benefits those involved in lawful armed conflict is one that has its basis in some of the oldest naturalistic scholarship, and has occasionally (and recently, more frequently) raised its voice.[146] It is seen, on the other hand, to be a tenet of positive law that international humanitarian law applies equally to both sides.[147] It was therefore no real surprise that the majority in the case had little truck with those arguments: in true positivistic style, the majority retorted that having what might be regarded as a 'just cause' was not a defence, although a good motive might be relevant to sentencing in general:

> International humanitarian law specifically removes a party's political motive and the 'justness' of a party's cause from consideration. The basic distinction and historical separation between the *jus ad bellum* and *jus in bello* underlies the desire of States to see that the protections afforded by *jus in bello*. . . . The political motivations of a combatant do not alter the demands on that combatant to ensure that their conduct complies with the law. . . . Consideration of political motives by a court applying humanitarian law not only contravenes, but would undermine a bedrock principle of that law.[148]

This strong rejection of just war/naturalism may seem to be excessive, however, it is a response to the defence, and the fact that their views clearly had purchase with one of the Judges. President King was in favour of accepting that owing to the fact that in his view Fofana and Kondewa were fighting on the 'just' side, they ought to be exempt from punishment.[149] He denied that he was engaging in just war reasoning, although it is difficult to escape the conclusion that that was precisely what he was doing, and drawing, on the most generous interpretation, on naturalism to do so, since the positivistic approach inevitably leads to the position of the majority. Any attempt to introduce just war thinking into positive international law proved subject to all the critiques of naturalism when some States attempted (partially successfully) to include it in positive law (in Article 1(4) of Additional Protocol I to the Geneva Conventions) in the 1970s.[150] Judge King's opinion was that of a judge, not a State, and therefore is a fortiori subject to such critiques.

9.3.1.4 The International Criminal Court

The dominant philosophy that can be seen in relation to both the Rome Statute and the early practice of the ICC is legal positivism, with a strict understanding of legality (*nulum crimen sine lege*) on the part of the drafters on one hand, and a concern with giving the

---

Judge Winter from the Deliberations in the Preliminary Motion on the Recruitment of Child Soldiers, SCSL-2004-04-14-PT, 28 May 2004.

145 *Prosecutor* v *Fofana and Kondewa*, Judgment, SCSL-04-14-A, 28 May 2008.

146 See the discussion in Alexander Orakhealshvili, 'Overlap and Convergence: The Interaction Between *Jus ad Bellum* and *Jus in Bello* (2007) 12 *Journal of Conflict and Security Law* 157.

147 *US* v *List* (1948) 15 *Annual Digest* 632.

148 *Fofana and Kondewa*, *supra* n. 145, paras 531–532, 534.

149 *Ibid.*, Partially Dissenting Opinion of Judge George Gelaga King, paras 26–31, 90–94.

150 For a useful overview of the debate in relations to Article 1(4) of Additional Protocol I see Anthony Cullen, *The Concept of Non-International Armed Conflict in International Humanitarian Law* (Cambridge: CUP, 2010) pp. 63–81.

drafters what they wanted, rather than setting out their own view of international justice on the part of the judicial branch of the Court (at least in the Appeals Chamber).

When the Rome Statute was being drafted, it was clear that some delegates wished to hem in the discretion of the judges, hence (unlike in the ICTY) there was, *inter alia*, a closed list of war crimes.[151] In the more general parts of the Statute, though, a highly positivistic approach is also visible.[152] To take Article 22 as an example, whilst the recitation of the *nullum crimen sine lege* principle in paragraph 1 is not especially controversial, the second paragraph is indicative of a very stern view of the appropriate ambit of judicial discretion: 'the definition of a crime shall be strictly construed and shall not be extended by analogy. In case of ambiguity, the definition shall be interpreted in favour of the person being investigated, prosecuted or convicted.' Whilst the prohibition of analogy is not, in itself, overly controversial, the express inclusion was clearly a strong nod towards the most restrictive interpretation of *nullum crimen sine lege*, perhaps positivism's strongest suit in criminal law. Given the fact that at times the ICTY had adopted a more naturalist, progressive, approach to the law (which admittedly then later on occasion found favour with states (and at times not)) it was clear that the drafters of the Rome Statute were more sceptical about the acceptability of such an approach. At least where judges might expand the law on such grounds without the close superintendence of States when they may assert jurisdiction over their own nationals.[153] Hence, a very rigid positivism (certainly more rigid than required by the European Court of Human Rights)[154] was adopted. It cannot be ignored that the approach to (the philosophy of) law adopted by States is not unaffected by whether or not their nationals are a possible subject of that law.

Article 22 is not the only place in which such an approach is manifest. It is also present in Article 21, which provides the applicable sources of law and thus provides the bedrock of the approach the Court is entitled to take.[155] Article 21 reads (in relevant part) that

> The Court shall apply:
> (a) In the first place, this Statute, Elements of Crimes and its Rules of Procedure and Evidence;
> (b) In the second place, where appropriate, applicable treaties and the principles and rules of international law, including the established principles of the international law of armed conflict;
> (c) Failing that, general principles of law derived by the Court from national laws of legal systems of the world including, as appropriate, the national laws of States that would normally exercise jurisdiction over the crime, provided that those principles are not inconsistent with this Statute and with international law and internationally recognized norms and standards.[156]

---

151 See Cryer, *supra* n. 9, chapter 5; Bruce Broomhall, 'Article 22' in Triffterer *supra* n. 44, 713, p. 714.

152 On positivism and codification of the criminal law see Jeremy Horder, 'Criminal Law and Legal Positivism' (2002) 8 *Legal Theory* 221.

153 This is the theme of Cryer, *supra* n. 9, chapters 5–6. See also Timothy L.H. McCormack, 'The Reticence of States to Try Their "Own Nationals" for International Crimes' in Mark Lattimer and Philippe Sands (eds), *Justice for Crimes Against Humanity* (Oxford: Hart, 2003) 107.

154 See *supra* n. 53.

155 See also van Schaack, *supra* n. 52 p. 189.

156 See generally Margaret McAuliffe deGuzman, 'Article 21' in Triffterer *supra* n. 44, 701. For critique of the provision in practice, see Robert Cryer, 'Royalism and The King: Article 21 of the Rome Statute and the Politics of Sources' (2009) 12 *New Criminal Law Review* 390.

This provision was intended to relate to the *nullum crimen* principle, and does so by setting up a clear hierarchy of sources.[157] At the top, the Statute, Rules of Procedure and evidence and (although they are only guidance) the Elements of Crimes.[158] A clear preference for written law (emanating from the drafters) is clearly visible. Even customary law (which is not to form the basis of criminal liability itself (owing, *inter alia* to the exclusive nature of the lists of offences in Articles 6–8 and the strictures of Article 22) and 'applicable treaties' are relegated to second place. The more controversial references to custom, and then general principles (which are where judicial discretion, and perhaps natural law,[159] could enter into the equation) are relegated to secondary and tertiary roles respectively.[160] Indeed, the tertiary role given to general principles of international law is redolent of the stern positivism of the Soviet approaches to international law, which largely rejected the legal nature of such principles.[161] It is the case, though, that such theoreticians go further than the Rome Statute, and general principles have tended to be, in practice, resorted to by international tribunals when treaties and custom have not served to answer the relevant question. The strictures of Article 21, however, are further evidence of the underlying (and not necessarily always unconscious) influence of strict legal positivism on the drafters of the Rome Statute.[162]

A third area in which the highly positivist approach taken to the law, in contrast to earlier international criminal tribunals such as the Nuremberg and Tokyo IMTs, can be seen in relation to the crime of aggression. As is well known, at Rome the drafters could not agree upon a definition of that crime. Hence the provision for jurisdiction over that offence in Article 5(1) of the Statute, but with the proviso that the Court was not to exercise jurisdiction over that offence unless and until the Statute was amended to include a definition of aggression.[163] The preference for written law over custom,[164] judicial discretion and, arguably (if one is to believe the prosecution at the Tokyo IMT), natural law is clear. In spite of the political debates that surrounded the crime of aggression, this does not undermine the point that the preference adopted taken is not apolitical, States were willing in Nuremberg and Tokyo to leave it to others to define the crimes. This was not the case in Rome. Strict positivism served State interests at the Rome negotiations; it did not in the drafting of the Nuremberg and Tokyo IMT Statutes, and States behaved

[157] deGuzman, *supra* n. 156 p. 702.

[158] On the normative status of the Elements see Schabas, *supra* n. 42, pp. 258–268.

[159] Ian Brownlie, *Principles of International Law* (Oxford: OUP, 7th edn., 2008) p. 16.

[160] deGuzman, *supra* n. 156, pp. 708–10. See also Fabián O. Raimondo, *General Principles of Law in the Decisions of the International Criminal Courts and Tribunals* (Leiden: Martinus Nijhoff, 2008) pp. 149–157.

[161] Grigory Tunkin, William E. Butler (trans.), *Theory of International Law* (London: George, Allen and Unwin, 1974) chapter 4.

[162] On a similar point, as Hersch Lauterpacht said, 'If governments are not prepared to entrust with legislative functions bodies composed of their authorised representatives, they will not be prepared to allow or tolerate the exercise of such activity by a tribunal enjoined by its Statute to apply the existing law' *The Development of International Law by the International Court* (London: Stevens, 1958) p. 76.

[163] Schabas, *supra* n. 42 pp. 109–115.

[164] Aggression is a crime in customary international law, *R* v *Jones, Milling et al* [2006] UKHL 16.

accordingly. The recent adoption of a definition of aggression that may be included in the Rome Statute (if it achieves a sufficient number of ratifications) is an instantiation of this approach, not a confounding of it.[165] Approaches which allowed the participants to draw on naturalism were considered acceptable in Nuremberg and Tokyo, but were not thought acceptable for the ICC, which might assert jurisdiction over the nationals of the drafters.

Even with the crimes upon which definitions could be agreed in Rome, this was not enough for some delegations[166] who wanted, for various reasons – some principled, some political, some presentational – greater specificity in the definition of offences.[167] This led to Article 9 of the Rome Statute, which provided for the drafting of Elements of Crimes, a very detailed set of requirements for conviction, that practically amount to a 'check-list' of the necessary parts of offences that needed to be proved. Although many States found the process useful,[168] as William Schabas has said, these Elements were an extraordinary example of an 'obsessive' legal positivism on the part of some of the drafters.[169] Again, the contrast with earlier Tribunals is striking, but can be explained on the basis that the drafters were aware that the ICC was an 'unsafe' Tribunal, which could exercise jurisdiction over its own nationals, whereas the Tribunals that had gone before largely were not expected to.[170] This affected their approach to the *nullum crimen* principle, which, in this instance, was a metonym for their more general, if rarely expressed, political/philosophical approach.[171]

The judges (at least the appellate judges) of the ICC have largely adopted the positivistic inclinations of the drafters. In part, owing to Article 21, they did not have much of a choice.[172] Nonetheless, the ICC is fully aware that, as a court of voluntary rather than compulsory jurisdiction, if it is to attract ratifications to the Statute, cooperation and financial support, it needs to not scare States too much, whose approach to international law tends towards the positivist, at least in its presentational form.[173] This can be seen by the reaction of the Appeals Chamber to the one attempt by a Pre-Trial Chamber to import teleological reasoning into their approach. This was in the *Democratic Republic*

---

165 On the debate see Roger S. Clark, 'Amendments to the Rome Statute of the International Criminal Court Considered at the First Review Conference on the Court, Kampala, 31 May–11 June 2010' (2010) 2 *Göttingen Journal of International Law* 689; Robert Heinisch, 'The Crime of Aggression After Kampala: Success or Burden for the Future?' (2010) 2 *Göttingen Journal of International Law* 713.

166 In particular, the United States.

167 For some of them see Schabas, *supra* n. 52, pp. 258–261.

168 Roy S. Lee, 'Introduction' Roy S. Lee *et al* (eds), *The International Criminal Court: Elements of Crimes and Rules of Procedure and Evidence* (Ardsley, Transnational, 2001) lv, pp. lv–lviii.

169 William Schabas, 'Interpreting the Statutes of the *ad hoc* Tribunals' in Vohrah *et al* (eds) *supra* n. 92, p. 887.

170 Cryer, *supra* n. 9, chapters 5–6.

171 As might be surmised from the above, the two are not usually so separate.

172 Although they have at times gone beyond what even Article 21 requires in this regard, Cryer *supra* n. 156.

173 Michael Struett, 'The Politics of Discursive Legitimacy: Understanding the Dynamics and Implications of Prosecutorial Discretion at the International Criminal Court' in Steven Roach (ed.), *Governance, Order, and the International Criminal Court: Between Realpolitik and a Cosmopolitan Court* (Oxford: OUP, 2009) 107, p. 107.

of the Congo decision.[174] The Trial Chamber had taken the view that relevant criteria for the determination of gravity of a case included '[i]s the conduct which is the object of a case systematic or large scale (due consideration should also be given to the social alarm caused to the international community by the relevant type of conduct)?'[175] The latter test, that of 'social alarm' does not appear in the Statute, and, in part on this basis, but also on more methodological grounds, the Appeals Chamber made sure it stamped on such approaches to the Statute, returning strictly to the Statute and the tests it set out, not allowing more subjective, moralistic judgments to enter into the equation.[176]

Furthermore, the textual reading the Appeals Chamber gave of Article 17(1)(d) was firmly based in the intentions of the drafters. They looked at the text, and the *travaux,* not to more vague (and more threatening to States) teleological approaches to base their decision on. This is in many ways what might be expected of a court, attempting to show States, both parties and non-parties, that it is 'sound' in the vernacular of British international law.[177] In other words, the Appeals Chamber was attempting to signal to States that they would get what they asked for, not what a chamber invents. It is no surprise that the President of the Appeals Chamber at this point was Judge Philippe Kirsch, Chairman of the Committee of the Whole at the Rome Conference, and an ex-diplomat. As such, it should not be a shock that he not only is a fan of using the *travaux*, but also has a keen sense of what States would like to see.[178]

Their reasoning for rejecting the Trial Chamber's view reads a little like a potted critique of naturalism in judicial reasoning:

> As to the 'social alarm caused to the international community by the relevant conduct . . . the Pre-Trial Chamber has not explained from where it derived this criterion, it is not mentioned in the Statute at all . . . the criterion of social alarm depends upon subjective and contingent reactions to crimes rather than upon their objective gravity. The crimes listed in articles 5 to 8 of the Statute, have been carefully selected. . . . The subjective criterion of social alarm therefore is not a consideration that is necessarily appropriate for the determination of the admissibility of a case.[179]

It is true that when Pre-Trial Chambers and Trial Chambers have dealt with the law, they have not always been as positivistically inclined,[180] but the Appeals Chamber has been fairly consistent on point, at least at this early stage.

---

174 Judgment on the Prosecutor's Appeal against the Decision of Trial Chamber 1 entitled 'Decision on the Prosecutor's Application for Warrants of Arrest, Article 58', ICC-01-04, 13 July 2006 (made public 23 September 2008).

175 *Ibid.*, para 64.

176 *Ibid.*, paras 73, 78, 79, 91.

177 Meaning, largely, in the UK context, consistent with a positivist approach to international law, whether identified or not.

178 Generally speaking, it is probably fair to say that the *lingua franca* of debate between States on international law is that of positivism.

179 Situation in the Democratic Republic of the Congo, *Judgment on the Prosecutor's Appeal against the Decision of Trial Chamber 1 entitled 'Decision on the Prosecutor's Application for Warrants of Arrest, Article 58*', ICC-01-04, 13 July 2006 (made public 23 September 2008) para 72.

180 Although they have at times been exactly that, see Cryer *supra* n. 156.

9.3.2 Positivism and Naturalism in Academic Scholarship

Although it is controversial whether or not international law is simply what international lawyers do and/or say, it is undoubtedly the case that in international criminal law scholars have had an impact far in advance of that that Article 38(1) of the ICJ Statute might imply. This is not to say that they have always been theoretically informed.[181] For many years the majority of theoretical commentaries (some of which are mentioned above) reacted to practice in international criminal law, and reflected the philosophical predispositions of the authors rather than counting towards contributions from theory to attempt to advance international criminal law. This is not to denigrate the approach adopted by those scholars, although as discussed above, for some practitioners[182] their approach to the law was more tactical than principled.

This has changed in the past decade or so, in particular under the influence of a small number of philosophers who have sought to explain the international nature of the core international crimes, and their ambit, with reference to philosophy. The most notable of these, as mentioned above, is Larry May, who seeks to explain aggression, war crimes, genocide and crimes against humanity with respect to a Grotian (i.e. mixed positivist and natural law) approach that also relies expressly on just war theory and his previous philosophical work on groups.[183]

There are others, including David Luban,[184] who have also undertaken such work and made considerable contributions to thought in the area, and attempted to influence the debate on point. It would be quite impossible in a chapter of a book to do justice to the nuances of these works without excluding too many other approaches to international criminal law. One of the important contributions that such works have made is to integrate discussion about what the law is, how it might be defended on philosophical grounds, and where a coherent application of (what the relevant scholar considers to be) the underlying philosophical commitments that have inspired pre-existing international criminalisation ought to lead to. There are very significant works in this area, and the cases they make may be morally quite convincing. Nonetheless, it is important, at an empirical level, not to overstate the extent to which coherence has always had a place in States' approaches to international criminal law. Although, as was seen above, such (naturalist-inspired) reasons have had an influence, at times they have been ignored, and for reasons that probably cannot be referred back to jurisprudence rather than political expedience.

---

181 Equally, the works of M. Cherif Bassiouni are a notable contribution to the literature which have been informed by the author's theoretical approach (which is from the Yale/policy school).

182 In particular those in the Prosecution and Defence at the Nuremberg and Tokyo IMTs, and the drafters of the Rome Statute.

183 *Supra* n. 6.

184 David Luban, 'A Theory of Crimes Against Humanity' (2004) 29 *Yale Law Journal* 85. See also Christopher Macleod, 'Towards a Philosophical Account of Crimes Against Humanity' (2010) 21 *European Journal of International Law* 281.

9.4 OTHER PHILOSOPHICAL APPROACHES TO INTERNATIONAL CRIMINAL LAW

There are various other philosophical approaches to international criminal law, although they have not all affected the practical application of international criminal law to the same extent. This part of this chapter will seek to survey some of them, in particular those that have been more influential either intellectually, or have impacted upon the practical implementation of international criminal law.[185] It is worth bearing in mind that these approaches tended to arise after international criminal law had established itself as an academic enterprise in and of its own right as a subject worthy of study, i.e. in the 1990s. That said, the approaches described below did not exist in any real way at the time of the Nuremberg and Tokyo IMTs.[186]

9.4.1 Critical Legal Studies, Feminism and Third World (TWAIL) Approaches[187]

To begin with what is the most difficult to define, in the abstract, set of scholars: those who can be seen as falling into the general descriptor of critical legal scholars, whether or not they would accept the appellation. Critical legal studies (CLS), with its concentration on the malleability of rules, the influence of politics on the notionally objective approaches to law, and interest in the way in which, as a result, rhetoric, personal, and moral positions (identified or otherwise) impact on the law, in many ways is a natural place for appraisal of international criminal law. International criminal law was probably first subjected to a significant critical critique by Gerry Simpson in 1997 in his 'War Crimes: A Critical Introduction'. Simpson looked at how international criminal law was not a coherent intellectual endeavour at the time,[188] how the politics have determined who

[185] As such, this chapter will not deal with, for example international relations theory and international criminal law, or law and economics approaches to international criminal law, as they are not, in themselves, philosophical approaches to international criminal law per se; although for an example of such approaches see Kenneth W. Abbott, 'International Relations Theory, International Law, and the Regime Governing Atrocities in Internal Conflicts' in Ratner and Slaughter (eds), *supra* n. 46; Mary Ellen O'Connell, 'New International Legal Process' in *ibid.*, 79; Jeffrey L. Dunoff and Joel P. Trachtmann, 'The Law and Economics of Humanitarian Law Violations in Internal Conflict' in *ibid.*, 211. There is little sophisticated Marxist theorising on international criminal law, although there is no reason why there ought not be. The same could be said about Queer theory. There has nonetheless been some very sophisticated work on sexual offences against men in armed conflict, see Sandesh Sivakumaran, 'Sexual violence against men in armed conflict' (2007) 18 *European Journal of International Law* 253–276; Sandesh Sivakumaran, 'Lost in Translation: UN Responses to Sexual Violence against Men and Boys in Situations of Armed Conflict' (2010) 92 *International Review of the Red Cross* 259.

[186] With the arguable exception of Judge Pal at the Tokyo IMT, *supra* n. 75.

[187] Although some might question whether these approaches could be taken as 'philosophical', Critical Legal Studio draws in depth upon continental philosophy, and both feminist and Third World Approaches draw quite directly on similar sources. Some liberal feminists and first (and perhaps second) wave TWAIL scholars may disagree on point, much of the literature discussed here does so. There is simply no space to engage in detail in the genealogy of the relevant approaches here.

[188] G. Simpson, 'War Crimes: A Critical Introduction', in McCormack and Simpson (eds), *supra* n. 9, 1. It is a legitimate question now whether international criminal law has become more, or less, coherent in the last decade.

is, and is not, prosecuted for international crimes, and how the inevitable selectivity of international criminal prosecutions raises questions about the idea of a coherent idea of international criminal law. Given the strong, albeit sympathetic, critique that Simpson offered, it is worth noting that he was also a member of the Australian delegation to the Rome Conference. The two roles are not inconsistent.[189] The same can be said with respect to another critical commentator who was also a member of a State's delegation to the Rome Conference, Immi Tallgren. In a series of articles Tallgren, who was a member of the Finnish delegation to that conference, offered not only a CLS approach to the concept of complementarity,[190] but also a personal appraisal of the negotiations, which is clearly influenced by David Kennedy's work on human rights activism.[191]

Indeed, the doyen of critical scholars in international law, Martti Koskenniemi has, upon occasion, expressed views on international criminal law. Not only has he engaged in debate about the difficulty in treading the path between impunity and show trials,[192] he has also spoken insightfully of the history of international criminal law.[193]

Furthermore, perhaps in a fashion exemplary (in both ways) of CLS's uncovering of *aporias* in legal reasoning, Koskenniemi has noted of the broad reading of the customary law applicable to crimes against humanity, liberated from the link to armed conflict in the Nuremberg IMT and ICTY Statutes, given in the *Tadić* 1999 Appeal:[194]

> Why would that be the correct interpretation? Would not regular principles of criminal law rather have spoken in favour of a more limited standard – *in dubio pro reo*? Surely the Tribunal framed its interpretation not by wishing to follow standard techniques of criminal law – after all, everything about the ICTY was 'standard' – but in view of the bias to guarantee as wide a scope for prosecution as possible. Again, the point is not that this was 'wrong' or 'political' – the opposite interpretation would have been no less so – but that the interpretative choices remain just that – choices – that refer back to formal sources and techniques of interpretation that seek to canvass a plausible notion of what people (such as the framers) may 'intend' but which remain undetermined by them.[195]

Much of this comment could be similarly applied to the 'humanising' the ICTY has engaged with,[196] and as was discussed above, it would be totalising to characterise the

---

189 Martti Koskenniemi, for example was a legal advisor to the Finnish government when he wrote the seminal *From Apology to Utopia* (Cambridge: CUP, reprinted 2005, original edn. 1989).

190 Immi Tallgren, 'Completing the "International Criminal Order": the Rhetoric of International Repression and the Notion of Complementarity in the Draft Statute for an International Criminal Court' (1998) 67 *Nordic Journal of International Law* 107.

191 Immi Tallgren, 'We Did It? The Vertigo of Law and Everyday Life at the Diplomatic Conference on the Establishment of an International Criminal Court' (1999) 12 *Leiden Journal of International Law* 683.

192 Martti Koskenniemi, 'Between Impunity and Show Trials' (2002) *Max Planck Yearbook of International Law* 1.

193 *Supra* n. 14.

194 *Prosecutor* v *Tadić*, Judgment, IT-94-1-A, 15 July 1999. A pure positivist would note, on the other hand, that this was *obiter*, and therefore would not have altered the result in the specific case.

195 Martti Koskennniemi, *From Apology to Utopia: The Structure of International Legal Argumentation* (Cambridge: CUP, Reissue with new epilogue, 2005, originally published 1989) p. 585.

196 Humanism and sovereignty are perhaps the international criminal law versions of the apology and utopia of which Koskenniemi spoke *ibid.*

judgments of the court as always going one way or the other. Or where the law is sufficiently clear one way or the other, that the Tribunal has not simply followed what the tolerably uncontroversial law is on point. Not all of the decisions are politics all the way down.

Moving on, feminism was a relative latecomer to international legal theory, appearing on the intellectual scene in the late 1980s and early 1990s. It has, nonetheless, had considerable influence on international criminal law, primarily in the developing recognition of gender-based crimes.[197] Although rape and other sexual offences have been war crimes for a very considerable period of time, the social reality surrounding such offences in wartime was considerably different, and prosecutions were rare, and often euphemistic, being for 'outrages on personal dignity' rather than rape or sexual assault, or based on outmoded chivalric concepts of 'honour' that fail to express the nature of the wrongs that need to be expressed by international criminal law.[198]

The ICTY and ICTR were clearly influenced by the increasing concern about gender-based crimes that came about in the late 20th century, at least in part owing to feminist scholarship.[199] Indeed, in the ICTR's first case, the presiding judge, Navanethem Pillay, asked for the indictment to be amended to include rape charges when evidence of such offences emerged at trial.[200] When the Rome Statue was being negotiated, NGOs such as the Women's Caucus for Gender Justice played a considerable role in ensuring that the Statute gave attention to gender crimes.[201] The action of the Office of the Prosecutor in the ICC in appointing the well-known feminist scholar Catherine MacKinnon as a special adviser on gender crimes implies that the influence of feminism is likely to continue on international criminal law.

Some consider the influence of feminism has already largely responded to the critiques that early feminist works had of international criminal law.[202] Others see much more work to do, to counter sexist stereotypes that are structured within the law, and to emphasise that sexual offences are always wrong, not just in the context of genocide, crimes against humanity and war crimes, and that more structural problems exist in recognising the gendered nature of international law.[203]

Some of the most recent contributions to the theory of international criminal law are

---

[197] Hilary Charlesworth, Christine Chinkin and Shelley Wright, 'Feminist Approaches to International Law' (1991) 85 *American Journal of International Law* 613.

[198] Christine Chinkin, 'Rape and Sexual Abuse of Women in International Law' (1994) 5 *European Journal of International Law* 329; Kelly Dawn Askin, *War Crimes Against Women: Prosecution in International Tribunals* (The Hague: Martinus Nijhoff, 1997); Judith Gardam, 'Women and Armed Conflict: Why the Silence?' (1997) 46 *International and Comparative Law Quarterly* 55.

[199] Hilary Charlesworth, 'Feminist Methods in International Law' in Ratner and Slaughter, *supra* n. 46, 159, p. 171.

[200] *Akayesu, supra* n. 138, para 6. On Pillay and gender crimes see Daniel Terris, Cesare P. Romano and Leigh Swigart, *The International Judge: An Introduction to the Men and Women who Decide the World's Cases* (Oxford: OUP, 2007) pp. 42–46.

[201] 'ICC Prosecutor appoints Prof. Catharine A. MacKinnon as Special Adviser on Gender Crimes', Press Release ICC-OTP-20081126-PR377, 26 November 2008.

[202] Noëlle Quénivet, *Sexual Offences in Armed Conflict and International Law* (New York: Transnational, 2008).

[203] Charlesworth, *supra* n. 199, pp. 171–179.

from the Third World.[204] There is a relatively small, but increasing, body of literature on point. Although the tradition in TWAIL is diverse, much of the concern of the scholarship on international criminal law from this approach concentrates on the lived reality of international criminal law of those in the Third World.[205] Concern is often expressed about the 'civilizing mission' represented by international law, and how past injustices and structural violence are downplayed or marginalised.[206] TWAIL scholars such as Anghie and Chimni also express concern about how the international legal process marginalises Third World States, and how this is reflected in the content of international criminal law.[207]

Other critiques have focused on how international tribunals have dealt with the Third World, particularly in relation to African conflicts. Some, for example, see the ICC as an imposition of Western concepts of justice, which do not map onto African concepts of justice and cognate practices.[208] Others have noted how international tribunals can misunderstand culture and that some of the norms (for example on child soldiers) reflect a Western bias.[209] Sometimes States express views consistent with TWAIL, in particular in the context of the ICC and its early focus on Africa. To take one example, the representative of Sudan, on the occasion of the situation in Dafur being sent to the ICC, said that:

> While the Council is keen on holding my country to account and to urge it to hold trials and achieve security and stability and overnight, in a territory whose area approximates that of Iraq, we find that very same Council continuing to use the policy of double standards . . . [and that it] . . . exposed the fact that this criminal court was originally intended for developing and weak States, and that it is a tool for the exercise of the culture of superiority and to impose cultural superiority. It is a tool for those who believe that they have a monopoly on virtues in this world, rife with injustice and tyranny. . . . The Council even goes so far as to affirm that exceptions are only for major powers and that this Court is simply a stick used for weak States and that it is an extension of this Council of yours, which has always only adopted resolutions and sanctions only against weak countries, while major Powers and those under their protection ride roughshod over the Resolutions of the Council, cynically disregard them and consider them a dead letter.[210]

There are some TWAIL ideas here, but these are more political statements than a self-conscious application of TWAIL and many TWAIL scholars would not agree with the Sudanese arguments. Scholars who adopt a TWAIL view often criticise selective application of the law (as do others), but those who do so generally do not claim that this is an argument in favour of impunity.[211] Indeed, it is important to remember that although, as it stands, the ICC is only publicly actively investigating situations in Africa,

---

204 Arguably Judge Pal's dissent at Tokyo could be seen as an example of this, see Kopelman, *supra* n. 75.

205 Anthony Anghie and B.S. Chimni, 'Third World Approaches to International Law and Responsibility for Atrocities in Internal Armed Conflict' in Ratner and Slaughter, *supra* n. 46, 185.

206 *Ibid.*, pp. 197–9.

207 *Ibid.*, pp. 201–202.

208 Drumbl, *supra* n. 48; Kamari Maxine Clarke, *Fictions of Justice: The International Criminal Court and the Challenge of Legal Pluralism in Sub-Saharan Africa* (Cambridge: CUP, 2009).

209 Tim Kelsall, *Culture Under Cross Examination: International Justice and the Special Court for Sierra Leone* (Cambridge: CUP, 2009).

210 UN Doc. S/PV.5158, at p. 12 (Mr Erwa).

211 See, e.g., Anghie and Chimni *supra* n. 205.

these have been (other than in Kenya), based on references from the States themselves, or the Security Council. Admittedly, though, there are grounds here for worry; TWAIL approaches are not hostile to international criminal law, but seek to improve it and ensure that it reflects a global approach to social problems.

9.4.2 Criminal Law Theory and International Criminal Law

One of the other approaches that can be identified in the theory of international criminal law is the trend towards theorising the substantive crimes in international criminal law. There are various approaches to such an inquiry. In the German-influenced school of thought about international criminal law much has been made in the context of taxonomical debate about the nature of international crimes and the principles of liability which apply to them.[212] Such analyses draw on the German *dogmatische* tradition,[213] which finds its roots in philosophers such as Cesare Beccaria, Immanuel Kant and Georg W.F. Hegel. It appraises international criminal law from the point of view of categories drawn from the sophisticated distinctions drawn by those theorists. In so doing, some exceptional contributions to the literature in the area have been made. Critics have taken the view that such contributions externalise concepts created at the domestic level, at times with specific municipal matters in mind. Furthermore, at times it could be argued that international crimes and domestic crimes are not subject to all the same concepts and principles,[214] and international law and domestic law do not have the same sources, therefore such transposition is inapposite. One response which has some purchase is that some principles developed in particular in Germany (by Claus Roxin) were designed specifically to deal with international crimes, and accurately reflect their frequently collective nature.[215]

In more common law-influenced works, work has focused perhaps more on what ought to be an international crime, the question of fair labelling, and the harm principle.[216] Larry May, for example, bases the case for the existence of international criminal prosecutions on an international version of the harm principle.[217] Such work tends to come from within, but not solely from, the liberal political tradition of political philosophy.[218]

---

[212] For examples see e.g. Héctor Olásolo, *The Criminal Responsibility of Senior Political and Military Leaders as Principals to International Crimes* (Oxford: Hart, 2009); Claus Kreß, 'The Crime of Genocide under International Law' (2006) 6 *International Criminal Law Review* 461 Ambos, *supra* n. 5.

[213] 'Dogmatic' in such debates does not have the derogative connotation it has in its English translation, and means something closer to conceptually coherent.

[214] Not least as some of the principles of liability used are simply different.

[215] Claus Kreß, 'Claus Roxin's Lehre von der Organisationsherrschaft und das Völkerstrafrecht' (2006) *Goltdammers Archiv für Strafrecht* 304; Devin Pendas, *The Frankfurt Auschwitz Trial 1963–1965: Genocide, History and the Limits of Law* (Cambridge: CUP, 2006).

[216] See, e.g. Robert Cryer, 'General Principles of Liability in International Criminal Law' in Dominic McGoldrick, Peter Rowe and Eric Donnelly (eds), *The International Criminal Court: Legal and Policy Issues* (Oxford: Hart, 2004) 233.

[217] May, *supra* n. 6, chapter 5.

[218] See, e.g. David Nersessian, *Genocide and Political Groups* (Oxford: OUP, 2010); Douglas Lackey, 'Postwar Environmental Damage: A Study *Jus Post Bellum*' in May and Hoskins (eds),

The approaches are sometimes avowedly normative, in that they suggest the creation of new crimes that cause similar harms to those that international criminal law has already accepted as worthy of criminalisation. These, of course, are subject whether justifiably or not to the other critiques, such as they are simply reflective of their own traditions that were developed domestically, and in the West. Attempts to read back criminal law theory into international law more generally have also proved controversial.[219]

Perhaps the most ambitious attempt as it stands to bring the two approaches together has been engaged in by one of the few scholars with the language skills to be able to do so fully,[220] George Fletcher. Fletcher's work on domestic criminal law was amongst the first to introduce philosophical investigation into criminal law in the English speaking world, whilst also integrating the civilian conceptual tradition.[221] He has turned his hand in recent years to understanding the fundamental 'grammar' of criminal law, which encompasses both domestic and international criminal law.[222] As, so far, only the first volume in the proposed triptych has been published, it would be premature to evaluate the project as a whole.[223]

9.4.3 Theoretical Approaches to the Foundations, Aims and Objectives of International Criminal Law

Fletcher has also engaged in other areas of debate in relation to international criminal law, probably the most important from our point of view is his investigation into individual and collective guilt in international criminal law.[224] This is only one of the contributions that scholars have made to the foundations of international criminal law, and the aims it has, or ought to have. In criminal law, the battle between deontologists and utilitarians has raged at the domestic level. The same has occurred at the international level, with both sides entering the fray.[225] On the retributive side scholars, and often the ICTY, have taken the view that in view of the seriousness of the offences, the

---

supra n. 48, 141; David Marcus, 'Famine Crimes in International Law' (2004) 97 *American Journal of International Law* 245.

219 George P. Fletcher and Jens D. Ohlin, *Defending Humanity* (Oxford: OUP, 2008), on which see Yoram Dinstein, 'The Hazards of Interdisciplinary Pollination: Some Critical Comments on *Defending Humanity*' (2009) 7 *Journal of International Criminal Justice* 517; although see Richard V. Meyer, 'A Plea for Defending Humanity' (2009) 7 *Journal of International Criminal Justice* 521.

220 See Kai Ambos, 'Toward a Universal Grammar of Criminal Law: Comments on George Fletcher's Grammar of Criminal Law' (2007) 28 *Cardozo Law Review* 2647, p. 2647.

221 George P. Fletcher, *Rethinking Criminal Law* (New York: Little, Brown & Co., 1979).

222 George P. Fletcher, *The Grammar of Criminal Law: Volume I* (Oxford, OUP, 2006).

223 Although for a symposium on the first volume see (2007) 28 *Cardozo Law Review* 2401–2738.

224 George P. Fletcher, 'The Storrs Lectures: Liberals and Romantics at War: The Problem of Collective Guilt' (2002) 111 *Yale Law Journal* 1499.

225 Again, there are also those who query whether retribution and deterrence can be translated across to international criminal courts and tribunals: Mirjan Damaška, 'What is the Point of International Criminal Justice?' (2008) 83, *Chicago-Kent Law Review* 329, p. 339. Some are also sceptical that there is currently a coherent theory of international criminal law: Drumbl, 'A Hard Look', *supra* n. 48. See, more optimistically, David Luban, 'Fairness to Rightness: Jurisdiction, Legality and the Legitimacy of International Criminal Law' in Besson and Tasioulas, *supra* n. 4, 569, pp. 574–575.

only appropriate response can be punishment, as desert for such offences.[226] There is instinctive appeal here, but many have drawn upon Hannah Arendt's critique of the *Eichmann* trial, that his evil was, in fact 'banal',[227] to argue that 'sometimes a tragedy may be so great, a series of events of such political or even metaphysical significance, that punishing an individual does not come close to measuring up to it'.[228] Others have responded, though, that this is the case with many domestic crimes too, and does not provide a reason to do what can be done, a position with which Arendt would probably not have disagreed.[229]

From the (utilitarian) deterrence side, the idea that the prevention of further crimes is the primary goal of international criminal law has been made,[230] however, there is considerable scepticism about whether the ideas of rational calculation that underlie deterrence theories apply in the situations in which international criminal law applies.[231] Some scholars have suggested that with high-level leaders, though, there may be something to assumptions of rational calculation.[232] There have been other suggested utilitarian/consequential aims for international criminal law, in particular rehabilitation and the contribution to peace that prosecutions can bring (often summed up in the slogan 'no peace without justice' or, perhaps more sophisticatedly, 'no lasting peace without justice').[233]

Against this, scholars such as the philosopher Anthony Duff have sought to provide a detailed defence of the existence of international criminal law from the point of view of denunciation of conduct.[234] This function, which has deontological roots, is designed to express the wrongfulness of the conduct. The ICTY has at times taken this view, on the basis that:

---

[226] Graham T. Belwitt, 'The Importance of a Retributive Approach to Justice' in David A. Blumenthal and Timothy L.H. McCormack (eds), *The Legacy of Nuremberg: Civilising Influence or Institutionalised Vengeance?* (The Hague: Nijhoff, 2008) 39. *Prosecutor* v *Aleksovski,* Judgment, IT-95-14/1-T, 24 April 2000, para 185.

[227] Arendt, *supra* n. 34; although see Antonio Cassese, 'Eichmnan: Is Evil so Banal?' (2009) 7 *Journal of International Criminal Justice* 645.

[228] Koskenniemi, *supra* n. 192, p. 2.

[229] Mark Osiel, 'Why Prosecute? Critics of Punishment for Mass Atrocity' (2000) 22 *Human Rights Quarterly* 118, p. 2.

[230] Payam Akhavan, 'Can International Criminal Justice Prevent Future Atrocities?' (2001) 85 *American Journal of International Law* 7.

[231] Damaška, *supra* n. 225, p. 344; Jan Klabbers, 'Just Revenge: The Deterrence Argument in International Criminal Law (2001) 12 *Finnish Yearbook of International Law* 249; Leslie P. Francis and John G. Francis, 'International Criminal Courts, the Rule of Law and the Prevention of Harm: Building Justice in Times of Injustice' in May and Hoskins (eds), *supra* n. 48, 58.

[232] Stephen Roach, 'Justice of the Peace? Future Challenges and Prospects for a Cosmopolitan Court' in Stephen Roach (ed.), *Governance, Order and the International Criminal Court* (Oxford: OUP, 2009) 225, pp. 226–9.

[233] Frederick Harhoff, 'Sense and Sensibility in Sentencing – Taking Stock of International Criminal Punishment' in Ola Engdahl and Pål Wrange (eds), *Law at War: The Law as it Was and the Law as it Should Be: Lieber Amoricum Ove Bring* (Leiden: Brill, 2008) 121, p. 131 (on rehabilitation); Priscilla Hayner, *Unspeakable Truths: Confronting State Terror and Atrocity* (London: Routledge, 2nd edn., 2011) chapter 12 (for some scepticism on whether this can be the case).

[234] E.g. Antony Duff, 'Can we Punish the Perpetrators of Atrocities?' in Thomas Brudholm and Thomas Cushman (eds), *The Religious in Responses to Mass Atrocity: Interdisciplinary Perspectives* (Cambridge: CUP, 2009) 79.

> Among the grievous crimes this Tribunal has the duty to punish, the crime of genocide is singled out for special condemnation and opprobrium. The gravity of genocide is reflected in the stringent requirements which must be satisfied before this conviction is imposed. These requirements – the demanding proof of specific intent and the showing that the group was targeted for destruction in its entirety or in substantial part – guard against a danger that convictions for this crime will be imposed lightly. Where these requirements are satisfied, however, the law must not shy away from referring to the crime committed by its proper name.[235]

Such an approach, critics assert, requires there to be some form of communication with the accused, and an acceptance by both sides of a shared moral community, such that calling that person to account by that community can be considered to have the right to do so, may empirically be absent. Duff accepts that to call someone to account, a polity must have the right to do so, but his response is that membership of humanity probably suffices, and just as the message is unlikely to be received, that does not mean that there should be no attempt to transmit it.[236] In a similar vein, Mirjan Damaška has said that, even where the audience is not just the perpetrator, but the society from which that perpetrator comes, 'international judges should not be swayed by hostile local responses to their decisions if they are generated by values or attitudes whose transcendence is the pedagogic aim of international criminal justice', although care has to be taken to look to local sensitivities, which may be more liberal than some of the broader inculpatory doctrines of international criminal law.[237]

There has also been work on the challenges to international criminal law that arise from sovereignty, some supportive of international criminal law, others less so.[238] There has also been very interesting work done on how universal jurisdiction and international criminal tribunals can be justified in a world in which States do have some standing.[239] Finally, still others have looked, from a philosophical point of view, at what can be done to confront evil, or whether such crimes are forgivable.[240] Space contraints sadly militate against detailed discussions of these contributions.

9.5 CONCLUSION

This chapter cannot claim to do any more than provide the most superficial scratch of the surface of the interrelationship of international criminal law and philosophy. What perhaps can be hoped is that this chapter provokes further thought, and has provided some of the tools to work within this area. There is a rich literature in the area, and it is to

---

235 *Prosecutor* v *Krštić*, Judgment, IT-98-33-A, 19 April 2004, paras 36–7.

236 Duff, *supra* n. 234, pp. 85-100; Duff, *supra* n. 234, pp. 597–602.

237 Damaška, *supra* n. 225, pp. 348–356.

238 On the side of international criminal law see Kristen Hessler, 'State Sovereignty as an Obstacle to International Criminal Law' in May and Hoskins (eds), *supra* n. 48, 39. For critique see Rubin, *supra* n. 43. For sophisticated defences of such prosecutions see Luban *supra* n. 225, pp. 577–580; May, *Crimes Against Humanity, supra* n. 6, chapters 4–5.

239 Alejandro Chehtman, *The Philosophical Foundations of Extraterritorial Jurisdiction* (Oxford: OUP, 2011).

240 Card, *supra* n. 49; Griswold, *supra* n. 49; Thomas Brudholm, 'On the Advocacy of Forgiveness after Mass Atrocities' in Brudholm and Cushman, *supra* n. 234.

be hoped that this chapter has shown that philosophy, whether expressly or impliedly, has played a notable role in the development of international criminal law. Sometimes it is at an academic level, but also, whether directly identified or not, jurisprudential approaches have been instantiated through the work of government actors and judges.

Beyond this, ethicists, psychologists, pure philosophers and sociologists also have a great deal to add to the debate here, and interdisciplinary work, when it is not simply touristic in nature, may be one of the most fruitful lines of inquiry in international criminal law, which could now be seen as a subject in its own right, rather than just a child of its two main constituent areas; international law and criminal law. Those who can draw on the philosophy of both will be in a strong position to bring the debate forward.

10 International law and EU law: between asymmetric constitutionalisation and fragmentation

Katja S. Ziegler

Both international law and EU law[1] are undergoing a process of constitutionalisation. The development of EU law is itself a symptom of the constitutionalisation of international law. EU constitutionalism in the dimension *between the EU and its Member States* is characterised by supranational rule-making, the Court of Justice's (CJEU) compulsory jurisdiction and the prominence of individual rights which are enforceable in an international court as well as, through direct effect, in national courts. More generally, the EU legal order is constitutionalised through a complex intertwining of EU and national law and a hierarchisation of the relationship of the two legal orders through substantive remedies and procedural mechanisms (in particular the reference for a preliminary ruling). EU constitutionalisation *within the EU legal order* is reflected in, amongst other aspects, the gradual expansion of qualified majority voting in the Council and the co-decision procedure (now ordinary legislative procedure) for EU legislation giving the European Parliament a veto right, the creation of EU human rights as standards of review, culminating in their codification in the EU Charter on Fundamental Rights, as well as a general maturing towards a more 'complete' legal order[2] with an internal hierarchy of norms.[3] International law likewise shows several, albeit less developed, signs of constitutionalisation, both in an institutional and in a substantive dimension: institutionally, although still rudimentary, the powers of the Security Council and its increased reach towards individuals (rather than only states) may be recalled as well as detailed normative and institutional frameworks and enforcement mechanisms in specific areas of international law (*Teilrechtsordnungen*, such as international human rights law, world trade law, the law of the sea, etc, and their respective dispute settlement bodies). The existence of secondary norms (such as those of the law of treaties or state responsibility) and emergence of formal normative hierarchies are another feature of international constitutionalisation. Normative hierarchies are created classically through the notion of *ius cogens*. But

[1] On a terminological note: in the following 'European Union' or 'EU' is used in its post-Lisbon meaning to refer to the one (consolidated) legal entity (established and governed by the Treaty on European Union (TEU) and the Treaty on the Functioning of the European Union (TFEU), (2010) OJ C 83, comprising what used to be the EC (and previously EEC) and EU, governed by the respective (EC and EU) Treaties. Reference will be made to 'the Court' where the substance of the text applies both to the ECJ and the renamed CJEU, to 'the EU Courts' where the substance may refer to both ECJ/CJEU and CFI/General Court. Reference to the ECJ and CFI will be made in relation to specific cases where this is historically the precise terminology.

[2] See, e.g. the claim that the EU has a 'complete system of legal remedies', C-50/00P *Unión de Pequeños Agricultores v Council of the European Union* [2002] ECR I-6677, para 40.

[3] See below p 353.

other mechanisms, such as international standards of legality and legitimacy, e.g. derived from human rights, democracy and the rule of law as well as the normative force of the existence of multilateral treaties with widespread, if not universal, membership, are linked to emerging normative hierarchies.[4]

The result of these developments is that constitutionalisation of the EU is at the same time a feature of constitutionalisation of international law. However, these constitutionalisation processes are asymmetrical and at times competing. Paradoxically and logically at the same time, both in spite of this and as a consequence of these constitutionalisation processes, the relationship between international law and EU law is often one of conflict when it comes to reconciling the two claims and processes of constitutionalisation.

This chapter will examine the relationship between EU law and international law in the light of the constitutionalisation of both. It will not concern itself with revisiting the monist or dualist relationship of the EU legal order with the international legal order in a technical sense.[5] It would be entirely possible for the EU Treaties to provide for one or the other, and each choice would have benefits and disadvantages, mainly for coherence or enforcement of (general international law). Instead, this chapter seeks to answer the question how far the EU is still open to, intertwined with and embedded in international law. It will also suggest from a theoretical perspective what the relationship should look like when considered in a substantive context, irrespective of institutional competition and conflict.

10.1 PERSPECTIVES ON THE RELATIONSHIP BETWEEN INTERNATIONAL LAW AND EU LAW AND THE NEED FOR COHERENCE

Many perspectives are possible on the relationship between international and EU law, and those perspectives have varied over time. The perspectives are generally informed by preconceptions of a universal or particularistic legal order and underlying notions of what is more relevant to make a legal order, its formal sources with an ultimate rule of recognition or its substantive authority and effectiveness.[6] The question raises what international relations theory refers to as the 'level-of-analysis problem'.[7] Public international

---

[4] See, e.g. E de Wet, 'The International Constitutional Order' (2006) 55 *International and Comparative Law Quarterly* 51, 59 ff and eadem, 'The Emergence of International and Regional Value Systems as a Manifestation of the Emerging Constiutional Order' (2006) 19 *Leiden Journal of International Law* 614 ff; A Paulus, 'The International Legal System as a Constitution' in JL Dunoff and JP Trachtman (eds), *Ruling the World? Constitutionalism, International Law and Global Governance* (CUP, Cambridge 2009) 69, 90 ff.

[5] For a detailed account see for example A Peters, 'The Position of International Law within the European Community Legal Order' (1997) 40 *German Yearbook of International Law* 9.

[6] J Nijman and A Nollkaemper, 'Beyond the Divide' in J Nijman and A Nollkaemper (eds), *New Perspectives on the Divide Between National and International Law* (OUP, Oxford 2007) 341, 354.

[7] JD Singer, 'The Level-of-Analysis Problem in International Relations' in K Knorr and S Verba (eds), *The International System: Theoretical Essays* (Princeton University Press, Princeton 1961) 77.

lawyers[8] generally presume the application of public international law and the character of the EU as an international organisation (i.e. focusing on its formal sources), while EU lawyers[9] tend to adopt the perspective of the EU as an autonomous legal order or even a self-contained regime, stressing its *sui generis* nature, allowing the substantive perspective to prevail in the evaluation.[10] But the 'level-of-analysis problem' also operates much more at ground-level. Perspectives on the legal nature of the EU (and on what it should do in case of conflict with other international law) depend on which focus the author takes. An analysis that starts from the international law foundations of the EU[11] is likely to lead to different results from one that focuses on a realist or empirical analysis of EU constitutionalism today.[12] The reception of the *Kadi and Al Barakaat* judgment of 2008,[13] in which the ECJ's Grand Chamber expressed its view on the relationship of international law and EU law in prominent terms, finding that the EU legal order was autonomous[14] from international law, seems to confirm this.[15] The decision amounted to an important

[8] P-M Dupuy, 'L'unité de L'ordre juridique international' (2002) 297 *Recueil des Cours* 1438; idem, 'A Doctrinal Debate in the Globalisation Era: On the Fragmentation of International Law' (2007) *European Journal of Legal Studies* (issue 1) at http://www.ejls.eu/1/4UK.pdf; A Pellet, 'Les fondements juridiques internationaux du droit communautaire' (1994) V-2 *Collected Courses of the Academy of European Law* 193, 221 ff; J Klabbers, 'The Changing Image of International Organizations' in J-M Coicaud and V Heiskanen (eds), *The Legitimacy of International Organizations* (2001) 221, 224; P Hilpold, 'EU Law and UN Law in Conflict: The *Kadi* Case' (2009) 13 *Max Planck Yearbook of United Nations Law* 141.

[9] T Tridimas, 'Terrorism and the ECJ: Empowerment and Democracy in the EC Legal Order' (2009) 34 *European Law Review* 103; T Tridimas and JA Gutierrez-Fons, 'EU Law, International Law, and Economic Sanctions against Terrorism: The Judiciary in Distress?' (2008–9) 32 *Fordham International Law Journal* 660; P Eeckhout, 'Community Terrorism Listings, Fundamental Rights, and UN Security Council Resolutions: In Search of the Right Fit' (2007) 3 *European Constitutional Law Review* 183, 205; S Douglas-Scott, *Constitutional Law of the European Union* (Longman, Harlow 2002) 260; Peters (n 5) 10 f. See however also B de Witte, 'European Union Law: How Autonomous is its Legal Order' (2010) 65 *Zeitschrift für Öffentliches Recht* 141; G de Búrca, 'The European Court of Justice and the International Legal Order after *Kadi*' (2009) 51 *Harvard International Law Journal* 1; KS Ziegler, 'Strengthening the Rule of Law, but Fragmenting International Law: The Kadi Decision of the ECJ from the Perspective of Human Rights' (2009) 9 *Human Rights Law Review* 288.

[10] B Simma and D Pulkowski, 'Of Planets and the Universe: Self-contained Regimes in International Law' (2006) 17 *European Journal of International Law* 483, 505 f; de Witte (n 9) 146; cf also Pellet (n 8) 203 f, who distinguishes different degrees of radicalism in regard to the relationship between international and EU law.

[11] See, for example, T Hartley, 'International Law and the Law of the European Union – A Reassessment' (2001) 71 *British Yearbook of International Law* 1.

[12] E.g. E Stein, 'Lawyers, Judges and the Making of a Transnational Constitution' (1981) 75 *American Journal of International Law* 1.

[13] Joined Cases C-402&415/05 P *Yassin Abdullah Kadi and Al Barakaat International Foundation v Council and Commission of the European Union* [2008] ECR I-6351.

[14] *Kadi and Al Barakaat* (n 13) para 317.

[15] See on the one hand, Tridimas and Gutierrez-Fons (n 9) 661, 681 et passim; P Eeckhout, 'Kadi and Al Barakaat: Luxembourg is Not Texas – or Washington DC', EJIL TALK!, 25 Feb. 2009, http://www.ejiltalk.org/kadi-and-al-barakaat-luxembourg-is-not-texas-or-washington-dc/; Kunoy and Dawes, 'Plate Tectonics in Luxembourg: The Ménage à Trois between EC Law, International Law and the European Convention on Human Rights following the UN Sanctions

cornerstone in defining the relationship between EU and international law,[16] at both a practical and a theoretical level.

The case has been reviewed extensively,[17] so a brief outline for the purposes of this chapter shall suffice. Kadi and Al-Barakaat challenged an EC Regulation which implemented UN Security Council Resolutions laying down targeted sanctions against suspected terrorists. The ECJ annulled the EC Regulation in the exercise of a full domestic/constitutional judicial review because it violated EU human rights, considering the EU as an 'internal and autonomous legal order'[18] in which human rights as part of primary EU law ranked more highly than obligations from an international agreement, which would only rank more highly than secondary EU law.[19] It also adopted a dualist position in that it found the EU not to be under a direct obligation to implement the Security Council Resolutions (it is implied that this is because the EU was not a party to the UN Charter), and it did not find that it was bound via the Member States.[20] However, it made a nod to the requirement to respect international law and to interpret the EC Regulation in the light of the Resolution.[21] Further, it paid no deference to the international level because the constitutional values of the EU's 'basic constitutional charter' were at stake.[22] The ECJ thus overruled the CFI which had held the EU to be bound by Security Council Resolutions by virtue of succession into Member States' obligations.[23] It had found them to be applicable in the EU legal order by virtue of EU law through the combined effect of Member States' obligations (Art 351 TFEU/ex-307 EC) under the UN Charter and Art 103 of the UN Charter.[24] It then paid deference to the Security Council in finding the Resolutions and implementing regulations not to be justiciable, the only exception being a review for violations of *ius cogens*[25] which *in casu* was too high a threshold for the invalidity of the Regulation.

While *Kadi and Al Barakaat* may be criticised for its antagonistic approach towards international law,[26] the decision has received generally positive commentary, either from the perspective of human rights and the rule of law[27] or, at a more theoretical level, from the perspective of legal pluralism, as potentially influencing the development of international rules at UN level.[28] However, the relationship between international and

---

Cases' (2009) 46 *Common Market Law Review* 73; on the other hand Hilpold (n 8) 165; de Búrca (n 9); Ziegler (n 9).

16 It has even been called the 'most important judgment ever delivered by the ECJ on the relationship between Community and international law', Tridimas (n 9); Tridimas and Gutierrez-Fons (n 9) 661; de Búrca (n 9).

17 See above (n 9).

18 *Kadi and Al Barakaat* (n 13) para 317.

19 The ECJ 'supposed' (i.e. assumed for argument's sake only) that the UN Charter was applicable, cf *Kadi and Al Barakaat* (n 13) para 308.

20 *Kadi and Al Barakaat* (n 13) para 299.

21 *Kadi and Al Barakaat* (n 13) paras 291, 297.

22 *Kadi and Al Barakaat* (n 13) paras 281 f, 285, 305, 318 ff.

23 T-315/01 *Kadi v Council and Commission* [2005] ECR II-3649, paras 196 ff, 203.

24 *Kadi* (n 23) paras 181 ff.

25 *Kadi* (n 23) paras 212, 227 ff.

26 Mainly international lawyers, cf Hilpold (n 8), but see also de Búrca (n 9); Ziegler (n 9).

27 Tridimas (n 9).

28 D Halberstam and E Stein, 'The United Nations, the European Union, and the King of

EU law, even after *Kadi and Al Barakaat,* still has many more facets, some of which may make the ruling appear to be less divisive. For example, the Court has consistently, even in the *Kadi and Al Barakaat* case, expressed a strong commitment (at least verbally) to international law; it has accommodated international law within the EU legal order, for example through interpretation; it has used international law as a tool when applying EU law, most notably borrowing from it when interpreting general principles of (EU) law, on which EU human rights have been founded exclusively for decades;[29] and it uses international law as standards in the external policies of the EU. In contrast, however, two further decisions of 2008 on the interaction with international law, the *FIAMM and Fedon*[30] and the *Intertanko* judgments, confirm the direction the Court has taken in *Kadi and Al Barakaat* and might establish a new direction in the case law, seemingly as part of a trend that stresses 'domestic constitutionalism' over internationalism (or 'international constitutionalism'). While this may be explicable and perhaps inevitable because the EU acts in its self-interest of establishing its legal identity more strongly vis-à-vis the Member States in particular, there are both opportunities and risks in this 'constitutionalisation' from the perspective of international law: opportunities, because the EU remains an example of a particularly effective international law[31] or even a 'laboratory', which may have directly or indirectly positive effects on the rest of international law;[32] risks because fragmentation, which may be considered the flipside of dealing with the effects of globalisation,[33] reduces the coherence of the international legal order and international law, thus undermining the very foundations on which the EU rests.

10.1.1 Perspectives on the Relationship between EU Law and International Law

The following perspectives on the relationship between international and EU law may be distinguished: firstly, from an international law perspective, the EU is a creature of international law and an international organisation created by treaties establishing a regional sub-set of international rules which, because of its particular shape, is at the same

---

Sweden: Economic Sanctions and Individual Rights in a Plural World Order' (2009) 46 *Common Market Law Review* 13; Tridimas (n 9); JA Kämmerer, 'Das Urteil des Europäischen Gerichtshofs im Fall "Kadi": Ein Triumph der Rechtsstaatlichkeit?' (2009) *Europarecht* 114, 121 f; 128 f; Ziegler (n 9).

29 B de Witte, 'International Law as a Tool for the European Union' (2009) 5 *European Constitutional Law Review* 265.

30 Joined cases C-120/06 P and C-121/06 P *FIAMM and Fedon v Council and Commission* [2008] ECR I-6513; C-308/06 *Intertanko et al. v Secretary of State for Transport* [2008] ECR I-4057.

31 Pellet (n 8) 268.

32 C Tomuschat, 'Artikel 281 EGV: Rechtspersönlichkeit der Gemeinschaft' in H von der Groeben and J Schwarze (eds), *Kommentar zum EU-/EG-Vertrag* (6th edn, Nomos, Baden-Baden 2003, para 46; C Walter, 'International Law in a Process of Constitutionalization' in J Nijman and A Nollkaemper (eds), *New Perspectives on the Divide Between National and International Law* (OUP, Oxford 2007) 191, 214; C Tomuschat, 'Obligations Arising for States Without or Against Their Will' (1993 IV) *Recueil des Cours* 195, 329, 356.

33 Fragmentation, has been described as 'an academic *leitmotiv* in an era of globalization'. P-M Dupuy, 'A Doctrinal Debate in the Globalisation Era: On the "Fragmentation" of International Law' (2007) *European Journal of Legal Studies* (issue 1) 1, 19 (text after n 57) at http://www.ejls.eu/1/4UK.pdf.

time an example for a particularly effective set of rules of international law and a part of international law where law making and enforcement of international law have reached new levels. EU law can serve indirectly and directly as an amplifier and reinforcer of international law:[34] indirectly, by providing an example of very effective international law that may influence how international law is perceived generally; and directly, where EU law attaches its own dogmatic principles of enforcement to specific rules of international law which benefit from the more developed instrumentarium in EU law.

Secondly, and linked to the previous point, are perspectives that identify a distinctly European approach to international law or a distinctly 'European' international law. This 'European' approach comes in several varieties. It is considered by some to be identical with the effectiveness and enforcement mechanisms in EU law as a part of international law. The EU treaty system and the interaction of the EU institutions and the Member States, particularly in the external dimension, are as such identified as a 'European' system of public international law.[35] Others identify a more widely construed 'European approach', as opposed to what is thought to be a distinct US approach, to international law.[36] Such perspectives focus on antagonists in the compliance debate of 'right' v 'might', law-abidance v power politics, idealism v realism, etc. Support is drawn from the different approaches to the International Criminal Court, the Kyoto Protocol and to some extent also the diverging interpretation of the right to self-defence in Art 51 of the UN Charter. Yet another angle is taken by those who see the European element represented in the allegedly Western (European) origins of international law.[37]

A third perspective might look at how, on a practical, if not on a theoretical level, EU law and international law interact and are closely intertwined, in spite of the insistence of the ECJ in *Kadi and Al Barakaat*. This intertwining has two dimensions: the EU as a norm-receiving and a norm-generating organisation, which both 'receives' norms of public international law and provides impetus for and input into their creation. The first

---

[34] Cf Pellet (n 8) 269 quoting the example of the French Conseil d'Etat and the Belgian Cour de Cassation strengthening also the effect of international law in domestic law.

[35] B de Witte, 'The Emergence of a European System of Public International Law: The EU and its Member States as Strange Subjects' in J Wouters, A Nollkaemper and E de Wet (eds), *The Europeanisation of International Law: The Status of International Law in the EU and its Member States* (Asser Press, The Hague 2008) 39.

[36] Cf sceptical J Pauwelyn, 'Europe, America and the "Unity" of International Law' in J Wouters, A Nollkaemper and E de Wet (eds), *The Europeanisation of International Law: The Status of International Law in the EU and its Member States* (Asser Press, The Hague 2008) 205–225, 213 ff, (with further references in n 31); JL Goldsmith and EA Posner, *The Limits of International Law* (OUP, Oxford 2005); A Linklater, 'A European Civilising Process', in C Hill and M Smith (eds), *International Relations and the European Union* (OUP, Oxford 2005) 367–387; cf A Peters, 'Compensatory Constitutionalism: The Function and Potential of Fundamental International Norms and Structures' (2006) 19 *Leiden Journal of International Law* 579, 583; M Koskenniemi, 'International Law in Europe: Between Tradition and Renewal' (2002) 16 *European Journal of International Law* 113; A-M Slaughter and W Burke-White, 'The Future of International Law is Domestic (or, The European Way of Law)' in J Nijman and A Nollkaemper (eds), *New Perspectives on the Divide Between National and International Law* (OUP, Oxford 2007) 110.

[37] Highly critical from a universal perspective, A Orakhelashvili, 'The Idea of European International Law' (2006) 17 *European Journal of International Law* 315.

of these dimensions, focusing on the impact of international law on EU law from the norm-receiving perspective, may be called the *internationalisation*[38] *of EU law.*[39]

Accordingly, the fourth perspective may look at the intertwining in the reverse direction, namely from the impact of the EU and EU law on international law in a norm-generating dimension which may be termed the *Europeanisation*[40] *of international law.* This perspective might focus on both the legal and the practical impact of the EU as an 'actor' on the international plane,[41] which it has increasingly become. This perspective goes beyond the realm of law into international relations and diplomacy.

Fifthly and finally, the relationship between EU and international law gives rise to theoretical questions beyond the positive law or international practice. The examination of the relationship of the EU with its Member States has already raised the question about the nature of the EU and its legal order, locating it on a continuous scale of different degrees of sovereignty or ultimate authority (exclusive, shared, none) as identified by statehood, federation of states and international organisation, or as something *sui generis* altogether. A discussion of the relationship of the EU and international law would not be complete without at least touching[42] upon this theoretical dimension of the nature of the EU. The relationship has become a new testing ground for pluralist theories of law. Originally developed in the context of the relationship between the EU and its Member States, they may be transposed to the characterisation of the relationship between international law and EU law more widely. Furthermore, the question of the relationship also raises the question of the function of the international legal order/community in a fragmented or pluralist international law which may also undergo a process of deformalisation of international law. A focus on shared fundamental values may mitigate these processes and provide one ground to answer questions of legitimacy of both international and EU law. Thus the traditional, rather schematic theories of monism and dualism increasingly become superseded by either pluralist theories or constitutionalist theories. Constitutionalist theories of international law, focusing on the notion of an international community and the UN as its closest institutional expression, have been around for a while and encountered a particular revival after the end of the Cold War and the proverbial 'New World Order' declared by then US President George Bush (senior). More modestly today they focus on expressions of international constitutionalism – functional, substantive and institutional.[43]

---

38 Likewise Hartley (n 11) 10, 17. It may be noted that the same effect is called 'Europeanisation' by J Wouters, A Nollkaemper and E de Wet (eds), *The Europeanisation of International Law: The Status of International Law in the EU and its Member States* (Asser Press, The Hague 2008), whereas here the term 'Europeanisation' is used specifically in regard to the effect of the EU and Europe on international law, see below 10.3.2, pp 310 ff.

39 See text around n 38 and 10.3.1 below, pp 283 ff.

40 Although 'Unionisation' would be more precise, it is less self-explanatory as a term and might lead to the confusion with the more technical aspect of international law becoming EU law by automatic or specific incorporation, by which it technically becomes EU law – and therefore benefits from the enforcement instruments of EU law. For the latter use (then called 'Communitarization') see Peters (n 5) 34 f.

41 E Cannizzaro (ed), *The European Union as an Actor in International Relations* (Kluwer Law International, The Hague 2002).

42 The scope of this chapter precludes more than a mere superficial treatment.

43 See in detail A-M Slaughter, *A New World Order* (Princeton UP, Princeton 2004); J Klabbers,

#602 20-03-2023 08:18PM
Item(s) checked out to Hashem Munim, Muh

TITLE: Research handbook on the theory a
BARCODE: 38008005260012
DUE DATE: 27-03-23

libraryservices.city.ac.uk

The analysis in this chapter will focus *firstly* on the interaction and mutual influence of EU law and international law. It will concentrate on the third perspective (internationalisation of EU law).[44] Only a short excursion into the vast and largely empirical fourth perspective (Europeanisation of international law) will be possible within the scope of this chapter.[45] *Secondly*, this chapter will attempt to sketch out how normative conflicts ought to be resolved,[46] acknowledging both the institutional and substantive problems of fragmentation as well as its positive and negative sides.[47] In as much as conflicts arise between different (territorial, sectoral or functional) sets of norms of international law, there is nothing special or *sui generis* about the EU legal system. The development of quasi-objective dimensions is considered to be a paradox inherent in all legal orders.[48] Although norms may be considered to be founded on a 'contractual' basis in the broadest sense (consensus, social assent) initially, once constituted, they develop quasi-objective dimension[49] (or in other words constitutionalise). This is as much true for the EU as for general international law and indeed domestic law. Dynamics can be discerned which are characterised by '"lesser polities" beginning to develop a sovereign world-view, and of others beginning to take them seriously'.[50] However, whereas competition may be fruitful, a minimum of coherence and unity of international law is essential in several respects:[51]

10.1.2 The Need for Coherence

Firstly, there is the technical aspect of a *common frame of reference or language*. As Dupuy has expressed it 'we cannot have an international community governed effectively by law if there is not a common understanding of its terms'.[52] However there is a more fundamental implication beyond accepted concepts and terminology. Challenging the unity of international law amounts to challenging its very *existence and survival*,[53] and hence the *foundations* of all 'fragmented' international law.

A Peters and G Ulfstein, *The Constitutionalization of International Law* (Oxford University Press, Oxford 2009); Paulus (n 4); M Kumm, 'The Cosmopolitan Turn in Constitutionalism: On the Relationship between Constitutionalism in and beyond the State' in JL Dunoff and JP Trachtman (eds), *Ruling the World? Constitutionalism, International Law and Global Governance* (CUP, Cambridge 2009) 258 ff; Walter (n 32); de Wet (n 4); E de Wet, 'The Emergence of International and Regional Value Systems as a Manifestation of the Emerging Constiutional Order' (2006) 19 *Leiden Journal of International Law* 611.

[44] See below 10.3.1, p 283.

[45] See below 10.3.2, p 310.

[46] See below 10.4, 10.5, pp 315 ff, 318 ff.

[47] Cf Report of the Study Group of the International Law Commission on 'Fragmentation of International Law: Difficulties Arising from the Diversification and Expansion of International Law', UN Doc. A/CN.4/l-702 of 18 July 2006, paras 8–9.

[48] Dupuy (n 33) 12 (text after n 41).

[49] Dupuy (n 33) 12 (text after n 41); M Virally, 'Sur un pont aux ânes: les rapports entre droit international et droits internes' in M Virally (ed), *Le droit international en devenir – essais écrits au fils des ans* (Presses Universitaires des France, Paris 1990) 103, 108.

[50] N Walker, 'The Idea of Constitutional Pluralism' (2002) 65 *Modern Law Review* 317, 347.

[51] Dupuy (n 33) 12 (text after n 41).

[52] Dupuy (n 33) 13 (text after n 44).

[53] See also fifth reason, text after n 59 below; p 276 f below.

Secondly, international law serves also as *fall-back position* and has a *gap-filling function* or 'tool box' function. Where other norms 'run out', international law can be used to fill the gap. For example, when all treaties are repudiated, it is possible to reject specific norms, but it is not possible to abolish at the same time the system of which all states and international organisations form part. This residual function is fulfilled within international law where international courts draw from general international law,[54] even in respect to national law, which, for example, may refer to international human rights where it turns out that there are gaps in the domestic protection of human rights.[55]

Thirdly, international law may *compensate* for a loss of constitutionalism at the national level.[56] One might counter that EU law functions in the same way and that the capacity to compensate highly depends on the state of development of international law, and in fact may be more likely to work in the opposite direction – international law borrowing from national law. However, even if some compensation for the loss of constitutionalism at national level is achieved through the EU itself, the EU is double-faced in this regard: it is a type of international law, but at the same time, because of its high degree of constitutionalisation, also like a domestic legal system and therefore also in need of compensatory constitutionalism. Gaps have been known to exist even within the realm of EU law, for example in the judicial protection under the pre-Lisbon standing rules[57] or in the old second and third pillars.[58] Compensatory mechanisms are even more relevant in other areas of international cooperation among the Member States where less effective constitutional structures replace or thin out domestic control mechanisms. Cutting off the possibility of such compensation in the area of EU law will have a wider impact. Besides, the legitimacy of the EU is enhanced through the existence of and compliance with external legal standards which also apply to primary (Treaty) law.[59] In that way international law could also promote internal constitutionalism both 'horizontally' within the EU and 'vertically' in regard to the Member States.

Finally, there is a normative reason, namely that without maintaining a substantive or value-based rootedness in universal aspects of international law, fragmented international law might lead to *relativism*. This long-term effect was feared by those who equated the ECJ's resistance to international law in *Kadi and Al Barakaat* with that of the US Supreme Court[60] in its *Medellin* decision.[61] Unless tying into a (minimum) of universal

---

54 Paulus (n 4) 84.

55 Cf *Minister of State for Immigration and Ethnic Affairs v Teoh* 104 ILR 460; (1994–5) 183 *Commonwealth Law Reports* 272 (High Court of Australia).

56 Peters (n 36).

57 *Unión de Pequeños Agricultores* (n 2); for a criticism see Opinion of AG Jacobs in the former case and the CFI in T-177/01 *Jégo-Quéré v Commission* [2002] ECR II-2365.

58 See S Peers, 'Salvation Outside the Church: Judicial Protection in the Third Pillar after the Pupino and Segi Judgments' (2007) 44 *Common Market Law Review* 883; G de Baere, *Constitutional Principles of EU External Relations* (OUP, Oxford 2008) 219 ff; A Hinarejos, *Judicial Control in the European Union: Reforming Jurisdiction in the Intergovernmental Pillars* (OUP, Oxford 2009).

59 See e.g. review by the ECtHR, no. 24833/94 *Matthews v United Kingdom* [1999] 28 EHRR 361.

60 See however dissent by Justice O'Connor, finding that the VCLT was a self-executing treaty, *Medellin,* 544 US at 689–90.

61 De Búrca (n 9) 2 f, 49; Halberstam and Stein (n 28) 67; Hilpold (n 8) 174.

values, the dissociation from international law may lead to relativism in the long term which will undermine the binding force of international law even if, as in *Kadi and Al Barakaat*, an adequate solution arguably is found *in casu*.

10.1.3 Outline

Against this backdrop of reasons for coherence and a certain degree of unity, the interaction of the two systems will be examined more closely. Thus, indirectly, the extent of fragmentation of international law by EU law and counteracting mechanisms will be examined. While the *Kadi and Al Barakaat* decision of September 2008 suggests fragmentation to an extent that the umbilical cord that ties EU law to international law is cut, this judgment has to be seen in its overall context in order to assess the relative weight of its individual or general aspects. On the one hand the ECJ seeks to decide the individual case adequately with the seemingly easiest and strongest argument. The necessary context of a court having to decide the case and to give reasons for it might require us to draw less absolute conclusions from the *Kadi and Al Barakaat* case. On the other hand, the broader picture might reveal that there is method, or at least that it is part of a wider trend.

This will be done in the widest sense by looking at the interaction of the two rule sets (section 10.3). The chapter will develop in section 10.3.1 how EU law receives international law (*internationalisation of EU law*). The reception of international law is understood in a broad sense to include both formal and informal interactions in order to assess its openness to international law. This is the dimension of the import of international law or, in other words, the EU as a norm-recipient. Section 10.3.2 of this chapter will take the opposite perspective: in how far does international law become Europeanised by interaction with EU law? This is the dimension of export of EU law to international law, or in other words, the EU as a norm-generator and actor of international law. Sections 10.4 and 10.5 will build on this and assess how the two systems deal with fragmentation and pluralism and how they ought to deal with it (section 10.5). In this context the legal nature of the EU will be discussed on the basis of foundational and institutional characteristics and substantive normative hierarchies (section 10.4). In this context, it is important to recall that talking about the relationship of EU law and international law is really a shorthand. The picture needs to be complemented by the dimension of the EU Member States. Much of the EU's approach to international law and the international legal order will be influenced by the three- or multi-dimensional situation which will therefore be addressed in section 10.2 before turning to analysis of the interaction of the EU with international law.

10.2 THE (NOT SO INVISIBLE) THIRD MAN: A MULTI-DIMENSIONAL RELATIONSHIP BETWEEN INTERNATIONAL LAW, THE EU AND THE MEMBER STATES

When mapping out the relationship between EU and international law, it is of utmost importance to bear in mind the third party in that relationship, which is a multi-dimensional relationship between EU, international and national law and the respective players. Daniel Bethlehem has astutely described the interaction of the three jurisdictions as:

> both complex and diffuse. Each system constantly acts upon, and interacts with, the other systems. . . . It is therefore . . . entirely artificial to describe these systems as distinct or separate from one another or as intersecting only marginally at the level of obligation. The practice, therefore, argues against a dualist conception of the relationship between the systems, even if specific interactions retain dualist qualities. Equally, however, to characterise the relationship between international law, Community law and national law, or even between any two of them, in monist terms, with its emphasis on a hierarchical relationship in which rules and principles of one or other system prevail over those of the others, is to mis-describe the reality of the practice. In practice, the relationship between the systems is characterised by constant interaction . . .[62]

Not only has the EU assumed a double-faced nature in regard to Member States and international law. The consideration of the Member States will be a relevant factor in how the EU reacts in its external dimension. At least from the perspective of European law and the Court of Justice, the relationship between national and EU law will have an impact on how individual cases involving international law are resolved and more generally conceptually on how the EU conceives its relationship with international law. Before considering the underlying motives for one or the other approach of the EU to international law, its relationship with the Member States will be recapitulated briefly.

10.2.1 Direct Effect and Supremacy of EU law in National Law and the Pluralist Equilibrium

The fundamental legal doctrines of direct effect and supremacy[63] shape the relationship between the EU and its Member States and will influence the interaction of the EU with (other parts or institutions of) international law. Through these doctrines, the EU legal order pushes far into national legal systems and mixes and hybridises with them. As is well known, the Court of Justice has since the early days of European integration constructed a vertical legal order between the EU and its Member States by developing the principle of direct effect of EU law with certain characteristics (generally, irrespective of its formal qualification, EU law that confers individual rights which are sufficiently clear and precise and do not require further implementing measures).[64] The direct effect or applicability of EU law within the legal orders of the Member States was the precondition for the claim to supremacy of EU law over national law. These two principles, together with the third principle of Member State liability for breaches of EU law, form the principal basis for the deeper degree of integration in the EU if compared with other

[62] D Bethlehem, 'International Law, European Community Law, National Law: Three Systems in Search of a Framework' in M Koskenniemi (ed), *International Law Aspects of the European Union* (Martinus Nijhoff Publishers, Leiden 1998) 165, 194.

[63] Now 'primacy', see Declaration concerning Primacy appended to the Lisbon Treaty.

[64] Case 26/62 *NV Algemene Transport- en Expeditie Onderneming van Gend & Loos v Netherlands Inland Revenue Administration* [1963] ECR 1, 13; 6/64 *Flaminio Costa v E.N.E.L.* [1964] ECR 585; 42/74 *Van Duyn v Home Office* [1974] ECR 1337; M Dougan, 'Sources, Supremacy and Direct Effect of Community Law' in D Wyatt and A Dashwood (eds), *European Union Law* (5th edn, Sweet & Maxwell, London 2004) 125, 150.

international organisations. They are also the basis for claims of the EU's *sui generis* nature, implying that these characteristics are not just about a deeper degree of integration but are the basis of a qualitative leap to a different category,[65] as summarised by the following passages from *van Gend en Loos* and *Costa v E.N.E.L.*:

> . . . and the Community constitutes a new legal order of international law for the benefit of which the states have limited their sovereign rights, albeit within limited fields, and the subjects of which comprise not only Member States but also their nationals. . . .[66]
>
> by contrast with ordinary international treaties, the EEC Treaty has created its own legal system which, on the entry into force of the Treaty, became an integral part of the legal systems of the Member States and which their courts are bound to apply . . .[67]

For the question of the relationship with international law, the justifications for the (judge-made) recognition of the principles of direct effect and supremacy are significant. In doing so, the Court claimed that the principles of direct effect and supremacy are rooted *in the Treaties*, so ultimately in the Member States' consent under international law. It may be noted that the 'new legal order' is one 'of international law'. This is explicit at least in the early judgments.[68] *Because* the Member States have created this special organisation which confers rights on individuals and provides for integration of an intensity that was hitherto unknown, it must be presumed that they intended to make it effective, and hence the Treaty must be interpreted in such a way as to have presumed direct effect and supremacy.

> The integration into the laws of each Member State of provisions which derive from the Community, and more generally, the terms and the spirit of the Treaty, make it impossible for the States, as a corollary, to accord precedence to a unilateral and subsequent measure over a legal system accepted by them on a basis of reciprocity. Such a measure cannot therefore be inconsistent with that legal system . . .[69]

The lack of supremacy 'would amount to a corresponding denial of the effectiveness of obligations undertaken unconditionally and irrevocably by Member States pursuant to the Treaty and would thus imperil the very foundations of the Community'.[70]

As is well known, the Court of Justice's claim to supremacy did not go totally uncontested by the Member States. A first wave of objections came from old Member States' constitutional or supreme courts (France, Germany, Italy), followed by a second wave of constitutional courts of new Member States following the eastern enlargement of 2004 (Poland, Czech Republic, Hungary, Estonia).[71] The challenges to the supremacy of EU

---

[65] Cf R Barents, *The Autonomy of Community Law* (Kluwer Law International, The Hague/London 2004). Critical of this analysis also J Klabbers, *Treaty Conflict and the European Union* (CUP, Cambridge 2009) 147 f; de Witte (n 9) 151.

[66] *Van Gend* (n 64).

[67] *Costa v E.N.E.L.* (n 64).

[68] The reference to international law was dropped later. Views about the significance of this verbal alteration range from proving the dissociation from international law to a mere technical abridgement. For the latter see de Witte (n 9) 147.

[69] *Costa v E.N.E.L.* (n 64).

[70] 106/77 *Amministrazione delle Finanze dello Stato v Simmenthal SpA* [1978] ECR 629, para 18.

[71] W Sadurski, '"Solange, chapter 3": Constitutional Courts in Central Europe – Democracy – European Union' (2008) 14 *European Law Journal* 1; A Albi, 'Supremacy of EC Law in the New

law had in common that they were based on fundamental constitutional principles, such as the rule of law (encompassing an effective human rights review) or democracy. They were put to rest when Member States implicitly entered into the *Solange II* understanding with the EU. By that understanding they accepted *de facto* (if not *de iure*) the supremacy of EU law, 'so long as' the EU generally protected fundamental rights adequately,[72] reaching an equilibrium with the EU, which, however, will remain potentially fragile. The Member States' threats were of the type of an *ultima ratio* emergency break and remain a Damocles sword pending over the EU. But it has to be said that it remains a sword that has not been used. Therefore, 'on the ground', supremacy is operational, subject to a carefully constructed judicial equilibrium which has been conceptualised by pluralist and multi-level governance theories about the relationship between the EU and its Member States.[73]

10.2.2 The Impact of the Relationship between the EU and its Member States on the EU's Approach towards International Law

Because supremacy over national law attaches to all directly effective EU law in the Member States' legal orders, it will also attach to international law when it is given direct effect by EU law. As will be shown in more detail below, subject to the specific norms at issue, both customary international law and international treaties to which the EU is a party are capable in principle of direct effect (and supremacy).[74] Through the duty of loyal cooperation these effects are extended also to mixed agreements.[75] This is in addition to the effects of more formal incorporation of international law through EU legislative acts. This extension of the principles of EU law is important in at least two ways: it is an important example of how EU law *reinforces* international law substantively and procedurally:

Member States: Bringing Parliaments into the Equation of "Co-operative Constitutionalism"' (2007) 3 *European Constitutional Law Review* 25.

[72] German Federal Constitutional Court, *Wünsche Handelsgesellschaft*, 22 October 1986, 73 BVerGE 339, translation at [1987] 3 CMLR 225 ('Solange II'): 'In view of these developments, it must be held that, so long as the European Communities and in particular the case law of the European Court, generally ensure an effective protection of fundamental rights as against the sovereign powers of the Communities which is to be regarded as substantially similar to the protection of fundamental rights required unconditionally by the Constitution, and in so far as they generally safeguard the essential content of the fundamental rights, the Federal Constitutional Court will no longer exercise its jurisdiction . . . and will no longer review such legislation by the standard of fundamental rights contained in the Constitution.'

[73] Walker (n 50); D Halberstam, 'Pluralism in Marbury and Van Gend' in MP Maduro and L Azoulai (eds), *The Past and Future of EU Law* (Oxford, Hart Publishing 2010) 26; I Pernice, 'Multilevel Constitutionalism in the EU' (2002) 27 *European Law Review* 511. Cf also J Griffiths, 'What is Legal Pluralism' (1986) 24 *Journal of Legal Pluralism* 1; N Krisch, 'The Pluralism of Global Administrative Law' (2006) 17 *European Journal of International Law* 247.

[74] Cf J Wouters and D van Eeckhoutte, 'Giving Effect to Customary International Law Through European Community Law', Working Paper no 25 (Institute for International Law, KU Leuven 2002) 28; HG Schermers, 'European Remedies in the Field of Human Rights' in C Kilpatrick, T Novitz and P Skidmore (eds), *The Future of Remedies in EU Law* (Hart, Oxford 2000) 205.

[75] E Neframi, 'The Duty of Loyalty: Rethinking its Scope through its Application in the Field of EU External Relations' (47) 2010 *Common Market Law Review* 323, 335.

international law benefits from the special enforcement instruments of EU law. It is also potentially important for the way and manner in which the Court of Justice conceptualises the effect of international law in EU law. It might be more sensitive to Member States' concerns than in a situation where it enforces 'pure' EU law. It might not be as willing to risk antagonising Member States and the fragile pluralist equilibrium obtained in the struggle for supremacy where 'merely' general international law is at issue. Hence the EU's and its courts' approach to international law may be influenced by a complex web of underlying motives and interests, some of them conflicting.

One motive may be *to accommodate Member State's concerns or interests*. An example of this can be found in *Elgafaji*, where the ECJ held that it had to interpret a provision of EU law independently from international law.[76] The underlying question was whether the protection afforded to refugees by the Qualification Directive[77] in cases of indiscriminate violence in an area went beyond the protection granted under Art 3 of the European Convention on Human Rights (ECHR). One reason revealed in the Advocate General's Opinion is that the higher level of protection guaranteed by some Member States could not be disregarded,[78] making it an example of an upward regulatory spiral of harmonisation; but concerns are also likely to relate to the anticipated response of dualist Member States to the direct application of international law, which might be perceived as too far-reaching. Such concerns will most certainly influence the approach of the EU and of its courts to international law. The interaction and relationship between Member States' domestic law and EU law differs from that between domestic law and international law, both in intensity and in its heterogeneity. Whereas Member States' interaction with EU law is uniform and deeply intertwined ('supranational'), it is heterogeneous and as a rule less deeply intertwined when it comes to general international law (which is more likely to be approached in a dualist way and to be used as a softer tool through interpretation). There is a strong parallel between the heterogeneous, diverse and sometimes inconsistent way domestic legal systems approach international law and the approach the EU takes to international law. Inconsistencies in the EU's approach to international law may directly result from the three-way relationship between the Union, the Member States and international law. The EU may not only be mindful of the diversity of approaches of the Member States to international law. It will also take into account the impact which 'integrating' international law more generally into the Member States' legal systems might have on the position of the EU vis-à-vis the Member States because such integration is likely to result in more directly effective international law in the Member States' legal systems than they ordinarily would allow for. The three-dimensional situation may therefore have an impact on the EU's (and its courts') approach, as (various) Member States' approaches to international law are taken into account. The EU needs to do so both from the perspective of the diversity of approaches and from the perspective of attaching EU law status to international law because this potentially alters international

---

[76] C-465/07 *Elgafaji v Staatssecretaris van Justitie* [2009] ECR I-921, para 28.

[77] Council Directive 2004/83/EC on minimum standards for the qualification and status of third country nationals or stateless persons as refugees or as persons who otherwise need international protection and the content of the protection granted (2004) OJ L304/12.

[78] Opinion of AG Maduro in *Elgafaji* (n 76) para 27.

law's status within the legal order of the Member States,[79] giving direct effect to international law in EU law. And the effect of this might influence the Member States' attitude towards the EU in a pluralist equilibrium.

Other motives might more directly relate to the *Union interest*: for example, international law might be more positively received into the Union legal order, where it helps to bolster EU law, for example by *extending* de facto *the scope of application of Union rules* or rules similar to EU rules where parallel or similar provisions are contained in international law. For example, in *van Duyn*, the Court refers to the international obligation of states to admit their own nationals to their territory[80] in order to strengthen EU free movement rules based on the principle of non-discrimination. The case law on direct effect of free trade, association, partnership and cooperation agreements and decisions of association councils demonstrates this further. Giving direct effect to these norms and decisions will expand the application of what substantively are EU rules, but the impact will be primarily on the Member States.[81] A more general aspect would be *establishing or extending the competence* of the EU in the external dimension, derived from its internal competences and the competences of Member States under international law.[82] In contrast the Court might be more inclined to *shield the EU (legislator) from different international standards,*[83] or itself from competing adjudication by other international tribunals,[84] or at least *to preserve political flexibility domestically* even in the light of international commitments.[85]

In a more general or indirect way, the Union interest is served by *constitutionalisation of the Union legal order*. Even (self-)limiting the exercise of Union powers – to the exclusion of international law – as was the case in *Kadi and Al Barakaat*,[86] may in principle still serve the Union interest if it seems necessary for its coherence in the light of its expanded scope of activity. The carefully balanced, but fragile, *Solange II* equilibrium with the Member States[87] about supremacy and fundamental rights protection,[88] reveals the tightrope walk for the European Union between expansion and self-limitation of its competence and the potential challenge of its authority by the Member States. Constitutionalisation of the

---

79 Peters (n 5) 26 f.

80 *Van Duyn* (n 64) para 22.

81 See overview of the case law by P Eeckhout, *External Relations of the European Union* (OUP, Oxford 2004) 283–292.

82 Joint Cases 3/76, 4/76 and 6/76 *Cornelis Kramer and others* [1976] ECR 1279, para 30/33–34.

83 *Intertanko* (n 30).

84 C-459/03 *Commission v Ireland (MOX plant)* [2006] ECR I-4657; I Govaere, 'Beware of the Trojan Horse: Dispute Settlement in (Mixed) Agreements and the Autonomy of the EU Legal Order' in C Hillion and P Koutrakos (eds), *Mixed Agreements Revisited: The EU and its Member States in the World* (Hart, Oxford 2010) 187, 188; Opinion 2/94 [1996] ECR I-1759; S Douglas-Scott, 'A Tale of Two Courts: Luxembourg, Strasbourg and the Growing European Human Rights Acquis' (2006) 43 *Common Market Law Review* 629, 650 f pointing out that the ECJ only referred to the jurisprudence of the ECtHR for the first time in 1996 in C-13/94 *P v S* [1996] ECR I-2143, whereas it had been referring to the ECHR for over 20 years at the time.

85 *FIAMM and Fedon* (n 30).

86 *Kadi and Al Barakaat* (n 13).

87 See above, p 280.

88 See above, n 72.

EU legal order in its self-limiting dimension[89] was reinforced in *Kadi and Al Barakaat,* and thus a Union interest was served in this regard. At the same time, the Court may, however, be more reluctant to actually use international law as a standard for direct judicial review or incidental review of the validity of its own acts (in contrast to rulings on the compatibility of Member States' acts) in a preliminary ruling procedure.[90] It thus displays a less open approach to international law in order *to maintain control over the standards by which it exercises legality review*,[91] i.e. out of autonomy considerations. This may be seen as part of bolstering EU constitutionalism vis-à-vis the Member States. Even if it in principle accepts that international law limits Union action and may serve as a standard of legality review, it must be further scrutinized for whether there is bias in the application of this principle.

10.3 THE INTERTWINING OF INTERNATIONAL LAW AND EU LAW: 'INTERNATIONALISATION' OF EU LAW AND 'EUROPEANISATION' OF INTERNATIONAL LAW

10.3.1 Internationalisation of EU Law

The internationalisation of EU law, or 'international law in EU law', may be discussed in two dimensions. In a foundational dimension, the EU has been created by and as a subject of international law, governed by it. A second dimension looks at the effect of international law by virtue of EU law.

10.3.1.1 Foundational dimension: the EU as a creature of international law

It is commonplace that the EU is founded on international law because it is created by treaty. Further, international law is not just the basis of the international legal personality of the EU, but also for the consequences of its being a subject of international law. Finally, because of the derived international subjectivity of the EU, Member States' obligations under international law further shape the EU as a creature of international law.

10.3.1.1.1 The Treaty Basis of the EU

The treaty basis of the EU has been much reviewed[92] and had some relevance to the debate about the constitutional nature of the failed so-called European Constitution. It is the most obvious factor which clearly positions the EU as an international organisation. It can be summarised as follows: The EU was created by a treaty by sovereign states, and the consent of all the Member States remains the ultimate rule of recognition. Pending a change of rule of recognition, which is possible but has not occurred thus far,

---

89 See for the distinction of enabling, constraining and supplementary constitutionalism, JL Dunoff and JP Trachtman, 'A Functional Approach to International Constitutionalization' in JL Dunoff and JP Trachtman (eds), *Ruling the World? Constitutionalism, International Law and Global Governance* (CUP, Cambridge 2009) 3, 12.

90 *Intertanko* (n 30).

91 Peters (n 5) 64.

92 E.g. Hartley (n 11) 17 ff; Pellet (n 8) 211 ff; Dupuy (n 8) 438–450.

the EU owes its validity to international law and, more specifically, the international law of treaties, so the international rules of the law of treaties apply to it. Admittedly, the rules laid down in the EU Treaties (now TFEU and TEU) are more detailed, more developed[93] and more deeply integrated into the Member States' legal orders than any other international law.[94] In other words, the EU is more constitutionalised both in its own legal order and in its relationship with the Member States. Nevertheless, it essentially continues to reflect the characteristics of an international organisation established under international law. Substantive constitutionalism is accorded less relevance and weight than formal or foundational internationalism.[95] The argument is supported by the fact that the rules of change or amendment of the EU Treaties require a revision treaty concluded by governments,[96] the possibility of dissolving or withdrawing from the EU[97] and the way the EU deals with conflicting international obligations of the Member States.

From the perspective of international law the *lex posterior* rule (including implied repeal) in principle is applied where the parties to a later treaty are identical to those of the EU treaties. However, the *lex posterior* rule is not non-derogable. Where a Treaty provides for its own amendment procedure, it is a reasonable interpretation that states would, for example, not intend to repeal the mechanism unless they clearly express such a wish.[98] In spite of a duty of loyal cooperation of the Member States under Article 4(3) TEU (ex Art 10 EC), it cannot be concluded at the current state of integration that the Member States have lost the power to amend the Treaties, but they have restricted the form and procedure by which they can do so.[99] The ordinary rules of change and

---

93 In particular with regard to the power to issue secondary legislation, a supranational legislative procedure, majority voting in the Council, the standing of individuals before an international court according to Article 263 TFEU and the development of Union human rights as well as a binding codification in the form of the EU Charter on Fundamental Rights.

94 Through the doctrines of direct effect, supremacy and Member State liability for breach of EU law and procedurally through the preliminary reference procedure.

95 Cf the distinction of formal and substantive constitutionalism by Dupuy (n 8) 399.

96 Article 48(4) TEU. The state consent principle is preserved in the simplified revision procedures (Art 48(6) subpara 2 and (7) subpara 4 TEU).

97 Article 50 TEU, newly created by the Treaty of Lisbon. Although meant as a provision allaying Member States' fears of EU federalism, regulating withdrawal, it actually led to newly created procedural restrictions (negotiation of an exit agreement). However, as the clause that 'failing that, two years after notification' the treaties will cease to be applied to that state, shows, this is unlikely to be an attempt to codify something that eludes regulation at this stage of integration but bowing to legal realism.

98 Cf 43/75 *Defrenne v Sabena* [1976] ECR 455, para 58 (a Directive was presumed not to change the Treaty).

99 For an argument that there cannot be an implied amendment to the EU treaties see HG Schermers and NM Blokker, *International Institutional Law: Unity within Diversity* (4th edn, Martinus Nijhoff, Leiden 2003) para 1164. In contrast: T Hartley, 'National Law, International Law and EU Law – How do they relate?' in PE Capps, M Evans and S Konstadinidis (eds), *Asserting Jurisdiction* (Hart, Oxford 2003) 65, 72 f. A test case would be a case brought against all Member States for a violation of a duty of loyalty to the EU (because the Court would not have jurisdiction to 'annul' an 'illegal' amendment of the Treaty). Here, it would become relevant whether the CJEU would apply international law rules in conjunction with EU law or exclusively EU law. If in this (so far) theoretical case the CJEU found that collectively the Member States

amendment of treaties are derogable if all parties/Member States agree to it.[100] Where the parties are not identical, Art 351 TFEU (ex Art 307 EC) is intended to preserve prior obligations and requires that the traditional mechanisms of international law be used to resolve or eliminate the conflict. Furthermore, in principle, secondary norms of international law (for example of the law of treaties or state responsibility) remain available as a subsidiary fall-back position,[101] because the EU Treaties foresee no mechanism beyond the penalty payments in Art 260 TFEU (ex Art 228 EC), leaving scope, for example, for the suspension of the Treaty in regard to a Member State according to Art 60(2) lit. a) VCLT which is in material breach of an obligation.[102] This implies that the EU is not a fully self-contained regime.[103]

10.3.1.1.2 International Personality of the EU

The EU has international legal personality according to Art 47 TEU. By virtue of its international legal personality, the EU is bound by international law, both customary[104] and treaty law; it is responsible for breaches of international law and may be under an obligation to react in a certain way to breaches by other subjects of international law.[105] Its personality is limited in several ways: it is conferred by the Member States in the Treaty, and hence not 'original' but derived. In regard to third states and international organisations its personality remains *res inter alios acta:* it depends also on the recognition of other subjects under international law, such as third states and other international organisations.[106] However, with a sufficient amount of recognition, it may be capable of acquiring an objective dimension.[107] It is not all-encompassing, but functionally limited by the competences of the EU, as is the case with any international organisation.[108] This

---

violated their obligations under the EU Treaties, a revolution in regard to the rule of recognition would take place.

[100] Cf Articles 39–40 VCLT.

[101] Hartley (n 11) 14–17; Tomuschat (n 32) para 46; Simma and Pulkowski (n 10) 516 ff.

[102] Tomuschat (n 32) para 46; Simma and Pulkowski (n 10) 518.

[103] Simma and Pulkowski (n 10) 519.

[104] C-162/96 *Racke v Hauptzollamt Mainz* [1998] ECR I-3655, para 45 f; C-432/92 *Anastasiou* [1994] ECR I-3116, para 46 f. *Interpretation of the Agreement of 25 March 1951 between the WHO and Egypt* Advisory Opinion of [1980] ICJ Reports 73, 89 f; F Hoffmeister, 'Die Bindung der EWG and das Völkergewohnheitsrecht der Verträge' (1998) *Europäisches Wirtschafts- und Steuerrecht* 365, 366.

[105] Vienna Convention on the Law of Treaties between States and International Organisations or between International Organisations; Tomuschat (n 32) paras 40, 47.

[106] Tomuschat (n 32) para 3; for the shortcomings of the sole application of the 'will theory' and the 'objective theory' and issues of recognition see in detail J Klabbers, 'Presumptive Personality: The European Union in International Law' in M Koskenniemi (ed), *International Law Aspects of the European Union* (Martinus Nijhoff Publishers, Leiden 1998) 231–253, 234–243; I Seidl-Hohenveldern and G Loibl, *Das Recht der internationalen Organisationen einschliesslich der supranationalen Gemeinschaften* (6th edn, C Heymanns, Cologne1996) para 0321.

[107] Schermers and Blokker (n 99) para 1565 f; D McGoldrick, 'The International Legal Personality of the European Community and the European Union' in M Dougan and S Currie (eds), *50 Years of the European Treaties: Looking Back and Thinking Forward* (Hart Publishing, Oxford 2009) 181, 185, 188 and 190.

[108] Schermers and Blokker (n 99) para 209 f; Seidl-Hohenveldern and Loibl (n 106) paras 0307, 0310, 0314.

contrasts with states, which naturally have all-encompassing personality under international law following from their sovereignty.[109]

Contrary to original subjects under international law, regulating the relationship with international law is not at the free disposition of the EU.[110] It follows from the only derived international personality of the EU that the competence to decide on the relationship between international law and its own legal order lies with the Member States. The question therefore must be: what have the Member States agreed upon – or what do the Treaties provide? However, as the Treaties do not make an explicit statement on the relationship, it practically fell to the EU Courts to define the relationship.[111] The absence of a provision in the founding Treaties can be explained by several possible reasons. One of them could be that the Member States simply did not see a need because EU law was just a result of a treaty regime.[112] Very much in line with the EU's constitutional narrative, it is not surprising that the EU Courts mirror constitutional approaches that can be found in the domestic legal orders of its Member States. However, from a foundational perspective, such a claim contradicts the derived international legal personality of the EU which only exists because of a transfer of sovereignty by the Member States. It has therefore been said that the EU is 'estopped' from raising sovereignty-related arguments against the incorporation of international law in its own legal order.[113] In practice, however, absent a Treaty requirement, the EU can decide on the effects within the EU legal order of each treaty it concludes – by virtue of its separate international personality. If no provision is made in the agreement, it practically falls to the Court to decide as a matter of interpretation of the agreement.[114] The EU Courts are also the sole arbiter of the effects of customary international law in EU law.

10.3.1.1.3 Member States' Obligations under International Law

Member States' obligations under international law are relevant for the delimitation of EU competences even beyond formalised rules of conflict such as Art 351 TFEU. Member States' obligations do not only matter at a practical level at which the EU will seek to maintain coherence and practical cooperation in order to avoid creating conflicts of obligations for its Member States.[115] They matter also legally, firstly because of the

109 See also Dupuy (n 8) 17.

110 See, however, in contrast, equating the EU and a domestic legal order, C Tietje, 'The Status of International Law in the European Legal Order: The Case of International Treaties and Non-binding International Instruments' in J Wouters, A Nollkaemper and E de Wet (eds), *The Europeanisation of International Law: The Status of International Law in the EU and its Member States* (Asser Press, The Hague 2008) 55, 57.

111 This does not neglect the fact that who is the arbiter has a bearing on the substantive answer to the question. Art 351(7) TFEU does not lay down the principle of monism or transform international law into the EU legal order. Rather, as Eeckhout (n 81) 277 has shown, the provision regulates the binding nature of agreements not just for the Union but also for the Member States.

112 Others could be mere oversight or the lack of consensus between Member States which approach international law in a variety of ways in their domestic legal orders, cf Peters (n 5) 22.

113 A Marschik, *Subsysteme im Völkerrecht: Ist die Europäische Union ein "Self-contained Regime"?* (Duncker & Humblot, Berlin 1997) 213 ff; Peters (n 5) 30.

114 Eeckhout (n 81) 285.

115 See, for example, the 'dialogue' with the European Court of Human Rights in this regard as a conflict-avoiding strategy reflected in C-94/00 *Roquette Frères SA v Commission* [2002] ECR

scope of EU competence, and beyond that because of the duty of loyal cooperation of the EU institutions towards the Member States.[116] Further, the following considerations from general international law about Member States' obligations will be relevant to the determination and interpretation of the scope and content of EU law:

(i) Non-delegation principle: no evasion of obligations by delegation of functions Just as Member States were internally constitutionally limited when they transferred aspects of their sovereignty to the EU, they could not transfer powers they did not have under international law. The Member States remain bound and responsible internationally. Therefore, they cannot 'delegate away' responsibility by transferring powers or functions that were already limited.[117] This would be in a sense an *ultra vires* use of their powers (*nemo plus iuris transfere potest quam ipse habet*).[118] However, because of the derogable nature of large parts of international law, apart from non-derogable rules such as *ius cogens*, Member States can create conflicts of obligations if not all previously existing obligations are also imposed on the international organisation which they create. Interpretation may eliminate some conflicts because it may be presumed that States do not intend to derogate from (and breach) existing obligations. Remaining conflicts of (relative) obligations can be addressed by the law of state responsibility. However, the scope of non-derogable rules is practically wider than that of *ius cogens*. The factual lack of intention to derogate from an existing obligation becomes nearer a legal principle with the increasing number of parties to which it is owed: where multilateral treaties are concerned, moreover, where these are of a quasi-constitutional nature, such as the ECHR, the effect of a reciprocal commitment between a number of like-minded states (obligation *erga omnes partes*) is to strengthen the rule. It becomes the strongest where an obligation is owed to all states or the international community as a whole (*erga omnes*)

I-9011, paras 20, 29; in the reverse direction (conflict avoided by Strasbourg) see no. 45036/98 *Bosphorus v Ireland* (2006) 42 EHRR 1.

[116] The principle of loyal cooperation has been primarily analysed as a duty of the Member States towards the Union (and one another), Neframi (n 75). Although it will be of residual significance (A von Bogdandy, 'Artikel 10 EGV: Aufgaben und Pflichten der Mitgliedstaaten' in E Grabitz and M Hilf (eds), *Das Recht der Europäischen Union* (Beck, Munich 40th instalment 2009, para 83), it may, however, also be applied as a principle Member States could invoke against the Union: M Zuleeg, 'Artikel 10 EGV: Verpflichtungen der Mitgliedstaaten' in H von der Groeben and J Schwarze (eds), *Kommentar zum EU-/EG-Vertrag* (6th edn, Nomos, Baden-Baden 2003, paras 1, 11; K Mortelmans, 'The Principle of Loyalty to the Community (Article 5 EC) and the Obligations of the Community Institutions' (1998) 5 *Maastricht Journal of European and Comparative Law* 67; and P Eeckhout, 'Case note on C-308/06, *The Queen on the application of Intertanko and Others v Secretary of State for Transport*, judgment of the Court of Justice (Grand Chamber) of 3 June 2008' (2009) 46 *Common Market Law Review* 2041, 2051; 44/84 *Hurd v Jones* [1986] ECR 29, 81; C-62/98 *Commission v Portugal* [2000] ECR I-5171, para 50; C-339/00 *Ireland v Commission* [2003] ECR I-11 757, para 72.

[117] No. 24833/94 *Matthews v United Kingdom* [1999] 28 EHRR 361; no. 43844/98 *T.I. v UK* [2000] I.N.L.R. 211.

[118] Joined Cases 21-24/72 *International Fruit Co. NV v Produktschap Voor Groenten en Fruit* [1972] ECR 1219, para 11; *Kadi* (n 23) para 195; PJ Kuijper, 'International Responsibility for EU Mixed Agreements' in C Hillion and P Koutrakos (eds), *Mixed Agreements Revisited: The EU and its Member States in the World* (Hart, Oxford 2010) 208, 210 ff.

because of universal membership to a treaty such as the UN Charter[119] or because of the value it protects.[120]

An interpretative presumption follows both from the primary obligation and the threat of state responsibility that Member States did not intend to create a conflict of norms for themselves when transferring powers. This was confirmed by the ECJ in the *Biotech Directive* case in which it reviewed whether the Directive forced Member States to breach their obligations under international law.[121] Although this was found not to be the case *in casu*, it is implicit in the structure of the analysis that the EU, as a matter of EU law, is not allowed to legislate in breach of Member States' obligations under international law (in that case the TRIPs Agreement and the Convention on Biological Diversity).

(ii) Succession principle A further way for the EU to be bound by treaty obligations of the Member States is through succession into the Member States' obligations.[122] The ECJ in *International Fruit Company* thus famously justified that the Community was bound by the GATT, although it was not formally a party to the treaty, because it assumed powers previously exercised by the Member States.[123] The CFI followed that line in regard to the UN Charter, holding that although it was not directly bound by the Charter, '*in so far* as under the EC Treaty the Community has assumed powers previously exercised by the member States in the area governed by the Charter of the United Nations, the provisions of that Charter have the effect of binding the Community'.[124] It was therefore bound by virtue of the EC Treaty, first, 'not to infringe the obligations imposed by Member States by the Charter of the United Nations or to impede their performance, and second, . . . to adopt all the measures necessary to enable its Member States to fulfil those obligations'.[125]

However, the Court of Justice has interpreted the succession into obligations of the Member States restrictively in later cases. It denied, for example, distinguishing from GATT,[126] the succession into Member States' obligations under the UN Charter and MARPOL 73/78 with the argument that 'in the *absence of a full transfer of the powers* previously exercised by the Member States to the Community, the latter cannot, simply

119 As is reflected in Art 103 UN Charter which 'institutionalises' universal membership today.

120 For the difficult relationship between *ius cogens* and the notion of *erga omnes* obligations cf KS Ziegler, *Fluchtverursachung als völkerrechtliches Delikt* (Duncker & Humblot, Berlin 2002) 565–577.

121 C-377/98 *Kingdom of the Netherlands v European Parliament and Council of the European Union (Directive on Biotechnological Inventions)* [2001] ECR I-7079, para 55. The Directive also by its own terms (Article 1) did not intend to cause 'prejudice to the obligations of the Member States pursuant to international agreements'.

122 Hilpold (n 8) 160 ff; Tridimas and Gutierrez-Fons (n 9) 680; C Tomuschat, 'Case T-306/01, Ahmed Ali Yusuf and Al Barakaat International Foundation v. Council and Commission; Case T-315/01, Yassin Abdullah Kadi v. Council and Commission' (2006) 43 CMLRev 537, 542 f.

123 *International Fruit Co.* (n 118) paras 10 ff.

124 *Kadi* (n 23) para 203; T-306/01 *Yusuf and Al Barakaat International Foundation v Council and Commission* [2005] ECR II-3533, para 253 (emphasis added).

125 *Kadi* (n 23) para 204; *Yusuf* (n 124) para 254.

126 *Intertanko* (n 30) para 48.

because all those States are parties to Marpol 73/78, be bound by the rules set out therein, which it has not itself approved'.[127]

The Court has, therefore, limited succession into Member States' obligations to the situation where *all* powers in an area are now exercised by the EU. The full transfer of powers might be equated with exclusive competence. This raises the question where the boundaries of an area of regulation lie in order to determine whether the EU has assumed 'full' powers. Further, it may be asked whether the distinction between exclusive and shared competence is tenable, considering the rationale for succession.[128] According to *International Fruit Company*, the rationale of succession is to avoid a conflict of obligations for the Member States which 'could not withdraw from their obligations to third countries'[129] and which therefore 'showed the wish to bind it [the Union] by the obligations entered into' by them, an intention they have made explicit in what is today Art 351 TFEU (ex Art 307 EC).[130] If Member States' intentions are relevant, as the Court stated in *International Fruit Company*,[131] an argument that would be supported by Member States' obligations under Art 103 UN Charter with which they may be presumed to intend to comply, then surely that intention applies to all situations in which the EU could create a conflict of obligations (and therefore state responsibility) for the Member States because it has (whatever) competence to act.[132] Although from an institutional perspective the EU has practically replaced the Member States in the GATT with the agreement of the other parties, whereas it is only an observer at the UN,[133] this is neither relevant for its competences vis-à-vis the Member States, nor for the avoidance of a conflict of obligations. It would therefore be inappropriate to require a *de facto* replacement of the Member States in an institutional sense.[134] Nevertheless, if Member States' actual or hypothetical intentions are relevant, it is hard to distinguish the full-blown involvement from the more isolated exercise of powers by the EU. In *Kadi and Al Barakaat*, the Court – somewhat surprisingly – does not even bother to respond to the CFI, which had assumed a succession by virtue of EU law (not by virtue of international law) into the obligations under the UN Charter, including Security Council Resolutions.[135] This follows its logic to decide the case on the basis of a domestic law/dualist rationale[136] and of the higher rank of its constitutional principles. International obligations which are in conflict with

---

[127] *Intertanko* (n 30) para 49 (emphasis added). For Marpol see already without further reason C-379/92 *Criminal proceedings against Matteo Peralta* [1994] ECR I-3453, para 16.

[128] For the question whether an express competence is required or whether an implied competence is sufficient see respectively Opinion of AG Kokott in *Intertanko* (n 30) para 43 and Eeckhout (n 116) 2051.

[129] *International Fruit Co.* (n 118) para 11.

[130] *International Fruit Co.* (n 118) para 15.

[131] *International Fruit Co.* (n 118) paras 12–15.

[132] In favour of transposing the arguments from *International Fruit Company* to UN SC Resolutions also Eeckhout (n 81) 438.

[133] Opinion of AG J Kokott in *Intertanko* (n 30) para 44.

[134] Para 14 of *International Fruit Co.* (n 118) may be interpreted as laying down a condition of replacement. But the wording 'has assumed the functions inherent in the tariff and trade policy, progressively . . .' is rather loose and leaves open how far a 'replacement' is in fact required. Cf. Eeckhout (n 81) 439.

[135] *Kadi* (n 23) para 203; *Yusuf* (n 124) para 253.

[136] Likewise Hilpold (n 8) 160.

basic constitutional principles are simply put aside, and with them the consideration for the conflict norm of Art 103 UN Charter with which the ECJ would have had to engage otherwise.[137] This might be short-sighted. It may be added that apart from a Member State interest that has been expressed in the Treaty, there is also a separate Union interest. A conflict of obligations between EU law and Member States' obligations 'is likely to undermine the practical effectiveness of the relevant provisions of Community law and/ or of international law'.[138]

10.3.1.1.4 Objective Elements in International Law

There are many instances in which obligations arise for states and other subjects of international law which go beyond the consent principle which dominates international law. The latter is most prominently visible in the way international norms are generated by treaty and customary international law and in the consensual nature of compulsory jurisdiction under international law. The clearest example of obligations which have reached an objective character are norms of *ius cogens*. Furthermore, the possibility of objective obligations resulting from the notion of an international community has been mooted.[139] This is not the place to embark on the merits of a legal (rather than political) concept of international community. Instead, what may be called 'building blocks' or isolated manifestations of such a notion will be discussed briefly: firstly, obligations of non-members under the UN Charter and secondly, objective dimensions of multilateral treaty regimes.

In regard to the former, there is a (largely uncontested) claim by UN organs, most notably the Security Council, to create obligations also for non-members. The Security Council intended to bind third (i.e. non-member) states as well as non-state parties by obligations under the UN Charter and by UN Security Council Resolutions under Chapter VII.[140] By the same rationale and by virtue of the EU's international legal personality, the EU may be considered to be bound. Art 39 of the UN Charter is not addressed only to UN members, and its drafting history supports an application to third states.[141] It is now widespread practice of the UN Security Council to address 'all States'

---

137 See, however, below in regard to interpretation of EU law in the context of international law.

138 Opinion of AG Kokott in *Intertanko* (n 30) para 78.

139 C Tomuschat, 'Die internationale Gemeinschaft' (1995) *Archiv des Völkerrechts* 1; B Fassbender, 'The United Nations Charter as Constitution of the International Community' (1998) 36 *Columbia Journal of Transnational Law* 529; A Paulus, 'The Emergence of the International Community' in J Nijman and A Nollkaemper (eds), *New Perspectives on the Divide Between National and International Law* (OUP, Oxford 2007) 216; Walter (n 32).

140 Tomuschat, 'Obligations' (n 32) 252 ff; Tomuschat, 'Artikel 281 EGV' (n 32) para 59; C Tomuschat, 'Crimes Against the Peace and Security of Mankind and the Recalcitrant Third State' in Y Dinstein and M Tabory (eds), *War Crimes in International Law* (Martinus Nijhoff, The Hague/London 1996) 41; J-D Kühne, 'International Economic Sanctions and Third States' (1992) *Archiv des Völkerrechts* 86; K Hailbronner, 'Sanctions and Third Parties and the Concept of International Public Order' (1992) *Archiv des Völkerrechts* 2; T Stein, 'International Measures Against Terrorism and Sanctions By and Against Third States' (1992) *Archiv des Völkerrechts* 38; D Thürer, 'UN Enforcement Measures and Neutrality. The Case of Switzerland' (1992) 117 *Archiv des Völkerrechts* 69; S Bohr, 'Sanctions by the United Nations Security Council and the European Community' (1993) 4 *European Journal of International Law* 256.

141 Tomuschat (n 32) 254.

in its resolutions under Chapter VII. For example it called on 'all states' to enforce the embargo against Iraq after its illegal occupation of Kuwait,[142] or, more recently, to impose and enforce anti-terrorist measures such as the asset freezes of suspected terrorists.[143] Because of practically universal membership of the UN, the significance of calling on all states has decreased. But the Security Council has also called on non-state actors and international organisations, addressing 'all parties to the conflict and all others concerned'[144] or 'all parties, movements and factions'[145] and 'all States and international organizations to act strictly in accordance with' the embargo against Iraq.[146] Such practice has gone unchallenged or was even accepted.[147] Incidentally, the UK's position in the *Kadi and Al Barakaat* litigation regarding the 'special status of resolutions' of the UN Security Council and the primacy of Charter obligations support this argument.[148] To a lesser degree, the Court's willingness to interpret its regulations implementing UN Security Council Resolutions in the light of the latter, considering them to be of high normative weight in this process, while at the same time not considering itself to be bound through UN membership, also points into this direction.[149]

The second quasi-objective effect results not truly from legal but from the political constraints of membership in a universal organisation such as the UN. Where the price to pay for not being part of it is so high that leaving is not acceptable, the distinction between political pressure and legal obligation becomes blurred. In that sense obligations resulting from the UN may be considered stronger than from the EU as it can be expected to be even less an option for States to leave the UN than it is to leave the EU, as demonsrated by the example of Greenland leaving and Norway's long-term torn position in regard to becoming a member.

10.3.1.2 The effect of international law in the EU legal order: how open is the EU to international law?

This section will examine the 'internationalisation of EU law'. The extent of openness of EU law to international law will be analysed by looking at the effect of international law within EU law by virtue of EU law. There are at least two different possible analytical perspectives which can run across these categories. Firstly, along the traditional *formal* distinction, a perspective of the source of the international law rule will be adopted, in other words, the effect of international treaties and customary international law in the

---

142 SC Resolution 670 (1990), op paras 1, 3, 4, 6–10; similarly in regard to Yugoslavia and Libya, see S Bohr, 'Sanctions by the United Nations Security Council and the European Community' (1993) 4 *European Journal of International Law* 256 ff.

143 SC Resolution 1267 (1999), op paras 3–5, 7; SC Resolution 1333 (2000), op para 4 f; SC Resolution 1373 (2001), op paras 1–3, 6.

144 SC Resolution 788 (1992), op para 5 and 752 (1992), op para 1, regarding Liberia and Bosnia respectively.

145 SC Resolution 794 (1992), op para 1.

146 SC Resolution 687 (1991), op para 25.

147 In the case of Switzerland (while not yet a UN member) in regard to its obligations under Chapter VII the Iraqi invasion of Kuwait, Tomuschat (n 32) 256; D Thürer, 'UN Enforcement Measures and Neutrality. The Case of Switzerland' (1992) 117 *Archiv des Völkerrechts* 69.

148 *Kadi and Al Barakaat* (n 13) para 276, see also paras 262, 268.

149 See also below p 305.

Union legal order will be analysed. Secondly, the interaction will be considered from the *substantive* perspective of the effect of international law in EU law, namely the type of effect (direct effect, interpretation and substantive 'borrowing' from international law) which will give more room to the subject matter of international law interacting with Union law, such as trade law, human rights, the UN Charter, and other international law. At this point it is worth recalling that the effect within the EU legal order is distinct from the question whether the EU is bound by public international law on the international plane. The EU Courts have always held that the EU is bound (internationally) by the rules of international law when exercising its competence,[150] a consequence that follows from the international legal personality.

The distinction of interaction by source (treaty or custom) provides an initially useful analytical prism by which to approach and to compare national legal orders' rules of interaction with international law because it provides a grid that reduces complexity and increases comparability. However, it is inevitably an incomplete reduction of the real picture. The interaction of national law with international law is much more complex 'on the ground' and influenced by policy considerations which will introduce a strong contextual element. Similarly, the EU's approach to international law is not schematic, but guided by its internal constitutionalism, especially in the dimension of the expansion of Union competence known from the relationship between the EU and its Member States. Where the EU, as represented by the EU Courts, could use international law to constitutionalise the EU legal order, it was open to it. Where there were risks involved, either because the EU Courts would be subjected to the authority of another dispute settlement body or because Member States might fear the widespread impact of international law through the EU law principle of direct effect,[151] it has proven to be much more reluctant. Within this internal rationale, the Court has been unsurprisingly wary of competing international legal orders with an advanced constitutionalism themselves – such as WTO, UN and UNCLOS, and more open to the very sectoral ECHR system.

Starting from a general self-image of the EU as open and receptive of international law (10.3.1.2.1), the details of the interaction will be considered from two perspectives: the source of the international norm (10.3.1.2.2); and the effect of the international norm in the EU legal order (10.3.1.2.3).

10.3.1.2.1 A General Principle of Friendliness and Openness of the EU Legal Order Towards International Law?

While the *Völkerrechtsfreundlichkeit* of the EC and EU Treaties was discussed mainly by German scholars,[152] extrapolating from a general principle of openness towards

---

[150] *Racke* (n 104) para 45; *Poulsen* (n 156) para 9 f; C-405/92 *Mondiet* [1993] ECR I-6133, paras 13–15; *Intertanko* (n 30) para 51.

[151] Cf, for example, the concerns of Denmark, Germany, France and the UK about direct effect of an international agreement in 104/81 *Kupferberg v Hauptzollamt Mainz* [1982] ECR 3641, paras 10, 15 f.

[152] Tomuschat, 'Artikel 281 EGV' (n 32), para 65; Hoffmeister (n 104) 366; U Everling, 'Sind die Mitgliedstaaten der Europäischen Gemeinschaft noch Herren der Verträge?' in R Bernhardt et al. (eds), *Völkerrecht als Rechtsordnung – Internationale Gerichtsbarkeit – Menschenrechte Festschrift für Hermann Mosler* (Springer, Berlin 1983) 173, 180; KM Meessen, 'The Application of Rules

international law derived from the German Constitution,[153] there was no explicit reference in the original treaties. On the contrary, if anything, the objective of the Union 'to assert its identity on the international scene' referred to in Art 2 EU (pre-Lisbon version) appeared to be more aggressively outward- than inward-looking. In contrast, Article 3(5) TEU, as amended by the Lisbon Treaty, envisages a more open relationship with international law:

> In its relations with the wider world, the Union shall uphold and promote its values and interests and contribute to the protection of its citizens. It shall contribute to peace, security, the sustainable development of the Earth, solidarity and mutual respect among peoples, free and fair trade, eradication of poverty and the protection of human rights, in particular the rights of the child, *as well as to the strict observance and the development of international law*, including respect for the principles of the United Nations Charter.[154]

It is noteworthy that the EU is not just described as a passive recipient of international law norms, but on the contrary, to take an active role in its development, thus recognising the role the EU plays as an actor of international law.[155]

The EU Courts have stressed time and again that the EU 'must respect international law in the exercise of its powers',[156] even when in effect it did not do so in the case under consideration.[157] Furthermore, it held that the competences in the area of development cooperation 'must be exercised in observance of the undertakings given in the context of the United Nations and other international organisations', as well as in the preservation of peace and security under the UN Charter.[158] Moreover, by finding that international law forms 'an integral part of the Community law'[159] the Court at least signalled openness in principle to international law, in that international law is incorporated into EU law

of Public International Law within Community Law' (1976) 13 *Common Market Law Review* 485, 499; E-U Petersmann, 'Auswärtige Gewalt, Völkerrechtspraxis und Völkerrechtsbindungen der Europäischen Wirtschaftsgemeinschaft' (1975) 35 *Zeitschrift für ausländisches öffentliches Recht und Völkerrecht* 213, 274; Peters (n 5) 28 f; Tietje (n 110) 68; see however also P Eeckhout, 'A Panorama of Two Decades of EU External Relations Law' in A Arnull, P Eeckhout and T Tridimas (eds), *Continuity and Change in EU Law. Essays in Honour of Sir Francis Jacobs* (OUP, Oxford 2008) 323, 330.

[153] C Tomuschat, 'Die staatsrechtliche Entscheidung für die internationale Offenheit' in J Isensee and P Kirchhof (eds), *Handburch des Staatsrechts*, Bd VII (CF Mueller, Heidelberg 1992) 483, 485 ff; K Vogel, *Die Verfassungsentscheidung des Grundgesetzes für die internationale Zusammenarbeit* (Mohr, Tübingen 1964).

[154] Emphasis added.

[155] For the wider question of a specifically European international law or European approaches to international law see n 36 above.

[156] *Racke* (n 104) para 45; C-286/90 *Ankagemyndigheden v Peter Michael Poulsen and Diva Navigation Corp* [1992] ECR I-6019, para 9 f; C-405/92 *Mondiet* [1993] ECR I-6133, paras 13–15; *Kadi and Al Barakaat* (n 13) 291 ff; *Intertanko* (n 30) para 51.

[157] *Kadi and Al Barakaat* (n 13) para 291 f; *Intertanko* (n 30) para 51.

[158] *Kadi and Al Barakaat* (n 13) para 292; C-91/05 *Commisison v Council (ECOWAS)* [2008] ECR I-3651, para 65. See also Art 220 TFEU (ex Art 302 EC), mentioning the relationships with the UN and international organisations.

[159] 181/73 *Haegemann v Belgium* [1974] ECR 449, para 5; *Kupferberg* (n 151) para 13; *Intertanko* (n 30) para 38.

either automatically[160] or through an (unwritten) blanket transformation of international law.[161] However, the proof is in the practical application and depends on the analysis of each individual norm of an international treaty and customary law which determines what effect a rule of international law has in the EU legal order (for example, direct effect or an effect on the interpretation of EU law).[162] The finding that it is an 'integral part' of the EU legal order does not say anything about its status within the EU legal order, and therefore on its own its value as an indicator of openness is limited. Moreover, it could be said that the principal motive for this openness is that it is the basis for the EU Courts' jurisdiction over norms of international law and therefore over the question what effect they have in the EU legal order, and in particular in the relationship with the Member States. In this spirit, the Court has held that the effect of agreements

> in the Community may not be allowed to vary according to whether their application is in practice the responsibility of the Community institutions or the Member States and, in the latter case, according to the effects in the internal legal order of each Member State which the law of that state assigns to international agreements concluded by it. Therefore it is for the Court, within the framework of its jurisdiction in interpreting the provisions of the agreements, to ensure their uniform application throughout the Community.[163]

This logic of uniformity and effectiveness, in a striking parallel, was also used to establish direct effect and supremacy of EU law in the Member States' legal orders.[164] By saying that international law is an integral part of EU law, the Court means it is within (or part of) the scope of EU law. A further parallel is striking: just as the Court has founded (and expanded) its jurisdiction over Member States' acts coming within the scope of EU law, it expands its jurisdiction in the context of international law.[165] As the logic applies both to agreements concluded by the EU and mixed agreements, it is unsurprising that the Courts have not distinguished between categories of agreements when determining their effects within the EU.[166]

---

160 This seems to be the prevailing opinion following the Court's judgments in *Haegemann* (n 159) para 5; *Kupferberg* (n 151) para 13. Tomuschat (n 101), para 48; C Kaddous, 'Effects of International Agreements in the EU Legal Order' in M Cremona and B de Witte (eds), *EU Foreign Relations Law: Constitutional Fundamentals* (Hart, Oxford 2008) 291, 293, 311.

161 This has the advantage of better explaining how agreements are fully reviewable as acts of the Member States, see Peters (n 5) 21 ff, esp 34 f; Kaddous (n 160) 293, fn 11.

162 Without being an 'integral part' of the EU legal order either there might not be scope for a principle of interpretation in conformity with international law at all, cf AG M Poiares Maduro in *FIAMM and Fedon* (n 30) para 39, or it would have to be based on another internal rule, such as a general rule of interpretation so as to avoid international responsibility.

163 *Kupferberg* (n 151) para 14.

164 See 10.2 above, pp 277 ff.

165 'Within the scope' has been interpreted very broadly as being wider than competence or the scope of application of an individual Treaty provision: Thus famously in C-60/00 *Mary Carpenter v Secretary of State for the Home Department* [2002] ECR I-6279, paras 36 ff; C-109/01 *Secretary of State for the Home Department v Akrich* [2003] ECR I-9607; E Spaventa, 'Fundamental Rights' in *Wyatt and Dashwood's European Union Law* (Sweet & Maxwell, London 2006) 257, paras 8-010 ff.

166 Peters (n 5) 21; Kaddous (n 160) 296.

10.3.1.2.2 The Formal Dimension: Interaction of International Law and EU Law by Source

The relationship between the EU and other international law within the EU legal order in principle could be regulated by the contracting states in a wide variety of ways, including in the form of an entity autonomous or separate from international law, subject to compliance with non-derogable rules of *ius cogens.* That means theoretically there are very few limits to the rules governing the relationship of international and EU law. However, the EU Treaties do not regulate the interaction of international law and EU law. This is particularly the case for customary international law but also for international treaties. *Prima facie* Art 216(2) TFEU, which provides that international agreements are 'binding' on the institutions of the EU and the Member States, seems to give a clue. However, at best the provision would leave it textually open whether treaties are not just binding but also directly effective. Because direct effect was not originally a concept of the E(E)C Treaty it seems to stretch the meaning of Art 216(2) TFEU to interpret it as laying down a monist approach to international law.[167] It is more convincing to interpret Art 216(2) TFEU as laying down the binding effect of treaties concluded by the Union *also on Member States* (who may not be a party unless for mixed agreements).[168] Further, there are (declaratory) rules of conflict for pre-existing treaties in Art 351 TFEU (ex Art 307 EC), but again, they do not govern the relationship of the EU and international law comprehensively, but only one specific aspect, namely the temporal one. The provision deals with treaties concluded before the entry into force of the EEC Treaty (for the original Member States), or – more relevant – before the accession to the EU. Naturally, such treaties are not binding on the EU and the Court has no jurisdiction over their substance.[169] In the interest of third states, obligations resulting from such treaties have priority over obligations owed to the EU.[170] Not unlike in many legal systems of the Member States, the relationship of international and EU law has therefore been developed by judges who borrowed from the Member States' approaches in search of the common denominator.

The Court has held in general terms that 'the powers of the Community must be exercised in observance of international law, including provisions of international agreements

---

[167] In the same vein Eeckhout (n 81) 277; see however S Lorenzmaier, in E Grabitz, M Hilf and M Nettesheim (eds), *Das Recht der Europäischen Union* (up to date as of 40th instalment of October 2009), Art 300, paras 89 ff.

[168] *Kupferberg* (n 151) para 13; *Commission v Ireland (MOX plant)* (n 84) para 175 f; Eeckhout (n 81) 276; Neframi (n 75) 331 f.

[169] A notable exception was the GATT which was held to be binding on the Community by virtue of a substitution theory. However, this approach seems no longer relevant after the creation of (and EU membership in) the WTO.

[170] C-118/07 *Commission v Finland* [2009] ECR I-10889, para 27. However, Member States are required to take appropriate steps to eliminate potential incompatibilities (Art 351(2) TFEU). Although they are free as to the choice of means, exceptionally termination of the treaty may be required, Case C-62/98 *Commission v Portugal* [2000] ECR I-5171, paras 48–49; Case C-84/98 *Commission v Portugal* [2000] ECR I-5215, paras 57–8. C-118/07 *Commission v Finland* [2009] ECR I-10889, para 28–35; C-249/06 *Commission v Sweden* [2009] ECR I-1335; C-205/06 *Commission v Austria* [2009] ECR I-1301. For details see M Cremona, 'Defending the Community Interest: The Duties of Cooperation and Compliance' in M Cremona and B de Witte (eds), *EU Foreign Relations Law* (Hart Publishing, Oxford 2008) 125–169, 131 ff; Neframi (n 75) 344 f for the view that the specific provision is a reflection of a general principle of loyal cooperation. See also p 298 below.

in so far as they codify customary rules of general international law'.[171] Furthermore, both customary and treaty law have been found to be an 'integral part' of EU law, and capable of direct effect.[172] The capacity for direct effect is unqualified for customary international law but subject to further requirements in the case of treaties.

(i) Customary international law Customary international law has been applied by the Court.[173] Significantly, cases concern the operation of secondary norms – on the creation, operation and validity of primary norms under customary international law as reflected in cases involving principles of the law of treaties (as codified in the Vienna Convention on the Law of Treaties)[174] or the delimitation of jurisdiction.[175] In that sense the Court uses international law as a common framework and fragmentation is limited by these mechanisms. But the Court also uses primary norms derived from international law, for example regarding nationality of natural persons[176] or ships.[177] Although the Court has used customary international law as a standard of assessment for the validity of an EU measure, thereby showing that also customary international law ranks above secondary EU law,[178] there appears to be no successful challenge on grounds of customary international law so far, leaving some doubt as to the Court's willingness to apply customary law directly as a ground for invalidity of an EU act.[179] The leading case is still *Racke*, which concerned an unsuccessful challenge of the validity of a Council regulation suspending a preferential trade agreement as part of the sanctions against the Federal Republic of Yugoslavia in 1991. As a result, Racke was charged a higher, non-preferential customs rate by the customs authorities. Both parties invoked rules of

---

[171] *Intertanko* (n 30) para 51; *Poulsen* (n 156) para 9; *Racke* (n 104) para 45.

[172] *Racke* (n 104) para 46.

[173] *Poulsen* (n 156) paras 12 ff; *Racke* (n 104) para 46. See in detail J Wouters and D van Eeckhoutte, 'Enforcement of Customary International Law through European Community Law' in JM Prinssen and A Schrauwen (eds), *Direct Effect. Rethinking a Classic of EC Legal Doctrine* (Europa Law Publishing, Groningen 2002) 183–234; P Koutrakos, *EU International Relations Law* (Hart Publishing, Oxford 2006) 244 ff; PJ Kuijper, 'Customary International Law, Decisions of International Organisations and Other Techniques for Ensuring Respect for International Legal Rules in European Community Law' in J Wouters, A Nollkaemper and E de Wet (eds), *The Europeanisation of International Law: The Status of International Law in the EU and its Member States* (Asser Press, The Hague 2008) 89, 88 ff.

[174] C-70/09 *Hengartner and Gassner v Landesregierung Vorarlberg* [2010] ECR I-(nyr), para 36; C-386/08 *Brita GmbH v Hauptzollamt Hamburg-Hafen* [2010] ECR I-(nyr), paras 44 f; *Kadi* (n 23) paras 222, 227; T-231/04 *Greece v Commission* [2007] ECR II-63, paras 85, 98; *Racke* (n 104); T-115/94 *Opel Austria GmbH v Council* [1997] ECR II-39.

[175] 89, 104, 114, 116, 117 and 125–129/85 *Ahlström Oy v Commission* [1988] ECR 5193 ('Woodpulp'); *Poulsen* (n 156) paras 12 ff.

[176] C-200/02 *Chen v Secretary of State for the Home Department* [2004] ECR I-9925, para 37; C-135/08 *Janko Rottmann v Freistaat Bayern* [2010] ECR I-nyr, paras 39, 48, 53 where the Court quotes customary international law rules on the conditions for acquisition or loss of nationality to support its finding that the withdrawal of a nationality conferred by a Member State due to fraud may amount to a justifiable restriction of Union citizenship.

[177] *Poulsen* (n 156).

[178] J Kokott and F Hoffmeister, 'A. Racke GmBH & Co. v Hauptzollamt Mainz, Case C-162/96' (1999) 93 *American Journal of International Law* 205, 207.

[179] Kuijper (n 173) 94.

customary international law: the *clausula rebus sic stantibus* as a customary law norm (codified in Art 62 VCLT) on the one hand and the customary law principle of good faith (codified in Art 26 VCLT) in performing the treaty obligations and in applying *rebus sic stantibus* by Racke on the other hand. The ECJ applied both norms directly, referring to the substantive criteria of Art 62 VCLT[180] and accepting customary international law as a standard for the legality review of a Community act. At the same time, however, the challenge remained unsuccessful and was watered down by the Court's curiously selective approach. It did not apply the procedural obligations (such as the requirement of prior notification) because they were not part of customary law, and it watered down the standard of review to 'manifest errors of assessment'.[181] Interestingly, in contrast to the requirement for direct effect of agreements after *FIAMM*,[182] the Court did not require the rule of customary international law (good faith), which could be said to apply only in relations between states, to confer rights on individuals in order to be invoked.[183]

(ii) Treaty law Art 216(1) TFEU and Art 37 TEU provide for the EU's power to conclude treaties; the provisions have to be supplemented by the relevant provisions on substantive competences.[184] As a result of the EU's treaty-making power, Member States' powers are limited externally. They can no longer unilaterally conclude treaties where the EU has exclusive competence (e.g. in the area of common commercial policy). Where they conclude treaties in areas of shared competence they are bound by a duty of loyal cooperation.[185] They have insofar given up or 'pooled' their sovereignty.[186]

International agreements could be presumed to be directly effective and to have primacy over secondary legislation in the EU, which could be reviewed for its validity and compatibility with EU law against the standard of international agreements.[187] Doubts have been cast on this presumption following the *Intertanko* judgment of 2008[188] which raised the threshold of direct effect of treaty norms, as will be discussed in further detail below.[189] Further doubts result from what appears to be an increasingly strict approach to the duties of Member States under Art 351 TFEU in regard to treaties pre-dating their EU membership. In a line of cases concerning bilateral investment treaties, the Court held that even where there was only a potential future conflict with EU law (e.g. the potential future adoption of harmonising measures regarding free movement of capital), a possible future renegotiation, suspension or termination of the treaty – which were the already

---

180 Albeit arguably erroneously, raising the question of the dangers of errors in the application of general international law by specialised tribunals.

181 *Racke* (n 104) paras 59 and 52 respectively.

182 See below text after n 216, p 302.

183 In the same vein (direct effect of customary law), although the ECJ verbally made a different assertion Eeckhout (n 81) 332; Wouters and van Eeckhoutte (n 74) 40, 43, 47 ff.

184 Arts 216 ff TFEU now applies to all Union competences (after the merging of the EC and EU by the Lisbon Treaty), including what was traditionally a second or third pillar matter. Special rules for the CFSP are however retained.

185 *Commission v Ireland (MOX plant)* (n 84) paras 169–171, 175–181; Neframi (n 75).

186 De Witte (n 35) 49.

187 See overview by Eeckhout (n 81) 281 ff.

188 *Intertanko* (n 30).

189 Below text after nn 199 and 210, pp 299 and 301.

far-reaching requirements in the past[190] – was insufficient.[191] The effectiveness of EU law required immediate implementation if a rule of EU law were to be adopted in the future. Therefore, Art 351 TFEU required that Member States negotiate a special reservation clause even before there actually was conflicting EU law, pre-empting a future clash between obligations under the bilateral investment treaty and EU law.[192] Although the very strict approach may have to be seen in the light of an anticipated expansion of the EU's competence provided by the Lisbon Treaty, the further tightening of the already quite strictly applied conflict rule of Art 351 TFEU is further evidence for a less open approach to international (treaty) law.

10.3.1.2.3 Interaction by Effect

This section will shift from form to effect and examine the interaction of international and EU law from the perspective of the effect of international law *within* the Union legal order. The different effects and mechanisms by which international law enters EU law serve as a focal point, namely the scope of direct effect in regard to treaties and customary international law, the interpretation in conformity with international law and 'substantive borrowing' from international law. The latter two methodological tools to a large extent allow the formal or categorical approaches to treaty and custom to be overcome.[193]

(i) Direct effect Although the question of direct effect is one that concerns both customary and treaty law, due to the few cases relating to customary international law it features in the case law mostly in regard to treaties, primarily those to which the EU[194] is a party.[195] It is, however, acknowledged by the Court that customary international law is directly effective in the EU legal order.[196] Direct effect of international norms in the EU legal order is one important factor in assessing its openness towards international law because it is the most far-reaching form of interaction. Direct effect may be loosely defined as the question whether individuals can invoke these norms before EU Courts

---

[190] C-473/93 *Commission v Luxembourg* [1996] ECR I-3207; C-62/98 *Commission v Portugal* [2000] ECR I-5171.

[191] C-205/06 *Commission v Austria* [2009] ECR I-1301; C-249/06 *Commission v Sweden* [2009] ECR I-1335; C-118/07 *Commission v Finland* [2009] ECR I-10889.

[192] C-205/06 *Commission v Austria* [2009] ECR I-1301, paras 36–40.

[193] Cf *Teoh* (n 55); Order of the German Federal Constitutional Court of 14 October 2004 – 2 BvR 1481/04, (2004) 111 *BVerfGE* 307 (*Görgülü*) at <http://www.bundesverfassungsgericht.de/entscheidungen/rs20041014_2bvr148104en.html>.

[194] With the Lisbon Treaty, the distinction between Community (Art 216 TFEU, ex Art 300 EC) and Union (EU) agreements (Art 37 EU, ex Art 24 EU) is abolished.

[195] However, there may be an indirect interaction between EU law and international law where a Member State is required to resolve a conflict between EU law and a pre-existing treaty; according to Art 351 TFEU, the Member State regularly must eliminate the conflict; however, depending on the issue in question, this might exceptionally entail that the EU as such eliminates the conflict – as happened occasionally where the scope of protection of the ECHR was wider than that under EU law, e.g. regarding the scope of protection of business premises under Art 8 ECHR and the right not to incriminate oneself. See below p 309 and n 264.

[196] Bases for this assumption are the judgments in *Haegeman* (n 159) para 5; *Kupferberg* (n 151) para 13; *Racke* (n 104) para 45 and *Poulsen* (n 156) para 9. Tomuschat, 'Artikel 281 EGV' (n 32), para 48. See also above, n 173.

and the courts of Member States.[197] Answering the question of the direct effect of international law in the EU legal order theoretically still leaves open the further question whether it is directly effective as EU law or as public international law, but the Court's emphasis on a uniform interpretation of directly effective international law presumes that it is directly effective as *Union law*[198] and therefore enforced in the same way as EU law. Direct effect in itself also does not say anything about the hierarchical rank of international law in the EU legal order.

The Court developed a two-stage test for direct effect. It examined firstly, whether the individual provision was suitable to be applied directly, namely whether it was sufficiently clear and precise and unconditional, that is, it was in that sense 'perfect' or 'complete' so that it could be applied directly within the EU legal order. Secondly, direct effect was not to be precluded by the 'nature and structure' or 'broad logic' of the agreement.[199] Until 2008, the Court applied this two-stage test by way of presumption: where the norm was 'complete', it was presumed to be directly effective.[200] Moreover, the only case in which the Court had excluded an agreement because of its 'nature and structure' from direct effect was the GATT/WTO Agreement.[201] This was widely considered to be an exception to the rule which was criticised by some to be inconsistent with the Court's approach to treaties generally.[202] In different contexts, such as association, partnership and free trade agreements and even their secondary acts, such as EFTA and association council decisions,[203] the Court very widely allowed for direct effect.[204] The principal reasons for the restrictive approach with regard to the WTO Agreement are considered to be that it is still characterised by great flexibility, an underlying principle of negotiation on the basis of reciprocity and that it was therefore not in the nature and spirit of the Agreement to be directly effective. As other states which are trading partners of the EU do not accord it direct effect, the EU would lose its political freedom and scope for negotiation if it granted direct effect to WTO rules. Academic opinion over the appropriateness of direct effect of the GATT/WTO remains divided.[205] With those who welcomed the Court's

---

197 Cf overview in Opinion of AG Poiares Maduro in *FIAMM and Fedon* (n 30) paras 23 ff; P Koutrakos, *EU International Relations Law* (Hart Publishing, Oxford 2006) 217 ff.

198 Peters (n 5) 31 f.

199 *FIAMM and Fedon* (n 30) para 110; *Intertanko* (n 30) para 45. For a summary of the case law see Opinion of AG Poiares Maduro in *FIAMM and Fedon* (n 30) paras 27 ff; Eeckhout (n 81) 301 ff.

200 Eeckhout (n 81) 301; P Koutrakos, *EU International Relations Law* (Hart Publishing, Oxford 2006) 251 ff. See also the cursory discussion, suggesting such a presumption in C-344/04 *IATA* [2006] ECR I-403.

201 See, e.g. *International Fruit Co.* (n 118) para 25 f; C-149/96 *Portugal v Council* [1999] ECR I-8395, para 47.

202 See, for example, N Lavanos, 'The Chiquita and Van Parys Judgments: An Exception to the Rule of Law' (2005) 32 *Legal Issues of European Integration* 449.

203 C-188/91 *Deutsche Shell AG v Hauptzollamt Hamburg-Harburg* [1993] ECR I-383, para 17; C-192/89 *Sevince v Staatssecretaris van Justitie* [1990] ECR I-3461, para 10.

204 Eeckhout (n 81) 283–292; Tomuschat, 'Artikel 281 EGV' (n 32) para 50 f; Kaddous (n 160) 302; e.g. 87–75 *Conceria Daniele Bresciani v Amministrazione Italiana delle Finanze* [1976] ECR 129, para 25.

205 Critical of the lack of direct effect PJ Kuijper and M Bronckers, 'WTO Law in the European Court of Justice' (2005) *Common Market Law Review* 1313; S Peers, 'Fundamental Right or

stance,[206] in the past it could at least be said that the lack of direct effect could be justified as an exceptional case. In three cases in 2008, the presumption of direct effect, which was considered to be a sign of openness of EU law and the Court towards international law, was shattered profoundly.

FIAMM and Fedon

In *FIAMM and Fedon* the Court confirmed and extended its constant line of jurisprudence as to the lack of direct effect of the GATT/WTO substantive rules to decisions of its Dispute Settlement Body (DSB) even after the expiry of a reasonable time for their implementation.[207] FIAMM and Fedon were caught up in the EU–WTO bananas dispute. The companies were affected by US countermeasures which were authorised by the WTO DSB because the EU had failed to fully implement a WTO DSB decision by the specified deadline.[208] They claimed damages for unlawful, and failing that, lawful conduct of the EU because it breached its obligations under WTO law. The ECJ reiterated the reasons given in its previous case law on the lack of direct effect of the substantive obligations under the WTO Agreement generally and applied them to decisions of the DSB, finding them also not to be directly effective. There are serious doubts about the transferability of the reasons (reciprocity, flexibility, political negotiations) that are given for the lack of direct effect of obligations under the WTO Agreement to decisions of the DSB: the EU–WTO bananas dispute had been settled when the damages actions were brought, so EU negotiating power could not be impaired.[209] The effect of the ruling in *FIAMM and Fedon* thus was to shield the EU legal order from its international obligations and to give the EU a license to breach international treaty obligations without sanction: the cost of the sanction was in effect 'privatized' because it was born by the affected traders. This approach follows a similar dualist logic as in *Kadi and Al Barakaat.* In contrast to *Kadi and Al Barakaat,* this ruling can hardly be considered to promote the rule of law even within the EU (the constitutional dimension). Hence its predominant effect is to undermine, in its international dimension, the legally binding nature of international obligations and decisions of international tribunals such as the DSB, let alone the credibility of the EU in its international relations more generally, making it open to the criticism of applying double-standards.

Intertanko

Since June 2008 the GATT/WTO is no longer the inconsistent exception to the general presumption of direct effect of international treaties. In *Intertanko* the ECJ precluded a further treaty from direct effect because of its 'nature and structure', namely the UN

Political Whim? WTO Law and the European Court of Justice' in G de Búrca and J Scott (eds), *The EU and the WTO: Legal and Constitutional Aspects* (Hart, Oxford 2001) 111.

206 Eeckhout (n 81) 302 ff; M Dani, 'Remedying European Legal Pluralism: The FIAMM and Fedon Litigation and the Judicial Protection of International Trade Bystanders' (2010) 21 *European Journal of International Law* 303, 310, 325.

207 *FIAMM and Fedon* (n 30) paras 108 ff, 121 ff, 133.

208 The DSB declared preferential treatment for bananas from ACP countries as incompatible with the WTO rules and required implementation of its decision by 1 January 1999.

209 Dani (n 206) 310.

Convention on the Law of the Sea.[210] The Council's argument made in this regard in the litigation was called 'surprising' by Advocate General Kokott, in particular in the light of previous case law.[211] It is also surprising considering the nature and fundamental status of UNCLOS as a multilateral treaty which is considered to be an 'objective legal order' as the 'constitution of the sea'.[212]

Intertanko was a challenge to an EC Directive on ship-source pollution which tried to address concerns about the inadequate levels of protection by international instruments after the major oil spill caused by the tanker *Prestige*. The Directive raised the standard of liability of ships in the territorial sea and broadened the circle of those responsible beyond the owners or masters of a ship to the cargo owner, classification societies and 'any other persons involved'. The applicants, a consortium of operators of the international shipping industry, argued that various aspects of the Directive violated international law (the International Convention for the Prevention of Pollution from Ships (MARPOL) and UNCLOS 1982 in particular). They challenged the Directive's stricter standard of liability ('serious negligence') as incompatible with standards contained in MARPOL because it applied to certain categories of persons beyond the territorial sea; it lowered the liability threshold in cases of accidental discharge and widened the categories of persons responsible. They also claimed that the stricter test amounted to a violation of the right to innocent passage under UNCLOS. The Court and Advocate General Kokott found the Directive to be compatible with international law. The Advocate General did so on substantive grounds whereas the Court rejected the argument that the international rules in question were applicable standards for the legality review in the first place because they lacked direct effect. The Court characterised UNCLOS as primarily state-centred in the traditional public international law sense, stressing that it 'seeks to strike a fair balance' e.g. between the interests of coastal and flag states, in order to then deny direct effect by its 'nature and broad logic'.[213] It then uses what is traditionally part of the second limb[214] of the test for the direct effect of international agreement, namely the sufficiently clear and precise character of a provision conferring individual rights, to support further its argument as to the nature of UNCLOS: individuals were not granted (subjective) independent rights and freedoms by virtue of the Convention because they require a nationality link with the (flag) state. Rights, therefore, at best were seen to attach to ships, but not to the individuals linked to those ships (e.g. owners).[215]

With such a requirement of individual rights as truly subjective rights in *Intertanko*, the Court narrowed the notion of direct effect in the international law context significantly. The alternative conception of direct effect simply asks whether individuals can invoke the

---

210 *Intertanko* (n 30) para 65.

211 Opinon of AG J Kokott in *Intertanko* (n 30) para 50. Cf *Poulsen* (n 156) paras 12 ff.

212 Opinion of AG Kokott (n 30) para 55. The law of the sea was one of the candidates for objective regimes envisaged by the ILC's Special Rapporteur Sir Humphrey Waldock in the then Draft Articles on the Law of Treaties that later became the Vienna Convention, Art 63, 1964 II *Yearbook of the International Law Commission* 5, 26 f.

213 *Intertanko* (n 30) paras 54, 58, 65.

214 Although the Court fudges the two limbs, both were argued separately in the proceedings. See also Eeckhout (n 116) 2054.

215 *Intertanko* (n 30) paras 59, 61. N.B. that many, if not most, rights in EU law require a nationality link in the form of EU citizenship too.

international rule,[216] which means it needs to be a 'complete norm' but not necessarily one that confers subjective rights.[217] While the requirement of an individual right as a subjective right for direct effect seems accepted for the direct effect of EU law in the Member States, this has not been clearly identified or settled for international law. And while it seems *prima facie* plausible to interpret direct effect identically in relation to Member States' legal orders and in relation to the Union legal order[218] precisely because of the effect that international law will have on the Union legal order, this does not withstand further scrutiny because the notion of direct effect is in fact wider than that of a subjective right in the EU-Member State dimension.

Typically, direct effect in a Union-Member State scenario implies that an individual right conferred by EU law serves as the cause of action *in the Member States' legal orders* – a Treaty provision, a regulation or a directly effective directive is invoked in order to replace or disapply conflicting national law. Direct effect is flanked by the alternative principles of incidental and indirect effect where the conditions of direct effect are not met. Both principles allow individuals to invoke norms of EU law for the purposes of striking out conflicting national law (exclusionary effect) and of interpreting national law in conformity with EU law. Direct effect proper in an EU-Member States scenario requires that a provision of EU law confers an individual right, sometimes described as a negative obligation, and is 'a 'complete' or 'perfect' norm so that it can be applied (i.e. sufficiently clear and precise and not in need of further implementing measures).[219] However, even in an EU-Member States context individuals can rely on provisions which seemingly have an objective thrust,[220] that is the notion of 'individual right' is interpreted very loosely. This is congruent with the dual rationale for direct effect in the first place, founded on the one hand on the rationale of individual rights (Member States should not deprive an individual of a right because of the significance of the individual right), on the other hand on the rationale of estoppel (Member States are estopped from invoking their own failure to comply with an international obligation).[221] Furthermore, even in an indirect (and more so in a direct) challenge to the legality of an EU measure, objective

---

216 AG Maduro rightly pointed out the factual differences between scenarios of direct effect of EU law in the Member States and of international agreements in the EU legal order which makes it preferable to speak of the 'ability to rely' on an international agreement: Opinion of AG Maduro in *FIAMM and Fedon* (n 30) para 28 f – albeit with a different conclusion from the one drawn here. In favour of a wider conception of direct effect as mere invocability by individuals, see K Lenaerts and T Corthaud, 'Of Birds and Hedges: The Role of Primacy in Invoking Norms of EU Law' (2006) 31 *European Law Review* 287, 298; M Mendez, 'The Legal Effect of Community Agreements: Maximalist Treaty Enforcement and Judicial Avoidance Techniques' (2010) 21 *European Journal of International Law* 83, 100 ff.

217 Cf C-377/98 *Kingdom of the Netherlands v European Parliament and Council of the European Union (Directive on Biotechnological Inventions)* [2001] ECR I-7079, para 54; Opinion of AG Kokott in *Intertanko* (n 30) para 66, who, however, assumes that the freedom of navigation amounts to an invidual right under customary international law, ibid para 67.

218 Opinion of AG Maduro in *FIAMM and Fedon* (n 30) para 28 f.

219 Case 26/62 *NV Algemene Transport- en Expeditie Onderneming van Gend & Loos v Netherlands Inland Revenue Administration* [1963] ECR 1; Case 106/77 *Amministrazione delle Finanze dello Stato v Simmenthal SpA* [1978] ECR 629.

220 See Lenaerts and Corthaud (n 216) 298.

221 148/78 *Pubblico Ministero v Ratti* [1979] ECR 1629, para 22.

norms such as the legal bases (or provisions allocating competence) may be invoked.[222] The directly effective EU law may or may not confer a subjective right in the strict sense. As a result the individual right is often more the consequence than the cause of direct effect in EU law.

In *Intertanko* the Court applied a stricter test to international law and precluded the invocability of provisions of UNCLOS by individuals. This was regardless of the fact that the situation was comparable to that of legality review of EU measures for which objective standards may be invoked.[223] In addition, a further consideration is relevant for international law. Although subjective rights of individuals are increasing, individual rights in a strict sense are not at all common in international law, even if many norms are designed to benefit individuals. In the case of international law, insisting on individual rights in the narrow sense, rather than on the notion of invocability, leads to gaps in enforcement and review in the EU legal order because the EU legal order itself does not contain all the procedural remedies that exist in the relationship between the EU and its Member States (such as preliminary references triggered by rights or enforcement actions under national law). But should direct effect be merely a tool for enforcement of international law?[224] Even if this may not be answered in the affirmative in general terms, the interest protected by an international provision should be decisive, even if no full-blown subjective rights are created under international law. Should, for example, the breach of humanitarian law not be invocable in EU Courts because it largely imposes obligations on states, but, in contrast to human rights law, does not confer subjective rights *stricto sensu*?

As mentioned, although accepted in principle,[225] the case law on direct effect of customary international law is sparse. One might read a restrictive trend also in regard to the notion of customary law in the judgment of *Intertanko.* Although the Advocate General embarked on an intensive analysis of the substance of the UNCLOS, the Court, in denying it direct effect as a treaty, brushed off in the same stroke the application of *parallel* customary international law. At the very least a more careful reasoning could have been expected here.

Kadi and Al Barakaat

As discussed in the context of succession into treaties concluded by Member States,[226] it follows from the ECJ's logic that it did not consider itself bound by the UN Charter internationally. And respect for international law more generally was not enough for the Charter and Security Council Resolutions to apply *within* the EU domestic legal order. The Court therefore purportedly only conducted a domestic review of a domestic act (an EC Regulation) on the basis of domestic constitutional standards. Even if the claim to be a legal order entails the notion of autonomy, the dualist approach of the Court with

---

[222] See, for example, the challenge of the EU's competence to adopt the relevant regulation in *Kadi and Al Barakaat* (n 13).

[223] Opinion of AG Kokott in *Intertanko* (n 30) para 66, who in addition finds that there was a genuine subjective right under customary international law, at para 67; Eeckhout (n 116) 2054.

[224] For an answer in the negative cf Eeckhout (n 81) 313 f.

[225] Wouters and van Eeckhoutte (n 74) 48.

[226] See above, p 288.

regard to international law gives the autonomy notion a new thrust, closing up the EU's openness to international law significantly.

The decision rests on a second leg, namely the hierarchy of the EU norms. As mentioned, international treaties rank more highly in the EU legal order than secondary legislation but not higher than EU primary law (the Treaties).[227] So, even if the Court had considered that the EU succeeded into the Member States' obligations under the Charter[228] or indeed that it had to 'acknowledge' in a softer form the significance of the UN Charter (as it did[229]), it would have reached the same result because EU fundamental rights as general principles of EU law rank at Treaty level,[230] and hence above international law which only ranks more highly than secondary legislation.[231] In fact fundamental constitutional principles were found to enjoy an even higher rank than 'ordinary' Treaty provisions. Whereas the ECJ pointed out that market freedoms are exceptionally derogable in accordance with Art 351 TFEU (ex Art 307 EC), 'any derogation from the principles of liberty, democracy and respect for human rights and fundamental freedoms enshrined in Article 6(1) EU as a foundation of the Union' was not permitted.[232] This would be correct on the basis of approaching the UN Charter (and equating UN Security Council Resolutions to the UN Charter[233]) as any other treaty. An argument can be made, however, that the Member States actually have resolved the interaction between EU law and the UN Charter when drafting the Treaty through a combined effect of Art 351 TFEU (ex Art 307 EC) and Art 103 of the UN Charter, giving the UN Charter a higher rank (expressive of *international* constitutionalism) than any rule stemming from the EU Treaties which runs counter to the constitutional rationale applied by the Court.[234] The autonomous reading of the EC Treaty, however, enabled the Court to exclude Art 103 of the UN Charter from its analysis.

(ii) Interpretation in conformity with international law Direct effect of, and interpretation in conformity with, international law are not always clearly identifiable as separate mechanisms where the EU Courts follow the international rule. Where they merely take the international rule 'into account', the difference becomes more obvious. Interpretation in conformity with international law occurs in the following situations:

Firstly, where the Union is bound by a treaty to which it is a party, sole or 'mixed',[235] and which, therefore, is an 'integral part' of the Union legal order, and where the treaty

---

227 Tomuschat, 'Artikel 281 EGV' (n 32) para 43.

228 Cf *Kadi and Al Barakaat* (n 13) para 307 '*supposing* it to be applicable to the Charter of the United Nations' (emphasis added), implying that the Court supposes (for argument's sake) that the Charter was binding on the EU.

229 *Kadi and Al Barakaat* (n 13) paras 292–7.

230 *Kadi and Al Barakaat* (n 13) paras 283 f, 326, 330.

231 *Kadi and Al Barakaat* (n 13) para 307.

232 *Kadi and Al Barakaat* (n 13) para 303; see already in this regard Ziegler (n 9) 297.

233 Likewise Eeckhout (n 81) 436 ff.

234 In the same vein Hilpold (n 8) 161.

235 C-53/96 *Hermès* [1998] ECR I-3603, para 32; C-392/98 *Dior and Others* [2000] ECR I-11307, para 47 f. The reason for the jurisdiction of the Court over the interpretation of mixed agreements in their entirety is that the respective spheres of competence between the Member States and the Union cannot be readily and clearly separated and to preserve uniform application.

is not directly effective, the Court requires interpretation of EU secondary legislation 'as far as possible' in the light of the EU's international obligations, in accordance with the primacy international rules enjoy over secondary EU legislation. There is widespread practice of interpretation in the light of the GATT or WTO Agreement.[236]

Secondly, even in the case of a treaty concluded by Member States only, to which the EU is not a party and where it has not succeeded into the obligations of the Member States, the Court applies the interpretative principle. In *Kadi and Al Barakaat*, somewhat inconsistent with its autonomy approach and its approach in regard to the (lack of) succession into Member States' obligations,[237] the ECJ went out of its way to stress its openness to international law and the UN Charter, in particular in the interpretation of EU law. It stated that its powers 'must be exercised in observance of the undertakings given in the context of the United Nations and other international organisations', to which 'it is necessary for the Community to attach special importance' in the light of the Security Council's 'primary responsibility . . . for the maintenance of peace and security at the global level' under Chapter VII of the UN Charter.[238] Therefore, it concludes, 'the Community is to take due account of the terms and objectives of the resolution concerned and of the relevant obligations under the Charter of the United Nations'.[239] Furthermore it stated that in 'the interpretation of the contested regulation, account must also be taken of the wording and purpose' of the relevant Security Council Resolution.[240] Thus not only the treaty (UN Charter), but also resolutions are relevant for the interpretation of EU law.[241]

The case of the UN Charter might be considered to be special. However, the EU Courts also used other international treaties to which the EU is not a party to guide their interpretation of EU law. They have referred to and interpreted other international treaties and have interpreted EU law in line with international norms which are not formally binding on the Union. The most well-known example is that of the ECHR. Other examples are the International Covenant on Civil and Political Rights (ICCPR) and the Convention on the Rights of the Child (CRC),[242] the Geneva Convention on the Status of Refugees of

---

[236] E.g. *Hermès* (n 235) para 28; C-61/94 *Commission v Germany* [1996] ECR I-3989, para 52 ('International Dairy Arrangement').

[237] This would suggest – contrary to what the ECJ says – that Resolutions are not an 'integral part' of the EU legal order. However, the consideration of resolutions is consistent with the implementation of the UN Security Council Resolutions by EC Regulation under Articles 60 and 301 EC, following the logic of 'implementation' of international law. See also above, p 291 and Kuijper (n 173) 100.

[238] *Kadi and Al Barakaat* (n 13) paras 292, 294.

[239] *Kadi and Al Barakaat* (n 13) para 296.

[240] *Kadi and Al Barakaat* (n 13) para 297. See also C-84/95 *Bosphorus Hava Yollari Turizm ve Ticaret AS v Minister for Transport, Energy and Communication and Others* [1996] ECR I-3953, paras 13–15.

[241] See already C-177/95 *Ebony Maritime SA and Loten Navigation Co. Ltd v Prefetto della Provincia di Brindisi and others* [1997] I-1111, paras 3, 20; C-84/95 *Bosphorus Hava Yollari Turizm ve Ticaret AS v Minister for Transport, Energy and Communication and Others* [1996] ECR I-3953, para 14; see also I Canor, 'Can Two Walk Together, Except They Be Agreed? – The Relationship Between International Law and European Law' (1998) 35 *Common Market Law Review* 137.

[242] C-244/06 *Dynamic Medien v Avides Media* [2008] ECR I-505, paras 39–41; C-540/03 *Parliament v Council (Family Reunification Directive)* [2006] ECR I-5769, para 37.

1951 as well as its Protocol and other relevant treaties concluded by the Member States as Art 63(1) EC refers to it,[243] the European Convention on Nationality and the Convention on the Reduction of Statelessness, the Universal Declaration of Human Rights[244] and the International Covenant on Economic, Social and Cultural Rights (ICESCR). For example, it found in *Bressol* that the equal treatment obligation of Member States under EU citizenship rules was compatible with provisions of the ICESCR.[245] However, such interpretation is not always free-standing, but operates through the vehicle of the notion of general principles of EU law. Therefore, there is also an overlap between interpretation in conformity with EU law and mere substantive 'borrowing' from international law.[246] General principles are of particular prominence in the area of human rights in which the import of standards of the ECHR through interpretation of the general principles is well established. However, the fact that the Court remained open and referred also to other, newer human rights instruments such as the CRC shows a genuine openness to international human rights law. Beyond the UN Charter and human rights treaties it has claimed jurisdiction over a dispute arising from a Convention to which only Member States are parties. However the CJEU has explicitly not embarked on a substantive interpretation of the international instrument but referred it back to the referring national court in *TNT Express*.[247] The exemplary list of case law demonstrates a somewhat eclectic use of international treaties by which the EU is not formally bound.

Thirdly, the Court has interpreted EU law in the light of customary international law and general principles of international law, such as the customary law rules on nationality of persons and ships, *pacta sunt servanda*, the *rebus sic stantibus* rule and interpretation in good faith in the law of treaties.[248] Here the line between direct effect and interpretation is particularly blurred. For example the *Opel Austria* case[249] is used to demonstrate both direct effect of customary law in EU law and the interpretation of EU law (the notion of legitimate expectations) in the light of customary international law.[250]

Against the backdrop of the recent series of case law sketched out above,[251] which conveys a more restrictive approach to international law, the question may be asked whether the Court is also more restrictive in regard to the interpretation of EU law in the light of international law, or whether, on the contrary, a wider use of the interpretative

---

243 Joined Cases C-175, 176, 178 & 179/08 *Salahadin Abdulla and Others* [2010] ECR I-(nyr), para 52 f; C-31/09 *Bolbol v Bevándorlási és Állampolgársági Hivatal* [2010] ECR I-(nyr), para 38; M Bronckers, 'The Relationship of the EC Courts with Other International Tribunals: Non-committal, Respectful or Submissive?' (2007) 44 *Common Market Law Review* 601, 602.

244 C-135/08 *Rottmann v Freistaat Bayern* [2010] ECR I-(nyr), para 52 f.

245 C-73/08 *Bressol and Others v Gouvernement de la Communauté francaise* [2010] ECR I-(nyr), para 85 f; see in detail Opinion of AG Sharpston, paras 135 ff.

246 See below (iii), p 308.

247 C-533/08 *TNT Express Nederland BV v AXA Versicherung AG* [2010] ECR I-(nyr), para 56, in respect of the Geneva Convention on the Contract for the International Carriage of Goods by Road of 19 May 1956.

248 See already above, p 296; *Intertanko* (n 30) paras 51–52; Eeckhout (n 81) 325 ff; Kuijper (n 173) 92 f.

249 T-115/94 *Opel Austria GmbH v Council* [1997] ECR II-39, paras 90 ff.

250 Eeckhout (n 81) 327.

251 See 10.3.1.2.3(i), p 298 above.

method compensates for a more restrictive use of the more formal methods. It may be recapitulated that the Court demonstrated a more restrictive attitude in regard to the direct effect of international treaties (UNCLOS in *Intertanko* and decisions of the WTO Dispute Settlement Body in *FIAMM and Fedon* and, arguably, the UN Charter and customary international law in *Kadi and Al Barakaat*). In the latter case the Court in particular also stressed in a dualist way the separateness and autonomy of the EU legal order vis-à-vis international law, which may be underlying the decisions in the other cases as well, if not as obviously.

The principle of interpretation is demonstrated in *Intertanko* in both respects mentioned above. The Court referred both to the interpretation in conformity with customary international law and with MARPOL, a convention concluded by all Member States, but to which the EU is not a party, and UNCLOS, which the EU has ratified but which, because of its 'nature and broad logic', was held to lack direct effect.[252]

> In those circumstances, it is clear that the validity of Directive 2005/35 cannot be assessed in the light of Marpol 73/78, even though it binds the Member States. The latter fact is, however, liable to have consequences for the interpretation of, first, UNCLOS and, second, the provisions of *secondary law* which fall within the field of application of Marpol 73/78. In view of the customary principle of good faith, which forms part of general international law, and of Article 10 EC, it is incumbent upon the Court to interpret those provisions *taking account of Marpol 73/78*.[253]

In principle, this reflects the traditional open approach. However, neither comes to bear in the case. The Court neither finds that there are parallel rules of customary international law, nor does it even attempt to reconcile the Directive and MARPOL by interpretation. In regard to UNCLOS the Court does not even pay lip-service to consistent interpretation of EU law in the light of the Convention. This is remarkable because it is in stark contrast with the Opinion of Advocate General Kokott who had recommended the same outcome as the Court eventually reached, but on the basis of an extensively argued, detailed harmonising interpretation of the international obligation and the EU Directive, which she found to be compatible with MARPOL.[254] There may be reasons for the absence of interpretation, such as the nature of the argument in the litigation or that the Court thought that conform-interpretation was impossible.[255] However, in the light of the extensive coverage and the weight of the arguments in the Advocate General's Opinion, such absence appears to ignore rather than 'take into account' international law. Such an approach contributes to an overall picture of reluctance in reviewing an act of the EU against international law[256] and the status of international law in EU law. The Advocate General had laid out that on the basis of the hierarchy of norms in EU law, international agreements had primacy over secondary legislation, that '[a]ccordingly, interpretation in conformity with international law must be given priority over other

---

252 *Intertanko* (n 30) paras 51–52.

253 *Intertanko* (n 30) para 52 (emphasis added).

254 AG Kokott, paras 80 ff, esp 93, 96, 101, 111; critically as 'excessively charitable towards the drafting of the Directive', E Denza, 'A Note on Intertanko' (2008) 33 *European Law Review* 870, 874.

255 Cf Eeckhout (n 116) 2056.

256 *Intertanko* (n 30) para 51.

methods of interpretation' and that conform-interpretation was only limited by 'rules and principles which take precedence over the Community's obligations under international law', such as 'general legal principles and in particular the principle of legal certainty' which precludes a *contra legem* interpretation.[257]

The reasoning in *Kadi and Al Barakaat* left no scope for a harmonious interpretation of the Security Council Resolution and the EC Regulation which allowed preservation of the fundamental rights of the EU legal order: there was an irreconcilable conflict. By its own rationale the EU was not bound by UN Charter and therefore it was not an 'integral part' of EU law, although it paid what in the overall context of the judgment can only be called lip-service to the importance of observing the Charter, which can be taken as a reference to guiding interpretation – in principle. The logic of Art 351 TFEU (ex Art 307 EC) and Art 103 UN Charter would still have required interpreting the Treaty as if the Member States had actually regulated the conflict in the Treaty in such a way as to avoid conflicts of obligations for them; the EU institutions, including the Court, are bound by these Treaty rules. This conundrum created by the Court could have been overcome in at least two different ways that would have preserved the unity of international law without changing the outcome: the first one is – with the CFI – to resort to the concept of *ius cogens* as Member States cannot through the EU Treaty (Art 351 TFEU) authorise the breach of such rules.[258] A second option would have been to interpret Art 351 TFEU in line with Art 31 VCLT flexibly and dynamically: Member States did not foresee the conflict of international law with fundamental constitutional principles and therefore would not have given the conflict rule such a broad scope. After all, as litigation around the implementation measures of targeted sanctions at state level shows, the Member States face the same problems domestically as indirectly through the EU and which the EU itself faces.[259] A third option would have been to resolve the conflict by (also) pointing to the conflict of norms at international level. There would have been more potential for interpretation of the standards of review by relying on other obligations of international law, such as international human rights law (which is said to be part of the general principles of EU law), as well as the norms of *ius cogens* (which the Court deliberately avoided).[260] The Court could have thus demonstrated more openness and could have embedded its decision better in international law, thereby avoiding an antagonistic signal. Admittedly, however, this would have made its decision more complicated.

(iii) Borrowing substantive standards from international law Famously, the EU legal order borrowed from international law (as well as national constitutional law) to fill its gap in the protection of fundamental rights.[261] In doing so, the EU has powerfully

---

257 AG Kokott, para 107 f.

258 Art 53 VCLT.

259 See, for example, *Her Majesty's Treasury v Ahmed and al Ghabra and R (Youssef) v Her Majesty's Treasury* [2010] UKSC 2; *Hay v HM Treasury* and *Secretary of State for Foreign and Commonwealth Affairs* [2009] EWHC 1677 (Admin); for a comparable case in the Federal Court of Ontario, Canada, cf *Abdelrazik v The Minister of Foreign Affairs and the Attorney General of Canada* [2009] FC 580.

260 *Kadi and Al Barakaat* (n 13) para 329.

261 See overview by A Williams, *EU Human Rights Policies. A Study in Irony* (OUP, Oxford

demonstrated the function and need for a minimum of coherence of the international legal order to compensate for emerging gaps in other legal orders.[262] Although once an initial muddling of the formal and substantive sources of EU human rights law had been overcome, the ECJ relied on general principles of law or of EU law as the formal source of human rights in EU law; it substantively explicitly imported and implemented mostly faithfully international standards, at times affording a more extensive protection than that at international level.[263] This was especially the case for the ECHR, where the ECJ corrected the interpretation of EU fundamental rights where it had fallen below the ECHR minimum standard as it developed its casuistic human rights protection.[264] The EU Courts have used the principles of legitimate expectations and proportionality in a similar way as general principles.[265] Borrowing requires the legal order to have a certain degree of openness. Although 'borrowing' leaves much scope for autonomy and selectivity,[266] such openness is not self-understood. One might recall debates about the appropriateness of reasoning including non-domestic standards by courts in a comparative perspective, and more specifically, the US debate on whether the use of and reference to 'international' (including foreign) decisions is lawful under the US Constitution.[267]

2004) 145–157; P Alston (ed), *The EU and Human Rights* (OUP, Oxford 1999); de Witte (n 29); A Peters, 'Supremacy Lost: International Law Meets Domestic Constitutional Law' (2010) 3 *Vienna Online Journal on International Constitutional Law* 170.

[262] Other examples are the creation of an extraordinary complaint based on violation of ECHR rights of prisoners in Germany, in spite of the fact that generally the ECHR does not have direct effect in Germany, see F Hoffmeister, 'Germany: Status of European Convention on Human Rights in Domestic Law' (2006) 4 *International Journal of Constitutional Law* 722. Cf also the strong interpretation of Australian law in the light of the unincorporated Convention on the Rights of the Child by the High Court of Australia in *Minister of State for Immigration and Ethnic Affairs v Teoh* (1994–5) 104 International Law Reports 460; see also G Griffith and C Evans, 'Teoh and Visions of International Law' (2001) 21 *Australian Yearbook of International Law* 75.

[263] C-60/00 *Mary Carpenter v Secretary of State for the Home Department* [2002] ECR I-6279; C-109/01 *Secretary of State for the Home Department v Akrich* [2003] ECR I-9607; C-127/08 *Metock and Others v Minister for Justice, Equality and Law Reform* [2008] ECR I-6241.

[264] See for the protection of business premises under Art 8 ECHR Joined Cases 46/87 and 227/88 *Hoechst AG v Commission* [1989] ECR 2859, para 17 f which was followed by the ECtHR in no. 13710/88 *Niemietz v Germany* [1992] 16 EHRR 97, para 29 and led to a correction of the ECJ's previous interpretation in C-94/00 *Roquette Frères SA v Commission* [2002] ECR I-9011, para 29; similarly, in regard to the right not to incriminate oneself, contrast T-112/98 *Mannesmannröhren-Werke AG v Commission* [2001] ECR II-729, paras 66 f, 77 f and C-374/87 *Orkem v Commission* [1989] ECR 3282, para 30 with 10828/84 *Funke v France* [1993] 16 EHRR 297 and 43/1994/490/672 *Saunders v UK* [1996] 23 EHRR 313; Douglas-Scott (n 84) 640 ff, 649.

[265] Case 112/77 *Töpfer* [1978] ECR 1019; Case 120/86 *Mulder* [1988] ECR 2321; Case 114/76 *Bela-Mühle* [1977] ECR 1211; T Tridimas, *The General Principles of EU Law* (2nd edn, OUP, Oxford 2006) 141 ff and 251 f.

[266] See also Douglas-Scott (n 84) 655 ff.

[267] Cf *Atkins v Virginia*, 536 U.S. 304 (2002), where the majority held that the death penalty for mentally ill persons amounted to cruel and unusual punishment prohibited by the Eighth Amendment. The majority used views from other jurisdictions in their argument. This was heavily criticised by Justices Scalia, Thomas and Rehnquist. This led subsequently to a proposal of a resolution of the House of Representatives (no 372, introduced in 2007), intended to express 'that judicial determinations regarding the meaning of the Constitution of the United States should not be based on judgments, laws, or pronouncements of foreign institutions unless such foreign judgments,

10.3.2 Europeanisation of International Law

The large topic of Europeanisation of international law or the impact of EU law on international law merits a survey on its own and cannot be covered extensively in this chapter. It has several dimensions: export of European rules, enforcement of international norms through the EU, and influence over the enforcement and creation of international law more generally as an actor on the international plane.[268] The dimensions are not always neatly separable where European and international rules go in tandem. For example the accession criteria used by the EU for candidate countries (Copenhagen criteria[269]) are part both of the EU and of wider international law (CSCE Final Act of 1975). It shall suffice for our purposes to sketch out some of these dimensions by giving examples.

The EU has become a prolific exporter of norms, and in particular human rights norms, in its enlargement process,[270] and in its association agreements and the European Neighbourhood Policy[271] and trade agreements, incorporating human rights values and conditionality.[272] More indirectly it facilitated the pre-emptive reception of norms by states that remain outside the Neighbourhood, such as Ukraine.[273] One example in this regard are provisions to protect and to facilitate integration of the Roma contained in accession agreements with many Eastern European states.[274] Furthermore, it included human rights

---

laws, or pronouncements inform an understanding of the original meaning of the Constitution of the United States'. See also *Roper v Simmons* [2005] 125 S.Ct. 1183, 1200 (per Kennedy J); see also C McCrudden, 'Judicial Comparativism and Human Rights' in E Örücü and D Nelken (eds), *Comparative Law Handbook* (Hart, Oxford 2007) 371, 380 ff for further examples and critique.

268 F Hoffmeister, 'The Contribution of EU Practice to International Law' in M Cremona (ed) *Developments in EU External Relations Law* (OUP, Oxford 2008) 37; L Lazarus, N Ghanea, C Costello and K Ziegler, *The Evolution of Fundamental Rights Charters and Case Law: A Comparison of the European and the United Nations Systems* (European Parliament, Directorate General for Internal Policies 2011) at http://www.europarl.europa.eu/activities/committees/studies/download.do?language=en&file=34751.

269 Requiring 'stability of institutions guaranteeing democracy, the rule of law, human rights and respect for and protection of minorities, the existence of a functioning market economy as well as the capacity to cope with competitive pressure and market forces within the Union', Conclusions of the Presidency at the Copenhagen Council 1993, para 13.

270 Art 49 TEU.

271 The Commission describes the European Neighbourhood Policy as the 'Community rulebook' which 'is gradually being adopted across large parts of the European continent. Beyond this, the EU is emerging as a global rule maker', Commission Staff Working Document 'The External Dimension of the Single Market Review', SEC(2007)1519, 20–11-2007, p 5.

272 M Cremona, 'External Relations and External Competence: The Emergence of an Integrated Policy' in P Craig and G de Búrca (eds), *The Evolution of EU Law* (OUP, Oxford 1999) 137–175; M Cremona, 'Human Rights and Democracy Clauses in the EC's Trade Agreements' in N Emiliou and D O'Keefe (eds), *The European Union and World Trade Law* (John Wiley & Sons, Chichester 1996) 62; M Cremona, 'The European Neighbourhood Policy: More than a Partnership?' in M Cremona (ed) *Developments in EU External Relations Law* (OUP, Oxford 2008), ch 7; P Leino and R Petrov, 'Between "Common Values" and Competing Universals – The Promotion of the EU's Common Values through the European Neighbourhood Policy' (2009) 15 *European Law Journal* 654.

273 K Wolczuk, 'Integration without Europeanisation: Ukraine and its Policy towards the EU' (2004) *EUI Robert Schuman Centre for Advanced Studies Working Papers* No 2004/15.

274 E.g. Czech Republic, Romania, Bulgaria. For a critical view in regard to EU action for the protection of minorities post-accession see Williams (n 261) 89 f and more generally on an

in its development policy, taking a broad approach which reflects a willingness of the EU to involve itself in the definition and enforcement of human rights.[275] While general international legal instruments (Universal Declaration of Human Rights, UN Charter, ICCPR, ICESCR) are in the foreground,[276] the conventions of international humanitarian law as well as the 1948 Genocide Convention and the 1951 Refugee Convention as well as other treaties and customary law are used.[277] In a regional context, EU integration made an impact on the way the European Court of Human Rights (ECtHR) is willing to exercise judicial review over acts of the Member States. Thus, in *Bosphorus v Ireland*, the ECtHR – deplorably from the perspective of human rights protection – took back its review, mirroring a *Solange II*-type approach,[278] so long as the EU offered equivalent protection,[279] in effect applying a presumption of conformity of acts of the EU with the ECHR. In contrast, it is also due to a more progressive approach of the ECJ that the ECtHR changed its position in regard to transsexuals' right to marry.[280]

From an institutional perspective, the EU (previously EC) is party to many treaties,[281] especially in subject areas where it has exclusive competence. On the basis of its competences, the EU has developed a substantial international treaty practice, being a party to over 50 UN multilateral agreements.[282] Examples are WTO, the Kyoto Protocol, the *Codex Alimentarius* Commission in the Food and Agriculture Organization (FAO) framework, UNCLOS, and regional fisheries commissions such as the North West Atlantic Fisheries Organisation and the Indian Ocean Tuna Commission, to name but a view.[283] The Lisbon Treaty provides finally for a competence to accede to the ECHR.[284] Within the UN system, it mainly enjoys observer or special participant status due to the lack of special provisions in

---

internal-external incoherence 79 ff, 196 ff.

275 Williams (n 261) 51.

276 Commission Report on the Implementation of Measures Intended to Promote Observance of Human Rights and Democratic Principles (for 1994), COM(95) 191 final, p 17bis; Council Regulation (EC) No 975/1999 of 29 April 1999 laying down the requirements for the implementation of development cooperation operations which contribute to the general objective of developing and consolidating democracy and the rule of law and to that of respecting human rights and fundamental freedoms, [1999] OJ L120/1, preamb para 6.

277 Council Regulation 975/1999 (n 276) para 8.

278 See above, p 280.

279 No. 45036/98 *Bosphorus v Ireland* (2006) 42 EHRR 1, paras 152 ff, esp 154–156.

280 No. 28957/95 *Goodwin v UK* (2002) 35 EHRR 447, para 100; C-13/94 *P v S* [1996] ECR I-2143; C-117/01 *K.B. v National Health Service Pensions Agency and Secretary of State for Health* [2004] ECR I-541, para 33; Douglas-Scott (n 84) 640 ff, 646; J Callewaert, '"Unionisation" and "Conventionisation" of Fundamental Rights in Europe: The Interplay between Union and Convention Law and its Impact on the Domestic Legal System of the Member States' in J Wouters, A Nollkaemper and E de Wet (eds), *The Europeanisation of International Law: The Status of International Law in the EU and its Member States* (Asser Press, The Hague 2008) 109, 124 ff; Lazarus et al (n 268) 202 ff.

281 Membership is achieved either by a treaty special clause for the EU, e.g. ECHR, or by a general treaty clause allowing the participation of regional (economic) organisations, e.g. WTO.

282 McGoldrick (n 107) 189.

283 See Hoffmeister, 'Outsider or Frontrunner? Recent Developments under International and European Law on the Status of the European Union in International Organizsations and Treaty Bodies' (2007) 44 *Common Market Law Review* 41 ff for a comprehensive overview.

284 See Art 6(2) TEU and Art 59 ECHR, as amended by Protocol no 14 of 13 May 2004 (entered into force 1 June 2010).

the relevant treaties, e.g. WHO, UNESCO, UN General Assembly.[285] Beyond the UN it has participant status in the ICAO, OECD and the Council of Europe. It became a full member of the FAO in 1991 as the first UN specialised agency that made the necessary modifications.[286] While a more detailed study of the impact of the EU as an actor of international law is beyond this chapter,[287] it may be assumed that participation translates into influence and that the EU shapes international law as an actor on the international plane.[288] A very visible example of influencing the substance of international law were the EC Guidelines on the Recognition of New States in Eastern Europe and the Soviet Union and a Declaration on Yugoslavia[289] which provided a strong impulse to change the customary rules on recognition: the then prevailing declaratory theory of recognition did not accord any constitutive relevance to the recognition of a state. Decisive were the effectiveness of government over a defined territory and defined population.[290] The EC Guidelines provided new state practice and possibly *opino iuris* for a modification of the declaratory theory in the recognition of new states by allowing legitimacy criteria to compensate – at least to an extent – doubts about the full presence of one of the objective criteria of statehood.[291]

10.3.3 Evaluation

As sketched out above, international and EU law are intertwined in a complex manner with the EU being both at the norm-receiving and at the norm-generating end. While EU institutions and in particular the Courts take pains to convey an image of openness towards international law, the picture is more ambiguous from a perspective of detail. The EU seems more open to international law where it allows for an expansion of the scope of EU law in the domain of the Member States, in effect extending the *acquis communautaire* to nationals of third states, as can be seen in its approach to the widely available direct effect of trade and association agreements and decisions of association councils under an association agreement.[292] However, it is still reluctant to use international law as a limit on EU competences where the validity or legality of EU measures was raised by a conflict with international law by taking a more restrictive approach to direct effect, in particular the requirement of an individual right.[293] It has been acknowledged in principle in *Racke*

---

[285] Also ECOSOC and most UN Specialised Agencies, e.g. ILO; OSCE.

[286] For an overview see F Hoffmeister and PJ Kuiper, 'The Status of the EU at the United Nations: Institutional Ambiguities and Political Realities' in J Wouters, F Hoffmeister and T Ruys (eds), *The UN and the EU – An Ever Stronger Partnership* (Asser Press, The Hague 2006) 9–34.

[287] See in greater detail, for the participation of the EU in UN human rights treaty bodies, KE Smith, 'Speaking with One Voice? European Union Co-ordination on Human Rights Issues at the United Nations' (2006) 44 *Journal of Common Market Studies* 113 and KE Smith, 'The European Union at the Human Rights Council: Speaking with One Voice but Having Little Influence' (2010) 17 *Journal of European Public Policy* 224.

[288] In detail Hoffmeister and Kuiper (n 286); McGoldrick (n 107).

[289] Reprinted in (1991) 62 *British Yearbook of International Law* 559 or (1993) 4 *European Journal of International Law* 72.

[290] As codified in the Montevideo Convention on the Rights and Duties of States, 1933.

[291] See e.g. I Brownlie, *Principles of Public International Law* (7th edn, OUP, Oxford 2008) 86–88; J Crawford, *The Creation of States in International Law* (2nd edn, OUP, Oxford 2006) ch 1.

[292] Kaddous (n 160) 312; see also Kuijper (n 173) 97 f.

[293] Cf Peters (n 5) 63.

that international law can serve as a standard of the validity review of EU law.[294] But in practice we find an imbalance between a less frequently activated self-limiting dimension and a more readily applied dimension in which international law is used to expand the scope of EU law vis-à-vis the Member States which resembles similar imbalance in regard to the application of EU human rights within the EU legal order.[295] Incidentally, the decision of *Kadi and Al Barakaat* is laudable in that it reinforces the self-limiting function of human rights, in line with EU constitutionalism, although it is problematic with regard to its treatment of international law. Relying on limits that are derived from domestic standards may be linked to the still relatively early state of development of the EU legal system. But if the system reaches greater maturity, it could also overcome this inward-looking, paradoxical approach and take its role as norm-generator in international law seriously, a role that it has assumed in different contexts where it exports norms.

The Court is also guarding its own sphere of jurisdiction from other tribunals that have jurisdiction over the same matters as the EU Courts in mixed agreements,[296] a motivation that has been suspected to be behind its 'self-denial' of competence to accede to the ECHR without a Treaty amendment.[297] Furthermore, direct effect and scope given to international law more broadly depends on policy considerations in other respects. Subject matter is one. In the area of international human rights norms, the Court appears to be more receptive to international norms even where the EU is not a party to an instrument than in trade law (GATT/WTO) or internal market law.[298] This openness is in contrast to the dualist foreclosure of international human rights in *Kadi and Al Barakaat* where they would have been used as (or reinforced) for the validity review of an EU measure.

In the position as norm-receiver, the approach of the EU and the ECJ/CJEU to international law thus has mirrored increasingly the approach of its Member States to international law. At least with regard to the constitutional status of international treaties, these are mostly characterised by dualist or flexible approaches to their reception in national law. This is understandable at many levels. Firstly, Member States' common denominator in approaching international law is a plausible way of looking for their (fictitious) regulation of the issue in the founding treaties of the EU. Secondly, a greater openness of the EU to international law than that of the Member States might be perceived as opening the 'floodgates' to international law further than Member States do themselves. This argument rests on the combined effect of the principles of direct effect and supremacy in EU law when attached to international law.[299] On the one hand, these lead to a greater enforcement of international law through EU law. On the other hand, it is exactly this effect that complicates the picture and may be one of the reasons behind the greater reluctance of the Court to give direct effect to international norms. Recent

---

294 Above, pp 296 f.

295 Williams (n 261) 94 ff.

296 *Commission v Ireland (MOX plant)* (n 84); M Bronckers, 'The Relationship of the EC Courts with Other International Tribunals: Non-Committal, Respectful or Submissive?' (2007) 44 *Common Market Law Review* 601, 613; see also Douglas-Scott (n 84) 652 for the reluctance of the ECJ and ECtHR to explicitly discuss one another's case law.

297 Opinion 2/94 [1996] ECR I-1759.

298 See above, p 298 in regard to bilateral investment treaties.

299 Cf Peters (n 5) 34 f.

case law concerning direct effect seems to be characterised by a more cautious and selective approach. By relying more on the principle of interpretation instead of direct effect in its interaction with international law, the Court retains flexibility as to the effect of international law in the EU and Member States' legal order.[300] Thirdly, the statist ideal and focus on autonomy in the international dimension[301] provides an 'easy way out' of unwanted influences, a quick fix for what are perceived to be legitimate decisions in individual cases without regard for overall coherence – from the perspective of a quasi-domestic constitutional court. The Court, however, replicates a model that has become increasingly outdated even with regard to states. Although references to globalisation and international interdependence are prone to be clichéd, the Court's approach seems untimely and backward looking in its method and in its orientation towards a statist model of the EU where at the same time sub-national, regional and sectoral or functional constitutional orders are on the rise[302] and the sovereign state on the decline. One would hope that this might not be more than a temporary lack of creativity in the absence of a clear example. However, there are at least two disadvantages, one of them being immediate for the EU legal order.

The first disadvantage concerns the general impact on the international legal order. A severance might amount to an attempt by the EU to pull itself out of the realm of international law by its own bootstraps, an endeavour that is condemned to fail as it undermines international law more generally. Even if the EU legal order has become a special case of international law, it has not been able to sever itself completely by replacing its treaty-based ultimate rule of recognition through a legal revolution. Being still part of international law will mean it will also be likely to feel the repercussions of a general challenge to the compliance with international law.

The second disadvantage results from a possible direct challenge of the EU's legal order from the Member States. It is one thing to claim direct effect and supremacy of EU law on the basis of – albeit fictitious – consent of the Member States to the effectiveness of the 'new legal order of international law'. It is an altogether different matter to weaken the link to international law generally because it weakens at the same time the reliance on the consent of Member States. Weakening the roots in international law may therefore be the indirect route to a formal replacement of the EU's ultimate rule of recognition in the form of the consent by its Member States. Of course that does not mean that an alternative is readily available. One option would be a technocratic, functional acceptance of a working reality by the Member States which has become detached from its original treaty basis. The alternative is, however, for the EU to proclaim its original source of legitimation to lie not any more in states but in the peoples of Europe – a pattern that is not unprecedented.[303] Besides, considerations for the rule of law, fundamental rights and, one might add, democracy are already part of the constitutionalising rationale of the EU.

---

300 As demonstrated, e.g. in *Intertanko* (n 30).

301 As demonstrated, e.g. in *Kadi and Al Barakaat* (n 13) and *FIAMM and Fedon* (n 30).

302 Cf de Wet (n 4) 53, 75.

303 Reference to 'the peoples' and their 'intermediary', the European Parliament can already be found in Case 26/62 *NV Algemene Transport- en Expeditie Onderneming van Gend & Loos v Netherlands Inland Revenue Administration* [1963] ECR 1, being reminiscent of the direct legitimation of US federal power from 'We the people' (rather than the states).

10.4 THE LEGAL NATURE OF THE EU – SOME REFLECTIONS FROM THE PERSPECTIVE OF ITS RELATIONSHIP WITH INTERNATIONAL LAW

Let us turn from the more practical question of the interaction of EU and international law to the underlying theoretical question about the legal nature of the EU. Does the relationship between the EU and the international legal order add relevant factors to questions about the legal nature of the EU? It may be recapitulated that the disjunction between the more consent-based or (intergovernmental) institutional or foundational dimensions of the EU and its substantive legal order (more state-like) has given rise to a debate about what the EU is: is it still an international organisation or (already)[304] a state(-like) entity, or, as has been suggested as it is 'clearly' not a state, a *tertium*, a *sui generis* creature?[305] Much depends on what is, in the eye of the beholder, the relative weight given to formal as opposed to substantive characteristics of the EU on the one hand; and on the other hand what is the beholder's view with regard to the continued existence and future necessity of sovereignty and ultimate authority in the late[306] (or post-) national state or legal order, in which sovereignty is no longer exclusive and may be divided into functional and sectoral divisions of autonomy which cut across traditional spatial/territorial ones.[307] However, the emphasis on the 'autonomy' of the EU legal order, not just in the relationship with the Member States but in a dualist variety externally towards international law, follows a constitutionalising paradigm. This seems at least *prima facie* to reinforce a move away from an ordinary international organisation on a continuum towards a statist paradigm, thus supporting *sui generis* theories.

Why does the question about the nature of the EU matter?

It might be helpful at this point to stop and ask: why does the legal nature of the EU matter at all? Firstly, it might give us a better understanding of the aim (or the *finalité*) of the EU, and on the basis of this an understanding of where it stands today. The overall aim of the EU is all but clear today, or, in Maduro's words, although 'its body is well known, its soul is still to a large extent a mystery'.[308] There is no consensus about the destination of the journey. While federal intentions were expressed in the EEC's founding phase, and are still written into the Preambles of the TFEU and EU Treaty ('Determined to lay the foundations of an ever closer union among the peoples of Europe'[309]), they have largely been lost due to a lack of consensus. It is, therefore, even more important to pick up trends, to make them transparent and to be able to put them into context. A very

---

304 The linear progression to statehood, which frequently underlies the debate, may be questioned in itself.

305 Dougan (n 64) 132: 'developed form of international organisation which displays characteristics of an embryonic federation'.

306 Walker (n 50) 347.

307 Walker (n 50) 334, 345 f.

308 MP Maduro, *We the Court* (Hart, Oxford 1999) 8; similarly MP Maduro, 'The Importance of Being Called a Constitution: Constitutional Authority and the Authority of Constitutionalism' (2005) 3 *International Journal of Constitutional Law* 332, 340.

309 TFEU: see preamb para 1; TEU: preamb para 13 and Art 1(2) TEU.

practical reason why the question of the legal nature matters is its relevance for the interpretation, especially teleological interpretation, of the Treaty. The – at least perceived – clearer perspective in the early days of European integration might, therefore, explain at least the assertiveness of the ECJ in 'constitutionalising' the Community in its early days.

Secondly, the nature matters for the 'yardstick' question. By which yardstick – or standards – should we assess the EU? Linked to the yardstick question is the question of the legitimacy of the EU itself, which is reflected in the debate about its actual or alleged democratic deficit. By which standards can we assess the legitimacy of the EU? Does the EU need to be democratic and observe the rule of law? The question itself may not be an altogether innocent or disinterested one, either way. There is a tendency to use automatically national constitutionalism and models of democracy as the ideal form of constitutionalism, and of course in this comparison the EU will fall short in many ways.

Two responses may be made: firstly, the legitimacy benchmark for a state may not necessarily be very different from that for an international organisation anymore due to the increased powers of international organisations. Secondly, the state is not what it used to be (if it ever was). In other words, the question of legitimacy is not so closely linked any more to the formal characterisation of an entity as state or international organisation. In both scenarios, the complexity (and diversity) of legitimating features and processes has increased. It is not so much 'the nature' of the EU that matters as its impact, in particular on individuals.

For an international organisation, it is the substantive constitutionalisation that triggers the need for greater legitimacy through democratic accountability and observance of the rule of law. The EU is not unique in developing its own – constitutional – dynamics, a further argument against its *sui generis* nature.[310] Other international bodies have claimed to be autonomous to dissociate their rulings from general international law,[311] or have stepped up their direct impact on individuals, as targeted sanctions by the UN Security Council powerfully demonstrate. One could even say that constitutionalism of other international organisations is in some respects more 'developed', as mentioned above[312] with regard to the right and practical possibility to exit from an international organisation in a UN–EU comparison, where it may be said that this is less conceivable in the case of a universal, but less integrated, organisation like the UN.

At the same time, adjustments in regard to the classic legitimating features have to be made for the late national state, which derives legitimacy from a range of mechanisms. The late national state has been characterised poignantly as disaggregating both 'upward' (by international integration and a more diverse picture of actors on the international plane) and 'downward' (by various phenomena such as regionalisation, autonomy claims and again, the more diverse picture of actors).[313] As a consequence, sovereignty and ultimate authority as the traditional legitimating features in a hierarchically oriented

---

310 Walker (n 50) 347; Hartley (n 99) 70.

311 ICTY, case no. IT-96-21-A *The Prosecutor v Zejnil Delalic, Zdravo Mucic, Hazim Delic and Esad Landzo* (*Celebici* case), paras 9 f, 24 f.

312 See above p 291.

313 See e.g. A-M Slaughter, 'International Law in a World of Liberal States' (1995) 6 *European Journal of International Law* 503; A-M Slaughter, 'Disaggregated Sovereignty: Towards the Public Accountability of Global Government Networks' (2004) *Government and Opposition* 159.

legal order are much more dispersed even in states. Multilevel constitutionalist theories respond to this phenomenon:

> 'Multilevel constitutionalism' is meant to describe and understand the ongoing process of establishing new structures of government complementary to and building upon – while also changing – existing forms of self-organisation of the people or society. It is a theoretical approach to explaining how the European Union can be conceptualised as a matter and creature of its citizens as much as the Member States are a matter and creature of their respective citizens. The same citizens are the source of legitimacy for public authority at the European as well as – regarding their respective Member State – at the national level, and they are subject to the authority exercised at both levels. The European Constitution would, thus, be composed by the national constitutions and the European Treaties in a bi- or multi-level constitutional system.[314]

Ultimate authority in the form of a rule of recognition and notions of hierarchy of norms are still common at state level.[315] However, the concepts have weakened, if they ever adequately described authority even at state level, by notions of shared sovereignty, condominium and pluralism within states' legal orders.[316] Yet constitutionalist models are still useful in explaining and organising authority and in preventing it from becoming completely relative. Although the relevance of the foundational and institutional perspectives based on ultimate rules of recognition (such as consent to international treaties creating an international organisation) may weaken due to subsequent developments, they cannot be entirely ignored from a theoretical perspective which seeks coherence. Theoretical coherence requires some sort of rule of recognition and hierarchy to resolve conflicts of norms.

Finally, the view on the future necessity of conceptions of sovereignty, ultimate authority or hierarchy will also depend on the actual or perceived merits of alternative conceptions which focus on the impact of a legal order on an individual (substantive constitutionalism) rather than on its formal legal nature (foundational and institutional perspective).

The above does not provide a clear answer to the legal nature of the EU from the way the ECJ has positioned itself towards international law. Although the 'autonomy' and new legal order claim might imply that the ECJ considers the EU as a non-internationl legal order, the ECJ does not actually claim *not* to be an international organisation.[317] It merely claims certain special effects of its 'new legal order'. One may ask, however, whether claiming these effects not just to assert authority over the Member States but also against other international law makes the EU less of an international organisation – less of an *aequus inter pares*. However, the general situation of fragmentation of international law[318] again does not seem to make it special or *sui generis* in this regard either. Potentially any international organisation could be characterised as *sui generis*. Yet stressing the international law pedigree of EU above everything else misses the degree and intensity of

---

314 Pernice (n 73) 512.

315 Cf the classics by H Kelsen, *Reine Rechtslehre* (2nd edn, Deuticke, Vienna 1960 (reprint 1967)) and HLA Hart, *The Concept of Law* (2nd edn, Clarendon Press, Oxford 1994).

316 It could be said that in the UK constitutional order a conflict exists between the rule of law and the sovereignty of Parliament which is balanced in an equilibrium between Parliament not doing anything egregious and the courts exercising a certain restraint.

317 De Witte (n 9) 147.

318 Dunoff and Trachtman (n 89) 6 ff.

the constitutional account.[319] If, however, with legal pluralist theories we encounter a shift from form to substance (e.g. hierarchies resulting from the substance of norms as new organising principles, as will be detailed below[320]), this might in itself be an answer that would fit better with *sui generis* approaches – if not for the fact that the phenomenon applies also to traditional states. The answer to the question of the nature of the EU may therefore lie in a challenge to the question: it presumes a neatness of legal constructs that does not exist (any more).

10.5 WHAT PLURALISM? – THE CONFLICT SCENARIO: TOWARDS A NORMATIVE THEORY OF CONSTITUTIONAL PLURALISM

10.5.1 What Pluralism?

The relationship between the EU and its Member States has been described as heterarchical rather than hierarchical,[321] characterised by competing claims to ultimate authority. In other words, the relationship is characterised by legal (or constitutional) pluralism. The ECJ's *Kadi and Al Barakaat* decision reinforces a pluralist conception of the international legal order, while constitutionalising the European legal order. Further, the pluralist conception is confirmed not just by one case but by what seems to be more of a trend, looking at the attempts to remain or establish an 'autonomous' legal order made in *FIAMM and Fedon* and *Intertanko*,[322] or more restrictive or flexible approaches to direct effect and the interpretation in conformity with international law. So far, the picture seems utterly familiar. The assertion of autonomy based on a 'new legal order' strongly echoes the earlier establishment of the new legal order vis-à-vis the Member States. However, subsuming the relationship between international and EU law under a pluralist paradigm does not lead us any further. The question must be: what sort of pluralism? Here, so it seems, the ECJ has taken a much more uncompromising apodictically dualist stance, which is the reason why the ECJ's *Kadi and Al Barakaat* judgment has widely been considered to be the seminal decision about the relationship between EU law and international law.[323] Pluralism can imply simply competition and power struggle and result in disengagement between competing authorities or those claiming to be authorities (closed or disengaged pluralism – or simply fragmentation).[324] Or it can incorporate a notion of openness and engagement with other authorities (open or engaged pluralism). Disengaged pluralism puts the ball in the other side's court and might be considered a demonstration of strength. It is still pluralism

---

319 Walker (n 50) 322.

320 Section 10.5.

321 Cf Halberstam and Stein (n 28); N Krisch, 'The Case for Pluralism in Postnational Law' in G de Búrca and JHH Weiler (eds), *The Worlds of European Constitutionalism* (CUP, Cambridge forthcoming, LSE Working Paper 12/2009, p 2.

322 Above, n 30.

323 See above, n 16.

324 Cf M Nettesheim, 'U.N. Sanctions against Individuals – A Challenge to the Architecture of European Governance' (2007) 44 *Common Market Law Review* 567, 581 f.

rather than hegemony if competing claims to authority are recognised as such, at least in their own sphere. Engaged pluralism, in contrast, will need to persuade substantively. It may, therefore, be more likely where the relationship between competing authorities is more fragile or evenly balanced.[325] And it might lead to better reasoning.

In its relationship to the Member States, the ECJ has opted for open pluralism. The equilibrium reached in the struggle for supremacy led to a judicial dialogue over fundamental rights, in the course of which the EU legal order absorbed human rights from the constitutional traditions of its Member States and international law.[326] The EU may be described as 'benefiting' from pluralism in this relationship as it weakens the foundational, constitutional claim of the Member States. Although only time will allow us to cast a final judgment, it appears that in its external dimension, the ECJ opted for disengaged pluralism by relying simply on its 'basic constitutional charter'.[327] However, the question must be asked whether the recent case law that indicates a retreat of the ECJ from openness to international law can still be called a pluralistic response or a constitutional one. It can be described as pluralistic as it makes competing claims of authority. But because it seals off at the same time the EU legal space from international law, it is also constitutionalising its own legal order internally, strengthening its position in the pluralistic equilibrium with the Member States on a continuum towards constitutionalisation in the internal dimension. Pluralism thus can be shown to be the tool of the (initially) weak actor to potentially *gradually* achieve a revolution in regard to the rule of recognition through creeping constitutionalisation. That could imply that pluralism is self-defeating.

However, it is not by extrapolating the 'new' and 'autonomous' legal order from the relationship with the Member States to the relationship with international law generally that is novel and concerning. The leap lies in the simultaneous restrictive approach to international law taken by this (not so) 'new legal order' which does not fit with the ECJ's earlier approaches to international law. It created a logical paradox, as aptly described by Eeckhout writing in 2004 before the ECJ's *Kadi and Al Barakaat* decision which generally reflects how the relationship between EU and international law was seen then.

> It would be hardly appropriate for EU law to develop an attitude of hostility towards other international treaties or agreements, which, of course, do not create a new legal order, but and nonetheless in essence identically legal instruments. On the other hand, precisely because of the distinction between the EU's own new legal order and classic international law, it is appropriate that direct effect should not be automatic, and that there may be agreements which in the light of the nature and structure, cannot produce such effect.[328]

It cannot be denied that this decision, as has been shown, fits into a trend of greater 'confidence' and assertion of the EU legal order in respect to general international law. However, not all hope is lost (yet). The *Kadi and Al Barakaat* case also has a strong

---

[325] Some might consider only the open version of pluralism as true pluralism, cf Halberstam and Stein (n 28) 58–60.

[326] See above 10.2.1, pp 278 ff.

[327] *Kadi and Al Barakaat* (n 13) para 281. Because of the ECJ's dualistic approach, opinions are divided over the question whether it left the door open for a *Solange* type dialogue, cf Ziegler (n 9) 299 f.

[328] Eeckhout (n 81) 301.

contextual element. Leaving tactical calculations about the constitutionalising effect in the EU's relationship with the Member States aside, the ECJ has, by asserting its own constitutional standards, taken what must have appeared to be the most economical and solid reasoning for the outcome in the individual case. It cannot be criticised for the short-term outcome from a casuistic perspective. The substantive and procedural human rights mechanisms at international level and, more specifically, the UN Security Council sanctions mechanism, were clearly deficient. Nevertheless, it can be criticised for a disregard of the precedential effect of the decision as well as the wider impact of this disjunctive reasoning. As pointed out by de Wet, unilateralism and the untimely insistence on statist paradigm may lead to the outcome that the 'fragile international community glued together and guided by a core of fundamental values will be lost' and with it a framework that binds together post-national political decision making.[329]

10.5.2 The Conflict Scenario: Towards a Normative Theory of Constitutional Pluralism

Even with a more positive view on fragmentation,[330] the question is raised how conflicts are best resolved. In the following, a model based on normative hierarchies both in international and national constitutional law (and the constitutional law of the EU) will be sketched out. It will be founded on a duty to engage with general international law and on a normative argument from what may be called a universal core of substantive constitutional standards.

Conflicts of norms may arise substantively as a result of inconsistent rules or inconsistent interpretation of rules and procedurally/institutionally through the multiple exercise of jurisdiction:[331]

- *Inconsistent rules*: different international fora, such as the EU and the WTO or UN, may each apply their own rules which might be inconsistent;[332]
- *Inconsistent interpretation*: different tribunals applying the same *rule*, but interpreting it differently;[333] another variant is the interpretation of rules from other regimes by different tribunals, raising the question of their relationship, in particular whether one of them has *lex specialis* character;[334]

---

329 De Wet (n 4) 76.

330 Cf M Koskenniemi and P Leino, 'Fragmentation of International Law? Postmodern Anxieties' (2002) 15 *Leiden Journal of International Law* 553; R Higgins, 'The ICJ, the ECJ, and the Integrity of International Law' (2003) 53 *International and Comparative Law Quarterly* 1; B Simma, 'Fragmentation in a Positive Light' (2003–4) 25 *Michigan International Law Journal* 845.

331 Dunoff and Trachtman (n 89) 6 ff.

332 E.g. the Bananas dispute, or the divergence over targeted sanctions.

333 E.g. the different interpretation of the rules of attribution in the law of state responsibility by the ICJ and the ICTY, see *Prosecutor v Tadic*, Case No. IT-94-1-A, Judgment of 15 July 1999, para 145 on the one hand, and *Military and Paramilitary Activities in and against Nicaragua (Nicaragua v United States of America)* [1986] ICJ Reports 14; *Case concerning the Application of the Convention on the Prevention and Punishment of the Crime of Genocide (Bosnia and Herzegovina v Serbia and Montenegro)* [2007] ICJ Reports 91, paras 404, 406 on the other hand.

334 E.g. no. 10328/83 *Belilos v Switzerland*, Series A 132, departing from the rules on reservations in the VCLT for human rights treaties. See in this context also General Comment 24.

- *Multiple fora of adjudication*: different tribunals are the institutional and practical side of fragmentation, in particular, through interpretation.

Resolution of conflicts in the different dimensions may occur either in an institutional or in a substantive way.[335] The institutional dimension, building on formal hierarchies, is even weakening at national level, as described above. At international level institutional hierarchies are very little developed, and indeed might not be preferable over a pluralist system that provides more flexibility for future developments and is more in line with the evolutionary nature of international law. However, substantive hierarchies or hierarchies of norms and principles which cut across different levels of governance would be able to provide a framework to preserve a minimum of coherence. Coherence is not only of formalistic relevance for lawyers to be able to overcome 'chaos' readily accepted by pluralism. A minimum of coherence is necessary to maintain the force of law as law, among other things.[336] It thus goes to the very question of the binding force of law, and international law in particular. In the light of this, the International Law Commission's Report on Fragmentation of International Law[337] has identified various existing methods of how to resolve conflicts of norms and thus to strengthen unity of international law. Unity can be enhanced not only through form, but also through substance,[338] namely: prioritisation (e.g. *lex posterior* and *lex specialis* rules), hierarchisation (the existence of *ius cogens* and of the distinction of primary and secondary norms[339]) and interpretation that is oriented towards maintaining coherence.[340] Theories of legal pluralism tend to focus on fragmentation (or diversity) and therefore tend to neglect 'the desirability or possibility of bringing hierarchy to the resulting (dis)order.'[341] These are all substance-oriented mechanisms. In the following, an attempt will be made to sketch out how engaged or open substantive constitutional pluralism might reduce the relative nature characteristic of pluralist theories.

Substantive hierarchies of norms are already reflected in the international legal order, most notably in the concept of *ius cogens*. Those norms are capable of being reinforced and informed by core values which are present both in international law and in national

---

335 Besson speaks of material and formal constitutions of IL: S Besson, 'Whose Constitution(s)? International Law, Constitutionalism and Democracy' in JL Dunoff and JP Trachtman (eds), *Ruling the World? Constitutionalism, International Law and Global Governance* (CUP, Cambridge 2009) 381, 389 ff, but pointing to the insufficiency (at p 406), from the perspective of democratic legitimacy, of only substantive constitutions.

336 See above, p 275.

337 M Koskenniemi (Special Rapporteur), Fragmentation of International Law: Difficulties Arising From the Diversification and Expansion of International Law. Report of the Study Group of the International Law Commission, UN Doc. A/CN.4/L.682 (13 April 2006).

338 Paulus (n 4) 88.

339 Dupuy (n 8) 215-245. The ILC, and especially one of its Rapporteurs on State Responsibility, Roberto Ago, dedicated extensive study to the distinction of primary and secondary norms in the long and complicated drafting process of the Articles of State Responsibility, see Report of the International Law Commission on the work of its twenty-first session, 2 June – 8 August 1969, paras 80-81, U.N. Doc. A/CN.4/220 (1969); KS Ziegler, *Fluchtverursachung als völkerrechtliches Delikt* (Duncker & Humblot, Berlin 2002) 82.

340 Paulus (n 4) 85.

341 Dunoff and Trachtman (n 89) 34; Cf Walker (n 50) 337–339.

(or EU) constitutional law, where they are likely to be more developed. In that way, a common core of norms may be identifiable and evolve which is accepted to be of prime importance. In tandem with a framework derived from secondary norms (such as about the formation and violation of norms, e.g. the law of treaties and state responsibility), such a core may serve as a skeleton of coherence for a fragmented international order.[342] It may serve as a basis for a unified discourse that draws from norms and values across the different constitutional 'sites' or 'entities' and through the mechanisms of international law becomes such a (rudimentary) framework – from which the practice of states draws and into which it feeds back, and thus reinforces it.[343] A unified discourse is a precondition for the common core of norms to be considered of special importance.

Of course it will be difficult to identify the precise content of a common core of or converging constitutional principles. Even for *ius cogens,* there is no consensus as to the scope of the concept beyond an accepted minimum of the prohibition of the use of force, genocide, the most fundamental rules of human rights and humanitarian law and the right to self-determination. In particular, the extent to which international environmental law rules or human rights in a wider sense form (already) part of *ius cogens* is debated.[344] Beyond *ius cogens*, i.e. in the original domain of national constitutional law, it is even more problematic to clearly identify what norms or principles would belong to a common core of constitutional principles.[345] Paulus considers democracy, the rule of law, the principle of separation of powers, protection of basic rights of states (analogous to a federal system) and potential for equality and solidarity rights[346] as the most basic principles of domestic constitutional orders which might be transferable to the international level.[347] Whatever their precise content and scope at the level of detail may be, human rights, the rule of law and the principle of democracy reflected in many of the world's constitutions would currently be counted among them.[348] They are numerously codified and invoked at domestic and international level and indeed also across levels[349] as legitimating principles,[350] and they are increasingly required by or from international institutions such as the ECJ or the Security Council. These processes attest to a deformalisation of law in favour of more informal substantive cross-fertilisation between legal orders from the national to the international and vice-versa, and also between different

---

342 Paulus (n 4) 88; Walter (n 32) 194 ff; Dunoff and Trachtman (n 89); de Wet (n 43); eadem (n 4); Kumm (n 43) 272 ff; Peters (n 36) 599 f.

343 Walker (n 50) 357; Peters (n 36) 597 f.

344 See in detail A Orakhelashvili, *Peremptory Norms in International Law* (OUP, Oxford 2006) 50 ff, in particular 53 ff, 65 ff; A Orakhelashvili, 'The Acts of the Security Council: Meaning and Standards of Review' (2007) 11 *Max Planck Yearbook of United Nations Law* 143, 181 ff.

345 Cf the variance between the authors quoted in n 342.

346 Paulus (n 4) 106.

347 Paulus (n 4) 92 f, 101, 105.

348 Peters (n 36) 601; W van Gerven, 'Two Twin-Principles of EU Law: Democracy and Accountability, Consistency and Convergence' in U Bernitz, J Nergelius and C Cardner (eds), *General Principles of EC Law in a Process of Development* (Wolters Kluwer, Alphen aan den Rijn 2008) 25, 30 ff counts democracy and the rule of law among the general principles of EU law.

349 See in greater detail Peters (n 261).

350 Cf Art 6 TEU and the need for restrictions to be founded on what is necessary in a democratic society in, e.g. Art 8(2) ECHR.

national legal orders.[351] For example, the widely called-for reduction of the democratic deficit at EU level attests to the transfer of the discourse about the principle of democracy to an international level. Furthermore, phenomena cutting across levels of governance, such as the democratic representation of the peoples of Europe through the European Parliament or inter-parliamentary cooperation of national parliaments point to the emergence of structures which are both international and cutting across levels. The protection of human rights both internationally and domestically and in the EU demonstrates most strongly that a common value lies in the principle of limited government and the rule of law. This has been powerfully demonstrated by the ECJ in *Kadi and Al Barakaat*. It not only held that 'any derogation from the principles of liberty, democracy and respect for human rights and fundamental freedoms enshrined in Articles 6(1) EU as a foundation of the Union'[352] was constitutionally prohibited. It also affirmed the hierarchically higher status of these principles within the EU legal order, representing a non-derogable core of constitutional foundations.[353] Furthermore, a discourse based on international constitutional values would also reflect the shift from actor-centrism focused on states of the international legal order to subject-matter orientation[354] and be able to accommodate the phenomenon of non-state actors, amongst them individuals, under international law.

How then should the existence of substantive normative hierarchies, evidenced both at domestic and international level, influence the resolution of conflicts between these levels and fragmented sectoral or regional international laws? Point of departure in a normatively charged pluralist system must be that each player is clear about their own hierarchy of values, such as democracy, the rule of law, dignity, non-discrimination, diversity, multiculturalism, etc., as these are the basis of the 'terms of engagement'.[355]

The first and foremost rule of an open pluralism based on a substantive hierarchy of norms would be a requirement to genuinely and seriously engage with the conflicting norm and not to ignore it or shut it out. For example, instead of invoking the artificial statist notion of autonomy of the EU legal order based on a dualist conception, the ECJ should embrace its responsibility, not just as a constitutional actor but also as an international actor, to engage with other rules of international law and thus enforce and develop them further. This responsibility may be considered to be particularly strong considering the foundational roots of the EU in international law. How this responsibility is discharged could be left to the quasi-constitutional entity, ranging between direct effect, interpretation in conformity to mere 'taking into account'. Instead of taking a sectoral, level or autonomy approach, a substance- or value-oriented approach should be taken

---

351 HH Koh, 'The 1998 Frankel Lecture: Bringing International Law Home' (1998) 35 *Houston Law Review* 625; Peters (n 261). This is well illustrated by the ECtHR: 'Admittedly, these case-law principles laid down by the Convention institutions concern the domestic legislation of States party to the Convention . . ., the Court cannot see any major obstacles to their application to the acts of an international legal order, like the one concerned in the present case', nos 6422/02 and 9916/02 *Segi and Gestoras Pro-Amnistiia and Others v 15 EU Member States*.

352 *Kadi and Al Barakaat* (n 13) para 303.

353 Ziegler (n 9) 297. It will be interesting to see whether the ECJ will implement the implied hierarchy of Treaty provisions under EU law in the domestic dimension.

354 As aptly pointed out by Walter (n 32) 194, 203.

355 Cf M Kumm, 'Constitutional Democracy Encounters International Law: Terms of Engagement' in S Choudhry (ed) *The Migration of Constutional Ideas* (CUP, Cambridge 2007) 256.

to resolving normative conflicts, i.e. less reliance on the level of regulation (hierarchy) or formalisation of a rule and more focus on a problem-oriented approach based on substantive values existing across sectors or levels. For example in a case of conflict between an international (or internationally derived) norm and a 'domestic' norm, instead of relying on the constitutional autonomy and exclusively domestic standards of review, such as the rule of law and human rights, a more open pluralism could engage with and rely upon the presence of the same values at international level together with the domestic (EU) standards.

More specifically, using the *Kadi and Al Barakaat* case as an example for this approach, the ECJ could and should have reached the same result, that is, an annulment of the EC Regulation implementing UN Security Council sanctions violating fundamental rights. But instead of relying on the autonomous legal order and in effect taking a dualist position, the Court could have (a) acknowledged the international obligation more clearly and (b) relied on the values of fundamental rights and the rule of law not just internally (as it did), but by relying on the unity of these principles in international law and, for that matter, Member States' domestic legal orders from which it has drawn so heavily in the context of human rights, as well as its own – EU – legal order, as summarised in the following passage:

> [A]ccording to settled case-law, fundamental rights form an integral part of the general principles of law whose observance the Court ensures. For that purpose, the Court draws inspiration from the constitutional traditions common to the Member States and from the guidelines supplied by international instruments for the protection of human rights on which the Member States have collaborated or to which they are signatories. In that regard, the ECHR has special significance[356]

Because of the open pluralism of the EU in regard to the substance of EU human rights, the Court would need to develop its current approach to human rights only a little further by incorporating international standards and their hierarchical position in regard to other international law, if it needed to rely on them where international law is directly or indirectly reviewed. Thus, such a value-oriented approach would still open up the scope for judicial review if EU Treaty law gave primacy to the UN Charter and Security Council Resolutions which – arguably – would have been the correct interpretation of the interplay of Art 103 of the UN Charter and Art 351 TFEU (ex Art 307 EC).

One might object that this reasoning would have been a much bolder move by the Court because it would have been a more direct conflict with the UN Security Council. Thus it might be perceived as more damaging to its authority than the reliance on the purely domestic nature of the EU implementing regulation. However, considered from a substantive perspective and not from a purely formalistic angle of different legal orders, the conflict at issue *was* between the normative force of Security Council Resolutions and fundamental rights of EU law. Nevertheless, the ECJ avoided the conflict by exclusively focusing on its own legal order.[357] It is therefore doubtful whether the technical

---

[356] *Kadi and Al Barakaat* (n 13) para 283.

[357] Cf Y Shany, *Regulating Jurisdictional Relations between National and International Courts* (OUP, Oxford 2007) 197 f for an analysis that this is in effect an 'avoidance' tactic.

difference of an open versus an indirect conflict would make a significant difference in regard to the degree of upholding or undermining the authority of the Security Council. It would, however, have made a difference for the authority of international law more widely, which arguably is more important than the institutional authority, even of the UN Security Council, in an individual case. The Court cast doubt over the status of general rules of international law and customary international law in the EU legal order. It even rejected a substantive hierarchy or value-based approach based on *ius cogens* in excluding already the applicability of *ius cogens* in the EU legal order (in contrast to the CFI), which could have supported its reasoning. Whether *ius cogens* is a special kind of customary international law or a special kind of general principle – or both – such an exclusion of even *ius cogens* norms from the EU legal order undermines the authority of international law and therefore the observance of international law more widely. As far as general principles are concerned it is outright contradictory with the EU's own approach to general principles as transcending the boundaries of legal orders.

This model does not deny that there will be conflicts with norms that are perceived to be so fundamental that a legal order will want to draw a line and is unable to adopt a harmonising interpretation.[358] However, it does not deny this possibility because the strengthening and developing of international law will result from the engagement, even if the outcome is not to follow a Security Council Resolution, on the basis that it is, in the eyes of the adjudicatory body, in fundamental conflict with the rule of law both at international and at 'domestic' level. The situation of a 'domestic' court having to rely exclusively on domestic norms would in all likelihood be a very rare last resort where supporting international rules may (yet) be unavailable. In the case of a court acting at international level, such an approach undermines not only the normative force of international law but also its own foundations.

Why should international (and national) courts apply this model?

But what's in it for the 'domestic' entity, the EU, *in casu*, a realist might ask? Why should the CJEU/ECJ not let considerations of procedural efficiency in regard to discharging a judgment in an individual case prevail over consciousness and responsibility of its wider impact, as indeed is more prominent with national courts?[359] In the case of the CJEU/ECJ a direct answer can be given from the Treaty: the Court has a constitutional responsibility to contribute to the 'strict observance and the development of international law'.[360] Beyond that, the legitimacy-enhancing effect of the model should be a further motivation. International law and domestic law, and, for our purposes, EU law, are in many ways engaged in the same processes and aims as general international law.[361] Cross-references

---

[358] Also Peters (n 261) 195.

[359] Cf the call for an informed and mutually respectful approach of international tribunals with regard to fragmentation, R Higgins, 'The ICJ, the ECJ, and the Integrity of International Law' (2003) 53 *International and Comparative Law Quarterly* 1, 19 f.

[360] Article 3(5) EU, see above, p 293. In a similar vein see the German Federal Constitutional Court in its *Görgülü* decision (n 193), para 36: 'The Basic Law is intended to achieve comprehensive commitment to international law, cross-border cooperation and political integration in a gradually developing international community of democratic states under the rule of law.'

[361] GL Neuman, 'Human Rights and Constitutional Rights: Harmony and Dissonance'

to one another are substantively legitimacy-enhancing in the domestic legal order. This becomes particularly visible in the protection of human rights. National human rights feed into the interpretation of international human rights and into the formation of customary international human rights law. International human rights, through doctrines of the margin of appreciation or their functional equivalents,[362] are open, within limits, for national human rights law; and national courts have become increasingly receptive not just of international but also of foreign human rights at least as a resource[363] for a legitimacy-enhancing argument.[364]

Enhancing legitimacy is not pure rhetoric. Cross-referencing to other legal orders is an inherent or internal mechanism of checks and balances which recognises that domestic constitutionalism is not the be all and end all. As the history of the 20th century has shown, national constitutional law should not be idealised either;[365] a result of its shortcomings were external checks and balances, such as in the founding of the UN, international human rights instruments and ultimately the EU itself. As internal struggles over minority rights, identity politics and their constitutional status (autonomy, independence) show today, constitutional tensions continue to exist.[366] Furthermore, legitimacy derived from international value discourse is able to compensate for the lack of 'linear' legitimacy derived from an ultimate rule of recognition, a benefit that might be assumed to be of particular attraction for the EU:

> it is precisely in order to prevail in this multi-dimensional world of overlapping boundaries and undercutting claims, and so also to ground or consolidate their internal legitimacy, that they typically seek a meta-authorisation – a deeper set of normative arguments for their position than would be required if, as in the one-dimensional state world, their constitutional constituency and mandate was purely self-contained.[367]

In sum, the ECJ missed an opportunity to shape the international legal system: although a tactical response and engagement on the international level – by the UN Security Council – might be the result in the individual case, it missed the opportunity of triggering more than a tactical response: namely the affirmation and development of international norms. By relying on merely domestic human rights, at the very least it does not positively affirm

---

(2003) 55 *Stanford Law Review* 1863; G de Búrca and O Gerstenberg, 'The Denationalization of Constitutional Law' (2006) 47 *Harvard International Law Journal* 243; de Wet (n 4) 74.

362 D Harris, M O'Boyle and C Warbrick, *Law of the European Convention on Human Rights* (OUP, Oxford 2009) 11–14; C-36/02 *Omega Spielhallen- und Automatenaufstellungs-GmbH v Oberbürgermeisterin der Bundesstadt Bonn* [2004] ECR I-9609.

363 And sometimes more, cf, for example, Art 39(1)(a) and (b) of the South African Constitution of 1996 formalised the requirement of using international law in the interpretation of constitutional rights in requiring that courts '(b) must consider international law; and (c) may consider foreign law'. See also Art 37(4)(b)(i) limiting a constitutional state of emergency by reference to international law.

364 C McCrudden, 'A Common Law of Human Rights? Transnational Judicial Conversation on Constitutional Rights' (2000) 20 *Oxford Journal of Legal Studies* 499, 502 ff; C McCrudden, 'Judicial Comparativism and Human Rights' in E Örücü and D Nelken (eds), *Comparative Law Handbook* (Hart, Oxford 2007) 371, 376.

365 See in this regard also Kumm (n 43) 318.

366 Kumm (n 43) 318 f.

367 Walker (n 50) 356.

opinio iuris in regard of the content of international human rights law and its status as customary law, although a ray of stimulus may result through the vehicle of general principles of law. Affirming a parallel rule of customary international human rights law would contribute to more powerful restraints on other international actors than the current tactical pre-emption by such actors which might result from a *Solange* paradigm – where it is doubtful whether the ECJ intended it at all in the first place. It can only be hoped that the ample interaction between international and EU law and the mutual influence will be reclaimed by the EU as something positive in the future and be to the mutual benefit of all three legal orders involved, or, in the words of Alain Pellet:

> On peut espérer que ce movement ira en s'accélérant et qu'il en résultera une 'banalisation' croissante du droit communautaire du fait de la 'communautarisation' progressive du droit international. Ce serait le signe réconfortant d'une meilleure intégration de la société internationale.[368]

[368] Pellet (n 8) 269.

11 International law, international politics and ideology

Alexander Orakhelashvili

11.1 INTRODUCTION

The interaction between legal and political arguments is based on the premise that while international legal science draws its data from the rules agreed upon by and binding on States, international relations theory has no such point of reference. This chapter is aimed both at taking stock of doctrinal approaches, and their reappraisal with a view to streamlining the argument on how the relationship between legal and political factors should be understood. This aim requires adopting an interdisciplinary focus, especially as the theory of international relations is (sub)consciously premised on the structural and sociological foundations of international law. The inter-disciplinary analysis in terms of mapping the joint discipline and constructing joint research agenda is legitimate and useful.[1]

The purpose of interdisciplinary analysis is to evaluate the working of the legal system and critically assess its merits. Social and political scientists are supposed to examine how crucial international law is for the existence of international society, how it may shape and transform this society, and how it influences the conduct of States. International relations theory does with international law what sociological and critical methods of legal science do in relation to the study of national legal systems. International relations theory has indeed developed 'instrumentalist' and 'normative' optics, the former allegedly underestimating the impact of shared norms on State behaviour, being challenged by the latter. The fundamental question theories pose is whether States care for reputation, or only calculation of interest and power really counts. This phenomenon could be viewed as a circular process of interaction where, in Keohane's words, 'interests shape institutions, which affect beliefs, including reputations, which in turn affect interests'.[2] But the further question is how these processes affect the content and applicability of established rules of law.

Social and political sciences have found a number of methods to examine the socio-political context of international law. The regime theory concentrates on the impact of international regimes, including international law regimes but also more informal

---

[1] The need for inter-disciplinary analysis has been affirmed by A-M Slaughter, A Tulumello and S Wood, 'International Law and International Relations Theory: A New Generation of Inter-Disciplinary Scholarship', 92 *AJIL* (1998), 367 at 369, 384, emphasising that such analysis focuses on converging themes such as international governance and social construction, and the range of options through which policy science focuses on international legal process.

[2] R Keohane, 'International Relations and International Law: Two Optics', 38 *Harvard ILJ* (1997), 487 at 494, 500.

political arrangements, on the conduct of States and development of international relations. Regimes are defined as 'sets of implicit principles, norms, rules, and decision-making procedures around which actors' expectations converge'.[3] The regime theory assesses how interests and power interact with institutions and thus covers part of the ground also addressed by the scholarship of international law. More recently, the interdisciplinary project of 'legalisation' has been developed, which examines international institutions in terms of the degree of their legalisation and identifies three criteria for determining the level thereof: obligation (legal commitment), precision (degree of clarity of rules in what they require, authorise or proscribe), and delegation (authority to apply rules and resolve disputes). Depending on that, the degree of legalisation of different international institutions and practices, ranging from the WTO dispute settlement framework to more informal balance of power arrangements, is ranked as high, moderate or low.[4] The degree of legalisation is particularly examined in the example of international tribunals, in terms of access to courts and impact of their decisions.[5]

Against this background, the legal reasoning proper focuses on what the legal regulation is, whether it has been properly established through its recognised sources, and how it applies to facts. As Oppenheim stated a century ago, 'the first and chief task is the exposition of existing recognised rules of international law – whether we approve or condemn it, whether we want to retain, abolish or replace it'. Rules can be criticised but even if supported by reason, equity and justice, they would not be legal rules unless expressed in the recognised sources such as treaties and custom.[6] As Simma and Paulus observe, 'moral and political considerations are not alien to law but part of it. However, formal sources remain the core of international legal discourse.' Lawyers' role is not to facilitate the decision-maker's dilemma between legal and political aspects of the issue, but to clarify the legal side of things.[7]

Interdisciplinary analysis requires a joint effort by scholars of international law and international relations, on the condition that each side understands the points of intersection of their own discipline with the other discipline. This is essentially different from arguing that the categories and requirements of one discipline could overtake those of the other. The key to this interdisciplinary analysis relates to identifying the fundamentals of the international society, its organising ideas, factors that cause and influence the existence of law and order in the international society, and the factors that influence the conduct of States, such as law, power, legitimacy, hierarchy and hegemony. Despite the abundance of writings, there is no contribution yet written that would assess the merit of all relevant doctrinal approaches by reference to the structural and systemic

---

3 S Krasner, 'Structural Changes and Regime Consequences', in Krasner (ed.), *International Regimes* (1983), 2.

4 K Abbott, R Keohane, A Moravscik, A-M Slaughter, D Snidal, 'The Concept of Legalization', 54 *International Organization* (2000), 401, 406.

5 R Keohane, A Moravscik, A-M Slaughter, 'Legalized Dispute Resolution: Interstate and Transnational', 54 *International Organization* (2000), 457.

6 L Oppenheim, 'The Science of International Law: Its Task and Method', 2 *AJIL* (1908), 313 at 314–315, 318, 329.

7 B Simma and A Paulus, 'The Responsibility of Individuals for Human Rights Abuses in Internal Conflict: A Positivist View', 93 *AJIL* (1999), 302 at 307–308.

characteristics of international law, which underlines the distinct originality of this contribution. This contribution is mainly about discourse and reasoning and how legal and policy arguments interact in this process, as opposed to the exposition of particular aspects of international law. The latter are adverted to for the sake of illustrating or verifying the patterns of discourse.

Theory of international law sometimes reflects the ideological perceptions and preferences as to the nature and (re)organisation of international society, and focuses on what international law should be, or is perceived to be, if it is to respond to those ideological perceptions and preferences, as opposed to what it actually is, being agreed upon and accepted by States. The aim of theory should be to (re)conceptualise and generalise the rules and patterns of international law, and closely relate to State practice. If divorced from these, theory becomes little more than the advancement of one's own ideology and perception.

A down-to-earth vision of theory is accepted by international relations scholars. According to Hans Morgenthau, theory must be consistent with facts and within itself, in order to bring order and meaning to a mass of phenomena, and reveal the rational essence in foreign policy.[8] There are inherent limits on what theory can deliver: 'even if a large-scale theory can be developed and appropriately tested, its predictions will be rather gross'. Empirical work holds the key to multiple issues.[9]

International relations theory attempts to identify laws focusing on variables and generating expectations through their repetition. Theories are sometimes understood as collections of such laws, but the difference between the two is that of degree not of kind. Another approach points to the qualitative difference between laws and theories, the former being identified through observation and the latter based on invented notions. Theoretical analysis alone does not prove anything. Theories are not sets of laws; they only explain laws. 'Laws remain, theories come and go.'[10] Any theory, as Waltz explains, 'leaves some things aside to concentrate on others', and makes predictions at the level of its generality.[11]

For the purposes of this analysis, we need to focus on international relations categories, such as power, interest and so on only to the extent necessary for grasping the interaction between legal and political factors. International relations reasoning has limits: it does not attempt duplicating the legal method, and thus generally eschews specific normative recommendations.[12] The value of pronouncements in international relations theory as to the nature and content of international law shall be judged by reference to the reflection in those pronouncements of the fundamental systemic and structural factors by which international law is shaped and guided. International relations theory can be very useful in

---

[8] H Morgenthau, *Politics among Nations: The Struggle for Power and Peace* (1948), 3.

[9] R Keohane, 'Theory in World Politics: Structural Realism and Beyond', in Keohane (ed.), *Neorealism and Its Critics* (1986), 188–189.

[10] K Waltz, 'Laws and Theories', in Keohane (ed.), *Neorealism and Its Critics* (1986), 27–28, 32–33.

[11] K Waltz, 'A Response to My Critics', in Keohane (ed.), *Neorealism and Its Critics* (1986), 344.

[12] KW Abbott, 'International Relations Theory, International Law, and the Regime Governing Atrocities in Internal Conflicts', 93 *AJIL* (1999), 361 at 362.

assessing sociologically the efficiency and performance of the international legal system, but its utility is very limited if it would attempt to come up with an alternative view of what international law is and what its rules require.

Just as in legal science, the positivist approach separating subject from object and focusing on the systemic connection between cause and consequence is also adopted in international relations theory.[13] Such positivism attempts to grasp the reality on the ground, formulating technically useful knowledge to help make predictions; is value-neutral; and can be tested through external evidence. But according to another approach, positivism can be committed to an ideology of its own and is premised on assumptions positivist science cannot question.[14] Even if this were the case, the utility of positivism could still not be questioned, because if anything can be questioned anytime and anywhere, there would be no firm foundation for a scientific analysis, and any subjective perception would be as good as focusing on objectively observable data.

11.2 THE SCOPE OF RELEVANCE OF POLITICAL FACTORS IN INTERNATIONAL LAW

Policy argument refers to the argument driven by policy or political factors.[15] As EH Carr points out, 'common usage applies the term "political" not to all activities of the State but to issues involving a conflict of power'.[16] Politics always relates to subjectively defined interest, perception and ideology aspiring to take over the public sphere. Debate on the interaction between law and politics is essentially about the impact of ideology and perception on the legal position.

According to Morgenthau, in resolving international conflicts law has to give way to politics, because 'what is at stake in conflicts of this kind is not who is right and who is wrong but what ought to be done to reconcile the particular interests of individual nations with the general interest in peace and order'. The actors involved in such conflicts are interested not in applying law but in changing it.[17] Dean Acheson asserted in the context of the Cuban missile crisis, which affected the 'power, position and prestige of the United States', that 'law simply does not deal with such questions of ultimate power'.[18] McDougal likewise disputed the rationality of distinguishing between legal and political questions because law is effectively shaped by political factors.[19]

---

13 R Cox, 'Social Forces, States and World Orders', in Keohane (ed.), *Neorealism and Its Critics* (1986), 242.

14 R Ashley, 'The Poverty of Neo-Realism', in Keohane (ed.), *Neorealism and Its Critics* (1986), 281–282.

15 Policy is defined as a course of action and a principle that influences one's behaviour; politics relates to activities related to gaining and maintaining power and status, *Compact Oxford English Dictionary* (Third edition 2005), 786–787.

16 EH Carr, *Twenty Years' Crisis* (2nd edn., 2004), 97.

17 H Morgenthau, 'Diplomacy', 55 *Yale Law Journal* (1945–1946), 1067 at 1079.

18 D Acheson, 'Remarks', 57 *AJIL* (1963), 13 at 14.

19 M McDougal, 'The Role of Law in World Politics', XX *Mississippi Law Journal* (1948–1949), 253 at 269–270; *cf.* also M Koskenniemi, 'The Politics of International Law', 1 *EJIL* (1990), 4 at 11, concluding that under this approach the binding force of law becomes an illusion.

Arguably international law is not the only system focusing on institutions and rules agreed between States. But it is unique in having binding force. Political factors are often appealed to for making an international legal argument. One could discuss only in an abstract manner what the impact of political factors on the legal position or the motivation behind the action of States is. When it comes to the resolution of a particular dispute, what matters is how the relevant facts are evaluated in the light of legal rules. The principal question is thus whether the consideration of political factors requires redefining international law as it is consistently understood within its own discipline.

The 'fusion' approach viewing law and politics as a single whole is opposed to positive framework of analysis, and is also a reaction against the political realists' view of law as the near-irrelevant 'other'. This approach advocates reconceptualising international law to embrace the policy argument.[20] Westlake asserts that political factors are important, even inseparable from the international legal process,[21] but without articulating the implications of this view. Kaplan and Katzenbach claim that political factors control the international legal process.[22] Slaughter's argument is that international law and international politics 'cohabit the same conceptual space',[23] which is a statement of the obvious. But this is not the same as the identity between international law and international politics. Identifying international law as an incidence of, or as taken over by, international politics effectively amounts to the denial of international law.

It is not easy to pronounce on such a line of reasoning because its proponents rarely spell out its implications for particular legal questions and mostly restrict their analysis to the issues of doctrinal agenda-setting. These are doctrinal attempts to 'reconcile' international law with power and politics and hopefully avoid the former's denial by the proponents of the latter. But this effectively entails the denial of the independent normative relevance of international law as the system of rules that can independently apply to facts and determine their legality. The traditional, now outdated, version of the denial of international law refers to structural factors such as the absence of international government. The denial of international law for our purposes refers to the denial of autonomous relevance of international law in regulating State conduct and determining its legality.

While policy factors are often appealed to in doctrine and practice, they should not be seen to encompass the consensual, legal factors. The borders of the legal system essentially determine where political reasoning ends and legal reasoning begins. Precisely for this reason the emphasis on political factors is often premised on professed or implied attempts to redefine international law in terms of ideology and politics. To illustrate,

---

20 *Cf.*, A-M Slaughter, 'International Law and International Relations Theory: A Dual Agenda', 87 *AJIL* (1993), 205 at 207, 209; similarly, Reus-Smit considers that separation from politics of law as a system of impartial rules seems increasingly anachronistic, and reconsideration of this approach is needed: C Reus-Smit, 'Introduction' in C Reus-Smit (ed.), *The Politics of International Law* (2004), 1–2.

21 J Westlake, *Collected Papers* (1914), 92–93.

22 M Kaplan and N de B Katzenbach, *Political Foundations of International Law* (1961), 8.

23 A-M Slaughter, 'International Law in a World of Liberal States', 6 *EJIL* (1995), 503.

Kingsbury contends that the concept of international law is essentially contested.[24] Others avoid emphasising the nature of international law as a body of binding rules.

The international relations scholarship acknowledges the categories of international law. EH Carr recognises that international law is a necessity of the political society of nations, because the bindingness of law is a precondition of the existence of that political society. Still, Carr proceeds from the distinction of international law from municipal legal systems in terms of the lack, by the former, of the legislature that can legislate for, and judiciary that can have jurisdiction over, all States. According to Carr, the fundamental question of why international law is binding is not a legal question. Carr denotes the natural law approach as utopian and the positive law approach as realist. This is at the root of the difference between regarding law as a branch of ethics or a vehicle of power. The positive character of law means divorcing it from ethics. Thus, 'in theories of international law, utopia tends to predominate over reality to an extent unparalleled in other branches of jurisprudence'. Carr challenges the thesis that law may be more moral than politics. Political remedy can be invoked against immoral or oppressive law.[25] But Carr does not clarify this issue further.

From the viewpoint of political realism that sometimes results in legal nihilism, it may very well be argued that, in the relevant circumstances, the insistence on the application of existing legal framework is utopian and idealist because it does not correspond to the power position and interest of politically dominant and powerful States. More subtle, but generically similar, is Henkin's argument that the realists should recognise the law's uses and idealists should recognise law's limitations.[26] Obviously, both substantive rules and enforcement venues under international law derive from consent of States and in this sense the whole system can validly be denoted as 'limited'. International law is limited to its field of regulation, but within that field it applies as law. The real issue for legal science is concentrating on what has actually been agreed by States and evaluating facts by reference to that. It is crucial for clarifying the relationship between international law and politics whether the emphasis on the nature of international law is a requirement or only one of the available options.

The mainstream way of explaining how international law is created and works is consensual positivism, which is the most suitable way of understanding the legal system operating between States that recognise no governmental authority above them.[27] Prescriptions of positive law are not as such based on ethics, but on consent. However, it is a completely different issue of ethics reinforcing the need to comply with international obligations once agreed upon. In other words, it is plausible to see an ethical dimension in positivism. Given that States are unlikely to accept international obligations they have not consented to, and to renounce the right to insist on compliance with consensually established international rules, denial of positivist premises raises questions that may have an ethical dimension, in the sense that such international law would not be workable

---

[24] B Kingsbury, 'Legal Positivism as Normative Politics: International Society, Balance of Power and Lassa Oppenheim's Positive International Law', 13 *EJIL* (2002), 401 at 432.

[25] EH Carr, *Twenty Years' Crisis* (2nd edn., 2004), 160–162, 163–166.

[26] L Henkin, *How Nations Behave: International Law and Foreign Policy* (2nd edn., 1979), 337.

[27] *Cf.* L Oppenheim, 'The Science of International Law: Its Task and Method', 2 *AJIL* (1908), 313 at 333.

in the inter-State legal community. It may be a matter for personal choice whether one sees an ethical dimension in this, but it is more plausible to see this as an existential argument referring to indispensable structural preconditions of the international legal system.

Still, there is doctrinal opinion both in international law and international relations theories that disputes the obvious foundational role of positivism. It is presumably right that legal scholars should ask why their method of studying international law is better than others.[28] A simple response in favour of positivism is that it is not simply *one's* method, but a *unique* method referring to what has actually been agreed as part of international law.

Morgenthau has objected to positivism and instead developed a functional approach that would see legal rules adapted to factual situations.[29] Kingsbury claims that international law depends on political conditions and social interpretations that are constantly changing, referring to 'the simple paradox that the positivist separation of law from moral argument and from politics is itself a moral and political position'.[30] But there is nothing inherently moral and political in the position that international law should be viewed as what States agree upon; and even if by professing positivism one were guided by a certain moral and political position, positivism still carries with it an advantage – not available to other doctrinal options – that it reflects the actual structure of international law created by sovereign and independent States on which no legal rules can be imposed without their consent. Positivism in international law is not a positivism just referring to objectively observable data, but a consensual positivism that refers to the rules States are *actually* agreed on. Following this does not involve any political stance. International law *is* consensual and there is no way around this.

Presumably positive international law cannot be absolutely self-sustaining. It has to rely on, and derive its legitimacy from, certain extra-positivist factors.[31] A system must rely on a principle – which in the case of positivism is consent – but the validity of this principle precedes what that principle requires. Basic premises of positivism do not deny that international law can contain non-consensual elements. Most if not all proponents of positivism have accepted that it is not without limits.[32]

11.3 THEORIES OF DENIAL OF INTERNATIONAL LAW

Legal analysis focuses on the way international legal rules are created; the way in which the content of international legal rules is ascertained by interpretation; the need to apply

---

28 S Ratner and A-M Slaughter, 'Appraising the Methods of International Law: A Prospectus for Readers', 93 *AJIL* (1999), 291 at 298.

29 H Morgenthau, 'Positivism, Functionalism, and International Law', 34 *AJIL* (1940), 260.

30 Kingsbury, *supra* n. 24, 403; similarly, Slaughter argues that 'the effort to uncover the political roots of positive law undermined the autonomous legal foundations of normative law'. A-M Slaughter, 'International Law and International Relations Theory: A Dual Agenda', 87 *AJIL* (1993), 205 at 216–217.

31 J Brierly, *The Basis of Obligation in International Law* (1958).

32 See A Orakhelashvili, 'Natural Law and Justice', *Max-Planck Encyclopedia of Public International Law* (2009).

rules to facts and the legal consequences, in terms of responsibility and remedies. The difficulty to reconcile the mainstream characteristics of the international legal system with the claimed normative impact of power and political factors seems to be responsible for the emergence of a number of theories, both in international law and international relations scholarship, that attempt to re-assess the principal characteristics of international law.

The principal discrepancy between international legal reasoning and international policy reasoning consists in the latter's focus on the actual impact of international legal regulation on the conduct of States: 'rules may exist, but they do not exert an independent influence on State behaviour'. Arguably, it would make better sense for policy scientists to study not international rules but the factors that actually affect the behaviour of States.[33] This attitude conveniently delimits the task of legal science from that of policy science. But the argument that the failure of the existing legal regulation to exert influence on the conduct of States could affect the existing legal regulation could effectively be a move towards the denial of the legal character of international law. In domestic law, criminal law may fail to exert an influence on rising crime, that is the conduct of criminals, which conduct might even be reinforced by societal patterns competing with legal requirements, but that could hardly be invoked against the study and analysis of criminal law as a discipline independent from the crime situation on the ground.

Denial of international law can take place not only through direct assertion that there is no such thing as international law,[34] but also by contesting that international law constitutes a legal system of agreed and binding rules and standards that regulate the conduct of States, provide the qualification for their actions, and prescribe the relevant legal consequences. Consequently, doctrinal options for the denial of international law encompass not only theories that straightforwardly deny that international law exists, but also theories contradicting the independent relevance of international law.

Some theories are vulgar and primitive, promoting the thesis that power will always get its way whatever the legal framework may require; other theories are subtler and maintain the appearance of following legal argument alongside the political one. Identifying the legal argument with the need to realistically assess the broader situation or policy context inherently risks reducing legal science to focusing on mutually exclusive and subjectively manipulable views, none of which will enjoy the legitimacy sufficient to enable it to prevail over the opposite view. On the other hand, no State will be willing to renounce its rights arising out of the sources of positive law just because it is alleged that having or exercising those rights does not accord with the broader real situation, or is conceptually unsuitable.

11.3.1 The New Haven Policy-oriented Approach

Policy-oriented approach contends that international law is a process of policy decisions, *not* a body of rules.[35] In other words, this approach stresses *some* predictability in

---

[33] Anthony Clark Arend, *Legal Rules and International Society* (1999), 4.

[34] See JR Bolton, 'Is There Really "Law" in International Affairs'? 10 *Transnational Law and Contemporary Problems* (2000), 1.

[35] M McDougal, 'International Law, Power and Policy: A Contemporary Conception', 82 *Recueil des cours* (I-1953). Westlake understood the international legal system as product and tool of Western/European liberal ideology. International law was thus described as human action of

international legal process, but does so at the cost of denying the essence and relevance of rules. The striking feature of this approach, inaugurated by its founder Myres McDougal is that in describing international law as policy process as opposed to rules, there has never been a consistent attempt to justify this thesis by reference to structural characteristics of international law. Instead, the policy-oriented school has been guided by certain purposes and foundational ideas – such as 'human dignity' – proclaimed without any major attempt to demonstrate that those purposes and ideas possess the required systemic relevance. This is the cardinal point at which the policy-oriented approach has diverged from the mainline task of legal science.

The New Haven approach – as its proponents proclaim – does not equate law with power, but instead sees it as a process of authoritative and controlling decisions, which is a very discrete part of social process at large.[36] Although McDougal has been denoted as a legal realist,[37] and has emphasised the relevance of power in understanding international legal process, he disagreed with the conception of power by political realism of Morgenthau and Kennan and proposed adopting 'a much more comprehensive notion of power than that of simple naked force applied by nation-State to nation-State'. The proper conception of power included, according to McDougal, not only naked force but also 'formal authority'. This authority shapes policies through treaties, resolutions, declarations and other rules. In other words, law is not divorced from power as classical realists see it, but is 'a continuous formulation and reformulation of policies and constitutes an integral part of world power process'.[38] The main question this reasoning begs is what the independent relevance of policy factors is given that the vehicles through which they are articulated already constitute sources and evidences of positive international law.

The policy-oriented approach necessarily presupposes the impact of ideology on the state of international law, which can be seen from McDougal's first contribution on this subject, stressing the constitutive relevance for 'world power process' of values of world democratic order.[39] The ideological input to construct the world power process of policy decisions as legitimating actions not justified under sources and rules of international law can be seen in McDougal's analysis of the legality of the US hydrogen bomb test around the Pacific islands under US trusteeship, involving the establishment of a 400 thousand square mile 'warning area' causing interference with navigation. McDougal starts by arguing that the international legal system is a process of continuous interaction, demand and response, a process in which competing claims are appraised, but then goes on to argue that 'technical terms' such as territorial sea, contiguous zone and jurisdiction are not inelastic prescriptions but 'flexible policy preferences, permitting decision-makers

---

politics, J Westlake, *Chapters on Principles* (1914), 393ff. The 'policy process' approach is seen as 'a commonplace' by M Kaplan and N de B Katzenbach, *Political Foundations of International Law* (1961), 231. But in fact, McDougal's Hague Lectures acknowledge that his policy-oriented approach went against the mainstream international law theory, see at 143–144.

36 S Wiessner and A Willard, 'Policy-Oriented Jurisprudence and Human Rights Abuses in Internal Conflict: Toward a World Public Order of Human Dignity', 93 *AJIL* (1999), 316 at 320.

37 S Anderson, 'A Critique of Professor Myres McDougal's Doctrine of Interpretation by Major Purposes', 57 *AJIL* (1963), 378.

38 M McDougal, 'Law and Power', 46 *AJIL* (1952), 102 at 10709, 111.

39 M McDougal, 'The Role of Law in World Politics', XX *Mississippi Law Journal* (1948–1949), 253 at 256.

a very broad discretion for adjusting particular controversies . . . for promoting major policies'. The United States was thus entitled to engage in such interferences in preparation for the defence of its allies and 'of all the values of a free world society'.[40] Thus, the principal policy-oriented thesis is that the entitlement follows from pursuing a particular ideological cause. McDougal and his disciples have not clarified what the legal relevance of those 'major purposes' would be if the action guided by them is criticised as illegal by other States; in other words, can 'major purposes' and policy goals imitate the alternative to consent and consensus?

In relation to specific issues, the policy-oriented approach has asserted the legality of State action where that action would not respond to the requirements of international law. For instance, the concept of 'substantive' as opposed to 'procedural' legality is developed to view certain unilateral actions, although impermissible within the institutional framework, as nevertheless lawful, mostly with a view to justifying humanitarian intervention;[41] or to see imperfect legal acts, such as unratified treaty or unadopted Security Council resolutions as producing legal effect and entitlements.[42] The 'major purposes' approach, in essence embodying ideological preferences, was employed by Reisman to justify the use of force even contrary to the text of Article 2(4) of the UN Charter where this promotes the cause of freedom and individual rights.[43] Earlier John Norton Moore more specifically observed in the example of the Vietnam War that the 'lawfulness of assistance to either faction must be determined by reference to genuine self-determination and the requirements of minimum world public order, not in blind reliance on black-letter rules as to which side, if any, can be aided in a civil war and sometimes suggesting an Alice-in-Wonderland search for neutral principles'. Thus, the US assistance to South Vietnam was 'consistent with fundamental community expectations respecting the lawfulness of the use of force'.[44] If, then, there are no neutral rules regulating intervention, every action could potentially be justified by 'major purposes' of ideology. But the absence of a link between that ideology and neutral rules deprives the former of any legitimacy apart from the mysticism of belief of those who profess that ideology, and provides no evidence as to why such ideological justification should be objectively better from what the opposite side can offer.

As Wolfgang Friedmann emphasised, the problem with Moore's argument was the 'method of thinking, the ambiguous use of terminology and the bias in the selection of facts', just as the US State Department briefs on the subject of the Vietnam war were

---

40 M McDougal, 'The Hydrogen Bomb Tests and the International Law of the Sea', 49 *AJIL* (1955), 356 at 357–361.

41 M Reisman, 'Unilateral Action and the Transformations of the World Constitutive Process: The Special Problem of Humanitarian Intervention', 11 *EJIL* (2000), 3.

42 M Reisman, 'Unratified Treaties and Other Unperfected Acts in International Law: Constitutional Functions', 35 *Vanderbilt Journal of Transnational Law* (2002), 729.

43 M Reisman, 'Coercion and Self-Determination: Construing Charter Article 2(4)', 76 *AJIL* (1984), 642. A passing remark is that if one tries to locate 'major community policies', whether or not they overlap with positive international law, the only venue to locate them is the resolutions of the UN General Assembly which represents the entire international community, as opposed to self-proclaimed 'major purposes' in doctrinal and political quarters.

44 JN Moore, 'The Lawfulness of Military Assistance to the Republic of Viet-Nam, 61 *AJIL* (1967), 1 at 24 and 31.

'designed to persuade, and therefore select or twist facts as required for the presentation of the case, while ignoring inconvenient facts'.[45] Friedmann adopted a legalistic approach in determining the legality of intervention, depending on 'who started violating the [ceasefire] agreement', and in more general terms stressed the necessity to search and resort to neutral principles, failing which '"minimum world public order" means, Humpty-Dumpty-like, what the policy-maker wants it to mean, a catch-all phrase to justify whatever action the writer wishes to justify'. The Vietnam War had clearly illustrated this, in the example of the US preference not to intervene when South Vietnam was proclaimed in breach of the 1954 Geneva Agreements, and not to regard this war as a civil war. This approach was not, according to Friedmann, based on international law, but on the hypothesis that the political objectives pursued by the United States were consistent with world public order because the United States stood for proper values while its opponents did not.[46] Similarly, Koskenniemi characterises the New Haven approach as 'illegitimate naturalism' which risks becoming just an apology of some States' policies. The 'base values' and 'major purposes' of New Haven is the alternative whereby this school attempts to replace the fundamental framework of sources of international law that forms the foundations of mainline positivism.[47]

The policy-oriented school emphasises the paramount importance of human dignity, but it is not generically similar to solidarism which emphasises the unity of humanity while the New Haven approach, like liberalism and other pertinent ideologies,[48] focuses on factors of ideology that divide the international community. Under this approach, the conduct of the 'better ones' has to be judged by different standards than that applicable to the conduct of others. Indeed, both the New Haven theory and its follow-ups demonstrate that the emphasis on 'human dignity' is meant not as a rigorous measure of State activity, but as a tool for the ideological upper hand. Effectively, the outcome of this approach is not that human dignity has to be preserved in individual instances, but that the actor perceived to be safeguarding the overarching goal of human dignity has to have its conduct justified, whatever the legal position.

The New Haven approach has repeatedly been disapproved. According to Simma and Paulus, the New Haven approach conflates law, political science and pure politics, and 'fails to provide the very guidance that real-life decision makers expect from their lawyers'. By not distinguishing clearly between norms and values, the New Haven approach ideologizes international law which is all too often based on minimal consensus of means and not of ends.[49]

It is most significant that McDougal's approach has been repeatedly disapproved in international relations theory, for instance by Hedley Bull and Michael Walzer. Bull criticises the policy-oriented attempt to 'liberate' law of logical and formal constraint and the attempt to merge legal reasoning with non-legal considerations. Viewing law as

---

[45] W Friedmann, 'Law and Politics in the Vietnamese War: A Comment', 61 *AJIL* (1967), 776 at 779.

[46] *Id.*, 781, 783, 785.

[47] M Koskenniemi, 'The Politics of International Law', 1 *EJIL* (1990), 4 at 11–13.

[48] See below sections 11.4 and 11.8 on liberalism and solidarism, respectively.

[49] B Simma and A Paulus, 'The Responsibility of Individuals for Human Rights Abuses in Internal Conflict: A Positivist View', 93 *AJIL* (1999), 302 at 305.

a process of 'authoritative decisions' deprives it of its independent focus and leads to its disappearance as an independent branch of international studies.[50] As Walzer explains, policy-oriented scholars are moral and political philosophers, would-be legislators, and it would be better if they presented themselves that way; they in fact aspire to restructuring the international society, but fail to explain its present structure.[51]

In methodological terms Kratochwil points out that McDougal's approach seems to be dictated by his particular point of view on US policy in the Cold War context, rather than by the method and theory of political science. As Kratochwil observes, 'the shift of focus away from rules to the decision process often makes a distinction between "law" and "politics" virtually impossible'. Law is not about legitimating ends, but also about legitimacy and illegitimacy of means. 'It is this specificity which distinguishes law from policy as well as from moral principles.' In addition, the reference to human dignity as a preferred ideology does not promote confidence. For, 'one of the main functions of law is to mediate between adherents of fundamentally different conceptions of the good life, or of human dignity'. The clash of interests and security concerns is part of international life; but aspiring to give certain interests an ideological upper hand neither leads to security nor enhances human dignity.[52]

As is clear from Kratochwil's analysis, the idea of human dignity postulated as the basis of McDougal's theory is aimed to be placed at the same level as the basic rule or rule of recognition would be placed under the positivist approach.[53] In this case the basic norm is defined in substantive or even ideological terms, as opposed to demonstrating its inherency in the legal system. This is especially clear as, in the 1940s and 1950s, when McDougal first developed the policy-oriented approach, the place of individual rights in international law was not as prominent as today, and the whole input of 'human dignity' appeared as merely ideological.

It has to be concluded that the authority behind arguments expounded by the policy-oriented school is little more than doctrinal and ideological preferences of authors. It could be argued that the working of international law, covering the creation, application and vindication of its rules, is indeed a process, which word would here be used in its most ordinary sense, as opposed to the New Haven mystification of 'process' as an alternative to rules. This opens the way for arguing that one's policy preference can easily translate into law and every policy action could potentially be justified as compatible with international law. The tool for that is precisely the 'authoritative process of policy decisions', even if sometimes seen as more consistent than the reliance on brute force, because it is in essence the set of subjectively defined ideological preferences.

11.3.2 The Cost-benefit Approach

As Louis Henkin explained, the cost-benefit calculation promotes the inclination of States to cooperate and observe international law, because legal rules and regimes can

---

50 H Bull, *The Anarchical Society* (1977), 144, 153–154.
51 M Walzer, *Just and Unjust Wars* (1977), 19.
52 F Kratochwil, *Rules, Norms and Decisions* (1989), 195–199.
53 Ibid., 195.

provide benefits outweighing those of unilateral action.[54] According to Goldsmith and Posner, international law is important but States comply with it only if and when it responds to their interests; international law has no inherent 'compliance pull'.[55]

The cost-benefit argument is essentially one-sided and partial. In order to understand this process properly, it is necessary to focus on the interest and perception of not only the law-breaker, but also that of the victims of the breach of international law. There is indeed merit in the thesis that States may forego temporary advantage they could derive from the breach of international law, in exchange for the more substantial benefit of preserving the whole system. It could not really be disputed that international law as a system is there because it responds to the fundamental interest of States to live in a predictable normative framework and not in chaos. But this approach can only explain motives; it cannot explain or reformulate the content of rules; it further cannot explain how international legal regulation can survive when a leading power no longer considers it to be in its interest, as the modern *jus ad bellum* has indeed done even against US attempts to revise this field of law in the context of its 'war on terror'.[56]

The factor of costs and benefits is undoubtedly relevant in the process of international law-making, and is further reflected in the reciprocal structure of the bulk of international law. But once the State agrees to an international rule or instrument, it shall be deemed to have already realised that giving such agreement is likely to bring benefits to it, in exchange for costs. The balance between costs and benefits is thus already resolved by the time the binding rule emerges. Before that happens, the State is not bound by anything on the particular matter and thus has the freedom to assess the potential costs and benefits before it takes its decision. But after the rule is in force the cost and benefit factor cannot imitate the alternative criteria replacing those of the legality of State action under international law. Illegal conduct is illegal whatever the cost-benefit considerations that may have motivated it. The point profoundly missing in the cost-benefit reasoning relates to legal consequences of illegal acts in the law of State responsibility. The cost-benefit theory has no distinct originality, for it merely restates the common sense that a thief benefits from goods he steals. But this does not make theft lawful.

Another weakness of the cost-benefit approach is that it is highly presumptive, claiming to be a theory of law, and operates with assumptions that need to be proved through the complex use of methods of political and economic sciences. It is widely assumed in some doctrinal quarters, both in international law and international relations, that the changes to the international system are due to the calculation by States whether the expected benefits will exceed expected costs. As Gilpin observes, however, 'these assumptions are abstractions from a highly complex political reality. They do not describe the actual decision processes of statesmen.' Furthermore, 'although one speaks of costs and benefits as if they were objective and quantifiable, both are highly

---

54 L Henkin, *How Nations Behave: International Law and Foreign Policy* (2nd edn., 1979); Arend (1999), 121, 123; R Bilder, 'Breach of Treaty and Response Thereto', *ASIL Proceedings* (1967), 193 at 199.

55 JL Goldsmith and EA Posner, *The Limits of International Law* (2006), 13.

56 See for detail A Orakhelashvili, 'Legal Stability and Claims of Change: The International Court's Treatment of *Jus ad Bellum* and *Jus in Bello*', 75 *Nordic JIL* (2006), 371.

subjective and psychological in nature'.[57] Thus, if the cost-benefit approach is accorded an independent relevance in the legal discourse, it will necessarily result in the denial of international law.

11.3.3 'Hegemonic' International Law

The current ethos of hegemonic international law follows from the perceived need, among others in journalism, to explain in legal terms the leading position of the United States in shaping and reshaping international law.[58] However, the idea of hegemony as related to international law has both earlier historical and inter-disciplinary origins. In principle, the argument that international law has been, or can be, dominated by a power or perception of one State or group of States (including the idea of European international law) is generically similar to the historical or political argument that the particular period of international history is marked by the hegemony of the relevant power. The division of the history of international law into Spanish, French, British and American periods runs parallel to the division of history in political science such as *Pax Britannica* and *Pax Americana*, which denote the periods dominated by the hegemony of the particular power.[59]

This approach is not always accurate. British hegemony (*Pax Britannica*) was based on Britain's sea power and liberal economic policies that were widespread at the time of the expansion of British prestige. Under this view, liberal economic values were universal rules and British sea power a potential enforcer. The image of British hegemony survived far longer than its actual hegemony. *Pax Americana* after the Second World War has also been understood as a form of hegemony. But already during the Cold War, there was a doctrinal argument that the United States could no longer act as the guarantor of the world order.[60] According to Detlev Vagts, the United States has no 'political and psychological infrastructure hegemony calls for'.[61]

The major problem with the hegemony approach is the assumption that if, at the particular period of international legal history, the relevant State has exercised political hegemony and the consequent influence on law-making, other periods of that history should be seen in the same perspective. But the patterns of hegemony have been diverse. *Pax Romana* was the domination by empire; *Pax Britannica* did not, at least in Europe, so much involve domination by Britain as its influence implied in the ability to tip the balance in the conflicts between other powers; *Pax Americana* was never an incontrovertible reality before 1992, that is the end of the bipolar world, and then it lasted only for a few years. The issue of hegemony is very much a matter of debate, premised upon the

---

57 R Gilpin, *War and Change in World Politics* (1981), 10–11, 51.

58 D Vagts, 'Hegemonic International Law', 95 *AJIL* (2001), 843, referring to, among others, the view of Charles Krauthammer in *Time*.

59 See P Taylor and C Flint, *Political Geography* (4th edn., 2007), referring to Modelski's cycles of hegemony. For attempts to locate this phenomenon in the history of international law, see W Grewe, *Epochen der Völkerrechtsgeschichte* (1988).

60 R Cox, 'Social Forces, States and World Orders', in Keohane (ed.), *Neorealism and Its Critics* (1986), 223–225, 229.

61 Vagts, *supra* n. 58, 845.

changing context of power allocation in the world and on whether it should be understood as unipolar or multipolar. It is unclear whether historical and political science has ever consistently defined the meaning of hegemony. It is even less clear whether, how and to what extent hegemony could translate into the international legal position, in a way defining or affecting the content of international rights and obligations.

Hegemony can imply a degree of unilateralism through which the hegemon shapes and influences the legal framework. The hegemon arguably provides the ideas and composes the agenda both for international political and international legal processes. In political terms, the hegemon often formulates potential outcomes of international controversies. But can the hegemon impose law on those who do not consent? If so, the hegemonic approach can be premised on the denial of the character of international law as the body of consensually agreed rules. To compose international law, it is not enough to have power; it is also necessary to obtain the consent of others.

Structurally, hegemony contradicts the nature of international law and its political foundations. Kingsbury emphasises 'an unavoidable tension between British advocacy of balance of power and hegemonic arguments for the Pax Britannica'.[62] Hegemony also contradicts the fundamental principle of sovereign equality of States. Oppenheim rejects the thesis that 'political hegemony exercised by the great powers rests on a legal basis'. States may be politically unequal but their legal equality 'must remain valid as long as the family of nations remains in existence'.[63]

Dominance by a powerful State can be a necessary but not a sufficient condition for hegemony.[64] The fact that the State has accumulated power within the international system confirms that the system is organised in a way to support this power position. The US accumulation of economic and military power in the aftermath of the Second World War, whether economic influence abroad, especially through international financial institutions, or establishment of military bases, has taken place consistently with international law. Thus the power-wielding State, if judging rationally, has to be interested in preserving the system and acknowledging the limits it may envisage for its power position. Power-accumulation takes place on the conditions prescribed under the system. Attempts to change the system may undermine the very power position of power-wielding-States. This is among other things why, during later stages of the Cold War, the enterprises such as the Vietnam War and 'war on terror' have not proved successful in terms of attracting legal approval.

Images of a particular hegemony certainly outlive its actuality. The reality of hegemony depends on the hegemon's interaction with the system where, as EH Carr has observed, *status quo* justifies the privileged position of dominant entities. Just as the domestic political class prays for domestic peace, so will internationally dominant entities seek to maintain peace in international affairs.[65] Thus the hegemon is supposed to want peace and continuity. The attitude of the United States towards a number of international legal

---

[62] Kingsbury, *supra* n. 24, 419.

[63] L Oppenheim, 'The Science of International Law: Its Task and Method', 2 *AJIL* (1908), 313 at 347.

[64] R Cox, 'Social Forces, States and World Orders', in Keohane (ed.), *Neorealism and Its Critics* (1986), 223.

[65] Carr, *supra* n. 24, 102–104.

questions aimed at changing international law certifies that, to use Henry Kissinger's classification,[66] the United States is a revolutionary power, attempting to change significant aspects of international law. Obviously there may be an argument that the hegemon actually uses force to manage the system. But this does not correspond to the attitude of international society towards the actions of the 'hegemon'. It is the system that makes a hegemon and not vice versa. Hegemony can survive only if the aspirations of the hegemon overlap with the basic requirements of the system. This is, among other things, why there can be no hegemonic international law: an entity, however major and powerful, cannot run the system. There is no government on an international plane and hegemons cannot imitate it.

11.4 REFLECTION OF THE NATURE OF INTERNATIONAL LAW IN INTERNATIONAL RELATIONS THEORY

It was a historian, AHL Heeren, who observed two centuries ago that international law is not just an aspect of international politics, but such a special aspect of it as predictably, even if strictly, allocated rights and duties of States.[67] This emphasises the special importance of international law – so understood from a non-lawyer's perspective. A significant attempt in international relations theory to capture the essence of international law is made by Hedley Bull. Bull takes a realistic view of international law in terms of its enforcement and emphasises the limits of this legal system, importantly capturing the legal character of international law as a normative system. Still, Bull emphasises that rules are there to ensure conduct consistent with the goals of international society,[68] which stresses the inherency of rules for the existence and survival of international society. According to Bull, reasoning about international law should be conducted on a normative as opposed to a factual and empirical plane. The interpretation of law has social, moral and political implications, but these should not determine international lawyers' exposition of the content of existing law.[69] Obviously socio-political considerations have to be considered, especially in terms of adapting law to changing circumstances. But if a distinction is not preserved between those rules of conduct which have the status of law and those which have not, international law cannot survive as a normative system at all.[70]

The normative aspect of rules is complemented by their sociological aspect. Where rules influence State conduct they are part of social reality. At times rules are broken, but 'if there were no possibility that actual behaviour would differ from prescribed behaviour, there would be no point in having the rule'. The efficacy of rules does not require the identity between prescribed and actual behaviour, that is the absence of violation, but there should be a very substantial degree of conformity. However, even this does

---

66 H Kissinger, *A World Restored: Metternich, Castlereagh and the Problems of Peace 1812–1822* (1957), 1.

67 *Cf.* C Graig and A George, *Power and Statecraft* (1995), 15–16.

68 Bull, *supra* n. 50, 64.

69 Bull, 123, 144.

70 Bull, 153.

not make international law a powerful motive behind international politics.[71] Thus the socio-political context of rules does not negate their normativity; instead, it conceptually nourishes that normativity as a phenomenon separate from factual and political reality. Bull illustrates that while the validity of rules and their political context shall be studied together, the two are essentially different phenomena, only the former belonging to the proper field of international law.

Although Bull does not profess so, his analysis of rules effectively subscribes to legal positivism. This is manifested by the thesis that rules must be made and communicated to those to whom they apply, and accepted by them as valid; the content of rules must be established through interpretation; and rules must be protected against developments in society that can undermine their operation; adapting rules to changing circumstances should happen through established procedures.[72] In conformity with positivism, Bull brilliantly captures the essence of international law to determine the limits on State action in situations where there is no consensus as to the desirability of the pertinent action. Rules limiting war apply in the context where opinions diverge as to which side is fighting just war; rules on sanctity of agreements apply where it is not agreed whether the particular agreement is desirable; rules on sovereign jurisdiction apply where there is no uniform opinion as to whether the intervention in internal affairs of States is justified. Where there is no consensus – presumably at political level – that the particular action is lawful and international society is divided, it would go not only against law but also against order to act as if that consensus existed.[73]

These are cardinal features of international law, emphasising the core of its independent relevance in international affairs, its independence from conflicting political interests. It is an irony that an international relations scholar has captured this particular aspect of international law better than has at times been done within the scholarship of international law.

To conclude, Bull's approach, which is a leading voice of international relations theory, certainly warns against idealism and views rules in the broader socio-political context in which they emerge and operate. But it also opposes rule-scepticism and inflating legal argument with political argument that would entail viewing law and policy as a fused whole. Bull's thesis that international law is not a principal motivation of international politics is perfectly compatible with the nature of this legal system: the function of international law is to impose certain limits on political action, not to motivate political action in general. Wherever free of legal restrictions, States can be guided by whatever motives they like.

Sometimes non-lawyers' perspective of international law can more accurately reflect the essence of this legal system than certain legal views do. While international lawyers take the 'inside' view of international law, their ideological orientation, or what they

---

71 Bull, 53, 123, 131, 133.

72 Bull, 54; the above ought to be considered as Bull's mainstream view, as opposed to some other ideas, *id.*, 88, that international law allows for sacrificing *status quo* without providing legislative mechanism to alter it, and even accepts the new situation brought about through the use of aggressive force. This view is outdated considering the state of international law and practice even at the time *The Anarchical Society* was first published.

73 Bull, 151.

view as incompleteness or failure of the system, induces them to advance extra-legal arguments. Political and social scientists, on the other hand, tend to see international law as one of the aspects of a broader international system, whose existence depends on international law. If compared to normal political patterns guided by diffuse and ever-changing interests, international law is the only factor that can predictably allocate rights and obligations. The insufficiency of political factors in explaining these processes is better realised by international relations scholars.

11.5 THE RELEVANCE OF POLITICAL FACTORS IN INTERNATIONAL LEGAL REASONING

According to Kratochwil, we need to distinguish between the legal order and the political system, but also emphasise interdependence between them:

> While the concept of a political system seems wider than that of 'law' – in that politics also includes law-making, bargaining, interest-articulation, etc. – the legal order is in another respect the wider concept. After all, it is through the constitutional provisions that law provides for the orderly *political process*. Precisely because the constitution is 'constitutive' of the political system, the conventional taxonomy of 'politics' and 'law' hides rather than illuminates important conceptual dimensions.[74]

Thus, the interaction between law and politics is multi-faceted and cannot be described in a primitive way of pronouncing that one determines or prevails over the other. There is not even a consensus as to what political factors mean in relation to international law. As Koskenniemi explains, 'political' elements of international law can emphasise either its dependence on political power, or its utopian political aspirations.[75]

The potential impact of political factors on international law can be twofold. In the first place, it can be claimed in particular situations that political factors affect or shape the content of rights and obligations of States in specific disputes, controversies and conflicts; or impact the validity, applicability and change of legal rules. Alternatively, in a more systemic perspective, the existence and operation of the system of international law is arguably premised on political factors. These arguments are qualitatively different and need to be addressed in turn. In doing so, it has to be remembered that the argument of the relevance of politics in international law has been developed over a century and has on occasions reflected legal positions which no longer characterise modern international law.

11.5.1 Claimed Impact of Political Factors on the Substance of International Law

EH Carr's analysis portrays law as a struggle between different political interests. Carr considers the need for certainty and predictability of international law, specifying that 'Law which is uncertain in its interpretation or capricious in its application fails to fulfil its essential function.' The essence of law is to promote stability and maintain the essential

[74] Kratochwil, *supra* n. 52, 251 (emphasis original).
[75] M Koskenniemi, 'The Politics of International Law', 1 *EJIL* (1990), 4 at 9.

framework of society. But Carr does not see stability and continuity as the only parts of political life. Radicals struggle to effect changes while conservatives try to maintain the *status quo*. According to Carr, the *status quo* is merely what suits the 'satisfied' powers.[76] If this is the only measure, there is no legitimacy differential between keeping the *status quo* and changing it, and *a fortiori* the factor of legality becomes irrelevant. If Carr's reasoning refers to politics and power as creating and changing law even in the absence of the required consensus then this reasoning ends up denying the binding force of international law to which Carr himself expressly subscribes. As for Carr's warning against law 'becoming a tool in the hands of the defenders of *status quo*', that's what it is for. What '*Status quo*' States have agreed upon by their free will is part of law. Questioning it will question the legitimacy of the entire system.

The models to follow this line of argument can be different. They can relate to directly arguing the irrelevance of the consensually established legal position; or that that legal position has been 'contracted out' in specific instances on a political basis; or that that legal position has changed or is changing. These are particular avenues for arguing the impact of politics and ideology on the legal position without providing the evidence to prove that the legal position is exactly that.

Obviously political factors are important in the calculation by the State whether or not to agree to a particular legal rule; to insist on implementing that rule or alternatively agree to its modification; to complain about the violation of that rule, including instituting judicial proceedings; and to take countermeasures.[77] Political factors may very well explain that the United States raises the issue of human rights violations in Myanmar and North Korea, but not, or not with the same vigour, in China. In certain cases States do not protest over violations of international law or insist on their rights, presumably due to the actual or perceived strength of other actors and the unwillingness to irritate and antagonise them. But it would be a step too far to suggest that the validity and content of the rules that States accept through their political decisions depend on those political factors.

There is an argument that legal rules are merely incidental to underlying power and political interest, and will be changed or disregarded if the latter change.[78] Although in doctrine the thesis of law-making as an incidence of political power has been developed by Charles de Visscher, his approach is complex, and pays sufficient attention to consensual legal factors in producing the legal regulation.[79] Legal rules and instruments often indeed fix power and political interest positions,[80] but having done so, they acquire and

---

[76] Carr, *Twenty Years' Crisis*, 166, 172, 289, 297.

[77] *Cf.* R Bilder, 'Breach of Treaty and Response Thereto', *ASIL Proceedings* (1967), 193 at 199.

[78] KW Abbott, 'International Relations Theory, International Law, and the Regime Governing Atrocities in Internal Conflicts', 93 *AJIL* (1999), 361 at 365.

[79] C de Visscher, *Theory and Reality in International Law* (1968), 153–156, 318–319, 327–329.

[80] As EH Carr demonstrates in the example of the 1925 Locarno Treaty, *Twenty Years' Crisis*, 99–100; or as Schwarzenberger observes in the example of treaties safeguarding the balance of power or extraterritorial rights and spheres of influence, *Power Politics*, 171–173. Last but not least, the voting arrangement in the UN Security Council under the UN Charter certainly reflected the power position of the victorious allies, but even as this power position changed, Article 27, subject to subsequent consensual understandings, retained its own independent validity separate from changing political interests and conditions. On the use of political argument to justify

maintain their independent validity separate from original political considerations. This among other things follows from the importance States-parties have accorded to those original political considerations by agreeing to endow them with legal standing. Political factors can ultimately undermine such treaty regimes but they would be relevant not only as political factors *per se* but as reflected in the legal framework of reciprocal non-compliance and changed circumstances, invocable in very limited conditions, strictly defined in Articles 60 and 62 of the 1969 Vienna Convention on the Law of Treaties.

Political factors, being undefined, uncertain and susceptible of subjective manipulation, cannot consistently explain international law. Because of the elusive and ever-changing nature of political factors and immeasurably diverse reactions of States, the reference to political factors cannot help to identify any coherent and predictable legal framework. The advantage of consensual approach is that once rules are verifiably agreed upon, they are deemed to apply to facts and determine their legality. States can thus safely rely on applicable law. Despite the element of political appreciation, the validity and operation of rules agreed between States, even if compliance with them is not insisted upon in some cases, continues unless and until they are modified in the same way as they were established. It has long since been accepted in international jurisprudence that renunciation of rights cannot be presumed but must be established through convincing evidence demonstrating the intention of the State to waive its right or entitlement.[81]

The argument that politics has primacy over law necessarily presupposes the distorted presentation of pertinent institutions of international law. To illustrate, Kaplan and Katzenbach, adhering to the policy-oriented approach, complain that sources of international law have become stereotyped, and warn against believing in impartial application of pre-existing rules.[82] Schwarzenberger argues that what he calls 'international law of power' provides for ways for the potential violator State to go back on its commitments if so required by its political interest:

> In order to avoid or mitigate such unpleasantness, international customary law offers a number of devices. On the level of auto-interpretation of international law by every sovereign State, all these devices provide convenient excuses of a quasi-legal character. The principles of self-preservation and self-defence and the *clausula rebus sic stantibus* are favourite tricks of the game.[83]

This statement confirms that the assertion of relevance of political factors necessarily attacks the structural foundations of international law, and also that those foundations are not necessarily arranged so as to reflect political interest to that extent. It hardly needs mentioning that self-preservation is not part of international law and the reliance on changed circumstances to terminate treaties is permitted under very limited circumstances as prescribed under Article 62 of the Vienna Convention on the Law of Treaties.

Policy approach thus promotes mixing legal argument and common sense. For a pure

---

circumventing the voting patterns of the Security Council see above section 11.3 on the New Haven school and Reisman in *Vanderbilt JTL*.

[81] *Clipperton Island* (France v Mexico), 26 *AJIL* (1930), 390; *Legal Status of Eastern Greenland*, PCIJ Series AB No 53, 46–47.

[82] M Kaplan and N de B Katzenbach, *Political Foundations of International Law* (1961), 231, 234.

[83] G Schwarzenberger, *Power Politics* (1964), 201.

policy approach there seems to be no threshold separating relevant arguments from irrelevant ones – the threshold that the relevant argument has to cross to qualify as a legal argument, in terms of relating to the verifiably established legal rule and its application to facts. At the same time, the doctrinal attempt to inflate legal reasoning with policy argument is not the same as the attempt of States to have the relevant legal position reappraised pursuant to their political argument. This is one of the aspects of international law-making. As Sir Arthur Watts has stated,

> There is room for the view that all that States need for the general purposes of conducting their international relations is to be able to advance a legal justification for their conduct which is not demonstrably rubbish. Thereafter, political factors can take over, and the international acceptability or otherwise of a State's conduct can be left to be determined by considerations of international policy rather than of international law. In this light, if politics is the art of the possible, then international law is merely art of the plausible.[84]

This argument could be interpreted as implying the primacy of politics over law, in the spirit of McDougal's approach that policy decisions are produced in the process of continuous interaction, demand and response. But the same thesis can also be located in the positivist context, where a legal argument that is not quite rubbish implies the claim of the State which makes it to change the law, or have itself exempted from the operation of the relevant legal rules. This can happen on political grounds but will have no effect unless consolidated through the legal process of claim, acceptance and consent. Other States may consent or object to the 'rubbish' claim on political grounds, but what will matter is not these political factors but that they consent, in the absence of which mere politics cannot add to the value of 'rubbish'. If other States will reject it, 'rubbish' will remain 'rubbish'. While the relevant processes are subsumable within the ordinary categories of international law-making and law-enforcement, the reference to political factors becomes moot.

States on occasions prefer not to engage in the legal argumentation as to their conduct, the legality of which is questionable, possibly with a view to concentrating on political acceptability of the relevant conduct and avoiding potentially damaging legal debate. Still, in State practice there is room for separating legal and political aspects of particular conduct from each other. For instance, in relation to Israel's use of force in the Entebbe incident to save its nationals' lives, Sweden observed in the Security Council debate that these motives arguably rendered the use of force politically acceptable, but by no means lawful. The US argumentation about the *Mayaguez* incident was also political, yet could not avoid condemnation from other States.[85] Similarly, during the 1999 NATO armed attack on Yugoslavia, only one NATO member-State argued in legal terms on humanitarian intervention, while others preferred to concentrate on the political and related context of humanitarian catastrophe. Yet this did not prevent the rejection of the lawfulness of humanitarian intervention by the prevailing majority of the international community within the Non-aligned Movement (132 States).

---

[84] Sir A Watts, 'The Importance of International Law', in Byers (ed.), *The Role of Law in International Politics* (2000), 5 at 8.

[85] J Green, 'Self-Defence: A State of Mind for States'? 55 *Netherlands ILR* (2008), 181 at 200–201.

One context in which legal argument diverges from political argument is the notion of so-called 'political' disputes. According to Morgenthau, 'the legalistic approach to essentially political problems is but an aberration from the true laws of politics'. Legal decisions cannot artificially separate international controversies from their broader political context, which cannot be captured by established rules of law.[86] Carr develops a view of 'political disputes' as allegedly different from legal disputes. Legal disputes are based on existing legal rights, and political disputes motivated by the desire to alter existing rights. Arguably, 'the essence of a political dispute is the demand that the relevant legal rule, though admittedly applicable, shall not be applied'. Such political disputes cannot be settled by tribunals applying law. Carr goes so far as to accuse the creators of the inter-war dispute settlement arrangements, such as the 1928 General Act, of attempts to force the essentially political function into legal process and thus make the judge a legislator.[87] Should the political disputes doctrine be followed, EH Carr's criticism could *a fortiori* be applied to judicial institutions such as the PCIJ and ICJ. As Sir Hersch Lauterpacht's analysis of the notion of 'political disputes' has demonstrated, this phenomenon does not really exist within the international legal system.[88] If the International Court's consistent treatment of political issues is considered, the basic task of international law is to apply to, determine the legality of, and sanction State conduct even if it is, or precisely because it is, undertaken for political reasons and self-interest.[89] Explaining the problem from the opposite side, Hurrell's observation is exactly to the point: 'if courts are asked to rule on particularly divisive political issues, this is a sign that something has gone wrong with the political, not the legal, system'.[90] Precisely for the reason that the cases before them may have heavy political connotations, international tribunals have to decide them on the basis of legal rules as the neutral and consistent basis for decision, to avoid being discredited for being a tool for a particular political interest under the guise of the administration of justice.

11.5.2. Political Foundations of International Law

It is hardly disputable that international law gives legal shape to political institutions such as war, diplomacy and balance of powers, and legal institutions such as treaties, claims and protests become indispensable elements of international politics.[91] Rules of international law derive, according to Carr, from a 'pre-legal political agreement'. Treaties express power politics. Every legal rule presupposes the initial political decision and thus the ultimate authority of law derives from politics. As Carr observes,

> respect for law and treaties will be maintained only in so far as the law recognises effective political machinery through which it can itself be modified and superseded. There must be a

---

[86] H Morgenthau, 'Diplomacy', 55 *Yale Law Journal* (1945–1946), 1067 at 1078–1079.

[87] Ibid., 184–186.

[88] *The Function of Law in the International Community* (1933), 159, 337, 379.

[89] See on detail A Orakhelashvili, *The Interpretation of Acts and Rules in Public International Law* (2008), chapter 2.

[90] A Hurrell, *On Global Order* (2008), 53.

[91] Kingsbury, *supra* n. 24, 407.

> clear recognition of the play of political forces which is antecedent to all law. Only when these forces are in stable equilibrium can the law perform its social function without becoming a tool in the hands of the defenders of *status quo*. The achievement of this equilibrium is not a legal, but a political task.[92]

According to Hedley Bull, consent of States as the basis of international law is 'prior to international law', and international law depends for its existence on pre-legal factors.[93] Similarly, Kratochwil considers that the basic rule conferring obligatory character to other rules has to be considered in extra-legal terms.[94] This could be so if the relevance of legal argument is restricted to positively stipulated law; but not inevitably so if it also includes the elements inherent in the international legal system necessary to enable it to function. As elaborated upon by JL Brierly, positive international law depends on pre-positive legal factors inherent in international society and reinforcing the binding force of rules, which is the principle of *pacta sunt servanda*.[95]

The antecedence of these political factors to law, or parallelism between legal and political factors, confirms the very point that both law and politics possess separate identities. But it is questionable how much practical utility is served by portraying consent as antecedent to or distinct from law. Conceptually, the extra-legal explanation of foundations of international law would depend on what the perceived basic norm is. Depending on what political or ideological factor one sees as reinforcing the projected basic norm, one can then project the legal position on particular matters as dictated not by any hard evidence of State consent and agreement, but by the ideological perception served by that basic norm,[96] for instance that of 'human dignity' of the New Haven school, or any related notion.

It is conceptually clear that international law may only be part of what organises international society: along with the rules agreed upon by States, international society is also governed by rules deriving from other objective factors. Kenneth Waltz refers to ordering principles of international society to explain how its parts are related to each other. Even more significantly, the question Waltz poses relates to the requirements for the functioning of international society, and patterns of behaviour deriving from the structural constraints of the system.[97] But the crucial task is to ascertain where 'other' ordering principles stand in relation to international law, to what extent they overlap with or contradict it. It should be examined what the role of international law, as part of the structure of the international system, is in comparison with its 'competitors' in impacting patterns of attitude and behaviour. The question is also whether the non-consensual,

---

92 Carr, *The Twenty Years' Crisis*, (2001) 166, 172, 180.

93 Bull, 66.

94 F Kratochwil, *Rules, Norms and Decisions* (1989), 189.

95 JL Brierly, *The Basis of Obligation in International Law* (1958), 11–12.

96 See further above section 11.3 on the New Haven approach.

97 K Waltz, 'Political Structures', in Keohane (ed.), *Neorealism and Its Critics* (1986), 73, 86. This neo-realist emphasis on structures shaping aspirations and conduct raises thoughts on certain tenets underlying both realism and constructivism. Similarly, Keohane suggests that States' interests depend on institutional context and power realities, R Keohane, 'Theory in World Politics: Structural Realism and Beyond', in Keohane (ed.), *Neorealism and Its Critics* (1986), 195. See below section11.6.

non-positivist, aspects of international law express the political foundations of international law.

On some views, political norms can be seen as competitors of international law. According to Morgenthau, politics is governed by objective laws that have their roots in human nature.[98] Focusing on these laws gives international relations a scientific dimension.[99] Wight focuses on political norms as an explanation of State conduct: 'A political law is a generalization about how political events recur. It may be a satisfactory generalization within a limited context, but become dubious in a wider context.'[100]

There is indeed some degree of normativity in certain political concepts and patterns underlying the field of international law. This is not a normativity in the sense of binding law, but a predictive normativity whereby the outcome of developments in international politics can be measured and explained. The underlying factors of such 'normativity' relate to the perceptions of States as to their status and interest in international relations, ranging between survival and domination. These perceptions generate reaction of States to events and processes. Such reaction can sometimes accord with international law and sometimes contradict it, but there can be a pattern of prediction and explanation with relative certainty as to how the relevant State is likely to behave in the relevant context. Now, it is possible to view these 'laws' as structural preconditions of international law and as political factors. But these 'political' factors would then be *preconditions* of international law, factors antecedent to it, not *the same as* international law.

'Political norms' such as balance of power, possibly hierarchy and spheres of influence, are not really norms in the sense of legal norms, but possess a broader systemic dimension. The notion of political norms also includes non-binding norms enshrined in political documents such as the Helsinki Final Act. These have no quality of legal norms either, but as an aspect of State practice and legal conviction, they can promote crystallisation of legal norms. In general, political norms cannot have distinct legitimacy because (a) they have no identifiable content and (b) they are not agreed upon as binding. It is unclear what the requirements of hierarchy or spheres of influence are: military implications, political, economic, or ideological; and consequently it is very difficult to demonstrate in individual cases that political norms such as hierarchy or spheres of influence are violated. All in all, political norms can be community policies depicting the possible direction of emergence of legal regulation through treaty or custom, but not more than that.

Not all 'political norms' or 'political laws' count as political foundations of international law. In this sense the balance of power possesses a unique systemic relevance, while most other 'political norms' merely interact with international legal process in occasional ways. Balance of power is sometimes seen as a law of nature.[101] According to Oppenheim, 'Law of Nations can exist only if there is an equilibrium, a balance of power, between the members of the Family of Nations. If the powers cannot keep one another

---

98 Morgenthau, *Politics among Nations*, 4.

99 S Burchill, 'Realism and Neo-Realism', in Burchill *et al.*, *Theories of International Relations* (2001), 78.

100 M Wight, *Power Politics* (1979), 179.

101 K Waltz, 'Anarchic Orders and Balances of Power', in Keohane (ed.), *Neorealism and Its Critics* (1986), 116.

in check, no rules of law will have any force, since an over-powerful State will naturally try to act according to discretion and disobey the law.'[102] As Kingsbury observes, 'Oppenheim himself saw the intimate connection between balance of power as a norm (or principle) of international politics and the structure of international law, while being careful to keep these formally distinct.'[103]

As Waltz explains, balance of power can impose restraints on power aspirations of States who may aspire to domination under the guise of survival. In effect balance prevents the world hegemony.[104] As Bull states, balance of powers has served to prevent the international system from being transformed by conquest into a universal empire.[105] This factor alone signifies the crucial importance of balance of power, and is also premised on the diversity in international society as a necessary precondition for the survival of international law. Political realism that regards power as a paramount consideration emphasises the equally vital role of balance of power. According to Waltz, in international politics the unbalanced power constitutes a danger 'even if it is American power that is out of balance'.[106] Unipolar systems are very precarious.[107] Hegemony is thus not easily sustainable over the long term.

According to Bull, international law depends for its survival on balance of power, while the preservation of the latter can result in the violation of international law, which brings the imperatives of the balance of power into conflict with those of international law.[108] This reasoning emphasises the systemic relevance of balance as a 'constitutional' principle alternative to law, yet is firmly premised on the denial of the identity between legal and political factors. In a broader context, Bull considers the function of law in relation to order in world politics to identify one of the competing principles of universal political organisation and proclaim its supremacy over other competitors. Thus, where international law clashes with balance of power, it actually hinders order rather than maintains it. Preventive war is illegal in international law, but may be conducive to balance of power. After all, law is an instrumentality of the variety of political purposes and the promotion of order is only one of them.[109]

Given that positivist international legal science focused on political foundations and preconditions of international law earlier than international relations theory, these political preconditions of international law do not have to be viewed as factors limiting the relevance of international law; they bring international law into existence and allow it to operate. Balance of powers may to some extent have the same importance for international law as national State and government has for national law. The existence of national society and State is indispensable for any viable national legal system to exist

---

102 L Oppehneim, *International Law*, volume 1 (1911), 73.

103 Kingsbury, *supra* n. 24, 420–421.

104 K Waltz, 'Anarchic Orders and Balances of Power', in Keohane (ed.), *Neorealism and Its Critics* (1986), 119, 127.

105 Bull, 102.

106 Quoted in S Burchill, 'Realism and Neo-Realism', in Burchill *et al.*, *Theories of International Relations* (2001), 97.

107 Ibid., 98.

108 Bull, 104–105.

109 Bull, 135, 138, 139.

and operate. But this is not to argue that national law possesses no separate identity from that national society and State.

As Kingsbury argues, 'notions of a balance of power now usually enter legal debates not as formulations of positive legal norms, but as an element of the set of political and ethical norms that enable international society to function, and that inform the values and operation of international legal rules and institutions'. Furthermore, 'The too frequent neglect by international lawyers of such interrelationships between international law and non-legal international normative structures is in part the result of positivist conceptions of law as a specialized and pure field of inquiry.'[110] But Kingsbury does not suggest a straightforward method whereby international lawyers should consider these non-legal 'normative' structures. Balance of power does not interfere with positivist foundations of international law. It seems that the interrelationship between the two could most usefully be viewed in a systemic perspective, as a matter of framework analysis, in terms of preconditions of the functioning of international law. If international law is to maintain its autonomy, these non-legal 'normative' factors should not interfere with the process of the application of specific rules of international law to facts and conduct of States.

Balance of powers is possibly the only political law that explains the essence of international law. It could not possibly be a legal principle, because if it were it would interfere with the freedom of States to redistribute power through bilateral deals, which is inherent in their sovereign autonomy. In conceptual terms, balance of powers limits certain patterns permissible under international law, and at times does so for the sake of preserving international law.

Now, to what shall that balance of powers, or equilibrium, relate? The 'classical' understanding of equilibrium refers to the balance of physical power so that no State can become so powerful as to endanger the existence and vital interests of other States. The need to maintain such equilibrium in the 16th to 19th centuries justified, as a matter of political assessment, armed intervention to deal with threats to that equilibrium. While such balance of powers is necessary for the existence and functioning of international law, it also has a broader dimension. Given that international law is a system of rules deriving from the consent of States, the balance necessary for its existence implies not only the balance of physical power, but also, separately but in interdependence with it, the balance of ideas, perceptions and interests that ultimately motivate States to accept or reject the relevant rule of international law, or seek a change in that rule. If the perception and interest of one State or group of States were to overtake the process of international law-making and law-enforcement, the will of other States would no longer count in this process and the autonomy of international law would get diffused into patterns of political ideology. The maintenance of such equilibrium in a broad sense is necessary for preserving the legitimacy of international law as a system of rules deriving from the expression of autonomous will.[111]

---

[110] Kingsbury, *supra* n. 24, 420.

[111] To that extent, pluralism is crucial for maintenance of the autonomy of international law, but this is pluralism in the society and does not contradict the solidarist elements that may be discerned from that society upon appreciation. See below section 11.8.

11.6 INTERNATIONAL LEGAL ARGUMENT AND THEORIES OF INTERNATIONAL RELATIONS

The debate about interaction between legal and policy arguments is widely reflected in the theory of international relations. It is emphasised that the theory to which a scholar subscribes will influence, if not determine, his views of international law.[112] In addressing the potential impact of these theories on international legal reasoning, it is proposed to focus on three theories that deal with factors potentially affecting the content, observance or systemic survival of international law: realism, constructivism and liberalism.

11.6.1 Realism

Principal categories of realism are national interest and power. According to Bull, pursuit of power is the denominator of all foreign policy.[113] Obviously States seek survival, but they also seek a broad range of purposes going beyond that, including domination.[114] According to Waltz, *Realpolitik* is based on interest-based calculation in a competitive environment, 'and success is defined as preserving and strengthening the State'.[115] The basic categories of realism are often seen in terms of ideological purposes. National interest is not exclusively part of the realist argument, but also can have ideological connotations. Morgenthau focuses on the ideological interest of States, who try to promote their particular ideologies, which can meet power resistance from another end.[116] But the argument premised on ideology is no longer a realist argument. From the pure realist perspective the crucial point is not whether the State sees its interest to promote a particular ideology, but whether it has enough power to overcome the resistance it is likely to meet. It has been a reality of both Cold War and post-Cold War politics that the policy and interest in promoting a particular ideology is not always accompanied by the necessary amount of power to do so.

As Keohane suggests, realism is necessary for any coherent understanding of world politics, because it focuses on power, interest and rationality.[117] Realism is based on a presumption that States act rationally in a way comprehensible to others; realism does not argue this axiomatically, but merely presents this as an interpretative guide to statesmen's actions. The realist focus on rationality was crucial in creating the 'science' of international relations.[118] By contrast, according to Gilpin, realism should be seen as a set of philosophical dispositions rather than a scientific approach.[119] In any case, realists

---

112 Arend (1999), 112.

113 Bull, 105; see also S Burchill, 'Realism and Neo-Realism', in Burchill *et al.*, *Theories of International Relations* (2001), 75.

114 K Waltz, 'Political Structures', in Keohane (ed.), *Neorealism and Its Critics* (1986), 85–86.

115 K Waltz, 'Anarchic Orders and Balances of Power', in Keohane (ed.), *Neorealism and Its Critics* (1986), 115–116.

116 See further below 11.6.3 on liberalism.

117 R Keohane, 'Theory in World Politics: Structural Realism and Beyond', in Keohane (ed.), *Neorealism and Its Critics* (1986), 159, 191.

118 R Keohane, 'Neorealism in World Politics', in Keohane (ed.), *Neorealism and Its Critics* (1986), 7, 10.

119 R Gilpin, 'The Richness of the Tradition of Political Realism', in Keohane (ed.), *Neorealism and Its Critics* (1986), 304.

are unified in their scepticism on making the world just and peaceful, and hold that the principles of domestic politics cannot be applied to international affairs.[120] Realism at times has been understood as amoral, justifying war and atrocities; in other versions, it has been understood as having a moral dimension too. Not all realists are agreed on whether this approach regards the State as a supreme entity, free of moral constraints.[121]

Classical realism is deemed to be sceptical about international law, as appears from the writings of EH Carr and Hans Morgenthau: 'legalism' is understood as a 'utopian' thinking. Instead, classical realism sought to provide conceptual ground for US foreign policy in terms of rationalising the accumulation of power.[122] Neo-realists criticise Morgenthau's 'murky' concept of power with little focus on its discontents, which made his theory inconsistent.[123]

Despite the initial and substantial utility of realism, it has weaknesses and its grasp can never be complete. As Keohane explains, the concept of power is difficult to measure validly a priori, and interests are underspecified. Realism does not clarify how order can be created from anarchy without superordinate power, and how peaceful change occurs.[124] In other words, realism neither claims the monopoly on truth nor aspires to explain all aspects of international relations.

Efforts to define national interest a priori have been unsuccessful.[125] National interest derives from national identity, which can be defined as a condition in which a mass of people have the same identification with national symbols and mobilise to act as one psychological group when these symbols can be enhanced or where they are threatened, to defend the shared national identity. National interest is capable of triggering mass national mobilisation to defend or enhance national identity.[126]

However, the factor of mobilisation of the public to defend national interest can be caused by what the relevant elite, acting through politics and media, will present to the public as their national interest. If an identity-based, that is 'subjective', view of national interest is taken, then national interest can be anything the relevant nation perceives it at any given moment to be. On the other hand, the link between interest and identity is indisputable and the search for any objective standard of defining the State's national interest would be unsound. But this does not remove the problem of distinguishing the properly national interest from that of the ruler or elite group – this problem may be as acute today as a few centuries ago when the concept of interest-based *Realpolitik* began to evolve. Still, an 'external' exercise in defining the State's national interest is indefensible. The dilemma can be resolved by studying the considerations that place limits on interests in the international society when they conflict with international law as, for instance, the

---

120 S Burchill, 'Realism and Neo-Realism', in Burchill *et al.*, *Theories of International Relations* (2001), 70–71.

121 R Gilpin, 'The Richness of the Tradition of Political Realism', in Keohane (ed.), *Neorealism and Its Critics* (1986), 319–320.

122 R Keohane, 'Neorealism in World Politics', in Keohane (ed.), *Neorealism and Its Critics* (1986), 9.

123 Ibid., 11, 13.

124 Ibid., 191, 199.

125 Ibid., 182.

126 W Bloom, *Personal Identity, National Identity and International Relations* (1990), 52, 79, 83.

International Court of Justice observed in the *Congo-Uganda Armed Activities* case in terms of the claims of legal relevance of security interests of States.[127]

Power refers to capacities and resources that are instrumental in pursuing the national interest. Power is not fixed in time and space, and is difficult to measure. Its use does not always guarantee its impact in the particular context of international politics. Nor does the power status of a State necessarily translate into its ability to influence the relevant situation.

It could never be enough to take power for granted, as self-explanatory; it is also needed to define its parameters, and clarify to what extent these parameters can be established with scientific certainty. Classical realism understands the power factor as fixing the position of States in the sense that smaller States have to adapt to irresistible forces and tendencies, which they are unable to alter and which favour strong States' interests.[128] Under this approach, power politics, under which weaker States obey the will of stronger ones, translates effectively into that of hegemonic international law, under which stronger States effectively control law-making. One realist concept of power refers to resources that can be used to induce other actors to do what they would not otherwise do, in accordance with the desires of the power-wielder. The outcomes of power action refer to the result of economic or military conflicts, and to changes in rules and institutions that regulate inter-State relations.[129] This phenomenon is crucially important in understanding the normative implications of power.

Schwarzenberger defines power as

> capacity to impose one's will on others by reliance on effective sanctions in case of non-compliance . . . [and] to exercise compelling pressure irrespective of its reasonableness. If the group or individual passively involved in the power nexus submits to pressure, this is due to a desire to avoid disagreeable consequences of resistance.

Power can be used for self-interest or in the interest of international society,[130] distinguishing between which can be difficult in practice and certainly cannot be performed by reliance on the claimed motives of the power-wielder only.

Depending on what factors are included in the concept of power, the same political entity could be seen as more or less powerful. To Dean Acheson, 'power is that combination of population, resources, technology, and will which makes a national society dominant among other national societies'.[131] The realist implications of power are presented in two ways. Stronger States can get away with the violation of law as a matter of fact;

---

[127] *Case Concerning the Armed Activities on the Territory of the Congo* (Democratic Republic of the Congo v Uganda), Judgment of 19 December 2005, General List No. 116, para. 26 (the Court acknowledged that the case involved security interest implications, but observed that its task was to resolve the dispute in accordance with legal rules).

[128] S Burchill, 'Realism and Neo-Realism', in Burchill *et al.*, *Theories of International Relations* (2001), 76.

[129] R Keohane, 'Theory in World Politics: Structural Realism and Beyond', in Keohane (ed.), *Neorealism and Its Critics* (1986), 183.

[130] G Schwarzenberger, *Power Politics* (1964), 14–15.

[131] D Acheson, 'Foreign Policy of the United States', 18 *Arkansas Law Review* (1964–1965), 225 at 226–227.

States will do what they think is in their interest and if they are powerful, international law cannot provide remedies against this;[132] or if the argument is taken further, their violation can bring about the change in the pertinent legal position: stronger States determine the content of international law.

According to Gilpin, although international rules express the inter-State consensus, the primary foundation of rights and duties of States is the power interest of most powerful States.[133] Such construction of realism, if accepted without limits, is a denial of normativity of international law, because the foundation of rights and duties is consent not power. A more balanced version is suggested by Hurrell, suggesting that there are a number of options available to powerful States in the process of law-making:

> to determine which issues get negotiated via formal interstate bodies and which are, for example, managed via market mechanisms; to influence both the rules of the bargaining game and what is allowed onto the agenda; to deploy a wide range of sticks and carrots in the bargaining process, including the threat of direct coercion; and, finally, to walk away from any institution that becomes too constraining. Institutions are not just concerned with liberal purposes of solving common problems or promoting shared values. They are also sites of power and reflect and entrench power hierarchies and the interests of powerful states.[134]

Still, institutions are not just the reflection of power and interest; they are an *agreed* reflection of that. It is right that major institutional projects such as the United Nations were realised because of the backing by great powers. But this is not the only means of relationship between law and power. Many rules of international law have appeared or been re-appraised as a consequence of the concerted attitude of third world States, such as the principle of self-determination, rules of the law of the sea, rules on the treatment of foreign investment and so on. Thus either power should not necessarily be seen as impacting the relevant legal position, or a deeper, more multi-dimensional insight into the concept of power is required than some versions of realism provide.

Every society, whether national or international, is premised on the reality that the pertinent actors, whether States, individuals or their groups, refrain from doing certain things they can afford to do owing to their power position (just as unbridled power action in defiance of law takes place at least as often in national as international societies). Now, it is plausible that these actors refrain from using their power because doing so is in their interest; but then, societies are always arranged to reflect the interests of their constituent actors, because the latter prefer living in order as opposed to chaos, the inevitable premise of which is the restraint on the use of available power. This is among other things why the illegal use of power is (almost) always met with disapproval by the international community. Nobody can deny that power can affect things at a factual level, but it would be a step too far to suggest that the power action by itself entails normative implications.

Wight treats international law as qualification to international society being anarchic and as meant to modify the patterns of power politics. But 'while in domestic politics the struggle for power is governed and circumscribed by the framework of law and institutions, in international politics law and institutions are governed and circumscribed by the

---

132 Carr, 297.

133 Gilpin (1981), 35.

134 A Hurrell, *On Global Order* (2008), 38.

struggle for power. This is indeed the justification for calling international politics "power politics" *par excellence*.'[135] As Hurrell explains,

> the tremendous differences in the scale of inequality between domestic and international settings do have a crucial negative impact on the possibility of any centralized system of law and order as well as other less structured forms of governance. Inequality means that some states have far less need for the cooperation and forbearance of others, that the strength of the violators of law can easily come to exceed that of the upholders of law, and that, even if this is not the case, attempts at coercive sanctions against violators will involve large-scale conflict.[136]

While these considerations are legitimate, in national societies the power difference between the individual and the government and elite is often far greater than in international society. Conflicts between power groups happen in national societies as well, as is the case with rebels and various clans. As the experience of many countries confirms, if a power group within a State intends to turn its will or position into law, all it needs to do is to influence a few political leaders, which will then be reflected in voting in the legislature. The outcome will bind the entire population of the State. In international society, power of a 'hegemon' cannot be so easily translated into law, because law needs State consent, and no State is bound unless it has consented.

The predominance of power and violence is not, as Waltz clarifies, any inherent implication of the lack of government over States. Some of the worst cases of violence have been committed by the State within its boundaries against its own population. This reinforces the observation of Waltz that 'The distinction between anarchy and government does not tell us much.'[137] If the factors of power and violence affect the nature and normativity of law, then they must be seen as doing so in relation to all law, not international law specifically.

In addition, power alone is not enough to resolve international problems. As Hurrell explains,

> states need international law and institutions both to share the material and political costs of protecting their interests and to gain the authority and legitimacy that the possession of crude power can never secure on its own. All major powers face the imperative of trying to turn a capacity for crude coercion into legitimate authority. . . . Power is not self-justifying; it must be justified by reference to some source outside or beyond itself, and thus be transformed into 'authority'. For this reason, it is a mistake to view 'law' as something that is, or can be, wholly separated from some separate other thing called 'political interest'.[138]

This emphasises the interdependence between law and politics, in particular the dependence of viability of political institutions on the operation of international law. But this very interdependence implies a lack of identity between the two, that is the separate existence of both categories in relation to each other. The very essence of international law is to apply to power relations and specify which exercise of power is lawful and which

---

[135] M Wight, *Power Politics* (1989), 102.
[136] A Hurrell, *On Global Order* (2008), 30.
[137] K Waltz, 'Anarchic Orders and Balances of Power', in Keohane (ed.), *Neorealism and Its Critics* (1986), 98–99.
[138] A Hurrell, *On Global Order* (2008), 39, 78.

is not. The possibility of characterising power action as unlawful is inherent in the very idea of law. A unique vision of power in relation to international law specifically cannot be consistently adopted.

The relativity of power and its dependence on context is best illustrated by Cox's distinction between the basic nature of the actors (power-seeking) and their mode of operation (power-balancing).[139] Thus, even if the power factor has initial significance, its ultimate significance is to be an element of balance between different power-wielders. As Hurrell further explains,

> power is not simply about one state seeking to change or shape the actions of another—getting someone else to do what they would not otherwise have done. It cannot be reduced to the interactions of pregiven actors. It is also about the constitution of action and the material and discursive conditions for action. Such ideas can sometimes sound abstract and overly structural.[140]

In an even more complex way, Keohane articulates the notion of fungibitity of power, which means that across the variety of fields great powers would necessarily prevail over smaller powers. Still, the failures of great powers to control weaker States in some issue-areas could be explained by the fact that 'the States that are weaker on an overall basis have more power resources than their stronger partners, and that the use of power derived from one area of activity to affect outcomes in other areas (through "linkages") is difficult'.[141]

As historical experience indeed shows, power-wielders do not always get their way, as was the case with the war in Vietnam or US intervention in Somalia. The outcome of US-led wars in Iraq and Afghanistan is far from clear. The US/UK power engagement with Libya in the 1990s over the Libyan refusal to extradite to those countries two terrorist suspects who were its nationals did not, despite the prevailing power of the United States and the United Kingdom, make their policies succeed. Although Security Council sanctions were imposed on Libya, they were not effective, and the final outcome of the dispute reflected the original preference of Libya.[142] The normalisation of US/UK–Libyan relations took place on the basis of mutual compromise and through the means of international law.[143] In other cases, States in a disadvantaged power position can rely on the alternative power, as the examples of Cuba and more recently Zimbabwe demonstrate. Power indisputably matters, but it is often spread in such a way that puts limits on either the power-wielder's ability to project power, or the effect of the projected power, or causes the power-wielder to pay a higher political price than it would have foreseen.

Some aspects of international law-making can be explained by Cox's description of the relationship between the stronger and weaker States where the former (including

---

139 R Cox, 'Social Forces, States and World Orders', in Keohane (ed.), *Neorealism and Its Critics* (1986), 243.

140 A Hurrell, *On Global Order* (2008), 72.

141 R Keohane, 'Theory in World Politics: Structural Realism and Beyond', in Keohane (ed.), *Neorealism and Its Critics* (1986), 184, 187; 'No matter how carefully power resources are defined, no power model will be able accurately to predict outcomes.' Non-power factors are also important, *Id.*, 195–196.

142 A Aust, 'Lockerbie: The Other Case', 49 *ICLQ* (2000), 283.

143 J Schwartz, 'Dealing With a 'Rogue State': The Libya Precedent', 101 *AJIL* (2007), 553.

'hegemons') do not use power but make concessions to the latter to secure their acquiescence to their leadership.[144] Thus, power by itself does not produce or change law. This is more a process of bargaining than power domination. Bare power does not get one as far as is sometimes assumed.

Morgenthau is overall right that replacing general patterns of 'old' power politics and diplomacy based on national interest is not an implication of modern international law. International law does not produce legalistic diplomacy.[145] According to Bull, the special interests of the dominant powers in society determine the content of the rules limiting the resort to force, regulating the binding force of agreements and property rights. These dominant elements are expected not to withdraw from rules but have them changed according to their interest.[146] Cox argues that institutions reflect power relations at the time of their creation and at least initially they encourage collective images consistent with those power relations. There is a close link between institutionalisation and hegemony. Eventually, however, institutions take on their life.[147] This way realism acknowledges the separate identity of law.

Experience indeed shows that the rules Bull refers to on occasions contradict the interest of the 'dominant element' or 'hegemon', and they attempt to have them replaced or rewritten. But such attempts are not successful because the rest of international society does not acquiesce in that. In other words, certain rules, although at the time of their emergence presumably reflecting the interest of dominant powers, continue in their original shape even if that interest will subsequently contradict it. Validity of legal rules, because of its consensual foundation, is more robust than ever-changing political interest and power positions. International law is the only measure of what States regard as just and fair. If the exercise of power goes against that, the power-wielder is acting in an anti-systemic way. Breach of law causes loss of certain policy and power assets.

Power, in whichever modality, is a constitutive element of every society organised around certain values. Law is needed to fix power positions; to allow bargaining for securing the national interest. Without law, power could be counter-productive and potentially self-destructive. If the realist aim is to have an international society that works according to the expectations and interests of States, then such a society must necessarily adhere to some rules that define the required or expected standard of State conduct. The realist understanding of power is far more complex than simple assumptions of power as a tool to make others do one's will and get away with what one does. If power is seen as an organising factor, it simply cannot be viewed as an unlimited tool in any State's hand.

The engagement of realism with the international law argument is a necessary precondition for the coherence of realism as a theory to understand international relations. The acceptance of the starting-point that legal rules are indispensable if national interest and power positions are to be maintained and safeguarded – that is if power and national interest can succeed in the conditions of order as opposed to anarchy – necessarily

---

144 R Cox, 'Social Forces, States and World Orders', in Keohane (ed.), *Neorealism and Its Critics* (1986), 219, 246.

145 H Morgenthau, 'Diplomacy', 55 *Yale Law Journal* (1945–1946), 1067.

146 Bull, 53.

147 R Cox, 'Social Forces, States and World Orders', in Keohane (ed.), *Neorealism and Its Critics* (1986), 219.

requires a realistic reappraisal of how far political power can and should be used in breach of international law for it not to undermine the fundamental premises of international society and order that maintain and nourish the viability of that very power and the position of power-wielders. Anarchy in the literal sense undermines both power and national interest: the assets gained through power position can be maintained only if order is maintained in the first place. Order in its turn cannot exist without law.

International law does not inherently mind States maximising their power, because it is premised on States as power bases, organised as territorial entities with territorial supremacy and authority over the content of international law, which enables them to safeguard their interests in the process of international law-making. Much of international law is about the patterns of the exercise of economic and military power, e.g. the law of countermeasures under the law of state responsibility, or the rules on the use of force. In these cases international law appears as the regulator defining the permissible uses of power. National interest motivates introducing the international legal regulation on a number of subjects. A number of rules on jurisdiction, trade and economic law, law of the sea, and reprisals are designed precisely to enable the State to keep itself powerful, wealthy and influential. If the rules of international law would go against the national interest of States, the latter would never agree upon them. In short, international law is premised on national power and interest.

On the other hand, international law places restrictions on the range of means through which national interest can be pursued, e.g. not to perpetrate aggression, not to bomb civilian objects, or not to commit genocide, in order to preserve the values on which the international community is united. In this sense international law does not aim to equalise the power and influence of States. It only reflects the fact that while free to pursue national interest, States live in a society which, if it is to avoid descending into anarchy, inherently requires the presence of limitations on national power.

As is commonly accepted, national interest can be either primary and fundamental, or context-dependent and even occasional and transitional.[148] If an interest is permanent and vital, essential for the State to survive and exist, and needs to be maintained in the context of international relations, then presumably most or all States have such an interest. This makes it more likely that international law will reflect this interest as a normative principle. In this sense, international law is an agreed and consensual reflection of what sort of interest States are reasonably expected to have, and how these interests should be ranked.[149] In this sense, national interest, although to some extent expressing the selfish aspirations of States, is nevertheless a structural and societal phenomenon: States can only desire as much as is compatible with their being part of the international society. The assertion of national interest in such unlimited sense can be not only illegal but also – which matters more from the policy perspective – anti-societal, with repercussions for the holder of the pertinent national interest.

International law exists in the environment of power relations. It coexists with power politics. Yet it is not the same as mere incidence of power; it is possible only because

---

[148] TW Robinson, 'National Interest', in JN Rosenau (ed.), *International Politics and Foreign Policy* (1969), 182 at 184.

[149] Constructivism may indeed have a point in this respect, see below 11.6.2.

there is a limit on power. The fact that international law has survived so far in the power politics environment is due to the fact that power is not all that matters in international relations. Although power can achieve short-term or long-term factual change, power per se cannot change the legal position. The latter can take place only through agreement between States and he who has power necessary for factual change has to have the power necessary to induce those who are opposed to that change to recognise the validity of that change. If power of such extent is lacking, the opposition to the legal change is not overridden and the 'old' legal position continues. While the violation does not change the legal position, the violator compromises not only the pertinent legal rule but also the legal system that, in the final analysis, gives sense to its power. It thereby compromises its own power position.

As is acknowledged in realist quarters, realism would be useless if dogmatically viewed as a set of answers to problems faced in world politics. It is especially weak in explaining change.[150] Hardly any version of realism has argued in absolute and axiomatic terms that power is the only and most important factor that explains international events. There are two factors enabling realism to embrace the relevance of international legal argument: limits on realism in explaining things and implications of unaccountable power. To conclude, what is realistic and what is not can point to different outcomes in different situations and hence cannot provide a coherent guide as to how international rights and obligations have to be seen or applied. On the other hand, the enduring relevance of realism is caused by its lack of ideological foundation,[151] and its ability to argue on the basis of necessity and rationality.[152] Whatever the merits of particular points of realism, it is firmly based within the realm of science and not of ideology. Given that realism's overall argument is incomplete and partial, the 'legalist' argument can likewise comment on realism only in such partial terms.

11.6.2 Constructivism

Constructivism assumes that the structure of the international system is social and not strictly material. Shared ideas, beliefs and values possess structural characteristics and shape the identity and interest of actors. This happens through imagination, communication and constraint. The pertinent norms and ideas work through their moral force in the relevant context. The language of justification provides the constraint of action.[153] Reality depends on how States perceive their material conditions.[154] As Hurrell describes the constructivist approach, 'Institutions are not about ways of helping actors achieve pregiven interests; rather interests and identities are shaped and reshaped by ongoing interaction, by institutional enmeshment, and by the processes of legal, administrative,

---

150 R Keohane, 'Theory in World Politics: Structural Realism and Beyond', in Keohane (ed.), *Neorealism and Its Critics* (1986), 159.

151 Ibid., 182.

152 S Burchill, 'Realism and Neo-Realism', in Burchill *et al.*, *Theories of International Relations* (2001), 98.

153 C Reus-Smit, 'Constructivism', in Burchill *et al.*, *Theories of International Relations* (2001), 217–219.

154 Arend (1999), 125, 127.

and cognitive internalization to which this gives rise.'[155] Constructivism seems to point to the role of international law as shaping and impacting the choice and interest of States. Thus, States might continue observing the rules of international law even if that would no longer respond to their interests.[156]

Much of identity and interest of a State derives from how it identifies itself and what need it feels to support its existence, survival and development. Shared ideas and beliefs come on the top of that, which explains that constructivism can explain only part of international politics. Still, there may be an inherent merit in the argument that by becoming members of international society, States accept some impact of this process on their identity and interest.

To some extent constructivism contradicts realism, as can be illustrated by Hans Morgenthau's vision of the United Nations system as not transforming the patterns of power politics, but as itself becoming an arena for that.[157] But even so, it is implausible that being part of the UN system has absolutely no impact on States' perception of their interests and identity. Instead, such processes should be seen as reciprocal interaction between the States' self-perceived identity and interest, and the context in which States aspire to pursue those interests. The latter obviously does not reform the substance of the former, but still has some effect on it, the precise extent of which should be ascertained in particular cases.

Although on its surface constructivism looks more international law-friendly, it does not as such explain the essence of the international legal system. The task of international legal reasoning is not to examine how international law shapes the identity and conduct of States on a general plane, but to assess the legality of specific conduct of States in the light of prescriptions of international law. However, the constructivist approach can be useful for the policy analysis of how international law works.

The partial value of constructivism is well illustrated by Hurrell, suggesting that 'Constructivism, with its emphasis on norms and rules, is often associated with a more optimistic view of international relations. But a constructivist view of power and of the problem of power is potentially more troubled, even tragic, than that of the comfortingly rationalist vision of the neo-realists.'[158] This is quite understandable as constructivism, just like realism, is focused only on part of international political processes and cannot be the best at explaining that in which it possesses no comparative advantage. Still, given that realism focuses only on the power part of international relations, constructivism is certainly useful in voicing the role of non-material factors, within which international law certainly falls, as constraining the interests and choices of States.

11.6.3 Liberalism

Applying liberal ideas to international relations presupposes that the world consisting of liberal democracies would have less incentive for wars. According to the liberal

---

155 A Hurrell, *On Global Order* (2008), 71.
156 Arend (1999), 131.
157 H Morgenthau, 'Diplomacy', 55 *Yale Law Journal* (1945–1946), 1067 at 1069–1070.
158 A Hurrell, *On Global Order* (2008), 36.

internationalist tradition from Kant onwards, States are not the principal rationale of the international system but the tools to achieve lasting peace and prosperity. On the other hand, liberal ideas have been promoted internationally to advance pragmatic national interest, as the United States used the free trade slogan as a tool to promote the access of its companies to foreign markets and achieve the position of world financial hegemony. Similarly, Britain did not hesitate in the 19th century to use force to protect its industries from foreign competition.[159] The sustainability of independent relevance of liberal ideas in international affairs is not obvious.

Liberals state their opposition to sovereign equality of States as accepted since the times of Grotius, and instead focus on the ideological type of the State to determine its status.[160] The liberal approach tries to see international law redesigned according to ideological premises: 'Liberals distinguish among States on the basis of their regime type.'[161] It is asserted that liberal market democracy is an internationally sanctioned legitimate model of domestic governance.[162] But in order for this to be so, the agreement of States to this effect ought to be demonstrated. Linking liberal ideology to the content of international law contradicts the nature of international law as the body of rules established through the agreement of States not subject to any overarching sovereign.

Liberalism can make sense in national societies where the protection of individuals is the fundamental aim of domestic constitutions, which no doubt is a heritage of classical liberal thought developed over the 18th to 19th centuries. In the inter-State legal order an ideology like liberalism cannot determine the character of the system. Liberal ideas and patterns face stiff opposition in international affairs from a number of States that do not want to embrace liberal ideology.[163]

Liberal theory is effectively an attempt to redefine international law and discover its broader concept,[164] which goes hand in hand with liberals' refusal to acknowledge the dividing line between law and politics. This further emphasises the similarity between liberal theory and the policy-oriented approach. Slaughter's emphasis on behavioural difference between States is generically similar to McDougal's reference to 'human dignity', among others in the hydrogen bomb test case. Further similarity with the New Haven School is visible from the opposition of liberalism to the basic structure of international law. As Slaughter claims, 'territorial boundaries become increasingly meaningless, so that situs analysis cedes its place to interest analysis'.[165] Both the New Haven School and

---

159 S Burchill, 'Liberalism', in Burchill *et al.*, *Theories of International Relations* (2001), 31, 52–53.

160 A-M Slaughter, 'International Law and International Relations Theory: A Dual Agenda', 87 *AJIL* (1993), 205 at 226–228.

161 A-M Slaughter, A Tulumello and S Wood, 'International Law and International Relations Theory: A New Generation of Inter-Disciplinary Scholarship', 92 *AJIL* (1998), 367 at 373.

162 I Clark, *Legitimacy in International Society* (2007), 180.

163 S Burchill, 'Liberalism', in Burchill *et al.*, *Theories of International Relations* (2001), 36–37, 43.

164 As conceded by liberal authors, A-M Slaughter, A Tulumello and S Wood, 'International Law and International Relations Theory: A New Generation of Inter-Disciplinary Scholarship', 92 *AJIL* (1998), 367 at 378.

165 A-M Slaughter, 'International Law and International Relations Theory: A Dual Agenda', 87 *AJIL* (1993), 205 at 236.

liberalism aspire to giving non-State entities a greater role than that envisaged within the positivist framework,[166] and provide ideological reasons for justifying humanitarian intervention that has no standing within the international legal system.

The internal inconsistency of the liberal theory has been exposed by the analysis of Jose Alvarez, demonstrating not only the evidence contradicting the premises of the liberal theory, but also that the behaviour of liberal States is not as conducive to peace and compatible with international law as the liberal theory imagines. 'Liberal' States are still keen on their sovereign autonomy, often contrary to the imperatives of liberalism.[167]

The internal inconsistency of the liberal theory is manifested when, if taken to its logical conclusion, it becomes an ideological tool for power struggle and an enhancement of political interest in the most classical pattern of *Realpolitik*, by helping one political interest to gain the ideological upper hand over other political interests. If that scheme were to be given effect, States would see their sovereign rights curtailed or nullified because they are not liberal democracies. That is why international law resists liberal ideology to matter per se, as a systemically impossible option. Non-liberal States could reciprocate; without reciprocity there could be no international law.

This is where liberalism fails to grasp the nature of the international legal system. States have rights, and those rights can be exercised to the extent allowed by international law, whatever the ideological dimension. In essence the liberal ideology, if given full effect, would entail abolition of international law as we know it. The ideology of promoting liberal values is in effect what Kant understood as a perpetual peace under universal empire. In this sense liberalism goes hand in hand with territorial expansion eventually aimed at universal domination.[168] Universal international law does not have to rely on universal moral, ethical and cultural traditions. It instead exists because States with different cultures and traditions have over centuries come to realise the need for coexistence to a degree that is reflected in particular rules of international law.

That the liberal theory is effectively an ideological antithesis to the nature of international law is demonstrated by the possibility of a similar ideological approach being taken on other sides. For instance, in 1960 the GDR communist leader Walter Ulbricht asserted that while the U2 reconnaissance flights conducted by the United States was spying, the similar collection of information by what he denoted as 'peace-lovers' was a 'humane duty'.[169] This is not qualitatively different from asserting the humane responsibility to intervene militarily for protecting human rights.

The inherent weakness of liberalism can be exposed if Morgenthau's thesis as to the inexistence of universally recognised moral and ethical principles is recalled. Political leaders often cast their argument in moral and ideological terms but in reality they are guided by considerations of national interest and power. Moral language is used for the sake of gaining political advantage.[170] Morgenthau rejects the idea of universalising one's

---

166 S Wiessner and A Willard, 'Policy-Oriented Jurisprudence and Human Rights Abuses in Internal Conflict: Toward a World Public Order of Human Dignity', 93 *AJIL* (1999), 316 at 323.

167 J Alvarez, 'Do Liberal States Behave Better? A Critique of Slaughter's Liberal Theory', 12 *EJIL* (2001), 183.

168 *Cf.* Wight (1979), 144.

169 Wight (1979), 119–120.

170 H Morgenthau, *Politics among Nations*, 5, 12.

moral and ethical principles.[171] Dependence of liberal ideology on power is also explained by Hurrell:

> the end of the Cold War ushered in a new distribution of power centered on the United States and the developed world, ending the challenges to Western conceptions of international society that had previously come from both the East and the South. The stability and legitimacy of liberal solidarism therefore cannot be divorced from the historical context of the highly unequal power relations from which it emerged.[172]

Thus, change in the power relations at the relevant historical stage will affect the standing of liberal ideology in international relations. Liberal theory has no independent conceptual explanation as far as international relations are concerned. Liberal ideology is in essence a repetition of earlier ideologies of colonialism and empire based on the superiority of one particular civilisation over others; liberal ideology is always premised on the superiority of power of liberal States that will help them to overcome the ideology of non-liberal States.

11.6.4 Evaluation of Theories

As Keohane suggests, international politics can be best understood through multidimensional analysis.[173] In this writer's view, different theories of international law are not mutually contradictory but mutually complementary, each of them focusing on the aspect of international politics unaddressed, or incompletely addressed, by other theories. In other words, each theory may possess comparative advantage in focusing on particular elements of international politics which are not the principal focus of other theories. This partial nature of each theory should be considered when its reflection of international legal argument is studied.

Lawyers, not always familiar with details of realism, often assume straightforward realist premises and treat them as limits on the legal argument. But realist international relations scholars do not treat realism as a set of unquestionable truths or a theory providing answers across the board. Realists acknowledge that the power factor cannot explain as many things as is often believed.

Liberalism and realism to some extent contain hidden appeal to each other, the former appealing to liberal ideology as a justification of the use of power, and the latter appealing to the power position of liberal States. There is no pure liberal theory of international law or international relations. What is professed as liberalism often supports the *Realpolitik*. Similarly, there is no pure realism because it is at times explained on the grounds of ideology.

A fusion argument would be that international law is what Western liberal powers would desire and enforce through their prevailing power. This is not frequently articulated by writers, but several doctrinal approaches seem to be premised on this perception. Crucial questions to be answered in this process are: do Western States have enough

---

171 S Burchill, 'Realism and Neo-Realism', in Burchill *et al.*, *Theories of International Relations* (2001), 80.

172 A Hurrell, *On Global Order* (2008), 75.

173 R Keohane, 'Theory in World Politics: Structural Realism and Beyond', in Keohane (ed.), *Neorealism and Its Critics* (1986), 200.

power to impose their international law on others? Are non-Western States likely to agree to that? What does the historical and empirical perspective have to say on these points?

Historically, liberalism justified colonialism,[174] which in its turn was among the rationales reinforcing the idea of European international law in the 18th and 19th centuries.[175] The liberal ideology in international law and relations is based on the same premise as underlies the idea of European international law, propagating priority and exclusivity based on culture and ideology. As Koskenniemi clarifies in analysing Slaughter's liberal theory, we have already been here when Schmitt and Morgenthau focused on power politics in an ideological context.[176] But this is only part of the truth. In fact, we have been there more than once: before Schmitt and Morgenthau, that is in times when the ideology of European international law was promoted; and after Schmitt and Morgenthau, when the policy-oriented school promoted the idea of differential treatment of the rights of States in terms of their ideological position.

The realist emphasis on power is often mixed with ideological and value judgments and prescriptive analysis. European international law, Cold War ideologies such as New Haven, post-Cold War liberalism, and the George W Bush doctrine of use of force and exporting democracy are essentially the same, even if not identical, phenomena. Their common gist is that some who are believed to have a superior power position are better and more rightful than others, more civilised, and should be seen as entitled to induce others to accept their vision and values, presumably even against their will; or suffer from the overwhelming power. All these ideologies presuppose the centrality of Europe/the West in creating and applying international law, without adducing the evidence to prove this position.

Viewing liberalism as determining the ways for the development of law in international society whose mainstream processes are still based on power and national interest effectively means according distinct legitimacy to the will and vision of power-wielders. In other words, liberalism can become an ideology justifying the position of hegemons if this will be supported by the patterns of allocation of power. If those patterns point to multipolarism under which power is shared between liberal and non-liberal States, liberalism would have no original significance for and impact on international affairs. On the other hand, the realist focus on national interest can help to explain the consensual nature of the international legal system. Precisely because States have national interest to care for, they will not accept a legal system imposing legal regulation on them where they have not consented.

Liberalism and constructivism also contain a hidden appeal to each other, if the argument is made that the ideology that shapes the interests and identity of States is the liberal ideology. An ideological edge of constructivism is demonstrated by the suggestion that being a liberal democracy encourages an intolerance of authoritarian regimes and a preference for free-market capitalism.[177] On balance, the utility of liberalism should

---

[174] See Kingsbury, *EJIL* (2002), 413.

[175] *Cf.* Orakhelashvili, 'The Idea of European International Law', 17 *EJIL* (2006), 317–345.

[176] M Koskenniemi, 'Carl Schmitt, Hans Morgenthau and the Image of Law in International Relations', in M Byers (ed.), *The Role of Law in International Politics* (1999), 16 at 33–34.

[177] C Reus-Smit, 'Constructivism', in Burchill *et al.*, *Theories of International Relations* (2001), 217.

be seen not as original and self-explanatory, but preferably through the prism of factors that constructivism perceives as relevant. Certain liberal values have indeed penetrated into the international legal system, notably through human rights law. This body of law is legally binding on States and presumably this factor affects the perception by States of their interests and identity. But this is not the same as the independent impact of liberal ideology on international affairs, which every State remains free to accept or reject save to the extent of obligations it has assumed.

11.7 INTERNATIONAL AND WORLD SOCIETY

Both international law and international relations address the problem of the ultimate point of reference and constitutive element in the international system. International legal theory asks whether sovereign States determine the nature of the international legal system; or whether, conversely, the system itself confers the quality of statehood and sovereignty to the relevant entities. International relations theory likewise asks the question of whether the nature of international society is determined by the identity and interest of States, or vice versa. In this respect, it has to be clarified whether international society refers to a group of States united around a particular ideology, or to that governed by the common set of rules.

Institutions and rules of international society reflect its nature and structure.[178] Kingsbury is right in emphasising that the factor of international/world society as the basis and precondition of international law constitutes an alternative to viewing law as a sovereign command.[179] Social necessity indeed makes international law possible; but it is another question to what extent it shapes the content of international law.

There is no commonly accepted definition of international order, much as it may seem to encompass more than international law. Bull defines international order as a pattern of activity that sustains the elementary goals of the society of States. As for international society, it 'exists when a group of States, conscious of certain common interests and common values, . . . conceive themselves to be bound by a common set of rules', such as respect for each other's independence, honouring agreements and limits on the use of force.[180] Thus, whatever Bull's perceived scepticism as to international law, his definition of 'society of States' is premised on legal rules. International law is essential in organising international society, as every society is founded on understandings about security against violence, observance of agreements, and rules on property rights.[181] Bull's 'anarchy' in the international system is not anarchy proper because it presupposes, indeed is premised on, the existence of order. Anarchy here means merely the absence of centralised government. Buzan characterises Bull's approach as a 'highly rational, contractual, rule-based conception of society'.[182] According to Wight, 'the most essential evidence for the existence of

---

178 Wight (1979), 111.
179 Kingsbury, *supra* n. 24, 409.
180 Bull, 8, 13, 19.
181 Bull, 53.
182 B Buzan, *From International to World Society? English School Theory and the Social Structure of Globalisation* (2004), 52.

an international society is the existence of international law', because every society has law that defines the rights and duties of its members.[183]

Denoting the international system as society, order or anarchy is descriptive. What matters in the end is the content of the rules agreed between States. Bull considers that world society, encompassing not only States but also processes within States, is more important than international order that focuses on States, because the former order is about safeguarding the values of humanity as a whole, and the latter order is just instrumental to it. In terms of allocating the priorities of international society and order, Bull suggests that international society has treated the preservation of States as a goal subordinated to peace and preservation of that society itself. This is an argument that opens up ways for debating the legitimacy of various actions performed on the international plane and affecting rights and duties of States. Bull's prioritisation of 'world society' has more ideological connotation than is deducible from any firm evidence.[184]

Bull's approach also locates the conflict between the evidentiary approach and ideological perception. Although acknowledging that the reference to Western or European values is not sufficient for providing legitimacy, Bull still argues that if international society has any cultural basis, it is Western modernity.[185] Thus Bull's analysis does not clarify the question of how a set of values that enjoys on its own no international legitimacy can provide the cultural background for international society. The key to understanding the organising patterns of international society rests not only with how the essence of this society is perceived by a doctrinal observer, but also with what the attitude of that society is on particular issues of international affairs.

The structure of international society inherently derives from legal ideas. As Ruggie observes, the rediscovery from Roman law of the concept of absolute private property inspired and explained the simultaneous emergence of mutually exclusive territorial State formations. Private property rights and sovereignty are analogous in differentiating the mode of possession and exclusion of others. They thus establish social relations. The basic structure of property rights characterises the entire social formation.[186] In other words, legal concepts determine what international society is. It cannot be unconditionally argued that society and order are antecedent to law.

While international/world society is necessary for international law to exist, the factor of society does not by itself constitute, determine or influence the rules of international law. The society factor can presuppose and necessitate some structural rules of international law required to operate if international law is to function at all, such as *pacta sunt servanda*, residual sovereignty, good faith, territoriality of jurisdiction and State activity

---

183 Wight (1979), 107.

184 Bull, 17, 21, 23–24, and indeed, Bull's further analysis focuses on concepts of world society in a Kantian liberal or Hobbesian realist sense, one focusing on national interest and the other on trans-national social bonds.

185 Bull, 37.

186 JG Ruggie, 'Continuity and Transformation in the World Polity', in Keohane (ed.), *Neorealism and Its Critics* (1986), 144–145, 149. Similarly, those who would dispense with sovereignty in the context of growing interdependence in international society must show why the idea of private property rights should not have been dispensed with in capitalist societies where they are often invaded on the basis of common social good, ibid., 146.

as clean ideologically as they could be, being instead based on the explanation of the rationale of law in international relations. Lauterpacht has certainly shown sympathy for Grotius, especially his thesis of the subjection of the totality of international relations to the rule of law,[197] but has not in his own major works accepted the thesis that international law is all-embracing. Although not positively professing to be an orthodox or mainstream positivist, Lauterpacht does not contradict the thesis that international law is best explainable through value-neutral positivism. The originality of his approach consists not in contradicting the consensual factor in law-making but in requiring the analysis as to what we understand the agreed rules of international law to mean. This is even clearer from stating the credo: 'the desire of generations of international lawyers to confine their activity to a registration of the practice of States has discouraged any determined attempt at relating it to higher legal principle, or to the conception of international law as a whole'.[198] This attitude enables international lawyers to separate legal analysis from politics, which Lauterpacht himself has championed, to view international law as more than incidence of power, and develop a consistent approach towards securing the outcomes dictated by the Rule of Law.

Pluralism and solidarism are purely intellectual constructs, and if international society is solidarist it cannot be pluralist. But it can also be argued that pluralism can explain a part of international relations, while the rest can be explained by solidarism. Unless substantiated by reference to legal framework, these approaches do not actually tell us much in terms of legal reasoning.

Consensualism *Lotus*-style reflects, in legal terms, the inherent pluralist element in international society. In theoretical terms, much of the solidarist values depend for their survival on the 'pluralist' structure of international order. The consensual and decentralised structure of the international legal system resolves the debate that the pluralist/ solidarist debate aims to resolve by depicting the balance of interests and values as well as ways to respond to global threats. Protection of human rights under international law is possible only if States as territorial sovereign entities undertake requisite obligations and are held accountable for their violation. Responding to global threats such as terrorism and proliferation of weapons of mass destruction is also firmly premised on the inter-State structure of international law. Only States that control territory can take measures adversely affecting terrorist networks in terms of movement, training and recruitment, and finance. The 'pluralist' framework of sovereign States is thus an indispensable premise for resolving 'solidarist' tasks.

In this sense, Huber's observation in the *Island of Palmas* case that sovereignty over a portion of the globe implies the responsibility for whatever goes on within that territory holds the key to the solution of the debate.[199] The 'pluralist' category of sovereignty is structurally necessary to see States as responsible for maintaining global values and responding to global threats, and inherently includes a 'solidarist' dimension of responsibility towards external actors for the exercise of 'pluralistically' defined sovereign

---

197 H Lauterpacht, 'The Grotian Tradition in International Law', 23 *BYIL* (1946), 1.

198 *The Function of Law* (1933), 438.

199 *Island of Palmas case,* Netherlands v USA, Sole Arbitrator Huber, The Hague, April 4, 1928, 2 *RIAA* 829.

powers. Thus, the doctrinal line dividing pluralism from solidarism is not very accurate. It is dictated by doctrinal considerations only, and fails to take into account the inherent structure of international law which any accurate analysis of international society needs to reflect.

If not inherently, then potentially, solidarist and communitarian approaches risk being exploited for the purposes of the ideology of one part of the world being imposed on others. The idea that producing solidarism depends on States being internally alike is rejected.[200] As Hurrell puts it, 'solidarists set themselves an impossible task and risk undermining the limited degree of consensus and order that has been achieved within the society of states'.[201] If not conceptually, then in practice, solidarism can support hegemony aspirations and thus go against international law. This could happen if the ideology of one group of States is sold as that of the whole international society. In fact, if there are such common ideas, there is no better place to look for them than in the rules and principles of international law expressing the agreement of international society.

11.9 LEGITIMACY AND FAIRNESS

Legitimacy as a concept is resorted to in legal and political sciences as a category providing an impartial justification for policies and conduct. It can be understood as part of international law, or external to it. According to Clark, legitimacy refers to the boundaries of legality, morality, and constitutionality. What proves to be legitimate at any time provides an essential explanation of State conduct.[202]

Legitimacy could be focused upon in terms of where it comes from (law, power, tradition), and defined by reference to factual power patterns, morality, or agreed normative requirements. In terms of content, legitimacy can refer to recognised patterns of international relations: law, equality, balance and so on. Franck views legitimacy as an alternative of coercion in providing an orderly functioning of the international community, and develops the concept of legitimacy in the international system in terms of the interaction of rules and States' perceived self-interest, as well as the capacity of rules to affect State conduct. By defining legitimacy as deriving legal rules from the right process encompassing not only valid sources but also socio-anthropological and philosophical insights,[203] Franck thus introduces extra-legal, presumably ideological, aspects into the concept of legitimacy of international rules, and further specifies that legitimacy in its turn forms a procedural justice element of the broader concept of fairness, which also includes distributive justice referring to consequential elements of law which cause the pertinent actors to voluntarily comply with law or seek its reform.[204] According to Clark, 'Core principles of legitimacy articulate a willingness to be bound, both to certain conceptions of rightful membership of society, and to certain conceptions of rightful conduct within it. This is what defines international society.' In terms of the interaction between

---

200 *Cf.* Buzan (2004), 60.
201 A Hurrell, *On Global Order* (2008), 78.
202 I Clark, *Legitimacy in International Society* (2007), 15, 19.
203 T Franck, 'Legitimacy in the International System', 82 *AJIL* (1988), 705–706, 710.
204 T Franck, *Fairness in International Law and Institutions* (1995), 7–8.

legitimacy and power, Clark does not subscribe to the perspective 'where legitimacy is reduced to the preferences of those hegemonic forces that are thought to manufacture it in the first place'. But 'legitimacy cannot be divorced from power. Legitimacy constrains power, while also being an important element of it. Power also impacts upon the practice of legitimacy, and contributes to the substance of the principles of legitimacy that come to be accepted. It is, in any case, only within the context of power relations that legitimacy becomes relevant at all.'[205] Still, Clark does not specify how legitimacy, being dependent on power, evades being defined by hegemons (to the extent such exist).

As Clark's analysis further demonstrates, 'legitimacy' aspires to playing the same role as liberal theory in terms of defining which States can be rightful members of international society due to their ideological orientation and organisation, giving rise to the assumption that revisionist, or not mainstream States somehow need to be reintegrated into international society.[206] From the viewpoint of international law, the status, sovereignty, rights and privileges of States depend not on ideological premises, or on whether the State in question is a pariah or not, but on policy-neutral, ideology-neutral elements of the international legal process, which define how the State comes into being and what its rights are. That's how States understand their rights and status. The 'pariah' State can be internationally isolated, for instance through multilateral sanctions, but this process has to be explained not as any inherent ideological implication of 'legitimacy', but as an incidence of consensually established institutions that adopt the respective decision resulting in the isolation of the pertinent State. For instance, the regimes of Milosevic and Sadam Hussein were (potentially) as 'outlaw' as the regimes in Myanmar or Zimbabwe. Still, punitive measures were applied to the former but not to the latter, among other reasons because there has been no comparable agreement on their 'punishment'.

More often than not, the factors responsible for denoting certain States as 'pariah' or 'outlaw' are the interest of the relevant powers in seeing regime changes happen; in other words, their desire to obtain benefits in terms of access to the territory, natural resources and market of the relevant 'pariah' or 'outlaw' State. The interaction between the 'liberal wing' of international society and 'pariah' States is hardly different from normal patterns of power politics.

Proponents of 'legitimacy' have not suggested the criterion of originality of this notion to add, in the legal sense, to the criterion of legality, without attempting to complement it with extra-legal socio-political considerations. If 'legitimacy' is used as a socio-political category to explain why States comply with international law, it could play a useful role; but it could cause misunderstandings as to the nature of international law, and aggravate rather than resolve conflicts in practice, if it were to be viewed as a normative alternative where international law does not provide for the outcomes desired in some political or ideological quarters. The concept of legitimacy can work only if it reflects the basic and commonly shared characteristics of international society and the international legal system, namely the absence of the sovereign over States and law-making by consent. Legitimacy cannot form an alternative to legality. To illustrate, although the Kosovo

---

205 I Clark, *Legitimacy in International Society* (2007), 20, 23.
206 Clark, 172–189.

Commission found NATO air strikes against Yugoslavia to be illegal but legitimate,[207] the international community, through the statement of non-aligned governments supported by 132 States, overwhelmingly rejected the concept of humanitarian intervention.[208]

11.10 CONCLUSION

Presumably no single theoretical approach can explain the nature of international legal relations. There is no strict dividing line between international legal and international relations theories in explaining international law. While some international law approaches show contempt or nihilism towards international law, other approaches view it as inevitable and understand its function perfectly well.

In some cases, policy approach, adopted by legal or political scientists, is essentially an attempt to confer legitimacy to constructs through which States can be denied of their legal rights, or have their conduct justified even if this is not supported by the pertinent legal position.

The best way of explaining the interaction between international law and politics is to avoid viewing them as fused into each other. Politics can be relevant for the existence, creation and change of international law in a number of ways. But politics is not the same as law; it certainly matters in terms of States agreeing to a rule or instrument, but it does not influence the content of already established legal rules, nor prejudice the separate existence of law. Mixing international politics with international law effectively equals the denial of the independent relevance of international law as a legal system. An interdisciplinary analysis that fuses legal argument with political ideology and lets political argument take over the legal reasoning inevitably risks misrepresenting the pertinent legal position. As Koskenniemi eloquently puts it, 'the interdisciplinary call cannot be divorced from the kinds of valid law and thus leads lawyers to contemplate an agenda that is posed to them by an academic intelligentsia that has been thoroughly committed to smothering the paths of the hegemon'.[209]

---

207 International Commission on Kosovo, *Kosovo Report: Conflict, International Response, Lessons Learned* (2001), 4.

208 *Cf.* I Brownlie, *Principles of Public International Law* (2003), 712.

209 M Koskenniemi, 'Carl Schmitt, Hans Morgenthau and the Image of Law in International Relations', in M Byers (ed.), *The Role of Law in International Politics* (1999), 16 at 34.

PART III

HISTORY OF INTERNATIONAL LAW

12 Periodization and international law

William E. Butler

Periodization may be understood as an analytical prism through which times past are organized into meaningful clusters in order to better understand the reasons for the occurrence of events or trends. In its most basic sense the past might be divided into the categories by which we measure the passage of time: seconds, minutes, hours, days, weeks, months, years, centuries, millennia, and so on. This is not normally feasible or even necessarily helpful in understanding larger issues of the past, however. More helpful, and assuredly more widely practised, is grouping periods of the passage of time for analytical purposes into segments or blocks that distinguish one from the other.[1]

With respect to the law of nations it is suggested that there are three separate domains that require their own analytical separation and periodization[2] in order to be meaningfully comprehended. These are: the origins and development of individual rules or norms; the origins and development of the recognition by subjects of international law of these individual rules or norms to constitute a *system* of law; and the origins and development of conceptions or ideas of the law of nations devised or elaborated by individual natural persons in the form of doctrines of international law. These domains would all fall into what Philip Allott has characterized as the 'intrinsic' history of international law.[3]

12.1 ON THE ROLE OF PERIODIZATION

The general literature on periodization as such is not as substantial as might be expected and not surprisingly has occupied the attention principally of general historians.[4] The present writer touched upon the issue with respect to Soviet doctrines of international

[1] 'To think history is certainly to divide it into periods, because thought is organism, dialectic, drama, and as such has its periods': B. Croce, *Theory and History of Historiography*, transl. D. Airshe (1921), p. 112.

[2] The term 'periodization' is encountered less often than one might expect in international legal writings. Equivalent terms include 'epochs', 'stages of development', 'historical periods', among others. While each of these designates a 'period', they do not necessarily constitute a periodization in the meaning suggested above.

[3] P. Allott, 'International Law and the Idea of History', *Journal of the History of International Law*, I (1999), p. 1 [hereinafter abbreviated as: *JHIL*].

[4] Among general works, see Jerry H. Bentley, 'Cross-Cultural Interaction and Periodization in World History', *American Historical Review*, CI (1968), pp. 749–770; L. L. Besserman, *The Challenge of Periodization* (1996); Marshall Brown, 'Periods and Resistance', *Modern Language Quarterly*, LXII (2001), pp. 309–316; William A. Green, 'Periodizing World History', *History and Theory* XXXIV (1995), pp. 99–111; R. Koselleck, *The Practice of Conceptual History* (2002); G. H. Nagel, 'Periodization', *International Encyclopedia of Social Sciences*, XI (1968), p. 581; P. Stearns, 'Periodization in World History Teaching', *The History Teacher*, XX, no. 4 (1987), pp. 561–580.

law.[5] It continues in non-Marxian writings to be the case that periodization has no accepted theoretical function. The identification of periods is seen to be an arbitrary and subjective exercise, a reflection of the individual historian's mind, or, a non-event as contrasted with historical facts or persons. Nonetheless, leaving aside those historians, including historians of international law, who do believe that society evolves in cycles or generations or similar units, in conformity to laws of societal development, the remainder find it difficult to dispense with temporal subdivisions. One must begin and stop somewhere, stress certain elements in the passage of time at the expense of others. This I characterize as pedagogical periodization: a useful convention for demarcating terminal and intermediate points in the subject matter being investigated.

One general historian exploring the concepts of feudalism and secularization as concepts demarcating the Middle Ages came to a view having considerable implications for the history of international law (although she does not pursue this): 'the history of periodization is juridical, and it advances through struggles over the definition and location of sovereignty'.[6]

Marxian scholarship took a more robust view of periodization. History is divided into five basic periods, each corresponding to stages in the development of productive forces and the social relations arising therefrom: primitive communalism; slavery; feudalism; capitalism; and socialism (communism). Each period is said to have its own laws of societal development. Although mankind is postulated not to pass through each period simultaneously, the periods are held to be applicable to all human society. 'Scientific periodization,' one Soviet scholar wrote, 'is constructed in accordance with the objective laws of nature and society.'[7] This approach continues to be widely accepted in post-Soviet Russian international legal doctrine.[8]

Periodization has been found to be helpful in organizing the literature on the subject. Macalister-Smith and Schwietzke chose this approach and identified the following periods:[9] Antiquity (from time immemorial to 475 AD); Middle Ages (476 to 1492); 16th

---

[5] See W. E. Butler, 'Some Reflections on the Periodization of Soviet Approaches to International Law', in D. D. Barry, W. E. Butler, and G. Ginsburgs (eds), *Contemporary Soviet Law: Essays in Honor of John N. Hazard* (1974), pp. 213–225. I develop a number of points pursued in that article herein.

[6] Kathleen Davis, *Periodization and Sovereignty: How Ideas of Feudalism and Secularization Govern the Politics of Time* (2008), p. 6.

[7] «Периодизация» [Periodization], Большая советская энциклопедия [Great Soviet Encyclopedia] (2nd edn.), XXXII, p. 432. For a thoughtful consideration of periodization by an English Marxian historian, see G. Leff, *History and Social Theory* (1969), pp. 130–151. Leff begins with the proposition: '. . . periodization is indispensable to historical understanding of any kind'.

[8] See R. A. Kolodkin, in V. I. Kuznetsov and B. R. Tuzmukhamedov, *International Law: A Russian Introduction*, transl. W. E. Butler (2009), p. 3. Also see L. N. Levina, История международного права [History of International Law] (2005), p. 3: 'Some scholars believe that international law arose simultaneously with the origin of States and formation of relations between them. The majority of Russian and post-Soviet international lawyers share this position.' Not all Soviet international lawyers, however, accepted uncritically a formalistic approach to the correlation between Marxian views on the stages of societal development and international law. See, for example, Iu. Ia. Baskin and D. I. Feldman, История международного права [History of International Law] (1990), pp. 11–13.

[9] P. Macalister-Smith and J. Schwietzke, 'Literature and Documentary Sources Relating to

century (1493 to 1648); Hugo Grotius; 17th and 18th centuries (1649 to 1815); and 1815 to the present. It is rather odd to see a single natural person identified as a 'period'.

12.2 PERIODIZATION IN GENERAL HISTORIES OF INTERNATIONAL LAW

It might be instructive to ask who first developed a periodization of the history of the law of nations.[10]

Ward. Among the early candidates must be Robert Plumer Ward (1765–1846), the jurist, politician, and novelist. Periodization was transparent in the full title of his two-volume study;[11] he was confining himself to Europe, disregarding any developments prior to Greece and Rome, and ending with the Age of Grotius. The reasons for these temporal limitations he discussed in his Preface. Initially inclined towards the view that the law of nations must be universal in its extent and application, he concluded upon reflection that:

> . . . we expected too much when we contended for the *universality* of the duties laid down by the Codes of Law of Nations; that, however desirable such a universality might be, the whole world were not susceptible of that intimacy and closeness of union . . . that it falls into different divisions or *sets* of nations, connected together under particular religions, moral systems, and local institutions, to the exclusion of other divisions or sets of nations; . . . in fine, that what is commonly called the Law of Nations, falls very far short of universality . . . .[12]

Ward returns to this theme, devoting the entire Chapter IV to 'That the Law of Nations, Is Not the Law of the World'.[13] Much of his periodization is literally chronological. Dispensing with the Greeks and the Romans as a single era, and then discussing how 'different classes of nations may be distinguished', he touches briefly upon the 'Scandinavian law of nations' before turning to the law of nations in Europe to the eleventh century. Subsequent chapters are devoted to blocks of time: from the eleventh to the fifteenth century, from the fifteenth to the seventeenth century, and a brief concluding chapter dedicated to the Age of Grotius.

The defining features of the period from the fall of Rome to the eleventh century appertain to the 'Dark Ages', although Ward does not use that term. In these years, Ward says, the law '. . . is nothing but a chain of the most cruel maxims; and as all ideas of principles or science, seems to have been banished, or rather never to have been entertained . . .', the

---

the History of Public International Law: An Annotated Bibliographical Survey', *JHIL*, I (1999), pp. 145–148.

10 Philip Allott notes that Hesiod (8th century BC) initiated a historiography based upon a progression of 'ages', commencing with a 'golden' age. See Allott, note 3 above, p. 12, n. 25.

11 R. P. Ward, *An Enquiry into the Foundation and History of the Law of Nations in Europe, From the Time of the Greeks and Romans, to the Age of Grotius* (1795).

12 Ibid., I, pp. xiii–xiv.

13 His view was shared by Henry Wheaton: 'Hence the international law of the civilized, Christian nations of Europe and America, is one thing; and that which governs the intercourse of the Mohammedan nations of the East with each other, and with Christians, is another and a very different thing.' H. Wheaton, *Elements of International Law with A Sketch of the History of the Science* (1836), I, p. 51, citing Ward for this proposition.

law of nations had become a 'series of bloody and savage customs'.[14] To Ward, the Age of Grotius constituted the restoration of a regime of ideas based on principles and science.

Wheaton. Henry Wheaton (1785–1848) initially produced a treatise on the law of nations[15] and was later inspired to devote a work specifically to the history of international law by a prize competition arranged by the Academy of Moral and Political Sciences in the Institute of France on the subject: 'Quels sont les progres qu'a fait le droit des gens en Europe depuis la Paix de Westphalie?'. The outcome for the English-speaking world was a work whose full title likewise encompassed a concept of periodization.[16]

For Wheaton the term 'earliest' meant the Greeks and the Romans, as was the case for Robert Ward. His observations for the period from the Greeks through to 1648 were introductory in nature, ranging from the laws of war, the international morality of the Greeks, the conduct of the Spartans and Athenians, Cicero's theory of international morality, Roman fecial law and *jus gentium*, through to the influence of Roman law in forming the modern law of nations and the influence of canon law and the writings of the casuists. In Wheaton's perception 'The peace of Westphalia, 1648, may be chosen as the epoch from which to deduce the history of the modern science of international law.'[17] His reasons were several: that peace terminated the long series of wars growing out of the religious revolution accomplished by Luther and Calvin and the struggle against the political preponderance of the house of Austria; it established the equality of the three religious communities of Catholics, Lutherans, and Calvinists in Germany and opposed

---

[14] Ibid., I, p. 211.

[15] Wheaton, note 13 above. The 'Sketch' is brief indeed, although the central points anticipate his fully-fledged history nine years later: 'The foundation of the modern science of international law may be traced to a period nearly coincident to that memorable epoch in the history of mankind – the revival of letters, the discovery of the new world, and the reformation of religion' (I, pp. 10–11). No special mention is made of the Peace of Westphalia or of the French Revolution, and he refers to the 'science' of international law, not the law of nations itself.

[16] H. Wheaton, *History of the Law of Nations in Europe and America; From the Earliest Times to the Treaty of Washington, 1842* (1845). A French edition, however, appeared several years earlier and the Harvard Law School records a 'Memoire' which may or may not be related to this work, undated but ascribed to ca. 1838. For the French edition, see H. Wheaton, *Histoire des progrès du droit des gens en Europe, depuis la paix de Westphalie jusqu'au Congrès de Vienne, avec un précis historique du droit des gens Européens avant la paix de Westphalie* (1841).

[17] Ibid., p. 69. Wheaton will be among those responsible for perpetuating what a substantial body of modern international legal scholarship now regards as the 'Westphalian myth',

> . . . which holds that the Peace Treaties of Westphalia of 1648 laid the foundations for the sovereign states system and constitute the formative acts of the law of nations that went along with it. It has been claimed and repeated that the main features and principles of that system were introduced into the law of nations at Westphalia . . . none of the . . . claims proved to have a foothold in the texts of the treaties themselves . . . and the treaties do nothing to constitute a European legal order.

See R. Lesaffer, 'International Law and its History: The Story of an Unrequited Love', in M. Craven, M. Fitzmaurice, and M. Vogiatzi (eds), *Time, History and International Law* (2007), p. 39 and literature cited. This deconstruction of Westphalian events has left the principal historian of the conflict unmoved: these important points '. . . do not detract from Westphalia's significance as a general marker for international development. Europe . . . was clearly moving towards a secular order based on more equal, sovereign states.' See P. H. Wilson, *The Thirty Years War: Europe's Tragedy* (2009), p. 754.

a perpetual barrier to further religious innovations and secularizations of ecclesiastical property; it rendered the status of the Holy Roman Empire almost independent of the emperor; it arrested the progress of Germany towards national unity under the Catholic banner. Westphalia, Wheaton continued, confirmed the political revolutions by which the Swiss Cantons and the United Provinces of the Netherlands had been severed from the former link with the Holy Roman Empire, in effect recognizing the principle of the right of popular resistance to intolerable oppression on the part of rulers. And, Wheaton observed, the Peace of Westphalia formed the basis of the treaty law of Europe, being constantly renewed and confirmed in every successive treaty of peace to the French Revolution.

In substantial measure this last observation was the central thesis of Wheaton's history. To him the central periods in the history of the law of nations were the successive peace treaties between 1648 and the French Revolution: Utrecht (1713); Paris and Hubertsburg (1763). Thereafter the French Revolution set in motion a reordering of the law of nations in Europe which Wheaton carried down to the Treaty of Washington (1842). Since his book originated in an essay for a French prize competition, it may be no accident that the French Revolution played such a central role and the Congress of Vienna did not.

Gardner. Daniel Gardner (1799–1863) wrote more or less at the same time as Henry Wheaton but could not have been familiar with Wheaton's history. He is among the earlier writers to consider the law of nations in Antiquity. He speculated that Antiquity had little knowledge of international law and 'made little progress prior to the Christian era'. Nonetheless, the 'dawn of human society is our point of departure'. He imagined that a nomadic warlike state continued for many ages during which, by degrees, the Egyptians, the Phoenicians, the Assyrians, the Chinese, the Etruscans, the Greeks, the Jews, the Persians, the Romans, and certain other nations prior to the Christian era acquired fixed habitations. However, Gardner was reluctant to ascribe this era and the institutes of behaviour that arose (respect paid to heralds and ambassadors, ransoming of persons and cities) as evidence of the existence of international law 'until it arose in Europe since the dark ages'.[18] Antiquity, Gardner said, was the 'era of force – brute force'.[19]

Oppenheim. Lassa Francis Lawrence Oppenheim (1858–1919) held to and elaborated a thesis which many regarded as the classic statement for the twentieth century: international law as a law between 'sovereign and equal States based on the common consent of these States is a product of modern Christian civilization, and may be said to be about

---

[18] D. Gardner, *A Treatise on International Law: A Short Explanation of the Jurisdiction and Duty of the Government of the Republic of the United States* (1844), p. 16.

[19] Ibid., p. 28. Discussion of the law of nations in Antiquity has been transformed by Bederman's study of the subject. Bederman argued there is an 'essential unity in the nature of State behavior in ancient times' but no '. . . historic continuity between the ancient and modern worlds . . .'. See D. Bederman, *International Law in Antiquity* (2001), pp. 3–4. Also see Starodubtsev, who wrote: 'It is naïve to suppose that the early norms of international law arose in a vacuum. Inter-tribal rules of behavior which already existed were the basis thereof.' See G. S. Starodubtsev, История международного права и его науки [History of International Law and its Science] (2006), p. 10. Both views find support in A. Altman, 'Tracing the Earliest Recorded Concepts of International Law', *JHIL*, VI (2004), pp. 153–172; VII (2005), pp. 115–136; X (2008), pp. 1–34; XI (2009), pp. 125–186, 333–356.

four hundred years old' (writing in 1920). The roots of international law Oppenheim traced 'very far back' into history in the form of 'rules and usages' observed by different nations of Antiquity in their external relations. The conception of a 'family of nations' was not part of the 'mental horizon' of the ancient world, although no nation could avoid coming into contact with other nations; this in turn gave rise to 'certain fairly congruent' rules to be observed.[20]

For Oppenheim 'far back' in human history meant beyond the Greeks and Romans, although he was not specific. He did identify a 'foreboding and presentiment' among the Jews of a future when 'all the nations of the world should be united in peace', an ideal which the Jews gave 'to the Christian world' and which was the same ideal that in bygone times 'inspired all those eminent men who have labored to build up' an international law. Totally different from this Jewish contribution was that of the Greeks to a future international law, who were prevented from 'raising the standard of their relations with neighbouring nations above the average level' of Antiquity.[21]

Vinogradoff. Sir Paul Vinogradoff (1854–1925) was among the first to pursue the concept of 'historical types of international law'. He identified five: (1) the tribe; (2) the city; (3) the Church; (4) the contractual association; and (5) the collectivistic organization. His inference is compelling that '. . . the evolution of these groups is bound to assume some form of international intercourse, alliances, and federations. For purposes of defence as well as for trade peoples in the most varied geographical surroundings and in entirely different ethnographical combinations develop similar forms of self-help, arbitration, religious sanction'. Thus, he concluded, '. . . in every stage of civilization we meet with characteristic features of international law'.[22]

The classification of early human history into the category of 'Antiquity' hardly does justice to his proposition. Only our ignorance of early human history, constantly enriched by the advances of archaeology, will sustain such a broad periodization. Perhaps the true value of his perception is to remind us that the modern State is a comparatively recent development and that the law of 'nations' or of 'peoples', to fall back on the pre-Bentham terminology, requires us to revisit the 'subjects' of the rules concerned. If current trends persist and the individual natural or juridical person increasingly acquires autonomous international legal personality, the lineage of individual rules and existence of earlier international legal orders acquires a relevance that goes far beyond mere interest in the past.

Butler/Maccoby. Sir Geoffrey Gilbert Butler (1887–1929) and Simon Maccoby collaborated to produce a work intended to supersede Wheaton and complete the project started by Thomas Alfred Walker (1862–1935) but never brought to fruition.[23] The periodization employed is as much literary as historical and has little in common with the law of nations per se. The book is divided into three parts: The Age of the Prince; The Age of the Judge; and The Age of the Concert. Effectively, this means that the history of international law

---

20 L. F. L. Oppenheim, *International Law: A Treatise*, ed. R. F. Roxburgh (3rd edn., 1920), I, pp. 48–49.

21 Ibid., I, p. 52.

22 See W. E. Butler (ed.), *On the History of International Law and International Organization: Collected Papers of Sir Paul Vinogradoff* (2009), pp. ix, 67.

23 T. A. Walker, *A History of the Law of Nations* (1899). Only volume one appeared.

commences from the sixteenth century, when the chief preoccupation, in the authors' view, was the study of the law of war.[24] The element of the 'judge' is humanitarian sentiment, a set of intangible factors that cause human beings to mollify harshness, seek principles to temper the harsh logic of positive rules, and protect the weak. The 'concert' represented efforts to mobilize the efforts of leading States to address common problems on a multilateral basis, including by means of convening international congresses for this purpose. It is evident that for Butler/Maccoby the development of individual international legal rules, growing perception of an international legal system, and maturing of international legal doctrines were but part of, for them, a much larger picture related to international relations.

Numelin. Ragnar Julius Numelin (1890–19?) doubted that diplomacy originated in classical Antiquity (noting that some writers traced the origins of diplomacy to God himself, who created angels to be His legates). Defined as the 'maintenance of peaceable relations between tribes and nations', diplomacy can be 'traced back to primitive surroundings' whose roots may be sought in the 'stone age inhabitants' of the Australian steppes, the island-dwellers of Oceania, the primitive peoples in Asia, the Negroes in Africa and the Indians of North and South America. 'As long as human communities have existed side by side without living in a permanent state of enmity – and sometimes even then – there have evolved certain rudimentary forms of diplomatic usage.'[25]

The rise of 'at least certain forms' of international law, Numelin suggested, is not 'conditioned by the existence of societies with written laws, but of societies which have entered into peaceful relations with each other, no matter whether these relations originate in magic and religious pressure, fear of external pressure, or commercial or political motives'.[26] The difference between earlier and later international law, itself a periodization, seems to be that social custom is the source of earlier international law and the results of fixed agreements constitute later international law. Numelin is, in other words, seeking the origins of international law as expressed in diplomacy among not 'historical' peoples whose existence is documented, but among peoples without a written history. He seems not to have been aware of Vinogradoff's work, although his argument is consistent with the views advanced by Vinogradoff.

Nussbaum. Arthur Nussbaum (1877–1964) produced a concise history of the law of nations that has dominated the field in the United States during the second half of the twentieth century.[27] After giving a few paragraphs to the 'primitives', the Ancient Orient, Greece, and Rome and mostly dismissing their contribution to the law of nations as indirect or negligible, Nussbaum uses a combination of general historical, regional, and 'treaty' criteria to single out the Middle Ages in West and East; Modern Times to the Thirty Years' War; the Peace of Westphalia to the Congress of Vienna, the Congress of

---

[24] G. G. Butler and S. Maccoby, *The Development of International Law* (1928), p. 3.

[25] R. J. Numelin, *The Beginnings of Diplomacy* (1950), p. 13.

[26] Ibid., p. 14.

[27] A. Nussbaum, *A Concise History of the Law of Nations* (rev. edn., 1954). A German translation appeared in 1960. Nussbaum lost his post at the University of Berlin in September 1933 by reason of being a Jew; his appointment at Columbia University dates from 1934, and he became Research Professor of Public Law there in 1939. A fine edition was printed for the Legal Classics Library in 2008.

Vienna; to the First World War; and the Treaty of Versailles to the Second World War as his main periods. This is a periodization which, despite certain differences in naming the periods, Grewe considered to be consistent with his own perceptions. More than most writers, however, Nussbaum gives great attention to the development of international legal doctrine from the Middle Ages onwards, sparring with James Brown Scott (1865–1943) in an Annex over the importance of the Spanish School vis-à-vis Hugo Grotius.

Verzijl. The most substantial history of international law in modern times is the lifetime's work of Jan Hendrik Willem Verzijl (1888–1987).[28] He addressed periodization in laconic fashion, reproducing in his treatise as Chapter 17 an English translation of an address made in 1951 at the University of Utrecht devoted to 'A Panorama of the Law of Nations'.[29] In 'very early time' he saw 'some customs' observed and honoured between nations or their rulers, few in number and 'rather monotonous' in content. A similar culture, he believed, was essential for a more comprehensive and richer international law, and that culture he saw as originating in the 'ancient Greek period'. Verzijl was sceptical that one could speak '. . . of a direct continuity of development between the legal institutions of those days and our own'.

He saw emerging out of the mists of the past two distinct bodies of rules loosely connected and often confused with one another. One was a collective of positive rules, few in number and slight in substance, but more or less generally observed. The other was a body of ideal concepts originating in the human mind and 'assumed to have an autonomous authority which enabled them to govern the relations between States'.[30] Not until the eighteenth century did for the first time, Verzijl suggested, a true positive law of nations gradually free itself from the embrace of moral and religious concepts to emerge as an independent law in the sense that one speaks of municipal law. Sharing some of the perceptions of Robert Ward, Verzijl concluded that, just as the political structures of various States differed from one another and during different epochs, the various international orders have been attended by their inseparable and appropriate type of international law. It would, he said, have been impossible 'for the international law of the Roman Empire to have resembled that of the Hellenic community of city states', and the feudal mediaeval community could not be ruled by the same law as that of the subsequent community of sovereign States. The international law of Islamic States differed in many characteristics from that of Christian powers in Western Europe or Byzantium.

Verzijl did, however, recognize that individual rules of international law were of varying ages. He accepted that some might trace their lineage back to the Middle Ages 'without having changed to any great extent in the course of their existence', whereas others that came into existence long ago have drifted and altered in response to political and historical events.[31] No specific periodization of these was undertaken.

Preiser. A German specialist, Wolfgang Preiser (1903–1987), addressed periodization in part as a conflict between 'chronological' and 'regional' subdivision in the history of international law. He is certainly correct to observe, as demonstrated by the examples

---

28 J. H. W. Verzijl, *International Law in Historical Perspective* (1968–98). 12 vols.
29 Ibid., I, pp. 379–399.
30 Ibid., I, p. 383.
31 Ibid., I, p. 386.

of periodization above, that the '. . . history of international law follows political history when dividing into periods'.[32] The question is whether the historian of international law should follow political history, accepting that there may be good reason from time to time for the general historian and the historian of international law to share coincident elements of periodization. Insofar, for example, as elements of periodization turn upon systemic changes in international relations that have a direct impact upon individual institutes of international law, the system of international law, or doctrines of international law, such coincidence would be appropriate and expected. Otherwise one would expect that the periodization of international legal history would turn upon occurrences within the law or doctrine themselves.

For the purposes of his contribution, Preiser confined himself to periods that in his view have proved to be of importance for modern international law. To this end he surveyed the history of the law of nations first from ancient times to 1648, distinguishing among 'ancient times (from 3000 B.C. to A.D. 400); the transition from Antiquity to the Middle Ages (A.D. 400 to 800); the Early and High Middle Ages (800 to 1300); the Late Middle Ages (1300 to 1500); and the Spanish Age (1500 to 1648)'. The next benchmarks were the Peace of Westphalia (1648) to the Congress of Vienna (1815), and then from 1815 to the First World War. The interwar period was the next period (two decades), and the balance of the periodization is from 1945 until the present. Periodization in other parts of the world outside Europe (Eastern and Western) and North America are addressed under the rubric of 'regional developments', four of the regions being geographical and one, oddly, religious (Islam). Within each of these major divisions there are sub-periodizations.

His periodization as a whole is based on the general views expressed by Grewe (see below) in the 1984 German edition of Grewe[33] and retained intact in the 'Library edition' of the *Encyclopedia of Public International Law*.[34] Grewe, in turn, was indebted to Preiser for the view that 'If one lays stress upon the point of time at which important institutions of modern international law emerged for the first time, one has to seek the beginnings of European international law in the later Middle Ages.'[35]

Grewe. Most of the best work on the periodization of international law has been produced by continental European jurists, a pre-eminent place being occupied by German

---

[32] W. Preiser, 'History of the Law of Nations', in R. Bernhardt, et al. (eds), *Encyclopedia of Public International Law* (1995), II, p. 721.

[33] W. G. Grewe, *Epochen der Völkerrechtsgeschichte* (1984).

[34] See Bardo Fassbender, 'Stories of War and Peace: On Writing the History of International Law in the "Third Reich" and After', *European Journal of International Law*, XIII (2002), p. 481. Grewe's periodization, Fassbender observed, also was adopted by K. H. Zigler, *Völkerrechtsgeschichte* (1994). A French jurist, while acknowledging the excellent discussion of periodization in Grewe, eschews the views there in favour of a chronology suggested by Bouthoul that is more consistent with the realities of international life and seems more correct. This approach divides the evolution of international law into 'theological', 'metaphysical', and 'positivist' phases. See D. Gaurier, *Histoire du droit international* (2005), pp. 20–21, following Gaston Bouthoul, *Traité de polémologie* (1991), pp. 11–13.

[35] W. Preiser, *Die Völkerrechtsgeschichte, ihre Aufgaben und ihre Methode* (1964), pp. 61ff; quoted in Fassbender, note 34 above, p. 485. On this view, Grewe excluded classical and preclassical Antiquity and most non-European legal communities. Preiser did include them in the *Encyclopedia* by resorting to accounts of regional systems of international law.

legal scholarship. Among these, pride of place, at least for the English-speaking world, must go to the superb reworking of the author's own translation by Michael Byers of the treatise on international law by Wilhelm Georg Grewe (1911–2000) which commences with an introduction dedicated to 'The Periodisation of the History of International Law'.[36] Grewe treats periodization as a 'morphological division', and the development of a system of 'typological categories' – a task 'seriously neglected in the study of international law', in contrast to other legal disciplines, and a problem that has 'either not been discussed at all' or treated in a very summary fashion.

Grewe offers a concise critique of his predecessors in this respect and concludes that insofar as 'there is agreement as to the periodisation of the history of international law, and above all as to the question of where one locates the limits of those periods', such agreement consistently follows the structure set out in his own book. Grewe does appeal for a sharp distinction to be drawn between the 'close connection' of 'legal theory' and 'State practice', which corresponds to my distinction between legal doctrine and individual rules of international law but which he also sees together as 'forms of expression of the . . . power [that] characterize the political style of an epoch just as much as its principles of social, economic and legal organization'. For Grewe, the law of nations and the international political system are cohesive, and 'the historical epochs of the modern law of nations are thus identified to those of the modern State system'. How, he asks, could it be otherwise, as the '. . . State system is necessarily the substrata which underlies the international legal order?'[37]

The periods of international law developed by Grewe had to meet certain 'test questions' in order to determine the basic features of the relevant legal system. Fassbender summarized these as follows: 'First, he inquired into the spiritual foundations of the community of nations in question, its composition and its spatial extension. Is this community occidental Christendom, the circle of "civilized nations" or, . . . a "universal community without common values"? How independent are the subjects of international law?' What requirements must be satisfied for a new member of legal society to be recognized? How does international law develop and to whom does it extend? Who may enforce compliance with this law? Grewe believed that the answers to these questions shed light on the particular stage of development of international law and therefore enter into the periodization of the subject. Each main chapter in Grewe's work contains a concise political history of the period.[38]

Grewe held that the epochs of the modern history of international law and those of

---

[36] W. G. Grewe, *The Epochs of International Law*, transl. and revised by M. Byers (2000), pp. 1–6. The insertion of the article 'The' in the title of the English-language edition of Grewe distorts the original German version, which omits the equivalent article and therefore does not commit Grewe to ostensibly all the epochs of international law. See Fassbender, note 34 above, p. 486. The same issue arose with my translation of G. I. Tunkin, *Theory of International Law* (1974); when asked whether the article 'The' should precede the word 'Theory', Tunkin replied that he entertained no pretensions of offering the definitive theory, but he also rejected the article 'A', preferring the ambiguity of having no articles whatsoever.

[37] For a critique of Grewe's periodization, see H. Steiger, 'From the International Law of Christianity to the International Law of the World Citizen – Reflections on the Formation of the Epochs of the History of International Law', *JHIL*, III (2001), pp. 180–193.

[38] Fassbender, note 34 above, p. 486.

the modern system of States coincided. Fassbender believes that Grewe's periodization of the history of international law followed that developed by Wolfgang Windelband (1886–1945) with important adjustments in a volume devoted to the foreign policy of the great powers in modern times.[39]

Butkevich. The Ukrainian international legal historian, Olga V. Butkevich, in her several works[40] has extended the thinking of Preiser and Grewe and offered her own trenchant criticisms of approaches to this subject. The periodizations of international law are, she suggests, too general and do not have regard to the distinctive features of international law itself. She attributes this to the fact that historians of international law have not developed a sufficient number of legal criteria to explain changes in historical periods and to the simple fact that the history of international law was ignored; it was easier to link international legal developments to the course of history generally without pursuing other explanations.

A particular strength of her exposition is the consideration of works that have not traditionally been considered by others, among them John Hosack (1809–1887), Amos Shartle Hershey (1867–1933), Franz von Liszt (1851–1919), Nguen Quoc Dinh, Thomas Joseph Lawrence (1848–1919), Werner Levi (b. 1912), Robert Redslob (b. 1882), George Grafton Wilson (1863-1951), James Edmund Sandford Fawcett (b. 1913), and a number of Russian international lawyers: Fedor Fedorovich Martens (1845–1909), Leonid A. Kamarovskii (1846–1912),[41] and Mikhail A. Taube (1869–1961),[42] for example. Vladimir E. Grabar (1865–1956) made notable contributions to periodization.[43]

Usenko. Evgenii Trofimovich Usenko (b. 1918) is among the few modern Russian international lawyers to address issues of periodization as such rather than merely to propose a scheme. Soviet doctrine, he wrote, 'proceeding from the mistaken conception that international law arose together with the origin of the State, divided the stages of its development according to the epochs of the development of human society into the international

---

39 W. Windelband, *Die auswärtige Politik der Grossmächte in der Neuzeit (1494–1919)* (1922); later editions appeared in 1925, 1936, 1937, and 1942. See Fassbender, note 34 above, pp. 505–506.

40 O. V. Butkevich, У истоков международного права [At the Sources of International Law] (2008); This Russian-language version distills in abridged form her three Ukrainian studies: Теоретичні аспекти походження і становлення міжнародного права [Theoretical Aspects of the Emergence and Formation of International Law] (2003); Міжнародне право стародавнього світу [International Law of the Period of Antiquity] (2004), reviewed in *JHIL*, VII (2005), pp. 107–112 (A. Kovler); Міжнародне право середніх віків [International Law of the Middle Ages] (2008).

41 See W. E. Butler and V. A. Tomsinov (eds), *Russian Legal Biography* (2007), I, pp. 260–271.

42 M. A. Taube, История зарождения современного международного права (Средние века) [History of the Birth of Modern International Law (Middle Ages)] (Spb., 1894). Only volume one was published. Taube confined himself to a periodization of the international community with a strong regional dimension present, rather than international treaties.

43 See V. E. Grabar (Hrabar), 'Esquisse d'une histoire littéraire du droit international du Moyen Age, du IV au XII siècles', *Revue de droit international privé et de droit pénal international*, XVIII (1936), pp. 7–39, 373–439. Grabar dated the origin of modern international law to the 'era of the migration of peoples', that is, to at least the fourth century AD. His personal archive in Tartu contains an outline setting out the periodization he had in view for his dissertation 'The Science of International Law in England Before the Reformation'. Grabar Archive, Tartu University, F. 38, s. 150; translated in W. E. Butler, *Russia and the Law of Nations in Historical Perspective* (2009), pp. 202–203.

law of slave-owning society, international law of feudal society, international law of a capitalist society, and contemporary international law'.[44] During the Soviet period, a major issue for Soviet doctrine was whether the October Revolution of 1917 constituted a benchmark in the development of modern international law, a proposition aggressively asserted by Soviet jurists from the late 1950s and still not entirely abandoned.[45]

Usenko rejects the proposition that international law would exist in primitive society. There could be no 'international relations' since the social community of a 'people' or a 'nation' did not exist. Peoples began to form only when the tribal kinship system gave way to the birth of statehood. International relations in a slave-owning society were regulated principally by municipal law, and in feudal societies relations were hierarchical and cannot be treated as being international legal relations. In Usenko's view, international law originated in the late Middle Ages as feudalism collapsed and capitalism formed in Europe. A precise dating is impossible, he believes; any periodization must depend upon criteria which underlie international law. Seeking 'universal' criteria, he suggests, would be 'unproductive', and he is concerned that elements of the 'prehistory' of international law would be mixed in with international law itself and lead to distortions. Usenko consequently prefers a systemic approach rather than concentrating upon individual rules or institutes of the law of nations dating from the 'prehistorical' era: '. . . we place at the base of periodization the stages of the origin and progressive development of international law as a definite, integral system'.[46] Accordingly, Usenko chooses the years 1555 to 1795 as his first period: the demise of the Holy Roman Empire, the origin of independent sovereign States as subjects of international law, and the forming of inter-State international relations as an object of international law. For him the major international legal acts are the peace treaties of Augsburg, Westphalia, and Utrecht; the period ends with the French Revolution, which resounded throughout Europe and influenced the progressive development of international law.

Usenko largely shares the Grewe approach, although he chooses different dates, most likely is unfamiliar with Grewe's work, and places a decidedly Russian spin on the significance of the First World War: 'The conditions for the commencement of the formation of such a qualitatively-new international law which we call contemporary arose only as a result of the grave crisis of the entire world system of capitalism caused by the First World War. The Great October Socialist Revolution in Russia laid the foundation for the origin thereof.'[47]

Johnston. Douglas M. Johnston (1931–2006) deployed periodization as a framework for narration in the form of 'dominant motifs', each 'eon' being presented as though it were dominated by a particular idealistic vision of the future.[48] The overriding theme is 'world order', with due recognition of the dangers of oversimplification and problems

---

44 E.T. Usenko, Очерки теории международного права [Essays on the Theory of International Law] (2008), p. 62.

45 For the view that the Soviet Revolution did bring transformations to the substance of international law, see J. B. Quigley, Jr., *Soviet Legal Innovation and the Law of the Western World* (2007).

46 Usenko, note 44 above, p. 64.

47 Usenko, note 44 above, p. 79.

48 D. M. Johnston, *The Historical Foundations of World Order: The Tower and the Arena* (2008), pp. xviii–xxi; reviewed in *JHIL*, XI (2009), pp. 187–201 (Carlo Focarelli).

of evidentiary rigour. He singles out the periods of early Antiquity in which a sense of primitive order is dimly perceived, including in the empires of Egypt and China. Classical Antiquity (ca. 600 BC and 400 AD) followed, an era in which human development had achieved a speculative stage and 'multi-ethnical conglomerations' permitted a system of 'universal order' to be at least imagined. Next came the 'pre-modern world' (ca. 400–1500 AD) during which Christianity and Islam created images of universal authority in their respective domains and early models of the modern State emerged. The early modern era (ca. 1500–1625) destroyed the notion of a universal authority within a single global system of religious belief and the Age of Discovery promoted the supremacy of sovereign entitlement rewarding materialistic ambition and entrepreneurship. Between 1615 and 1815 the law of nations emerged as a new kind of legal order buttressed by national consciousness and the expansion of State power based on colonization abroad. The following century from 1815 to 1905 represented the confluence of ideas and events traceable to the writings of Enlightenment philosophers and literary figures of Europe and America. And despite the appalling catastrophes of two world wars and the Cold War, the century from 1905 to 2005 Johnston saw as a period in which international law developed into an 'innovative and benevolent system of world community law'.

12.3 CONCLUSIONS

Periodization is enjoying a minor renaissance in the modern historiography of international law simply because some writers are expressly addressing the subject and its implications for the first time. Although periodization can be and has been used to demarcate 'international legal orders', which on the grand scale have been understood by some to encompass a 'law of nations in Antiquity' and a 'law of nations in the Middle Ages', the analytical prism being proposed here is less concerned with contextual features of an 'order' and more with the lineage of individual rules, systemic perceptions of those rules by the subjects of the system, and doctrines. There is an implication, deliberate, that lineage may transcend 'orders', and to that extent, the analytical time-limited conception of an 'international legal order' is not necessarily helpful.[49] In more general terms, a concentration upon intrinsic rather than extrinsic approaches to the history of international law may serve us better, although most writers have preferred the extrinsic approach.[50] Periodization is relevant to all approaches.

Grewe may be right to suggest that an international legal order 'can only be assumed to exist if there is a plurality of relatively independent (although not necessarily equal-ranking) bodies politic' linked to one another and not subject to a 'superimposed authority having comprehensive law-making jurisdiction and executive competence'.

---

[49] 'Despite cultural, religious, spatial, and temporal differences, we discover a remarkable unity of structure and coherence of different manifestations of the law of nations during Antiquity and the Middle Ages' ['Au-delà des différences culturelles, religieuses, spatiales et temporelles, nous découvrons une remarquable unité de structure et de cohérence des différentes manifestations du droit des gens durant l'Antiquité et le Moyen Age']. See S. Laghmani, *Histoire du droit des gens du jus gentium imperial au jus publicum europaeum* (2003), p. 7.

[50] On the distinction, see Allott, note 3 above.

He adds the further criterion that 'these bodies politic must observe norms . . . deemed to be binding on the basis of a legal consciousness rooted in religious, cultural and other common values'.[51] But when, so far as we can determine, has there ever existed on this planet anything other than a plurality of 'bodies politic' – which presumably must encompass pre-State formations dating back to the earliest manifestations of mankind. No Empire or similar structure, however powerful, has succeeded, or sought to succeed, in exterminating or subjugating all 'bodies politic' on the earth. While a degree of mutual inter-dependence may affect perceptions of the existence of an 'international legal order', mutual inter-dependence is not necessarily a prerequisite to perceptions of a rule of behaviour in mutual relations. Inter-dependence implies more of a systemic perception, albeit short of an 'order'; mere mutual relations, episodic and unstructured, may generate rules without inter-dependence being involved.[52]

Butkevich is compelling in her observations on the inadequacies of using major treaties as the foundation of periodization (Westphalia, Utrecht, Vienna, Versailles, and so on). These documents may or may not have constituted benchmarks in international relations, but that is an issue for the periodization of international diplomacy. Whether they contributed something to the development of the law of treaties is the issue, and they are almost never approached from this perspective. Our histories of international law, in other words, establish no causal relationship between particular events during the passage of time and the development of individual rules or institutes of the law of nations. We are strong in distinguishing context from one 'epoch' to another, but routinely we lose sight of the legal rules themselves and the dimension of continuity they may represent with the past.

At no time in its history has the international legal system established or imposed temporal requirements as to when particular norms or systems may have developed. In diplomacy or in international judicial or arbitral proceedings or in national courts the parties are at liberty to cite relevant evidence of international practice from any time period. International Law is an 'historical system of law'.

Discussions of periodization in the literature of international law are incidental and uncommon. The renewed interest in the history of international law and the desire to impose intellectual rigour upon the discipline are justly requiring that virtually everything done in the past be revisited and, in many cases, redone, even while counting our blessings for the labours of predecessors whose collective contributions have been invaluable. It seems clear that historians of international law must stand back from the histories of international relations and diplomacy, not to mention general universal histories,[53] and develop their own periodizations of the international legal phenomena which they investigate. This probably requires that different questions be asked of the evidence than have been asked in the past; we may have to rethink our perceptions about the causal

---

51 Presumably such a 'value' may include reciprocity.

52 A French jurist put the proposition well: 'The history of international law cannot be the history of politics or of diplomacy' ['L'histoire du droit international ne peut pas être l'histoire de la politique ou de la diplomatie']. See H. Legohérel, *Histoire du droit international public* (1996), p. 3.

53 There are strong views to the contrary. Starodubtsev believes that the 'periodization of world history must underlie the periodization of international law'. See Starodubtsev, note 19 above, p. 16.

relationship between rules of international law and the international system or order within which they operate. At a minimum, the causal link must be demonstrated to exist, and not merely assumed or inferred.

Confusion should be minimized between the history of State practice as evidence of the origin and existence of rules of international law and the history of ideas about international law (doctrine).[54] They are so commonly mixed, with the result that doctrinal writings are often regarded as the history of the legal system rather than of ideas about the nature and substance of the legal system. Moreover, if we are inclined to doubt the lineage of continuity of rules between one international order and another, as some historians of international law are, does the same standard apply to ideas (doctrinal views) generated in early periods of human civilization? Why should we dismiss the possibility or desirability of rules being transmitted from one 'world order' in, say, Antiquity to the present if we are willing to acknowledge the indebtedness of present generations to, say, the intellectual contributions of the early Greeks and Romans to Western civilization, including ideas about law and diplomacy?

The weaknesses in our histories of international law are cast in stark relief by a discussion of periodization. Chaos reigns; it may well be that we have no history of international law in written form at all, merely impressionistic discourses based on general histories of diplomacy, international relations, or human society – products of literary imagination rather than empirical research, products of unproven assumptions about the inter-relationship of law and diplomacy, foreign policy, international affairs, and the international system.

Our confusion of doctrine with law may lead us to confuse doctrine with history. Doctrine is defined in Article 38(1)(d) of the Statute of the International Court of Justice: '. . . teachings of the most highly qualified publicists of the various nations . . .'. This implies definition, logic, argument, contention, generalization, and ultimately, opinion to be used as evidence as to the existence and content of rules of international law. History may have doctrinal roots and use doctrinal writings as source material, but history does imply an objectivity of perception and presentation, a body of material fashioned according to the precepts of historical science, and not partisan advocacy. The fledgling discipline of the history of international law is afflicted by the absence of temporal orientators that reflect the causal components of the origins and development of the law of nations and, later, international law. The prerequisites for an explanatory periodization are lacking.

---

[54] See O. V. Butkevich, 'History of Ancient International Law: Challenges and Prospects', *JHIL*, V (2003), pp. 229–231.

13 Acculturation through the Middle Ages: the Islamic law of nations and its place in the history of international law

Jean Allain

Lassa Oppenheim was quoted with authority as late as 1948 stating that 'international law as a law between sovereign and equal states based on the common consent of those states is a product of modern Christian civilization, and may be said to be about four hundred years old'.[1] Such a statement might have held up to scrutiny in the early years of the United Nations organisation, which consisted of only 58 Member States and had yet to go through the decolonisation process. The last sixty years, by contrast, have seen membership of the United Nations grow more than threefold to 192; and has taken the State system, which was comprised in the main of European States and outposts of its progeny, to one which is truly worldwide. As a result might one not say that international law is a law between sovereign and equal states, which has only become fully functional with the end of the decolonisation process? Can one declare that international law, rightly understood as a State system including all peoples of the world, is barely twenty years old?

International law, as 'a product of modern Christian civilization', only gains traction with the age of discovery and the European colonial venture which lasted until European States looked to accommodate non-Christian States from the Treaty of Peace of 1856 (settling the Crimean War) onwards, via the medium of the construct of 'civilisation'. The year after the publication of the seventh edition of Oppenheim's *International Law*, the United Nations International Law Commission quietly decided to 'refrain from using the expression "civilized countries".'[2] More than sixty years after the first meeting of the International Law Commission it is clear that it, through its codification of international law – including framework treaties in such areas as the law of treaties, consular and diplomatic relations, and the law of the sea – allowed newly independent States the opportunity to participate in the progressive development of international law, and thus developed international law to become truly universal in scope and application.

That said, it must be acknowledged that basic tenets of international law which hold today are grounded in the European experience of not only the 1648 Peace of Westphalia but also the age of discovery inaugurated by the voyages of Columbus and de Gama. But it can hardly be maintained in the twenty-first century that the Spanish School of International Law – with the likes of Francisco de Vitoria and Francisco Suárez, having

[1] Hersch Lauterpacht (ed.), Lassa Oppenheim, *International Law: A Treatise*, 1948. Some 45 years later, the leading French text spoke of a 'total rupture' in the evolution of international law as between Antiquity and the Age of Discovery; noting that 'rare are the authors who would espouse a different opinion'; see Patrick Dailler and Alain Pellet's *Droit International Public*, 1994, p.45.

[2] United Nations, International Law Commission, *Yearbook of the International Law Commission 1949*, 1956, p.170.

lived in a Spain and been of the generation which witnessed the fall of Granada in 1492 and the end of Islamic rule in Andalusia – conjured international law into existence. Many of the elements of state practice regarding diplomacy (the conduct of embassies), sanctity of alliances, and the limits of warfare were already in evidence more than a millennium before the 'fathers of international law' made their imprints on the subject.[3]

As part of a research handbook, what this chapter seeks to achieve is to draw attention to an important phenomenon which transpired during the millennium between Antiquity and the Age of Discovery, that is: the creation and sustained existence of a self-encompassing system of international law meant to govern relations of the Islamic world and its 'other'. The chapter demonstrates that the Islamic law of nations took from its predecessors and, through acculturation, gave to those who came after it, so that the echoes of the *Siyar*, the Islamic law of nations, are to be recognised as having been heard in the development of the Christian law of nations continuing through to contemporary international law. What clearly emerges from this study is that much research needs to be undertaken to understand the Islamic law of nations which played out during the Middle Ages and its contemporary relevance both historically and normatively.

13.1 THE HISTORIOGRAPHY AND THE GAP OF INTERNATIONAL LAW THROUGH THE MIDDLE AGES

To date, much of what we know about international law in the Middle Ages emerges within an Oppenheim-esque paradigm which focuses on 'the contribution of the medieval canon lawyers to the formation of international law', taking its lead from the 'pioneering work of Ernest Nys during the last two decades of the nineteenth century'.[4] In considering the historiography of international law focused on the Middle Ages, Professor Emeritus James Muldoon of Rutgers University noted that Nys, along with Vanderpol and Holland, 'recognized that the medieval canonists did make a contribution, a minor one perhaps but a real one nevertheless, to the tradition which culminated with the publication of Grotius' *De jure belli ac pacis*'. Though Muldoon adds: 'Not being primarily interested in the canonists, however, none of these scholars clearly distinguished the work of the canonists from that of theologians and philosophers.'[5] While these – in Muldoon's words – pioneers in the study of pre-Grotian international law pointed to areas that

---

[3] Note the comment by Muhammad Hamidullah, *Muslim Conduct of State*, 1968, p. 63: 'Speaking of [the history of international law], writers habitually begin with the Greek City-States, describe the Roman period as immediately following, and then all of a sudden talk of modern times, neglecting the gap of almost a thousand years that intervenes and asserting that during the Middle Ages: [here quoting Oppenheim's 1928, 4th edition of *International Law*] "For an International Law there was . . . no room and no need"'.

[4] James Muldoon, 'The Contribution of Medieval Canon Lawyers to the Formation of International Law', *Traditio: Studies in Ancient and Medieval History, Thought, and Religion*, Vol. 28, 1972, p. 483. Note also James Muldoon, *Canon Law, the Expansion of Europe, and World Order*, 2009.

[5] *Id.*, 'The Contribution of Medieval Canon Lawyers to the Formation of International Law', p. 486. Of interest may be Theodor Meron, *Henry's War and Shakespeare's Laws: Perspectives on the Law of War in the Later Middle Ages*, 1993.

required further research, the very study of the history of international law in the early twentieth century was side-tracked by the work of James Brown Scott who, as general editor, produced the *Classics of International Law* series published by the Carnegie Endowment for Peace. As a result a schism developed amongst the proponents of the Protestant Grotius as the 'father of international law', and Scott's assertion that it was in fact the Catholic theologians of the Spanish School of International law – primarily Francisco de Vitoria – who should wear the mantle of the originators of international law.

This sterile debate deflected attention away from considerations of international law during the Middle Ages in favour of focus being placed on Christian sectarianism of the sixteenth and seventeenth centuries. As Muldoon relates, the 'overall effect of James Brown Scott's work was to block serious examination of the pre-Grotian development of international law and relations'.[6] For Muldoon, the likes of Regout, Moreau-Rebel, and Belch rescue the pre-Grotian era by emphasising that the development of international law during the Middle Ages should be understood in light of 'the notion of a universal society comprising all men'. For Pope Innocent IV in the thirteenth century, accommodation with non-Christians ('infidels') had to transpire. If not, then the view that 'legitimate power could exist only in the hands of Christians prevailed' and this would result in 'no international law or international relations'. With these considerations in mind, James Muldoon set out a research agenda which is worth considering. He noted, 'it might be better, at this stage of research, to assume that the writers of canonistic tradition from Innocent IV to Vitoria represent various abortive attempts to create from the canonistic elements of a rudimentary international law'. Muldoon noted that each of these writers 'share one important characteristic which supports this view. Each man was personally interested in European contacts with infidel societies.'[7]

For Pope Innocent IV, contact with infidels was a reality which emerged from the Crusades, wherein it had previously been argued that Christians possessed a right of *dominium* over all and thus the right to conquer all before them. By contrast Innocent IV argued that the 'legitimacy of the crusades rested on the fact that the Muslims had taken land from Christians unjustly and so Christians had a right to reclaim them'. Where Muslim lands had not been taken from Christians, it was to be 'safe from Christian attack'. As Muldoon notes in a more recent piece, the importance of Innocent IV was not restricted to theorising about the relationship between Christianity and its 'other'; as Pope, 'he dispatched the first mission to Mongols in an attempt to find some basis of peaceful relations with the Mongols who were devastating eastern Europe'.[8] The significance of the approach of Innocent IV is that the debate between those that advocated and those that opposed *dominium* in relation to 'infidels' would be at the heart of debates which would transpire during contact with and conquest of the New World and beyond during the sixteenth and seventeenth centuries. The legitimacy of conquest, wrapped up in the concept of *dominium*, necessitated the '*Requerimento*, a document that the conquistadores in the Americas

---

6 Muldoon, 'The Contribution of Medieval Canon Lawyers to the Formation of International Law', p. 493.

7 Ibid., p. 497.

8 James Muldoon, "Medieval Canon Law and the Formation of International Law', *Zeitschrift (der Savigny-Stiftung) für Rechtsgeschichte: Kanonistische Abteilung*, Vol. 81, 1995, p. 69.

were expected to read to the Indians before attacking them', for fear of being heretical in denying the *dominium* of the native population.[9] Thus, the consideration of Vitoria and the Spanish School (and not to forget Las Casas and Sepúlveda) owe 'a great debt to the work of the canonist' in shaping the debates which would give rise to what in Europe has traditionally been recognised as the advent of international law.[10]

Yet, it should be recognised that the history of international law has been written by the victors. Despite this, the decolonisation period and the advent of an international society worthy of that name means that new voices are appearing. Most obviously that of TWAIL: the Third World Approach to International Law. Where the Middle Ages are concerned, a fruitful area of research may well be that of 'European contacts with infidel societies'; and more so the interaction between the Medieval world of both Western and Eastern Christianity with that of the Muslim world and vice versa. As such, the study of the history of international law during the millennium which was the Middle Ages must first and foremost centre itself on the Islamic law of nations which was an effective system which materialised and sustained itself through this time period.

13.2 THE ISLAMIC LAW OF NATIONS AND MUHAMMAD SHAYBANI'S *SIYAR*

The life of the Prophet Muhammad (570–632 CE) was the catalyst which precipitated an Arab conquest 'whose scale was unparalleled in world history' and which, by the early eighth century, 'encompassed the largest empire the world had yet seen'.[11] Islam was, for the millennium under consideration, 'the greatest and most influential of the world's monotheistic religions', constituting the leading civilisation of the epoch, and including 'many of the world's great cities and some of its most productive agriculture'.[12] At the height of those conquests, a number of Islamic jurists had devoted themselves to the law of nations as a separate field of legal inquiry. Thus, some eight hundred years before Grotius brought together the various tenets of European public law *qua* Christian law of nations into one text, an Islamic jurist, Muhammad ibn al- Hasan al-Shaybani, had done the same with regard to the Islamic law of nations. In the writings of Shaybani we have an acknowledgement of what must be recognised as a self-encompassing regime of international law which, like its European counterpart some eight hundred years later, had aspirations of universal application.

Muhammad Shaybani was born in Wasit, Iraq, in 750 CE.[13] He grew up in Kufa, Iraq, a city which, during Shaybani's lifetime, played a fundamental role in the development of *Sharia* – or Islamic law – as it was from here that Abu Hanifi developed what would become his eponymous school of jurisprudence which, along with the Shafi, Maliki, and Hanbali Schools, forms the core of legal thinking within Sunni Islam. Having studied

---

[9] Ibid., p. 73.

[10] Ibid., p. 68.

[11] Clive Ponting, *World History: A New Perspective*, 2000, pp. 305–306.

[12] Ibid., p. 301.

[13] Or, based on the Islamic Calendar: 132 AH; re: *Anno Hegirae*, ie: the emigration of Muhammad from Mecca to Medina known in Arabic as the *Hijri*.

under Hanifi until his mid-teens, Shaybani would then become a disciple of Abu Yusuf, before embarking on his noteworthy career as a legal scholar and, for a short period of time, a judge.

The Islamic law of nations, or *Siyar*, developed as a sub-field of *Sharia* worthy of independent study only after Shaybani's fundamental writing brought it to the fore. Although Shaybani's magnum opus, the *Kitab al-Siyar al-Kabir*, is lost to history, its memory lives on in two surviving commentaries written some three hundred and five hundred years after its first appearance.[14] As for Shaybani's writings, what survives today is his *Kitab as-Asl*, a text translated into English by Majid Khadduri in 1966.[15] This earlier consideration of the *Siyar* by Shaybani is, in actuality, a text which re-enacts a discourse between Abu Yusuf and his pupil, wherein the opinions of first and foremost, Abu Hanifi, then Abu Yusuf, and then Muhammad Shaybani, on the law of nations is set out.

The *Siyar*, like contemporary international law, was meant to be universal in scope, though it sought to create a *Pax Islamica*. As set out by Shaybani, his *Siyar* was 'the product of Islamic juridical speculation at the height of Islamic power', the so-called Islamic classical period of the Abbasid dynasty.[16] As such, Shaybani's approach to the *Siyar* is a ninth-century vision of a perpetual peace once the ongoing Arab conquest brought all of humanity under the banner of Islam. The *Siyar* is very much a self-encompassing system of the law of nations, premised on a fundamental dichotomy between those within the territorial sphere of Islam and those yet to be incorporated. Whereas the Christian law of nations until 1856 was in essence interested in the common public law of Europe, a millennium before saw the *Siyar* set out a method and understanding of action for the nation of Islam with those nations beyond its borders.

Emanating from a starting point which was the proselytisation of non-believers, the *Siyar* was not based on reciprocity or consent, but was meant to be imposed on certain non-Muslims, both outside the abode of Islam, and within, with regard to non-Islamic religious communities. Despite schisms developing within Islam during its early years, most notably between Sunni and Shia, there was recognition that Islam was 'not merely a set of religious ideas and practice but also a political community' and, as such, conceptually does not venture too far from the modern conception of the 'State'.[17] The Islamic Caliphate – that territory where Islamic authority was sovereign – was known in Siyarian Islamic theory as *dar al-Islam*, literally the abode of Islam. This was juxtaposed to *dar al-harb*, the abode of war – another concept developed by Islamic jurists – which in combination formed the fundamental dichotomy of the *Siyar*. Unlike the division which existed in international legal scholarship up until very recently as between volumes devoted to war and to peace, the very essence of the *Siyar* was more than academic, it was the pivot upon which the Islamic law of nations functioned. The pivot was in the main about war.

However, incorporation through agreement rather than military conquest transpired,

---

[14] Commentaries by Muhammad bin Ahmad Al-Sarakhsi (10th century CE) and al-Jamal al-Husayri (13th century CE).

[15] See Majid Khadduri, *The Islamic Law of Nations: Shaybani's Siyar*, 1966. Note that Khadduri translated from a manuscript dated 1240 CE/638 AH.

[16] Ibid., 1966, p. 19.

[17] Ibid., p. 10.

in 638 CE, when, for instance, the second successor to the Prophet Muhammad, Umar ibh al-Khattab, accepted the surrender of the city of Jerusalem on the following terms:

> In the name of God, the Merciful, the Compassionate. This is the assurance of safety [*aman*] which the servant of God Umar, the Commander of the Faithful, has given to the people of Jerusalem. He has given them an assurance of safety for themselves, for their property, their churches, their crosses, the sick and healthy of the city and for all the rituals which belong to their religion. Their churches will not be inhabited by Muslims and will not be destroyed. Neither they, nor the land on which they stand, nor their cross, nor their property will be damaged. They will not be forcibly converted. [. . .].
> The people of Jerusalem must pay the taxes [*jizya*] like the people of other cities and must expel the Byzantines and the robbers. Those of the people of Jerusalem who want to leave with the Byzantines, take their property and abandon their churches and crosses will be safe until they reach their place of refuge. [. . .]
> If they pay their taxes according to their obligations, then the conditions laid out in this letter are under the covenant of God, are the responsibility of His Prophet, of the caliphs and of the faithful.[18]

Where the *Siyar* concerned itself with *dar al-Islam*, was with regard to the management of *dhimmis*, so-called 'People of the Book', those religious communities which possessed scriptures and, finding themselves within the abode of Islam, had accepted its sovereignty. Unlike Muslims who benefited from full citizenship rights within the abode of Islam, *dhimmis* status entitled individuals to the protection of their person and property, and rights related to professing their religions, though not in a way which might offend Muslims. *Dhimmis* were required to wear distinctive dress and were precluded from building new houses of worship, riding horses or bearing arms. The incorporation of *dhimmis* into *dar al-Islam* was predicated on submission to Muslim sovereignty, though for preferring to maintain their own religion at the expense of converting to Islam, *dhimmis* were required to pay the *jizya*: an annual protection tax levied against each able-bodied man of military age as compensation for their exclusion from military service.[19]

Where foreigners were concerned, entry into *dar al-Islam* was possible, based on the issuing of a safe-conduct (an *aman*) either by a representative of the State, these being issued to visiting emissaries so as to facilitate negotiations, or by any Muslim within *dar al-Islam* for, what in essence, was private ends. An *aman* was meant to last for one year, as beyond that, the annual poll tax would have to be paid and the foreigner then would become a *dhimmis*. Such safe-conducts provided for the protection of one's family and property during a sojourn and allowed for the possibility of commerce and trade. When foreigners entered Islamic territory from *dar al-harb*, the abode of war, the requirement of a safe-conduct was essential as failing this, the penalty was death unless one converted to Islam. Marcel Boisard argues that the 'very liberal Muslim legislation facilitated the passage of foreigners across the Muslim world and that of Muslims to the outside'. This,

---

[18] Hugh Kennedy, *The Great Arab Conquest: How the Spread of Islam Changed the World We Live In*, 2007, pp. 91–92. Note that Kennedy raises the spectre of the authenticity of the text as emanating from the hand of the Caliph Umar or emerging as a demonstration as to what, in contemporary terms, might be considered 'best practice' as to what should be included in such agreements.

[19] See generally Majid Khadduri, *War and Peace in the Law of Islam*, 1955, pp. 175–201.

in turn, allowed for trade links to establish themselves, thus creating the 'embryo of an international commercial law'.[20]

Where the law of treaties is concerned, Arthur Nussbaum, in his seminal *A Concise History of the Law of Nations*, writes, that this 'forms an impressive part of Islamic doctrine'.[21] The first successor to Prophet Muhammad, Abu Bekr, gave the following orders to his soldiers: 'Let there be no perfidy, no falsehood in your treaties with the enemy, be faithful in all things, proving yourselves upright and noble and maintaining your word and promises.' As will be noted in Shaybani's own writing, to be considered below, abrogation of treaties had to be preceded by notice being given. 'On the whole', Nussbaum writes, 'the record of Islam is definitely good on this score. The crusaders, although aggressors, proceeded on the principle that no faith need be kept with infidels.' Says the noted English historian, Lane-Poole, with an eye to the Crusaders, 'the virtues of civilization were all on the side of the Saracens [re: Muslims]'.[22]

Turning now to give voice to Shaybani's text, *Kitab as-Asl*, it will be recalled that the text reads as a conversation between Shaybani and his mentor Abu Yusuf. The dichotomy between *dar al-Islam* and *dar al-harb* is manifest in this passage where Shaybani asks:

> If some of the inhabitants of the territory of war enter [*dar al-Islam*] under an *aman* for trade and some of them were indebted to others, do you think that any of them would be held liable for a debt contracted in the *dar al-harb*.
> [Abu Yusuf] replied: No.
> I asked: Why?
> He replied: Because they entered *dar al-Islam* under an *aman*, and any arrangement that they may have entered into in the *dar al-harb* is none of our concern.[23]

Khadduri, the English-language translator of Shaybani's *Siyar*, notes that the *aman* 'served a useful purpose for both Muslims and non-Muslims in making possible the establishment of temporary peace relations', as the normal state of affairs under the Islamic law of nations was perpetual war as between the territories of *dar al-Islam* and *dar al-harb*.

As the very basis of the Islamic law of nations, as first set out by Shaybani in the seventh century, was the goal of perpetual peace through the incorporation of humanity into *dar al-Islam*, the regulation of foreigners and *dhimmis* within the abode of Islam was secondary to the ever-expanding Islamic State at the expense of its neighbours. It was here within the abode of war, *dar al-harb*, that a permanent state of war existed. This took place under the mantle of *jihad*, the obligation, during this era of Islamic expansion, to take the war to the enemy as a means of incorporating more territory into *dar al-Islam*, if those within that territory failed to convert or submit by becoming *dhimmis*.[24] This 'lesser' *jihad* was predicated on converting pagans to Muslims, by force if necessary, but

---

20 Marcel Boisard, 'On the Probable Influence of Islam on Western Public and International Law', *International Journal of Middle East Studies*, Vol. 11, 1980, p. 432.

21 Arthur Nussbaum, *A Concise History of the Law of Nations*, 1962, p. 53.

22 Ibid., pp. 53 and 54.

23 Majid Khadduri, *The Islamic Law of Nations: Shaybani's Siyar*, 1966, p. 171.

24 See generally, Shaheen Sardar Ali and Javaid Rehman, 'The Concept of *Jihad* in Islamic International Law', *Journal of Conflict and Security*, Vol. 10, 2005, pp. 321–343. For a history of the reinvigoration of *jihad* from the 19th century onwards, see Stephen Neff, *War and the Law of Nations*, 2005, pp. 378–382.

through persuasion if possible, and differs from the 'greater' *jihad*, the Quranic imperative of a spiritual inner struggle against one's demons. For Khadduri, the lesser 'jihad was therefore employed as an instrument of both the universalization of religion and the establishment of an imperial world state'.[25]

Jihad, as a war of proselytisation, was incumbent on all able-bodied men and served both to provide a unifying basis and rallying point for an ever-growing Muslim community; and to shift the battleground from Arab inter-communal and tribal warfare during the pre-Islamic era towards the outside world as a means of propagating the faith. A type of Hobbesian 'state of nature' existed during the expansionist periods as those within *dar al-Islam* did not recognise any capacity to interact as equals with foreign powers. The dichotomy was such that you were 'either with us or against us'; that the precepts of Islam were that foreigners failed to meet the religio-ethical standards required to be deemed equal. Shaybani's *Kitab as-Asl* deals in large part with conduct of hostiles and the spoils of war. Here Abu Yusuf in speaking to Shaybani, relates the thoughts of the leader of the Hanifi School of jurisprudence, Abu Hanifi, as to these issues in general. Shaybani asks:

> If the army attacks the territory of war and it is a territory that has received a invitation to accept Islam, it is commendable if the army renews the invitation, but if it fails to do so it is not wrong. The army may launch the attack [on the enemy] by night or by day and it is permissible to burn [the enemy] fortifications with fire or to inundate them with water. If [the army] capture any spoils of war, it should not be divided up in the enemy territory until [Muslims] have brought it to a place of security and removed it to the territory of Islam.
> Abu Yusuf said: I asked Abu Hanifi [his opinion] concerning the food and fodder that may be found in the spoil and whether a warrior in need may take from that spoil [before division] any of the food for himself and fodder for his mount.
> He [Abu Hanifi] replied: there is no harm in all that.[26]

With regard to the spoils of war, Shaybani seeks to deal with the difficult cases:

> I ask: In dividing the spoil, how much, do you think, should be given to a horse-rider and how much to a foot-warrior?
> [Abu Yusuf] replied: The horse-rider should be given two shares [one for the mount and one for himself] and the foot-warrior one. [. . .]
> I asked: Why do you think that the horse-rider should be given two shares and the foot-warrior one?
> He replied: Because it has been related to us that this was the practice of [the Caliph Omar bin al-Khattab]. This was also the opinion of Abu Hanifi. [. . .]
> I asked: If a man entered the territory of war as a mounted warrior with the army and if his horse died of exhaustion or was hamstrung, so that when the spoil was taken to a place of security [*dar al-Islam*] he was a foot-warrior – though it was recorded in the [army list] that he had a horse – or if he had brought a horse before entering the territory of war and it died of exhaustion in the dar [*al-Islam*], should he be allotted the shar of a horse-rider?
> He replied: Yes.[27]

As originally conceived the perpetual war as between *dar al-Islam* and *dar al-harb* had to give way to accommodation as the early success of Arab conquest failed to manifest

---

[25] Majid Khadduri, *War and Peace in the Law of Islam*, 1955, p. 51.
[26] Ibid., p. 96.
[27] Ibid., p. 107.

itself into the universalisation of Islam. Working within the Islamic binary system of international relations, accommodation was manifest in peace treaties which suspended hostilities for, at most, ten years and thus deemed the non-Islamic party to the agreement to be temporarily part of *dar al-Islam*.[28] More than anything peace treaties from the Islamic perspective were temporary by their very nature, meant to suspend war, in essence, to allow a regrouping before a state of war would once more become the norm. Here Shaybani is interested in the possibility of abrogating a peace treaty, as he asks:

> If some of the inhabitants of the territory of war asked the Muslims to make peace with them for a specified number of years without paying tribute, do you think that the Muslims should grant the request?
> He [Abu Yusuf] replied: Yes, provided the Imam has considered the situation and has found that the inhabitants of the territory of war are too strong for the Muslims to prevail against them and it would be better for the Muslims to make peace with them.
> I asked: If (the Imam) made peace with them and found upon reconsideration it was disadvantageous for Muslims since it was made without any tribute being paid to him, can he give notice, abrogate the peace agreement, and attack them?
> He [Abu Yusuf] replied: Yes.[29]

13.3 ACCULTURATION, ACCOMMODATION AND THE ECHOES OF THE *SIYAR*

It must be emphasised that Shaybani's exposition of an Islamic law of nations in the *Siyar* was written during the classical period of Islam, when very little thought was being given to other polities, as the Arab conquest, continuing, as it were, unabated, was focused on incorporating new territories and populations. Yet, as a recent study by Hassan Khalilieh shows, by the eleventh century this was no longer possible; instead accommodation was required, though acculturation transpired. As Khalilieh notes:

> It is a truism that the formulation of international law arises from confrontation of alien cultures and their struggle to forge common principles with which to govern interactions between their peoples. In the cases where one culture subjugates another and institutes its legal system in place of its predecessor's, some degree of assimilation of the legal practices and customs of the subjugated culture inevitably occurs and establishes its contribution to the ongoing development of the jurisprudence of the region over which it ruled.[30]

In Khalilieh's consideration of the recently discovered *Treatise concerning the Leasing of Ships and the Claims between (Contracting) Parties* by Muhammad Ibn Umar, written

---

28 Note that according to some (though a minority of) classic Islamic jurists the possibility existed of a third territorial situation: *dar al-ahd* (territory of covenant) or *dar al-sulh* (territory or peaceful arrangement) wherein by treaty annual tributes were paid in exchange for recognition, but this territory was to be considered as independent from *dar al-Islam*. Note also the granting of neutral status to Ethiopia as being 'voluntarily declared to be outside of the bounds of [Islam's] area of expansion'. Majid Khadduri, *War and Peace in the Law of Islam*, 1955, p. 258.

29 Majid Khadduri, *The Islamic Law of Nations: Shaybani's Siyar*, 1966, pp. 154–155.

30 Hassan Khalilieh, *Admiralty and Maritime Laws in the Mediterranean Sea (ca. 800–1050): The Kitab Akriyat al-Sufun vis-à-vis the Nomos Rodioan Nautikos*, 2006, p. xi.

in the tenth century, he juxtaposes it against the contemporaneous Rhodian Maritime Law of the Byzantine Empire by saying that 'it is unconvincing to take for granted that medieval maritime laws owed their origins to Roman law'.[31]

In his study, Khalilieh considers treatises which are not so much about the governing of the Mediterranean sea in the sense of the law of the sea, but rather about private maritime commercial law. What Khalilieh shows is that those Christians who were incorporated into *dar al-Islam* of the Southern Mediterranean as *dhimmis* 'preserved the maritime laws instituted in the [Justinian] Digest, as well as local customs, for over a century'. However, with the consolidation of Islam and its Schools of jurisprudence 'from the eighth century onwards, many canonical regulations and practices were "Islamicized"'.[32] Khalilieh's explanation of this process is then given over to the great Islamic historian, Ibn Khaldun:

> The condition of the world and of nations, their customs and sects, do not persist in the same form or in a constant manner. . . . Such is the case with individuals, times and cities, and it likewise happens in connection with regions and districts, periods and dynasties. . . . The new power, in turn, is taken over by another dynasty and customs are further mixed with those of the new dynasty. More discrepancies come in, so that the contrast between the new dynasty and the first one is much greater than between the second and the first one. Gradual increase in the degree of discrepancy continues. The eventual result is there is this continued succession of different races to royal authority and government, changes in customs and institutions will not cease to occur.[33]

Although limited evidence exists, Marcel Boisard's tentative consideration of the 'probable influence' of Islam on international law speaks to acknowledging that acculturation must have transpired over the near millennium of dominance which the Arab conquest maintained. 'It appears impossible, in fact', Boisard writes,

> that the Spanish canon scholars (read: Vitoria and Suárez), and Grotius who succeeded them, should not have borrowed anything from the Muslim civilisation whose power in the Mediterranean maintained itself until the end of the sixteenth century. In the field of international relations, we can imagine that there was a real contribution, since 'international law' was an integral part of Muslim legal science and must not have been unknown to European universities.[34]

Boisard goes further by pointing to the eleventh century *Las Siete Partidas* of Alphonse X of Castile – the first codification of law in Europe – and its consideration of armed conflict 'both in form and content as a direct adaptation of Muslim law'.[35]

Even over the period of Shaybani's lifetime, the rise of Islam had to accommodate itself

---

[31] Ibid., p. 256.

[32] Ibid., p. 250.

[33] Ibid., p. 253. See also J. Dawood (ed.), *Ibn Khaldun: The Muqaddimah*, (Franz Rosenthal translator), 1989, pp. 25–26.

[34] Marcel Boisard, 'On the Probable Influence of Islam on Western Public and International Law', *International Journal of Middle East Studies*, Vol. 11, 1980, p. 441.

[35] Here Boisard makes reference to a rather obscure text entitled the *Villayet*. See Boisard p. 435; and repeated in Frédéric Mégret, 'A Cautionary Tale from the Crusades? War and Prisoners in Conditions of Normative Incommensurability', in Sibylle Scheipers (ed.), *Prisoners in War*, 2008, p. 31, though this time as '*Villiyet*'. Firmer ground may be found in Arthur Nussbaum, *A Concise History of the Law of Nations*, 1962, p. 52, where Nussbaum states: 'Booty had to be delivered

to situations where it bumped up against other polities which could defend themselves against attempts to impose *dar al-Islam*. As the tide of conquest turned, and *dar al-Islam* came under threat throughout the eleventh to thirteenth centuries by Christian Crusaders and Tartar and Mongolian invaders, the very nature of the Islamic law of nations was reinterpreted from being offensive in nature to defensive by necessity. Thus, as Ann Elizabeth Mayer relates, Muslim states 'had to begin to adjust their ambitions and practice to the realities of their declining prowess and to enter into permanent peace treaties'.[36] This transpired at a time when the Islamic Empire, having grown so vast, started to fragment into its component parts; while Cordoba in Spain would govern Andalusia, a more fundamental schism developed between Ottoman Turks (Sunni Islam) and Persia where Shia Islam was the basis of proto-state formation. The Shafi School of jurisprudence, for its part, recognised the establishment of a category between *dar al-Islam* and *dar al-harb*, that of *dar al-sulh* where peaceful coexistence based on 'armistice, diplomatic ties, or peace agreements' transpired. As Onder Bakircioglu notes, *dar al-sulh*, 'despite its controversial and impermanent status, was adopted in accordance with the Muslim realisation once again that the obligation of military *jihad* could not be maintained actively against all external enemies who were much stronger than those faced during the rise of the Islamic faith'.[37] It might be noted that the binary nature of *dar al-Islam* and *dar al-harb* provided for the possibility of being excluded from the abode of war, through a recognition of neutrality in the Islamic war of conquest. Ethiopia for one, so near the epicentre of Islam, was immune from military *jihad* in recognition of the sanctuary it offered to early followers of the Prophet Muhammad.[38] By the fourteenth century, the ability to sustain an offensive *jihad* was no longer sustainable; in its wake, Islamic jurists such as Ibn Taymiya reconstituted *jihad* as 'a defensive war against unbelievers whenever they threatened Islam'.[39]

Where acculturation may be most evident as between Christian Europe and Islam is during the Crusades wherein Christian forces were required to interact with Islamic forces in the carrying out of protracted warfare. Javaid Rehman notes that Islamic law, from its onset, developed 'clear rules relating, *inter alia*, to, notice of commencement of hostilities, effects of war, methods of warfare, organisation of the army and navy, modes of fighting, time of fighting, preparation, discipline and regulation of the army.'[40] In general terms Islamic law made a distinction between combatants and non-combatants;

---

to [Islamic] authorities for distribution, the treasury keeping one-fifth of it – a rule adopted, surprisingly enough, by the *Siete Partidas* of Alphonse X of Castile.'

[36] Ann Elizabeth Mayer, 'War and Peace in the Islamic Tradition and International Law', in John Kelsay and James Turner Johnson (eds), *Just War and Jihad: Historical and Theoritical Perpectives on War and Peace in Western and Islamic Traditions*, 1991, p. 196. Note also Ahmed El-Kosheri, 'History of the Law of Nations: Regional Developments: Islam', *Encyclopedia of Public International Law,* Vol. 2, 1995, p. 810. John Kelsay, *Arguing the Just War in Islam*, 2007.

[37] Onder Bakircioglu, 'A Socio-Legal Analysis of the Concept of Jihad', *International and Comparative Law Quarterly*, Vol. 59, 2010, p. 21.

[38] See the chapter on neutrality in Majid Khadduri, *War and Peace in the Law of Islam*, 1955, pp. 251–267.

[39] Majid Khadduri, *The Islamic Law of Nations: Shaybani's Siyar*, 1966, p. 59. See also Sheikh Wahbeh al-Zuhili, 'Islam and International Law', *International Review of the Red Cross*, Volume 87, 2005, p. 277.

[40] Javaid Rehman, *International Human Rights Law*, 2010, p. 767.

this is manifest in Shaybani's *Siyar* where the question is posed: 'do you think that the blind, the crippled, the helpless insane, if taken prisoners of war or captured by the warriors in a surprise attack, would be killed?', to which the answer from Abu Yusuf came back in the negative: 'they should not be killed'.[41] Likewise where prisoners of war are concerned, Boisard points to Christian acculturation, stating that 'to our knowledge, it is only from the time of the Crusades that the West seems to have been preoccupied with this problem'.[42] If we look to the Graeco-Roman literature and law in antiquity, there is little resemblance to what emerges from the Spanish School of International Law, or later Grotius, where hostilities are concerned.[43] However, the various tenets of Islamic law governing armed conflict point to an inter-cultural socialisation process taking place wherein those elements seen to be useful in inter-state relations were taken up and, in the opposite fashion of the *dhimmis* fishermen of the Southern Mediterranean, the elements of the *Siyar* were over time 'Christianised'.

We get a sense of an Islamic approach to issues of warfare from a set of instructions given by the Abbasid Caliph Qudamah ibn Jafar in 922 CE, which include the following:

> He has commanded him to prevent his troops from staying in the house of any subject [. . .], except if it is by his permission and willingness, and also from trampling on the cultivation and making it treaded by animals or rendering it a path to reach his destination. He should not take straw for fodder from those who possess it except on the payment of the price and the willingness of the owners.[44]

Beyond this, Muhammad Ashraf enumerates provisions found in Islamic law governing, *inter alia*, forbidden acts, spies, uniforms, flags of truce, enemy property and treatment of the dead.[45] These items and their content are not dissimilar from the provisions governing the same elements of the laws of war today. And yet, in their contemporary guise, the roots can be recognised through acculturation. Boisard notes:

> It is in the law of war that we find the best elaborated rules of the West as influenced by the East. Indeed, various institutions of European medieval civilisation bore an indelible imprint, if not purely and simply of their oriental origin, at least of their strong dependence on the analogical military institutions of the Muslim East. This influence, in a period when war played a particularly important role, affected the general atmosphere as much as the specific dispositions for dealing with the defeated and the attitudes towards combatants and certain technical clauses, such as the exchange of prisoners and care for the wounded. The transmission of influence naturally took place where Islam and Christianity confronted each other on the field of battle; in Spain and in the Palestine of the Crusades. Westerners, who had scarcely any code of warfare, found that their enemies had extremely elaborate rules of conduct, whether concerning the declaration of war or means of damaging the enemy. The psychological impact was such that, for a while, there were two kinds of Christian warrior: those who had been impressed by the chivalric

---

41 Majid Khadduri, *The Islamic Law of Nations: Shaybani's Siyar*, 1966, p. 101.

42 Marcel Boisard, 'On the Probable Influence of Islam on Western Public and International Law', *International Journal of Middle East Studies*, Vol. 11, 1980, pp. 432.

43 For the conduct of hostilities in antiquity, see David Bederman, *International Law in Antiquity*, 2001, pp. 207–266.

44 See Form of Instructions to the Commander of Succours and of War, as found in Muhammad Ashraf, *Muslim Conduct of State*, 1968, p. 313.

45 See ibid.

spirit during their previous encounters with Muslims and those who only knew of the barbaric practices of the Middle Ages.[46]

For Khadduri, the turning point of the *Siyar* from being offensive in nature to being accommodating in reality, is the 1535 Treaty of Alliance between the Ottoman Sultan and the King of France. In Khadduri's 1956 article published in the *American Journal of International Law* he notes that fundamental tenants of *Siyar* – those elements not touched by Quranic imperatives – were reinterpreted so as to allow for the liberalisation of trade in the face of the opening of the European trade route to Asia via the Cape of Good Hope during the Age of Discovery at the expense of the traditional overland route through *dar al-Islam* via the South-East Mediterranean.[47] Thus, accommodation manifested itself in the Sultan negotiating a treaty which recognised a formal equality between the parties and opened the possibility of such agreements being offered to other Sovereigns. Further, that peace could only be limited to a ten-year period was put aside in the 1535 Treaty to allow for the life of the instrument to run parallel to the lives of the rulers. French subjects were exempt from the local jurisdiction and from the annual tax required for *dhimmis*. The 1535 Treaty was thus not only a break with the past, but the start of the capitulation regime which would persist in areas where European colonialism was not able to secure a footing.[48]

While the 1535 Treaty points to a shift in the power relationship between the Islamic world and Europe which had, by this time, embarked on its Age of Discovery, it should come as little surprise that the elements of capitulation did not simply appear on the scene in the sixteenth century, but had been in evidence for some time as creating a link between East and West. The loss of jurisdiction over *dhimmis*, in the guise of nascent consular protection, was to evolve over the latter part of the Middle Ages wherein accommodation made economic sense in the Mediterranean basin, where a modus operandi emerged between the Italian cities of Genoa, Pisa, and most importantly Venice, as well as Byzantine ports, and Muslim rulers. Having gained *capitula* or brief chapters outlining specific unilateral grants set out in a treaty, merchants were able to settle in *dar al-Islam*. The head of foreign merchant enclaves, the 'consul', would carry out juridical and administrative functions with regard to his fellow citizens. Thus through acculturation by accommodation we witness 'the foundations of still existing consular privileges'.[49]

---

[46] Marcel Boisard, 'On the Probable Influence of Islam on Western Public and International Law', *International Journal of Middle East Studies*, Vol. 11, 1980, p. 442.

[47] Majid Khadduri, 'Islam and the Modern Law of Nations', *American Journal of International Law*, Vol. 50, 1956, p. 360; as reproduced in Mashood Baderin (ed.), *International Law and Islamic Law*, 2008, p. 5.

[48] For a consideration of the *Siyar* into modern times see: Christopher Ford, 'Siyarization and its Discontents: International Law and Islam's Constitutional Crisis', *Texas International Law Journal*, Vol. 30, pp. 499–533; as reproduced in Mashood Baderin (ed.), *International Law and Islamic Law*, 2008, pp. 19–53.

[49] Thomas Alfred Walker, *A History of the Law of Nations: From the Earliest Times to the Peace of Westphalia*, 1648, p. 116.

13.4 CONCLUSION

The basis of international law beyond its European public law *qua* Christian international law roots remains shrouded in mystery. The pervasive dominance of the West over the last five hundred years has meant that little energy has gone into encouraging research into international law before the Age of Discovery. As this study is part of a research handbook, an attempt has been made to give sense to the Islamic law of nations, which dominated the millennium between Antiquity, and a Europe emerging from the Dark Ages. It would be difficult to imagine an area of international law which requires more research and focus of study; and by the same token has yet to be investigated in any systematic or even meaningful manner. For those with the linguistic tools necessary, there are libraries in the Islamic world, including the New Bibliotheca Alexandrina, and beyond, awaiting the type of work which Majid Khadduri and Hassan Khalilieh have done in bringing ancient texts to life and to the attention of wider audiences. Sources relating to the Crusades, or related to Andalusia and specifically at the heart of the renaissance of international law, at the University of Salamanca, should be investigated.

It has now been twenty years since Marcel Boisard spoke of a 'probable influence of Islam' on international law. Today, we have progressed but a short distance indeed. The fact that the only known law of nations, beyond the one currently in force, which had universal aspiration and was fully operational was the *Siyar* – the Islamic law of nations, remains shrouded and obscured. This despite the fact that for close to a millennium the Islamic law of nations governed the largest swaths of the known world. What influence Muhammad Shaybani's *Siyar* might have had on the Spanish School or Grotius in concrete terms has yet to be investigated in any true fashion and thus remains conjecture. That said, it would appear that acculturation could not have failed to transpire during the Middle Ages in the sphere of law. The histories of mathematics, astronomy, and medicine have all acknowledged their debt to the Islamic world.[50] The emphasis of the existence of an Islamic law of nations in a research handbook of this type is but a first step in bringing to light an area of study which must be recognised as suffering from a severe limitation of primary sources and thus holds out the promise of research worthy of time and dedication.

---

50 Consider, for instance, the more than a dozen volumes of the *Zeitschrift für Geschichte der Arabisch-Islamischen Wissenschaften*.

14 The classical law of nations (1500–1800)

Randall Lesaffer

14.1 FROM *RESPUBLICA CHRISTIANA* TO *JUS PUBLICUM EUROPAEUM*[1]

14.1.1 The Collapse of the *Respublica Christiana*

Since the 19th century, international lawyers and historians of international law generally have defended the view that modern international law roots back to the sovereign States system of Early-Modern Europe (1500–1800). The first publication by the Dutch humanist Hugo Grotius (1583–1645) of his seminal work *De jure belli ac pacis libri tres* (1625)[2] and the Peace Treaties of Westphalia (1648),[3] ending the Thirty Years War (1618–1648),

[1] For surveys of the law of nations in Early-Modern Europe: Dominique Gaurier, *Histoire du droit international. Auteurs, doctrines et développement de l'Antiquité à l'aube de la période contemporaine* (Rennes, 2005) pp. 143–479; Wilhelm G. Grewe, *The Epochs of International Law* (Berlin etc., 2000) pp. 137–424; Slim Laghmani, *Histoire du droit des gens du* jus gentium *impérial au* jus publicum europaeum (Paris, 2003) pp. 61–223; Arthur Nussbaum, *A Concise History of the Law of Nations* (New York, 1947); A. Pillet (ed.), *Les fondateurs du Droit International* (Paris, 1904); Wolfgang Preiser, 'History of the Law of Nations: Ancient Times to 1648', in Rudolph Bernhardt (ed.), *Encyclopaedia of Public International Law* (Amsterdam, 1995) vol. 2, pp. 722–49; Ernest Reibstein, *Völkerrecht. Eine Geschichte seiner Ideen in Lehre und Praxis* (Freiburg and Munich, 1957) vol. 1; Heinhard Steiger, 'Ius bändigt Mars. Das klassische Völkerrecht und seine Wissenschaft als frühneuzeitlichte Kulturerscheinung', in Ronald G. Asch, Wulf Eckart Voss and Martin Wrede (eds), *Frieden und Krieg in der Frühen Neuzeit. Die europäische Staatenordnung und die aussereuropäische Welt* (Munich, 2001) pp. 59–85; Antonio Truyol y Serra, *Histoire du droit international public* (Paris, 2005) pp. 47–95; Stephan Verosta, 'History of the Law of Nations: 1618 to 1815', in Bernhardt, *Encyclopaedia of Public International Law*, vol. 2, pp. 749–67; Karl-Heinz Ziegler, *Völkerrechtsgeschichte. Ein Studienbuch* (2nd edn., Munster, 2007) pp. 117–68. For a bibliography of relevant sources and secondary literature: Peter Macalister-Smith and Joachim Schwietzke, 'Literature and Documentary Sources Relating to the History of International Law', *Journal of the History of International Law*, 1 (1999) pp. 136–212.

[2] Maurice Bourquin called Grotius the father of the law of nations: 'Grotius est-il le père du droit des gens?', in *Grandes figures et grandes œuvres juridiques* (Geneva, 1948) pp. 77–99. Over the years, his title has been challenged, e.g. by Grewe and Haggenmacher, while Ziegler considered it justified: Wilhelm G. Grewe, 'Grotius – Vater des Völkerrechts', *Der Staat*, 23 (1984) pp. 161–78; Peter Haggenmacher, *Grotius et la doctrine de la guerre juste* (Paris, 1983) p. 622; idem, 'Grotius and Gentili: A Reassessment of Thomas E. Holland's Inaugural Lecture', in Hedley Bull, Benedict Kingsbury and Adam Roberts (eds), *Grotius and International Relations* (2nd edn., Oxford, 1992) pp. 133–76; Karl-Heinz Ziegler, 'Hugo Grotius als Vater des Völkerrechts', in Peter Selmer and Ingo von Münch (eds), *Gedächtnisschrift für Wolfgang Martens* (Berlin and New York, 1987) pp. 851–58; idem, 'Die Bedeutung von Hugo Grotius für das Völkerrecht – Versuch einer Bilanz am Ende des 20. Jahrhunderts', *Zeitschrift für Historische Forschung*, 13 (1996) pp. 354–71.

[3] E.g.: 'The peace of Westphalia 1648, may be chosen as the epoch from which to deduce the history of the modern science of international law', in Henry Wheaton, *History of the Law*

were often indicated as the very birth certificates of the classical law of nations that preceded and preconfigured modern international law.

First, the view that the history of international law only became relevant for the understanding of current international law with the birth of the sovereign State in Early-Modern Europe has been rightly challenged for being reductionist.[4] Scholars have indicated the significance for the development of modern international law of earlier legal systems and traditions, more particularly those of Greek and Roman Antiquity,[5] and of international legal developments outside Europe, more particularly in relation to Europe's confrontation with the outer-European world during the Early-Modern Age.[6] Second, already at the end of the 19th century, some scholars argued that the roots of the sovereign State system and the classical law of nations needed to be traced back beyond the first half of the 17th century. Some authors, most prominently the American

---

of Nations in Europe and America from the Earliest Times to the Treaty of Washington (New York, 1845) p. 69. Recently the 'Westphalian myth' has come under attack: Stéphane Beaulac, 'The Westphalian Legal Orthodoxy – Myth or Reality?', *Journal of the History of International Law*, 2 (2000) pp. 148–77; Derek Croxton, 'The Peace of Westphalia of 1648 and the Origins of Sovereignty', *International History Review*, 21 (1999) pp. 569–91; Heinz Duchhardt, 'Westfälischer Friede und internazionale Beziehungen in Ancien Régime', *Historische Zeitschrift*, 249 (1989) pp. 529–43; idem, 'Westphalian System. Zur Problematik einer Denkfigur', *Historische Zeitschrift*, 269 (1999) pp. 305–15; Arthur Eyffinger, 'Europe in the Balance: An Appraisal of the Westphalian System', *Netherlands International Law Review*, 45 (1998) pp. 161–87; Peter Haggenmacher, 'La paix dans le pensée de Grotius', in Lucien Bély (ed.), *L'Europe des traités de Westphalie. Esprit de diplomatie et diplomatie de l'esprit* (Paris, 2000) pp. 67–79; Randall Lesaffer, 'The Westphalian Peace Treaties and the Development of the Tradition of Great European Peace Settlements prior to 1648', *Grotiana*, new series 18 (1997) pp. 71–95; Andreas Osiander, 'Sovereignty, International Relations and the Westphalian Myth', *International Organization*, 55 (2001) pp. 251–87; Meinhard Schröder, 'Der Westfälische Friede – eine Epochengrenze in der Völkerrechtsentwicklung?', in Meinhard Schröder (ed.), *350 Jahre Westfälischer Friede. Verfassungsgeschichte, Staatskirchenrecht, Völkerrechtsgeschichte* (Schriften zur europäischen Rechts- und Verfassungsgeschichte 30, Berlin, 1999) pp. 119–37; Heinhard Steiger, 'Der Westfälischen Frieden – Grundgesetz für Europa?', in Heinz Duchhardt (ed.), *Der Westfälische Friede. Diplomatie, politische Zäsur, kulturelles Umfeld, Rezeptionsgeschichte* (Munich, 1998) pp. 33–80; Karl-Heinz Ziegler, 'Die Bedeutung des Westfälischen Friedens von 1648 für das europäische Völkerrecht', *Archiv des Völkerrechts*, 37 (1999) pp. 129–51; idem, 'Der Westfälischen Frieden von 1648 in der Geschichte des Völkerrechts', in Schröder, *350 Jahre Westfälischer Friede*, pp. 99–117.

4 Randall Lesaffer, 'International Law and its History: The Story of an Unrequited Love', in Matthew Craven, Malgosia Fitzmaurice and Maria Vogiatzi (eds), *Time, History and International Law* (Leyden and Boston, 2007) pp. 27–41; Heinhard Steiger, 'From the International Law of Christianity to the International Law of the World Citizen. Reflections on the Formation of the Epochs of the History of International Law', *Journal of the History of International Law*, 3 (2001) pp. 180–93; Paul Vinogradoff, *Historical Types of International Law* (Leyden, 1923).

5 David Bederman, *International Law in Antiquity* (Cambridge, 2001) p. 6; Wolfgang Preiser, *Der Völkerrechtsgeschichte. Ihre Aufgaben und Methoden* (Wiesbaden, 1964); idem, 'Die Epochen der antiken Völkerrechtsgeschichte', *Juristenzeitung*, 23/24 (1956) pp. 737–44; Heinhard Steiger, 'Probleme der Völkerrechtsgeschichte', *Der Staat*, 26 (1987) pp. 103–26.; Karl-Heinz Ziegler, 'Die römische Grundlagen des europäischen Völkerrechts', *Ius Commune*, 4 (1972) pp. 1–27; idem, *Völkerrechtsgeschichte*, pp. 1–4.

6 Antony Anghie, *Imperialism, Sovereignty and the Making of International Law* (Cambridge, 2004); Yasuaki Onuma, 'When Was the Law of the International Society Born?', *Journal of the History of International Law*, 2 (2000) pp. 1–66.

James Brown Scott and the Belgian Ernest Nys, have put the spotlight on the so-called precursors of Hugo Grotius from the 16th and early 17th centuries, such as the Spanish scholastics Francisco Vitoria (c. 1480–1546) and Francisco Suarez (1548–1617) and the jurists Baltasar de Ayala (1548–1584) and Alberico Gentili (1552–1608).[7] Under the impact of the reappraisal of the cultural, social and political revival of the 12th and 13th centuries – known as the 'Renaissance of the Twelfth Century' –[8] some international legal historians moved back the origins of the modern State system to the Late Middle Ages.[9]

The latter view certainly has merit. The emergence of the sovereign State in Europe was a long and gradual process that started in the Late Middle Ages and would only come to full fruition after the French Revolution (1789). But this does not justify considering the long period from 1300 or one or two hundred years earlier, as a long phase of continuous growth of the sovereign State and of modern international law. In the history of the international legal order of Europe, an important caesura needs to be laid around 1500. The decades around the turn of the 16th century were marked by the collapse of the old medieval order of Europe.

Before the 16th century, the Latin West could still be considered a kind of political and legal unity. Although the Latin West had fallen apart into scores of kingdoms, secular and spiritual principalities and lordships as well as city-republics and consisted of literally thousands of legal circles, each with its own laws and courts, it also formed a hierarchical continuum of which all these numerous and diverse political and juridical entities were part. This order, to which, since the Renaissance, the term *respublica Christiana* was applied, stood under the supreme authority of the emperor and the pope. Since the High Middle Ages, the authority of the emperor had been effectively limited to the Holy Roman Empire – the Kingdoms of Germany and Italy – although other princes and kings granted the emperor a symbolic precedence. The pope was still the supreme spiritual leader of the Latin West, an authority which extended into many aspects of the political and juridical life of Europe, including important matters of 'international' relations such as war and peace. In the *jus commune*, that amalgam of learned Roman law, canon law and some feudal law, the Latin West also had a common jurisprudence. For many matters of international relations, jurists, diplomats and rulers would refer to the learned texts of Roman, canon and feudal law. During the Middle Ages, there was no autonomous jurisprudence or literature of *jus gentium*. But many aspects of the relations between political entities that would later fall under the law of nations were dealt with

---

[7] Ernest Nys, *Le droit de la guerre et les précurseurs de Grotius* (Brussels, 1882); James Brown Scott, *The Spanish Origin of International Law. Francisco de Vitoria and his Law of Nations* (Oxford and London, 1934). Scott included these and other precursors of Grotius in The Classics of International Law (Carnegie Institution, 40 vols., from 1911), in which their major treatises, with an English translation, were reproduced.

[8] Charles H. Haskins, *The Renaissance of the Twelfth Century* (Cambridge, Mass. and London, 1927).

[9] Wolfgang Preiser suggested 1300 as a starting point: 'Über die Ursprünge des modernen Völkerrechts', in Erich Bruel (ed.), *Internationalrechtliche und staatsrechtliche Abhandlungen. Festschrift für Walter Schatzel zum 70. Geburtstag* (Düsseldorf, 1960) pp. 373–87; idem, 'Völkerrechtsgeschichte', in Karl Strupp and Hans-Joachim Schlochauer (eds), *Wörterbuch des Völkerrechts* (2nd edn., Berlin, 1962), vol. 3, pp. 693–5; idem, 'History of the Law of Nations: Ancient Times to 1648', pp. 736–67.

by the glossators and commentators of Roman and canon law. Inasmuch as there was a jurisprudence of *jus gentium*, it was part and parcel of the *jus commune*, or the law at large. Whereas Roman law was mostly a professorial law and was almost nowhere in Europe applicable law, canon law was the law of the Church and was applied throughout the Latin West by all ecclesiastical courts. Inasmuch as the Church claimed and held jurisdiction in many issues relating to international relations, such as the justification of war, the enforcement of treaties sworn by oath and princely marriages, there was an effective *jus gentium*, enforced by the ecclesiastical courts, and in particular by the highest Church authorities, the pope and the papal court.[10]

Between 1450 and 1550, three major changes brought the medieval legal order of Europe down. First, the decades before and after 1500 were marked by the rise of some major dynastic power complexes, foremost among which were Valois France and Habsburg Spain. By the end of the 15th century, France and Spain, then under the Catholic Monarchs Ferdinand VI of Aragon (1479–1516) and Isabella of Castile (1474–1504), were locked in a battle for hegemony over Italy, which in time was to expand into a struggle for hegemony in Western Europe. The Franco–Spanish great power conflict would remain one of the linchpins of the fabric of European politics until deep into the 17th century. The decades around 1500 also saw the revival of the crusader ideal and the call for unity of the Latin West in the face of the Ottoman threat. The conquest of Constantinople in 1453 had been the beginning of seven decades of westwards expansion by the Ottomans with the destruction of much of the Venetian maritime empire in Greece in the 1470s and 1480s, the conquest of Mameluk Syria and Egypt in 1516–1517, the conquest of Rhodes in 1522 and the conquest of Hungary in 1526 ending with the failed siege of Vienna in 1529. In this context, the old medieval ideal of 'universal monarchy' was revived. Some of the French kings as well as Charles V, Emperor, King of Spain and Lord of the Burgundian Netherlands (1516–1558), at some point claimed to be the secular head of the Latin West and therefore to be entitled to lead the external war effort of Christianity against the common enemy, the Turks. Hegemony over Italy, 'the garden of empire' in the words of the great Florentine poet Dante Alighieri (1265–1321), the seat of Christianity in the West as well as the logical launching base for any counter-offensive against the Turks, was the necessary precondition to vest and impose such a 'universal monarchy'. But with their rivalry over who was to lead the Latin West in a common war against the Turks, the two leading monarchs of the early 16th century, Charles V and Francis I of France (1515–1547), saw the last serious attempt of restoring unity to failure

---

10 Randall Lesaffer, 'The Medieval Canon Law of Contract and Early-Modern Treaty Law', *Journal of the History of International Law*, 2 (2000) pp. 178–98; idem, 'The Grotian Tradition Revisited: Change and Continuity in the History of International Law', *British Yearbook of International Law*, 73 (2002) pp. 103–39, at pp. 110–15; idem, 'Peace Treaties from Lodi to Westphalia', in Randall Lesaffer (ed.), *Peace Treaties and International Law in European History: From the End of the Middle Ages to World War One* (Cambridge, 2004) pp. 9–41, at pp. 9–13; James Muldoon, 'The Contribution of the Medieval Canon Lawyers to the Formation of International Law', *Zeitschrift der Savigny-Stiftung für europäische Rechtsgeschichte, kanonistische Abteilung*, 81 (1995) pp. 64–82, Ziegler, Römische Gründlagen; idem, 'The Influence on Medieval Roman Law on Peace Treates', in Lesaffer, *Peace Treaties and International Law*, pp. 147–61.

and destroyed the final vestiges of imperial authority.[11] Henceforth, 'universal monarchy' would become a buzzword in the mouths and writings of those who opposed the ambitions to European hegemony by the leading great power of the age, first Spain (1530s to the Peace of the Pyrenees, 1659) and then France (after 1659).[12]

Second, there was the Reformation. By the second half of the 16th century, the unity of the Latin Church was lost. The northern half of Europe had rejected the authority of the pope and had been converted to one of the Protestant denominations. Religion, which for almost a millennium had been the fundament of the unity of the Latin West, was now the main cause of dissension. In some of the major countries of Europe, including the German Empire, France and the Netherlands, Catholics and Protestants became locked in a fierce battle for political control, quickly making religion one of the main dividing lines at the international level as well. On the legal side, the religious conflict destroyed one of the main fundaments on which the medieval order of the *respublica Christiana* had rested: that of the universal authority of canon law and of the ecclesiastical and the papal courts. As in the context of the learned *jus commune,* particularly so in matters of *jus gentium*, Roman, canon and feudal law had become inextricably bound to one another, this also jeopardized the usefulness of the secular learned law as a source of authority. Moreover, under the influence of Protestant and humanist jurisprudence – which in many countries such as France and the Netherlands were closely intertwined – a more national approach to 'Roman' law was taken, weakening its 'universal' character and uses.[13]

Third, the discoveries by the Spanish and the Portuguese and their conquest of territories in the East Indies and in the Americas put new challenges in the field of international relations. The claims to monopoly over navigation and commerce by the Spanish and Portuguese and their conquest of native lands in the Indies raised new questions for which new answers needed to be articulated. Moreover, existing European customs and doctrines which were vested in a common history and on the authority of Roman and canon law were irrelevant to the relations with the newly discovered peoples with whom there was no common past and who were neither Roman nor Christian. The need arose for a new common basis to vest international legal relations on.[14]

By the second half of the 16th century, the medieval order of the *respublica Christiana* had collapsed and the Latin West was thrown into a deep political and legal crisis. Many of the old customs and doctrines relating to war and peace, diplomacy, foreign trade and

---

11 John M. Headley, 'The Habsburg World Empire and the Revival of Ghibellinism', *Medieval and Renaissance Studies,* 7 (1978) pp. 93–127; idem, *The Emperor and his Chancellor: A Study of the Imperial Chancellery under Gattinara* (Cambridge, 1983); Randall Lesaffer, 'Charles V, *monarchia universalis* and the law of nations (1515–1530)', *Legal History Review*, 71 (2003) pp. 79–123.

12 Franz Bosbach, *Monarchia universalis. Ein politischer Leitbegrif der frühen Neuzeit* (Göttingen, 1988).

13 Donald R. Kelley, *Foundations of Modern Historical Scholarship: Language, Law and History in the French Renaissance* (New York, 1970); idem, 'Civil Science in the Renaissance: Jurisprudence in the French Manner', *Journal of the History of Ideas*, 3 (1981) pp. 261–76; idem, 'Law', in John H. Burns (ed.), *The Cambridge History of Political Thought 1450–1700* (Cambridge, 1991) pp. 66–94; Peter Stein, 'Legal Humanism and Legal Science', *Legal History Review*, 54 (1986) pp. 297–306; J. Witte, *Law and Protestantism: the Legal Teachings of the Lutheran Reformation* (Cambridge, 2002).

14 Anghie, *Imperialism, Sovereignty and the Making of International Law*, pp. 17–23; Steiger, 'From the International Law of Christianity', pp. 185–6.

navigation might still be applied among European princes, but the common authority on which they were founded had crumbled. The authority of the pope and of ecclesiastical courts was less and less invoked in matters of war, peace and diplomacy. Treaty practice offers a clear illustration thereof. During the Late Middle Ages, the interpretation and enforcement of treaties, especially of treaties ratified by oath, fell under the application of canon law and the jurisdiction of the Church. In many treaties, direct reference was made to ecclesiastical and papal authority and ecclesiastical sanctions were invoked in case of a breach of treaty. Whereas it remained customary until the late 17th century to ratify treaties by oath, by the end of the 16th century almost all references to the jurisdiction of the pope and ecclesiastical institutions and sanctions had disappeared from treaty practice, also among Catholic princes. Rarely, if ever, did princes appeal again to the papal courts to rule over a case of breach of treaty.[15]

14.1.2 Jus Publicum Europaeum

The collapse of papal and ecclesiastical authority in the field of international relations had made the great princes and republics externally sovereign. In the absence of any higher authority of law making or law enforcement, they were now thrown upon their own devices to articulate a new legal order and to uphold it. It took more than a century for this to happen. Only after Westphalia did the new order, that of the *jus publicum Europaeum* (*droit public de l'Europe*) emerge. It took until the 18th century for it to be accomplished.

The century between 1550 and 1650 was an age of turmoil for the Latin West. Some of the major countries of Europe were plagued by political instability, civil unrest and even civil war. Some of the major conflicts of the period, such as the Eighty Years War (1567–1648) between Spain and its rebellious provinces of the Northern Netherlands, the French Wars of Religion (1562–1598) and the Thirty Years War (1618–1648) had political as well as religious causes. Over the 16th and 17th centuries, in most countries of Europe, with the exception of the Empire, kings and their governments were successful at strengthening the power of central government and the gradual elimination of old local and regional elites as independent power brokers and contenders for government. In most countries, this process of centralisation went through a series of political clashes and outright civil war. The 1640s and 1650s were particularly ripe with elite rebellions and other forms of civil war. Several of the major countries of Europe, including England (Civil War, 1641–1649), France (Fronde, 1648–1653), Spain (Catalonia 1640–1653), Portugal (1640–1668), and Naples (1647–1648) fell victim to armed revolt. These revolts, however they ended, would prove to be the last convulsions of protracted armed resistance by local elites against the centralisation of power. In all, during the century after 1550, conditions were hardly conducive for a new stable, international order to emerge. It would take until the second half of the 17th century before the conditions for this were sufficiently present.[16]

---

15 Lesaffer, 'Peace Treaties from Lodi to Westphalia', pp. 33–34.

16 Peter Zagorin, *Rebels and Rulers, 1500–1660* (2 vols., Cambridge, 1982).

The Peace Treaties of Westphalia (1648)[17] have been widely acclaimed as the turning point and the very constitution of the 'Westphalian' order of the sovereign States system and of the classical law of nations. Claims have been made to the extent that the Peace of Westphalia introduced and laid down the basic principles of the sovereign States system and its law of nations, such as the principle of the sovereignty and equality of States, the religious neutrality of the international order and the balance of power.[18] The truth is that none of these principles were introduced, or even appear as principles of international relations in the Westphalia Peace Treaties. At best, some related ideas can be found in the context of the internal political, constitutional and religious settlements among the Emperor and the Estates of the Empire that were part of the treaties. But these did not reflect on the law of nations, had little to do with State sovereignty and were hardly innovative.[19] Yet the Peace of Westphalia is an epochal event because it marked the end of the last great religious war and brought a relative form of stability to Central Europe, one of the main battlefields of the great powers of the age. As such, the Peace of Westphalia, together with the settlement of the great civil wars of the 1650s and 1660s assured the conditions of stability necessary to construct a new international legal order. It was rather *after* than *at* Westphalia that the 'Westphalian' order was born.

The classical law of nations, or the *jus publicum Europaeum*, was laid out in the decades between Westphalia and the Peace Treaties of Utrecht (1713). Its main sources were customs and treaties. The peace treaties coming out of the great multilateral peace conferences of the age, such as those of Nijmegen (1678/1679), Rijswijk (1697), Utrecht (1713), Vienna (1738) and Aachen (1748),[20] were particularly important and laid down or incorporated the main principles of the political and legal order of Europe. Later treaties often referred to older treaties as the fundament for the new peace and expressly

---

[17] The Westphalia Peace Treaties that ended the Thirty Years War were the Treaty of Munster of 24 October 1648 between the Emperor and the Estates of the Holy Roman Empire and the King of France and the Treaty of Osnabruck of that same date between the Emperor and the Estates of the Holy Roman Empire and the Queen of Sweden. On 30 January 1648, at Munster, the Spanish and the Republic of the United Provinces of the Northern Netherlands had also made peace, thus ending the Eighty Years War. Fritz Dickmann, *Der Westfälische Friede* (7th edn., Munster, 1998); J.J. Poelhekke, *De Vrede van Munster* (The Hague, 1948).

[18] E.g. Richard A. Falk, 'The Interplay of Westphalia and Charter Conceptions of International Legal Order', in Richard A. Falk and Cyril E. Black (eds), *The Future of International Legal Order* (Princeton, 1968) vol. 1, pp. 43–48; Leo Gross, 'The Peace of Westphalia, 1648–1948', *American Journal of International Law*, 42 (1948) pp. 20–41; Andrea Rapisardi Mirabelli, 'Le congrès de Westphalie. Ses négociations et ses résultats au point de vue de l'histoire du droit des gens', *Bibliotheca Visseriana Dissertationum Ius Internationale Illustrantium*, 20 (1929) pp. 7–18.

[19] See footnote 3.

[20] Whereas as the peace conferences were multilateral in the sense that many of the European powers participated, they resulted in a series of bilateral peace treaties. The first important exception to that was the Peace of Aachen (1748), ending the War of Austrian Succession. Heinz Duchhardt, 'Friedenskongresse im Zeitalter des Absolutismus – Gestaltung und Struktur', in Konrad Repgen (ed.), *Forschungen und Quellen zur Geschichte des Dreissigjährigen Krieges* (Munster, 1981) pp. 226–39; Krystyna Marek, 'Contribution à l'étude de l'histoire du traité multilatéral', in Emanuel Diez et al. (eds), *Festschrift für Rudolf Bindschedler* (Bern, 1980) pp. 17–39. See J.A.H. Bots (ed.), *The Peace of Nijmegen – 1676–1678/79 – La Paix de Nimègue* (Amsterdam, 1980); Heinz Duchhardt (ed.), *Der Friede von Rijswijk 1697* (Mainz, 1998); Thomas R. Kraus, *'Europa sieht ten Tag leuchten . . .': der Aachener Friede von 1748* (Aachen, 1998).

confirmed them. In the series of treaties thus named, the Westphalia Peace Treaties were only included in treaties relating to the Empire.[21]

The classical law of nations was a law premised on the sovereignty of the State. It was designed to regulate the external relations of the sovereign princes and city-republics of Europe. As such, the classical law of nations could only emerge and unfold on the rhythm of the emergence of the sovereign State. State sovereignty has two dimensions, an external and an internal one. External sovereignty can be defined negatively as the absence of any higher authority. External sovereignty can be either absolute or relative. Absolute external sovereignty implies the absence of higher authority in relation to every aspect of public authority; relative external sovereignty means that it is limited to some parts of public authority, such as the right to wage war or make peace. The collapse of the *respublica Christiana* of the early 16th century had assured the main princes and city-republics of external authority in all important aspects of international political life. By 1550, Europe did exist out of a few dozen externally sovereign powers.

But it would take more than another century for the main States of Europe to be well underway to becoming internally sovereign and it would take until the French Revolution (1789) and the 19th century for internal sovereignty to be truly accomplished. Internal sovereignty can be defined as the situation in which the sovereign power within the State – e.g. the king – is the sole source of all public authority; all other public institutions hold their power through delegation from the sovereign. Again internal sovereignty can be either absolute or relative, in the sense that it is limited to certain aspects of public authority. In his *Les six livres de la République* (1576), the French jurist Jean Bodin (1530–1596) considered a prince to be sovereign if he held exclusive power over seven essential State functions.[22] As regards international relations, internal sovereignty means that the central government monopolises all external relations of the State, such as the right to send or accredit diplomats, to make treaties and to make war.

With few exceptions, the major political entities of Early-Modern Europe were monarchies. Some of the leading ones, such as France, Spain, Sweden or the Habsburg-Austrian complex, were composite monarchies. They consisted of several realms that were held in personal union by their common prince. Between 1500 and 1800, in most countries, princes and their governments gradually succeeded in strengthening the political and legal unity of their territories and enhancing their control over the different parts of their 'empires'. In some countries, such as England, this went much farther than in others. In the process, the old local and regional political and military elites were eliminated as independent power brokers at the national level and were absorbed in the apparatus of State.[23]

After the revolts of the mid 17th century, central governments more or less monopolised the external relations of the State. This dramatically changed the setting of

---

[21] Steiger, 'Grundgesetz für Europa', pp. 58–66.

[22] Julian Franklin, *Jean Bodin and the Rise of Absolutist Theory* (Cambridge, 1973); idem, 'Sovereignty and the Mixed Constitution: Bodin and his critis', in Burns (ed.), *Cambridge History of Political Thought 1450–1700*, pp. 299–344.

[23] Richard Bonney, *The European Dynastic States, 1494–1660* (Oxford, 1991); Nicholas Henshall, *The Myth of Absolutism: Change and Continuity in Early Modern European Monarchy* (London and New York, 1992).

'international relations'. Whereas during the Late Middle Ages, literally hundreds of the most different sorts of actors, from the emperor to kings, princes, lords of all kinds, bishops and abbots to city and town governments, were involved with matters of war, diplomacy and international trade, now these issues became the preserve of a few dozen princes and city-republics and their agents. Whereas during the Late Middle Ages, the law of nations had formed an integral part of the law at large, as it applied to all kinds of rulers and institutions, now it became the preserve of the sovereign holders of the highest public authority. As such, it became a distinct category of law, and of public law at that. This meant that concepts and rules of private law, which before were applied directly to international relations, now needed to be transferred from the domain of private law to that of the law of nations through a conscious process of analogy or adaptation.

State sovereignty might be the linchpin of the system of Europe of the late 17th and 18th centuries, but it is wrong to interpret the evolution of the law of nations from 1650 to 1800 one-sidedly in terms of the emergence of the sovereign State. The classical law of nations was as much an attempt to organise the system of sovereign States and limit the free arbiter of States as to accommodate them. The dynamic tension that came with this was inherent to the system. The fact that princes and States sometimes got away with the most blatant acts of aggression, such as in the case of the Prussian invasion and conquest of Silesia in 1740 and the Polish Partitions (1774, 1792 and 1795), indicates a failure of the system to reign in the ambitions of States but does not imply that it was not attempted or that these actions went undisputed.

What were, apart from State sovereignty, the main characteristics of the classical law of nations? First, the sovereign princes and rulers felt themselves to be part of a wider community. That community was by and large limited to Western, Central and Northern Europe as well as the Christian parts of Southern Europe. During the 17th and 18th centuries, it expanded to the east to include Russia. Whereas some European powers had extensive trade and diplomatic relations with the Ottoman Empire, the latter was not truly part of the European legal order.[24] Treaties and other diplomatic documents continued to make reference to overriding common interests and values to which the sovereign princes stated their adherence. Between 1500 and 1800, changes took place in relation to the terminology used in treaties to indicate the community of princes and these overriding interests and values. Until the end of the 17th century, Europe was referred to as *Christianitas, orbis Christiana or respublica Christiana.* Only during the 18th century did these direct references to Christianity fade away and make place for the term 'Europe'. In the preambles of many peace treaties of the 16th and 17th centuries, the desire to stop the shedding of Christian blood and thus to restore the unity of Christianity was voiced. Until the end of the 16th century, reference was made to the interests of religion and the Church as well as to the necessity of unity in the face of the Turkish threat. Over the 17th century, the latter two references disappeared; what was left was the expression of a vague desire to restore the peace and unity of Christianity. In 18th-century treaties, a new phrase was coined to refer to the overriding common interests and values to which princes had to submit. In many preambles and in some of the main articles of peace

---

24 Karl-Heinz Ziegler, 'The Peace Treaties of the Ottoman Empire with the European Christian Powers', in Lesaffer, *Peace Treaties and International Law*, pp. 338–64.

treaties of the 18th century, it was held that the conditions under which peace was made were instrumental to the upholding of the 'tranquillity and security of Europe'. In some cases, this was more than lip service to a noble ideal. More than once during the 18th century, dynastic interests or even constitutional rules were set aside for the overriding purpose of attaining a stable peace.[25]

Second, during the 18th century, the balance of power became one of the leading principles of the international order. Only a few treaties made direct reference to the 'équilibre de l'Europe', but it was covered by the far more frequently voiced interest of safeguarding the 'tranquillity and security of Europe'. Safeguarding the balance of power was a precondition to the peace and the security of the sovereign States of Europe. The doctrine of the balance of power implied that no State would be allowed to become so powerful that it might outstrip any likely coalition of opponents and become hegemonic, at the European level or at the level of a subsystem. This balance was not to be achieved through actual equality between all States, but through the formation of equilibrated coalitions. When the balance was disrupted, the liberty and sovereignty of all States was felt to be at risk. The doctrine was inextricably linked to the concept of State sovereignty. It also served to justify war, and even preventive war. But at the same time, the doctrine could also serve to reign in the freedom of States. The most famous example thereof was the compromise from the Peace of Utrecht (1713) on the Spanish succession, whereby the French and Spanish Bourbons had to accept the curbing of their dynastic rights in the name of European peace and the balance of power.[26]

Third, the sanctity of treaties remained an overriding principle of the law of nations. Faith to the given word was considered the basic fundament of the international order and the breaking of treaties one of the most perfidious acts, which was not lightly committed. The Swiss diplomat Emer de Vattel (1714–1767) was not alone in considering the upholding of treaties a 'sacred' duty, in which all nations had an interest. The perpetrator was to be considered 'a public enemy which attacks the foundations and the common peace and security of Nations'.[27] So, when princes went to war, they were very meticulous in explaining that they did not act in contravention of an existing peace treaty, but were

---

[25] Lesaffer, 'Peace Treaties from Lodi to Westphalia', pp. 29–34; idem, 'Paix et guerre dans les grands traités du dix-huitième siècle', *Journal of the History of International Law*, 7 (2005) pp. 25–43.

[26] Peace Treaty of Utrecht between France and Great Britain of 11 April 1713, Art. 6 in Clive Parry, *Consolidated Treaty Series* (Dobbs Ferry, 1969, further CTS) vol. 27, pp. 482–83; Peace Treaty of Utrecht between Great Britain and Spain of 13 July 1713, Art. 2 in CTS, vol. 28, pp. 299–300. On the balance of power: Herbert Butterfield, 'The Balance of Power', in Herbert Butterfield and Martin Wight (eds), *Diplomatic Investigations: Essays in the Theory of International Politics* (London, 1966) pp. 132–48; Heinz Duchhardt, 'The Missing Balance', *Journal of the History of International Law*, 2 (2000) pp. 67–72; Evan Luard, *The Balance of Power: The System of International Relations, 1648–1815* (Basingstoke, 1992); Arno Strohmeyer, *Theorie der Interaktion. Das europäische Gleichgewicht der Kräfte in der frühen Neuzeit* (Vienna, Cologne and Weimar, 1994); Martin Wight, 'The Balance of Power and International Order', in Alan James (ed.), *The Bases of International Order* (London, 1973) pp. 85–115.

[27] Emer de Vattel, *Le droit des gens ou principes de la Loi naturelle* (1758, ed. and transl. Albert de La Pradelle and Charles G. Fenwick, The Classics of International Law, 3 vols., Washington, 1916; for another English edn., Béla Kapossy and Richard Whatmore, *Natural Law and Enlightenment Classics*, Indianapolis, 2008) 2.15.222.

resorting to war either because their opponent had first broken the conditions of the peace or that they did so for a cause which did not contravene existing treaty relations or obligations.

Fourth, many peace and alliance treaties of the late 17th and of the 18th centuries also provided for third-power guarantees. Under the provisions thereof, third powers promised to safeguard and help enforce the conditions of a treaty by rendering aid to the victim of a breach of treaty. In some major peace treaties of the 17th century, the power which had mediated the treaty was invited apart from other powers which were not expressly nominated.[28] Later, the role of guarantor was more generally assumed by the great powers, regardless of their having played a formal role of mediator during the peace conference. Over the 18th century, some multilateral alliances were made with the specific purpose of upholding pre-existing peace treaties. The Triple, later Quadruple Alliance of 1717/1718 to uphold the Peace of Utrecht is the main example thereof.[29]

Fifth, the doctrine of the balance of power and the guarantee system reflected the recognition of the special role of the great powers in the upholding of the 'tranquillity and security of Europe'. In taking on the role of guarantor of the European peace order, the great powers assumed and were granted a special responsibility for the European order and special rights to intervene, including through the use of force, to do so. To some extent, this prefigured the 'Concert of Europe' of the 19th century under which the five great powers of Europe assumed the role of guaranteeing and managing the order of Europe as laid down at the Congress of Vienna (1814/1815).[30]

14.2 THE LAW OF NATIONS AS AN AUTONOMOUS DISCIPLINE

14.2.1 Scholastics and Humanists

Before the 16th century, there was no autonomous jurisprudence of the law of nations with its own text canon and literature. Since the 11th century, the glossators and commentators of Roman and canon law had written numerous glosses, commentaries, legal opinions and even some treatises on matters relating to diplomacy, war, trade and navigation but they had not forged it into a self-standing branch of the law. As these matters were the concern of numerous and very diverse political players, ranging from kings to petty lords, the *jus gentium* was not yet the preserve of just one category of political entities.

---

[28] Treaty of Nijmegen between France and the Republic of 10 August 1678, Art. 20, CTS vol. 14, p.365; Treaty of Rijswijk between France and the Republic of 20 September 1697, Art. 20, CTS vol. 21, p.347; Treaty of Rijswijk between France and Spain of 20 September 1697, Art. 36, CTS vol. 21, p.453; Treaty of Rijswijk between the Empire and France of 30 October 1697, Art. 54, CTS, vol. 22, p.5.

[29] Treaty of The Hague of 4 January 1717, in CTS vol. 30, p.65; Treaty of London of 22 July 1718, CTS vol. 30, p.415.

[30] Andreas Osiander, *The States System of Europe 1640–1990: Peacemaking and the Conditions of International Stability* (Oxford, 1994); Gerry Simpson, *Great Powers and Outlaw States: Unequal Sovereigns in the International Legal Order* (Cambridge, 2004).

This was only to change after the sovereign State had emerged and after central governments had monopolised the State's external relations. Before this, the writings of Roman and canon lawyers relevant to diplomacy, war, trade and navigation were fully part of the law at large. They were to be found spread through their glosses and commentaries on the Roman and canon law sources. Concepts, principles and rules of Roman, canon and feudal law, as well as of private and public law were used without much discretion to address questions relating to *jus gentium*. The learned doctrine had a direct impact on international practices and was a major source of law as it was invoked in numerous cases before ecclesiastical courts or arbiters; Roman law was directly applied to matters of trade and navigation. Apart from Roman and canon lawyers, theologians also dealt with matters of war and peace in their writings. For some subjects, one could distinguish between a theological and a Romanist tradition, with the canon lawyers often in the middle. The main difference between these traditions was that the theologians, and canon lawyers, were more concerned with the effects of human behaviour upon one's immortal soul, whereas the Roman lawyers, and canon lawyers, were more concerned with its effects here and now. So the theologians would ask the question what the consequences for waging an unjust war were for one's salvation or damnation, whereas Roman lawyers would look at the rights one could or could not acquire through unjust war.

The collapse of the religious unity of Europe during the first half of the 16th century destroyed much of the authority on which the doctrine, and thus the practices, of the *jus gentium* had rested. This had two paradoxical consequences. On the one hand, after 1500, doctrine lost much of its direct impact on the practices of international relations. Far fewer disputes between princes and republics were settled in courts or through arbitral practice, where appeal to jurisprudence used to be made. An important exception needs to be made for the continuous role played by prize courts and courts of admiralty over cases of maritime warfare, privateering, piracy and matters of navigation in general; in these courts, Roman law continued to have its impact felt. Also, some cases about diplomatic immunity made it into court.[31]

On the other hand, the 16th and 17th centuries saw the emergence of the law of nations as an autonomous scholarly discipline with its own literary tradition. Before 1500, few self-standing treatises were written on matters pertaining to the *jus gentium*. Several Roman and canon lawyers wrote treatises on subjects of war, peace and diplomacy, but their scope was rarely limited to these issues.[32] During the 14th and 15th centuries, some treatises were written with a more exclusive focus on the laws of war and peace.[33]

---

[31] Charles de Martens, *Causes célèbres du droit des gens* (2 vols., Leipzig, 1827) and idem, *Nouvelles causes célèbres du droit des gens* (2 vols., Leipzig, 1843).

[32] Most of these treatises are to be found in the great collection of treatises from Venice, 1583–1586 known as the *Tractatus Universi Juris* (18+4 vols.) and in the collection of treatises which were censured out because of their association with Protestantism, see in particular: *Tractatus Universi Juris Extravagantes, vol. 1: De dignitate et potestate seculari* (Venice, 1548; Naples, 2005).

[33] The canon lawyer Giovanni da Legnano († 1383) wrote a treatise on war, reprisals and duels: Giovanni da Legnano, *Tractatus de bello, de represaliis et de duello* (1360, ed. and transl. Thomas E. Holland, The Classics of International Law, Oxford, 1917). In *Tractatus Universi Juris,* vol. 16, three treatises on war (*De bello*) were included, namely those by Johannes Lupus, Martinus Garatus Laudensis and Francisco Arias. Garatus Laudensis (15th century) also wrote a treatise on treaties,

Outside the field of the learned law, some treatises were written on the code of chivalry.[34] Humanist jurisprudence had given a great stimulus to the writing of treatises as autonomous monographs which dealt with a subject of law in a more or less exhaustive and systematic way. From the middle of the 16th century onwards, this spilt over into the field of the law of nations as an increasing number of self-standing treatises on aspects of the laws of war and peace were written and published.

Modern scholars have classified the writers of the law of nations of the 16th and early 17th centuries by pitting scholastic against humanist writers. The – Spanish – theologians and jurists of the Second Scholastic, or the School of Salamanca, continued the Aristotelian tradition of Thomas Aquinas (1225–1274). The two main protagonists were two theologians, the Dominican Francisco Vitoria and the Jesuit Francisco Suarez. In two famous *Relectiones* from the 1530s, *De Indis* and *De jure belli*, Vitoria addressed the question of the justice of the Spanish conquests in the Americas.[35] Suarez laid out his doctrine of natural law and the law of nations in several works, including his *opus magnum, De Legibus ac Deo Legislatore* (1612).[36] Other important scholastics include the Dominican theologians Juan de la Peña (1513–1565), Domingo de Soto (1494–1560), the Salamanca theologian and canon lawyer Diego de Covarruvias (1512–1577), the jurist Fernando Vazquez de Menchaca (1512–1569) and the Jesuit theologian Luis de Molina (1535–1600).

Under the terms 'humanists' and 'humanism' fall a far wider group of scholars and a far wider range of views. The humanist tradition includes men of letters such as Desiderius Erasmus (c. 1469–1536) and Justus Lipsius (1547–1606), the earliest political writers who took some of their ideas from classical texts and humanist philosophy, such as Nicolo Machiavelli (1469–1527) and Jean Bodin, protagonists of humanist jurisprudence such as Andrea Alciato (1492–1550) and François Hotman (1524–1590) and jurists who were influenced by humanism such as Baltasar de Ayala and Alberico Gentili. Ayala, a military judge in the Spanish Army of Flanders during the early stages of the Eighty Years War, wrote a substantial treatise on the laws of war and military discipline.[37] Gentili, a Protestant jurist who had to flee Italy and became Regius Professor of Civil Law at Oxford, was the author of three treatises on matters of the law of nations. His *De jure belli libri tres* was the main exposition of the laws of war and peace before Grotius's *De jure belli ac pacis*.[38] Another main treatise on the laws of war and military discipline, written

---

De confoederatione, pace et conventionibus principum (ed. Alain Wijffels, in Lesaffer, *Peace Treaties and International Law*, pp. 412–447).

34 Most famously, Honoré de Bonet, *L'arbre des batailles* (c. 1386, transl. G.W. Coopland, Liverpool, 1949).

35 Edn. 1696, ed. and transl. Ernest Nys and John P. Bate, The Classics of International Law, Washington, 1917; ed. and transl. Anthony Pagden and Jeremy Lawrance, *Vitoria: Political Writings*, Cambridge Texts in the History of Political Thought, Cambridge, 1991, pp. 231–327.

36 Transl. Gwladys L. Williams, Anna Brown and John Waldron, The Classics of International Law, 2 vols., Oxford and London, 1944.

37 Baltasar de Ayala, *De Jure et Officiis Bellicis et Disciplina Militaris* (1584, ed. and transl. John Westlake and John P. Bate, 2 vols., The Classics of International Law, Washington, 1912).

38 Alberico Gentili, *De legationibus libri tres* (1594, ed. and transl. Ernest Nys and Gordon J. Laing, The Classics of International Law, 2 vols., Oxford, 1924); idem, *De jure belli libri tres* (1598, edn. 1612, ed. and transl. Coleman Philippson and John C. Rolfe, 2 vols., The Classics of

in the 16th century, was that by the Italian jurist Pierino Belli (1505–1575), who still belonged to the Bartolist tradition of Roman law and was less influenced by humanism.[39]

One should be careful not to take the distinction between scholastics and humanists too far. It is true that, inasmuch as they were mainly theologians, the Spanish scholastics continued in the tradition of Aristotelian and Thomist theology, but they also made ample use of late-medieval Roman and canon law texts and, particularly the Jesuits Molina and Suarez, were not untouched by humanist ideas. The humanists, especially the jurists among them, made references to the medieval legal rather than the theological tradition, but they too did not throw away the whole Aristotelian-Thomist tradition, which had become deeply imbedded in medieval legal thought.[40] The main innovative push of their thought came, however, from classical rhetorical (Cicero, Quintilian), philosophical (Platonism and Neo-Platonism, Stoicism), and historical (Livy, Tacit) texts and traditions.

Recently, some authors have attempted to map out the main differences between the views of Spanish scholastics and humanists.[41] Although these attempts have some merit, one should be careful not to overstate the opposition between the two groups. These were not two monolithic schools but broad, and at times, overlapping traditions.

The Spanish scholastics reached back to the Thomist concept of natural law. According to Vitoria, all mankind formed a natural community which has been preordained by divine will and was premised on the common good of all mankind. It was ruled by the principles of natural law (*jus naturale*), which was inherent to human nature, was considered common to all mankind and offered common ground to base legal relations among all nations of the world on. The law of nations (*jus gentium*) was derived from it. The law of nations did, however, also contain rules which could not be directly derived from it but were man-made. These rules derived from the consent of the greater part of the world (*consensus maioris partis totius orbis*), a consent based on a shared concern for the common good and a common understanding of the rationality of the maxims of natural law. This law of nations was to be found in customs and treaties, but was ultimately subject to the law of nature. Suarez's theory was far more radical as he rejected the notion of a natural world community to which States were subject. The law of nations, which was to be found in customs and treaties, was founded on the consent of States, but this was not dictated by the maxims of natural law. Suarez introduced a truly positive law of nations. This raised the question of the binding character of the law of nations. How could the binding character of a rule be guaranteed if it was based on voluntary consent? The answer to this, provided by Suarez, was that natural law stipulated the

International Law, Oxford and London, 1933); idem, *Hispanicae Advocationis libri duo* (1613, edn. 1661, ed. and transl. Frank Frost Abbot, The Classics of International Law, Oxford, 1921).

[39] Pierino Belli, *De re militari et bello tractatus* (1563, ed. and transl. Arrigo Cavaglieri and Herbert C. Nutting, 2 vols., The Classics of International Law, Oxford and London, 1936).

[40] James Gordley, *The Philosophical Origins of Modern Contract Doctrine* (Oxford, 1991).

[41] Diego Panizza, 'Political Theory and Jurisprudence in Gentili's *De Iure Belli*: The great debate between "theological" and "humanist" perspectives from Vitoria to Grotius', *International Law and Justice Working Papers* 15/5 (2005), at www.iilj.org/publications/2005-15Panizza.asp.; Richard Tuck, *The Rights of War and Peace: Political Thought and the International Order from Grotius to Kant* (Oxford, 1999).

binding character of promises, and thus of rules based on consent. In this way, natural law underpinned the positive law of nations.[42]

Many of the humanist jurists also put human nature and natural law centre-stage in their thought, but under the influence of the Roman rhetorical tradition and Tacitism, some of the more radical humanists had a more relaxed view on the impositions made on human behaviour by natural law. According to Richard Tuck and other writers, 'humanists' held self-preservation as the primary dictate and duty of natural man. As the law of nations was the law of nature applied to princes and States and the State thus became the embodiment of natural man – a conceptual leap which was only really made by Grotius but was already lurking in the thought of jurists such as Alciato and Gentili – self-preservation and not the dictates of the common good became the foremost purpose of the State. By consequence, some humanists had an easier time at finding justification for preventive war or European imperialism than the Spanish scholastics had, although these too devised a justification for the Spanish and Portuguese expansion in the Indies and the Americas. Whereas this is true for some humanists such as Alciato or Gentili, one should be careful not to generalise too much. Though one can discern a 'humanist' tradition from the commonality of source and methods some writers used, there was no such thing as a common substantial humanist doctrine of the law of nations.[43]

14.2.2 Naturalists and Positivists

The Dutch humanist Hugo Grotius authored two important treatises on the law of nations. In 1604, he published *De jure praedae*, a treatise on the law of plunder in defence of the capture by the recently founded Dutch East-India Company (V.O.C.) of a Portuguese ship in the East Indies. From this, he in 1609 extracted his *Mare Liberum,* in which he argued for the freedom of navigation on the high sea. In 1625, while living as an exile in France, he published *De jure belli ac pacis libri tres*.[44] As opposed to *De jure*

---

42 Camilo Barcia Trelles, 'Francisco Suarez (1548–1617), *Receuil des Cours de l'Académie de Droit International*, 43 (1933) pp. 385–551; Yves de la Brière, *La conception de droit international chez les théologiens catholiques* (Paris, 1930); J.A. Fernandez-Santamaria, *The State, War and Peace: Spanish Political Thought in the Renaissance 1516–1559* (Cambridge, 1977); Heinz-Gerhard Justenhoven, *Francisco de Vitoria zu Krieg und Frieden* (Cologne, 1991); Joseph Kohler, 'Die spanische Naturrechtslehrer des 16. und 17. Jahrhunderts', *Archiv für Rechts- und Wirtschaftsphilopsophie*, 10 (1916/1917); James Brown Scott, *The Spanish Origin of International Law: Francisco de Vitoria and his Law of Nations* (Oxford and London, 1934); Jozef Soder, *Die Idee der Völkergemeinschaft und die philosophische Grundlagen des Völkerrechts* (Frankfurt, 1955); idem, *Francisco Suarez und das Völkerrecht. Grundgedanken zu Staat, Recht und internationalen Beziehungen* (Frankfurt, 1973); Antonio Truyol y Serra, *Die Grundsätze des Staats- und Völkerrecht bei Francisco de Vitoria* (Zürich, 1947); Laurens Winkel, 'The Peace Treaties of Westphalia as an Instance of the Reception of Roman Law', in Lesaffer, *Peace Treaties and International Law*, pp. 222–37.

43 Benedict Kingsbury and Benjamin Straumann (eds), *The Roman Foundations of the Law of Nations: Alberico Gentili and the Justice of Empire* (Oxford, 2010); Tuck, *The Rights of War and Peace*, pp. 16–50.

44 Hugo Grotius, *De jure praedae commentarius* (1604, transl. Gwladys L. Williams, The Classics of International Law, 2 vols., Oxford and London, 1950; for another English version, ed. Martine van Ittersum, Natural Law and Enlightenment Classics, Indianapolis, 2006); idem,

praedae, the text of which was lost until 1864 – except for *Mare Liberum* – this book went through many re-editions and became the most influential textbook on the law of nations until the middle of the 18th century. It was this work that won Grotius the – disputed – title of 'father of the law of nations'.[45]

Whereas his 'precursors' only dealt with some aspects of the law of nations or discussed the law of nations in the context of a more general work, Grotius's *De jure belli ac pacis* was the first somewhat comprehensive treatise on the law of nations. Apart from the laws of war and peace properly speaking – the latter word referring to the law of peacemaking after war – Grotius also discussed other subjects such as treaty law and diplomatic law. The exposition was, however, not strictly limited to law applicable to rulers and States, but was imbedded in a general exposition of natural law, applicable to individuals as well. In this sense, Grotius's treatise was a precursor to the great treatises *De jure naturae et gentium* by the main natural law philosophers of the late 17th and early 18th centuries. With Grotius as with other writers, many concepts and rules from the medieval tradition of canon and Roman (private) law found their way into the new law of nations through the mediation of natural law, which consisted of the main principles and most common precepts of property, contract and tort law.

For decades, modern students of Grotius have been debating whether Grotius was indebted to humanism or to early-modern scholasticism. The truth of the matter is that Grotius was eclectic in the use of his sources and was not concerned with this labelling. Being a renowned man of letters and a humanist himself, he made ample use of the humanist classical text canon and of the writings of humanist jurists, but he also made ample use of medieval theological, canonist and Romanist literature and of the writings of some of the early-modern scholastics.[46]

Grotius's merit was not to have 'invented' a new law of nations. He was above all a brilliant eclectic and system-builder. His main contribution is therefore to have constructed a more or less consistent and logical system of the law of nations out of the inheritance of Antiquity, the medieval traditions of theology, canon law and Roman law and the writings of the humanists and scholastics of the century before.

Whereas Grotius's thought about the substance of natural rights and obligation

---

Mare liberum (1609, for an English version, ed. David Armitage, Natural Law and Enlightenment Classics, Indianapolis, 2004); idem, *De jure belli ac pacis libri tres* (1625, edn. 1646, transl. Francis W. Kelsey, The Classics of International Law, 2 vols., Washington, 1913; for another English version, ed. Richard Tuck, Natural Law and Enlightenment Classics, 3 vols., Indianapolis, 2005).

45 On the life of Grotius: C.S. Edwards, *Hugo Grotius, The Miracle of Holland: A Study in Political and Legal Thought* (Chicago, 1981); Henk Nellen, *Hugo de Groot. Een leven in strijd om de vrede, 1583–1645* (Amsterdam, 2007); C.G. Roelofsen, 'Grotius and the International Politics of the Seventeenth Century', in Bull, Kingsbury and Watson, *Grotius and International Relations*, pp. 95–131; Martine van Ittersum, *Profit and Principle: Hugo Grotius, Natural Rights Theories and the Rise of Dutch Power in the East Indies (1595–1615)* (Leyden and Boston, 2006). On the relation between *De jure praedae* and *De jure belli ac pacis*, Benjamin Straumann, *Hugo Grotius und die Antike. Römisches Recht und römische Ethik im frühneuzeitlichen Naturrecht* (Studien zur Geschichte des Völkerrechts 14, Baden Baden, 2007).

46 See, in particular, his references in the *Prolegomena* to *De jure belli ac pacis* 38–56. Robert Feenstra, 'Quelques remarques sur les sources utilisées par Grotius dans ses travaux de droit naturel' in *The World of Hugo Grotius (1583–1645). Proceedings of the International Colloquium . . . Rotterdam 6–9 April 1981* (Amsterdam and Maarssen, 1984) pp. 65–81.

and about the laws of war and peace is permeated by the humanist concern with self-preservation,[47] for his formal system of the law of nations he was deeply indebted to the scholastic tradition of natural law. Grotius distinguished the law of nations from the law of nature. Whereas the latter was applicable to all, the former was only applicable to nations and their rulers.[48] Grotius further distinguished between two laws of nations, according to their sources. The *jus gentium naturale* or *primarium* derived from the law of nature, and thus ultimately, from divine will. The *jus gentium voluntarium* or *secundarium* was based on the consent of the peoples. The binding character of these rules was vested in the binding nature of promises under natural law ('pacta sunt servanda'). The *jus gentium voluntarium* was positive, man-made law but it was not a completely autonomous category of law. Just as Vitoria before him had done, Grotius acknowledged that the general consent of all the nations would never be given to a rule that contradicted the rationality of the law of nature. Moreover, the positive law of nations could never allow what the law of nature prohibited.[49]

The distinction between natural and positive law of nations was there to remain and became one of the linchpins of the doctrine of the law of nations. To Grotius, as to many of his successors of the 17th and 18th centuries, the natural law of nations was the domain in which the precepts of natural justice and reasonableness reigned supreme. The positive law of nations was founded on the consent of nations and was to be found in customs and treaties. The precepts of natural law were only binding in conscience and on the eternal soul (*in foro interno*). Reckoning would only follow at the Final Judgment before God's court. To religious men such as Grotius and many of the rulers, diplomats and writers of the 17th and 18th centuries, this was the forum that counted. The voluntary law of nations was binding upon men in the present and was externally enforceable through human sanctions. Whereas it could, at least according to some writers, including Grotius, not cut itself completely loose from the exigencies of natural justice, it could relax its impositions to a more realistic level and have a more pragmatic intake. As such, the dichotomy between natural and positive law continued between medieval theologians and lawyers and between Spanish scholastics and humanists.[50]

---

47 Panizza, 'Political Theory and Jurisprudence in Gentili's *De Iure Belli*'; Tuck, *The Rights of War and Peace*, pp. 78–108.

48 Grotius, *De jure belli ac pacis*, Prol. 1.

49 Roberto Ago, 'Le droit international dans la conception de Grotius', *Receuil des Cours de l'Académie de Droit International*, 182 (1983) pp. 375–98; Alfred Dufour, Peter Haggenmacher and Jiri Toman (eds), *Grotius et l'ordre juridique international* (Paris, 1985); Grewe, *Epochs of International Law*, pp. 194–95; Peter Haggenmacher, *Grotius et la doctrine de la guerre juste* (Paris, 1983); Hartmut Schiedermair, 'Hugo Grotius und die Naturrechtsschule', in Bodo Börner and Hermann Jahrreis (eds), *Einigkeit und Recht und Freiheit. Festschrift für Karl Carstens* (Cologne, 1984–1985) vol. 2, pp. 477–96; Antonio Truyol y Serra, 'Grotius dans ses rapports avec les classiques espagnols du droit des gens', *Recueil des Cours de l'Académie de Droit International*, 182 (1983) pp.431–51; W. van der Vlucht, 'L'œuvre de Grotius et son influence sur le développement du droit international', *Recueil des Cours de l'Académie de Droit International*, 7 (1925) pp.399–509; Hans Wehberg, 'Die Unteschiedung von Natur- und Völkerrecht in der Lehre von H. Grotius', in Hans Kruse and Hans G. Seraphim (eds), *Mensch und Staat in Recht und Geschichte. Festschrift für Herbert Kraus* (Kitzingen and Main, 1954) pp. 227–32.

50 Randall Lesaffer, 'Gentili's *jus post bellum* and Early-Modern Peace Treaties', in Kingsbury and Straumann, *Roman Foundations*.

Some of the major treatises on the law of nations of the 17th and 18th centuries were written by the leading representatives of the Modern School of Natural Law. Among these Samuel Pufendorf (1632–1694), Gottfried Wilhelm Leibniz (1646–1716), Johann Gottlieb Heineccius (1681–1741), Jean Barbeyrac (1674–1744), Jean-Jacques Burlamaqui (1694–1748) and Christian Wolff (1679–1754) need to be mentioned. Pufendorf was one of the most radically consequential naturalists. Grotius, Leibniz and others sought the precepts and rules of natural law in the examples of the ancients, in the classical text canon and/or in Roman and canon law. They considered these sources to be *ratio scripta* (written reasonableness) and thus to embody natural reason and justice. Pufendorf made much less use of external sources and attempted to mentally construct the laws of nature and of nations through a purely rational process of deduction. Moreover, Pufendorf rejected the existence of a binding positive law of nations. The law of nations was to be directly derived from natural law, and it was binding upon States as it was on men.[51]

Christian Wolff's great treatise on the laws of nature and of nations, *Jus naturae methodo scientifica pertractata* (1740–1748),[52] was translated into French, amended to include some of his own ideas and made more accessible for the general public by the Swiss diplomat Emer de Vattel. His *Le droit des gens ou principes de la loi naturelle* (1758) quickly drove the work of the great German philosopher into the shadows and was added to the works of Grotius and Pufendorf as one of the seminal textbooks of the law of nations in Europe. Vattel's work would have a great impact on the emerging discipline of international law in the United States and would remain influential until deep into the 19th century.[53]

Wolff's and Vattel's work represent the mainstream in many of the debates on the law of nations of the 18th century. Their system held on to the dualism that was essential to the jurisprudence of the law of nations since Grotius, that of a distinction between a natural and a positive law of nations, between a sphere of natural justice and one of externally enforceable law. Vattel (and Wolff) distinguished four categories of law of nations. First, there was the natural or necessary law of nations. This was the law of nature as applied and adapted to nations. Second, there was the voluntary law of nations. It was general in application, common to all nations. Vattel ranked this together with the other two categories as positive law, but it was not truly that. It found

---

51 Samuel Pufendorf, *Elementorum Jurisprudentiae Universalis libri duo* (1660, edn. 1672, ed. and transl. Hans Wehberg and William A. Oldfather, The Classics of International Law, 2 vols., Oxford and London, 1931); idem, *De jure naturae et gentium libri octo* (1672, edn. 1688, ed. and transl. Walter Simons and C.H. and William A. Oldfather, The Classics of International Law, 2 vols., Oxford and London, 1934); idem, *De officio hominis et civis juxta legem naturalem* (1673, edn. 1682, ed. and transl. Walther Schücking and Frank G. Moore, The Classics of International Law, 2 vols., Oxford 1927; also ed. and transl. James Tully and Michael Silverthorne, *Samuel Pufendorf. On the Duty of Man and Citizen According to Natural Law,* Cambridge Texts in the History of Political Thought, Cambridge, 1991 and eds Ian Hunter and David Saunders, Natural Law and Enlightenment Classics, Indianapolis, 2003).

52 Christian Wolff, *Jus gentium methodo scientifica pertractatum* (1749, edn. 1764, ed. and transl. Otfried Nippold and Joseph H. Drake, The Classics of International Law, 2 vols., Oxford and London, 1934).

53 Mark W. Janis, *America and the Law of Nations 1776–1939* (Oxford, 2010).

its expression in the common behaviour of States, but it was also constrained by natural law. Its legal basis was the common consent of States, which was presumed, not established. It could modify and thus deviate from the necessary law of nations, but it could not contradict it. If it did, consent could not be presumed, so Vattel implied.[54] Next came the two categories of arbitrary law of nations, which were particular in application and thus only applied to those States which had given their consent: conventional law of nations, to be found in treaties, based on express consent and customary law of nations, based on tacit consent. These were truly positive law as they were based on the free arbiter of States.[55]

From the second half of the 17th century onwards, a growing number of treatises on the positive law of nations, as it appeared in treaties and customs, was published. Modern scholars have often distinguished between natural lawyers and positivists among the writers of the 17th and 18th centuries. Mostly, the positivists are styled as opponents of the natural lawyers because of their alleged rejection of natural law and justice. In truth, most of the authors of treatises on the positive law of nations acknowledged the existence and the relevance of natural law and justice and even gave them a place in their system, but they simply had their focus elsewhere. Richard Zouche (1590–1661), one of the successors of Gentili to the Regius Chair of Civil Law in Oxford, the German diplomat Samuel Rachel (1628–1691), the German professor Johann Wolfgang Textor (1638–1701), the Dutch magistrate Cornelius van Bynkershoek (1673–1743), the French cleric Gabriel Bonnot de Mably (1709–1785), the German professor Johann Jakob Moser (1701–1785) and the German professor and statesman Georg Friedrich von Martens (1756–1821) rank among the foremost 'positivist' writers of the classical law of nations. Another, important consequence of the turn to the positive law of nations was the publication of collections of treaties and other diplomatic documents from the end of the 17th century onwards. The German philosopher and jurist Leibniz, himself a protagonist of the School of Natural Law, in 1693 published a collection of European treaties ranging from 1096 to 1497, to which he added a supplement in 1700.[56] His work, like of others, was surpassed by the huge collection by Jean Dumont (1666–1727) of European treaties since the Early Middle Ages.[57] Over the late 17th and 18th centuries, several national treaty collections were published. At the end of the century, Martens started with a collection of treaties since 1761.[58]

---

54 Vattel, *Le droit des gens, Préliminaires*, 21 and 26.

55 Vattel, *Le droit des gens, Préface*, pp. x–xi, *Préliminaires*, 7, 21, 24–27. Emmannuelle Jouannet, *Emer de Vattel et l'émergence doctrinale du droit international classique* (Paris, 1998).

56 Gottfried Wilhelm Leibniz, *Codex juris gentium diplomaticus* (Hannover, 1693); idem, *Mantissa codicis juris gentium diplomatici* (Hannover, 1700).

57 Jean Dumont, *Corps universel diplomatique du droit des gens* (8 vols., Amsterdam and The Hague, 1726–1731; 5 supplements, 1739).

58 Georg Friedrich von Martens, *Recueil des principaux traités d'alliance, de paix, de trêve, de neutralité, de commerce, de limites, d'échange, etc. . . . depuis 1761 jusqu'à présent* (7 vols., Göttingen, 1791–1801), supplemented by other different series.

14.3 THE SOVEREIGN STATE AS A WAR MACHINE

14.3.1 The *Jus Ad Bellum*

War was an endemic feature of life in Early-Modern Europe. The Early-Modern sovereign States were first and foremost war machines, designed to mobilise as many resources as possible for waging war, spending the majority of the public budget on the military even in times of peace. The drive behind this was dynasticism. At the beginning of our period, most of the dynasties that ruled the major countries of Europe only had a tenacious hold on their lands. Military glory and expansion, and the resources and opportunities this created to enhance royal power and to buy the support of the noble elite, were central to the survival and stability of the monarchy. The military revolution of the 16th and 17th centuries, with the generalisation of the use of gun power and the introduction of the *trace italienne* in fortress building, increased the scale and costs of warfare on land and sea manifold. This certainly helped kings and princes to break the military power of local and regional power brokers and to monopolise warfare and, with time, international relations to the exclusion of all other powers within the State. But it also forced them to set up an ever stronger and more effective bureaucracy and fiscal apparatus, further enhancing the financial needs of the State and bringing them on a collision course with local and regional elites. The consequence of this was a kind of vicious circle according to which princes had to strengthen their military and bureaucratic apparatus, leading to an increase of the likelihood and the scale of internal conflict and of international war, making it necessary further to expand the State apparatus. The rising costs of war also enlarged the scale and scope of war in yet another way. Whereas during the Middle Ages, wars had been fairly limited affairs between rulers and their armies, war now became the affair of the whole State. As the costs of war rose, the need to recuperate part thereof from the enemy grew and systematic plundering, looting and taxing the enemy became one of the crucial occurrences of war. Moreover, the economy of the enemy was much more targeted than before, on land and particularly on the sea.[59]

By consequence, war became far more disruptive than it had been before. By the late 16th century it had become customary at the inception of a war to take a series of measures putting an end to normal relations with the enemy, his vassals and subjects. These included an appeal to all subjects to harm the enemy and his subjects, the prohibition of trade and navigation, the seizure of all enemy property – public and private – within one's own territory, the arrest or expulsion of enemy subjects, the revocation of all passports, and the issuing of general reprisals or letters of marque against all enemy property found

59 On the Military Revolution(s): Jeremy Black, *A Military Revolution? Military Change and European Society 1550–1800* (London, 1991); idem, *European Warfare 1494–1660* (London and New York, 2002); idem, *European Warfare 1660–1815* (London, 1994); John A. Lynn, *Giant of the* Grand Siècle*: The French Army, 1610–1715* (Cambridge, 1997); Geoffrey Parker, *The Military Revolution: Military Innovation and the Rise of the West 1500–1800* (Cambridge, 1984); idem, *The Army of Flanders and the Spanish Road 1567–1659* (2nd edn., Cambridge, 1990); David Parrott, *Richelieu's Army: War, Government and Society in France, 1624–1642* (Cambridge, 2001); Michael Roberts, *The Military Revolution, 1560–1660* (Belfast, 1956); Guy Rowlands, *The Dynastic State and the Army under Louis XIV: Royal Service and Private Interest, 1661–1701* (Cambridge, 2002).

inside and outside one's own territory.[60] Whereas before, in the Middle Ages, warfare did not disrupt all peaceful relations between the belligerents and their subjects, now it did. In the Late Middle Ages, wars could be considered as a string of separate acts of hostility. In Early-Modern Europe, war was considered as a state of war, distinct and different from the state of peace. To the state of peace, the laws of peace applied; to the state of war, the laws of war applied and with time, for third States, the laws of neutrality. The Dutch humanist Hugo Grotius (1583–1645) was the first famously to define war as a state (*status*). By the time he wrote this, in 1625, the evolution towards war as a state of affairs was already well under way, as Grotius acknowledged.[61]

The most elaborate and important treatises in the field of the law of nations of the 16th century dealt with the laws of war and peace(making). The subject also formed the hardcore of Grotius's more comprehensive treatise on the law of nations – as the title made clear – and of most treatises of the 17th and 18th centuries. In his *De jure belli libri tres*, the jurist Gentili had treated systematically in three books with what he considered the three main parts of the *jus belli ac pacis*. In modern terms, these were the *jus ad bellum* (the law on the conditions under which one could wage war), the *jus in bello* (the laws of war properly speaking, applying to the state of war), and the *jus post bellum* (the rules about the ending of war and the restoration of the laws of peace).[62] Whereas few later authors would treat with these three subjects in such a systematic and balanced manner as Gentili had, this threefold division became classic and remains so today.

The just war doctrine, which had been moulded into its classical form by the theologians, canon lawyers and civil lawyers of the Late Middle Ages, still played a crucial role in the writings on the *jus ad bellum* between 1500 and 1800. Under the just war doctrine, war was perceived as an instrument of justice. It was the forcible self-help of a wronged party against the perpetrator of a prior injury (*executio juris*). Under the just war doctrine, war was discriminatory. Only one side had a right to wage war; only this side could benefit from the *jus in bello,* and more particularly the *jura belli* (the rights of war), such as the right to loot, conquer or to hold and be held for ransom. At the end of just war

---

60 See the declarations and manifestos of war of the 17th and early 18th centuries published in Dumont, *Corps universel diplomatique* or in *A General Collection of Treatys, Declarations of War, Manifestos, and other Publick Papers, Relating to Peace and War, Among the Potentates of Europe, from 1648 to the Present Time* (4 vols., London, 1710–1732). See Bernd Klesmann, *Bellum solemne: Formen und Funktionen europäischer Kriegserklärungen des 17. Jahrhunderts* (Mainz, 2007); Stephen Neff; 'Peace and Prosperity: Commercial Aspects of Peacemaking', in Lesaffer, (ed.), *Peace Treaties and International Law*, pp. 365–81, at pp. 365–70; idem, *War and the Law of Nations: A General History* (Cambridge, 2005) pp. 102–15.

61 'Sed usus obtinuit ut non actio, sed status eo nomine indicetur, ita ut sit Bellum status per vim certantium qua tales sunt: quae generalitas omnia illa bellorum genera comprehendit': Hugo Grotius, *De jure belli ac pacis libri tres* (Paris, 1625), 1.1.2.1: 'But Custom had so prevailed, that not the Act of Hostility, but the State and Situation of the Contending Parties, now goes by the Name; so that War is the State or Situation of those (considered in that Respect) who dispute by Force of Arms.' Translation by John Morrice (1738) of the French edition by Jean Barbeyrac, reprinted as Hugo Grotius, *The Rights of War and Peace*, ed. Richard Tuck (Natural Law and Enlightenment Classics, 3 vols., Indianapolis, 2005). Also 3.21.1.1.

62 On Gentili, Diego Panizza, *Alberico Gentili, giurista ideolog nell'Inghilterra Elisabettiana* (Padova, 1981); G.H.J. van der Molen, *Alberico Gentili and the Development of International Law: His Life and Times* (Amsterdam, 1937).

came just peace. This peace too was discriminatory. The just belligerent should see the rights for which it had fought vindicated and could seek compensation for the losses and costs of the war, and even inflict a punishment.[63]

The demise of papal and ecclesiastical authority in the field of war and peace and the rise of the sovereign State made the discriminatory character of war an untenable proposition. In the absence of a clear common body of law against which to weigh the opposing claims of princes and of a neutral superior authority to judge on these claims, it became impossible to decide with any semblance of objectivity who represented the just side in a war.

The writers of the law of nations of the 16th century wrestled with the problem of the uncertainty of the justice of a war and tried to adapt the just war doctrine by compromising on the discriminate application of the *jura belli*. For this, two different approaches were tried. There was the approach of the Roman lawyers, such as Ayala and Gentili. They focused on the legal effects rather than on the justice of war by saying that it sufficed for a war to be legal, and thus the laws of war to apply, if the belligerent was sovereign and the war had been formally declared. This did not mean that they pushed the just war doctrine aside, but only that they neutralised its effects on the *jus in bello* and the *just post bellum*. Gentili held that, because it was most often impossible to know who was in the right, it had to be accepted that both sides had a right to wage war. As such, the laws of war needed to be applied indiscriminately to both sides and the peace agreement could not be based on a judgment on the justice of the cause of the belligerents, but on the outcome of the war itself. To him, war was an instrument to solve a dispute in the absence of the possibility to render judgment. Gentili also accepted the possibility of a war to be just on both sides.[64] With their concept of 'legal war,' Ayala and Gentili stepped in the footsteps of some of the commentators of Roman law, among whom Bartolus de Sassoferrato (1314–1357). Bartolus had already accepted the indiscriminatory application of the *jura belli* to both sides in a war.[65] The commentator Raphael Fulgosius (1367–1427) as well as the humanist Alciato had acknowledged that a war could be just on both sides so that all belligerents could benefit indiscriminately from the *jura belli*. In this, Fulgosius had been somewhat more radical than Alciato, who underscored that the cause should not be manifestly unjust and thus implicitly presumed good faith on the parts of the belligerents.[66]

Alciato thereby came close to the solution advanced and preferred by the Spanish

---

63 Jonathan Barnes, 'The Just War', in Norman Kretzmann et al. (eds), *The Cambridge History of Later Medieval Philosophy* (Cambridge, 1982) pp. 750–84; Haggenmacher, *Grotius et la doctrine de la guerre juste*; Maurice H. Keen, *The Laws of War in the Late Middle Ages* (London, 1965) pp. 63–81; Theodor Meron, *Henry's Wars and Shakespeare's Laws: Perspectives on the Law of War in the Later Middle Ages* (Oxford, 1993) pp. 17–63; Neff, *War and the Law of Nations*, pp.45–82; Frederick H. Russell, *The Just War in the Middle Ages* (Cambridge, 1975).

64 Ayala, *De jure et officiis bellicis*, 1.2.34; Gentili, *De iure belli*, 1.6.48.

65 Bartolus, *Digestum novum in tertium tomum Pandectarum commentaria Secunda super Digesto novo* (Basel, 1562), ad. D. 49.15.24; Haggenmacher, *Grotius et la doctrine de la guerre juste*, pp. 280–81.

66 Raphael Fulgosius, *In Pandectas* (Lyon, 1554), ad D.1.1.5; Andrea Alciato, *Commentarii in Pandectas* (Lyon, 1550), 1.1.5 and *Paradoxorum iuris civilis* 2.21, in *Opera Omnia* (4 vols., (Basel, 1549), iii: 'utraque parte optimo iure belligerari arbitramur' ('we find that it is possible to wage

scholastics. Vitoria and some of his followers introduced a distinction between the objective and subjective justice of the war. Whereas Vitoria clung to the view that a war could, objectively speaking, not be just on both sides, he acknowledged that each side could be excused, on the basis of an invincible error, from believing in good faith that he was waging a just war. Thus Vitoria introduced the '*bellum justum ex utraque parte*' (war just on both sides) on the subjective level. Through the application of two concepts from Roman contract law – *bona fides* and *error* – Vitoria opened the door to a non-discriminatory conception of war, in which both sides had a right to wage war and enjoy the benefits of the laws of war.[67]

To Grotius has fallen, again, the merit of making a synthesis between the two doctrines. Grotius used the dichotomy between the natural and voluntary law of nations to solve the problem of the discriminatory character of war under the just war doctrine. The question of the justice of war he relegated to the sphere of natural law of nations; here, the just war doctrine applied and war could only be just on one side. In the sphere of the voluntary law of nations, the concern was with the legal effects of war. Here, Grotius introduced the notion of 'legal war', or in his terminology, 'war in due form' (*bellum solemne*). For a war to have legal effects, it only needed to be waged under sovereign authority and needed to be formally declared.[68] The Grotian solution was adopted by most writers of the law of nations after him until the late 18th century. It still stood at the centre of the *jus ad bellum* of Wolff and Vattel.[69] Thus, doctrine acknowledged the right of sovereigns to resort to war at will under the positive law of nations, while keeping the ideal and language of justice alive under the natural law of nations.

With this dual approach to the problem of war, doctrine did more than paying lip service to an old idea; it reflected the duplicity that was endemic in early-modern State practice. In practice, as in doctrine, the just war proved very resilient. During the whole Early-Modern Age, and even after, princes and governments took great care, when resorting to war, to justify themselves to their officials, military, subjects, and allies and to neutral States. The justice of war was a matter of conscience, but that did not make it unimportant. Formal declarations of war were often substantial texts in which the reasons for war were explained; these, as well as the less formal manifestos of war were widely distributed and sometimes published in several languages. For these justifications, the rudiments of the just war doctrine were used. Most generally, war was justified as an act of defence against an attack, or at least against a serious violation or most likely a series of violations of the rights, and from the 18th century onwards, increasingly also the interests, of the State or its allies. The need to justify a war in terms of defensive action was of great practical importance as one of the main sinews of the security network of any State in Early-Modern Europe were its alliance treaties with other States. The vast majority of these alliances where defensive; the ally would only

---

war with the best of right on both sides', my transl.); see Haggenmacher, *Grotius et la doctrine de la guerre juste,* 203–12.

67 Vitoria, *De jure belli*, 2.4–5.

68 Grotius, *De jure belli ac pacis*, 1.3.4.1, 3.3.4–5 and 3.3.12–13; Haggenmacher, *Grotius et la doctrine de la guerre juste*, pp. 568–612.

69 Vattel, *Le droit des gens*, 3.3.24–28 and 39–40; Wolff, *Jus gentium*, 6.617 and 633–635, 7.777–778 and 888.

be forced to stand up to its obligation in case its ally could prove a *casus foederis* and was acting in defence.

Often, it was argued why it was necessary to resort to a full and formal war, as opposed to a more limited military action in the sense of what later would be called a 'measure short of war'. The main thrust of early-modern justifications was that war was the last resort after all alternatives had failed and that it was absolutely necessary because of the proven obstinacy of the enemy. Only in the 19th century would doctrine develop more different categories of 'measures short of war' such as self-defence, reprisal and intervention, but some of this already existed before. Self-defence, as a natural right, had been known since Roman times. It formed part of early-modern State practice as a limited use of force against a prior attack by the enemy. Furthermore, early-modern practice and doctrine distinguished between the role of belligerent and auxiliary. An auxiliary in war was an ally, which, while not a belligerent itself, was not neutral but supported the war effort of its ally, including through the means of subsidies and of lending troops.[70]

But whereas the just war doctrine continued to reign supreme for the need to explain why a State went to war, it had lost all relevance for the way the war was waged or ended. Regardless of their claims to fight a just war – and the enemy therefore an unjust war – with few exceptions, belligerents applied the *jus in bello* indiscriminately to all sides in the war. Moreover, in no peace treaty between sovereigns was judgment rendered on the justice of war or were concessions made on the basis of the justice or injustice of the war. When early-modern princes went to war, they waged a just war; when they were fighting it or ended it, they fought or ended a war in due form.

14.3.2 The *Jus In Bello* and the Laws of Neutrality

The writers of the classical law of nations perceived of war as a state, and not as a set of separate acts of hostility. War was the state to which the laws of war applied; peace the state to which the laws of peace applied. One of the functions of formal declarations of war and formal peace treaties was to indicate the point at which the state of war began and ended. As war became ever more disruptive, the laws of war needed to become more detailed and elaborate. The same went for the laws applicable to the relations between belligerents and non-belligerents. Over the 18th and 19th centuries, these would grow into a third category, that of the laws of neutrality. Both the laws of war and those of neutrality consisted of a growing body of customary and treaty rules.

Before going into some aspects of the laws of war and neutrality, a general remark needs to be made. Over the 16th and 17th centuries, the *jus in bello* emancipated itself from a broader category of laws *de bello* that had also included matters of military discipline. In other words, the 'international' laws of war became separated from the 'national' laws and customs of military discipline. Whereas the former pertained to the reciprocal rights and duties of military and subjects from two different States, the latter pertained to the internal organisation of the armed forces of a single sovereign and the discipline

---

[70] Klesmann, *Bellum solemne*; Randall Lesaffer, 'Defensive Warfare, Prevention and Hegemony. The Justifications for the Franco-Spanish War of 1635', *Journal of the History of International Law*, 8 (2006), pp. 91–123 and 141–179; Neff, *War and the Law of Nations*, pp.95–158.

enforced upon these by and in the name of the sovereign. This dualism between an internal and an 'international' sphere of law was a consequence of the monopolisation of war and the military by the sovereign State.[71]

From the late 17th century onwards, central governments and military commands started to promulgate legislation and military codes to impose and enforce a stricter discipline on their armed forces, both on land and sea. This was part of a gradual process of 'nationalisation' of the armed forces, by which foreign mercenaries had to make place for armies consisting of own nationals. The – often noble – members of the officer corps continued to feel part of an international warrior elite. Instead of the code of chivalry, which had embodied the laws and customs of war of the Middle Ages, came a new body of laws. This started off as the professional code of a warrior elite of mercenary captains and entrepreneurs, and their soldiers. As armies were brought under State control, agreements about the conduct of war in a particular theatre were increasingly negotiated and made in the name of princes, thus becoming the subject of regular treaties. Also, the laws of war were implemented in national legislation and national military codes.

One of the main thrusts in the evolution of the laws and customs of war during the Early-Modern Age were the attempts by governments and military commands to regulate the rights of officers and soldiers to plunder as well as to appropriate a share of the profits for the treasury. Under traditional law, the ownership of movables captured during war fell to the individual captor. Under the code of chivalry, this also applied to ransom taken from prisoners of war. As of the 16th century, many peace treaties included stipulations to the effect that prisoners of war would be mutually released. Whereas at first the treaties still provided for the payment of ransoms already agreed on, over the 17th century, the release became unconditional. Another example of the growing State monopoly over war was the levying of contributions. These were tributes, in money or goods, to be paid to occupying forces which were fixed in written compacts or treaties and which were considered a substitute for the right to plunder. These allowed appropriating the profits of war for the army's upkeep or the prince's treasury.[72]

Siege warfare was a central feature of early-modern warfare. Under the traditional laws of war, a town or fortress taken by storm could be sacked and plundered. The beleaguered lost the right of capitulation once the enemy artillery had been raided. Over the 17th century, this rule was relaxed and it now became customary to allow surrender until a breach was made and the artillery of the besiegers had approached within a hundred yards of the breach. From the other side, surrendering a town or fortress too quickly could give rise to prosecution of the garrison commander for treason by his own command or government. In any case, the vast majority of sieges were ended with

---

71 Barbara Donagan, 'Codes of Conduct in the English Civil War', *Past and Present*, 118 (1988) pp.65–95, at pp.75–76 and 82–84. See also Keen, *The Laws of War*; Meron, *Henry's Wars*; Robert C. Stacey, 'The Age of Chivalry', in Michael Howard, George J. Andreopoulos and Mark R. Shulman (eds), *The Laws of War: Constraints on Warfare in the Western World* (New Haven and London, 1994) pp.27–39.

72 Philippe Contamine, 'Un contrôle étatique croissant. Les usages de guerre du XIVe au XVIIIe siècle: rançons et butins', in Philippe Contamine (ed.), *Guerre et concurrence entre les Etats européens du XIVe au XVIIIe siècle* (Paris, 1998) pp.199–236; Geoffrey Parker, 'Early Modern Europe', in Howard, Andreopoulos and Shulman, *Laws of War*, pp.40–58.

a formal capitulation. In many cases, generous conditions were granted to the defeated garrison and the citizens. Mostly, the garrison were allowed to depart with their lives. Often they were granted the right to leave with all honours of war, carrying their weapons and enough food, and sometimes they were even allowed to take deserters along. But, of course, conditions could be harsher and sometimes towns were sacked. From the early 18th century onwards, in an increasing number of cases, separate capitulations were made with the commanders of the defeated garrison for their soldiers and the town government for its citizens. Under these agreements, the citizens would be guaranteed their lives, property and liberties.[73]

The disruption of the enemy's maritime trade became one of the main features of economic warfare during the Early-Modern Age. During war, but also during times of peace, government licensed private entrepreneurs as privateers to capture enemy merchants and disrupt the maritime trade of the enemy as much as possible. The legal origins of privateering lay in the medieval institution of particular reprisal, by which an individual was granted by his sovereign the permission to seek compensation for an injury suffered from a foreigner by appropriating the goods of a compatriot of the foreigner. Under civilian doctrine, reprisal could only be obtained after one had unsuccessfully sought redress through normal judiciary procedures.[74] Early-modern peace treaties often stipulated that no reprisals would be granted for the future, except in case of manifest denial of justice. Out of these particular reprisals grew the custom of granting general reprisals. This entailed an appeal to one's own subject to inflict as much harm to the enemy as possible. General reprisals could already be promulgated during peacetime, e.g. in the run-up to a war. General reprisals were granted through 'lettres of marque and reprisal' to certain entrepreneurs to equip privateers and harass the enemy's maritime trade. As States navies grew, men-of-war began to play an ever increasing role in maritime prize taking. Consequently, governments developed rules about the distribution of prizes among the government, officers and sailors.

The laws of maritime warfare tied in with the laws of neutrality. An international body of customary law developed about the mutual rights of belligerents and non-belligerents in relation to 'neutral' shipping; that is the merchants of non-belligerent States. The issue fell subject to a lively and ongoing debate about four main questions. First, there was the question what constituted contraband. Which goods could not be transported to a belligerent because they were a direct aid to the war effort and could thus be stopped regardless of the nationality of the owner of the goods or of the ship they were transported in? Second, there was the question of what constituted a blockade, preventing all shipping movements. Should this be the effective, permanent blockade of a harbour, or did a more distant blockade by cruising a coastline suffice? Third, there was the question of the status of neutral goods on enemy ships or of enemy goods on neutral ships. Could these be taken as prize? Fourth, there was the question how far the rights of belligerents to stop and search neutral

---

73 Randall Lesaffer, 'Siege Warfare in the Early Modern Age: a Study on the Customary Laws of War', in Amanda Perreau-Saussine and James B. Murphy (eds), *The Nature of Customary Law: Legal, Historical and Philosophical Perspectives* (Cambridge, 2007) pp. 176–202; John Wright, 'Sieges and Customs of War at the Opening of the Eighteenth Century', *American Historical Review*, 39 (1934) pp. 629–44.

74 Bartolus of Sassoferrato, *Tractatus represaliarum* (1354).

ships reached. These questions would give rise to severe conflicts over the late 17th and 18th centuries, even leading up to war. The Anglo-Dutch Wars of the late 17th century (1652–1654, 1665–1667, 1672–1674) and the Armed Neutrality (1780) stand out.

The position of non-belligerents also underwent a more conceptual change over the 17th and 18th centuries. Under the discriminatory concept of just war, it was illogical for a non-belligerent to be truly impartial as he fell under the moral duty to support the just belligerent. Although there would remain a middle category between belligerent and neutral, that of auxiliary, the shift to a formal concept of war made room for strict impartiality. The traditional laws of war did not generally provide for specific rights and duties of non-belligerents; these had to be agreed on in particular agreements with the belligerents or enforced from a position of strength. Some 18th-century writers, among them Bynkershoek, Vattel and Martin Hübner (1723–1795), caught the wind of time and articulated a doctrine of the rights and duties of neutrals, implying a duty of strict impartiality and a right to see their interests, territory, trade and property protected.[75] In reality, the position of neutrals remained the subject of particular treaty regulations. It would be the last decades of the 18th century and the first of the following century before general rules of customary law grew out of this practice.[76]

14.3.3 The *Jus Post Bellum*[77]

Under a consequential application of the just war doctrine, a just war needed to end in a just peace. Wolff and Vattel spelled out the multiple, far reaching consequences thereof. First, it meant that the unjust belligerent lost his claim to the object for which the war was fought. Second, he was liable for all the damages and costs suffered by the just belligerent because of the war. Third, also the just belligerent was liable for his unjust wartime actions, that is actions that went against the necessary laws of war.[78]

To Wolff and Vattel, the justice of peace, like the justice of war, pertained to the necessary law of nations, and was thus only operative *in foro interno*. As, *in foro externo*, claims to justice were to be considered irrelevant to the conduct of the war, logically, they were also irrelevant when making peace. The non-existence of an impartial authority to render

---

[75] Cornelius van Bynkershoek, *Quaestionum juris publici libri duo* (1737, ed. and transl. J. de Louter and Renney Frank, The Classics of International Law, 2 vols., Oxford and London, 1930); Martin Hübner, *De la saisie des bâtiments neuters; ou, Le droit qu'ont les nations belligérantes d'arrêter les navires des peuples amis*, 2 vols., The Hague, 1759.

[76] John B. Hattendorf, 'Maritime Conflict', in Howards, Andreopoulos and Shulman, *Laws of War*, pp.98–115; Phili Jessup and Francis Deak (eds), *Neutrality: Its History, Economy and Laws* (4 vols., New York, 1935–7); Carl J. Kulsrud, *Maritime Neutrality to 1780: A History of the Main Principles Governing Neutrality and Belligerency to 1780* (Boston, 1936); Stephen C. Neff, *The Rights and Duties of Neutrals: A General History* (Manchester, 2000); C.G. Roelofsten, *Studies in the History of International Law: Practice and Doctrine in Particular with Regard to the Law of Naval Warfare in the Low Countries from circa 1450 until the Early 17th Century* (Utrecht, 1991).

[77] Christine Bell, *On the Law of Peace: Peace Agreements and the Lex Pacificatoria* (Oxford, 2008); Jörg Fisch, *Krieg und Frieden im Friedensvertrag. Eine universalgeschichtliche Studie uber Grundlagen und Formelemente des Friedenschlusses* (Stuttgart, 1979); Lesaffer, *Peace Treaties and International Law*; Heinhard Steiger, 'Friede in der Rechtsgeschichte', in Wolfgang Augustyn (ed.), *Pax. Beiträge zu Idee und Darstellung des Friedens* (Munich, 2003) pp. 11–62.

[78] Vattel, *Le droit des gens*, 4.2.18; Wolff, *Jus gentium*, 8.986.

judgment over the justice of the war – both in terms of *jus ad bellum* and *jus in bello* – made it undesirable as well as impossible to construe peace as an act of justice. It could only be a political compromise, an agreement between equal partners, the validity of which did not lie in its justice, but in their consent. Under the voluntary laws of nations, the *jus post bellum* could not but take into account the very basic assumptions that underlay war 'in due form': that, in terms of its external effect, it was to be considered 'just' on both sides; that both parties had the same rights; and that the voluntary law of nations granted impunity to the unjust side.[79] Both just war as well as war in due form had their complement: just peace and compromise peace, which one could also call formal peace.

With this, Wolff and Vattel, as others had done before them, capitulated before the realities of the sovereign States system. The basis for the legal solution to a war was not its justice, but its outcome. According to Gentili, this could either be determined by the victor of the war – in case of a complete victory over the enemy – or by consent in a peace treaty. The vast majority of wars in Early-Modern Europe ended in compromise peace along the lines of what Vattel understood under it. This was different for many peace treaties made between European States and indigenous people outside Europe. In the East Indies as well as in the Americas, the European powers often styled peace treaties as unilateral grants of peace. The treaties laid the blame for the war, which was labelled a rebellion, at the doorstep of the indigenous peoples. Amnesty was a unilateral act of mercy, which had to be paid for through cessions and tributes.[80]

None of the peace treaties between European sovereigns of the Early-Modern Age rendered judgment on the war and contained an attribution of guilt to one of the belligerents. In the preambles of peace treaties, the signatories most often limited themselves to deploring the war and the hardship it had brought in the most general of terms. The refusal to judge was not restricted to the level of the *jus ad bellum*, but also extended to the *jus in bello*. From the 16th century onwards, it became customary for the signatories to include a clause of amnesty in the treaty. This implied that the signatories waived all claims for damages and costs because of the war, for themselves as well as for their subjects and adherents. By the beginning of the 19th century, these clauses disappeared but by then it had been long since accepted that they were automatically implied.[81] The amnesty clause tied in with another common stipulation from early-modern peace treaties, that relating to the restitution of private property. During the Early-Modern Age, it was customary for the belligerents to seize and confiscate the property of enemy subjects found on their territory. Under the doctrine of war, this was done to safeguard the future payment of the damages and the costs of war caused by the unjust enemy belligerent. As peace treaties did not render judgment on the justice of war, it was impossible to consider these seized goods as compensation for damages and costs, so that the legal basis for their seizure collapsed. Therefore, logically, most peace treaties included a general clause of automatic restitution. To this general standards provision, treaties also made a standard exception, namely for all movables. There were sound reasons to do so. First, under traditional law, captured

---

79 Vattel, *Le droit des gens*, 3.12.190–192.

80 Fisch, *Krieg und Frieden im Friedensvertrag*, pp. 139–204.

81 Grotius, *De jure belli ac pacis*, 3.20.15; Vattel, *Le droit des gens*, 4.2.20; Wolff, *Jus gentium*, 8.990.

movables went to the capturer, and not to the State – although this rule had lost much of its practical application by the early 18th century. Second, the retrieving and restitution of movables would be far more complex than for immovables and would cause a multitude of disputes and court cases that would make a speedy solution to the war impossible. These two general clauses were often supplemented with dozens of more detailed stipulations.

Between 1500 and 1800, peace treaties became increasingly extensive, growing into documents containing dozens, and with time hundreds, of often detailed political and legal stipulations. In general, one can distinguish three categories of peace treaty clauses. First, there were the political concessions made and won by the belligerents. Second, there were the clauses aimed at ending the state of war and dealing with its consequences. Third, there were the clauses aimed at restoring the state of peace and regulating the future, peaceful relations between the signatories. This last category also included provisions for guaranteeing that the peace would be endurable and stable. As war became an ever more encompassing state of affairs and the normal peaceful relations between the belligerents were thoroughly disrupted, an increasing number of matters needed to be dealt with to end the state of war and restore the state of peace. Over the Early-Modern Age, an extensive body of law regarding peacemaking was developed in peace treaty practice. As regards the end of the state of war, peace treaties generally stipulated an end to the hostilities, a general amnesty, the revocation of reprisals and letters of marque, restitution of all seized realty without, however, income from that property that had lapsed during the time of its seizure, the revocation of all sentences rendered against absent enemy subjects, the conditions under which to restore territories, cities and fortresses and their future legal status, the suspension of prescription before the courts for the duration of the war, the mutual release of prisoners of war and the inclusion of allies and adherents in the peace. With regards to the restoration of peaceful relations for the future, the treaties stipulated perpetual peace and friendship among the principals and their subjects, free movement of persons, the right to trade, the promise for equal treatment of one another's subjects before the courts, the promise not to grant new reprisals or letters of marque, the protection of enemy subjects and property at the inception of a new war and, finally, the recognition that an infringement by a subject would not break the peace but only lead to sanctioning the perpetrator himself.[82] From the late 15th century onwards, peace treaties provided for an increasing number of stipulations with relation to trade and navigation. By the 18th century, it had become customary to deal with matters of trade and navigation in separate treaties, which were made at the same time or shortly after peace was made, the so-called Treaties of Friendship, Commerce and Navigation.[83]

A final word needs to be said about the perpetual character of peace treaties. In early-modern treaties, the signatories normally stipulated that the peace would be 'perpetual'. As such, a peace treaty differed from a truce, which was only made for a limited period of time. The perpetuity of peace was, however, qualified. It did not imply that the signatories promised never to resort to war against one another again. It only meant that the peace treaty exhausted their right to resort to war for the disputes over which the war

---

[82] Lesaffer, 'Peace Treaties from Lodi to Westphalia', pp. 29–42; idem, 'Gentili's *iust post bellum*'.

[83] Stephen C. Neff, 'Commercial Aspects'.

had started – or which had later during the war been added as an additional cause – and which had been settled by the peace treaty. A signatory thus only broke the peace if he resorted to war, on the use of force in general, over the same dispute, but not if he resorted to war for another cause alien to the treaty. A truce only suspended the right to wage war and reserved the rights of States to take up arms again over the same dispute once the stipulated period had passed.[84]

14.4 *THE SOVEREIGN STATE AND ITS REPRESENTATIVES*[85]

Early-modern diplomatic practice was marked by the rise of standing diplomacy. The use of permanent residents first originated in Italy in the 15th century. Before, diplomats had only been used on temporary assignments. During the Middle Ages, some rulers held *procuratores* on a more permanent basis in Rome with the papal courts. These were lawyers especially assigned to represent their rulers in cases pending before the papal courts. The rise of standing diplomats was a by-product of the attempts by the leading powers of Italy to stabilise peace and form long-standing alliances among one another, particularly after a 25-years peace was made at Lodi (1454). From Italy, the practice slowly spread over Europe during the 16th, 17th and 18th centuries, to become a common practice. This did not exclude the use of temporary diplomats on particular assignments, such as treaty negotiations or participation in peace conferences.

Standing diplomacy put different demands on the laws of diplomacy, in particular in relation to diplomatic immunity. Diplomatic immunity is almost as old as diplomacy itself. The works of the early-modern writers on the law of diplomacy such as those of Gentili and Grotius abound with examples of its violation or upholding from biblical or ancient Greek and Roman times. Already in Antiquity, it was generally acknowledged that the physical integrity of foreign representatives should be respected and protected. The canon and civil lawyers of the Late Middle Ages developed a jurisprudence of diplomacy and diplomatic immunity. The Roman private law contract 'mandate' (*mandatum*) formed the doctrinal basis under the laws of diplomacy. Furthermore, diplomats were not only considered to be the promoters of their principals' interest, but also promotors of the common good of the whole Latin West. This made diplomats more vulnerable to attacks from their hosts. Therefore, and also in view of the limited extension and duration of their mandate, diplomatic immunity was restricted to what was necessary for the exercise of the assignment. Diplomats were therefore liable for actions which fell outside their mandate. They could thus be prosecuted for common crimes and for the payment of their debts.

Over the Early-Modern Age, immunity became more absolute and extensive. For this,

---

[84] Belli, *De re militari et bello tractatus*, 5.2.3. and 10.2.27–28 and 35; Gentili, *De jure belli*, 2.12.302–305, 3.14.590 and 3.24.708–711; Grotius, *De jure belli ac pacis*, 3.20.27 and 3.21.5; Pufendorf, *De jure naturae et gentium*, 8.7.6; Vattel, *Le droit des gens*, 4.2.19; Wolff, *Jus gentium*, 8.987; Fisch, *Krieg und Frieden*, pp. 355–361.

[85] E.A. Addair, *The Extraterritoriality of Ambassadors in the Sixteenth and Seventeenth Centuries* (New York, 1929); Myres S. Anderson, *The Rise of Modern Diplomacy 1450–1919* (London and New York, 1993); Lucien Bély, *Espions et ambassadeurs au temps de Louis XIV* (Paris, 1990); Garrett Mattingly, *Renaissance Diplomacy* (Boston, 1955).

two main causes can be indicated. First, the collapse of the *respublica Christiana* and the rise of the sovereign State ended the duplicity inherent in the doctrine of medieval diplomacy. The diplomat now received the unequivocal acknowledgment that he was the representative and promotor of this ruler's interest and nothing but that. This gave ammunition to the doctrine that only that ruler could judge on the diplomat. Second, the more permanent presence of diplomats extended the reach of their activities and made their liability for common legal disputes ever more problematic. The problems of standing diplomacy were exacerbated by the Reformation as questions about the right of diplomats to practice their religion in a country adhering to another confession arose. Early-modern practice is ripe with examples of political and legal disputes on the extension of diplomatic immunity.

Gentili was one of the first modern writers to delve into the subject from a legal perspective. He still upheld that diplomats could be prosecuted for common crimes and in civil disputes, but he did away with the idea that they were also the servants of the common good of Christianity. Gentili was, famously, consulted in the case of the Spanish ambassador in England, Bernardino de Mendoza (1541–1604), who was involved in the so-called Throckmorton plot of 1584 to assassinate Queen Elizabeth (1558–1603) and to put Mary, Queen of Scots (1542–1587) on the English throne. Gentili held that the ambassador could not be prosecuted, not because of an immunity but because natural law did not allow the punishment of an attempted crime and because diplomats could not be judged under municipal law, but only under the (natural) law of nations.

It fell to Grotius to bring about a revolution in diplomatic doctrine. The Dutch humanist defended the doctrine of extra-territoriality. In essence, this comes down to the fiction that diplomats do not find themselves on the territory of the host land and thus do not fall under that country's jurisdiction. By consequence, they fall solely under the jurisdiction of their own sovereign. The host can thus only appeal to the diplomat's sovereign to act or is left with the option of expelling the diplomat. In practice, the exact boundaries of the immunity of a diplomat and his followers varied with time and place and were subject to negotiations and disputes. But in general, in practice as in doctrine, a more absolute and extensive interpretation of immunity arose.

14.5 THE EXPANSION OF EUROPE[86]

The Early-Modern Age is the age of Western Europe's first worldwide imperialism. Between the late 15th and the 18th centuries, several Western European States conquered

---

[86] Anghie, *Imperialism*; Joshua Castellino and Steve Allen, *Title to Territory in International Law: A Temporal Analysis* (Aldershot, 2003); Jörg Fisch, *Die europäische Expansion und das Völkerrecht. Die Auseinandersetzungen um den Status der überseeischen Gebiete vom 15. Jahrhundert bis zur Gegenwart* (Stuttgart, 1984); Lewis Hanke, *The Spanish Struggle for Justice in the Conquest of America* (Dallas, 2002); Edward Keene, *Beyond the Anarchical Society: Grotius, Colonialism and Order in World Politics* (Cambridge, 2002); Randall Lesaffer, 'Argument from Roman Law in Current International Law; Occupation and Acquistive Prescription', *European Journal of International Law*, 16 (2005) pp. 25–58; Anthony Pagden, *Lords of All the World: Ideologies of Empire in Spain, Britain and France c. 1500 – c. 1800* (New Haven and London, 1995);

and built overseas empires spanning the globe. The Portuguese, later followed by the English, French and Dutch, built a maritime and commercial empire in the Eastern Indies with trading and staging posts along the coasts of Africa. The Spanish destroyed and took over the great empires of the Aztecs, Mayas and Incas in Mexico and Peru and formed settler colonies there. The Portuguese, and more temporarily the Dutch, did the same with Brazil as did several other European nations, mainly the Spanish, French and English, in Northern America and the Caribbean.

Colonisation and empire-building raised the question of the justification of conquest and occupation by the European powers, both in relation to the people and rulers overseas as in relation to European competitors. The first European empire-builders, the Spanish and Portuguese, were quick to claim a monopoly on navigation, trade and colonisation outside Europe and the Mediterranean and to base their claims on papal investiture. In his bull, *Dum diversas* of 1452, Pope Nicholas V (1447–1455) granted the Portuguese king the right to explore and conquer all heathen lands. The bull *Romanus Pontifex* (1455) defined the geographical extent of this grant more precisely but also made it exclusive to the Portuguese. After Christopher Columbus (1541–1506) made his first voyage to America in 1492–1493, Pope Alexander VI (1492–1503) promulgated the bull *Inter Caetera* (1493) by which the Spanish kings were invested with exclusive rights to the lands and seas 100 miles west of the Azores and the Cape Verde Islands, thus dividing the world between the two Iberian powers. With the Treaty of Tordesillas (1494), both powers agreed to fix the line 270 miles more to the west. After the first circumnavigation of the world (1519–1522), the need arose to fix a second line through the Pacific, which was done at the Treaty of Saragossa (1529).[87]

The Portuguese discovery of a trade route to the Indies around Africa (1495) and the Spanish discovery of America (1492) were the outcome of their earlier expeditions in the Northern Atlantic and along the Atlantic coast of Africa, which in turn were a next step in the expansionist drive that came from the *Reconquista* of the Iberian peninsula from the Arabs and the Moors and the many overseas contacts, peaceful and not, with Northern Africa. The papal investiture of the Portuguese and Spanish with the right to explore, navigate, rule and exploit the lands and seas to be discovered outside Europe is to be explained from a missionary and Crusader's perspective. The Portuguese and Spanish kings were acknowledged to be the Church's defenders and champions in the spreading of the faith. The conquest and submission of lands and peoples and the exploitation of natural resources was held to be necessary because it was instrumental thereto; other European princes had to respect the Spanish and Portuguese kings' monopoly because they were acting for the common cause of Christianity.

The Spanish and Portuguese strategy came quickly under attack, including from inside Spain. Vitoria famously rejected the authority claimed by the pope to grant secular rights over non-Christians – or any other people for that matter. He appealed to natural law and the classical just war doctrine to justify the Spanish conquests in the Americas. Vitoria

---

Karl-Heinz Ziegler, 'Völkerrechtliche Aspekte der Eroberung Lateinamerikas', *Zeitschrift für Neuere Rechtsgeschichte*, 23 (2001) pp. 1–29.

[87] For these and other related texts: Frances G. Davenport (ed.), *European Treaties bearing on the History of the United States and its Dependencies to 1648* (4 vols., Washington, 1917).

recognised the empires and political entities of the natives for being 'perfect communities' or organised, political societies with their own laws. But natural law, which was common to all men, stipulated some rights, such as the right to communicate, to trade and to spread one's faith. The violation of these rights gave just cause for war, the outcome of which could then be the conquest and submission of the unjust enemy.

The doctrines of Vitoria and other representatives of the Spanish School of Salamanca did not greatly impact the practices of their government, but set natural law centre-stage in the doctrinal debates of the 16th to 18th centuries on the issues of the freedom of navigation and the acquisition of territories outside Europe. From the early 16th century onwards, the Iberian claims to exclusive rights over the oceans and lands outside Europe were challenged by other powers, in particular France, and later the Dutch Republic and England. French jurists argued that the papal grants did not impinge upon pre-existing rights of other Christian princes in areas where the Portuguese and Spanish had not effectively ventured first. The Protestant powers rejected all papal claims right away. At the Truce of Vaucelles (1556), the French king conceded that his subjects could not navigate or trade in the Spanish Indies (mainly Spanish America) without permission of the Spanish king. Although a concession by the French, it also left room for the interpretation defended by the French and others that the Iberian exclusive rights were limited to the areas they had effectively under control. In later peace treaties, Spain could not again attain such a concession from France. In peace treaties with France and other powers from the late 16th and the 17th centuries, mutual claims about the Indies were often left unsettled. This did not imply, as some scholars have claimed, that the peace treaty did not apply to the Indies and that a permanent state of war raged there, but only that it contained no settlement of opposing claims.[88]

Grotius and other Protestant writers also took inspiration from Vitoria and the Spanish scholastics. Grotius confirmed the existence of natural and thus universal rights of navigation and trade. He turned the argument, however, against the Iberian claims to monopolisation. Grotius, as others before and after him, used the concept of *occupatio* of a *res nullius* from the Roman *jus gentium* to justify the acquisition of land by European colonisers from the natives. Just as the first appropriation of a thing that belonged to nobody (*res nullius*) confers title of ownership, so the first occupation of unoccupied land (*terra nullius*) confers title. Crucial to Grotius's doctrine was the claim that uncultivated land was unoccupied. Nomadic people held no title to their lands. Under the same reasoning, in his *Mare Liberum*, Grotius defended the impossibility of vesting title over the sea, as it could not be occupied.

The doctrine of occupation would grow into one of the leading doctrines for the justification of European colonisation. It would also be used in practice, mainly in the era of Second Imperialism (19th–20th centuries) and in Australia and Africa. But treaties with the local rulers and people became the main instrument of European colonisation. Apart from outright conquest, cession of rights and lands by treaties formed the main legal underpinning of much of the European empire-building from the 15th to the 20th centuries.

---

[88] Grewe, *Epochs of International Law*, pp. 152–62; Carl Schmitt, *Der Nomos der Erde im Völkerrecht des Jus Publicum Europaeum* (4th edn., Berlin, 1997).

15 The 19th-century life of international law

Alexander Orakhelashvili

15.1 INTRODUCTION

The principal questions raised by the 19th-century framework of international law relate to the understanding by States of the general essence and relevance of treaty obligations; the relationship between treaty obligations and national interest, as particularly displayed in the example of continuous attempts and policies of great powers to acquire and maintain spheres of influence; and the relationship between treaties and general interest, that is the collective interest dimension in treaty-making.

The 19th-century life of international law had multiple faces. It witnessed strong trends towards multilateralism and collective decision-making. Certain political, informal, quasi-legal yet arguably semi-constitutional normative principles developed and gained generally accepted character: the principle of the balance of power became universalised and institutionalised; the mutual encounter of empires produced the doctrine of spheres of influence. At the same time, this multilateralism served as yet another tool for *Realpolitik* in terms of legitimising colonial acquisitions and spheres of influence.

The 19th century was also a period which impressed different writers differently, and produced several mutually diverging doctrinal trends: the 'naturalism' of Phillimore and the 'pragmatism' of Westlake and Hall, mirrored by the Euro-centrist doctrine bordering on racism led by Lorimer and, last but not least, Lassa Oppenheim's positivism which has proved its conceptual value for a long time since the end of the 19th century. While Westlake, Hall and Lorimer are interesting only for a historical focus on the international legal doctrine, Oppenheim's positivism lives on as a mainstream of the modern international legal system reinforced by consensual positivist foundations of international law. It is an implication precisely of the multiple faces of the 19th-century life of international law that the same period of international legal developments has impressed the leading international law thinkers in such a different way.

Chronologically, the 19th century starts from 1801 and ends with 1900. David Kennedy has spoken of a long century running from 1789 until 1914.[1] The international lawyer's perspective could presumably accommodate both these perspectives. But, as the analysis below will demonstrate, for an international lawyer the 19th century is a *pattern* before it is a *period*.

Although including several major wars and crises, systemically and normatively the 19th century has been a period of political and legal stability. This has partly been due to capitalising on the accumulated experience in the period from the 16th to the 18th centuries, and partly due to the legal system being so flexible and adapting to underlying

[1] D Kennedy, 'International Law and the Nineteenth Century: History of an Illusion', 65 *Nordic JIL* (1996), 385 at 390.

systemic political patterns. The international lawyer's 'real' 19th century certainly has those crises and wars at its centre, but it is also a period of stability and routine – that very stability and routine which was backed by unchallengeable legitimacy, reflected in dusted records of experience over more than a century but which has profoundly failed at the end of its days to respond to and contain the ultimate challenge of World War I.

In political and economic terms the 19th century witnessed all that mankind had experienced before: wars, economic expansion, partition of States, dynastic inter-marriage, and large-scale massacres of undesirable populations have been part of world politics before, during and after the 19th century. Kennedy characterises the 19th century as 'largely a European story: the Concert in Europe, the balance of power, nationalism in Europe and Latin America, the Age of Empire, and the opening of Japan. There were imperial ambitions in Africa and Asia, and Great Power competition, an arms race, and ultimately, war.'[2] One significant novelty was the immediate face-to-face confrontation of empires, their competition for territory and the consequent emergence of the doctrine of spheres of influence. This is the experience that Sir Halford Mackinder generalised in his *Geographical Pivot of History* in 1904 as the driving factor of international politics, and which also gave impetus to multiple international legal developments.[3] Apart from that, all statesmen needed was the awareness of long-standing political patterns; all they counted upon was a universally shared quest for stability. The 19th century thus was the period in which States increasingly realised the role of international law, notably of treaties, as an inherent part of their *Realpolitik* and an essential if not indispensable precondition for their ability to conduct their foreign policies.

15.2 LAW AND COLLECTIVE INTEREST

One principal trend of the 19th-century life of international law was its routine incorporation of the culture of multilateralism and a collective approach to threats and problems that States would collectively view as common threats and problems. As one early manifestation of this approach, the 1805 British Memorandum to the Russian Government has viewed the threat from Napoleonic France in broad communitarian terms. The rescuing from the dominion of France of the countries it had subjugated, reducing France within its former limits, and such arrangements as would provide more effectual barriers against future French encroachments were viewed in conjunction with an effort 'to form, at the restoration of peace, a general agreement and guarantee for the mutual protection and security of different powers, and for re-establishing a general system of public law of Europe'.[4]

---

[2] Kennedy, 390.

[3] H Mackinder, 'The Geographical Pivot of History', 23 *The Geographical Journal* (1904), 421; see also, for analysis of these processes and their impact on international law, A Orakhelashvili, 'International Law and Geopolitics: One Object, Conflicting Legitimacies?' 39 *Netherlands Yearbook of International Law* (2008), 155–204.

[4] Official Communication made to the Russian Ambassador at London, on 19 January 1805, explanatory of the views which His Majesty and the Emperor of Russia formed for the deliverance and security of Europe, in CK Webster, *British Diplomacy 1813-1815 – Select Documents Dealing with the Reconstruction of Europe* (London 1921), 389ff.

The 1813 Memorandum of the British Government has demonstrated the understanding that legal safeguards were needed for maintaining peace and security in Europe. An increased awareness is manifested that peace in Europe cannot be secured by the reliance solely on national interests and policies, but that agreed international policies and arrangements, endowed with legitimacy precisely due to being agreed and shared, were needed for that purpose. The Treaty of Alliance would not terminate with the war but would contain defensive engagements with mutual obligations to support the powers attacked by France. The *casus foederis* would be an attack by France on the European dominions of any of the contracting parties. The *Memorandum on Maritime Peace*, forming part of the 1813 Memorandum, specified in broader policy terms that Britain stood ready to sacrifice some territorial possessions

> for the welfare of the Continent, being desirous of providing for her own security by a common arrangement, rather than by an exclusive accumulation of strength and resources. Her object is to see a maritime as well as military Balance of Power established amongst the powers of Europe, and as the basis of this arrangement she desires to see the independence of Spain and Holland as maritime powers effectively provided for. Upon the supposition that these two objects shall be obtained in the proposed arrangements, that the limits of France shall be reduced within proper bounds, and that the peace of the Continent shall be secured by an amicable understanding between the Allies, Great Britain will then be prepared also to return within corresponding limits and to throw her acquisitions into the scale of general interests.[5]

Article II of the 1814 Paris Treaty specified that France would retain its limits as they existed on 1 January 1792.[6] The Separate and Secret Articles to the Paris Treaty specified that 'a system of real and permanent balance of power in Europe' had to be established and 'shall be regulated at the Congress upon the principles determined upon by the Allied Powers among themselves, and according to the general provisions contained in the following Articles'. Those Articles specified the arrangements regarding the territorial status of Austrian and Sardinian Territories, Switzerland and Holland.[7] The Definitive Treaty of Paris of 20 November 1815 specified that French frontiers would return to the position in which they were in 1790.[8]

Another aspect of using international law to serve the general interest was related to the prohibition of the slave trade. Additional Articles to the 1814 Treaty specified that

> His Most Christian Majesty, concurring without reserve in the sentiments of His Britannic Majesty, with respect to a description of traffic repugnant to the principles of natural justice and of the enlightened age in which we live, engages to unite all his efforts to those of His Britannic Majesty, at the approaching Congress, to induce all the Powers of Christendom to decree the abolition of the Slave Trade, so that the said Trade shall cease universally, as it shall cease definitely, under any circumstances, on the part of the French Government, in the course of 5

---

5 Memorandum of Cabinet, 26 December 1813, and attached Memorandum on Maritime Peace, in Webster, 121–127.

6 Definitive Treaty of Peace between Great Britain &c., and France, signed at Paris, 30 May 1814, ratification exchanged at London, 17 June 1814, in M Hurst (ed.), *Key Treaties for the Great Powers*, Volume 1 (Newton Abbott 1972), 1–2.

7 1 Hurst (ed.), 13–14.

8 Definitive Treaty of Peace between Great Britain, Austria, Prussia, and Russia, and France, signed at Paris, 20 November 1815, in 1 Hurst (ed.), 128–129.

> years; and that, during the said period, no slave merchant shall import or sell slaves, except in the colonies of the State of which he is a subject.[9]

In 1815, Castlereagh was instructed by the British Government to press the representatives of other Powers in relation to the abolition of the slave trade, even with offers of territorial cessions and pecuniary sacrifices.[10] The Declaration regarding the abolition of the slave trade was then adopted on 8 February 1815 which, despite claims that it served the British economic interest, constituted one of the first major steps towards the humanisation of international law.

15.3 LAW AND THE ADJUSTMENT OF STRATEGIC POSITIONS OF STATES

The political patterns underlying inter-State relations in the 19th century – wars, spheres of influence – increasingly required reliance on treaties to protect the political positions of States. Assuming treaty obligations meant adopting, confirming or altering political positions, often of strategic importance, and turning these political positions into law.

At the beginning of the 19th century, Britain, France and Russia had been competing for influence on Iranian affairs. One principal British interest was to secure Iranian support if its Indian possessions were attacked. Treaty-making was one of the principal means to validate and secure political gains in these directions. In 1800 Captain John Malcolm arrived in Iran to win – that is buy – the friendship of the Shah in the form of a defensive treaty. Iran would not allow French military influence within its territory and would attack Afghanistan if the latter were to attack India. If Iran were attacked by the French or the Afghans, Britain would provide military assistance. These agreements were never formally ratified.[11] In about a year, Iran felt threatened by the southward expansion of Russia and requested help from Britain. Britain refused, as its treaty with Iran referred to threats from France and Afghanistan, not Russia. Iran nevertheless felt offended, and in 1807 signed a treaty with Napoleon's France, whereby it undertook to sever ties with Britain and allow the French passage to India through Iranian territory.[12] However, a subsequent treaty between Britain and Iran included a clause that, in return for the Iranians not allowing the French to use their territory to attack Indians, Britain would now assist Iran against unspecified invaders even it were at peace with them – with troops, arms and advisers. This effectively meant assisting Iran in the face of a potential conflict with Russia.[13]

The historical process of the Central Asian 'Great Game' demonstrated the reliance of statesmen on international law when the British annexation of Sind in 1843 and Punjab in 1849 brought the British Empire to the belt of territory beyond which lay Afghanistan. The British Government had to choose between asserting its interests by force or

---

9 1 Hurst (ed.), 16–17.
10 Speech of Castlereagh in the House of Commons (extracts), March 20, 1815, in Webster, 395.
11 P Hopkirk, *The Great Game – On Secret Service in High Asia* (Oxford 1991), 31–32.
12 Hopkirk, 32–33.
13 Hopkirk, 35–36.

attempting to obtain a friendlier understanding, formally defined. The British approach thus was to station garrisons as close as feasible to the Afghan border and adhere to the policy of not interfering with domestic affairs of this country. A series of treaties with Afghanistan followed, such as the 1855 Treaty whereby the East India Company undertook never to interfere with internal affairs of Afghanistan, and the 1857 Treaty whereby a subsidy was promised to the Afghan ruler and it was provided that British officers would reside in Afghanistan to control its employment.[14]

Another interesting example is offered by the 1833 Treaty of Unkiar Skelessi and the 1841 London Convention on Turkish Straits. The former treaty originated out of the situation of a military conflict between the Ottoman Sultan and the Egyptian Ruler who was deemed to be his vassal. Russia sent troops to support the Sultan, after which the 1833 Treaty was concluded. Article I of this Treaty specified that Russia and the Ottoman Empire would afford each other, in the event that either of them were attacked, 'substantial aid, and the most efficacious assistance'. The Separate Article appended to the Treaty, however, specified that the Russian Emperor,

> wishing to spare the Sublime Ottoman Porte the expense and inconvenience which might be occasioned to it by affording substantial aid, will not ask for that aid if circumstances should place the Sublime Porte under the obligation of furnishing it, the Sublime Ottoman Porte, in place of the aid which it is bound to furnish in case of need, according to the principle of reciprocity of the Patent Treaty, shall confine its action in favour of the Imperial Court of Russia to closing the Strait of the Dardanelles, that is to say, to not allowing any Foreign vessels of War to enter therein under any pretext whatsoever.[15]

The 1841 London Convention on Turkish Straits further institutionalised the principle that as long as the Ottoman Empire was at peace, it would admit no foreign war vessels into the straits of the Bosphorus and the Dardanelles.[16]

The context of the Crimean War brought with it complex international legal developments. By the 1854 Treaty of Constantinople, Britain and France undertook to render military aid to Turkey to assist them

> in repelling the Aggression which has been made by His Majesty the Emperor of All the Russias upon the territories of the sublime Porte, and Aggression by which the Integrity of the Ottoman Empire and the Independence of the Throne of His Imperial Majesty the Sultan are menaced; and their said Majesties being fully persuaded that the existence of the Ottoman Empire in its present Limits is essential to the maintenance of the Balance of Power among the States of Europe.

According to Article I, Britain and France ordered powerful divisions of their navies to proceed to Constantinople, and undertook to employ for these purposes such number of their land forces as would be necessary to attain the object of protection of Turkey. What is more important is that Article II of the Treaty provided for a collective approach in terms of confronting Russia, namely by an obligation of Turkey not

---

[14] AW Ward and GP Gooch, *The Cambridge History of British Foreign Policy 1783–1919* (Cambridge 1923), Vol. 3, 72–73.

[15] 1 Hurst (ed.), 226–228; the separate article was deemed to be part of the main treaty.

[16] 1 Hurst (ed.), 259–260.

to enter into any negotiation, armistice or a treaty of peace with Russia without the knowledge and consent of Britain and France. Article III provided that as soon as the objective of this Treaty was realised through the conclusion of the peace treaty, Britain and France would withdraw their forces.[17] A further convention concluded at London specified that Britain and France, 'being animated with a desire to maintain the Balance of Power in Europe, and having no interested ends in view, renounce beforehand the Acquisition of any Advantage for themselves from the events which may occur' (Article IV).[18]

After the war the General Treaty of Peace was concluded in 1856, Article II of which provided for the reciprocal evacuation of territories parties had occupied in this war. Under Article II Russia undertook to restore to Turkey the town and citadel of Kars as well as other parts of the Ottoman Empire possessed by Russia. Sebastopol and other Crimean places were restored to Russia. Article VII provided for the admission of Turkey to the European Concert, and Article XI specified that the Black Sea had to be neutralised.[19]

The tripartite Treaty of 25 April 1856 gave Great Britain the right to ask France to cooperate in preventing any appropriation of Turkish territory. But France, conscious of liabilities nearer home, had throughout made it clear that in no circumstances would she fight with Britain against Russia.[20] The relativism of the binding force of the 1856 Treaties has been articulated by the British Government as well. Palmerston did not believe that these treaty guarantees would last infinitely, as 'our interests alone are eternal and perpetual'. If, furthermore, 'a treaty be found injurious to the interests of a country, and some means of violating it are obvious, I do not know of what country in Europe we could predicate a strict observance of the treaty'. In fact when the Black Sea clauses were abrogated, evidence was submitted from several quarters that Palmerston never expected these guarantees to last longer than a few years.[21]

In fact the Russian decision to depart from the Black Sea clauses of the Paris Treaty has been a test case in relation to the binding force of international obligations. The British position was voiced by Lord Granville in relation to the Russian decision that 'the assumption contained in the Russian circular of the right of one Power to deal singly with a European treaty was one which was fatal to the validity of all international engagements'.[22] Lord Granville continued that

---

[17] Treaty between Great Britain, France, and Turkey, relative to Military Aid to be given to Turkey, signed at Constantinople, 12 March 1854, ratifications exchanged in London, 25 April 1854, in 1 Hurst (ed.), 299–301.

[18] Convention between Great Britain and France, relative to Military Aid to be given to Turkey, signed at London, 10 April 1854, ratifications exchanged in London, 15 April 1854 in 1 Hurst (ed.), 303–305.

[19] General Treaty of Peace between Great Britain, Austria, France, Prussia, Russia, Sardinia, and Turkey, signed at Paris, 30 March 1856, ratifications exchanged at Paris, 27 April 1856, in 1 Hurst (ed.), 317ff.

[20] 3 Ward and Gooch, 135.

[21] H Temperley, 'The Treaty of Paris of 1856 and Its Execution', 4 *Journal of Modern History* (1932), 523 at 529.

[22] Quoted in Lorimer, I, 45.

> If, instead of denouncing the special convention annexed to and embodied in the treaty of 1856, the Russian Government had asked her Majesty's Government, as well as the other Governments parties to that treaty, to consider whether there were not reasons which would justify some modifications being made therein, her Majesty's Government would, in conjunction with the other co-signatories, have taken into consideration the merits of such a request; and, by such a course on the part of the Russian Government, whatever might have been the result, they would have avoided the risk of future complications, and of making a precedent dangerous to all international engagements.

The Russian response by Prince Gorchakov was as follows:

> We regret to see that Lord Granville lays stress principally on the form of our communications. It was not chosen by us. Certainly we should have asked for nothing better than to obtain our purpose by an understanding with the signatories of the treaty of 1856. But the principal Secretary of State of her Britannic Majesty well knows that all attempts made, at different times, to assemble the Powers in common deliberations, with a view to remove the causes of complication which disturb the general peace, have repeatedly failed. The prolongation of the actual crisis, and the absence of a regular Power in France, removes still further the possibility of such concert.[23]

Under the 1871 London Protocol 'The plenipotentiaries recognise that it is an essential principle of the law of nations that no Power can liberate itself from the engagements of a treaty, nor modify the stipulations thereof, unless with the consent of the contracting Powers by means of an amicable arrangement.'[24] This declaration attracted diverse doctrinal comments. According to Lorimer,

> the circumstances in which the plenipotentiaries had met, on that very occasion, were sufficient to show how little reality there was in the 'amicable arrangement' by which they arrived at the 'unanimity' to which they no doubt formally attained. Nothing but a threat of war by Russia, supported as she was known to be by Germany, could have induced either France or England to accept her propositions.[25]

JS Mill, on the other hand, saw a certain degree of legitimacy in the Russian position, and focused on the general relationship between *pacta sunt servanda* and the principle that no excessively burdensome obligations should be imposed on a State. Mill observed that

> If a lawless act has been committed in the present instance, it does not entitle those who imposed the conditions to consider the lawlessness only, and to dismiss the more important consideration whether, even if it was wrong to throw off the obligation, it would still not be more wrong to persist in enforcing it. If, though not fit to be perpetual, it has been imposed in perpetuity, the question when it becomes right to throw it off is but a question of time. No time being fixed, Russia fixed her own time, and naturally chose the most convenient.

Mill further emphasised that nations 'should abstain from imposing conditions which, on any just and reasonable view of human affairs, cannot be expected to be kept'.[26]

---

23 In Lorimer, I, 45–46.
24 2 Hurst (ed.), 459.
25 Lorimer, vol 1, 45.
26 Cited in JL Brierly, *The Law of Nations* (Oxford 1949), 243.

In the wake of war between Russia and Turkey in 1877 and against the background of the growing instability of the Ottoman Empire, European great powers had been resorting to treaty-making to acquire or recognise territorial influences. On 16 April 1877 Russia and Rumania concluded a treaty regulating the passage of Russian troops through the Rumanian territory.[27] The Treaty of 1 January 1877 between the Russian and Austrian Empires agreed the recognition of Serbian territories as neutral, and in the Supplementary Convention of 18 March the two great powers agreed on territorial changes upon which they were to insist if the dissolution of the Ottoman Empire were to follow. Austria would receive Bosnia while Russia would receive Bessarabia from Rumania and discretion to acquire further territories in Asia Minor. Austria thus made the territorial gains it desired without any need to use military force.[28]

The Convention between Britain and Turkey of 4 June 1878 provided that if Russia retained parts of Asiatic Turkey it had occupied in the war of 1877–1878, 'England engages to join His Imperial Majesty the Sultan in defending them by force of arms.'[29] The failure to implement this obligation and its actual reversal through the 1878 Berlin Treaty[30] was politically responsible for the decisive alteration of the political orientation of Turkey, its alienation from Anglo-French forces and gradual engagement with the German Reich, with all the implications that World War I witnessed.

The case of the Russo-Turkish war of 1877–1878 and the treaties concluded after this war offers an interesting context for the conclusion, implementation and modification of treaties in the 19th century. As soon as it became certain that the war between Russia and Turkey would end in Russia's favour, Great Britain and Austria-Hungary had given both the belligerent powers to understand that no modification of the Treaties of 1856 and 1871 would be regarded as valid without consultation with the Signatory States.[31] The 1878 Treaty of San Stefano was effectively forced upon Turkey by Russia, and the principal bone of contention for the Western powers was that this Treaty envisaged the creation of a Greater Bulgarian Principality that would effectively have been a Russian ally, thus enhancing its influence over, possibly even leading to its domination of, the Balkan region. A diplomatic push for a broader peace conference was thus made, and the British position was that it would not send plenipotentiaries to Berlin or elsewhere just to confirm a *fait accompli* that existed on the ground. Therefore Britain claimed that the Treaty of San Stefano should be submitted in its entirety to the jurisdiction of the powers, whose duty and right it would be to determine how far it was inconsistent with the Treaty of 1856 and the Protocol of 1871, and to approve or reject any departures from these agreements according to their full discretion. The Russian position was, however, that the San Stefano Treaty should merely be communicated to the Congress and that Russia would not be bound by decisions of other powers.[32]

---

27 2 Hurst (ed.), 517.

28 3 Ward and Gooch, 116–117.

29 Convention of Defensive Alliance between Great Britain and Turkey, with respect to the Asiatic Provinces of Turkey, signed at Constantinople, 4 June 1878, 2 Hurst (ed.), 546–547.

30 Under Article LVIII of the 1878 Berlin Treaty, these territories were ceded by Turkey to Russia, in 2 Hurst (ed.), 574–575.

31 3 Ward and Gooch, 128.

32 3 Ward and Gooch, 128, 132–133.

This deadlock of legal approaches was somewhat mitigated by a political compromise when Britain communicated to Russia that as soon as the idea of Greater Bulgaria was abandoned, Britain would accept Russian positions in relation to Serbia, Montenegro and Russian acquisition of Bessarabia and of territories in Asiatic parts of the Ottoman Empire.[33]

The Berlin Congress in 1878 included only great powers and none of the small States whose interests were to be adjudicated was allowed representation.[34] In essence, the Treaty of Berlin adopted at the Congress ratified the outcome of territorial arrangements that had previously been obtained through a series of bilateral negotiations between the great powers. Article LXIII of the Treaty rather symbolically assured the continuance in force of the 1856 Paris Treaty and 1871 London Protocol as soon as these were not modified by the Berlin Treaty.

Collective treaty efforts and their 'public law' character were essentially undermined by the bargaining the great powers conducted on the sides, or even as part of that very treaty-making process. This 'public law' treaty-making process was used to enhance the geopolitical influence of great powers. Britain, for instance, was interested in acquiring a foothold in Egypt to secure its open way to India, and asked for French non-interference in that respect; in return, Britain would not object if France were to acquire Tunis.[35] The same approach was witnessed with the British approach in relation to the Russian acquisition of Bessarabia as described above, and the Austrian acquisition of a sphere of influence in Bosnia, which was also based on the Austrian–Russian compromise in the wake of the war between Russia and Turkey. It was this kind of relativism that compromised the stability of 'public law' treaties and effectively undermined their influence on the ground.

This duplication of policies was further corroborated as the Treaty of Berlin was essentially premised on the great powers' understanding of their contemporary state of international law as allowing the acquisition of territory by conquest. The Treaty kept being violated through a series of territorial changes introduced unilaterally by Bulgaria, Russia, Austria, Britain and France over the subsequent three decades.[36] The potential for this was already enshrined in the underlying philosophy of the Berlin Treaty, for if international law, on which the Treaty was based, allowed for unilateral and forcible territorial changes, it thereby relativised the legal force and effect of the Berlin Treaty itself and made it in principle admissible to take such steps even in defiance of its terms.

The 1887 Russian–German Reinsurance Treaty was a notable international legal development in terms of the use of treaties to regulate the issues of war and neutrality in great power relations. Article 1 of the Treaty provided that Germany and Russia would remain neutral in each other's wars unless Germany attacked France or Russia attacked Austria. The Treaty was concluded for three years, after which it lapsed and was not renewed. As the German refusal to renew the Reinsurance Treaty illustrates, the termination of a treaty regime fixing political expectations of great powers could substantially alter the entire political climate in Europe.

---

33 3 Ward and Gooch, 133, 138.
34 3 Ward and Gooch, 137.
35 3 Ward and Gooch, 136.
36 See for detail 3 Ward and Gooch, 143–144.

These events radically altered the European balance of power as Bismarck had envisaged and engineered it. With the Reinsurance Treaty safeguards gone, the Russian Government felt impelled to conclude political and military agreements with France, which radically altered the position of Germany and naturally forced reconsideration of British policies on this matter. Instead of being based on firm treaty-based expectations, 'for fully ten years European international relations were reduced to something like a state of flux. The old connections began to dissolve and on all sides there was an uncertain groping for a new stability.'[37]

In its turn, the German decision not to renew the Reinsurance Treaty presumably reflected the relevance of international law and obligations for foreign policies of great powers. This decision came amid the changes of German foreign policies and the German Government presumably felt compelled to duly announce the intention of effecting these changes through its refusal to renew the Treaty, as opposed to formally sticking to it and then breaching it when its political interest so demanded. In short, this case presumably demonstrates that the entitlement to breach treaty obligations to satisfy political needs was not, at that stage, imagined as part of the mainstream foreign policy thinking of governments.

This is further reinforced by the fact that after refusing to renew the Reinsurance Treaty, 'The German Government insisted that it would stand by its former attitude, even with respect to Russian policy in Bulgaria, yet it firmly refused to give even the most informal written declaration to that effect.'[38] This illustrates a clear understanding between a purely political statement of intention that brings no legal commitments with it, and the legal implications of making a promise in writing. The fact that the Russian Government was seriously confused by such course of action by the Germans illustrates that both Governments had properly understood that legal obligations were binding and that unilateral, politically motivated evasion of these obligations would not be reasonably, or regularly, intended by or expected of a government that had assumed these obligations.

The course of events that followed aptly illustrates the above thesis. In 1890, Germany gave up Bismarck's policy of abstention in Bulgarian affairs, and on a more general plane began pursuing the policy of rapprochement with Britain, the very policy that the Reinsurance Treaty was meant to prevent. On a different but related note, the issue of Germany's intention in relation to the Turkish straits was raised when the German and Russian Emperors met in Narva accompanied by their ministers. Russian minister Giers enquired into the German position in relation to the interpretation of the Straits Convention. German minister Caprivi admitted that the Russian view of the Straits Convention was the correct interpretation, but flatly rejected the suggestion of Giers that he should confirm this to the Russians in writing.[39]

This approach was also confirmed in another instance relating to proposals of Franco-Russian alliance. The French proposed in 1892 that, should there be a mobilisation of armed forces of Germany or the Triple Alliance, Russia and France should do likewise

---

37 WL Langer, *The Diplomacy of Imperialism 1890–1902* (Vol. I, NY 1935), 4.
38 Langer, 6.
39 Langer, 8–9.

without the need for prior agreement or notification. Russia would then be obliged to place all her forces at the frontier with Germany, except the forces needed to check Austria; the forces to be used against Germany would then attack the Germans to prevent them from transporting their troops to the West and crushing France. The Russian position was premised on mobilisation being regarded as 'the most decisive act of war.' In political and strategic terms, Russians estimated the prospect of such a deal as giving the French more advantage than themselves, and concluded that they should preserve their absolute freedom of action in this regard.[40]

This confirms that the political mainstream in Europe was not premised on a routine evasion of international obligations and primacy of State will over treaties. The way of maintaining the required degree of political freedom was to avoid entering into international obligations, as opposed to breaching them when political interests so demanded.

15.4 LAW AND COLONIALISM

International law was also relevant in terms of great powers' colonial policies. As explained, the basis of norms that underpinned colonisation between 1870 and 1914 'followed from the consensus in the preferences of the major powers of the period, preferences that fundamentally preserved a global system that awarded great benefits to the major powers. To deviate from these norms was to invite sanctions, imposed either unilaterally, by particularly offended metropolitan countries, or collectively, by the major powers in concert.' The collective suppression of the Boxer Rebellion in China in 1898 is an example of this phenomenon.[41]

The Treaty of Nanjing of 29 August 1842 was signed between Britain and China under the threat of an assault on Nanjing by British troops. It provided for the opening of five ports to British trade and residence and the cession of Hong Kong to Britain.[42] This was followed by the 1843 General Regulations for Trade at Five Ports and the Supplementary Treaty of the same year, to specify trade tariffs. The British example encouraged other European powers to obtain similar advantages from China and this led to the conclusion of similar treaties with the USA and France in 1844, and Sweden and Norway in 1847. The second round of unequal treaties was similarly concluded under threat of war in 1858 with Britain, France, the USA and Russia, and legalised the opium trade, allowed foreign merchant ships to navigate the Yangtze River, opened additional ports and allowed foreign warships to cruise along the sea coasts and be stationed in inland waters, and further developed the system of extra-territoriality.[43]

The essence of the extra-territorial system in China has been described thus:

---

[40] Langer, 34–35.

[41] DJ Puchala and RF Hopkins, 'International Regimes: Lessons from Inductive Analysis', in SD Krasner (ed.), *International Regimes* (Ithaca 1983), 61 at 73.

[42] Articles I–III, Treaty of Peace, Friendship, Commerce and Indemnity between Great Britain and China, 29 August 1842, Ratifications exchanged at Hong Kong, 26 June 1843, in 1 Hurst (ed.), 268–269.

[43] Wang Tieya, 'International Law in China: Historical and Contemporary Perspectives', 221 *RdC* (1990), 195 at 237–240; for further examples of unequal treaties see *ibid.*, 251.

> The régime was broad in scope and, under the régime, numerous special rights and privileges were granted. It included 19 powers, 14 of which were European countries, namely, Austria, Belgium, Denmark, France, Germany, Great Britain, Italy, the Netherlands, Norway, Portugal, Russia, Spain, Sweden and Switzerland, one from Asia, Japan, one from North America, the United States, and the remaining three were South American countries, Brazil, Mexico and Peru. They were called 'treaty powers' and enjoyed the special rights and privileges provided by unequal treaties. The special rights and privileges acquired by the powers were multitudinous. They may be listed as follows
>
> 1. the system of extraterritoriality including the foreign courts and the 'mixed court' at Shanghai;
> 2. fixed and low tariff provided by treaties;
> 3. foreign controlled settlements and concessions at the trade ports;
> 4. leased territories considered as 'disguised territorial cession';
> 5. foreign controlled Legation Quarter and legation guards at Beijing;
> 6. foreign troops at Tienjin and at points along the railway from Beijing to the sea;
> 7. foreign gunboats and naval vessels at coastal ports and on the Yangzi River;
> 8. foreign police along certain railways;
> 9. foreign administered maritime customs service, postal service and Salt Gabelle (tax agency);
> 10. coastal navigation (cabotage) and navigation on inland waters;
> 11. immunity from direct taxation;
> 12. payment of indemnities;
> 13. loans and their guaranties;
> 14. railway, mining and telecommunication concessions;
> 15. the right of issuing currency;
> 16. the right of missionaries to settle, acquire real property and proselytize throughout the country;
> 17. the establishment of educational institutions free from Chinese supervision;
>
> and the most-favoured-nation clauses, which were unilateral, unconditional and broad in scope, extended all these special rights and privileges to all countries which were in a treaty relation with China.[44]

Colonial policies were implemented through multilateral treaties as well. By the Treaty of 26 February 1884, Britain and Portugal claimed to regulate the status and navigation of the Congo without consulting other powers. An architect of this Treaty, Lord Granville, recognised that 'there could be no advantage in concluding a treaty which would not be accepted by other Powers whose acceptance would be indispensable before it could come into operation'.[45] The Congo Act of 25 February 1885 specified that there would be a freedom of navigation for all signatory European powers in the regions forming the basin of the Congo and the Niger.[46]

As for other decisions of the Berlin Conference, the European great powers essentially produced a collective decision to carve up the African continent between them. The respective provisions of the Berlin Act of 1885 stipulated that:

---

44 Wang Tieya, 252–253.
45 Ward and Gooch, 208–209.
46 Ward and Gooch, 209.

> XXXIV. Any power which henceforth takes possession of a tract of land on the coasts of the African Continent outside of its present possessions, or which, being hitherto without such possessions, shall acquire them and assume a protectorate . . . shall accompany either act with a notification thereof, addressed to the other Signatory Powers of the present Act, in order to enable them to protest against the same if there exists any ground for their doing so.
> XXXV. The Signatory Powers of the present Act recognize the obligation to insure the establishment of authority in the regions occupied by them on the coasts of the African Continent sufficient to protect existing rights, and, as the case may be, freedom of trade and of transit under the conditions agreed upon.[47]

One abortive attempt at colonisation was witnessed in treaty relations between Italy and Ethiopia. The 1889 Wichale Treaty was signed by the Ethiopian Emperor Menelik and Count Pietro Antonelli of Italy, and later ratified by the Italian king. The Italian version of Article 17 of the Treaty, according to its English translation, specified that 'His Majesty the King of Kings of Ethiopia consents to avail himself of the government of His Majesty the King of Italy for all negotiations of affairs which he might have with other powers or governments.' The Italian Government consequently announced to other great powers in Europe that it had been put in charge of the foreign relations of Ethiopia.[48]

It is suggested that the effect of Article 17 was not clear in establishing protectorate over Ethiopia, as arguably

> the Italian Government hardly ever used the word 'protectorate' in official documents, and on several occasions even denied that there was any question of a protectorate. When in later years Italian jurists wrote or spoke of a 'protectorate', they based this interpretation on the juridical consequences of Crispi's notification of 11 October 1889, in the sense of Article 34 of the General Act of Berlin, and of the acknowledgement of the notification by all the signatories to the Act, and not on Article 17 in and of itself. This acknowledgement, according to the interpretation given to Article 34 by the interested governments . . ., and not Article 17, created the Italian protectorate over Ethiopia.[49]

However, the protectorate existed in practice as well as in theory, manifested through '(a) Italian consular protection of Ethiopians, especially in Egypt and the Holy Land, and the authorization to grant them Italian passports; (b) the attributing of Ethiopia to the Italian sphere of influence in the Anglo-Italian agreements of 1891 and 1894'.[50] But this would not be the end of the story.

First clear indications that there might be a misunderstanding or disagreement on this fundamental issue came when the Ethiopian Emperor Menelik wrote to several of the European courts in December 1889 without using the Italian government as an intermediary. The German Emperor and the Queen of the United Kingdom responded that further diplomatic relations with Ethiopia would have to be conducted through Italy, on the basis of the Wichale Treaty. The Emperor stated that he would accept no

---

[47] For the French text see C Parry, *Consolidated Treaty Series with Index* 1648–1919, Oxford 1969, 485.

[48] S Rubenson, 'The Protectorate Paragraph of the Wichale Treaty', 5 *Journal of African History* (1964), 243 at 243–244.

[49] C Giglio, 'Article 17 of the Treaty of Uccialli', 6 *Journal of African History* (1965), 221 at 224.

[50] Giglio, 229–230.

such obligation, and accused Antonelli of having deceived him.[51] As has been pointed out, 'Even if one accepts that the Italian text constitutes sufficient basis for a claim (and this was seriously questioned even by the Italian Resident General himself), the Amharic certainly does not.'[52] Furthermore,

> Menelik signed the Italian text, trusting Antonelli, and convinced that it agreed with the Amharic. Antonelli himself never alleged that Menelik knew the meaning of the Italian text of Article 17, drawn up in a language which neither Menelik nor his interpreter understood, and had signed, therefore, in bad faith. Antonelli had in fact sufficient knowledge of Amharic to be aware of the difference between the two texts; moreover, he never denied knowing, except in one undocumented instance.'[53]

Therefore, 'the Italian government could base no legal claim to a protectorate over Ethiopia on Article XVII as such'.[54] This controversy would later be resolved in Ethiopia's favour – not through the legal process but on the battlefield, in the 1896 battle of Adowa.[55]

15.5 CONCLUSION

Multiple experiences have illustrated that the 19th-century life of international law relied on the relevance of common values and interests, the need for collective action, and collective decisions to regulate multiple aspects of international politics. But the same culture of multilateralism would also feed the pattern of colonialism and elevate it to the rank of the imagined system of the 'public law of Europe'. Collective decisions and actions were adopted not only to safeguard the general peace or pursue higher humanitarian goals, but also to enshrine collective positions and take collective action in terms of safeguarding the shared interest of great powers, often at the cost of the interests and welfare of other States.

Arguably, according to Kennedy, the 19th century inaugurated a disciplinary anti-intellectualism, a repeated practice of demonstrating the unsatisfactory nature of both positivist and naturalist answers to the questions of law's force in the world of sovereigns.[56] But precisely that pragmatism has also constituted – and demonstrated – fundamental problems of the 19th-century approach. The principal lesson from the 19th-century history of international law is that flexibility and adaptability are not what should be expected of this legal system in the first place. In fact, and in the longer run, it can generate more problems than it resolves.

International law in the 19th century, which to a great extent was an epoch of relativism, constituted a tool for *Realpolitik* as well as a check on it. There was no 'European international law' in the 19th century, and no tangible system of 'public law of Europe', yet

---

51 Rubenson, 246, 248–250.
52 Rubenson, 258.
53 Giglio, 228.
54 Rubenson, 258.
55 Rubenson, 282.
56 Kennedy, 400.

there was a reasonable degree of uniformity in the nature of major players in international politics, in terms of their political, strategic and economic interests and their consequent adoption of policies and agenda. Colonialism and related forms of expansion were one aspect in which the interests and aspirations of great powers coincided;[57] they could thus understand each other's positions, which in turn increased the room for mutual balancing and accommodation, among other things through international law. International law firmly became one of the principal tools whereby States could secure their political interest and define the acceptable limits on that political interest in a mutually shared and acknowledged manner. As long as the geopolitical environment of balance of power and Great Game lasted, so would the international law patterns of the 19th century survive and remain relevant. The insufficiency of those political patterns to prevent World War I naturally demonstrated the limitations of 19th-century international law patterns to secure peace and stability. The principal emphasis of 20th-century developments was thus on the need to provide for *institutional* safeguards for the international legal system to operate and for an increased focus on the rights and interests of non-State entities.

In the end all diverging doctrinal trends were accurate, albeit partial in reflecting the 19th-century life of international law. The natural law school noticed the articulation of the natural law argument; pragmatic approaches relied on the policies of great powers to adhere to their treaty obligations only to the extent their interests required; the 'European' international law school noticed the obvious policies of colonialism and imagined them as the factor underlying the essence of the whole legal system; finally, consensual positivism focused on the crucial relevance of consensual law-making to enable States to properly look after their national interest. This last factor – the binding force of treaties – was just about the only continuous contribution that the 19th-century life of international law made to the subsequent development of this legal system.

[57] As Puchala and Hopkins state, the Russian revolution in 1917 created a formally anti-imperialistic State, thus breaking a European consensus that supported the principles of colonialism, DJ Puchala and RF Hopkins, 'International Regimes: Lessons from Inductive Analysis', in SD Krasner (ed.), *International Regimes* (Ithaca 1983), 61 at 75.

16 International law between universality and regional fragmentation. The historical case of Russia

*Lauri Mälksoo**

16.1 INTRODUCTION

Russia's role in the history of international law has not yet become subject to extensive critical scrutinies. What do I mean by saying 'critical' scrutinies? My impression is that the historical work done on Russia's or Russian scholars' role in international law tends to be quite Eurocentric. The Eurocentrism comes in two versions: the Western European one and, perhaps surprisingly, the Russian one. The Western European version tends to marginalize or even stay relatively silent on any major independent Russian role in the history of international law. For example, when Carl Schmitt (1888–1985) wrote his *Der Nomos der Erde*[1], the historical case of Russia would have enabled him to make an even more extensive argument in terms of the history and geography of colonization. Schmitt's point was that *ius publicum europaeum* or the 'European law of nations' (as the 'classical international law' was often called in Europe) flourished especially because it was created to organize and control the European colonization of the world. Yet if Schmitt had included the history of the Russian colonization of Siberia, the Caucasus and Central Asia, he could have demonstrated that the normative language of Christian *mission civilisatrice* was at work not only in overseas colonization but also in conquering vast adjacent land masses in Asia.[2] If Schmitt had taken this phenomenon into account, he could have changed emphases in the overall evaluation of the historical process.

How does the Eurocentric approach result in the marginalization of Russia in the history of international law? Paradoxically, Russia's marginalization is reached by emphasizing Russia's legal-political connections with Europe in the history of international law. The result is inevitably that Russia is treated as a liminally (and sometimes failed) European country that has made some contributions to (Western-dominated) international law. In this approach, Russia has been part of Europe, at least from the early 18th century onwards, but the kind of Europe that mattered relatively little to the emergence and historial development of international law, at least when compared

* Research for this chapter was undertaken with the support of a Starting Grant of the European Research Council and grant No 8087 of the Estonian Science Foundation.

1 See Carl Schmitt, *Der Nomos der Erde im Völkerrecht des Jus Publicum Europaeum*, 4th edition, Berlin: Duncker & Humblot, 1997.

2 Schmitt further played on the geopolitical distinction between 'land' and 'sea' in his *Land und Meer: eine weltgeschichtliche Betrachtung*, Frankfurt: Klett-Cotta, 2008. See further on this colonization, Dominic Lieven, *Empire: The Russian Empire and its Rivals*, New Haven: Yale University Press, 2002.

to Western Europe. While Asia, Africa and even America clearly used to be objects of European colonization and/or settlement, Russia became an active subject quite early on yet remained a peripheral subject within Europe. The final account of this approach has been a not always so convincing story of how the Imperial Russia of St Petersburg emerged out of some kind of historical darkness in order to make contributions to European international law-making in 19th century Vienna, The Hague and Geneva. However, it was only with the advent of the United Nations at the end of World War II that a leading role of the Soviet Russian superpower seems to have found wide recognition in the West. Yet again in 1991 this superpower vanished in order to make space for a fledgling Russian democracy.

We learn about the world through the languages that we have access to. Vis-à-vis the West, language puts Russia into a weaker position. The reality is that the Russian language, albeit one of the six official languages of the United Nations, has never been widely read nor understood among the Western practitioners and researchers of international law. Yet most of the thinking on international law in Russia has naturally been published in the Russian language. Unfortunately, there is in the West a clear tendency to notice and take into account just these Russian international law voices who made themselves heard or were translated also into Western European languages, for example Fyodor Martens (1845–1909) in the Tsarist period and Grigory Tunkin (1906–1993) in the Soviet period. But even here the Western reception of the contribution of such scholars has been ambivalent. These authors may have been prominent but was it really *their* voice or that of the Russian government that one could hear? Arthur Nussbaum's (1877–1964) criticism of the qualifications and character of Fyodor Martens are quite characteristic in this sense. In a Cold War-era article, Nussbaum criticized Martens's proximity to the Tsarist power and the patriotic views expressed in his legal-political writings.[3] Yet was Nussbaum prepared to use the same high ethical standard towards the American or German international lawyers? Or was it particularly reproachable or only natural for an international lawyer to be close to power in *Russia*?

Yet paradoxically, the perhaps unavoidable Eurocentrism of Western Europeans has been matched by Russian scholars themselves. Have Westerners ignored or downplayed the role and contributions of Russia and the Russians in international law? Some Russian scholars have responded with the call: let us prove how wrong they were! An example would be Vladimir Hrabar's (Grabar's) (1865–1956) historical work which tends to measure the Russian achievements since Peter the Great in terms of how they matched with European standards of scholarship in international law.[4] However, notwithstanding Grabar's impressive erudition and certainly best intentions, his approach is also implicitly marked by Eurocentrism.

What is common to both the European and Russian branches of Eurocentrism is the

---

[3] See Arthur Nussbaum, *Frédéric de Martens. Representative Tsarist Writer on International Law*, XXII Acta Scandinavia juris gentium (Nordisk Tidsskrift for International Ret) 1952, pp. 51–66 at pp. 60 *et seq.*

[4] Vladimir Grabar, *The History of International Law in Russia, 1647–1917: A Bio-Bibliographical study*, translated and edited by William E. Butler, Oxford University Press, 1990. A bibliographically updated Russian version was further published by Butler in 2005: V.E. Grabar, *Materialy k istorii literatury mezhdunarodnogo prava v Rossii (1647–1917)*, Moscow: Zertsalo, 2005.

emphasis on the universality of international law. The approach that highlights the universality of international law at any cost, even against contradicting historical evidence, in fact builds on Eurocentric premises. The birth and development of international law are usually associated with the Peace of Westphalia in 1648, and intellectually with the Spanish school, Grotius, Pufendorf and other natural law scholars of Western Europe. Thus the thankless task of Hrabar was to demonstrate how successful and active Russia was in the reception of the Grotian international law. But no matter how intensely one is trying to prove that Russian contributions to the development of the Grotian international law were 'as important as those in Western Europe', one still remains only catching up with the European standard. How could it be otherwise? Hrabar's own Soviet biographers and disciples recounted that Hrabar himself, an international law researcher in late Tsarist Russia, discovered a number of mistakes in the celebrated textbook of Franz von Liszt (1851–1919) when he translated it into the Russian language. Then he communicated these mistakes to von Liszt who thankfully corrected them in the subsequent German edition as well. However, while this is a lovely story, it is unlikely that it makes any wider point, for example about the particularly high level of scholarship in pre-revolutionary Russia. But what if one were to look at Russia's history with international law without over-emphasizing how well Russia caught up with her historical teachers?

In this chapter, I will attempt to construct a non-Eurocentric reading of Russia's role in the history of international law. As will soon be obvious, this will not automatically imply that I will adopt a reading that is particularly sympathetic to Russia's history with international law. More specifically, I will approach the question of Russia's role in and contribution to international law through the general problem of universality of international law. It will be a useful exercise to see how the historical case of Russia fits into current debates about universality, Eurocentrism and fragmentation of international law.

16.2 THE PROBLEM OF UNIVERSALITY IN INTERNATIONAL LAW

The problem of universality continues to be one of the most pressing issues in contemporary international law. Normatively, international law is nowadays almost always constructed as universally applicable – in essence at least, 'one and the same thing for all States'. Yet in terms of sociological reality, there exist significant differences in the understanding and application of international law or, as the Harvard scholar David Kennedy has put it, 'international law is different in different places'.[5] This includes more than classical textbook examples that show certain countries have regulated the interrelationship between domestic and international law (e.g., the monist and dualist solutions). As a further example, take the key concept of classical international law – State sovereignty. In a number of conflict-ridden regions in the world (e.g., Afghanistan, Somalia), sovereignty is artificially and fictionally constructed and maintained. Tribal and ethnic cross-border allegiances de facto trump the power of nominal sovereigns. Or take another example

[5] David Kennedy, *The Disciplines of International Law and Policy*, 12 Leiden Journal of International Law 1999, p. 9 at 12.

– international human rights law. Empirically, it is quite clear that whatever human rights treaties States have signed and ratified, a number of them tend to interpret their commitments (to put it euphemistically) in quite idiosyncratic ways.

One cannot over-emphasize the importance of the question of universal applicability of international law. This question is about nothing less than whether the world, notwithstanding all objectively existing differences between nations, is still somehow 'one' at the normative level or, contrarily, is broken into normatively independent regions and spheres of influence. The question is whether the 'international community' truly exists,[6] and what is its definition and reach. International lawyers know in the back of their minds that the realist school of international relations theory maintains that any claims about the existence of 'international community' are utopian. Realists maintain that the true condition of international relations continues to be anarchy.[7]

The doctrine of contemporary international law accommodates the language of differences within the general unified structure of international legal relationships. This accommodation is conveniently achieved via the concept of regional international law. Privileged regional legal arrangements (e.g., EU, NATO, NAFTA, etc) are recognized in this scheme. They are seen as separate rooms in a larger house, for according to the prevailing doctrine, there cannot be regional international law beyond or outside the edifice of universal international law. For example, a regional treaty creating privileged relationships would still be a treaty within its universally recognized meaning, i.e. the 1969 Vienna Convention on the Law of Treaties.

There are good reasons why the doctrine of international law should uphold the claim of universality of international law. To put it dramatically, without the (normative) universality of international law, the world would be even more divided than it is. There would be European law, American law, maybe WTO law, NAFTA law, law of oceans, etc. Perhaps there would be inter-civilizational or inter-regional law instead of (universal) international law.

Yet at the same time, there remain two different levels of analysis: the world as it is and the world as we want it to be. The claim of universality of international law is nowadays at least as much normative as it is empirical. Empirically, scholars taking a more sociological/facts-based approach to the reality of international law have observed as much disunity and fragmentation as the mainstream of international legal scholarship continues to insist on universality and unity.[8]

In terms of research and scholarship, the question of functional fragmentation of international law has recently received more attention than the question of regional fragmentation. 'Functional fragmentation' labels the problem that sub-fields of international

---

[6] See further Andreas L. Paulus, *Die internationale Gemeinschaft im Völkerrecht*, Munich: Beck, 2001.

[7] See E.H. Carr, *The Twenty Years' Crisis 1919–1939: An Introduction to the Study of International Relations*, London: Palgrave, 2001; Hans J. Morgenthau, *Politics among Nations. The Struggle for Power and Peace*, New York: McGraw-Hill, 1993; Kenneth Waltz, *Theory of International Politics*, New York: McGraw-Hill, 1979; John J. Mearsheimer, *The Tragedy of Great Power Politics*, New York: Norton, 2001.

[8] See Adda B. Bozeman, *Future of Law in a Multicultural World*, Princeton University Press, 1971.

law such as international trade law (WTO law), human rights law, international environmental law, international criminal law, etc have occasionally shown tendencies to desire to free themselves from the 'constraints' of general international law. For example, the European Court of Human Rights (ECHR) in Strasbourg has in some cases had to deal with human rights issues stemming from the Soviet past of Latvia. In some cases where it has decided against Latvia and in favour of the petitioning individual(s), the ECHR has chosen to avoid the discussion on Latvia's legal status during the Soviet period.[9] (Latvia's argument in these cases was that the country was illegally occupied and annexed by the USSR from 1940–1991 and that this fact had already been recognized in 1991, at least by the Western states.) Essentially, the Strasbourg court switched off the question of the international legal status of Latvia for the purposes of solving such cases, considering the question of the country's status 'irrelevant'. But there are 'human rights' issues that cannot legally be solved in isolation from 'general international law' issues. If it no longer mattered whether annexation was illegal or not, it would put any practical relevance of (non-)recognition as an institute of general international law in doubt.

In a recent study on fragmentation and international law, the International Law Commission (ILC), led by the special rapporteur Martti Koskenniemi, took a relaxed approach towards the functional fragmentation of international law.[10] The ILC study makes the point that what is sometimes feared as functional fragmentation (most prominently, by the Presidents of the International Court of Justice) at the same time brings about more diversity and representation of different interests in international law. There is thus even a certain democratic quality to fragmentation. The ILC study comes to the optimistic conclusion that general international law has ways and mechanisms to cope with the phenomenon of fragmentation.[11]

The ILC study dedicates less space to the question of regional fragmentation. This probably reflects the fact that if there are some areas of consensus in contemporary international law, one is that regional fragmentation as such does not or should not endanger the universality of international law. Intellectual speculation about the validity of the premise of the universality of international law can be seen as dangerous as such. They may also take us back to divisive or violent times that most of the States or international law specialists do not want international law to go back to. It has become a part of the prevailing professional ethos of international lawyers to emphasize unity rather than disunity – for there are already too many politicians, diplomats and scholars in the world who thrive on, and make careers out of, the world's differences and divisions.

Yet as already noted above, there remains the is/ought problem: when contemporary international law claims universality, is it a normative (desired) or sociological (descriptive) position or both? Is modern international law universal or ought it to be? This chapter will take a historical look at the problem of universality/regional fragmentation, demonstrating that from the historical perspective, international law's effective claim to universality is a relatively recent one. But even so, one needs to remain realistic about

---

[9] See e.g. the ECHR's case of *Kononov v. Latvia* (Application No 36376/04), Judgment, 24.07.2008.

[10] See ILC (finalized by Martti Koskenniemi), *Fragmentation of International Law: Difficulties arising from the Diversification and Expansion of International Law*, A/CN.4/L.628, 13.04.2006.

[11] *Ibid.*, conclusions.

the depth of universality. Of course, the future and present are not necessarily historically determined. (From the fact that international law did not used to be seen as truly universal does not follow that it may not be universal today or become so in the future.) Nevertheless, the history of the (thinness of) universality will help us at least to better understand the challenges contemporary international law faces 'on the ground'.

Another point of clarification that must be made relates to the very notion of universality. When exactly is it that we can historically speak of 'universality' of international law and conversely, when is it justified to prioritize regionalism and fragmentation? Sometimes international legal theory has been outspokenly clear about this. For example, 19th-century international law was universal only within the West (including Russia). However, even if the theory does not 'officially' attack the universality of international law, the State practice may sometimes give out tendencies of regional fragmentation at the costs of universality. (Formally attacking the idea of universality may be politically too costly for States.) In sum, we can find evidence about universality/fragmentation both in the State practice and in the predominant theories of international law.

A major epistemological question remains: how do State practice and international legal theory relate to each other? For example, Vladimir Hrabar and William E. Butler have dedicated a major study to the literature of international law in Tsarist Russia.[12] But what exactly was the role of such international legal works in their time? To what extent was such a role an independent one? Maybe the role of some international legal works was to deceive the reader in the State's interest?[13] It is sometimes (self-)critically said that international lawyers tend to mistake the history of international legal writings for the history of international law as such. It seems that the history of international legal theory cannot be understood in isolation from the State's political history, especially in historical contexts where the State has tended to be all-powerful such as in Russia. Hrabar's tragedy was that, writing in the Stalinist period, he had to analyse the international legal writings in Russia like an isolated island – which it of course never was nor could be. To analyse a 19th-century Russian author on international law without discussing the role of the Russian *raison d'état* and the question what, politically, was the role of international legal arguments in the country in the first place, simply does not make sense. The conclusion is that in the historical evaluation, one needs to keep in mind the interaction between State practice/interests and legal theories. Seldom have they existed in complete isolation from each other.

16.3 DID RUSSIA KNOW 'INTERNATIONAL LAW' BEFORE PETER THE GREAT?

One of the main narratives within the history of international law is the story about how the law of nations 'became universal'. The story, at least as classically told, goes something

---

[12] See supra at footnote 4.

[13] See for a further discussion Lauri Mälksoo, *The Science of International Law and the Concept of Politics. The Arguments and Lives of the International Law Professors at the University of Dorpat/Iur'ev/Tartu 1855–1985*, 76 British Yearbook of International Law, Oxford University Press, 2005, pp. 383–502 at pp. 392 *et seq.*

like this: there were traces of international law in major ancient civilizations and cultures yet the crucial time for the birth of international law as we know it today was the late mediaeval period[14] and early Modern Age.[15] Especially the Peace of Westphalia of 1648 created 'a new world order'.[16] The principle of sovereign equality of States was accepted, instead of previous universalist claims of the (Roman) Emperor. Initially, the circle of nations that developed the Westpahlian order was identical with the group of Western and Central European (Catholic and Protestant) nations. In essence, the sovereignty-centred order of the Peace of Westphalia replaced the mediaeval *respublica Christiana*.

The story then goes on to describe how the 'international community' extended from Western and Central Europe to the rest of the world. The European states were initially reluctant to extend the law of nations to other, non-European nations. On the contrary, the law of nations in a sense was used as an ideological weapon against the non-European nations. The theory that was put forward was that only civilized/European/Christian nations could understand and comply with international law. Uncivilized/non-European/non-Christian nations were not considered capable of providing reciprocal legal relationships to civilized/European nations.

As far as non-European/non-Christian powers are concerned, the standard historical account tells us that Turkey was accepted as member of the 'civilized family of nations' only after the Crimean War ended in 1853 with the conclusion of the Paris Peace Treaty. Moreover, the same account continues to tell the story of Japan – how Japan was finally accepted into the same 'family of civilized nations' in 1905 when the Treaty of Portsmouth ended the Japanese-Russian war.

There is a certain irony in the fact that both of these non-European nations – Turkey and Japan – gained recognition as full members of the 'family of nations' only after their respective victorious wars against Tsarist Russia. (One must add, as a footnote, that in the Crimean War, Britain and France contributed, for balance of power reasons, decisively towards the victory and new status of Turkey.) Not all participants in these wars could have been aware of the irony that not so long ago, in the early 18th century, it had been Russia herself who had waged the same battle for the recognition of her status as a civilized country on the eastern coasts of the Baltic Sea.

When in 1700 Russia initiated the Great Nordic War against Sweden, then the predominant power on the Baltic Sea, Tsar Peter commissioned the Vice Chancellor of his Empire, Petr Shafirov, to write a moral-legal defence of the war from the Russian perspective. Shafirov's pamphlet became the first known Russian argument in the framework of the European law of nations.[17] It is interesting to see how Shafirov's/Peter's

---

14 See V. Hrabar, *Rimskoe pravo v istorii mezhdunarodno-pravovykh uchenii: elementy mezhdunarodnogo prava v trudakh legistov XII-XIV vv*, Iur'ev (Tartu): Mattiesen, 1901.

15 See Wilhelm G. Grewe, *The Epochs of International Law*, translated and edited by Michael Byers, Berlin, New York: de Gruyter, 2000.

16 Karl-Heinz Ziegler, *Völkerrechtsgeschichte – Ein Studienbuch*, Munich: C.H. Beck, 1994.

17 See P.P. Shafirov, *A Discourse concerning the Just Causes of the War between Sweden and Russia: 1700–1721*, with an introduction by William E. Butler, Dobbs Ferry, NY: Oceana Publications, 1973; P.P. Shafirov, *Rassuzhdenie, kakie zakonnye prichiny Petr I, tsar i povelitel vserossiiskii, ka nachatiu voiny protiv Karla XII, korlja shvedskogo, v 1700 godu imel*, Moscow: Zertsalo, 2008.

argument that Russia was both legally and morally right to wage war against Sweden was intertwined with the argument that Russia was a civilized/Christian/European nation. Moreover, in the same breath that Shafirov argued Russia to be a civilized/Christian/European country, he insisted on the continued exclusiveness of the club of 'civilized nations'. Namely, Shafirov passionately argued that since Turkey was a Muslim nation, the (European) law of nations could not apply to it and, correspondingly, Turkey should not raise any legal-moral objections against the activities of Russia. In this sense, the 'international community' that Russia joined in the early 18th century, was constructed as culturally-regionally limited and exclusive. It was humiliating to enter such a system of argumentation established elsewhere (i.e., in Western Europe) but successful entry into the system at least offered the prospect of humiliating others who remained in the realm of the non-civilized. One could always find consolation in the fact that even if one's 'civilizedness' was put in doubt, one could point at others who were even less 'civilized'.

The language of international law was used by Muscovy in a pragmatic and functional way in the context of the Great Nordic War (1700–1721). If Western Europeans needed proof of civilizedness, Shafirov's goal was to provide it. In any case, Shafirov had good reasons to be upset about the fact that Europeans thought of Russia as an uncivilized/non-European country. In any case, there did not appear to be any evident exclusive link between international law and European civilization to the effect that international treaties would have been unknown to non-European countries. Most of the elements of 'European' international law such as treaties between States were also known to Muscovy. Muscovy had concluded peace treaties even before Peter, e.g. with Poland in 1667. The fact that China was not a Christian nation, did not prevent the conclusion of the Russo-Chinese Nerchinsk peace treaty in 1689.[18]

Wherein consisted the ultimate success of the argument of Petr Shavirov? It was in the Russian *fait accompli* and the logic that a country could not be un-civilized if it managed to win a war against Sweden which had been a prominent and advanced member of the 'community of civilized nations' in Northern Europe. In the last resort, the proof of Russia's civilizedness consisted in the success of her arms. Moreover, Shafirov emphasized that Russia was a Christian country and in that way appealed to the unity of Christian nations. This was certainly a new line of argumentation from the Russian point of view because throughout the late Middle Ages and in the time of early modernity, the Orthodox and Latin branches of Christianity tended to relate to each other in rather hostile ways. Animosity rather than unity of the two separate Christian traditions had been the political reality.

Eminent historians of international law such as Onuma Yasuaki from Tokyo have recently revisited the question 'when did international law become universal?', offering alternative readings to the Eurocentric narrative of the 'extension of the international community' over the late 19th and 20th centuries.[19] A main insight of Professor Onuma

---

[18] See Henning Scheu, *Das Völkerrecht in den Beziehungen Chinas zu den europäischen Seemächten und zu Russland. Ein Beitrag zur Geschichte des Völkerrechts*, Dissertation, Frankfurt, 1971.

[19] See Yasuaki Onuma, *When was the Law of International Society Born?*, 2 Journal of the History of International Law 2000 No 1, pp. 1–66. See also Gerrit W. Gong, *The Standard of 'Civilization' in International Society*, Oxford University Press, 1984.

is that other, non-European civilizations did not necessarily linger in normative darkness before the European concept of international law was 'extended' to the rest of the world, usually with conquest and/or arm-wrestling. Onuma focuses in his examples on East Asia (which was governed by the Sinocentric world order) and the Islamic world. It is Onuma's argument that the international law that finally became successful as universal was solely a specific (i.e., European) type of international law that was essentially made universal by force and the success of European colonization.

It seems promising to follow this line of argumentation and make a link to Russia's history as well. In fact, this line of thinking has already been attempted in the past. Namely, Baron Michael von Taube (1869–1961) and Sir Paul Vinogradoff (1854–1925), both Westernized representatives of Russian legal scholarship, argued in the early 20th century that Byzantine and Russia used to have their own 'historical types of international law'.[20] But what in their minds constituted such a separate 'type'? The keyword here is the intensity of normatively significant historical contacts – who communicated with whom and on what terms. For example, the Grand Princes of Kievan Rus concluded at least four peace treaties with Byzantium – in 907, 911, 944 and 971. These offer insight into penal practices and judicial procedure, the status of foreigners, the law of shipwreck, the ratification of treaties and the legal status of envoys.[21] Of course certain States of ancient Rus also had contacts, including legal contacts, with Western Europe. For example, Novgorod concluded commercial treaties with German towns in 1195, 1257 and 1270. Thus, the geographic and temporary limits of the separate 'historical type of international law' as argued by Taube are somewhat difficult to establish. Moreover, even if ancient Rus had its own historical type of international law, this did not imply that legal communication was impossible with representatives of other traditions, as Novgorod's contracts with Hanseatic towns prove.

We cannot understand the birth of 'classical international law' without understanding the importance of religion and religious debates in late mediaeval Europe. The mediaeval European man was deeply religious and the debates about religion that had come to divide the Christians were simultaneously central normative debates.[22] The princes of Kievan Rus accepted the baptism of their lands from Byzantium. Thus, the Russian lands continued to formally adhere to the Orthodox version of Christianity after the schism between Rome and Constantinople was finalized in 1054. Another important event was the Florentine consilium in 1439 where the Roman and Byzantine clerics reached an agreement about the reunification of the Eastern and Western Christian churches. However, the representatives of the Moscow patriarchate – which at that time had already become de facto independent from the patriarchate in Constantinople – refused to accept the deal reached in Italy. Rather, the Muscovite clerics went on to construct Muscovy as the last stronghold of unspoiled Christianity. This positition was

---

[20] See Michel de Taube, *Etudes sur le développement historique du droit international dans l'Europe orientale*, 11 Recueil des Cours (1926-I), p. 341; Paul Vinogradoff, 'Historical Types of International Law', in: *The Collected Papers of Paul Vinogradoff* (1928), ii, at 248–318.

[21] See further William E. Butler, *Russia and the Law of Nations in Historical Perspective*, London: Wildy, Simmonds and Hill, 2009, pp. 3–4.

[22] See e.g. Donald W. Treadgold, *The West in Russia and China. Religous and Secular Thought in Modern Times*, Volume I, Russia 1472–1917, Cambridge University Press, 1973.

further strengthened when Constantinople indeed fell under the rule of victorious Turks in 1453.

So what made up the Russian historical type of international law? First of all, Baron Taube argues that the domestic normative situation determined the outlook to the international arena. Byzantium upheld the concept of the absolute power of the emperor (basileus). In Latin Europe and in contrast to the situation in Byzantium, the Catholic Church developed a considerable independence from the emperors and even successfully challanged their power. In Byzantium, the prevailing constitutional idea was that the emperor was the representative of God on Earth. His power was thus, at least conceptually speaking, completely unchecked. In Catholic Europe, the 'balance of power' between emperor and pope in fact created a normative revolution of its kind,[23] laying a different foundation to such fundamental problem areas as separation of powers and property rights.[24]

Following this element, Taube argued that the *bellum justum* (just war) doctrine that inspired the later field of *ius ad bellum* emerged in Catholic Europe and was virtually unknown in Byzantium and ancient Rus'.[25] If the Emperor was an unchecked representative of God on Earth, who would have been in the position to discuss the 'justness' of his wars? As a consequence of the lack of *bellum justum* doctrine in the Byzantine tradition, Taube insisted that the wars between the Russian Princes were 'more cruel and more lawless' than the wars in mediaeval Western Europe. However, it is somewhat doubtful whether such a conclusion can be reached with any historical accuracy.

On the other hand, Taube praised the high development of ambassadorial (diplomatic) law and the art of diplomacy in Byzantium. Thus, according to Taube, it turned out that while mediaeval Catholic Europe was more advanced in *ius and bellum* Byzantium was leading in the art of diplomacy.

However, perhaps the practically most important aspect of the specific Orthodox/Russian 'type of international law' was the idea that Muscovy inherited from Byzantium: the claim that it was entitled to protect Orthodox Christians abroad.[26] Thus, the Orthodox *Grossraum*, to make a parallel to the later terminology of Carl Schmitt, was a concrete order of privileged interests in territories inhabited by Orthodox believers. Muscovy claimed the right to 'protect' them – notwitshanding the issue of the 'sovereignty' of others.

Taube's general argument seems significant – of course, that Russia knew 'international law' before Peter the Great broke the window to (Western) Europe. It just happened to be a partly different kind of 'international law'. Of course much depends on our definiton of international law. Does the existence of 'international law' presuppose a developed or at least somehow articulated doctrine? Or is it necessary that the principle of sovereign equality between nations be recognized? The legal historians representing the view that modern international law was born in or around 1648 would claim so.

---

23 See Harold J. Berman, *Law and Revolution II. The Impact of the Protestant Reformations on the Western Legal Tradition*, Cambridge, Mass: Harvard University Press, 2003.

24 See also Richard Pipes, *Russia under the Old Regime*, 2nd edition, London: Penguin Books, 1993.

25 See Taube, *Etudes* . . ., pp. 366–368.

26 See also Nussbaum, *op. cit.*, p. 52.

However, this view is also implicitly the Eurocentric one because it ties the very concept of international law to the way international law came to be constructed in the Westphalian Europe. If legal arguments historically proceeded from moral-religious ones, it fixates a certain time period to distinguish 'law' from 'non-law'. Another – broader – definition of international law would focus on normative contacts with others more broadly. When there was a binding theory about the normative status of others, in war and in peacetime, we could talk about a version of 'international law'.

In the context of normative thinking in East Asia, Professor Onuma points out the hierarchical nature of the regional normative thinking. There could have been no equality between the most civilized centre of the world, China, and normatively dependent nations which made up vassal states in various degrees.[27] Moreover, the Chinese emperors were not interested in conquering the world because they considered the rest of the world less civilized than China itself.

Some parallels to Muscovy can be drawn here. To start with, the Russian lands were the prey of the Muslim conquerors of the Golden Hord from 1240–1480. They were thus cut off from political and legal developments in Western Europe. Even after the Mongol yoke was thrown off, Russia was not regarded as part of the *respublica Christiana*. Nor did the rulers of Muscovy want to be that: they adopted the interpretation, according to which only Muscovy knew pure and unspoiled Christian faith, i.e. orthodoxy. Why should there be normative unity with heretics? Another aspect of Muscovy's development was its type of absolutism. As the Harvard historian Richard Pipes has explained, the Tsar's political power went closely together with his property rights to all Russia.[28] To be the Russian Tsar meant to own Russia in a way that was never or no longer the case in England, France or Germany. An interesting normative exchange took place in the 16th century between Muscovy's Tsar Ivan Grozny and the English Queen Elizabeth I. Namely, Ivan Grozny wrote to Queen Elizabeth that he felt disappointed about her status as ruler – he had realized that her power in her country was not entirely unchecked.[29] How in such circumstances could Elizabeth expect equality with a ruler such as Ivan himself who 'had it all' and was fully entitled to it?

Thus, when Peter the Great 'broke the window' to Europe, Russia had already developed a particularly strong type of autocracy. The question was whether and if so, to what extent, the type of civilization or domestic regime type influenced the country's understanding of international law, and continued to be topical throughout the 19th and partly even 20th centuries. What then was Russia's role in international legal discourse, which was so dominated by Western European powers and thinkers? Was Russia liminal Europe, which had been unfortunate enough to be cut off from the rest of the Old World? Or perhaps Russia was the first non-Western power to successfully internalize the language of international law and start to use it in its own favour? In any case, at least officially, Peter's Russia abandoned Ivan Grozny's language of a priori religous-political superiority vis-à-vis other nations.

---

[27] See further Rune Svarverud, *International Law as World Order in Late Imperial China. Translation, Reception and Discourse, 1847–1911*, Leiden/Boston: Brill, 2007.

[28] See Pipes, *Russia under the Old Regime*.

[29] See *ibid.*

16.4 'CIVILIZED' VS THE 'UNCIVILIZED': INTERNATIONAL LAW IN TSARIST RUSSIA

In the 18th century, the Russian Empire became the leading power in Northern Europe. Domestically, the all-pervasive project was that of Europeanisation. As it was understood, Europeanness also meant the study of European legal and political thought. Peter the Great had a high opinion of the works of Samuel Pufendorf and Catherine the Great demonstrated deep interest in leading French Enlightenment thinkers. Yet in terms of political and legal reforms, many of the progressive ideas of the Enlightment were not implemented easily in Russia. Most notably, serfdom was abolished only in 1861. As the often used expression has it, Russia continued to 'lag behind' Western Europe. Another question was to what extent the European-oriented Russian court around the emperors reflected the identity of the Russian people at that time.

In European diplomacy and treaty practice, Russia made a number of significant contributions in the late 18th and early 19th centuries. Catherine II's Declaration of Armed Neutrality of 1780 influenced the development of the law of sea and was directed against the interests of the predominant sea power, England.[30] Russia's role in defeating Napoleon's France is well known[31] as is Russia's rise to a leading position in the European Concert at the Congress of Vienna in 1815. Politically, the Russian monarchy represented reactionary anti-democratic ideas in the European balance of power politics, especially in the Holy Alliance.

In terms of the study and scholarship of international law, the few and relatively obscure Russian writings on natural law of the 18th to early 19th century did not leave a lasting mark and remained largely unnoticed, both within and especially outside Russia. By and large, Russia remained at the intellectual receiving end of European writings of and debates on international law.[32] A change occurred in the mid-19th century and was driven by Baltic German scholars or Russian scholars of Baltic German origin at the Universities of St Petersburg and Dorpat (today: Tartu). Russian authors such as Dmitry Kachenovsky (1827–1872) and Mikhail Kapustin (1828–1899) at the universities of Moscow and Kharkov made interesting contributions[33] but in terms of impact and reception of their works, they remained in the shadow of Baltic German/Livonian authors such as August Bulmerincq (1822–1890) and especially Friedrich Martens (1845–1909).

The fact that scholars originating from the Russian Baltic Sea provinces of Estonia and Livonia would dominate the Russian scene of international law in the late Tsarist period has been an interesting historical phenomenon. The Balts seemingly enjoyed

---

[30] Carl Bergbohm, *Die bewaffnete Neutralität 1780–1783. Eine Entwicklungsphase des Völkerrechts im Seekriege*, Berlin: Weidmannsche Buchhandlung, 1884.

[31] See Dominic Lieven, *Russia against Napoleon: the True Story of the Campaigns of War and Peace*, New York: Viking Press, 2009.

[32] For Russian legal scholarship more generally at that time, see Arkadi Kornev/Aleksandr Borisov, *Pravovaya mysl v dorevoljutsionnoi Rossii*, Moscow: Eksmo education, 2005.

[33] See *Zolotoi fond Rossiiskoi nauki mezhdunarodnogo prava. Tom I. D. Kachenovski, Kurs mezhdunarodnogo prava, M. Kapustin, Mezhdunarodnoe pravo, N. Korkunov, Lektsii po mezhdunarodnomu pravu*, Moscow: Mezhdunarodnye otnoshenia, 2007.

their double position of representing 'genuine Europeanness' in Russia and at the same time translating Russian state interests into the language of international law. Because the Russianized Baltic Germans were perceived as most genuinely 'European' among the Russian subjects, they were naturally catapulted to the top of their field at the pro-European Tsarist courts at St Petersburg.

Let us look at the international legal theory of the most outstanding representative of international law in Tsarist Russia, Friedrich Martens (1845–1909). The focus of this chapter does not allow us to dedicate much attention to all noteworthy aspects in the theory of Martens, e.g. the concept of international administrative law that he had borrowed from Lorenz von Stein (1815–1890) and developed further.[34] The most crucial element in his theory of international law was the normative distinction between civilized and uncivilized peoples. While Martens had already dealt with these ideas intensely in his doctoral dissertation on consular jurisdiction,[35] he generalized his views in his 1882 textbook of international law, the first original one to appear in the Russian language.[36] Martens held that only civilized/European/Christian nations (or nations established by European settlers such as the US) could be subjects of international law.[37] At the same time, non-civilized/non-European/non-Christian nations, at least in their stage of development at that time, had to remain outside the inner circle of the subjects of international law. According to Martens, a more primitive type of natural law did apply to uncivilized peoples (i.e., they were not entirely without rights either, for instance they could not have been killed 'just like that'). Yet Martens argued that the international law of civilized nations had to be based on reciprocity which was practically impossible in the relationships between 'civilized' and 'uncivilized' peoples.

It would be an intellectual mistake to dismiss Martens as simply a typical 19th-century European racist and nothing else. Of course, he may have been that as well but not only that. To start with, most other European scholars of the time made the same crucial distinction between 'civilized' and 'uncivilized' nations – James Lorimer (1818–1890) in Britain, Henry Wheaton (1785–1848) in the US and others.[38] Their views reflected the consensus at the time among statesmen, diplomats and educated public.[39]

---

34 The concept of 'global administrative law' has recently been developed by international law scholars working at or associated with NYU School of Law. See e.g. a symposium edited by Benedict Kingsbury, Nico Krisch and Richard Stewart in 17 European Journal of International Law 2006.

35 See Friedrich Martens, *Das Consularwesen und die Consularjurisdiction im Orient*, translated by H. Skerst, Berlin: Weidmann, 1874.

36 See Fyodor Martens, *Sovremennoe mezhdunarodnoe pravo tsivilizovannykh narodov*, 2 volumes, Moscow: Yuridicheski kolledzh MGU, 1996.

37 See *ibid.*, pp. 143–145, 157.

38 See further Martti Koskenniemi, *The Gentle Civilizer of Nations. The Rise and Fall of International Law 1870–1960*, Cambridge University Press, 2001 and Antony Anghie, *Imperialism, Sovereignty and the Making of International Law*, Cambridge University Press, 2005.

39 The editor of this book, Alexander Orakhelashvili, has argued in an earlier article how wrong 19th-century European international lawyers were on this point; that international law was, in fact, universal. I have an epistemological difference with Dr Orakhelashvili on this point. To me, international law is and has been a social construction not an objectively existing reality that a majority of observers can misread or misinterpret. Therefore, I cannot follow the logic that most influential international lawyers of a certain period could have been *wrong* about the nature of their subject.

Moreover, upon closer examination, the ideas of Martens do not necessarily look so out of touch with international legal debates in the early 21st century. Martens was certainly a Russian imperialist but not, it seems, a *völkisch* type of nationalist. His definition of civilization was the respect for (European) liberal values and human rights.[40] He postulated – in Russia's domestic context quite subversively – that a country's approach to international law followed from its domestic regime type.[41] When a state respected the rights and freedoms of its 'subjects', it was also more likely to respect the treaties that it had concluded with other states. Conversely, if the rulers did not respect the rights of their citizens, how could they have been respectful of international law? This is what the distinction on a civilizational basis meant for Martens.

Of course, the governments of many countries to which Martens wanted to grant a special status in international law, including Tsarist Russia, were not at all so respectful of the rights of their 'subjects'. In this sense, the theory of civilized states was manifestly misused in the practice. Scholars and diplomats such as Martens are responsible for their parts in these misuses.

However, if we adopt the ideas of Martens in our times and replace the concept of 'civilization' with the concept of 'human rights', we discover that we have substantively quite similar normative debates today.[42] Europe defines itself politically – via the European Union and the Council of Europe – through the concepts of human rights and democracy. In terms of the policy of international law, it remains one of the most debated and controversial questions whether international law should distinguish between democracies and dictatorships, countries that predominantly respect human rights and others that do not. A number of current Western scholars and policy makers, particularly in the US, have followed in the footsteps of Martens, sometimes probably not being fully aware of their intellectual and political predecessors.[43] Anne-Marie Slaughter's idea of international law of liberal states is ultimately not so different from Martens's idea of international law of civilized states – especially since for Martens, 'civilization' translated into respect for individual rights.

In highlighting the need to distinguish between civilized and uncivilized nations, Martens even 'surpassed' his international law colleagues in the West. Perhaps this can be psychologically explained by the phenomenon that new converts to a belief system tend to be the most eager proselytizers, or as an expression has it, even 'more Catholic than the Pope'. Many 19th-century Western European intellectuals and politicans continued to look down at Russia as an only partly European/civilized country with a largely agrarian economy whose backward political regime pushed it almost

---

Whether one politically or ethically approves or disapproves of certain views, is an entirely different matter. See Alexander Orakhelashvili, *The Idea of European International Law*, 17 European Journal of International Law 2006, No 2, pp. 315–347.

[40] See Martens, *op. cit.*, pp. 8–9.

[41] See Martens, *op. cit.*, pp. 8, 27.

[42] See also Jack Donnelly, *Human Rights: a New Standard of Civilization?*, 74 (1) International Affairs 1998, pp. 1–24.

[43] See Anne-Marie Slaughter, *International Law in a World of Liberal States*, 6 European Journal of International Law 2005, pp. 503–538; Fernando R. Tesón, *A Philosophy of International Law*, Boulder: Westview Press, 1998; Robert Kagan, *The Return of History and the End of Dreams*, New York: Knopf, 2008.

naturally into a position of 'gendarme of Europe'. What would be a better psychological self-help against the demeaning rhetoric of the others than to make the language of the defence of the (European) civilization one's own and add a particular intensity to it?

In the context of 19th-century Tsarist Russia, there was one more significant aspect to the distinctions made by Martens – domestic. To suggest here the *cui prodest*? question is probably influenced by the Marxist interest in what constituted the 'real reasons' (the hidden *Unterbau* rather than visible *Überbau*) of the distinction made by Martens. Besides internationally defending Russia's *droit de conquete* vis-à-vis 'uncivilized' Asian nations and peoples, Martens simultaneously maintained in the domestic context that Russia had to continue to learn 'from more enlightened European nations'. As the historical debate between Westernizers and Slavophiles evolved in 19th-century Russia, Martens and his fellow international lawyers at the country's universities were almost exclusively representing the Westernizing/Europeanizing cause. They expressed embarassment about the likes of Ivan Grozny because the 'Oriental style' of such Tsars had set Russia historically apart from Europe. But as far as the Baltic German scholars were concerned, it was also accidentally in their personal interest to advocate the Europeanness rather than 'Russianness' of Russia: for it was they who were to perform as naturally born middlemen between Russia and Europe. This brought along titles, positions and influence – and who on the path of such a worldly subject as international law seriously minded having these?

In concluding this section, let us come back to the main theme of this chapter – universality vs regional fragmentation in the history of international law. Russia in the Tsarist period from Peter the Great to Nicholas II (late 17th century until 1917) came to share entirely the same concept of international law as it was known in Western Europe. Russia was perceived as a European country, albeit a unique one. The inner-European contacts on dynastic levels were very intimate. For example, the Russian Tsar Nicholas II and the German Kaiser Wilhelm II, both relatives, addressed each other in private letters as 'Nicky' and 'Willy'. When Russia's treaties with Western and Central European powers were published under the editorship of Fyodor (Friedrich) Martens, the final product was not at all different from the treaty collection of his namesake in Germany in the late 18th to early 19th centuries.[44]

On the other hand, this unity of (Western) Europe and Russia at that time – also in terms of international law – may have been historically more conditioned than the success of the Hague Conferences in 1899 and 1907 (where Russia played a leading role) and other important conferences may have suggested. To start with, this was the time when the economic, military, scientific, etc power of Western Europe was at its absolute historical height. From the Russian perspective, this made it very reasonable to seek access to and equality with the privileged 'civilized world'. In order to 'survive' and modernize, Russia may not have had much choice other than to emphasize its political, cultural and

---

44 See Georg Friedrich von Martens, *Recueil des principaux traités d'Alliance, de Paix, de Trêve, de Neutralité, de commerce, de limites, dechange &c. conclus par les Puissances de L'Europe tant entre elles qu'avec les Puissances et etats dans d'autres parties du monde*, Göttingen, 1791; Fréderic de Martens, *Recueil des traités et conventions conclus par la Russie*, St Petersburg, 1885.

legal belonging to (Western) Europe, and suppress factors of normative difference. And this is what the Russian elite did.

However, part of the question is what price Russia had to pay in order to appear and be perceived as 'civilized'/European. A number of conservative Slavophile criticizers of the Tsarist government argued in the 19th century that the orientation of the Tsarist government had become too foreign – 'German' – sympathizing with Protestantism rather than Orthodoxy, etc. Nevertheless, in terms of Russia's greatness, the European orientation of Tsarist Russia and the normative unity with Europe worked. In terms of its conquests, Tsarist Russia was one of the most expansionist and successful European Empires. These successes must have helped to silence the conservative Russian critic who thought, as Dostoevsky did, that the Petrine Russia had served 'even more Europe's interests than its own'. It is also important to add that international law of the 18th and 19th centuries was quite helpful for Russia, as for any other European Empire, since it tolerated and accepted military conquests.

Yet it seems quite a noteworthy historical fact that when the Bolsheviks came to power in 1917, almost all leading Russian international law scholars and functionaries were forced to go into to exile.[45] The exiled scholars of the St Petersburg school in particular, had carried German rather than Russian family names – Taube, Nolde, Mandelstam, etc. Some German-speaking legal scholars from the Baltic provinces and associated with the university in Dorpat (Tartu) became particularly vehement intellectual opponents of Russian Bolshevism. Axel Freytagh-Loringhoven (1878–1942), a professor of law in the pre-1917 University of Tartu (then Iur'ev) and participant in the Russo-Japanese war of 1904–1905, even became a leading representative in the field of international law in the German Reich in the 1930s. Among other things, Freytagh-Loringhoven advocated the idea that the USSR should not be accepted as a member of the international community – for, he argued, it had turned its back on the values of European civilization (such as respect for private property). Baltic Germans such as Freytagh-Lorinhoven also became the collateral damage of Russia's historical and normative turn in 1917.

Finally, in terms of universality/fragmentation of international law one needs to once again emphasize the limits of any normative 'unity' in the 18th and 19th centuries. There was a unity and Russia belonged to it but it was still a regional-cultural unity. European and Russian scholars and diplomats of that period usually did not construct international law as universal. Instead, the law of nations was discriminatory, based on the ambiguous and all-permitting notion of 'civilization'. Thus, the nation states of the West and Russia belonged together as subjects of international law but nations in the non-Christian world did not.

[45] See further Grigori Starodubtsev, *Mezhdunarodno-pravovaya nauka rossiiskoi emigratsii (1918–1939)*, Moscow: Kniga i biznes, 2000.

16.5 A DIFFERENT IDEOLOGY FOR FRAGMENTATION: 'SOCIALIST INTERNATIONAL LAW' OF THE SOVIET PERIOD

An aspect that has been very actively debated with respect to 20th-century Russia and its law(s) is the question of breaks and continuities.[46] In the international legal sphere, the Bolsheviks emphasized that they had practically nothing in common with the rulers of Tsarist Russia. They gave their vocal support to the principle of self-determination of peoples[47] and denounced aggressive wars and so-called unequal treaties that had previously been concluded with 'uncivilized nations'. The Marxist-Lenininst theory of law emphasized the class element of law – all law was inevitably class law. In the capitalist countries, laws were made by the minority, the exploiting class. In Soviet Russia which was the first country where the workers took the power to themselves, the laws had to express the interests of the majority, the workers. At least this was hypnotically suggested to the world.

Fyodor Martens in his theory of international law had emphasized the connection between the nature of the domestic political regime and its international-legal 'performance'. The guiding criteria of Martens and his era were culture and civilization: how developed a country was (including in terms of its respect for individual rights domestically) determined its legal relationships and status internationally. The Bolsheviks adhered to a similar idea but turned it around: countries with a just socio-political order (Soviet and socialist countries) and countries with an unjust socio-political order (capitalist countries) could not simply continue to have the same international law as before 1917. Thus, the first and second generation of Soviet Russia's international lawyers – Yevgeni Korovin (1892–1964) and Fyodor Kozhevnikov (1905–1998) – emphasized the international legal break with the capitalist world, primarily that of the West.[48] They rejected the idea of the universality of international law and insisted instead that heavy regional fragmentation (as a temporary solution until socialism won everywhere) was inevitable. International law between the USSR and the capitalist West could be only a very basic and minimalist type of international law. Otherwise, the USSR and other socialist countries were entitled to build up, develop and defend their own international law, socialist international law. In that way, the element of class law was transferred to international relations. Instead of being European/civilized in order to qualify for privileged membership in the international community, a country now had to follow the footsteps of the Russian October revolution for the same purpose.

From the early 18th century until 1917, there had been a normative unity between

---

[46] See e.g. George K. Ginsburgs, *From Soviet to Russian International Law. Studies in Continuity and Change*, The Hague: Kluwer, 1998; Tarja Långström, *Transformation in Russia and International Law*, Leiden/Boston: Brill, 2003.

[47] See for a recent and perhaps slightly too enthusiastic interpretation of the Soviet views on this right Bill Bowring, *The Degradation of the International Legal Order: The Rehabilitation of Law and the Possibility of Politics*, London: Routledge, 2008.

[48] See Evgeni A. Korovin, *Das Völkerrecht der Übergangszeit. Grundlagen der völkerrechtlichen Beziehungen der Union der Sowjetrepubliken*, Berlin, 1929, pp. 7–8, 13; Fyodor I. Kozhevnikov, *Sovetskoe gosudarstvo i mezhdunarodnoe pravo 1917–1947 gg*, Moscow, 1948, p. 25.

the West and Russia. Russia counted herself and was counted by others as part of the 'civilized community of nations'. After the Russian October revolution of 1917, it was often emphasized, both in the West and in Russia, that the earlier normative unity had been broken.[49] But it also seems necessary to keep in mind that before the 18th century, there had been other times of normative disunity between Russia and Western Europe, such as between the 13th and 16th centuries. Slavophiles, Panslavists and other Russian conservatives had, throughout the 19th century, continued to argue that, with Peter the Great's reforms, the country's elite had 'sold out Russia's soul' and forced the country to join 'false Europe'. At first glance the Russian conservatives of the 19th century and the Bolsheviks of 1917 had nothing in common. Yet upon closer examination both of these streams had in common a certain Messianism, namely the belief that it was *Russia*'s fate to save Europe and the world. While the 19th-century conservatives based their hopes on the religious purity of Russian Orthodoxy, the Bolshevik revolutionaries of the early 20th century built on ideals of social justice and equality between men. The exiled Russian thinker Nikolai Berdyaev (1874–1948) provocatively considered the Bolsheviks to be a Christian-inspired movement/sect and interpreted the Bolshevik rise to power as an expression of Russia's historical Messianism.[50] In this interpretation, 1917 was not such an absolute break for Russia as the Bolsheviks themselves wished to believe. On some level, the Bolsheviks drew also from pre-Petrine traditions and reservoirs of normative energy. It was quite telling that the post-1917 Russian conservative exiles were often as anti-European as they were anti-Bolshevik. Thus, Count Trubetskoi and other emigrés in Prague laid foundation to the Russian 'Eurasianist' movement at that time.

Early Soviet international legal theory (especially Korovin) argued that the universality of international law had been broken because the universality of old international law was simply not worth preserving. Yet the suspicion between new Russia and the West was mutual. Essentially, the USSR still struggled in the 1920s and 1930s to gain full and formal international recognition. The US, for example, recognized the Soviet government only in 1933. Only in 1934 was the USSR admitted to the League of Nations and was then expelled from the organization in December 1939, because of its aggression against Finland in the Winter War.

In order to put Russia's 1917 'break' with Europe into perspective, we may compare two outliers of European civilization, Russia and the US, at this juncture. The French philosopher annd traveller Alexis de Tocqueville (1805–1859) had already made provocative comparisons between the two great countries. Messianism and a certain scepticism about 'old Europe' was characteristic of both. The US messianism was built on the critique of Europe's non-democratic political institutions and traditions.[51] In the 19th century, the US chose to be only conditionally connected with the normative world of Europe. On the one hand, it chose time and again distance vis-à-vis European affairs, on the other hand it claimed for itself special rights in the Western hemisphere (Monroe doctrine). The idea that there was a special 'American international law' was also expressed

---

49 See e.g. Krystyna Marek, *Identity and Continuity of States in Public International Law*, Geneva: E. Droz, 1954, p. 124.

50 Nikolay Berdyaev, *Istoki i smysle russkogo kommunizma*, Paris, 1955.

51 See Robert Kagan, *Dangerous Nation: America's Place in the World from Its Earliest Days to the Dawn of the Twentieth Century*, New York: A. Knopf, 2006.

in the 19th and early 20th centuries (e.g. by Alejandro Álvarez from Chile). Special institutes such as the non-recognition of illegitimate governments were developed in the Americas. The US international law doctrine had its own specific traits and features.[52]

In this sense, post-1917 Soviet Russia was not the first power to normatively rebel against 'old Europe' and the international community that had been built around it. It was a striking coincidence (or not) that Vladimir Lenin in Soviet Russia and Woodrow Wilson in the US proclaimed the right of peoples to self-determination almost simultaneously. Yet while the US again adopted in the 1920s an isolationist approach towards 'European' affairs, Soviet Russia was a clearly revolutionary power in terms of insisting that the world revolution would have to start in Europe.

Part of the Soviet Russian international legal thinking was that the Bolsheviks thought about Eastern Europe in terms of Russia's historic territory and sphere of influence. Although the Bolsheviks in Russia rejected in most ways the Tsarist legacy, they took quite seriously Tsarist Russia's historical borders. Treaties concluded in 1920 and 1921 with Finland, the Baltic republics (Estonia, Latvia, Lithuania) and Poland were treated as tactical; these treaties and the guarantees thay had given were soon unilaterally reversed when circumstances in international politics became more favourable to Moscow.

Final recognition of the legitimacy of the Soviet government was only achieved with the Allied victory in World War II and the decisive Soviet contribution to it. The USSR became one of the founding members of the United Nations and a veto-empowered permanent member of the UN Security Council. While the United Nations was founded in San Francisco, in terms of geopolitical divisions of Cold War Europe, the gentleman's agreements reached at Yalta in early 1945 were equally important. When the United Nations was founded, Soviet forces had already assumed control in the territories that soon came to be known as the Warsaw Pact countries. The conference of Yalta defined the Soviet *Grossraum*.

In terms of universality and fragmentation of international law, the USSR and the Soviet theorists implied that a special 'socialist international law' applied between the USSR and the other Warsaw Pact countries. But as the Brezhnev doctrine and the uprisings in East Berlin in 1953, in Hungary in 1956 and in Czechoslovakia in 1968 demonstrated, 'socialist international law' primarily translated as Moscow's sphere of control. In these territories, Moscow overruled the application of the universal norm of international law, Article 2 para. 4 of the UN Charter. Paradoxically, the very institute of veto power of the permanent members of the UN Security Council made sure that nothing could be done about the violations of Hungarian and Czechoslovak sovereignty.

The legal rhetoric of the Soviet governments and the theoreticians vis-à-vis the capitalist West changed somewhat over time. In fact, even Soviet legal theory had its own 'hardliners' (e.g., Fyodor Kozhevnikov) and 'liberals/softliners' (e.g. Grigory Tunkin) and periods dominated by the respective streams. However, it is evident that these shifts moved in parallel with the evolution of the Soviet governments' political emphases and orientations. Tunkin's rise in Soviet international law initially coincided with Khrushev's thaw. Tunkin's works published in the late Breshnev era were gloomier,

[52] See also Mark W. Janis, *American Tradition of International Law: Great Expectations, 1789–1914*, Oxford University Press, 2004.

again more antagonistic towards the West and reflected anxieties about nuclear war and US predominance.[53] In his works, Tunkin sometimes criticized what he called Western attempts to over-ideologize international legal theory.[54] Thus, notwithstanding the phenomenon of socialist international law (which he supported and advocated), he insisted on the universality of international law.[55] Moreover, Tunkin argued that it had been the Russian Revolution itself that had triggered the liberation of colonial territories and ultimately made international law truly universal.[56] Tunkin's disciples at Moscow State University, such as Rein Müllerson, became leading liberal representatives of late-Soviet (*perestroika*-era) international legal theory in the USSR.

In terms of Western research on Russia, particular attention was paid to Soviet treaty practice and theory.[57] Western international legal views on Soviet Russia reflected similar positions and variations as in the USSR. The hardliners were pessimistic about any possibility of legal normative cooperation with the USSR, even considering such cooperation harmful and counterproductive. If one trusted the Soviets, one got cheated, argued a US author plainly: 'While cheating is fully justified in Marxism-Leninism [. . .] its roots are to be found in the Russian tradition where deception is as natural a national characteristic as is freedom in the United States.'[58]

Yet another stream of Western legal scholars took a more conciliatory and engaging approach towards post-Stalinist Soviet Russia, attempting to emphasize the (often few) common features with the Soviets rather than the differences most people were daily aware of anyway. For example scholars educated at Harvard University's Law School, most prominently Harold J. Berman and William E. Butler, tried to understand Soviet Russia without pre-fixed negative ideological lenses. The more conciliatory attitudes may have been one of the reasons why Grigory Tunkin became relatively well known and respected in the West. Tunkin's talk about peaceful co-existence between the West and the East was appealing to international law circles outside the USSR. This appealed as 'mutual assurance of ideological non-destruction', as a doctrine of 'live and let others live'. The conciliatory efforts of these scholars recall the words of Vladimir Hrabar expressed at his inaugural lecture at the University of Iur'ev (Tartu) in 1893: 'international law is a science about peace'.[59]

Perhaps the biggest difference in the Soviet and Western interpretations of international law was that of human rights. The USSR had a quite ambivalent attitude towards human rights. Its government and leading lawyers tried to imitate the rhetoric of human rights and even make the point that human rights were better protected in the USSR than anywhere else in the world. However, eventually even they understood that

---

53 See e.g. Grigory I. Tunkin, *Pravo i sila v mezhdunarodnom sisteme*, Moscow, 1983.

54 Grigory I. Tunkin, *Ideologicheskaya borba i mezhdunarodnoe pravo*, Moscow, 1967.

55 Grigory I. Tunkin, *Voprosy teorii mezhdunarodnogo prava*, Moscow, 1962, pp. 24–25.

56 Tunkin, *Voprosy teorii mezhdunarodnogo prava*, p. 65.

57 See Jan F. Triska and Robert M. Slusser, *The Theory, Law and Policy of Soviet Treaties*, Stanford University Press, 1962.

58 Joseph D. Douglas, Jr, *Why the Soviets Violate Arms Control Treaties*, Washington: Pergamon-Brassey's, 1988, p. 62.

59 Vladimir Hrabar, Voina i mezhdunarodnoe pravo, in: *Uchenye zapiski imperatorskago Iur'evskago universiteta*, No 4, Iur'ev, 1893, pp. 23–24.

Soviet arguments about human rights did not come across as too convincing against the background of the Soviet reality. The USSR abstained from voting when the Universal Declaration of Human Rights was adopted in the UN General Assembly in 1948. Later on, Soviet diplomats attempted to establish the supremacy of social, economic and cultural rights over civil and political rights. That the UN's two human rights covenants of 1966 became two in the first place may be one of the most lasting influences of the USSR in treaty-making. Altogether, however, the USSR saw in the West's human rights rhetoric a great danger to its sovereignty. (Retrospectively, we may conclude: rightly so.) Only when the Helsinki Final Act of the European Conference on Security and Cooperation was adopted in 1975 did the USSR accept for the first time that there was at least some legally established window to discuss the situation vis-à-vis human rights in the USSR. This was used by Russian, Baltic and other dissidents who founded the Moscow Helsinki Group. Amazed Westerners later started to discuss the 'Helsinki effect', which led to Secretary General Gorbachev and *perestroika*.[60]

16.6 CONCLUSIONS

It is a trivial thing to say but the study of the history of international law helps us also to understand better some developments and conflicts in contemporary international law. For example, Europe and Russia are currently holding a grandiose, although partly hidden, normative debate about the importance of human rights and democracy in international law. In 1998, the Russian Federation ratified the European Convention on Human Rights. However, Russia's relationship within the Council of Europe system has been relatively strained. Of course, by now Russia seems to have been re-socialized to the European human rights protection system. However, this has not happened without costs to the effectiveness of the Strasbourg system. Moreover, leading Russian politicians have expressed their dissatisfaction with some Strasbourg judgments. While there has been no problem with Russia's compliance with the ECHR's judgments as such (the government always pays what the Court has ordered), compliance with commitments that were made when the country joined the Council of Europe has remained a problem. Most publicized of these issues has been the question of formal abolition of the death penalty. Segments of Russian public opinion and legal scholarship are increasingly resisting the idea that Russia should 'learn' human rights and democracy from the West. The 19th-century debates between Westernizers and nationalists have been revived and in this sense, the country has found its continuity with the pre-1917 period. Representatives of Russia's foreign policy elite continue to ponder over who Russia could 'save' this time.[61]

Another interesting phenomenon has been political discussions and claims about the 'terroritory of the former-URSS' and the 'near abroad'. For example, politically post-Soviet Russia has resisted the idea of the NATO enlargement of the territory of the

---

[60] See Daniel C. Thomas, *The Helsinki Effect. International Norms, Human Rights, and the Demise of Communism*, Princeton University Press, 2001.

[61] See Sergei Karaganov, *Will Russia Save the West?*, 23.12.2009, Project Syndicate, http://www.project-syndicate.org/commentary/karaganov13/English.

former USSR. While the argument never was (nor could it be) that NATO may not be enlarged in terms of international law, the argument nevertheless was that politically, morally, it should not. Essentially, the argument has still been a normative one, namely about Russia's privileged spheres of interest outside its borders in Eastern Europe.

Moreover, when the Kosovo conflict escalated in early 1999, many in the West considered Russia's insistence that military force could not be used against the regime of Milosevic in Yugoslavia (later Serbia) irrational and counterproductive. Yet knowing the history of international legal arguments in Tsarist Russia (not to meution Muscovy's spiritual predecessor, Byzantium), one could in 1999 detect the claim that Russia continued to see herself as the protector of the Orthodox population. The normative dimension and history of this claim was seldom properly understood in the West (because of a different historical-normative tradition, the one of emphasizing universal human rights). Even the Georgian–Russian conflict in South Ossetia may be understood in terms of claims to spheres of influence. In the field of collective security, Russia is making efforts to build up its alternative to NATO. In terms of economic cooperation, the customs union between Russia, Belarus and Kazakhstan is planned as an Eastern alternative to the EU.

In today's international law, Russia is a vocal supporter of the UN Charter and its rigid regulation of the use of military force. However, the universal language of the UN Charter is also capable of hiding behind its veil historical claims to spheres of interest, at least those of the permanent members of the Security Council. When a permanent member of the SC blocks with the veto an act that it considers hostile, such an act will be qualified as illegal. Incidentally, such a solution can help to maintain one's historically acquired *Grossraum*.

Nevertheless, in terms of the main thread in this chapter – universality vs regional fragmentation of international law, it is important to emphasize that nowadays, very few scholars or policy makers discussing international law make a conscious argument in favour of fragmentation and against universality. We have passed the eras of civilized vs uncivilized and capitalist vs socialist nations. Yet history and culture as such have proved more persistent factors in international legal affairs as it has seemed in more hopeful (or desperate) moments, for example when Mikhail Gorbachev demanded a 'common European house'. Nowadays, international law remains, at least rhetorically, 'the (universal) language of international relations'. But the dialects of this language can sometimes be very heavy. Some speakers of the common language of international law continue to have difficulties with understanding or trusting each other. The divisions in the UN's Human Rights Council (formerly Commission) continue to be a valid example.

Thus, the purpose of this chapter has not been to advocate fragmentation. Rather, the goal is to draw the attention of the reader to the point that successful long-term universality cannot be built on formalities and dreams. It can only be built on truly common values, which can only emerge if one takes a very realistic and honest look at one's own and others' identities, motives and actions.

17 International law in the 20th century

Carlo Focarelli

17.1 INTRODUCTION

What sort of international law was in place at the outset of the 20th century?[1] The slave trade had been abolished, paving the way for international law rules aimed at protecting human beings as such.[2] Humanitarian considerations, with a view to alleviating the gruesome effects of war, had also inspired the establishment of the Red Cross and the making in 1864 of the first ever Convention on the protection of the victims of war,[3] which in turn set in motion the process of codification of customary international law in general.[4] Humanitarian and cosmopolitan ideas had inspired the mission of the *Institut de droit international* founded in 1873.[5] A number of international institutions had been created, particularly in the course of the 19th century, such as International River Commissions and Administrative Unions,[6] as well as regional international organizations such as the Union of the American Republics.

These rules and institutions had emerged within the 'states system' originally built by equal, mutual-tolerating, secular European powers sharing a similar political, economic, social, religious and cultural background.[7] In the 19th century the system began to expand globally by spreading the 'state' model outside Europe. At that time international law was applied to 'civilized nations', namely to those states – essentially European, or of European descent and cultural background – that fulfilled a 'standard of civilization'

---

1 For an overall exposition of the history of international law in the 20th century see, *e.g.*, Wilhelm G. Grewe, *The Epochs of International Law* (Berlin/New York: Walter de Gruyter, 2000; original: *Epochen der Völkerrechtsgeschichte*, Baden-Baden: Nomos, 1984), Parts V–VII; Karl-Heinz Ziegler, *Völkerrechtsgeschichte* (Munich: Verlag C.H. Beck, 2007, 2nd edn.), Chapters 10–12; Douglas M. Johnston, *The Historical Foundations of World Order. The Tower and the Arena* (Leiden/Boston: Martinus Nijhoff Publishers, 2008), Chapter 9; Martti Koskenniemi, 'History of International Law, World War I to World War II', in EPIL, 2nd edn., at <http://www.mpepil.com>; *id.*, 'History of International Law, Since World War II', *ibid.*

2 See A.Y. Rassam, 'Contemporary Forms of Slavery and the Evolution of the Prohibition of Slavery and the Slave Trade under Customary International Law', 39 *Virginia Journal of International Law* (1999), pp. 303–352; David Weissbrodt, 'Slavery', in EPIL, 2nd edn., at <http://www.mpepil.com>.

3 See Martha Finnemore, *National Interests in International Society* (Ithaca and London: Cornell University Press, 1996), pp. 69–88.

4 For an historical overview of the codification process of international law cf. <http://www.un.org/law/ilc/index.htm>.

5 See Martti Koskenniemi, *The Gentle Civilizer of Nations: The Rise and Fall of International Law 1870 – 1960* (Cambridge: Cambridge University Press, 2002), pp. 12–19.

6 Paul S. Reinsch, *International Unions and Their Administration*, 1 AJIL (1907), pp. 579–623.

7 See Hedley Bull and Adam Watson (eds), *The Expansion of International Society* (Oxford: Oxford University Press, 1985).

ultimately reflecting secularized Judeo-Christian values.[8] While the Ottoman Empire, China and Japan were gradually accepted into the circle of civilized nations in the second half of the 19th century, European colonies, protectorates and informal suzerainty were maintained.[9]

Before examining the international law of the 20th century two methodological caveats are in order. First, while a history of international law may address a variety of questions ranging from historical events to major diplomatic deals, scholarship achievements or archaeologies (in Foucaultian terms)[10] of key structural concepts, the history outlined here is confined, for sake of space, to rules and to their more immediate contextualization. Other surrounding issues, such as theoretical developments, are treated elsewhere in this book, whereas historical and diplomatic events or political implications may easily be retrieved in general accounts of the political history of the 20th century. Secondly, a period larger than usual has been covered, starting from 1899 rather than from 1919.[11] This choice depends on the assumption that, while any division of history is artificial in some measure, the period spanning from the First Hague Peace Conference of 1899 could better capture international law as the law of a global community. It is submitted that the history of international law should be detached from diplomatic history and seen in its own terms.

17.2 UP TO THE END OF WORLD WAR I (1899–1918)

The most relevant developments of international law from the end of the 19th century to World War I mainly relate to the conclusion of a number of multilateral treaties both on the law of war and other war-related matters during the two Peace Conferences held in The Hague in 1899 and in 1907 and on the protection of individuals, either in armed conflict (wounded and sick) or in peacetime (trafficked white slaves). The Conventions,

---

8 Gerrit W. Gong, *The Standard of Civilization in International Society* (Oxford: Clarendon Press, 1984).

9 Jörn Axel Kämmerer, 'Colonialism', in EPIL, 2nd edn., at <http://www.mpepil.com>.

10 Michel Foucault, *The Archaeology of Knowledge* (London and New York: Routledge, 2002), translated from *L'Archéologie du savoir* (Paris: Gallimard, 1969).

11 Typically, Wilhelm G. Grewe, *The Epochs*, cit., starts the contemporary period from 1919, assuming that World War I marked the end of the 'classical' epoch, which developed from the end of the Middle Ages, and the opening of a 'post-classical' period. The periodization followed by Grewe (and many others, such as Karl-Heinz Ziegler, *Völkerrechtsgeschichte*, cit.) is based on three major turning points marked by well-known landmark treaties: the Treaties of Westphalia (1648), the Treaties of the Congress of Vienna (1815) and the Treaty of Versailles (1919), giving some weight to the Charter of the United Nations (1945). In Grewe's view these treaties marked the development of an international law as a law progressively dominated by Spain, France, Britain; then, after 1919, by a transitional Anglo-American Diarchy; and finally, after 1945, by the United States and the Soviet Union. This periodization, although perhaps acceptable in general diplomatic history, is open to criticism as far as international law is concerned. It depends inter alia on Grewe's underlying stance that international law is but a reflection of the most powerful nations, a view that might satisfy the historian and the political scientist but is hardly acceptable to the jurist, if only because it fails to clarify the diverse origins and developments of individual international law rules, apart from such an alleged monolithic entity as 'international law' taken as a whole.

having been concluded in The Hague, have subsequently inspired the label 'Hague law' to mean the law governing the conduct of hostilities and neutrality, while the Conventions on the victims of war, having been concluded at Geneva from 1864 on, have inspired the label 'Geneva law' to denote the law specifically dealing with humanitarian considerations. Today, these two traditional branches of *jus in bello* are regarded as forming one single complex system called international humanitarian law.[12]

It is worth noting that the outbreak of World War I took European intellectuals by surprise.[13] Few if any could imagine that an all-out war would break out between European 'civilized' nations. The abolition of the slave trade and the adoption of humanitarian international law rules aimed at protecting both the victims of war and the most gratuitous acts of warfare in the 19th century had convinced political leaders and public opinion that from then on the brutality of war would have involved only savage peoples outside Europe or a European power compelled to defend itself from a savage people's attack. What proved shocking was that the cruellest war ever waged broke out precisely in Europe, between European powers and for an apparently futile motive. One of the most insightful analyses of this sentiment is owed to Sigmund Freud in an outstanding essay written a few months after the outbreak of the war and published in 1915.[14]

17.2.1 The Hague Conventions and Regulations of 1899 and of 1907

After a number of treaties had been made in the second half of the 19th century aimed at codifying the laws and customs of war,[15] a breakthrough occurred around the turn of the century in the law of warfare by the two Hague Peace Conferences of 1899 and of 1907. The 1907 Conference, in particular, was attended by virtually all the states then existing, European and non-European, and may thus be considered the first genuine historical attempt at convening nearly all states of any cultural background to create a genuinely universal international law. Significantly, the major concern of the Conferences was not the end of a war and the making of a peace treaty as in the past, but rather the prevention of future wars. A Permanent Court of Arbitration, still existing today, was set up pursuant to Articles 20 to 29 of the 1899 Convention for the Peaceful Settlement of International Disputes.[16]

The First Hague Peace Conference of 1899 was convened on the initiative of the Czar of Russia Nicholas II 'with the object of seeking the most effective means of ensuring to all peoples the benefits of a real and lasting peace, and, above all, of limiting the

---

[12] *Legality of the Threat or Use of Nuclear Weapons*, ICJ, Advisory Opinion of 8 July 1996, para. 75, at <http://www.icj-cij.org/docket/files/95/7495.pdf>.

[13] For detailed information on World War I see <http://www.firstworldwar.com/index.htm>.

[14] Sigmund Freud, 'Zeitgemässes über Krieg und Tod', in *Das Unbehagen in der Kultur und andere Kulturtheoretische Schriften* (Frankfurt am Main: Fischer Taschenbuch Verlag, 2004); English translation: *Civilization and Its Discontents* (London: Penguin Books Ltd, 2002), also available at <http://www.panarchy.org/freud/war.1915.html>.

[15] *Supra*, note 3.

[16] The 'permanent' element of the Court was (and still is) a list of arbitrators from which the parties to a dispute might choose. Up to then arbitration was resorted to by making an agreement and establishing an arbitration panel at the very moment when the dispute arose. See Nisuke Ando, 'Permanent Court of Arbitration (PCA)', in EPIL, 2nd edn., at <http://www.mpepil.com>.

progressive development of existing armaments'.[17] The Conference failed to reach agreement on the limitation or reduction of armaments; however, three Conventions – among which at least the Convention Regarding the Laws and Customs of War on Land, with annexed Regulations is worth mentioning[18] – and other acts were adopted; six 'wishes' were also formulated on further matters to be discussed in a later Conference.[19] Of interest is a resolution adopted by the Conference whereby 'the restriction of military charges, which are at present a heavy burden on the world, is extremely desirable for the increase of the material and moral welfare of mankind'. This, coupled with the Martens Clause contained in the Preamble of the Land Convention,[20] was a first development eventually leading to transformation of international law from the 19th-century law of 'civilized nations' to the 20th-century 'global' law made by all states for the benefit of the whole of humankind.[21]

At the 1907 Conference, thirteen Conventions and one Declaration were concluded, ranging from the peaceful settlement of international disputes to land and maritime warfare.[22] The Drago-Porter Convention is worth mentioning as a first antecedent to the later prohibition of the use of force.[23] A Regulation annexed to the Fourth Convention was devoted to belligerent occupation. The Permanent Court of Arbitration was confirmed and its rules improved. It was affirmed that the treaties agreed upon were understood to be in the interest of mankind and the Martens clause was reiterated in the Preamble of the Fourth Convention. All the treaties adopted were designed to govern inter-state wars. No international law rules existed, nor were they created at that time, for the regulation of civil wars, which fell within states' domestic jurisdiction.

17.2.2 The Geneva Wounded and Sick Convention of 1906 and the Paris White Slave Traffic Treaties of 1904 and 1910

Several proposals had been made after 1864, especially by the International Conferences of the Red Cross Societies, for the revision of the 1864 Wounded and Sick Convention. In 1906, following a wish expressed in the Final Act of the 1899 Hague Conference, Switzerland convened a Conference to this end. Thirty-five states participated. A new, more detailed Convention was adopted, on the basis of proposals submitted to it by the

---

17 Russian note of 30 December 1898/11 January 1899, at <http://avalon.law.yale.edu/19th_century/hag99-02.asp>.

18 The International Military Tribunal at Nuremberg (*infra*, note 106) held in 1946 that 'by 1939 [the rules] laid down in the Convention were recognized by all civilized nations, and were regarded as being declaratory of the laws and customs of war', 41 AJIL (1947), pp. 248–249.

19 For the text of all relevant documents see <http://www.pca-cpa.org/upload/files/1899ENG.pdf> and <http://www.icrc.org/ihl.nsf/INTRO?OpenView>.

20 Antonio Cassese, 'The Martens Clause: Half a Loaf or Simply Pie in the Sky?', 11 EJIL (2000), pp. 187–216.

21 *Infra*, note 29.

22 For the text of all relevant documents see <http://www.pca-cpa.org/upload/files/1907ENG.pdf> and <http://www.icrc.org/ihl.nsf/INTRO?OpenView>.

23 Convention on the Limitation of Employment of Force for Recovery of Contract Debts of 18 October 1907, at <http://avalon.law.yale.edu/20th_century/hague072.asp>. See Wolfgang Benedek, 'Drago-Porter Convention (1907)', in EPIL, 2nd edn., at <http://www.mpepil.com>.

International Committee of the Red Cross (ICRC), replacing the 1864 Convention in the relations between the Contracting States.[24]

In 1904 the White Slave Traffic Agreement was signed at Paris.[25] A further White Slave Traffic Convention was signed at Paris in 1910, recognizing women trafficked for prostitution as victims of a contemporary form of slavery and marking a step towards protecting the vulnerable from being taken, trafficked and forced into prostitution or other exploitative situations.[26]

17.3 THE INTER-WAR PERIOD AND WORLD WAR II (1919–1945)

The major developments of international law in the inter-war period concerned the establishment of universal international organizations (in particular the League of Nations), self-determination of peoples, the protection of minorities and individuals, the regulation of air space, the partial prohibition of war and the peaceful settlement of disputes, further rules on the conduct of war and the protection of the victims of war, armed reprisals, an early attempt to regulate international terrorism, non-intervention (especially during the Spanish War),[27] and the articulation of a number of principles and rules by way of international jurisdiction and arbitration.

17.3.1 The End of World War I, the Bolshevik Revolution and the Great Depression

World War I was significant in several respects. First, the unexpected experience of an all-out war waged by European 'civilized' nations inflicted a blow to the notion of civilization as a standard for admission into the circle of the family of nations. The 'European Age', along with colonial expansion, was coming to an end, replaced by two non-European powers, the United States and the Soviet Union.[28] The decline of the European powers was also apparent in the gradual abolition of capitulations from 1899 on.[29] Universal concerns – regardless of religious, ideological, cultural and geographical considerations – took hold, a perception reflected in all major multilateral treaties, which often made reference to the 'benefit of mankind'. The idea itself of civilization became

---

24 Convention for the Amelioration of the Condition of the Wounded and Sick in Armies in the Field of 6 July 1906, at <http://www.icrc.org/ihl.nsf/FULL/180?OpenDocument>.

25 International Agreement for the Suppression of the White Slave Traffic of 18 May 1904, at <http://untreaty.un.org/English/CTC/ch_VII_7p.pdf>.

26 International Convention for the Suppression of the White Slave Traffic of 4 May 1910, at <http://untreaty.un.org/English/CTC/ch_VII_10p.pdf>.

27 Frances Lannon, *The Spanish Civil War, 1936–1939* (Oxford/New York: Osprey Publishing, 2002).

28 J.M. Roberts, *Modern History: From the European Age to the New Global Era* (New York: Oxford University Press, 2008).

29 See Maurits H. van den Boogert and Kate Fleet (eds), *The Ottoman Capitulations: Text and Context* (Rome: Istituto per l'Oriente, 2003); Maurits H. van den Boogert, *The Capitulations and the Ottoman Legal System. Qadis, Consuls and Beraths in the 18th Century* (Leiden: Brill, 2005); Mark S.W. Hoyle, *Mixed Courts of Egypt* (London: Graham & Trotman, 1991).

global when the 'civilizing mission' of the colonial powers was integrated into the mandates system of the League of Nations[30] and gradually evolved towards universal human rights.[31] Secondly, the war had left a world in transition with many hopes and very few certainties. Innumerable international attempts were made at promoting peace and a naive euphoria spread on the occasion of the establishing of some historic international treaties and institutions. Public opinion, lobbying associations and political leaders believed that international law could ensure international peace and security for humankind through the operation of a world organization. At the same time distrust between states was pervasive. Events in Italy and in Germany showed that public opinion could easily be manipulated and led to espouse totalitarianism. No wonder the experience of the inter-war period provoked the emergence of a new academic discipline, International Relations (IR), with a – realist and down-to-earth – proclivity to warn against utopianism, a sentiment that was later to be regarded as one of the major causes of World War II.[32] Thirdly, the dissolution of the Austro-Hungarian Empire and of the German Reich prompted the question of the colonies' fate. The principle of self-determination of peoples was upheld so as to ensure that governments were supported by their peoples. Several smaller (strongly nationalistic) states emerged in Central and South-Eastern Europe. Here, the protection of national minorities was thought to be vital to the maintenance of both domestic and international order.

Another key event was the 1917 Bolshevik Revolution. The revolution sparked an ideological confrontation that lasted until 1989–1991.[33] The Soviet Union, built on Marxism-Leninism principles – such as atheism, abolition of private property and progressive suppression of the state – harshly opposed the 'traditional' features of the European 'family of nations', which in principle shared the Christian religion as well as political and economic liberalism. The Soviet Union immediately challenged the very foundations of international law as it then stood. First, it threatened colonial powers by advocating the application of the principle of self-determination of peoples to both national groups in Europe and colonies overseas. Secondly, it claimed substantive equality between states and rejected economic coercion by the strongest, in particular unequal treaties. Thirdly, it pledged to intervene in internal affairs of other (especially capitalist) states in order to assist the working class and socialist political parties living therein and in principle subject to their rulers with a view to a worldwide revolution. Fourthly, it repudiated certain existing rules of international law, deemed to further 'bourgeois' interests, and denounced several treaties that were formally binding on Russia, particularly in the field of protection of foreign investments.[34]

A third key event that occurred a few years later at the end of World War I was the

---

30 *Infra*, note 46.

31 Edward Keene, *Beyond the Anarchical Society: Grotius, Colonialism and Order in World Politics* (Cambridge: Cambridge University Press, 2002).

32 Edward A. Carr, *The Twenty Years' Crisis 1919–1939. An Introduction to the Study of International Relations* (London: Macmillan, 1939; 2nd edn. reprinted by Houndmills: Palgrave, 2001).

33 Gabriel Gorodetsky, *Soviet Foreign Policy, 1917–1991: A Retrospective* (London: Routledge, 1994).

34 Antonio Cassese, *International Law* (Oxford: Oxford University Press, 2001), pp. 31–32.

Wall Street crisis of 1929 and the Great Depression. Faced with the apparent inability of markets to self-regulate, a belief began to spread that states should intervene in the economy to ensure full employment even at the cost of compromising the stability of exchange rates.[35] For example, shortly after becoming president of the United States in 1933, Frank D. Roosevelt created the New Deal, an unprecedented set of regulatory laws and agencies aimed, inter alia, at strengthening government's control of big corporations and banks. State interventionism soon provoked economic nationalism, prompting autarkist measures of a 'beggar thy neighbour' kind that rapidly escalated and contributed to precipitating war.

17.3.2 The League of Nations

While World War I was still underway, US President Woodrow Wilson promoted the idea of what was to become the League of Nations in his famous 'Fourteen Points' of 8 January 1918.[36] The idea of a universal 'federation of states' had a historical pedigree in the 'perpetual peace' projects – in particular Kant's *Perpetual Peace: A Philosophical Sketch* published in 1795[37] – that had been devised in the past to bring about peace between the then Christian European rulers.[38]

The legal nature of the League was soon widely debated. Some contended that the League was a groundbreaking move towards a cosmopolitan world federation. The Covenant was even conceived as 'higher law',[39] or a sort of international constitution, taking precedence over other conflicting treaties. Others replied that the League was nothing other than a particularly advanced form of international co-operation, if not just a classical instrument of the Anglo-American hegemony after the victory against Germany.[40]

The League Covenant did establish a series of principles that outlived the Organization. First, the Covenant unprecedentedly banned aggression.[41] Under Article 10 member

---

35 In particular, John M. Keynes's *The General Theory of Employment, Interest and Money* (London: Macmillan, 1936) challenged the earlier neo-classical economic paradigm and served as a theoretical justification for state interventionist policies.

36 At <http://avalon.law.yale.edu/20th_century/wilson14.asp>. On the Fourteen Points, see Joachim Schwietzke, 'Fourteen Points of Wilson (1918)', in EPIL, 2nd edn., at <www.mpepil.com>.

37 The text is available inter alia at <http://www.mtholyoke.edu/acad/intrel/kant/kant1.htm>.

38 For an historical exposition of perpetual peace projects from the Late Middle Ages to the 20th century see Dominique Gaurier, *Histoire du droit international. Auteurs, doctrines et développement de l'Antiquité à l'aube de la période contemporaine* (Rennes: Pr. Univ. de Rennes, 2005) pp. 435–510.

39 Hersh Lauterpacht, 'The Covenant as the Higher Law', 17 BYIL (1936), pp. 54–65. Under Article 20 of the Covenant in fact member states agreed that the Covenant 'is accepted as abrogating all obligations or understandings inter se which are inconsistent with the terms thereof' and undertook 'that they will not hereafter enter into any engagements inconsistent with the terms thereof'. In case a member state would have undertaken any obligations inconsistent with the terms of this Covenant before becoming a member thereof, it had the duty 'to take immediate steps to procure its release from such obligations'.

40 See Wilhelm G. Grewe, *The Epochs*, cit., pp. 619–624; Stephen C. Neff, *War and the Law of Nations* (Cambridge: Cambridge University Press, 2005), pp. 279–293.

41 Admittedly, the Covenant confined itself to subject war to a three-month cooling-off

states undertook to 'respect and preserve as against external aggression the territorial integrity and existing political independence of all Members of the League'. No definition of aggression was provided. The Covenant was thus regarded as a return to a discriminatory law of war[42] and, according to some, a revival of the Groatian tradition of *bellum justum*[43] or of the ideas of the French Revolution.[44] Article 16 provided for sanctions against aggressor states but those adopted against Italy for its aggression against Abyssinia (1935–1936) miserably failed.[45]

Secondly, the League took on the task of supervising the administration of the former colonies of the German Reich and of the Ottoman Empire by 'mandatory' powers.[46] Article 22 of the League Covenant set out a 'mandates system' providing that the well-being and development of colonies and territories 'which are inhabited by peoples not yet able to stand by themselves under the strenuous conditions of the modern world' form 'a sacred trust of civilisation' under the supervision of the League. A flexible system was devised with three classifications: 'A', 'B' and 'C' Mandates. Mandatary states had an obligation to submit to the Council an annual report in reference to the territory committed to their charge.

Thirdly, the prevention of 'secret diplomacy' in accordance with Wilson's First Point was sanctioned by Article 18 of the Covenant. Member states had an obligation to register '[e]very treaty or international engagement entered into hereafter by any Member of the League' as soon as possible, with a duty of publication. Interestingly, Article 18 added that '[n]o such treaty or international engagement shall be binding until so registered'. In fact, Article 18 was often construed in the sense that non-registered treaties could simply not be invoked before League bodies. This narrow, more realistic interpretation eventually inspired the drafters of the UN Charter in formulating Article 102.

Finally, the process of codification of customary international law continued under the auspices of the League, which convened in 1930 at The Hague the first Conference for the Codification of International Law to provide a codification of the existing rules on nationality, territorial waters and state responsibility for injuries to aliens. The Conference produced a Convention on certain questions relating to the conflict of

---

period and to a settlement procedure before either the League Council or the Permanent Court of International Justice (PCIJ) or an arbitral tribunal. As a result, war was still allowed after the expiry of the three-month period or against a state that had not complied with a unanimous report of the League Council, the PCIJ's judgment or the arbitral award, in case these instances had be resorted to. Nor did the Covenant ban measures short of war, in particular naval blockade, reprisal and intervention.

[42] See Wilhelm G. Grewe, *The Epochs*, cit., pp. 619–624; Stephen C. Neff, *War and the Law of Nations*, cit., pp. 279–293.

[43] Cornelis van Vollenhoven, *The Three Stages in the Evolution of the Law of Nations* (The Hague: Martinus Nijhoff, 1919), later to be resumed by Hersch Lauterpacht, *The Grotian Tradition in International Law*, 23 BYIL (1946), pp. 1–53.

[44] Alphonse Aulard, 'La société des nations et la révolution française' in Id., *Etudes et leçons sur la révolution française* (Paris, 1921), pp. 135–138, available at <http://galica.bnf.fr/ark:/12148/bpt6k54320969/f8.image.pagination>; Robert Redslob, *Histoire des grands principes du droit des gens depuis l'antiquité jusqu'à la veille de la grande guerre* (Paris: Rousseau, 1923), pp. 275 ff.

[45] See George W. Baer, *Test Case: Italy, Ethiopia, and the League of Nations* (Stanford: Hoover Institution Press, 1976).

[46] See Ruth Gordon, 'Mandates', in EPIL, 2nd edn., at <http://www.mpepil.com>.

nationality laws[47] and three Protocols on military obligations in certain cases of double nationality and on statelessness, but nothing else on the topic of territorial waters (except for some draft articles) and failed to adopt even a single recommendation on the subject of state responsibility.

17.3.3 Territorial sovereignty, domestic jurisdiction and the legal regime of air space and polar regions

In the 1928 *Island of Palmas* Arbitral Award, Judge Huber famously defined sovereignty in the relations between states as 'independence', pointing out that 'independence in regard to a portion of the globe is the right to exercise therein, to the exclusion of any other state, the functions of a state'.[48] A similar statement was made by the Permanent Court of International Justice (PCIJ) in its Advisory Opinion of 1931 in the *Austro-German Customs Union*.[49] The notion of statehood was defined in Article 1 of the Montevideo Convention on Rights and Duties of States of 1933, still today often quoted on the matter.[50]

Special problems arose with regard to the Arctic and Antarctica. The doctrine of effective occupation could hardly be invoked in the polar regions, given their physical features, and other titles were relied upon, including symbolic occupation, discovery, exploration, contiguity and division of claimed areas in sectors.[51] The notion that the test for statehood was effectiveness was affirmed with some qualifications in the *Island of Clipperton* Arbitral Award rendered in 1931.[52]

With the invention of airplanes and balloons the problem of what legal rules should govern cross-border air navigation inevitably arose. Relying on the analogy with maritime navigation two basic principles emerged: freedom of flight over land and sea spaces not subjected to national jurisdiction, similar to freedom of maritime navigation at high seas, and exclusive jurisdiction of the territorial state in the air space over its territory and territorial sea, similar to the jurisdiction exercised by coastal states over their territo-

---

47 Cf. 179 LNTS, p. 89.

48 2 UNRIIA, p. 838, available at <http://untreaty.un.org/cod/riaa/cases/vol_II/829-871.pdf>.

49 PCIJ, *Customs Regime Between Germany and Austria (Protocol of March 19th, 1931)*, Advisory Opinion of 5 September 1931 (Series A/B, No. 41), p. 45. In his famous individual opinion Judge Anzilotti argued that independence 'is really no more than the normal condition of States according to international law; it may also be described as *sovereignty* (*suprema potestas*), or *external sovereignty*, by which is meant that the state has over it no other authority than that of international law', *ibid.*, p. 57.

50 Inter-American Convention on Rights and Duties of States of 26 December 1933, at <http://avalon.law.yale.edu/20th_century/intam03.asp>.

51 Such claims were made by Canada in 1907, by the Soviet Union between 1916 and 1926, by Great Britain in 1917, 1923 and 1926, and by France in 1924. See Samuel W. Boggs, *The Polar Regions: Geographical and Historical Data for Consideration in a Study of Claims to Sovereignty in the Arctic and Antarctic Regions* (Buffalo, NY: Hein, 1991).

52 *Difference Relative to the Sovereignty over Clipperton Island* (*France* v. *Mexico*), Arbitral Award of 28 January 1931, 2 RIAA, p. 1110, at <http://untreaty.un.org/cod/riaa/cases/vol_II/1105-1111.pdf>. The Arbitrator held that while effective occupation is the rule in ordinary cases, a symbolic taking of possession was sufficient in uninhabited territories, as was that of France concerning the Island of Clipperton.

rial waters. These principles were laid down in the Aerial Navigation Convention signed at Paris in 1919[53] and later restated and expanded in the ICAO Convention adopted at Chicago in 1944.[54]

As to independence and non-intervention, Article 15(8) of the League Covenant prevented the Organization from interfering in the domestic jurisdiction of member states by stipulating that if a dispute raised by a member state against another 'is found by the Council to arise out of a matter which by international law is solely within the domestic jurisdiction of that party, the Council shall so report, and shall make no recommendation as to its settlement'. This provision was interpreted by the PCIJ in the *Nationality Decrees* Advisory Opinion of 1923 to the effect that member states' domestic jurisdiction included in principle matters in which they were free from international obligations.[55]

17.3.4 Minorities, Rights of Individuals and International Criminal Justice

Territorial sovereignty, independence and non-interference were aimed at protecting states in their mutual relations. A number of international law rules were created with a view to limiting the power of governments in the way they ruled their own populations. Such rules followed the example of European post-Westphalia treaty clauses governing religious freedom and were destined to propel the international human rights movement that boomed in the post-World War II period. A number of treaties were concluded for the protection of minorities within the states born from the dissolution of the Ottoman Empire. Individual members of minorities could submit to the League Council petitions alleging that a breach of a minority right had been committed by a Party.[56]

While in the 19th century only the slave trade was abolished, in the 20th century also the trafficking in women and children as well as slavery in itself was banned. Within the League of Nations a number of humanitarian committees dealt with slave trade, along with the fight against drug and women trafficking and pornography. In 1921 the Traffic of Women and Children Convention was signed at Geneva.[57] In 1923 the admission of Ethiopia to the League was conditioned, at the request of Great Britain, on the abolition of slavery and the slave trade.[58] On 25 September 1926 the Slavery Convention was signed at Geneva under the auspices of the League of Nations,[59] providing a definition of

---

53 Convention Relating to the Regulation of Aerial Navigation of 13 October 1919, 17 AJIL (1923) Supp., p. 195 ff.

54 Convention establishing the International Civil Aviation Organization (ICAO) of 7 December 1944, at <http://www.icao.int/icaonet/dcs/7300_cons.pdf>.

55 PCIJ, *Dispute between France and Great Britain as to the Nationality Decrees issued in Tunis and Morocco (French Zone)*, Advisory Opinion of 7 February 1923 (Series B, No. 4), pp. 23–24.

56 See Anna Meijknecht, 'Minority Protection System between World War I and World War II', in EPIL, 2nd edn., at <http://www.mpepil.com>.

57 International Convention for the Suppression of the Traffic in Women and Children of 30 September 1921, at <http://untreaty.un.org/English/CTC/ch_VII_2p.pdf>.

58 J. Allain, *Slavery and the League of Nations: Ethiopia as a Civilised Nation*, 8 JHIL (2006), pp. 213–244.

59 At <http://www2.ohchr.org/english/law/slavery.htm>. See Suzanne Miers, *Slavery in the Twentieth Century: The Evolution of a Global Problem* (California:AltaMira Press, 2003).

slavery that is still valid today. In 1933 the Traffic of Women Convention was adopted at Geneva.[60]

Other rules were introduced, along with the establishment of the International Labour Organization (ILO), for the protection of workers.[61] The League of Nations also operated in the field of refugees' protection.[62]

As for individual responsibility, Article 227 of the Treaty of Versailles provided that the Allied and Associated Powers 'publicly arraign[ed] William II of Hohenzollern, formerly German Emperor, for a supreme offence against international morality and the sanctity of treaties'.[63] It was provided that a special Tribunal was to be constituted to try the Emperor. Provision was made that the Allied and Associated Powers would address a request to the Government of the Netherlands for the surrender to them of the former Emperor in order that he might have been put on trial. The Netherlands however rejected the request.

In tracing the origins of crimes against humanity, later to be found in Article 6(c) of the 1945 Statute of the Nuremberg Tribunal,[64] of special interest is a joint declaration made by France, Great Britain and Russia on 28 May 1915 in protest at the mass killings of Armenians in the Ottoman Empire.[65]

17.3.5 Natural Resources and Foreign Investments

Before World War I, it was commonly agreed (at least among European powers) that the taking of foreign property by a state was allowed provided prompt and adequate compensation was paid. This consensus was first challenged by the Bolshevik government. The Soviet Union immediately issued a Decree, on 26 October 1917, that abolished private property in land, without any provision being made for compensation and in respect of all owners, whether nationals or aliens. In the next two years other sectors of the Soviet economy were nationalized without compensation. Public debt was also repudiated. While Western countries declared the Soviet measures against their nationals null and void and claimed compensation, the Soviet Union made counterclaims against the alleged Western intervention in the revolution. Discussions persisted over time but without results. Once the right to private property was denied to nationals, the standard of national treatment clearly no longer satisfied aliens and the need for an international standard, providing for a higher protection than national, became apparent.

A turning point in foreign investment during the inter-war period was marked by Mexican nationalizations subsequent to the Agrarian Reform of 1927. In this connection,

---

60 International Convention for the Suppression of the Traffic in Women of Full Age of 11 October 1933, at <http://untreaty.un.org/English/CTC/ch_VII_5p.pdf>.

61 See, e.g., the Convention No 29 concerning Forced or Compulsory Labour of 28 June 1930, at <http://www.ilo.org/ilolex/cgi-lex/convde.pl?C029>. Article 23 of the League Covenant was specifically devoted to social matters.

62 See Carlile A. Macartney, *Refugees: The Work of the League* (London: League of Nations Union, 1930); Dieter Kugelmann, 'Refugees, League of Nations Offices', in EPIL, 2nd edn., at <http://www.mpepil.com>.

63 At <http://avalon.law.yale.edu/imt/partvii.asp>.

64 *Infra*, note 106.

65 Antonio Cassese, *International Criminal Law* (Oxford: Oxford University Press, 2003), p. 68.

an important and well-known correspondence between US Secretary of State Cordell Hull and the Mexican Foreign Minister took place. In a diplomatic note of 21 July 1938, Hull stressed that the taking of property without compensation amounted to confiscation, despite the expressed Mexican intent to pay at some time in the future. The note added that a right to 'prompt and just compensation' reflected a 'universally accepted principle of international law, based on reason, equity and justice'. This being denied by the Mexican foreign Minister, Mr Hull famously replied on 22 August 1938 that no government was entitled to expropriate private property, for whatever purpose, without provision for 'prompt, adequate and effective' payment therefor,[66] a formula later to become – albeit resisted by other states, at least until the end of the Cold War – the standard required by Western countries.

17.3.6 Self-determination of Peoples

In the 19th century self-determination had been thought to imply (as a 'principle of nationalities') a right of nations to become independent states. Accordingly, only nationally homogeneous states were considered legitimate.

In his theses on *The Socialist Revolution and the Rights of Nations to Self-Determination*, published in 1916,[67] Lenin provided a broad definition of self-determination as an entitlement of ethnic or national groups to decide whether to secede and form a new state or to demand autonomy within the state where they lived. Shortly after, in his Fifth Point, US President Wilson championed self-determination as a right of peoples freely to choose their government.[68] While self-determination was not envisaged in the League Covenant, Wilson's proposal inspired a number of plebiscites held by the Allies in disputed areas and was inserted in minority. The League mandates system itself was a compromise between self-determination and the interests of the administrative powers. The 'principle of nationalities' was relied upon for the dismemberment of the Austro-Hungarian, Russian, and Ottoman Empires.[69]

17.3.7 The Kellogg-Briand Pact, the Stimson Doctrine and Armed Reprisals

A Pact for the Renunciation of War was made in 1928 on the initiative of the United States and France, the so-called Kellogg-Briand Pact.[70] The Pact consisted of only three Articles. Under Article 1, in particular, the parties condemned, in the names of their respective peoples, recourse to war for the solution of international controversies, and renounced it, as an instrument of national policy, in their relations with one another.[71]

---

[66] Cf. AJIL (1938) Supp., p. 192; G.H. Hackworth, *Digest of International Law* (Washington, 1940–1944), vol. 3, p. 658.

[67] Available at <http://www.marxists.org/archive/lenin/works/1916/jan/x01.htm>.

[68] *Supra*, note 36.

[69] See Daniel Thürer and Thomas Burri, 'Self-determination', in EPIL, 2nd edn., at <http://www.mpepil.com>.

[70] See Stephen C. Neff, *War and the Law of Nations*, cit., pp. 293–296. Further bibliographical references are available at <http://avalon.law.yale.edu/20th_century/kbbib.asp>.

[71] At <http://avalon.law.yale.edu/20th_century/kbpact.asp>.

The Pact impliedly assumed that states retained their right to self-defence, as evidenced in a correspondence between the United States and Great Britain.[72]

Some rather illusory optimism surrounded the making of the Pact, whose preamble solemnly proclaimed that it was aimed at 'uniting the civilized nations of the world'. In all, 57 states adhered to the Pact, including 48 members of the League of Nations, roughly the whole international community of the time. The Pact was binding on some states that were not members of the League of Nations, including the United States (which made reservations to note that its participation did not limit its right to self-defence or require it to act against signatories breaking the agreement). In fact, the Pact had little effect in stopping the rising militarism of the 1930s, and notably Japan's invasion of Manchuria in 1931, Italy's conquest of Ethiopia in 1935–1936, Germany's invasion of Poland in 1939, the Soviet Union's attack on Finland in 1939, and Japan's attack on the United States in 1940.

The Kellogg-Briand Pact was alluded to by US Secretary of State Henry L. Stimson when he enunciated in two identical notes dispatched on 7 January 1932 to Japan and China – in relation to the 1931 Japanese seizure of Manchuria – non-recognition of international territorial changes carried out by military force in breach of the Kellogg-Briand Pact.[73] The doctrine constituted a far-reaching change in the practice of recognition.[74] It was immediately accepted by the League of Nations[75] and by Latin American states,[76] but was not applied in respect of the Italian aggression towards Ethiopia in 1935. It is doubtful whether the doctrine reflected a general rule of international law in the inter-war period.[77]

Neither the League Covenant nor the Kellogg-Briand Pact dealt with measures short of war. It was generally held that such measures continued to be permitted. The well-known *Naulilaa* Arbitral Award of 1928 stated the law on reprisals and proved later considerably influential on state practice.[78]

---

72 Cf. <http://avalon.law.yale.edu/20th_century/kbbr.asp#no1> and <http://avalon.law.yale.edu/20th_century/kbbr.asp#no2>.

73 '[The United States] does not intend to recognize any situation, treaty, or agreement which may be brought about by means contrary to the covenants and obligations of the Pact of Paris of August 27, 1928, to which treaty both China and Japan, as well as the United States, are parties', in J.W. Wheeler-Bennett (ed.), *Documents on International Affairs 1932* (Oxford: Oxford University Press, 1933), p. 26. See David Turns, 'The Stimson Doctrine of Non-Recognition: Its Historical Genesis and Influence on Contemporary International Law', 2 *Chinese Journal of International Law* (2003), pp. 105–143. A precedent of the Stimson Doctrine is often seen in the Tobar Doctrine, concerning non-recognition of governments seizing power through revolution or *coup d'état*, which was included in the Treaty on the Recognition of New Governments concluded by the Central Republics on 20 February 1907 and amended in 1923 (19 AJIL (1925), p. 164).

74 Wilhelm G. Grewe, *The Epochs*, cit., p. 600.

75 An Assembly Resolution of 11 March 1932 stated that '[I]t is incumbent upon the members of the League of Nations not to recognize any situation, treaty, or agreement which may be brought about by means contrary to the Covenant of the League of Nations or to the Pact of Paris', LNOJ (1932), Spec. Supp., No. 101, p. 87.

76 Cf. Article 2 of the Inter-American Convention on the Prevention of War, Non-Aggression and Conciliation (so called Saavedra-Lamas Pact), signed at Rio de Janeiro on 10 October 1933, at <http://avalon.law.yale.edu/20th_century/intam01.asp>.

77 However, the doctrine was also endorsed in Article 11 of the Montevideo Convention on Rights and Duties of States of 1933 (*supra*, note 50).

78 2 UNRIAA, pp. 1011–1033, available at <http://untreaty.un.org/cod/riaa/cases/vol_II/

17.3.8 Conduct of War, Protection of the Victims of War and Disarmament

With regard to *jus in bello* the Hague Conventions and Regulations of 1899 and 1907 were expanded with a number of further instruments.

In 1922 five of the victorious Powers of World War I adopted the Treaty relating to the Use of Submarines and Noxious Gases in Warfare at Washington.[79] The Treaty never entered into force due to the failure of France to ratify it. In 1930 the same signing states concluded the Treaty for the Limitation and Reduction of Naval Armaments,[80] whose Article 22(1) provided that 'submarines must conform to the rules of international law to which surface vessels are subject'. Of some interest are also the 1923 Hague Rules on Air Warfare drafted by a Commission of Jurists charged with preparing such and other rules by the 1922 Washington Conference on the Limitation of Armaments, a private restatement of the law having per se no binding force.[81]

In 1929 a new Wounded and Sick Convention, which took into account the experience of World War I, was made.[82] The amendments adopted were of lesser importance than those of 1906.[83] The same day a Convention relative to the Treatment of Prisoners of War was adopted at Geneva.[84] Worth mentioning is also the Asphyxiating, Poisonous or Other Gases Protocol adopted in 1925 at Geneva.[85]

17.3.9 International Adjudication

In the inter-war period international adjudication generally proved successful and contributed to the clarification and development of international law. Especially prior to 1933 several arbitration treaties were concluded.

A breakthrough was the establishment of the PCIJ in 1921 and the introduction of the so-called compulsory jurisdiction. The Court operated as a standing international court with pre-existing judges and pre-established non-derogable procedural rules. While *ad hoc* arbitration continued to be resorted to, the ICPJ represented an institutional framework having virtually worldwide jurisdiction.[86]

1011-1033.pdf>). Two years later another arbitral award was rendered which restated *Naulilaa* in the *Cysne* case: *ibid.*, at 1035–1077 (at <http://untreaty.un.org/cod/riaa/cases/vol_II/1035-1077.pdf>). See Julia Pfeil, 'Naulilaa Arbitration (Portugal v Germany)', in EPIL, 2nd edn., at <http://www.mpepil.com>.

79 Treaty relating to the Use of Submarines and Noxious Gases in Warfare at Washington of 6 February 1922, at <http://www.icrc.org/ihl.nsf/FULL/270?OpenDocument>.

80 Treaty of London for the Limitation and Reduction of Naval Armaments of 22 April 1930, at <http://www.icrc.org/ihl.nsf/FULL/310?OpenDocument>.

81 At <http://www.icrc.org/ihl.nsf/0/b9ca3866276e91cfc12563cd002d691c?OpenDocument>.

82 Convention for the Amelioration of the Condition of the Wounded and Sick in Armies in the Field of 27 July 1929, at <http://www.icrc.org/ihl.nsf/FULL/300?OpenDocument>.

83 *Supra*, note 24.

84 Convention relative to the Treatment of Prisoners of War of 27 July 1929, at <http://www.icrc.org/ihl.nsf/FULL/305?OpenDocument>.

85 Protocol for the Prohibition of the Use of Asphyxiating, Poisonous or Other Gases, and of Bacteriological Methods of Warfare of 17 June 1925, at <http://www.icrc.org/ihl.nsf/FULL/280?OpenDocument>.

86 All PCIJ decisions are available at <http://www.icj-cij.org/pcij/index.php?p1=9>.

17.3.10 International Terrorism

Following the assassination of King Alexander I of Yugoslavia by Croatian ethnic separatists, the League of Nations took the first step towards defining and outlawing international terrorism. In 1937 the Convention for the Prevention and Punishment of Terrorism was adopted; however, while being signed by 23 states, it was only ratified by one state (India) and acceded to by one (Mexico) and never entered into force. The Convention contained a definition of acts of terrorism in Article 1(2) – which was later to be resumed – as 'criminal acts directed against a State or intended to create a state of terror in the minds of particular persons, or a group of persons, or the general public'.[87]

17.4 THE COLD WAR PERIOD (1945–1989)

It has been debated whether the end of World War II was a turning point in the history of international law.[88] Politically, the post-war period, known as the Cold War period (1947–1991),[89] was marked by a bi-polar system led by two superpowers, the United States and the Soviet Union. Legally, their rivalry actually paralyzed the UN Security Council owing to criss-cross vetoes. Eventually, the bi-polar system was somehow challenged by the Non-Aligned Movement (NAM),[90] a group of developing countries that considered themselves not formally aligned with or against any major power bloc.

The breach of fundamental rules of international law applicable to armed conflict and the commission of mass atrocities during World War II soon pressed for new international law rules aimed at protecting human rights. Another major development of the Cold War period was the decolonization process in the 1950s and 1960s, which gave birth to 'Third World' countries and brought to the fore the North–South divide, in addition to the existing West–East divide. A further sensitive area was the regulation of nuclear weapons and, more generally, of weapons of mass destruction. Nuclear Mutual Assured Destruction (MAD) made the prohibition of the use of force more plausible and acceptable, even a necessity in practical terms.[91]

Attempts at creating regional (or in any event geopolitically homogeneous) integrations and alliances proved successful. In the Western bloc NATO was established in 1949,[92] just as the Council of Europe.[93] In the 1950s the process of European integration peaked in the establishment of the European Communities. Quite a few international organizations, universal and regional, were set up and given an impressively wide range of competences in virtually all areas of life. In the Eastern bloc the Warsaw Pact was formed

---

[87] Cf. 19 League of Nations Doc. C.546M.383 1937 V. See Ben Saul, *The Legal Response of the League of Nations to Terrorism*, 4 *Journal of International Criminal Justice* (2006), pp. 78–102.

[88] See Wilhelm G. Grewe, *The Epochs*, cit., pp. 639–640.

[89] Ebrahim Afsah, 'Cold War (1947–91)', in EPIL, 2nd edn., at <http://www.mpepil.com>.

[90] Cf. <http://www.nam.gov.za/background/background.htm#4.4>.

[91] See Henry D. Sokolski (ed.), *Getting Mad: Nuclear Mutual Assured Destruction, Its Origins and Practice*, at <http://www.strategicstudiesinstitute.army.mil/pdffiles/PUB585.pdf>.

[92] At <http://www.nato.int/cps/en/natolive/index.htm>.

[93] At <http://www.coe.int/DefaultEN.asp>.

in 1955 as a response to NATO.[94] The economic analogue to the Warsaw Pact was the Council for Mutual Economic Assistance (CoMEcon). Other defensive alliances created in the Cold War period include the League of Arab States (LAS),[95] the Organization of American States (OAS)[96] and the Organisation of African Unity (OAU),[97] which were established in 1945, 1948 and 1963, respectively.

17.4.1 The United Nations

In 1945 the Organization of the United Nations was created with a view to replacing the League of Nations.[98] It was clear that the League had failed, but it was equally clear that the idea of a universal organization responsible for world peace and security was more necessary than ever. The United Nations' organs were modelled on the League's, with smaller overlaps of competences between the Council and the Assembly and far more power conferred on the Council. The Assembly was made up of all member states and all of them had one vote, but the Assembly (with very few exceptions) was endowed with only recommendatory powers. The Council consisted of 11 members (later to become 15, when in 1965 an amendment to this effect was adopted), of which five were permanent and enjoyed veto power (the United States, the Soviet Union, the United Kingdom, France and China), while the others were elected for a two-year period by the General Assembly. Not only was the Council composed of few members, it also had the decision-making power under Chapter VII of the Charter. It could make binding and/or coercive measures against states responsible for a threat to the peace, breach of the peace, or an act of aggression. In addition, the Council was given a wide, virtually unlimited discretion. Article 24 expressly stated that it was the Council that had the 'primary responsibility' in the maintenance of international peace and security.

In the *Reparation* Advisory Opinion of 1949 the ICJ held that the UN was an international legal person 'capable of possessing international rights and duties', including the right to bring international claims.[99] The question whether the UN Charter is a veritable constitution of the international community has been much debated since the inception of the Organization, thereby resuming the discussions entertained in respect of the League of Nations.[100]

The United Nations has been far more successful than the League of Nations in codifying customary international law. Article 13 of the Charter provided for both 'codification' and 'progressive development' of international law. To this end, the International Law Commission (ILC), an organ composed of 34 independent experts, was set up in

---

94 For the text cf. <http://www.fordham.edu/halsall/mod/1955warsawpact.html>.

95 At <http://www.arableagueonline.org/las/index_en.jsp>.

96 At <http://www.oas.org/en/default.asp>.

97 On 11 July 2000 the OAU was transformed into the African Union (AU), at <http://www.africa-union.org/root/au/index/index.htm>.

98 For a recent, general overview of the United Nations, see Thomas G. Weiss and Sam Daws (eds), *The Oxford Handbook on the United Nations* (Oxford: Oxford University Press, 2007).

99 *Reparation for Injuries Suffered in the Service of the United Nations*, ICJ, Advisory Opinion of 11 April 1949, p. 179, at <http://www.icj-cij.org/docket/files/4/1835.pdf>.

100 See Bardo Fassbender, *The United Nations Charter as the Constitution of the International Community* (Leiden: Martinus Nijhoff Publishers, 2009).

1947 with General Assembly Resolution 174 (II).[101] The Commission prepared a number of draft Conventions on a variety of areas of international law, some of which were approved by the states, including the law of the sea in 1958,[102] the law of diplomatic and consular relations in 1961 and 1963,[103] and the law of treaties in 1969, 1978 and 1983.[104]

The UN was part of a more general organizational 'system' made up of a number of Specialized Agencies – which were concerned inter alia with issues affecting people's daily life, such as labour (ILO), health (WHO) and education (UNICEF) – , Programmes and Funds.[105]

17.4.2 The Nuremberg and Tokyo Trials

On 8 August 1945 the Nuremberg International Military Tribunal (IMT) was established. Its Statute (the 'Charter') contained a number of provisions that have been resumed in later Statutes of post-Cold War international criminal tribunals.[106] In particular, Article 6 introduced two new categories of international crimes, in addition to war crimes: crimes against humanity – an expression that was traceable to the massacre of Armenians in 1915[107] – and crimes against peace (i.e. aggression). A similar trial was carried out at Tokyo by the International Military Tribunal for the Far East (IMTFE). The Tribunal

---

[101] Res.174(II)of21November1947,at<http://daccess-ods.un.org/access.nsf/Get?OpenAgent&DS=A/RES/174(II)&Lang=E&Area=RESOLUTION>.

[102] Convention on the Territorial Sea and the Contiguous Zone (at <http://untreaty.un.org/ilc/texts/instruments/english/conventions/8_1_1958_territorial_sea.pdf>), Convention on the Continental Shelf (at <http://untreaty.un.org/ilc/texts/instruments/english/conventions/8_1_1958_continental_shelf.pdf>), Convention on Fishing and Conservation of the Living Resources of the High Seas (at <http://untreaty.un.org/ilc/texts/instruments/english/conventions/8_1_1958_fishing.pdf>), Convention on the High Seas (at <http://untreaty.un.org/ilc/texts/instruments/english/conventions/8_1_1958_high_seas.pdf>). All Conventions were made on 29 April 1958. The UN Convention on the Law of the Sea (UNCLOS) (at <http://www.un.org/Depts/los/convention_agreements/texts/unclos/closindx.htm>) was not prepared by the ILC but resulted from the third UN Conference on the Law of the Sea which took place from 1973 through 1982.

[103] Vienna Convention on Diplomatic Relations of 18 April 1961 (at <http://untreaty.un.org/ilc/texts/instruments/english/conventions/9_1_1961.pdf>), Vienna Convention on Consular Relations of 24 April 1963 (at <http://untreaty.un.org/ilc/texts/instruments/english/conventions/9_2_1963.pdf>) and Vienna Convention on Special Missions of 8 December 1969 (at <http://untreaty.un.org/ilc/texts/instruments/english/conventions/9_3_1969.pdf>).

[104] Vienna Convention on the Law of Treaties of 23 May 1969 (at <http://untreaty.un.org/ilc/texts/instruments/english/conventions/1_1_1969.pdf>), Vienna Convention on Succession of States in respect of Treaties (at <http://untreaty.un.org/ilc/texts/instruments/english/conventions/3_2_1978.pdf>), Vienna Convention on Succession of States in respect of State Property, Archives and Debts of 8 April 1983 (at <http://untreaty.un.org/ilc/texts/instruments/english/conventions/3_3_1983.pdf>), Vienna Convention on the Law of Treaties between States and International Organizations or between International Organizations of 21 March 1986 (at <http://untreaty.un.org/ilc/texts/instruments/english/conventions/1_2_1986.pdf>).

[105] Cf. <http://www.un.org/docs/ecosoc/unagencies.html>.

[106] Agreement for the Prosecution and Punishment of the Major War Criminals of the European Axis, and Charter of the International Military Tribunal of 8 August 1945, at <http://www.icrc.org/ihl.nsf/FULL/350?OpenDocument>. See Christian Tomuschat, *The Legacy of Nuremberg*, 4 *Journal of International Criminal Justice* (2006), pp. 830–844.

[107] *Supra*, note 65.

was established on 19 January 1946 by a special proclamation of General MacArthur as the Supreme Commander in the Far East for the Allied Powers after approval of its Statute (the 'Charter').[108] It had jurisdiction over the Japanese leaders for crimes against peace, war crimes, and crimes against humanity committed during World War II.

Both Tribunals were controversial, either because only the victors were the judges and the defendants were only citizens of the defeated – thus justifying the charge of victors' justice – or because they judged the accused for crimes that did not exist as legal crimes at the time of the action. The Nuremberg Tribunal pointed out that '[t]he Charter is not an arbitrary exercise of power on the part of the victorious nations, but . . . it is the expression of international law existing at the time of its creation; and to that extent is itself a contribution to international law'.[109] The enduring legacy of the Nuremberg and Tokyo trials was the recognition of individual criminal responsibility under international law. Famously, the Tribunal held that 'Crimes against International Law are committed by men, not by abstract entities, and only by punishing individuals who commit such crimes can the provisions of International Law be enforced.'[110]

In 1946 General Assembly Res. 95 (I) affirmed 'the principles of international law recognized by the Charter of the Nuremberg Tribunal and the judgment of the Tribunal'.[111] By Res. 488 (V) of 12 December 1950 the General Assembly reiterated the 'principles of Nuremberg' and requested the ILC to prepare a draft code of offences against the peace and security of mankind.[112] The draft code would not be approved until 1996. Besides the 1948 Genocide Convention and the four 1949 Geneva Conventions,[113] worthy of mention is the Statutory Limitations Convention of 1968.[114] Moreover, a number of decisions were handed down during the Cold War period by domestic courts dealing with international crimes, among which the *Eichmann* Judgment by the Israeli Supreme Court of 1963 stands out.[115]

17.4.3 International Human Rights and International Humanitarian Law

Human rights are the most groundbreaking international law rules created in the post-World War II era. They have gradually changed international law as a whole in that they limit the power of rulers vis-à-vis the ruled. A similar rationale, but more limited in scope, also informs (as will be discussed below) the principle of self-determination of peoples to the extent that it prescribes to colonial rulers respect for the will of the colonized to become a state.

Human rights were mentioned in Articles 1(3), 13, 55(c), 62, 68 and 76 of the UN

---

108 At <http://www.jus.uio.no/english/services/library/treaties/04/4-06/military-tribunal-far-east.xml>.

109 At <http://avalon.law.yale.edu/imt/judlawch.asp>.

110 *Ibid.*

111 Res.95(I)of11December1946,at<http://www.icrc.org/ihl.nsf/FULL/355?OpenDocument>.

112 Res. 488 (V) of 12 December 1950, at <http://daccess-dds-ny.un.org/doc/RESOLUTION/GEN/NR0/060/86/IMG/NR006086.pdf?OpenElement>.

113 *Infra*, notes 118 and 132.

114 Convention on the Non-Applicability of Statutory Limitations to War Crimes and Crimes Against Humanity of 26 November 1968, at <http://www2.ohchr.org/english/law/warcrimes.htm>.

115 In 36 ILR, pp. 277–342.

Charter. The Charter also provided in Article 2(7) – a successor of Article 15(8) of the League Covenant[116] – that the Organization could not 'intervene' in matters essentially within the domestic jurisdiction of the member states. On the basis of these provisions the Universal Declaration of Human Rights was adopted in 1948.[117] The Declaration was not legally binding but has provided over time the model for subsequent binding rules. The day before the adoption of the Universal Declaration the Genocide Convention was also made.[118] At a regional level the European Convention on Human Rights (ECHR) was signed in 1950 within the Council of Europe with a view to protecting civil and political rights in Europe.[119] The European Social Charter was additionally made in 1961 to guarantee social and economic rights.[120] The European Convention was extraordinarily innovative in that it provided, besides a list of substantive rights, the creation of a European Commission and a Court of Human Rights for determining whether a violation of the Convention had occurred. Petitions against contracting states deemed to have violated the Convention from either contracting states or individuals were envisaged. The American Convention on Human Rights, modelled on the European Convention, was adopted in 1969.[121] The African Charter on Human and Peoples' Rights was concluded in 1981, providing for a Commission to monitor its application and observance.[122]

In the 1950s and 1960s UN organs, despite the wording of Article 2(7), began to condemn certain states for gross violations of human rights, in particular Southern Rhodesia and South Africa for their apartheid policies. This gave rise to a gradual erosion of Article 2(7) in the field of human rights, a trend that also affected self-determination of peoples. It took time, however, to finalize at the UN a general treaty on human rights. This did not occur until 1966 when two Covenants were concluded, one on civil and political rights and the other on economic, social and cultural rights.[123] The reasons for two separate treaties were the divergences between Western states (advocating civil and political rights) and Communist as well as developing states (championing economic rights). Other universal treaties on specific human rights – often providing for a monitoring committee, although endowed with different powers – have also been con-

---

116 *Supra*, note 55.

117 At <http://www.un.org/en/documents/udhr/>. See Johannes Morsink, *The Universal Declaration of Human Rights. Origins, Drafting & Intent* (Philadelphia: University of Philadelphia Press, 1999).

118 At <http://www2.ohchr.org/english/law/genocide.htm>. The Genocide Convention resumed General Assembly Res. 96 (I) of 11 December 1946, affirming that genocide was a 'crime under international law', at <http://daccess-dds-ny.un.org/doc/RESOLUTION/GEN/NR0/033/47/IMG/NR003347.pdf?OpenElement>.

119 European Convention on Human Rights of 4 November 1950, at <http://www.conventions.coe.int/Treaty/en/Treaties/Html/005.htm>.

120 European Social Charter, at <http://www.conventions.coe.int/Treaty/en/Treaties/Html/035.htm>.

121 American Convention on Human Rights of 22 November 1969, at <http://www.oas.org/juridico/english/treaties/b-32.html>.

122 African Charter of Human and Peoples' Rights of 1981, at <http://www.achpr.org/english/_info/charter_en.html>.

123 At <http://www2.ohchr.org/english/law/ccpr.htm> and <http://www2.ohchr.org/english/law/cescr.htm>.

cluded, in particular regarding slavery in 1953[124] and in 1956,[125] racial discrimination in 1965 (ICERD),[126] discrimination against women in 1979 (CEDAW),[127] torture in 1984 (CAT),[128] and children in 1989 (CRC).[129] Worthy of mention also are the 1951 Refugee Convention[130] and the 1954 Stateless Convention.[131]

Equally swift was the effort to establish rules on the protection of the victims of war. As early as 1949, on the initiative of the Red Cross, the four Geneva Conventions on the victims of war were concluded.[132] Significantly, common Article 3 of the Conventions specifically dealt with internal conflicts. In 1977 the Conventions were supplemented by two Additional Protocols concerning international and non-international conflicts, respectively. Developing countries succeeded in obtaining the inclusion in Article 1(4) of the First Protocol of a provision equalizing, under certain conditions, international conflicts to national liberation wars. Israel did (and has) not ratified the First Protocol for this reason and Article 1(4)'s correspondence to customary international law (hence its application to third party states) is contentious. The Cape Provincial Division of South Africa denied such correspondence in a decision of 1987 in the *Petane* case.[133]

In connection with the rules applying to hostilities, mention is to be made of the question of the legality of nuclear weapons. In a judgment of 1963 in the *Shimoda* case,[134] the District Court of Tokyo held that the atomic bombing of Hiroshima and Nagasaki in 1945 was in breach of the rules of international law governing aerial warfare. Only in 1968 was a Treaty on the Non-Proliferation of Nuclear Weapons (NPT) signed with a view to

---

124 Protocol amending the Slavery Convention of 1926, at <http://avalon.law.yale.edu/20th_century/slavprot.asp>.

125 Supplementary Slavery and Slave Trade Convention of 1956, at <http://avalon.law.yale.edu/20th_century/slave56.asp>.

126 International Convention on the Elimination of All Forms of Racial Discrimination of 21 December 1965, at <http://www2.ohchr.org/english/law/cerd.htm>.

127 Convention on the Elimination of All Forms of Discrimination against Women of 18 December 1979, at <http://www2.ohchr.org/english/law/cedaw.htm>.

128 Convention against Torture and Other Cruel, Inhuman or Degrading Treatment or Punishment of 10 December 1984, at <http://www2.ohchr.org/english/law/cat.htm>.

129 Convention on the Rights of the Child of 20 November 1989, at <http://www2.ohchr.org/english/law/crc.htm>.

130 Convention relating to the Status of Refugees of 28 July 1951, at <http://www2.ohchr.org/english/law/refugees.htm>. See also <http://www.unhcr.org/pages/49da0e466.html>.

131 Convention relating to the Status of Stateless Persons of 28 September 1954, at <http://www2.ohchr.org/english/law/stateless.htm>.

132 Convention (I) for the Amelioration of the Condition of the Wounded and Sick in Armed Forces in the Field, Convention (II) for the Amelioration of the Condition of Wounded, Sick and Shipwrecked Members of Armed Forces at Sea, Convention (III) relative to the Treatment of Prisoners of War, and Convention (IV) relative to the Protection of Civilian Persons in Time of War, all signed on 12 August 1949, at <http://www.icrc.org/ihl.nsf/INTRO?OpenView>.

133 *S.* v. *Petane*, Cape Provincial Division, Judgment of 3 November 1987, at <http://www.icrc.org/ihl-nat.nsf/46707c419d6bdfa24125673e00508145/50c59239e1b869edc1256b0500490120!OpenDocument>.

134 *Ryuichi Shimoda et al.* v. *The State*, District Court of Tokyo, Judgment of 7 December 1963, at <http://www.icrc.org/ihl-nat.nsf/46707c419d6bdfa24125673e00508145/aa559087dbcf1af5c1256a1c0029f14d?OpenDocument>.

limiting the spread of nuclear weapons.[135] It reserved the right to possess nuclear weapons to the five states that are permanent members of the Security Council, thus giving them a further privilege for reasons of global security.

Overall, there were considerable overlaps between international human rights, international crimes and international humanitarian law.

17.4.4 Decolonization and the New International Economic Order (NIEO)

The UN Charter enshrined the principle of self-determination of peoples in Articles 1(2) and 55. Self-determination was not originally intended as implying decolonization, i.e. as a right of colonies to become states, but presumably as non-interference between existing states. The Charter established in Article 73 a trusteeship system for non-self-governing territories which were assigned to UN members, similar to mandataries in the League of Nations. Moreover, Article 2(7) of the Charter prohibited the Organization from interfering in the domestic jurisdiction of member states, and no doubt at that time colonial rule fell within this reserved domain. Articles 73 and 2(7) were swept away by the practice of the Organization in the 1950s and 1960s.[136]

A landmark step towards the interpretation of self-determination as decolonization was General Assembly Res. 1514 (XV) of 1960, proclaiming the Declaration on the Granting of Independence to Colonial Countries and Peoples.[137] General Assembly Res. 1803 (XVII) of 1962 on permanent sovereignty over natural resources affirmed 'the status of permanent sovereignty over natural wealth and resources as a basic constituent of the right to self-determination'.[138] Eventually, the principle of self-determination was included in other international instruments, such as Article 1 of the two UN Covenants on Human Rights[139] and in General Assembly Res. 2625 (XXV) of 24 October 1970 proclaiming the Declaration on Friendly Relations and Co-operation Among States.[140] The ICJ affirmed and articulated the principle of self-determination in the 1971 *Namibia*[141] and in the 1975 *Western Sahara* Advisory Opinions.[142]

In the period from 1945 to 1970 a wave of expropriations and nationalizations took place in many countries, first in Eastern European states within the Soviet bloc

---

135 Treaty on the Non-Proliferation of Nuclear Weapons of 1 July 1968, at <http://www.un.org/events/npt2005/npttreaty.html>.

136 Benedetto Conforti and Carlo Focarelli, *The Law of the United Nations* (Leiden/Boston: Martinus Nijhoff, 2010, 4th edn.), pp. 165–170.

137 Res. 1514 (XV) of 14 December 1960, at <http://daccess-dds-ny.un.org/doc/RESOLUTION/GEN/NR0/152/88/IMG/NR015288.pdf?OpenElement>.

138 Res. 1803 (XVII) of 14 December 1962, at <http://www2.ohchr.org/english/law/resources.htm>.

139 *Supra*, note 123.

140 Res. 2625 (XXV) of 24 October 1970, at <http://daccess-dds-ny.un.org/doc/RESOLUTION/GEN/NR0/348/90/IMG/NR034890.pdf?OpenElement>.

141 *Legal Consequences for States of the Continued Presence of South Africa in Namibia (South West Africa) notwithstanding Security Council Resolution 276 (1970)*, ICJ, Advisory Opinion of 21 June 1971, paras. 52–53, at <http://www.icj-cij.org/docket/files/53/5595.pdf>.

142 *Western Sahara*, ICJ, Advisory Opinion of 16 October 1975, paras. 57–59, at <http://www.icj-cij.org/docket/files/61/6195.pdf>.

and eventually in former colonies after decolonization. Antagonism between capital-importing and capital-exporting states, the former advocating a national standard in the treatment of foreign investors (which were often nationals of former colonial powers) to be exclusively determined by national courts – in accordance with the so-called Calvo clause – and the latter claiming a higher international standard, prevented common rules from emerging. It was generally accepted, however, that states were allowed to proceed to nationalizations for the purposes of reforming their economic systems, providing that a number of conditions were met, including the existence of a public interest and the payment of compensation. What remained uncertain was the amount of compensation due. Most investment disputes were settled through lump-sum agreements providing for an amount that was never the value of the commercial worth of the property nationalized. Over time, however, developing countries took a pragmatic approach: while critiquing foreign investment at the international level and claiming economic sovereignty, they often concluded bilateral investment treaties (BITs) for the purposes of their economic development. In 1965 the International Centre for the Settlement of Investment Disputes (ICSID) was established to provide facilities for conciliation and arbitration of international investment disputes[143] and in 1985 the Multilateral Investment Guarantee Agency (MIGA) was created with a view to insuring investments against losses relating to various risks, including currency transfer restrictions, expropriations, war and civil disturbances.[144]

Attempts to govern corporate activities in host countries began within the UN in 1974 with the establishment of the Commission on Transnational Corporations (UNCTC). A series of drafts were produced without much success and the Commission gave up in 1992. The Organisation for Economic Co-operation and Development (OECD) issued Guidelines for Multinational Enterprises in 1976[145] and the ILO produced a Tripartite Declaration of Principles Concerning Multinational Enterprises in 1977.[146]

Most importantly, in 1974 the UN General Assembly adopted a Declaration, a Programme of Action and a Charter of Economic Rights and Duties of States on the establishment of a New International Economic Order (NIEO).[147] The Charter laid down a number of basic principles destined to introduce social justice in international affairs, including the principles of 'common heritage of mankind' (article 29) and of 'sustainable development' (article 30). All the efforts towards development peaked in 1986 when the UN General Assembly adopted Res. 41/128 on the right to development.[148]

---

143 Convention on the Settlement of Investment Disputes between States and Nationals of Other States of 18 March 1965, at <http://icsid.worldbank.org/ICSID/StaticFiles/basicdoc/partA.htm>.

144 Cf. <http://www.miga.org/>.

145 At <http://www.oecd.org/dataoecd/56/36/1922428.pdf>.

146 At <http://www.ilo.org/wcmsp5/groups/public/---ed_emp/---emp_ent/documents/publication/wcms_101234.pdf>.

147 Resolutions 3201 (S-VI) and 3202 (S-VI) of May 1, 1974, at <http://www.un.org/ga/search/view_doc.asp?symbol=A/9559&Lang=E>; Res. 3281 (XXIX) of December 12, 1974, at <http://daccess-dds-ny.un.org/doc/RESOLUTION/GEN/NR0/738/83/IMG/NR073883.pdf?OpenElement>.

148 Res. 41/128 of 4 December 1986, at <http://www.un.org/documents/ga/res/41/a41r128.htm>.

17.4.5 Proliferation of International Organizations

If decolonization brought about a multiplication and diversification of states, other international actors increasingly took an active part in international relations, in particular inter-governmental organizations (IOs), leaving aside some relevance of multinational corporations (MNCs) and non-governmental organizations (NGOs).

Soon after World War II, IOs, both universal and regional, blossomed. The object and purpose of IOs, far from creating a world government, was to enhance the co-operation between member states. Most of them, however, were given only recommendatory powers; a meaningful exception was the decision-making and coercive powers entrusted to the UN Security Council under Articles 41 and 42 of the UN Charter. The major problems of IOs were with their effectiveness and ability to direct member states' behaviour. Regional organizations worked better since they could profit from a relative homogeneity of their member states. Another problem was IOs' democratic deficit as their organs mostly consisted of delegates from national governments rather than from parliaments, let alone selected through a direct election. Only in the European Communities was direct election of the Parliament achieved in 1979, although the decision-making power remained in the hands of the national executives. Another feature that weakened IOs was their financial dependence on member states. The European Communities, given their ultimate federal objective, no doubt were the most advanced IOs created in the Cold War period.

17.4.6 National Claims to Control of Spaces and the Common Heritage of Mankind

Claims to rights of exploitation of natural resources, concomitant with scientific and technological advancements, were extended by coastal states to the sea at an increasing distance off the coast.

A landmark was US President Harry S. Truman's Proclamation No. 2667 of 28 September 1945 claiming the right of the United States to exclusive exploitation of natural resources of soil and subsoil of the continental shelf, as defined in geological terms and regardless of effective occupation.[149] Other states immediately followed suit and within a few years the legal regime of the continental shelf crystallized into general international law. Coastal states were given 'sovereign rights' beyond their territorial sea but only as far as the soil and sub-soil were concerned, while the freedom of fishing and navigation in the superjacent waters remained open to the use of all states. This regime was codified by one of the four Conventions adopted at the First UN Conference on the Law of the Sea.[150]

As far as the full control of coastal states to territorial waters was concerned, a Second Conference on the Law of the Sea was convened in 1960 by the UN to reach an agreement on the width of the territorial sea, an issue that had remained unsolved in 1958, again with no results.

The race to the natural resources of the oceans and the trend towards extending the

---

149 At <http://www.presidency.ucsb.edu/ws/index.php?pid=12332>.

150 For all conventions on the law of the sea cf. *supra*, note 102.

powers of coastal states continued thereafter. During the Third UN Conference on the Law of the Sea, which spanned from 1974 to 1982 and resulted in the UN Convention on the Law of the Sea of 1982 (ICLOS), the 'exclusive economic zone' (EEZ) took hold in state practice. The EEZ, advocated by developing countries, rapidly crystallized into a customary international law rule. As a result, the freedom of fishing, which in the past was typical of the high seas, was now excluded in this very large belt of sea off the coast.

The 1982 Convention also defined the width of the territorial sea – up to a limit not exceeding 12 nautical miles, measured from baselines – and provided an updated definition of continental shelf which took note of the case law developed by the ICJ with and after the *North Sea* Judgment of 1969.[151]

Part XI of the UN Convention, dealing with the 'Area', i.e. 'the seabed and ocean floor and subsoil thereof, beyond the limits of national jurisdictions', proved the most contentious point between developed and developing countries. It provided, in Article 136, that 'the Area and its resources are the common heritage of mankind'. The principle had first been launched by the Ambassador of Malta, Mr Arvid Pardo, in the UN General Assembly on 1 November 1967.[152] The Outer Space treaty, signed at the beginning of 1967, had already provided that outer space was 'the province of all mankind'.[153] The proposal was later included in Article 29 of the 1974 Charter of the Economic Rights and Duties of States and in the 1979 Moon Treaty.[154] Part XI of the Convention, resulting in the adopted 1982 text, was fiercely opposed by developed countries. It was only after the end of the Cold War, in 1994, that the Convention was modified through an *ad hoc* Implementing Agreement which introduced liberal principles into the legal regime of Part XI.[155] Only then was the Convention ratified by developed states and swiftly came into effect. With its entry into force, the International Tribunal for the Law of the Sea (ITLOS) was established under Annex XV of the Convention.[156]

Turning to outer space, on 4 October 1957 the Soviet Union launched *Sputnik* – the first Earth-orbiting artificial satellite, whose unanticipated announcement ignited the Space Race between the two superpowers – without asking for authorization of the states above whose territories the Sputnik orbited and without meeting with any protest. It became immediately clear that 'outer' space – i.e. the space beyond air space, although it was unclear where the dividing line lay – was subject to a different legal regime than air space. Outer space was instantly regarded as open to every state's exploration and use, a principle immediately laid down in a number of resolutions adopted by the UN General Assembly, including Res. 1962 (XVIII) of 1963, containing the Declaration of legal

---

151 *North Sea Continental Shelf (Federal Republic of Germany/Denmark)*, ICJ, Judgment of 20 February 1969, at <http://www.icj-cij.org/docket/files/51/5535.pdf>.

152 Cf. Arvid Pardo, *The Common Heritage: Selected Papers on Oceans and World Order 1967–1974* (Malta: Malta University Press, 1975).

153 *Infra*, note 159.

154 *Supra*, note 147, and *infra*, note 161. See Jennifer Frakes, 'The Common Heritage of Mankind Principle and the Deep Seabed, Outer Space, and Antarctica: Will Developed and Developing Nations Reach a Compromise?', *Wisconsin International Law Journal* (2003), pp. 409–434.

155 Agreement relating to the implementation of Part XI of the United Nations Convention on the Law of the Sea of 10 December 1982, at <http://www.un.org/Depts/los/convention_agreements/texts/unclos/closindxAgree.htm>.

156 At <http://www.itlos.org/start2_en.html>.

principles governing the activities of states in the exploration and uses of outer space.[157] In legal doctrine the notion of 'instant custom' was coined.[158] The principles governing outer space were finally translated into the Outer Space Treaty of 1967, whose Article 1 defined outer space as 'the province of all mankind'.[159] Other multilateral treaties, subsequently concluded on specific aspects of outer space,[160] were designed to detail some principles already set out in the Outer Space Treaty. As mentioned, the Moon Agreement of 1979 expressly stated, in Article 11, that 'the moon and its natural resources are the common heritage of mankind', a provision strongly contested by developed countries.[161]

As for Antarctica, seven 'claimant states' asserted sovereign rights over portions of the continent on the basis of the 'sector theory'. Some claims overlapped, causing friction. Claims were not generally recognized. Finally, claims and objections to them were all 'frozen' by the Antarctic Treaty made in 1959, to which all claimant states and major powers (including the permanent members of the UN Security Council) adhered.[162]

17.4.7 Recourse to Force

Chapter VII of the UN Charter established a system of collective security centralized in the Security Council and premised on the ban on the use of force. In the landmark *Nicaragua* Judgment of 1986 the ICJ held that the prohibition on the use of force set out in Article 2(4) reflected a rule of customary international law.[163] In the Charter the prohibition on the use of force was accompanied by two exceptions in Article 51 (individual and collective self-defence) and in Article 42 (armed operations carried out by the Security Council). Also self-defence was recognized by the ICJ in the *Nicaragua* Judgment as customary international law.[164] In fact, the system was inspired by an idealized, state-modelled approach that immediately proved hardly feasible.

The system provided that in case the Council found a threat to the peace, a breach of the peace or an act of aggression (Article 39), it could adopt measures either not involving the use of force, notably economic sanctions (Article 41), or involving the use of

---

157 Res. 1962 (XVIII) of 13 December 1963, at <http://daccess-dds-ny.un.org/doc/RESOLUTION/GEN/NR0/186/37/IMG/NR018637.pdf?OpenElement>.

158 Bin Cheng, 'United Nations Resolutions on Outer Space: "Instant" International Customary Law', 5 *Indian Journal of International Law* (1965), pp. 23–48.

159 Treaty on Principles Governing the Activities of States in the Exploration and Use of Outer Space, including the Moon and Other Celestial Bodies of 27 January 1967, available (along with all other treaties on outer space) at <http://www.unoosa.org/pdf/publications/STSPACE11E.pdf>.

160 Cf. the 1968 Agreement on the Rescue of Astronauts, the Return of Astronauts and the Return of Objects Launched into Outer Space, the 1972 Convention on International Liability for Damage Caused by Space Objects and the 1975 Convention on Registration of Objects Launched into Outer Space.

161 Agreement Governing the Activities of States on the Moon and Other Celestial Bodies of 1979.

162 At <http://www.ats.aq/documents/ats/treaty_original.pdf>. For further information see <http://www.ats.aq/e/ats_treaty.htm>.

163 *Military and Paramilitary Activities in and against Nicaragua (Nicaragua v. United States of America)*, ICJ, Judgment of 27 June 1986, pp. 277–278, at <http://www.icj-icj.org/docket/files/70/6503.pdf> (at para. 188).

164 *Ibid.*, at paras. 193–195.

force (Article 42). In the maintenance of international peace and security the Council was given the 'primary responsibility' and member states agreed that 'in carrying out its duties under this responsibility the Security Council acts on their behalf' (Article 24). The General Assembly had only recommendatory powers, although in 1950 it adopted Resolution 377 (V) called 'Uniting for Peace' claiming a power to adopt security measures in case the Council was paralyzed by the veto of its permanent members.[165] The question of criss-cross vetoes had already given rise to two advisory opinions of the ICJ, in 1948[166] and in 1950,[167] concerning admission of new members to the Organization.

The UN system presupposed that the Council had an army of its own and Article 43 of the Charter stipulated that agreements should soon have been made in order for member states to place military contingents at the disposal of the Council. Such agreements, however, were not made. As a result, the Council created 'peacekeeping' missions consisting of military observers and lightly armed troops with monitoring, reporting and confidence-building roles in support of ceasefires and limited peace agreements.[168] The Council also authorized the use of force once in 1950, on the occasion of the Korean War, taking advantage of the temporary absence of the Soviet delegate in protest at the failure by the Council to substitute Formosa for the People's Republic of China in the permanent seat.[169] Apart from a Council's mandate in 1948 to deploy military observers to the Middle East to monitor the Armistice Agreement between Israel and its Arab neighbours, the first peacekeeping mission was set up by the General Assembly in 1956 (UNEF I) on the basis of the 1950 *Uniting for Peace* Resolution[170] and served later as a model for all subsequent missions, which were invariably set up by the Council, beginning with ONUC in Congo in 1960.[171] The legal basis in the Charter of peacekeeping was initially and remained later obscure. Secretary-General Dag Hammarskjöld even referred to it as belonging to 'Chapter Six and a Half' of the Charter, placing it somewhere between peaceful methods of settling disputes (Chapter VI) and coercive action (Chapter VII), a rather unsatisfactory answer. The question was soon raised by a number of members that contested the legality of UNEF I and ONUC and refused to bear their costs. In the *Certain Expenses* Advisory Opinion of 1962 the ICJ held that both operations were in keeping with the Charter.[172]

It has been suggested that four 'seismic' developments transformed the world soon after the signature of the UN Charter and undermined the Charter provisions concerning the use of force: (a) the advent of the Cold War, which froze the UN Security Council's

---

165 At <http://www.un.org/Depts/dhl/landmark/pdf/ares377e.pdf>.

166 *Conditions of Admission of a State to Membership in the United Nations (Article 4 of the Charter)*, ICJ, Advisory Opinion of 28 May 1948, at <http://www.icj-cij.org/docket/files/3/1821.pdf>.

167 *Competence of the General Assembly for the Admission of a State to the United Nations*, ICJ, Advisory Opinion of 3 March 1950, at <http://www.icj-cij.org/docket/files/3/1821.pdf>.

168 Cf. <http://www.un.org/en/peacekeeping/>.

169 Res. 83 of 27 June 1950 and Res. 84 of 31 July 1950, at <http://daccess-dds-ny.un.org/doc/RESOLUTION/GEN/NR0/064/97/IMG/NR006497.pdf?OpenElement>.

170 Cf. <http://www.un.org/en/peacekeeping/missions/past/unefi.htm>.

171 Cf. <http://www.un.org/en/peacekeeping/missions/past/onuc.htm>.

172 *Certain Expenses of the United Nations (Article 17, paragraph 2, of the Charter)*, ICJ, Advisory Opinion of 20 July 1962, at <http://www.icj-cij.org/docket/files/49/5259.pdf>.

ability to guarantee collective security, (b) the state practice of indirect (rather than traditional direct) aggression through the sending by a State of armed bands, groups, irregulars or mercenaries, with a view to carrying out acts of armed force against another state, (c) the technological transformation of weaponry, which tended to make obsolete Article 51 and to justify anticipatory self-defence, and (d) the spread of human rights rules, their link to threats to the peace and the need for humanitarian intervention to repress tyrants.[173]

The paralysis of the Security Council was rarely avoided. This occurred on two occasions when the Council adopted sanctions under Article 41 of the Charter against Southern Rhodesia in 1966 and against South Africa in 1977 because of their policy of apartheid.[174] Indirect aggression 'of such gravity' as to amount to direct aggression or consisting in a 'substantial involvement therein' was listed among the acts amounting to aggression by the General Assembly in Article 3(g) of the Definition of aggression annexed to Resolution 3314 (XXIX) of 1974,[175] and as 'armed attack' for the purposes of self-defence under both Article 51 of the UN Charter and customary international law by the ICJ in the *Nicaragua* Judgment of 1986.[176] Admittedly, self-defence was routinely invoked in the Cold War period to justify almost any kind of military intervention. However, pre-emptive self-defence was generally condemned, as evidenced by Security Council Res. 487 of 1981 condemning the Israeli bombing of the Iraqi reactor *Osiraq*.[177] Also the US quarantine aimed at preventing the installation in Cuba of missile-launching ramps coming from the Soviet Union was, apart from its inevitability from a security perspective, generally condemned. Although there were a few instances of claimed humanitarian intervention, such as on the occasion of India's invasion of East Pakistan (later to become Bangladesh) in 1971, the general view was against its legality, as the ICJ had the opportunity to state in the 1986 *Nicaragua* Judgment.[178] As opposed to self-defence, armed reprisals were routinely condemned, both by the Security Council and by the General Assembly, although the criteria for distinguishing the two figures remained unclear.

On other occasions force was used to target terrorist bases in the territory of other states. For example, in 1985 Israel struck Tunis[179] and in 1986 the US struck Tripoli and Benghazi in Libya,[180] both with a view to targeting the POL's headquarters there. These actions were also generally condemned by the international community.

---

173 Thomas M. Franck, *Recourse to Force. State Action Against Threats and Armed Attacks* (Cambridge: Cambridge University Press, 2002), pp. 3–4.

174 See Res. 232 of 16 December 1966 and Res. 253 of 29 May 1968 against Southern Rhodesia (repealed by Resolution 460 of 21 December 1979) and Res. 418 of 4 November 1977 against South Africa (repealed by Res. 919 of 26 May 1994).

175 Cf. Declaration on the definition of aggression adopted by the General Assembly with Res. 3314 of 14 December 1974, at <http://daccess-dds-ny.un.org/doc/RESOLUTION/GEN/NR0/739/16/IMG/NR073916.pdf?OpenElement>.

176 *Supra*, note 163 (at para. 195).

177 Res. 487 (1981) of 19 June 1981, at <http://daccess-dds-ny.un.org/doc/RESOLUTION/GEN/NR0/418/74/IMG/NR041874.pdf?OpenElement>.

178 *Supra*, note 163 (at para. 267).

179 Cf. Security Council Res. 573 of 4 October 1985, at <http://daccess-dds-ny.un.org/doc/RESOLUTION/GEN/NR0/489/10/IMG/NR048910.pdf?OpenElement>.

180 Cf. UN Doc. S/PV.2674 and S/PV.2675.

17.4.8 Trade and Finance

At Bretton Woods the International Monetary Fund (IMF) and the Bank for International Reconstruction and Development (IBRD), commonly known as the World Bank, were established in 1944 with a view to avoiding the inward policies of the inter-war period. At first the World Bank was concerned with economic reconstruction in Europe; subsequently, it focused on development in general. The Bretton Woods arrangement also provided for the establishment of an International Trade Organization (ITO) for a multilateral system of trade liberalization. The ITO failed, inter alia, because of the United States' refusal to ratify its Statute. However, Part IV of the ITO Statute (the 'Havana Charter') was adopted in 1947 and temporarily applied as the 'General Agreement on Tariffs and Trade' (GATT) from 1 January 1948. The 'temporary' application of GATT, however, lasted until 1994, when GATT was included, as GATT 1994, within the Agreements managed by the new World Trade Organization (WTO).

In 1964 the United Nations Conference on Trade and Development (UNCTAD)[181] issued a 'Joint Declaration of the Seventy-Seven Countries' and founded the Group of 77 (G-77), a coalition of developing countries whose goal was to enhance their negotiating capacity in the UN especially by promoting trade for economic growth.[182] Shortly after its establishment UNCTAD became a subsidiary organ of the UN General Assembly.[183] As a result, in 1966 a new Part IV (devoted to 'Trade and Development') was included in the GATT, exempting developing countries from reciprocity, and in 1979 an 'enabling clause', introducing a 'Generalized System of Preferences' (GSP), was also made part of GATT with a view to making exports from developing countries more competitive relative to other countries.

In 1971 the world witnessed the collapse of the dollar exchange standard based on fixed currency rates, as established at Bretton Woods in 1944, and the gradual emergence of a new international economic order based on floating exchange rates. The 1971 crisis was in part due to the creation of the Organization of the Petroleum Exporting Countries (OPEC),[184] operating in a cartel-like fashion to control oil supply and prices. As runaway inflation and deep recession followed, Western governments began fully to embrace neoliberalism. The new international neo-liberal economic order was propelled by British Prime Minister Margaret Thatcher and US President Ronald Reagan when they upheld, in the 1980s, free trade, deregulation, privatization, along with spending and tax cuts ('Washington Consensus'). Tariffs had already been significantly reduced since 1948 as a result of the application of GATT. The neoliberal project was immediately endorsed by the IMF and by the World Bank inducing other states, in particular developing countries, to follow it for 'restructuring' their systems as a condition for obtaining loans and assistance.

---

181 At <http://www.unctad.org/Templates/Startpage.asp?intItemID=2068&lang=1>.

182 At <http://www.g77.org/>.

183 Res. 1995 (XIX) of 30 December 1964, at <http://daccess-dds-ny.un.org/doc/RESOLUTION/GEN/NR0/210/89/IMG/NR021089.pdf?OpenElement>.

184 Cf. <http://www.opec.org>.

17.4.9 Environment

In the 1960s the environmental issue came to the fore. Few if any international law rules existed in this field. The environment fell in principle within the domestic jurisdiction of states. One principle was uncontroversial enough, namely the duty of states not to allow their territory to be used in such a way as to damage the environment of other (in particular of neighbouring) states. The principle was famously stated in the *Trail Smelter* Arbitration in 1941.[185] It was later restated in more general terms by the ICJ in the *Corfu Channel* Judgment of 1949 in terms of 'every State's obligation not to allow knowingly its territory to be used for acts contrary to the rights of other States'[186] and, in connection with environmental protection, in a few soft law instruments, notably in Principle 21 of the Stockholm Declaration on the human environment of 1972,[187] and in Principle 21(d) of the 1982 World Charter for Nature.[188] Another principle on which there was general agreement was the duty of co-operation and consultation between the states concerned, as laid down in the *Lac Lanoux* Arbitration,[189] a principle later reiterated, for example, in Principle 24 of the Rio Declaration of 1972.

As for marine pollution the entire Part XII of the UN Convention on the Law of the Sea of 1982 was devoted to environmental protection. Article 192 provided an obligation to protect and preserve the marine environment and Article 197 stipulated a duty of co-operation. The Convention, however, for the reasons stated above,[190] entered into force only after the end of the Cold War period. Of interest also are treaties dealing with specific problems relating to marine pollution, such as the Brussels Intervention Convention of 1969, concluded after the *Torrey Canyon* incident of 1967 off the British coast,[191] the London Pollution Convention of 1973,[192] the London Dumping Convention of 1972,[193] the Geneva Transboundary Air Pollution Convention of 1979,[194] and many others.

As regards the protection of the global environment, the Vienna Ozone Layer Convention of 1985 is worth mentioning.[195]

---

185 In AJIL (1939), pp. 182–212, and (1941), pp. 684–734, at 716–717.

186 *Corfu Channel (United Kingdom of Great Britain and Northern Ireland v. Albania)*, ICJ, Judgment of 9 April 1949, p. 22, at <http://www.icj-cij.org/docket/files/1/1645.pdf>.

187 At <http://www.unep.org/Documents.Multilingual/Default.asp?DocumentID=97&ArticleID=1503>.

188 UN General Assembly Res. 37/7 of 28 October 1982, at <http://www.unep.org/Law/PDF/UNEPEnv-LawGuide&PrincN05.pdf>.

189 Cf. 24 ILR, pp. 101–142.

190 *Supra*, note 155.

191 International Convention Relating to Intervention on the High Seas in Cases of Oil Pollution Casualties of 29 November 1969, at <http://www.vilp.de/Enpdf/e280.pdf>.

192 International Convention for the Prevention of Pollution from Ships of 2 November 1973 (MARPOL), at <http://sedac.ciesin.columbia.edu/entri/texts/pollution.from.ships.1973.html>.

193 Convention on the Prevention of Marine Pollution by Dumping of Wastes and Other Matter of 13 November 1972, at <http://www.admiraltyguide.com/conven/dumping1972.html>.

194 Convention on Long-range Transboundary Air Pollution of 13 November 1979, at <http://www.unece.org/env/lrtap/full%20text/1979.CLRTAP.e.pdf>.

195 Convention for the Protection of the Ozone Layer, at <http://www.unep.org/ozone/pdfs/viennaconvention2002.pdf>.

Since the issuance in 1987 of the Brundtland Report *Our Common Future*, the link between economy and environment and the topic of 'sustainable development' – already stipulated in the NIEO Charter of 1974[196] – has come to the fore and has taken root in the international debate. According to the Report '[s]ustainable development is development that meets the needs of the present without compromising the ability of future generations to meet their own needs'.

17.4.10 International Terrorism

International terrorism during the Cold War period primarily referred to groups conducting wars for self-determination, especially the Palestinian Liberation Organization (PLO). Contingent (allegedly 'terrorist') incidents raised the question of creating new international law rules on international terrorism to face events similar to those that had occasioned such rules. Since the 1960s, a number of multilateral treaties were made against specific crimes that were usually associated with international terrorism,[197] including the 1963 Aircraft Convention,[198] the 1970 Unlawful Seizure Convention,[199] the 1971 Civil Aviation Convention,[200] the 1973 Diplomatic Agents Convention,[201] the 1979 Hostages Convention,[202] the 1980 Nuclear Materials Convention,[203] the 1988 Airport Protocol,[204] the 1988 Maritime Convention,[205] and the 1988 Fixed Platform Protocol.[206] As they dealt with specific crimes, these Conventions did not provide a general definition of terrorism. Other treaties were concluded at a regional level, such as the 1971 OAS

---

196 *Supra*, note 147.

197 All conventions are available at <http://treaties.un.org/Pages/DB.aspx?path=DB/studies/page2_en.xml&menu=MTDSG>.

198 Tokyo Convention on Offences and Certain Other Acts Committed on Board Aircraft of 14 September 1963, at <http://treaties.un.org/doc/db/Terrorism/Conv1-english.pdf>.

199 The Hague Convention for the Suppression of Unlawful Seizure of Aircraft of 16 December 1970, at <http://treaties.un.org/doc/db/Terrorism/Conv2-english.pdf>.

200 Montreal Convention for the Suppression of Unlawful Acts against the Safety of Civil Aviation of 23 September 1971, at <http://treaties.un.org/doc/db/Terrorism/Conv3-english.pdf>.

201 New York Convention on the Prevention and Punishment of Crimes against Internationally Protected Persons of 14 December 1973, at <http://treaties.un.org/doc/db/Terrorism/english-18-7.pdf>.

202 New York International Convention against the taking of hostages of 17 December 1979, at <http://treaties.un.org/doc/db/Terrorism/english-18-5.pdf>.

203 Vienna Convention on the Physical Protection of Nuclear Material of 3 March 1980, at <http://treaties.un.org/doc/db/Terrorism/Conv6-english.pdf>.

204 Montreal Protocol for the Suppression of Unlawful Acts of Violence at Airports Serving International Civil Aviation, supplementary to the Convention for the Suppression of Unlawful Acts against the Safety of Civil Aviation of 24 February 1988, at <http://treaties.un.org/doc/db/Terrorism/Conv7-english.pdf>.

205 Rome Convention for the Suppression of Unlawful Acts against the Safety of Maritime Navigation of 10 March 1988, at <http://treaties.un.org/doc/db/Terrorism/Conv8-english.pdf>.

206 Rome Protocol for the Suppression of Unlawful Acts against the Safety of Fixed Platforms Located on the Continental Shelf of 10 March 1988, at <http://treaties.un.org/doc/db/Terrorism/Conv9-english.pdf>.

Convention,[207] the 1977 European Convention[208] and the 1987 SAARC Convention.[209] These latter, by contrast, did provide a general, albeit obviously not universal, definition of international terrorism.

A universally accepted definition of international terrorism was not even reached when in 1972 the UN General Assembly set up an *ad hoc* committee to consider a Draft Comprehensive Convention on international terrorism. One of the major controversial points was whether liberation wars in Africa during decolonization constituted terrorism. Western countries confined terrorism to acts performed by individuals and groups, as well as state-sponsored individuals and groups, whereas non-Western states extended terrorism to cover acts performed by states and particularly by governments that oppressed peoples under colonial domination, apartheid or military occupation. Clearly one's terrorist was another's freedom fighter.

17.4.11 Conceptualizations of International Justice, Obligations *Erga Omnes* and *Jus Cogens*

Alongside decolonization, the prohibition of aggression and the protection of international human rights, new patterns were devised in state practice (in parallel to legal doctrine) to conceptualize basic values of the international community as a whole. Emphasis was placed on solidarity, 'welfarist', and ultimate social justice among all states and their peoples. This trend peaked in the 1970s.

As discussed earlier, in 1967 the concept of 'common heritage of mankind' was proposed by Mr Pardo.[210] The previous year the ICJ had disappointed Third World states in denying standing to Liberia and Ethiopia in the *South West Africa* cases.[211] On that occasion the Court had rejected the notion than an *actio popularis* was provided for by international law for the protection of common interests, such as in that particular case the cessation of the South Africa's trustee mandate over Namibia. In 1970, arguably as an apology, the ICJ pronounced the most famous words of its judicial history in introducing obligations *erga omnes*. In a dictum of the *Barcelona Traction* Judgment, the Court defined obligations *erga omnes* as 'obligations towards the international community as a whole' and gave as examples those deriving from the outlawing of acts of aggression and of genocide, as also the principles and rules concerning the basic rights of the human person, including protection from slavery and racial discrimination.[212] The concept,

---

[207] Washington Convention to Prevent and Punish Acts of Terrorism Taking the Form of Crimes against Persons and Related Extortion that are of International Significance of 2 February 1971, at <http://treaties.un.org/doc/db/Terrorism/Conv16-english.pdf>.

[208] European Convention on the Suppression of Terrorism of 27 January 1977, at <http://treaties.un.org/doc/db/Terrorism/Conv15-english.pdf>.

[209] Convention on Suppression of Terrorism of 4 November 1987, at <http://treaties.un.org/doc/db/Terrorism/Conv18-english.pdf>.

[210] *Supra*, note 152.

[211] *South West Africa (Liberia v. South Africa)*, Proceeding joined with *South West Africa (Ethiopia v. South Africa)* on 20 May 1961 *(Second Phase)*, ICJ, Judgment of 18 July 1966, para. 88, at <http://www.icj-cij.org/docket/files/47/4955.pdf>.

[212] *Barcelona Traction, Light and Power Company, Limited (Belgium v. Spain) (New Application: 1962)* of 5 February 1970, paras. 33–34, at <http://www.icj-cij.org/docket/files/50/5387.pdf>.

broadly understood, was not novel,[213] and the ICJ itself had somehow prefigured it in the *Reservations* Advisory Opinion of 1951;[214] but the historical context surrounding the ICJ's dictum in *Barcelona Traction* played a key role in spreading the feeling of a revolution in the structure of international law.

The previous year, in 1969, the concept of *jus cogens* had also been adopted, over the dissent of France, at the Vienna Conference on the Law of Treaties.[215] Article 53 of the Vienna Convention on the Law of Treaties equated *jus cogens* with 'a norm accepted and recognized by the international community of States as a whole as a norm from which no derogation is permitted and which can be modified only by a subsequent norm of general international law having the same character'.[216] The concept of *jus cogens* drew upon sparse doctrinal contributions made in the inter-war period,[217] which had revived some natural law hints at the concept of non-derogable law made by the Roman-law-inspired classics of international law, including Emer de Vattel.[218] *Jus cogens* was then conceptualized as a limit to the content of treaties: treaties *contra bonos mores* were thought to be null and void basically on the basis of a general principle of law.

Interestingly, during the Vienna Conference it was Socialist and Third World states that pressed for *jus cogens* – understood to cover self-determination of peoples and the prohibition of aggression, genocide, slavery, racial discrimination and apartheid, in short what was felt to be blameful of past European colonialism – while, justifiably, Western states took a sceptical stance at best. *Jus cogens* was regarded by non-Western states as a technical tool to supersede traditional (European, colonialist and capitalist) international law by new principles worked out by the whole of states,[219] or at least (from the Soviet perspective) to protect the principles underlying the doctrine of peaceful coexistence.[220] *Jus cogens* had inter alia the potential to cause the invalidity of past unequal treaties between European colonizers and former colonies. Western states naturally feared that *jus cogens* could be instrumentally used by non-Western states simply to bypass or to overwhelm undesired (but still 'positively' existing) rules, and to bring about a radical change in international law.[221]

---

[213] Maurizio Ragazzi, *The Concept of International Obligations* Erga Omnes (Oxford: Clarendon Press, 1997), pp. 18–42; Christian J. Tams, *Enforcing Obligations* Erga Omnes *in International Law* (Cambridge: Cambridge University Press, 2005), pp. 48–52.

[214] *Reservations to the Convention on the Prevention and Punishment of the Crime of Genocide*, ICJ, Advisory Opinion of 28 May 1951, p. 23, at <http://www.icj-cij.org/docket/files/12/4283.pdf>.

[215] See Alexander Orakhelashvili, *Peremptory Norms in International Law* (Oxford: Oxford University Press, 2006).

[216] *Supra*, note 104.

[217] Cf. Alfred Verdross, *Forbidden Treaties in International Law*, 31 AJIL (1937), pp. 571–577; Id., *Trattati* contra bonos mores, 29 *Rivista di diritto internazionale* (1937), pp. 3 ff.

[218] Cf. Emer de Vattel, *The Law of Nations or the Principles of Natural Law Applied to the Conduct and the Affairs of Nations and of Sovereigns* (Washington: Carnegie Institution of Washington, 1916; translation of the edition of 1758), Book II, Ch. 12, at para. 161.

[219] See, e.g., the statement at the Vienna Conference of Sierra Leone, in *United Nations Conference on the Law of Treaties*, First Session (Vienna, 26 March–24 May 1968), *Official Records*, Summary Records of the Plenary Meetings of the Committee of the Whole, p. 300, para. 9.

[220] See, e.g., the statements of Romania and Ukraine, *ibid.*, pp. 312–313, paras. 55–63, and p. 322, para. 6.

[221] The major opponent to *jus cogens* was France (*ibid.*, pp. 309–310, paras. 26–34). Doubts

The basic ideas underlying *jus cogens* and obligations *erga omnes* were later revived in Article 19 of the ILC Draft Articles on State Responsibility worked out in the 1970s on the initiative of Special Rapporteur R. Ago.[222]

17.4.12 International Adjudication

The Cold War period saw a decline in the commitment to international adjudication. States of the Soviet bloc, in particular, were against submission to the ICJ and other international courts and tribunals. However, the ICJ did deliver a number of important judgments and advisory opinions, although most the of latter remained a dead letter. Of relevance are the 1969 *North Sea*[223] and 1986 *Nicaragua*[224] Judgments with respect to the dualistic definition of international custom. Besides, in the 1950 *Haya de la Torre*[225] and in the 1960 *Right of Passage*[226] Judgments the Court developed the concepts and regional and bilateral international custom, respectively, while in the 1951 *Norwegian Fisheries* Judgment the Court admitted the concept of persistent objector.[227] As for other international law sources, the ICJ discussed error as a circumstance affecting the validity of treaties in the *Temple of Préah Vihéar* Judgment of 1962,[228] a statement later to be codified in Article 48 of the Vienna Convention on the Law of Treaties of 1969, and the legal relevance of unilateral acts in the *Nuclear Tests* Judgment of 1974.[229] At the regional level, a robust jurisprudence was developed by the European Commission and Court of Human Rights, as well as, again in the European context, by the Court of Justice of the European Communities.[230]

---

were also cast by Switzerland (*ibid.*, pp. 323–324, pp. 25–31). Other Western states were more accommodating, especially considering that *jus cogens* was bound to protect basic human rights that were deemed to be in common with Socialist and Third World states. In the end, *jus cogens* was accepted by Western states on condition that the ICJ be given compulsory jurisdiction over its determination, a clause that was included in Article 66(a) of the Vienna Convention.

222 See the Draft Articles adopted on First reading in 1996, at <http://www.lcil.cam.ac.uk/Media/ILCSR/articles_1996%28e%29.doc>.

223 *Supra*, note 151 (at paras. 74–81).

224 *Supra*, note 163 (at paras. 183–186).

225 *Haya de la Torre (Colombia/Peru)*, ICJ, Judgment of 13 June 1951, pp. 277–278, at <http://www.icj-cij.org/docket/files/14/1937.pdf>.

226 *Right of Passage over Indian Territory (Portugal v. India)*, ICJ, Judgment of 12 April 1960, pp. 39–40, at < http://www.icj-cij.org/docket/files/32/4521.pdf>.

227 *Fisheries (United Kingdom v. Norway)*, ICJ, Judgment of 18 December 1951, p. 131, at <http://www.icj-cij.org/docket/files/5/1809.pdf>.

228 *Temple of Préah Vihéar (Cambodia v. Thailand*, ICJ, Judgment of 15 June 1962, pp. 26–27, at <http://www.icj-cij.org/docket/files/45/4871.pdf>.

229 *Nuclear Tests (Australia v. France)*, ICJ, Judgment of 20 December 1974, at <http://www.icj-cij.org/docket/files/58/6093.pdf>; *Nuclear Tests (New Zealand v. France)*, ICJ, Judgment of 20 December 1974, at <http://www.icj-cij.org/docket/files/59/6159.pdf>.

230 Worthy of mention are, in particular, as a step towards the goal of shaping a European federation, the principle of supremacy of Community law over domestic law, the tendency to broaden the direct effect of Community law within domestic legal systems and the identification of a wide range of fundamental rights as an 'integral part' of the EC law.

17.5 THE POST-COLD WAR PERIOD (1989 TO DATE)

With the fall of the Berlin Wall in 1989, the ending of the Warsaw Pact on 1 July 1991 and the dismantling of the Soviet Union in December 1991, as well as the marginalization of the global South in the international decision-making process, the West – led by the USA, now the only remaining superpower – emerged as the key agenda-setter in the international arena. A belief spread that a 'new world order',[231] based on democracy and the rule of law,[232] was surfacing. The collective military response to the Iraqi occupation of Kuwait waged on 17 January 1991 with the green light of all five permanent members of the UN Security Council encouraged such a confidence. The conclusion of the Strategic Arms Reduction Treaty (START) between the United States and the Soviet Union on 31 July 1991,[233] a few months before the collapse of the latter, bolstered optimism. In subsequent years, all states of the former Soviet bloc, except for the Russian Federation, gradually joined NATO after the end of the Cold War.

Multinational corporations (MNCs) and transnational non-governmental organizations (NGOs) have become more and more influential and pervasive, raising the question of whether the world is ruled by a 'global governance' (as opposed to the old idea of a global government)[234] and of how 'private authority' is shaping states and international affairs.[235] In the Report *Our Global Neighborhood*, issued in 1995, the Commission on Global Governance (established in 1992 by UN Secretary-General Boutros Boutros-Ghali) defined global governance as 'the sum of many ways individuals and institutions, public and private, manage their common affairs'.[236] In fact, NGOs played a crucial role in inducing states to conclude the 1997 Landmine Convention[237] and the 1998 Statute of

---

[231] A decisive step towards a new world order was the landmark speech made by Mikhail Gorbachev to the UN General Assembly on 7 December 1988 ('Further world progress is now possible only through the search for a consensus of all mankind, in movement toward a new world order'). The term 'New World Order' was soon after used by US President George Bush Sr. on 11 September 1990 in a speech to the Congress relating to the military response to Iraq's invasion of Kuwait ('[The war in Iraq is] a rare opportunity to move toward an historic period of cooperation. Out of these troubled times . . . a New World Order can emerge') and on 21 September 1992 in a speech to the UN ('Nations should develop and train military units for possible U.N. peacekeeping operations . . . If multinational units are to work together, they must train together . . . Effective multinational action will also require coordinated command and control and inter-operability of both equipment and communications').

[232] See the implausible and often-critiqued thesis of Francis Fukuyama, *The End of History and the Last Man* (New York: The Free Press, 1992). A rather more sceptical theory was developed by Samuel P. Huntington, *The Clash of Civilizations and the Remaking of World Order* (New York: Simon & Schuster, 2003). For yet another reading see Robert Kagan, *Of Paradise and Power. America and Europe in the New World Order* (London: Atlantic Books, 2003). A neo-Marxist, 'imperial' theory was advanced by Michael Hardt and Antonio Negri, *Empire* (Cambridge, Mass.: Harvard University Press, 2002).

[233] Cf. <http://www.state.gov/www/global/arms/starthtm/start/start1.html>.

[234] James N. Rosenau and Ernst-Otto Czempiel, *Governance Without Government: Order and Change in World Politics* (Cambridge: Cambridge University Press, 1992).

[235] Rodney Bruce Hall and Thomas J. Biersteker (eds), *The Emergence of Private Authority in Global Governance* (Cambridge: Cambridge University Press, 2002).

[236] At <http://www.sovereignty.net/p/gov/ogn-front.html>.

[237] *Infra*, note 286.

the International Criminal Court.[238] In turn, the Multilateral Agreement on Investment (MAI), negotiated between members of the OECD to harmonize rules on foreign investment (in particular BITs), collapsed in 1998 as a result of protests from consumer groups and environmentalists who feared the treaty would have disabled national governments' ability to protect their own citizens from MNCs' demands.[239] NGOs have increasingly been linked to broad networks and coalitions that have rendered them far more effective than in the past. The power exerted by MNCs, especially on developing countries, has been in line with the current liberal system of global economy, enhanced by the establishment of the World Trade Organization (WTO) in 1994, but subject to some self-restraint in the name of a 'corporate social responsibility' to limit potential harm to workers, consumers, communities and the environment.[240]

After the collapse of the rivalry between the two blocs international conflicts and ethnic tensions erupted in many parts of the globe. Weak and failed states, often deriving from quasi-statehood,[241] have multiplied and raised the question of legal regimes applicable to spaces where no credible and effective (hence truly responsible) authority exists, including the use of force against non-state actors (criminals, rebels or terrorists),[242] let alone 'outlaw' states in which governments' proneness is precisely to provide criminals and terrorists with territory and other facilities to commit crimes elsewhere.[243] Peacekeeping, and occasionally peace enforcement and even complete state-building, have been deployed by the UN Security Council to safeguard institutional stability within states as the main strategy to maintain international peace and security. However, while in the 1990s humanitarian considerations appeared to displace the *raison d'Etat*, after the 9/11 attacks counterterrorism and security needs tended to prevail over human rights.

The UN codification process has moved forward and new instruments have been transformed into treaties. Among them the International Watercourses Convention of 1997[244] and the States Immunities Convention of 2004[245] are worth mentioning. Of utmost importance, although not translated into a binding treaty, are the Articles on State Responsibility approved by the ILC in 2001, probably the most important ILC achievement in the post-Cold War period. The Articles are generally considered by international and domestic courts, as well as in legal doctrine, as declaratory of customary international law.

---

238 *Infra*, note 279.

239 Cf. <http://www.oecd.org/daf/mai/index.htm>.

240 Jennifer A. Zerk, *Multinationals and Corporate Social Responsibility. Limitations and Opportunities in International Law* (Cambridge: Cambridge University Press, 2006).

241 Robert H. Jackson, *Quasi-States: Sovereignty, International Relations and the Third World* (Cambridge: Cambridge University Press, 1990).

242 I. William Zartman (ed.), *Collapsed States* (Boulder, CO: Lynne Rienner, 1995).

243 Gerry Simpson, *Great Powers and Outlaw States* (Cambridge: Cambridge University Press, 2004).

244 Convention on the Law of the Non-navigational Uses of International Watercourses adopted by the UN General Assembly on 21 May 1997, at <http://untreaty.un.org/ilc/texts/instruments/english/conventions/8_3_1997.pdf>.

245 United Nations Convention on Jurisdictional Immunities of States and Their Property adopted by the General Assembly on 2 December 2004, but (as of end 2009) not yet in force, at <http://untreaty.un.org/ilc/texts/instruments/english/conventions/4_1_2004.pdf>.

Finally, the dissolution of the Soviet Union, of the Socialist Federal Republic of Yugoslavia (SFRY) and of Czechoslovakia, as well as the 'reunification' of the two Germanies, brought to the fore a host of 'old' legal questions such as recognition of statehood, succession in respect of treaties and of foreign debt.

17.5.1 The Security Council Hyper-activity

With the fall of the Berlin Wall the UN Security Council has begun to act without being systematically blocked by criss-cross vetoes. The term 'threat to the peace' in Article 39 of the Charter has been broadly construed to include internal crises, such as apartheid and massive violations of human rights and of international humanitarian law, civil war, proliferation of nuclear weapons and international terrorism. As a result, the Council has adopted a large number of measures under Article 41 and, failing an army of its own, has authorized member states to use military force under Chapter VII of the Charter. The practice of authorizations began with the Gulf War of 1991 against Iraq and was later extended to internal situations, including, of late, even the repression of piracy.[246] Peacekeeping has evolved from preventing local conflicts from becoming drawn into the main superpower confrontation of the Cold War years to internal peace-building and democratization. Missions have been multiplied, extended to civil tasks, and occasionally organized as international administration of territories, such as in East Timor and in Kosovo in 1999. Two key documents of the post-Cold War period that envisaged such a major transformation in the nature of peacekeeping were the 1992 *Agenda for Peace* Report of UN Secretary-General Boutros Boutros-Ghali[247] and the 2000 'Brahimi Report'.[248] In this context the Peacebuilding Commission, established in 2005 as a common subsidiary organ of the Security Council and the General Assembly, is expected to play a key role. Security Council meetings and resolutions have expanded tremendously.[249] This hyper-activity, if compared to the Cold War period, has raised a number of questions of legitimacy under the UN Charter. In particular, the limits of the Security Council's powers have been widely debated, especially in the first years after the end of the Cold War and, more recently, when the Council has taken 'general' measures against international terrorism[250] and set up a public list of alleged terrorists against whom member states are under the obligation to adopt coercive measures which range from the freezing of assets to the ban of cross-border travelling.[251] No wonder the ICJ was soon called upon to determine, in the *Lockerbie* case, whether it could exercise a form

---

[246] Douglas Guilfoyle, 'Piracy off Somalia: UN Security Council Resolution 1816 and IMO Regional Counter-Piracy Efforts', 57 ICLQ (2008), pp. 690–699.

[247] *An Agenda for Peace*, Report of the UN Secretary General of 17 June 1992, at <http://www.un.org/Docs/SG/agpeace.html>.

[248] Report of the Panel on United Nations Peace Operations of 21 August 2000, at <http://www.un.org/peace/reports/peace_operations/>.

[249] Cf. <http://www.un.org/peace/peacebuilding/>.

[250] Res. 1373 of 28 September 2001, at <http://daccess-dds-ny.un.org/doc/UNDOC/GEN/N01/557/43/PDF/N0155743.pdf?OpenElement> and Res. 1540 of 28 April 2004, at <http://daccess-dds-ny.un.org/doc/UNDOC/GEN/N04/328/43/PDF/N0432843.pdf?OpenElement>.

[251] Cf. <http://www.un.org/sc/committees/1267/consolidatedlist.htm>.

of judicial review over resolutions adopted under Chapter VII of the UN Charter.[252] No univocal answer, however, was then given.

17.5.2 The Sovereignty Debate

The Report *Our Global Neighborhood* of 1995 was critiqued by both advocates and opponents of sovereignty.[253] It is unclear whether state sovereignty should be strengthened or weakened, or whether state sovereignty has *already* substantially vanished or, on the contrary, is stronger than ever.[254] Some have argued that in the current world system it is actually MNCs that 'rule the world'.[255] Since the end of the Cold War it has been systematically contended that state sovereignty is increasingly being undermined by a wide range of global and local challenges, including economic globalization, national disaggregation, international humanitarianism.[256] In particular, human rights activists are pressing for humanitarian intervention against tyrants in other countries on the basis of the sovereignty as responsibility concept[257] and notably the responsibility to protect doctrine.[258]

At the same time sovereignty has been sought by the new states that emerged from the dissolution of the Soviet Union, Czechoslovakia and Yugoslavia, as occurred in the 1950s and in the 1960s to former colonies. A claim to sovereignty (along with the safeguard of domestic democratic processes) is also made by No Global movements against alleged 'obscure' powers who make decisions outside the state in an undemocratic way, such as the WTO panels and Appeal Body or arbitrators that settle foreign investment disputes. Third World states also defend sovereignty as a guarantee of equality and generally resist the responsibility to protect doctrine.

---

[252] *Questions of Interpretation and Application of the 1971 Montreal Convention arising from the Aerial Incident at Lockerbie (Libyan Arab Jamahiriya v. United States of America)*, Request for the indication of Provisional Measures, ICJ, Order of 14 April 1992, at <http://www.icj-cij.org/docket/files/88/7085.pdf> and *Questions of Interpretation and Application of the 1971 Montreal Convention arising from the Aerial Incident at Lockerbie (Libyan Arab Jamahiriya v. United Kingdom)*, Preliminary Objections, ICJ, Judgment of 27 February 1998, at <http://www.icj-cij.org/docket/files/89/7249.pdf>.

[253] *Supra*, note 236.

[254] Linda Weiss, *The Myth of the Powerless State* (Ithaca, New York: Cornell University Press, 1998).

[255] See, e.g., David C. Korten, *When Corporations Rule the World* (Sterling/San Francisco: Kumarian Press and Berrett-Koehler Publishers, 2001, 2nd edn.).

[256] See Susan Strange, *The Retreat of the State. The Diffusion of Power in the World Economy* (Cambridge: Cambridge University Press, 1996).

[257] Francis M. Deng, Sadikiel Kimaro, Terrence Lyons, Donald Rothchild and I. William Zartman, *Sovereignty as Responsibility. Conflict Management in Africa* (Washington D.C.: The Brookings Institution, 1996); Kofi A. Annan, *Two Concepts of Sovereignty*, *The Economist*, 16 September 1999.

[258] See Carlo Focarelli, 'The Responsibility to Protect Doctrine and Humanitarian Intervention: Too Many Ambiguities for a Working Doctrine', 13 *Journal of Conflict & Security Law* (2008), pp. 191–213. For the latest developments cf. <http://www.un.org/ga/president/63/interactive/responsibilitytoprotect.shtml>. For a comment on the recent Libyan conflict, see Carlo Focarelli, 'Libya: a Turning Point for the Responsibility to Protect Doctrine?', available at <http://www.e-ir.info/?p=8091>.

17.5.3 The Global Commons and the Developments of *Jus Cogens* and Obligations *Erga Omnes*

The doctrines of sovereignty as responsibility and responsibility to protect, as susceptible to humanitarian intervention, are linked to obligations *erga omnes*. Some core values are felt so important as to create in all states a legal interest in their observance. All states are deemed to be entitled to invoke responsibility for violations of obligations *erga omnes*. If governments have obligations towards their own citizens and these cannot be expected to force their governments into abiding by them, then such obligations must necessarily be owed to all other states and imply a power of all other states to take effective (including military) measures against the defiant government. However, the practice shows that states are extremely reluctant to intervene and when they intervene this is because it is convenient to do so. In fact, only the strongest can intervene and they will do so only when there is a gain in sight[259].

A similar analysis applies to *jus cogens*. After the end of the Cold War *jus cogens* actually began to be extended to fields other than the law of treaties and relatively widely applied by courts. As the 1969 Vienna Convention did not specify which rules were peremptory, most interpreters endeavoured to identify peremptory rules. However, with the expansion of *jus cogens* in virtually all areas of international law the analysis should focus on the 'special' effects it entails.[260]

Article 19 on state crimes as worked out by the ILC in the 1970s was adopted on first reading by the ILC in 1996, but it was deleted in the Articles finally approved in 2001, as a result of opposition by the states. However, *jus cogens* and obligations *erga omnes* have remained.[261]

17.5.4 Prohibition of the Use of Force, Humanitarian Intervention and Anticipatory Self-defence

On 2 August 1990 Iraq invaded Kuwait. UN Security Council Resolutions 660 of 2 August and 662 of 9 August 1990 condemned Iraq's invasion and called for the immediate and unconditional withdrawal of Iraqi forces.[262] Economic sanctions were adopted by Res. 661 of 6 August 1990 under Article 41 of the Charter.[263] A UN ultimatum, contained in Res. 678, followed on 29 November 1990.[264] On 24 February 1991, US-led coalition ground forces began the attack (Operation 'Desert Storm'). On 27 February Kuwait City was liberated. The military response was in collective self-defence and backed by

---

[259] See Carlo Focarelli, 'Common Article I of the 1949 Geneva Conventions: A Soap Bubble?', 21 *European Journal of International Law* (2010) pp. 125–171, available at <http://ejil.oxfordjournals.org/content/21/1/125.full.pdf+html>.

[260] For such a discussion see Carlo Focarelli, 'Promotional *Jus Cogens*: A Critical Appraisal of Jus Cogens Legal Effects', 77 *Nordic Journal of International Law* (2008), pp. 429–459.

[261] See <http://untreaty.un.org/ilc/texts/instruments/english/draft%20articles/9_6_2001.pdf>.

[262] At <http://daccess-dds-ny.un.org/doc/RESOLUTION/GEN/NR0/575/11/IMG/NR057511.pdf?OpenElement>.

[263] *Ibid.*

[264] At <http://daccess-dds-ny.un.org/doc/RESOLUTION/GEN/NR0/575/28/IMG/NR057528.pdf?OpenElement>.

an authorization of the Security Council. It was the first time that the Security Council authorized a war, except for the rather extraordinarily case of the Korean War in 1950.[265]

In the following years humanitarian considerations inspired action taken in situations of internal conflict and massive violations of human rights. The Security Council deployed a peacekeeping operation in Somalia in 1992 (UNOSOM I) to monitor the ceasefire in Mogadishu and escort deliveries of humanitarian supplies to distribution centres in the city.[266] The mission was soon reinforced, in 1993, and changed into peace enforcement (UNOSOM II),[267] but with disastrous results. Subsequently, the Security Council authorized states (the United States, actually) to use force in Haiti in 1994 following a coup.[268] No action was taken in Rwanda in 1994 while the genocide was underway; nor could the United Nations do much to avoid genocide in Srebrenica in 1995.

In 1999, NATO decided to bomb the Federal Republic of Yugoslavia (FRY) for massive violations of human rights in Kosovo. The military operation was justified on humanitarian grounds. While hostilities were under way, on 24 April 2009, NATO adopted a 'New Strategic Concept' claiming the need to intervene beyond the hypothesis of self-defence as envisaged by Article 5 of the 1949 NATO Treaty, so as to confront risks of a wider nature than state attacks, including acts of terrorism, sabotage and organized crime (para. 24).[269] When the bombing of Kosovo ceased, an international integral administration was established in Kosovo.

The 9/11 terrorist attack on the United States prompted a 'global war on terror'. Security grounds and preventive self-defence became top priority and were seen to prevail over human rights and democratic guarantees. On 7 October 2001 a US-led coalition waged war on Afghanistan, as responsible for the attack, in self-defence. The Taliban government was soon defeated and overthrown. During the hostilities a number of alleged 'terrorists' were captured and transferred to the US Guantanamo military base, located in Cuba, and detained there as 'unlawful combatants', a designation that has been the subject of strong criticism by international human rights institutions. In 2002 the Bush administration upheld preventive self-defence in the National Security Strategy document, renewed in the 2006 document.[270]

In 2003 war was waged against Iraq invoking a variety of justifications: pre-emptive self-defence, pre-existing authorization of the Security Council, need to enforce previous Security Council resolutions, pro-democratic intervention. Unlike the war in Afghanistan in the aftermath of the 9/11 attack, several states were now overtly against war. The US insisted that Iraq had weapons of mass destruction in breach of previous Security Council resolutions. After the main military operations it was found that no weapons of mass destruction were present in Iraq. A few months later, Saddam Hussein was apprehended, tried, convicted, sentenced to death and executed. The United States

---

265 *Supra*, note 169.

266 At <http://www.un.org/en/peacekeeping/missions/past/unosomi.htm>.

267 At <http://www.un.org/en/peacekeeping/missions/past/unosom2.htm>.

268 Res. 940 of 31 July 1994, at <http://daccess-dds-ny.un.org/doc/UNDOC/GEN/N94/312/22/PDF/N9431222.pdf?OpenElement>.

269 Cf. <http://www.nato.int/cps/en/natolive/official_texts_27433.htm?selectedLocale=en>.

270 Cf. <http://georgewbush-whitehouse.archives.gov/nsc/nss/2006.pdf>.

and the United Kingdom were recognized by the Security Council, by Res. 1483 of 2003, as 'occupying powers' and asked to comply with international humanitarian law.[271] Instead, a number of regulations were issued by the Coalition Provisional Authority (CPA) and the whole institutional structure of the Iraqi state completely changed. The term 'transformative occupations' – in derogation from the traditional conservative principle – was then used.[272]

The 2001 Afghanistan War and the 2006 Israeli–Lebanese War raised the question of whether self-defence is permitted against non-state actors. The ICJ gave a negative answer in the 2004 Advisory Opinion on the *Israeli Wall*, holding that self-defence is an armed reaction by a state to an attack from another state, although the opposite view has been taken by a few judges in individual opinions and in legal doctrine.[273]

17.5.5 International Crimes and International Humanitarian Law

In 1993 and in 1994 the UN Security Council established the International Criminal Tribunal for the former Yugoslavia (ICTY)[274] and the International Criminal Tribunal for Rwanda (ICTR)[275] under Chapter VII of the Charter. The two *ad hoc* Tribunals were given a time-limited mandate and 'completion strategies' to end within 2010 were established by the Council in 2003[276] and in 2004.[277] The Statutes of the two Tribunals contained certain principles drawn from the Statute of the Nuremberg Tribunal. The two Tribunals constituted a partial step towards avoiding the criticisms that the Nuremberg Tribunal had attracted. A key question that both faced at the very beginning of their activity was about their very legality. In 1995 the ICTY held that the legal basis of its establishment was Article 41 of the UN Charter.[278] In 1997 the ICTR followed suit.[279] Since their inception the two Tribunals have produced a robust case law, thereby articulating the development of international humanitarian and criminal law to an extraordinary level.

---

271 Res. 1487 of 22 May 2003, at <http://daccess-dds-ny.un.org/doc/UNDOC/GEN/N03/368/53/PDF/N0336853.pdf?OpenElement>.

272 Adam Roberts, *Transformative Military Occupation. Applying the Laws of War and Human Rights*, 100 AJIL (2006), pp. 580–622.

273 *Legal Consequences of the Construction of a Wall in the Occupied Palestinian Territory*, ICJ, Advisory Opinion of 9 July 2004, para. 139, at <http://www.un.org/secureworld/>.

274 Res. 827 of 25 May 1993, at <http://daccess-dds-ny.un.org/doc/UNDOC/GEN/N93/306/28/IMG/N9330628.pdf?OpenElement>. See also <http://www.icty.org/>.

275 Res. 955 of 8 November 1994, at<http://daccess-dds-ny.un.org/doc/UNDOC/GEN/N95/140/97/PDF/N9514097.pdf?OpenElement>. See also <http://69.94.11.53/default.htm>.

276 Res. 1503 of 28 August 2003, at <http://daccess-dds-ny.un.org/doc/UNDOC/GEN/N03/481/70/PDF/N0348170.pdf?OpenElement>.

277 Res. 1534 of 26 March 2004, at <http://daccess-dds-ny.un.org/doc/UNDOC/GEN/N04/286/29/PDF/N0428629.pdf?OpenElement>.

278 *Prosecutor* v. *Dusko Tadić*, ICTY Appeal Chamber, Decision on the defence motion for interlocutory appeal on jurisdiction of 2 October 1994, paras. 34–36 <http://www.icty.org/x/cases/tadic/acdec/en/51002.htm>.

279 *Prosecutor* v. *Joseph Kanyabashi*, ICTR Trial Chamber, Decision on the Defence Motion on Jurisdiction of 18 June 1997, para. 27, at <http://69.94.11.53/ENGLISH/cases/Kanyabashi/decisions/180697.pdf>.

The most important advancement in international criminal law, and in international law in general, has been the establishment of the International Criminal Court (ICC) under the 1998 Rome Statute.[280] The Court is the first permanent international criminal court to prosecute perpetrators of the most serious crimes of concern to the international community. Unlike the ICTY and the ICTR, the Court is based on a treaty (joined as of end 2009 by 110 states) rather than imposed on all UN member states by the UN Security Council. The Court has jurisdiction over 'the most serious crimes of concern to the international community as a whole', namely, genocide, crimes against humanity, war crimes. The crime of aggression may fall within the jurisdiction of the Court if the Assembly of the Parties provides in the future a definition thereof. The establishment of the Court implies that political leaders may be prosecuted for their most serious breaches of human rights towards their own populations, a decisive step towards 'sovereignty as responsibility'.[281] Many, albeit certainly not all, the criticisms against the Nuremberg Tribunal and the *ad hoc* Tribunals have been positively overcome. In practice, however, eight years after the entry into force of the Statute occurred on 1 July 2002, the overall performance of the Court is far from encouraging.

Since 2000 a few 'hybrid' or 'internationalized' criminal tribunals have been established, thus apparently inaugurating a novel strategy to cope with both international crimes and serious domestically sanctioned crimes. They are called hybrid because they have both international (e.g., the majority of sitting judges) and domestic (e.g., the applicable law) elements. The Special Court for Sierra Leone (SCSL),[282] the Extraordinary Chambers in Cambodia in the Courts of Cambodia (ECCC)[283] and the Special Tribunal for Lebanon (STL)[284] are worth recalling. The UN has been always implicated in their creation, albeit in different ways and with different legal weight.

As for domestic courts, the *Pinochet* decision of 1999 delivered by the House of Lords made headlines, arguing for the denial of jurisdictional immunity to former heads of state charged with international crimes, such as torture. Ever since other former and even incumbent heads of state have been indicted for alleged commission of international crimes. However, the French Court of Cassation accorded immunity to Gaddafi, who was charged with international terrorism, inter alia as an incumbent foreign head of state. Slobodan Milosević was under trial before the ITCY when he died. Charles Taylor is being judged by the Special Court of Sierra Leone (SCSL). The ICC issued in 2009 a warrant of arrest against incumbent President of Sudan, Al-Bashir.[285] An approach similar to *Pinochet* was taken by the Italian Court of Cassation in the landmark *Ferrini* Judgment of 2004, as well as in other subsequent decisions. This jurisprudence has been resisted by other courts, including the House of Lords in the *Jones* decision of 2006, and was challenged in 2008 by Germany before the ICJ as inconsistent with the rule of cus-

---

280 At<http://www.icc-cpi.int/NR/rdonlyres/EA9AEFF7-5752-4F84-BE94-0A655EB30E16/0/Rome_Statute_English.pdf>.

281 *Supra*, note 257.

282 At <http://www.sc-sl.org/>.

283 At <http://www.eccc.gov.kh/english/default.aspx>.

284 At <http://www.stl-tsl.org/action/home>.

285 Ellen Lutz (ed.), *Prosecuting Heads of State* (New York: Cambridge University Press, 2009).

tomary international law imposing sovereign immunity for acts performed *jure imperii*.[286] After the end of the Cold War, a number of states have passed laws providing for universal jurisdiction over international crimes. These laws require, however, some minimum links between the crime and the forum state and expressly exclude foreign heads of states, prime ministers and ministers of foreign affairs.[287]

Finally, as regards international humanitarian law, worthy of mention are the 1997 Landmine Convention[288] and the 2008 Cluster Munitions Convention.[289] Their conclusion has greatly benefited from the powerful thrust of NGOs.

17.5.6 Human Rights, Rule of Law, Democracy and the Concept of Human Security

An important development within the UN in the field of human rights is the substitution, in 2006, of the Human Rights Commission with the Human Rights Council.[290] A few further human rights treaties have been concluded concerning specific categories of vulnerable peoples, including the Migrant Workers Convention of 1990 (ICRMW),[291] the Disappearances Convention of 2007,[292] and the Disabilities Convention of 2007 (CRPD),[293] all establishing a monitoring committee.

The notions of democracy, rule of law and good governance have spread worldwide as basic parameters of governments' performance and political legitimacy. Political conditionality based on them has been routinely applied by the Bretton Woods and other Institutions, as well as by the EU. Democracy, understood in terms of Western liberal democracies, has increasingly been seen as the best political system, almost regardless of the circumstances, even worthy of being exported and imposed by force.[294] Beginning with Namibia's 1989 vote, the United Nations and other organizations, either international (such as OSCE, EU, AU and the Council of Europe) or non-governmental (such

---

286 See for a discussion on this topic Carlo Focarelli, 'Case Report: Federal Republic of Germany v. Giovanni Mantelli and Others. Order No. 14201', 103 AJIL (2009), pp. 122–131.

287 See Wolfgang Kaleck, 'From Pinochet to Rumsfeld: Universal Jurisdiction in Europe 1998–2008', 30 *Michigan Journal of International Law* (2009), pp. 927–980.

288 Convention on the Prohibition of the Use, Stockpiling, Production and Transfer of Anti-Personnel Mines and on their Destruction, 18 September 1997, at <http://www.icrc.org/ihl.nsf/FULL/580?OpenDocument>.

289 Convention on Cluster Munitions of 30 May 2008, at <http://www.icrc.org/ihl.nsf/FULL/620?OpenDocument>.

290 At <http://www2.ohchr.org/english/bodies/hrcouncil/>. The Council was created by General Assembly Res. 60/251 of 3 April 2006 (at <http://www2.ohchr.org/english/bodies/hrcouncil/docs/A.RES.60.251_En.pdf>).

291 International Convention on the Protection of the Rights of All Migrant Workers and Members of Their Families of 18 December 1990, at <http://www2.ohchr.org/english/law/cmw.htm>.

292 International Convention for the Protection of All Persons from Enforced Disappearance of 6 February 2007, at <http://www2.ohchr.org/english/law/disappearance-convention.htm>.

293 Convention on the Rights of Persons with Disabilities of 30 March 2007, at <http://www2.ohchr.org/english/law/disabilities-convention.htm>.

294 For a critical analysis see Fareed Zakaria, *The Future of Freedom. Illiberal Democracy at Home and Abroad* (New York/London: W.W. Norton & Company, 2003); Colin Crouch, *Post-democracy* (Cambridge: Polity Press, 2004).

as Global Rights,[295] NED,[296] International IDEA,[297] and ICJ[298]) have been monitoring elections and providing supposedly unbiased electoral assistance in several post-conflict societies, weak democracies, democracies in transition and, of late, even long-standing democracies.[299] Election monitoring has often become an inherent part of a broader mandate of peacekeeping and peacebuilding.

Since 1989 the human rights movement has become so central that the new, potentially all-embracing concept of 'human security' has been developed. A milestone was UNEP's 1994 *Human Development* Report, challenging the traditional notion of national security and championing a global, people-centred (as opposed to a state-centred) view of security. It was premised on ensuring freedom from want and freedom from fear (i.e. physical and psychological safety, dignity and well-being) for all persons worldwide.[300]

With the privatization of traditional public services and with the growing role of individuals on the international stage, difficult questions have arisen in relation to respect for human rights by non-state actors and, in particular, by multinational corporations (MNCs). During the 1990s, reports about the negative impact of transnational companies proliferated. Publications and campaigns by international human rights NGOs brought to the fore the potential negative impact of corporate activity on human rights. Companies were now being scrutinized not only for alleged unequal hiring practices or adverse environmental effects, as in the past, but also for actions which could contribute to conflict and human rights' abuses committed by aligning with authoritarian governments, funding repressive military forces, hiring abusive private security, and paying bribes to illegal armed groups for security. A new generation of voluntary codes of conduct emerged. The UN launched the *Global Compact* in 2000.[301] In 1997, the UN Sub-Commission on the Promotion and Protection of Human Rights set up a five-expert Working Group on the Working Methods and Activities of Transnational Corporations. In 2003 the Working Group issued a 23-article non-binding code of conduct for transnational corporations called 'Norms on the Responsibilities of Transnational Corporations and Other Business Enterprises' that placed direct responsibility on MNCs as 'organs of society' to promote respect for a wide range of human rights listed therein. The 'Norms' received several criticisms and were soon set aside by the Commission of Human Rights. In 2005, UN Secretary-General Kofi A. Annan appointed a Special Representative with the mandate to 'identify and clarify' international standards and policies in relation to business and human rights and to submit 'views and recommendations' for considera-

---

295 At <http://www.hrlawgroup.org/>.

296 At <http://www.ned.org/>.

297 At <http://www.idea.int/>.

298 At <http://www.icj.org/>.

299 Cf. <http://www.un.org/depts/dpa/french/electoral_assistance/ea_content/ea_un_system.htm>.

300 At <http://hdr.undp.org/en/reports/global/hdr1994/chapters/>. See also <http://www.humansecurityreport.info/index.php?option=com_frontpage&Itemid=1>; the collection of comments by 21 authors to the question 'What is human security?' published in 35 *Security Dialogue* (2004), pp. 275–396; and Shahbanou Tadjbakhsh and Anuradha M. Chenoy, *Human Security. Concepts and Implications* (Abingdon/New York: Routledge, 2007).

301 Cf. <http://www.unglobalcompact.org/index.html>.

tion by the Commission. The Special Representative has hitherto submitted a number of reports to the Human Rights Council, the last of which on 21 March 2011.[302]

17.5.7 International Terrorism

While the end of the Cold War could suggest that a universally agreed definition of terrorism was at hand, after the 9/11 attacks on the United States international terrorism sparked a hot debate on world security.[303] The United States and its allies declared a global 'war on terrorism', presented as a sort of novel 'just war', and pressed IOs (in particular the UN) for a top-priority commitment to counter-terrorism. Ever since condemnation of international terrorism in all forms and manifestations has been universal; yet the question of what is meant by international terrorism has remained open.

In a Declaration contained in Res. 49/60 of 1994 the UN General Assembly provided a general definition of international terrorism.[304] As a result, with Res. 51/210 of 1996, the General Assembly set up an *ad hoc* committee to reach an accepted definition to be included in a Draft Comprehensive Convention on international terrorism.[305] The committee, however, is still debating the definition of terrorism.

The UN Security Council has generally avoided defining international terrorism in the abstract. It did not actually define terrorism in Resolutions 1368 and 1373 of 2001, adopted in the aftermath of the 9/11 attacks. Also the Counter-Terrorism Committee set up by Res. 1373 has generally avoided definitions, thus allowing states to rely on the (inevitably diverging in part) definitions of their national legislations. However, Security Council Res. 1566, adopted in 2004, exceptionally provides a definition of terrorism in Article 3.[306] In other resolutions and presidential statements the Security Council has confined itself to indicating specific persons and groups, or incidents, as terrorist.

A number of further multilateral counter-terrorist treaties have been entered into since 1989, including the Plastic Explosives Convention of 1991,[307] the Terrorist Bombing Convention of 1997,[308] the Terrorist Financing Convention of 1999,[309] the Nuclear

---

[302] All reports are available at <http://www.business-humanrights.org/SpecialRepPortal/Home/ReportstoUNHumanRightsCouncil>.

[303] See the collection of writings published in 4 *Journal of International Criminal Justice* (2006), pp. 891–1180.

[304] Res. 49/60 of 9 December 1994, at <http://daccess-dds-ny.un.org/doc/UNDOC/GEN/N95/768/19/PDF/N9576819.pdf?OpenElement>. The definition was later reiterated by the General Assembly in several subsequent resolutions: *e.g.* in Res. 50/53 of 11 December 1995, Res. 51/210 of December 17, 1996; Res. 52/165, of December 15, 1997; Res. 53/108 of December 8, 1998; Res. 54/110 of December 9, 1999; Res. 55/158 of December 12, 2000.

[305] Res. 51/210 of 17 December 1996, at <http://daccess-dds-ny.un.org/doc/UNDOC/GEN/N97/761/65/PDF/N9776165.pdf?OpenElement>.

[306] Res. 1566 of 8 October 2004, at <http://daccess-dds-ny.un.org/doc/UNDOC/GEN/N04/542/82/PDF/N0454282.pdf?OpenElement>.

[307] Convention on the Marking of Plastic Explosives for the Purpose of Detection of 1 March 1991, at <http://treaties.un.org/doc/db/Terrorism/Conv10-english.pdf>.

[308] International Convention for the Suppression of Terrorist Bombings of 15 December 1997, at <http://treaties.un.org/doc/db/Terrorism/english-18-9.pdf>.

[309] International Convention for the Suppression of the Financing of Terrorism of 9 December 1999, at <http://treaties.un.org/doc/db/Terrorism/english-18-11.pdf>.

Terrorism Convention of 2005,[310] the Maritime Safety Protocol of 2005,[311] and Platforms Safety Protocol of 2005.[312] At the regional level worth mentioning are the 1998 Arab Convention,[313] the 1999 Islamic Convention,[314] the 1999 OAU Convention,[315] and the 1999 CIS Co-operation Treaty.[316] Significantly, Article 3 of the OAU Convention points out that 'the struggle waged by peoples in accordance with the principles of international law for their liberation or self-determination, including armed struggle against colonialism, occupation, aggression and domination by foreign forces shall not be considered as terrorist acts'. A similar clause is found in Article 2 (*a*) of the Arab Convention and in the Preamble of the Islamic Convention. OAS, the Council of Europe, the EU and OSCE are silent on whether wars of national liberation constitute international terrorism

In fact, counter-terrorism measures, including the US-led 'war on terror', and emergency national steps taken by several states, have raised concerns about the protection of human rights of alleged terrorists. The question has also arisen whether terrorism should be seen as an 'armed attack' justifying a response in self-defence (whether anticipatory or successive) or an ordinary (serious) crime against which the traditional rules on the repression of organized crime are applicable, or even an autonomous international crime.[317] In fact, proposals to include international terrorism in the ICC Statute were rejected. Also the Special Tribunal for Lebanon, which has jurisdiction over an alleged terrorist attack against Prime Minister Hariri in 2005, is concerned with international terrorism as defined by domestic (as opposed to international) law.

17.5.8 Global Economy

The end of the Cold War marked a major shift to economic globalization. In 1994 the World Trade Organization (WTO) was established. The agreed-upon package comprised a set of agreements that extended liberalization from trade in goods (as originally envisaged in the GATT) to many other sectors, including services (GATS) and intellectual property rights (TRIPs Agreement), a move favourable to developed countries, which

---

[310] International Convention for the Suppression of Acts of Nuclear Terrorism of 13 April 2005, at <http://www.un-documents.net/icsant.htm>.

[311] Protocol to the Convention for the Suppression of Unlawful Acts against the Safety of Maritime Navigation of 14 October 2005, at <https://www.unodc.org/tlbd/en/2005_Protocol2Convention_Maritime%20Navigation.html>.

[312] Protocol to the Protocol for the Suppression of Unlawful Acts against the Safety of Fixed Platforms Located on the Continental Shelf of 14 October 2005, at <https://www.unodc.org/tlbd/pdf/Protocol%20Fixed%20Platforms%20EN.pdf>.

[313] Arab Convention on the Suppression of Terrorism of 22 April 1998, at <http://www.unhcr.org/refworld/docid/3de5e6646.html>.

[314] Convention of the Organization of the Islamic Conference on Combating International Terrorism of 1 July 1999, at <http://www.unhcr.org/refworld/docid/3de5e6646.html>.

[315] Organization of African Unity Convention of the Prevention and Combating of Terrorism of 14 July 1999, at <http://treaties.un.org/doc/db/Terrorism/OAU-english.pdf>.

[316] Treaty on Cooperation among States Members of the Commonwealth of Independent States in Combating Terrorism of 4 June 1999, at <http://treaties.un.org/doc/db/Terrorism/csi-english.pdf>.

[317] Antonio Cassese, *The Multifaceted Criminal Notion of Terrorism in International Law*, 4 *Journal of International Criminal Justice* (2006), pp. 933–958.

was accepted by developing countries in exchange for concessions in textiles and agriculture. A powerful mechanism of dispute settlement was also created. Of utmost importance was the admission of China to the WTO on 11 December 2001. Worth mentioning also is the boom of Bilateral International Treaties (BITs), as well as multilateral treaties, on foreign investment after the end of the Cold War.[318]

The Bretton Woods Institutions and WTO have proved unable to keep at bay global crises, in particular the 1997 South-East and 1999 Russian crises, as well as the 2008 financial crisis, which originated in the United States. In the aftermath of the 1997 and 1999 crises they were charged with disrupting local economies and, more generally, domestic democracies by forcing states into applying their economic and political conditionality polices. Protests from anti-globalization and civil-society movements erupted in the Seattle demonstrations of 1999 against the WTO and the Bretton Woods Institutions, and have persisted ever since, bringing the WTO negotiations to a standstill.

One of the major problems that faced the application of WTO Agreements was the relation between liberalization needs and non-trade values, especially those adversely affecting environment, labour, consumers, and human rights in general. The WTO basic prohibition of protectionist measures prevents member states from adopting legislation that penalizes production process methods having a negative impact on the environment or on human rights. Member states have actually ratified a great many Multilateral Environmental Agreements (MEAs) and Human Rights Treaties. As a result, many potentially conflicting multilateral legal regimes co-exist in contemporary international law, undermining its coherence and, indeed, workability. A debate on the 'fragmentation' of international law has followed, involving the entire structure of international law, but no satisfactory criteria appear at the moment in sight to provide agreed-upon solutions.[319]

17.5.9 Environment and Sustainable Development

The focus on the environment, notably on global warming and climate change, has considerably increased since the end of the Cold War. As mentioned, several Multilateral Environmental Agreements (MEAs) have been concluded.

In 1992, the UN Framework Climate Change Convention (UNFCCC) was signed with a view to stabilizing the amount of greenhouse gases in the atmosphere at a level that could prevent dangerous man-made climate changes. Since then, 193 countries have ratified the Convention and 15 Conferences of the Parties (CoP) have taken place, the latest in December 2009 in Copenhagen. In 1997, at the Third CoP, the Kyoto Protocol was adopted. Unlike the UNFCCC, the Kyoto Protocol set binding targets. Under the Protocol 37 industrialized countries plus the EU as a whole pledged to reduce their emissions of greenhouse gases by 5 per cent on average from the 1990 level. The targets applied from 2008 to 2012. The Protocol has attracted many criticisms, especially from

---

[318] See M. Sornarajah, *The International Law on Foreign Investment* (Cambridge: Cambridge University Press, 2010, 3rd edn.).

[319] See the Report of the Study Group of the ILC, established in 2002, *Fragmentation of International Law: Difficulties Arising from the Diversification and Expansion of International Law* of 13 April 2006 (UN Doc. A/CN.4/L.682).

the United States. States are still deeply divided and a new binding treaty replacing the Kyoto Protocol is awaited.

A number of rulings on environmental protection have been made in recent years by national and international courts, including the *Nuclear Weapons* Advisory Opinion of 1996,[320] the *Gabčíkovo-Nagymaros* Judgment of 1997,[321] the decision delivered in 1993 in the *Minors Oposa* case by the Supreme Court of the Philippines whereby the right to a healthy environment 'concerns nothing less than self-preservation and self-perpetuation . . . the advancement of which may even be said to predate all governments and constitutions' and can be 'assumed to exist from the inception of humankind'.[322] The notion that the right to a healthy environment is part of human rights has been upheld by international monitoring courts and bodies in interpreting other rights (especially the right to the respect for private life) laid down in human rights treaties.

As for Antarctica, the Convention on the Regulation of Antarctic Mineral Resources (CRAMRA) was adopted in 1988 but failed following a public pressure campaign launched by a coalition of international organizations to prevent any minerals development in the region. An alternative proposal was then made for a comprehensive regime to protect the Antarctic environment which eventually resulted in the Madrid Protocol of 1991 banning all mining in Antarctica and designating the continent as a 'natural reserve devoted to peace and science'.[323]

17.5.10 International Adjudication

The post-Cold War period has witnessed a spectacular revival of international jurisdiction and arbitration, in particular investment disputes arbitration. Former communist countries have largely accepted compromissory clauses and international tribunals have multiplied, giving rise to the problem of institutional fragmentation of international law.[324]

17.6 CONCLUSION

The key feature of current international law relative to the past is its concern with governing people's daily life *within* states (i.e. how rulers are expected to govern their populations) as opposed to classical *inter-state* relations. The 'diplomatic' conception of international law as a set of rules either of 'etiquette' for diplomats or of merely ideal (or moral) guidelines for governments in their mutual relations, albeit still deep-rooted,

---

320 *Supra*, note 12 (at para. 29).

321 *Gabčíkovo-Nagymaros Project (Hungary/Slovakia)*, ICJ, Judgment of 25 September 1997, paras. 53 and 140, at <http://www.icj-cij.org/docket/files/92/7375.pdf>.

322 *Oposa et al.* v. *Fulgencio S. Factoran, Jr. et al.*, Supreme Court of Philippines, Judgment of 30 July 1993, para. 20, at <http://www.elaw.org/node/1343>. The Court, in particular, endorsed the concept of sustainable development by stating that 'every generation has a responsibility to the next to preserve that rhythm and harmony for the full enjoyment of a balanced and healthful ecology'.

323 At <http://www.ats.aq/documents/recatt/Att006_e.pdf>.

324 *Supra*, note 319.

are in many respects outdated. Contemporary international law governs, directly or indirectly, the daily life of billions of people on earth and is increasingly taken account of by governments in respect of how they rule and by national courts in their routine judicial activity. This is not to imply that the world has attained a working universal law, capable of superseding national legislation in case of conflict, still less that the world has an effective and (generally perceived) just authority capable of dictating and administering common rules for the common good of humankind. The world is today, more than ever, premised on states that recognize no superior authority and that are the only actors credibly capable of enforcing rules and orders, including international law and decisions. Tensions and conflicts between states, within states, between states and non-state actors and even between non-state actors themselves are as frequent as ever. This urges both new rules and renewed efforts to obtain a greater degree of compliance with existing rules. Rules unilaterally or 'apologetically' imposed might perhaps be benevolent but will hardly work and, indeed, are no rules at all. There is by now increasing agreement that international law already affects in part, and *should* do so fully in the future, all people in their daily lives, beginning with subsistence and other basic needs. No doubt this marks a breakthrough compared to what was known as international law in its whole previous history.

Index